Portrait of a Priestess

Portrait of a Priestess

Women and Ritual
in Ancient Greece

Joan Breton Connelly

PRINCETON UNIVERSITY PRESS
PRINCETON AND OXFORD

This publication has been supported by a grant from Charles Scribner III in memory of his father, Charles Scribner, Jr., a past president and trustee of the Princeton University Press.

Library of Congress Cataloging-in-Publication Data

Connelly, Joan Breton, date.
    Portrait of a priestess : women and ritual in ancient Greece / Joan Breton Connelly.
       p.   cm.
    Includes bibliographical references and index.
    ISBN-13: 978-0-691-12746-0 (hardcover : alk. paper)
    ISBN-10: 0-691-12746-8 (hardcover : alk. paper)
    1. Greece—Religion.   2. Women and religion—Greece.   3. Women priests—Greece.
4. Greece—Antiquities.   5. Greece—History—146 B.C.–323 A.D.   I. Title.
BL795.W65C66   2007
292.6′10820938—dc22

                            2006013073

British Library Cataloging-in-Publication Data is available

This book has been composed in Adobe Jensen
Printed on acid-free paper. ∞
pup.princeton.edu
Printed in Canada
10 9 8 7 6 5 4 3 2 1

Front cover and spine, frontispiece: Attic white-ground phiale (detail). Plate 1
Back cover: Attic black-figure amphora (detail). Plate 12

Chapter details: chapter 1, detail of figure 1.2; chapter 2, detail of figure 2.2; chapter 3, detail of figure 3.4; chapter 4, detail of figure 4.9; chapter 5, detail of figure 5.12; chapter 6, detail of figure 6.12; chapter 8, detail of figure 8.5; chapter 9, detail of figure 5.24; chapter 10, detail of figure 6.14. Chapter 7, detail of marble relief. Berlin, Staatliche Museen Antikensammlung SK 881. Photo Antikensammlung, Staatliche Museen zu Berlin, Bildarchiv Preussicher Kulturbesitz

For Dorothy, Cacky, TA, and Kippy

Contents

CONTENTS

Acknowledgments

The idea for this book was born in Brunilde Ridgway's office in the Thomas Libary at Bryn Mawr College in 1988. Bruni had recently published her groundbreaking article "Ancient Greek Women and Art: The Material Evidence" in the *American Journal of Archaeology*. I had just published *Votive Sculpture of Hellenistic Cyprus*, bringing me face to face with my first Greek priestess (see pl. 14). Intrigued by this and other images of women shown holding temple keys, I resolved to study them next. I thank Bruni Ridgway, above all others, for standing behind this book from start to finish.

The foundations on which the book is built were set much earlier on. For this, I thank Mary Lefkowitz, who, at Wellesley College, first opened for me the world of ancient women and Greek myth. Her thoughtful insights have informed this work throughout its writing.

A lively interest in Greek religion stems from my undergraduate days, as well, when I was lucky enough to enjoy epic summer road trips to Brauron and Eretria with Lilly Kahil in her Citroën DS. When I began this book years later, she invited me to Paris as a foreign member at the *Lexicon Iconographicum Mythologiae Classicae* and helped in every way. Dorothy Thompson put the first terracotta votive figurine in my hand when I was twenty, and, throughout the decades that followed, guided me as the wisest and most generous of mentors. I am privileged to have been a member of Erika Simon's seminar "Festivals of Attica," during the year in which she delivered her memorable Flexner Lectures at Bryn Mawr. I owe an enormous debt to these excellent teachers and to the esteemed colleagues with whom I have discussed Greek religion during the years that have followed. I particularly thank Christiane Sourvinou-Inwood and Robert Parker for the generosity and insight with which they have shaped my understanding of the ancient past.

Much of what I have learned about Greek religion has come from the sanctuaries in which I have been privileged to excavate: Apollo at Corinth, Zeus at Nemea, Apollo Hylates at Kourion, Artemis on Failaka, and the island sanctuary of Yeronisos off western Cyprus where I have worked for the past sixteen years. I thank my extraordinary team and the Peyians and Paphians who have brought such joy to this labor. Theresa Howard Carter, director of our work in Kuwait, has been the best of mentors in the field and an inspiring friend, in the trenches and out.

A New York University Presidential Mellon Fellowship and National Endowment of the Humanities Travel to Collections Grant supported my research in its earliest years. I was thus able to begin my work at the Beazley Archive Database in Oxford, where I thank Donna

Kurtz, Thomas Mannack, and Melanie Mendoza. These grants also supported my research in Paris, where I had the privilege of attending seminars at the Centre Louis Gernet. As is evident throughout this book, the work of Stella Georgoudi, Alain Schnapp, Francois de Polignac, and Francois Lissarrague has greatly informed my approach. I warmly thank them for the rich scholarly exchange that continues through my participation with the research team on cult personnel for the *Thesaurus Cultus et Rituum Antiquorum*.

A MacArthur Foundation fellowship supported years of research and writing, and I am deeply grateful to the John D. and Catherine T. MacArthur Foundation, particularly to Adele Simmons and Catharine Stimpson, under whom the award was made. This enabled me to work at Oxford, where I enjoyed a number of visiting fellowships. I am indebted to the Warden and Fellows of All Souls College, where I spent a very happy year, as a result of the special kindness of Margaret Bent, John Ma, M. L. West, Peregrine Horden, Magnus Ryan, Julian Bullard, Patrick Reilly, Gunther Treitel, Jack McManners, John Landers, William St. Clair, and Patrick Neill. I am deeply grateful to Robert Parker for sponsoring me at New College, Oliver Taplin at Magdalen College, and Ewen Bowie at Corpus Christi College, and to the many scholars who enriched my time within each of these remarkable communities. I thank Michael Vickers, Emily Kearns, Nicholas Purcell, Beate Dignas, and Robin Osborne for their generosity in discussing specific aspects of my work. At Cambridge, I have benefited greatly from scholarly exchange with Anthony Snodgrass, Colin Austin, Nigel Spivey, James Diggle, and Louise and Martin Robertson.

I was privileged to spend a term at the Radcliffe Institute for Advanced Study, thanks to Mary Maples Dunn. I thank her, as well as Gregory Nagy, Ernst Badian, and Karen King, for making my time at Harvard both pleasant and productive. While finishing this book I returned to Bryn Mawr, where I enjoyed two terms as a research associate. I am indebted to Rick Hamilton, Stella Miller-Collett, Mabel Lang, Julia Gaisser, T. Corey Brennan, Radcliffe Edmunds, Karen Tidmarsh, and the best of librarians, Eileen Markson, for their generous help and friendship. Kippy Stroud and her Acadia Summer Arts Program have provided the ideal environment for thinking and writing at the close of so many perfect summers, and I thank her for cheering on this work at every turn.

I am indebted to the administration and faculty at New York University for supporting my research, especially Richard Foley, Mary Carruthers, Edward Sullivan, Matthew Santirocco, Kenneth Silver, Norbert Baer, and Dick Turner. I warmly thank Lillian Vernon, whose chair I have been honored to hold, for her generosity and for her example, which has inspired me greatly. I am indebted to my students at NYU for the lively questions and keen interest that helped to shape this book.

I thank the many scholars who kindly provided access to materials, photographs, and permissions to reproduce them, including Katerina Rhomiopoulou, Alcestis Choremi, Nikolaos Kaltsas, Charalambos Kritzas, Dina Peppa-Delmouzou, Petros Themelis, Dyfri Williams, Alex Truscott, Michael Vickers, Susan Walker, Brian Shefton, Annie Caubet, Fede Berti, Bodil Bundgaard Rasmussen, Irene Bösel, Michael Krumme, Michael Padgett, John Hermann, Florence Wolsky, Brigitte Freyer-Schauenburg, Jane Sattenau, Ilknur Özgen, Turhan Birgili, Orhan Atvur, Christopher Ratté, Brad Cook, John Traill, Aileen Ajootian, and Marina Thomatos.

Generous colleagues have given their time and expertise in reading parts or the whole of the manuscript. I am deeply indebted to them for their thoughtful insights, and thank Colin Austin, Roger Bagnall, Bruce Beck, Helene Foley, Stella Georgoudi, Janet Halley, Natalie Boyd Kampen, Mable Lang, Mary Lefkowitz, William T. Loomis, Lynn Meskell, Robin Osborne, Robert Parker, Kimberley Patton, Dimitris Plantzos, Brunilde Ridgway, Christiane Sourvinou-Inwood, Steven V. Tracy, and Rita Wright. I also thank the dear friends who have offered support of various kinds, including Joan Abrahamson, Nicholas Barber, Brigitte Bourgeois, John Brademas, Hans Gunther Buchholz, Horace A. Davies II, Brian DeLorey, Katherine Fischer, Pamela and Andrew Jacovides, Ruth Keshishian, Socratis Mavrommatis, Howland Murphy, Dinos Lordos, James Ottaway Jr., Dimitris Pandermalis, Jérôme Paolini, Mary Patterson McPherson, Elin Shriver, Susan F. Springer, Robert B. Stevens, Ted Rogers, Rita Severis, and Anastasia P. Vournas.

My editor at Princeton University Press, Ian Malcolm, has been an author's dream. I warmly thank him and the production editor, Sara Lerner; designer, Sarah Henry; and copyeditor, Romaine Perin, for their dedication to excellence. For assistance in research, editing, computer formatting, and other essential tasks I am deeply indebted to Jason Governale, Jie Yuan, Victoria Tsoukala, Brad Cook, Marina Thomatos, Jing An, Daisy Ki Nam, Margaret Rubick, Jill Lingenfelter, and Adam Peters. Bruce King painstakingly prepared the general index. George Marshall Peters has skillfully rendered the line drawings and I thank him, as always, for the talent he brings to all that he touches.

A generous subvention from Charles Scribner III has enabled this book to be richly illustrated and thoughtfully designed. I thank Charlie for the treasured friendship that has flourished since our undergraduate days at Princeton, and for the intelligence, care, and fun that he has brought to this endeavor.

This book was begun at Bryn Mawr and completed in Northeast Harbor, Maine. I am indebted to the excellent women from whom I learned so much along the way, especially Dorothy Burr Thompson, Catherine Ditulh Sharpless, Theresa Howard Carter, and Marion Boulton Stroud. I dedicate it to them with thanks and admiration.

March 2006
New York City

Abbreviations

ABV	J. D. Beazley, *Attic Black-Figure Vase-Painters*. Oxford 1956.
Add	L. Burn and R. Glynn, *Beazley Addenda: Additional References to ABV, ARV, and Paralipomena*. Oxford 1982.
Add²	T. H. Carpenter, *Beazley Addenda: Additional References to ABV, ARV², and Paralipomena*, 2nd ed. Oxford 1989.
AG	J. Bekker, *Anecdota Graeca* I–III. Berlin 1824–21.
APF	J. K. Davies, *Athenian Propertied Families*. Oxford 1971.
ARFV	J. Boardman, *Athenian Red-Figure Vases*. Oxford 1975.
ARV²	J. D. Beazley, *Attic Red-Figure Vase-Painters*, 2nd ed. Oxford 1963.
CEG	P. A. Allen, *Carmina epigraphica graeca saeculorum VIII–V a. Chr. n.* [vol. I] *and . . . saeculorum IV a. Chr. n.* [II].
CIG	A. Boeckhius, *Corpus Inscriptionem Graecorum*. Berlin 1828–77.
CIJ	J.-B. Frey, *Corpus Inscriptionum Judaicarum*. Rome 1936–52.
CIL	*Corpus Inscriptionum Latinarum*. Berlin 1862–.
CVA	*Corpus Vasorum Antiquorum*. [Various places of publication] 1922–.
EAA	*Enciclopedia dell'arte antica classica ed orientale*. Rome 1958–.
ED	M. Segre, *Iscrizioni di Cos*. Public Documents. Rome 1993.
FD	*Fouilles de Delphes III. Inscriptions*. Paris 1910–.
FGrH	F. Jacoby, *Die Fragmente der griechischen Historiker*. Leiden 1926–58, reprint 1954–60.
GAI	L. Threatte, *The Grammar of Attic Inscriptions*, vol. 1, Berlin 1980; vol. 2., Berlin 1996.
GHI I²	R. Meiggs and D. Lewis, *A Selection of Greek Historical Inscriptions* I². Oxford 1969 and rev. ed. 1988.
I.Cos	M. Segre, *Iscrizioni di Cos*. 2 vols. ed. G. Pugliese-Carratelli. Rome 1993.
ID	*Inscriptions de Délos*. 7 vols. Paris 1926–72.
I.Didyma	A. Rehm, *Didyma, Zweiter, Teil: Die Inschriften*. ed R. Harder. Berlin 1958.
I.Ephesos	H. Wankel et al., eds., *Die Inschriften von Ephesos*. 7 vols. Bonn 1979–81.
I.Erythrai	E. H. Engelmann and R. Merkelbach, eds., *Die Inschriften von Erythrai und Klazomenai*. 2 vols. Bonn 1972.
IG	*Inscriptiones Graecae*. Berlin, 1877–.
IG²	*Inscriptiones Graecae, editio minor*. Berlin 1913–.

IGSK	*Inschriften der Griechischen Städte aus Kleinasien.* Cologne 1972.
I.Knidos	W. Blümel, *Die Inschriften von Knidos I.* Bonn 1992.
ILCV	E. Diehl, *Inscriptiones Latinae Christianae Veteres.* 4 vols. Berlin, Dublin, and Zurich 1925–67.
I.Magnesia	O. Kern, *Die Inschriften von Magnesia am Mäander.* Berlin 1900.
I.Mylasa	W. Blümel, *Die Inschriften von Mylasa.* 2 vols. Bonn 1987, 1988.
I.Pergamon	M. Fränkel, *Die Inschriften von Pergamon.* 2 vols. Berlin 1890–95.
I.Priene	F. Hiller von Gaertringen, ed. *Inschriften von Priene.* Berlin 1906.
I.Stratonikeia	M. Ç. Şahin, ed., *Die Inschriften von Stratonikeia.* 2 vols. Bonn 1981, 1982.
LGPN	M. J. Osborne and S. B. Byrne, *Lexicon of Greek Personal Names,* vol. 2. Oxford 1994.
LGS	*Leges Graecorum Sacrae:* J. von Prott, pt. I, *Fasti Sacri;* L. Ziehen, pt. II, *Leges Graeciae et Insularum.* Leipzig 1896–1906.
LIMC	*Lexicon Iconographicum Mythologiae Classicae.* Zurich and Munich 1981–97.
LSAG	L. H. Jeffrey, *The Local Scripts of Archaic Greece.* Oxford 1990.
LSAM	F. Sokolowski, *Lois sacrées de l'Asie mineure.* Paris 1955.
LSCG	F. Sokolowski, *Lois sacrées des cités grecques.* Paris 1969.
LSJ	H. G. Liddell, R. Scott, and H. S. Jones, *A Greek-English Lexicon.* Oxford 1925.
LSS	F. Sokolowski, *Lois sacrées des cités grecques. Supplement.* Paris 1962.
MAMA	W. Calder, E. Herzfeld, and S. Guyer, *Monumenta Asiae Minoris Antiqua.* Manchester 1928–.
NGSL	E. Lupu, *Greek Sacred Law: A Collection of New Documents.* Leiden 2005.
OCD[3]	S. Hornblower and A. Spawforth, eds., *The Oxford Classical Dictionary,* 3rd ed. Oxford 2003.
PA	J. Kirchner, *Prosopographia Attica.* Berlin 1901–3.
Para	J. D. Beazely, *Paralipomena: Additions to Attic Black-Figure Vase-Painters and Attic Red-Figure Vase-Painters.* Oxford 1971.
PCG	R. R. Kassel and C. Austin, *Poetae Comici Graeci.* Berlin 1983–.
PLRE	A.H.M. Jones, *Prosopography of the Late Roman Empire.* Cambridge 1972–92.
RAW	S. I. Johnston, *Religions of the Ancient World.* Cambridge, MA, and London 2004.
RE	A. F. von Pauly, *Paulys Real-Encyclopädie der classischen Altertum swissenschaft.* Stuttgart 1894–1963.
SEG	*Supplementum Epigraphicum Graecum.* Leiden 1923–71. H. W. Pleket and R. S. Stroud, eds., Amsterdam 1972–.
SGDI	H. Colletz and F. Bechtel et al., *Sammlung der Griechischen Dialekt-Inschriften.* Göttingen 1884–1915.

Syll.³	W. Dittenberger, et al. ed., *Sylloge inscriptionum Graecarum,* 3rd ed., 4 vols., Leipzig 1915–24.
TAM	*Tituli Asiae Minoris.* Vienna 1901–.
TrGF	*Tragicorum Graecorum Fragmenta,* vol. 3, S. Radt, ed., *Aeschylus.* Göttingen 1985.

Plate 1
Attic white-ground phiale, the Painter of London D12. Boston, Museum of Fine Arts 65.908, Edwin
E. Jack Fund. Photograph © 2007 Museum of Fine Arts, Boston.

Plate 2
Attic red-figure oinochoe,
from Chuisi, the Triptolemos
Painter. Berlin, Staatliche
Museen Antikensammlung 2189.
Photo: Bildarchiv Preussischer
Kulturbesitz/Art Resource, NY.

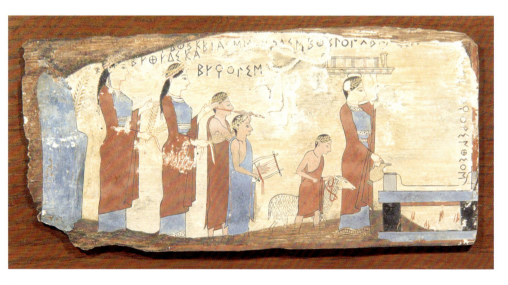

Plate 3
Painted wooden plaque, from Pitsa. Athens, National Archaeological Museum 16464. Photo courtesy Archaeological Receipts Fund (TAP Service).

Plate 4
Attic red-figure pelike, the Pan Painter. Newcastle, Shefton Museum of Greek Art and Archaeology 203, University of Newcastle upon Tyne. Photo courtesy Shefton Museum of Greek Art and Archaeology.

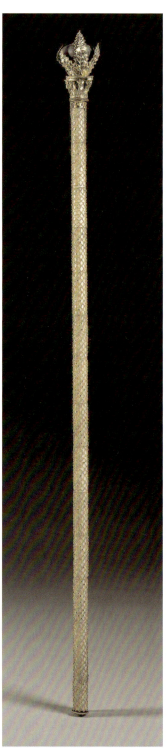

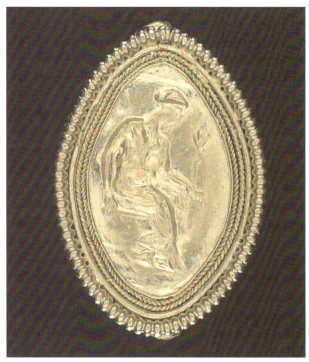

Plate 5 (opposite, top left)
Gold necklace, from Taras. London, British Museum 1952. © Copyright the Trustees of The British Museum Museum 1952.

Plate 6 (opposite, right)
Gold scepter, from Taras. London, British Museum 2090. © Copyright the Trustees of The British Museum.

Plate 7 (opposite, bottom left)
Gold ring, from Taras. London, British Museum 215. © Copyright the Trustees of The British Museum.

Plate 8 (above)
Attic white-ground cup, the Villa Giulia Painter. New York, Metropolitan Museum of Art, The Bothmer Purchase Fund, Fletcher Fund, and Rogers Fund, 1979 (1979.11.15). Photograph, all rights reserved. The Metropolitan Museum of Art.

Plate 9
Attic black-figure band cup. Private Collection.

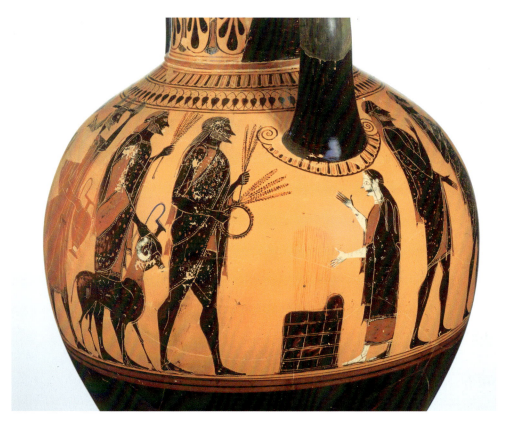

Plate 11
Attic black-figure amphora, the Affector. Munich, Staatliche Antikensammlungen und Glyptothek
1441. Photo: Staatliche Antikensammlungen und Glyptothek München, by Renate Kühling.

Plate 10
Attic black-figure band cup. London, British Museum 1906.12-15.1. © Copyright the Trustees of The British Museum.

Plate 12
Attic black-figure amphora. Berlin, Staaliche Museen Antikensammlung 1686. Photo: Bildarchiv Preussischer Kulturbesitz/Art Resource, NY.

Plate 13
Marble relief. Berlin, Staatliche Museen, Antikensammlung K 104. Photo: Bildarchiv Preussischer Kulturbesitz/Art Resource, NY.

Plate 14 (left)
Limestone statue, from Arsos, Cyprus. Larnaca Museum 663. Photo: J. B. Connelly.

Plate 15 (right)
Limestone statue, from Arsos, Cyprus. Larnaca Museum 663. Photo: J. B. Connelly.

Plate 16 (left)
Marble statue of Nikeso, from Priene. Berlin, Staatliche Museen Antikensammlung SK 1928. Photo: Bildarchiv Preussischer Kulturbesitz/Art Resource, NY.

Plate 17 (right)
Marble statue of the priestess Eirana, sanctuary of Artemis Ortheia at Messene. Messene Museum no. 242. Photo: J. B. Connelly.

Plate 18 (left)
Marble statue of the priestess Claudia Siteris, sanctuary of Artemis Ortheia at Messene. Messene Museum no. 243. Photo: J. B. Connelly.

Plate 19 (right)
Marble statue of girl, sanctuary of Artemis Ortheia at Messene. Messene Museum no. 244. Photo: J. B. Connelly.

Plate 20 (above, left)
Marble grave stele of the priestess Polystrate. Athens, Kerameikos Museum I 430. Photo: J. B. Connelly.

Plate 21 (above, right)
Marble grave stele of priestess, from Rhamnous. Athens, National Archaeological Museum 2309. Photo: J. B. Connelly.

Plate 22 (opposite, top)
Marble grave stele of priestess Chairestrate. Piraeus Museum 3627. Photo: J. B. Connelly.

Plate 23 (opposite, bottom)
Marble grave stele of Nikomache. Piraeus Museum 217. Photo: J. B. Connelly.

Plate 24 (left)
Marble funerary column of Mneso. Athens, Epigraphical Museum 11144. Photo: J. B. Connelly.

Plate 25 (right)
Marble funerary altar of Theomnasta. Thebes Museum. Photo: J. B. Connelly.

Plate 26
Limestone relief, Taras. Princeton, The Art Museum 1983-34. Museum Purchase, gift of the Willard
T. C. Johnson Foundation, Inc., and an anonymous donor.

Plate 27
Marble funerary relief of Menophila, from Sardis. Istanbul, Archaeological Museum I 4033. Photo:
Turhan Birgili.

Portrait of a Priestess

CHAPTER 1

Introduction
Time, Space, Source Material, and Methods

At the end of the second century B.C., Athenian worshippers set out in procession, marching from Athens to the sanctuary of Apollo at Delphi to celebrate the Pythais festival. The pageant was held in a grand manner "worthy of the god and his particular excellence." One individual stood out among the participants: Chrysis, priestess of Athena Polias. For her role in making the occasion one that befitted both Athens and Delphi, the people of Delphi bestowed upon Chrysis the crown of Apollo. The city also voted to grant her, as well as all her descendants, an impressive series of rights and privileges: status as a special representative of Athens to Delphi (*proxenos*), the right to consult the oracle, priority of trial, inviolability (*asylia*), freedom from taxes, a front seat at all competitions held by the city, the right to own land and houses, and all other honors customary for *proxenoi* and benefactors of the city.[1]

Back in Athens, Chrysis's cousins, Dionysios, Niketes, and Philylla, set up a statue of their famous relative on the Acropolis. They themselves were prominent Athenians from a family distinguished by its numerous cult officials. Chrysis had a great-great-grandfather who was a sacred supervisor (*epimeletes*) of the Eleusinian Mysteries and a grandfather who was a priest of Asklepios.[2] The decree set up by the people of Delphi and the statue base from the Athenian Acropolis provide a tantalizing glimpse into the life of an exceptional woman. While scores of inscriptions survive to honor men in this way, Chrysis stands out as one of the few women who received special privileges by decree.[3] Her public record brought substantial rights for her and all her descendants. She further enjoyed the honor of having her statue set up on the Athenian Acropolis, ensuring that she would be remembered always in her priestly status.

Despite wide contemporary interest in the role of women in world religions, the story of the Greek priestess remains elusive. Scattered references, fragmentary records, and ambiguous representations confound attempts to form a coherent view of women who held sacred offices in ancient Greece. Yet the scope of surviving evidence is vast and takes us through every stage on the path through priesthood. It informs us about eligibility and acquisition of office, costume and attributes, representations, responsibilities, ritual actions, compensation for service, authority and privileges, and the commemoration of priestesses at death. Only by gathering far-flung evidence from the epigraphic, literary, and archaeological records can we recognize larger patterns that reveal the realities of the women who held office. This evidence provides firm, securely dated documentation from which we can bring to life the vibrant story of the Greek priestess.

This narrative is particularly important because religious office presented the one arena in which Greek women assumed roles equal and comparable to those of men. Central to this phenomenon is the fact that the Greek pantheon includes both gods and goddesses and that, with some notable exceptions, the cults of male divinities were overseen by male officials and those of female divinities by female officials.[4] The demand for close identification between divinity and cult attendant made for a class of female sacred servants directly comparable to that of men overseeing the cults of gods. Indeed, it was this demand that eventually led to a central argument over the Christian priesthood, exclusively granted to male priests in the image of a male god. As Simon Price has stressed, the equality of men and women as priests and priestesses in ancient Greece was nothing short of remarkable.[5] In a world in which only men could hold civic office and enjoy full political rights, it would have been easy enough for cities to organize their priesthoods on the model of magistracies. But the power of gender in the analogy between sacred servant and deity was so strong that it warranted a category of female cult agents who functioned virtually as public-office holders. Price has challenged us to consider the deeper question of why the Greeks so emphasized both genders for their gods.[6] We will take up this line of inquiry in chapter 2.

Evidence for priestesses can be found in nearly all categories of Greek texts, from Linear B tablets to epic and lyric poetry, histories, tragedies, comedies, political speeches, legal documents, public decrees, and antiquarian commentaries.[7] Inscribed dedications attest to the generosity of priestesses in making benefactions to cities and sanctuaries, their pride in setting up images of themselves, and their authority in upholding sanctuary laws. Inscriptions also provide evidence that these women were publicly honored with gold crowns, portrait statues, and reserved theater seats. Priestesses are represented in nearly every category of visual culture, including architectural sculpture, votive statues and reliefs, funerary monuments, vases, painted shields, wooden plaques, and bronze and ivory implements. In the face of this abundant evidence it is hard to understand how the prominent role of the Greek priestess has, until recently, been ignored by modern commentators or, worse yet, denied.[8]

Never before has the archaeological evidence for priestesses been systematically examined within the broader context of what is known from the epigraphic and literary spheres. From the late nineteenth century, inscriptions have been the primary source for our understanding of ancient priesthoods.[9] In her dissertation of 1983, Judy Ann Turner brought together wide-ranging epigraphic evidence for feminine priesthoods, focusing largely on the acquisition of sacred offices.[10] In 1987, Brunilde Ridgway pioneered the study of material evidence for women in ancient Greece, including images of female cult agents.[11] Alexander Mantis's comprehensive monograph on the iconography of priesthood, male and female alike, followed in 1990.[12] This groundbreaking work brought together a wide corpus of images, many of which had been unknown. In the years that have followed, additional monuments representing priestesses have been published, and broader studies on women and religion have made some limited use of visual material.[13] In her important study of priesthoods, dedications, and euergetism, Uta Kron has called for the viewing of archaeological and epigraphic data together with and in contrast to what we know from literary sources.[14]

A central contribution of *Portrait of a Priestess* is the recognition of the authority of the archaeological record and its integration into our broader understanding of the women who served Greek cults. In this, I follow Anthony Snodgrass, Gloria Ferrari, Christiane Sourvinou-Inwood, and others who have emphasized the independent existence of the archaeological record from the textual tradition that has, in so many ways, subordinated it.[15] As the long-neglected visual material has its own history, its own "language," motivations, and influences, we should not expect it to illustrate facts recorded in texts. Instead, it will be seen to reflect aspects of priestly service not preserved elsewhere, significantly broadening our understanding of sacred-office holding. In many cases, it contributes evidence for periods and regions that do not have the benefit of a surviving textual heritage. Beyond this, archaeological and epigraphic evidence sometimes can be seen to contradict the picture given in literary sources. It thus provides an important correction to the distorting effects of the voice, intent, and context of the author, as well as the accidents of survival and the benefits of privilege that have focused our attention on only a fraction of the original corpus of texts.

Two important developments in scholarly thinking have made conditions ripe for a seasoned and comprehensive review of the evidence for Greek priestesses. One is a reassessment of the alleged seclusion of women in classical Athens and the implications of this for our understanding of their public roles. The other is a new questioning of the validity of the category of regulations called "sacred laws," long viewed as distinct and separate from the larger body of legislation within the Greek polis. This opens the way for understanding female cult agents as public-office holders with a much broader civic engagement than was previously recognized. These two paradigm shifts make for a fresh and forward-looking environment in which we can evaluate the evidence, one that allows for a new understanding of the ancient realities of priestly women.

First, let us track developments on the question of the "invisibility" of women. Over the past thirty years, it has become a broadly accepted commonplace that Athenian women held wholly second-class status as silent and submissive figures restricted to the confines of the household where they obediently tended to domestic chores and child rearing.[16] This has largely been based on the reading of certain well-known and privileged texts, including those from Xenophon, Plato, and Thucydides, and from certain images of women portrayed in Greek drama.[17] The consensus posture of this view has, to a certain extent, been shaped by the project of feminism and its work in recovering the history of gender oppression.

While there have been some voices of dissent from early on, the chorus of opponents to this oversimplified position has grown steadily over the years, gathering strength from the economic, political, and social/historical arenas.[18] Already in the 1980s, David Cohen stressed the importance of distinguishing between "separation" and "seclusion," and pointed out serious contradictions between cultural ideals and real-life social practices.[19] Edward Harris has now elucidated the active role of women in the economic sphere, where they exercised informal, but highly effective, methods for influencing decisions about money.[20] Lin Foxall has shown that women had considerable control over property within their households, particularly those women who brought large dowries, and took initiatives in economic matters in which they held a vested interest.[21] Examining archaeological remains from domestic contexts, Lisa Nevett and Marilyn Goldberg have offered a new understanding of gendered space and the regulation of social relations within the Greek household.[22] Josine Blok has shown that women's public speech in Athens had everything to do with where they were and when they were there.[23]

Jeffrey Henderson and Christiane Sourvinou-Inwood have made compelling cases for the presence of women at dramatic performances in Greek theaters, despite a modern reluctance to accept it.[24] Early on in the debate, Cynthia Patterson considered the possibility of citizen identity for women described as *hai Attikai*.[25] Josine Blok has now argued on linguistic grounds that Athenian women of citizen families were, in fact, recognized as citizens. Importantly, she has shown that their leadership roles in matters of cult were, in effect, political offices that directly engaged women with the broader enterprise of *politeia*.[26]

Even those who persist in maintaining an "invisibility" for Athenian women recognize that cult worship offered the single stage on which women could enjoy some measure of prominence. But this religious stage has too often been dismissed as secondary and peripheral to the political and economic nucleus of the polis. This attitude is clearly a product of our own contemporary cultural biases and has nothing to do with the realities of the ancient city. By marginalizing the importance of sacred-office holding, interpreters persist in presenting a pessimistic picture of the possibilities for Athenian women, subjected to utterly passive roles in an entirely secondary status.

This is why new developments in our understanding of so-called sacred laws are so important. Each sanctuary had its own rules and regulations to direct the behavior of worshippers and the functioning of cult. Often, these were inscribed on stone *stelai* set up for all to see. Such regulations were first designated as "sacred laws" more than a hundred years ago; the validity of grouping them together as a fixed category of thought has now come under review.[27] Robert Parker has demonstrated that these sacred laws differ in no way from other laws and decrees issued by ancient communities. Most meetings of the citizen Assembly at Athens had split agendas that first took up decisions on religious matters, followed by discussion of secular issues. Religious matters took up a large proportion of the Assembly's time, and the city spent great sums of money in financing cult affairs.[28] Parker clarifies for us that sacred laws are simply laws of the state concerned with religious action, no different except in subject matter from any other laws.[29]

The implications of Parker's insights are profound, particularly for our understanding of female officeholders. If the Greeks did not distinguish between "church" and "state," then the long-standing binary model of "sacred" and "secular" is an erroneous construct that has outlived its usefulness.[30] If things religious were not considered separate from things secular, then the positions of leadership held by priestly women were primary, not peripheral, to the centers of power and influence.

Just as the sacred/secular binary model is under review, so the construct of public/private will be revisited at several points in this study.[31] To be sure, we can recognize cases in which the public/private model provides a valid and useful lens through which the Greek experience can be considered. Still, there are ways of understanding a more complex reality than this construct allows. When it comes to ancient women, it may be not only impossible but also inappropriate to make hard-and-fast distinctions between public and private life.[32] Josine Blok has shown that public space and private space are relative concepts whose meanings are determined by use and, therefore, by time.[33] She tracks the mobility of Athenian women through their city and on their own schedules, in which time dictates their experience of public space. Lin Foxall has long questioned the privileging of power in the public sphere over that of the "less important" power of the domestic realm. She has shown that "use" is just as important as "possession" when it comes to household property. By shifting away from the public/private binary construct and the "subordination theory" way of managing these terms, we can appreciate the more complex realities that characterized ancient life.

A central theme of this book is directly related to the public/private quandary. This is the correlation between domestic ritual, in the care of the house, and public ritual, in the care of the temple. The agency of the women who circulated between these two spaces is paramount in this. Some interpreters view women's work in the ritual sphere as a mere "rehearsal" for the conventionally sanctioned female role of subservience within the Greek household.[34] But a case can be made that things actually worked the other way around. Since the temple was effectively the "house" of the cult statue, it needed to be cared for just like a private domestic space.[35] Much of this care involved the traditional household work of ancient women: cleaning, decorating, weaving, and cooking. Social behavior experienced at home was thus codified in public ritual performed within the formal setting of the sanctuary.[36] This process of codification will be examined in chapter 2.

Reconstructing the life experience of ancient priestesses from fragmentary texts and images is a daunting task. The job is made more difficult because, by its very nature, Greek priesthood does not lend itself to generalization. Our clearly defined modern Western view of Christian priesthood denies the plurality inherent in the ancient religious offices required by the existence of so many gods. Unlike what exists for our modern institutions, Greek religion had no sacred book that set down a universal system of beliefs and laws; no single, unified church with central authority; and no clergy to instruct in beliefs. Instead, religion was embedded in every aspect of life and was intensely local, highly dependent on regional tradition.[37] The Greeks did not even have a separate word for religion, since there was no area of life that lacked a religious aspect.[38] We are faced with what Angelos Chaniotis has called a "bewildering plurality" of terms given in the sources, not just for the cult associations that he has focused upon, but for virtually all aspects of Greek worship.[39]

I am deliberately adopting a broad and encompassing view to embrace this "bewildering plurality" and the full range of possibilities for women's agency that it reflects. I shall include examples of girls, maidens, and women who are not, strictly speaking, priestesses, but whose engagement in cult activity sheds light on the broader system within which priestesses functioned. The Greek priestess is best understood within the context of this system, which allows for more flexibility in the identification of sacred women than modern interpreters may like. I include cult agents of varying ages and ranks, not because I shy away from clearly defining my subject, but because I do not find the binary model priestess/nonpriestess a useful one in understanding the contradictions and complexities of the lived experience of Greek women.[40] Priesthood was, in most cases, a temporary status and women could move in and out of a number of priesthoods over the course of a lifetime. Methodologies drawn from anthropology and social archaeology are especially helpful here, as they focus on the ways in which life cycle, age, and gender structure social identities.[41] Much more will be said about the methodological framework of this study at the end of this chapter. But for now, let it be said that I will combine a variety of approaches and examine the widest range of material in order to gain the fullest understanding of the lived experience of Greek priestesses.

Chronological and Geographical Scope

I shall also adopt a broadly inclusive chronological scope with an aim to present the best-preserved evidence from the widest range of sources. This will include documentation for priesthoods from the Archaic through the Hellenistic periods and even into Roman Imperial times when I see useful points for comparison. I understand and accept the risks of this approach and the methodological difficulties that it invites. The long chronological view is by no means meant to create the impression of an unbroken continuity in practice from the Archaic through the Roman period. Quite the contrary, it illustrates that real change happened, often carefully designed as a return to tradition. We have benefited from a number of careful studies with well-defined chronological and regional limits.[42] But the long and broad view enables us to see what is not so apparent in narrowly focused studies. Rarely has the evidence from classical Athens been viewed within the larger context of later material from the wider Hellenized world. Never has the sculptural type of the standing draped female figure been viewed diachronically from its early appearance, for example, on the Archaic Athenian Acropolis through the later examples in Hellenistic and Roman sanctuaries of Asia Minor. This long view allows us to call into question whether the Archaic and classical periods, in fact, represent the golden age of ancient Greek religion. The abundance of cults, and opportunities to serve, that proliferated during the Hellenistic period may suggest otherwise. The profound changes in the organization of private worship, including the wide diffusion of voluntary cult associations, attest to a shift in focus to individuality and personal piety that is unattested in earlier periods.[43]

Fundamentally, this is a book about Greek cities. But I shall adopt a broad scope on the geographical front, again, allowing for useful points of comparison. The intention is to include the highest-ranking evidence from South Italy to Asia Minor, right across the Mediterranean basin. Again, the selection of evidence is not meant to argue for continuity. Rather, it is to balance a view that is inescapably Athenocentric in character, owing to the rich but disproportionately large body of material that survives from classical Athens. This is particularly true for visual culture, for which Athens has contributed such a significant corpus of images of women engaged in cult activity. It is vitally important to consider representations from the so-called periphery of the Greek world in order to balance this view. Limestone statues of key-bearing priestesses from Hellenistic Cyprus, jewelry from what might be the grave of a priestess at Taras in South Italy, and the large corpus of funerary reliefs for priestesses of Hellenistic Asia Minor give a more accurate picture of feminine priesthood across the Greek world. This material serves as a necessary control in evaluating evidence from "center" and "periphery" and checks a tendency to generalize from the more accessible examples.

The uneven nature of the evidence makes for a situation in which we know a great deal about certain priesthoods and very little about others. In chapter 3, we will take an in-depth look at a few priesthoods of prominence for which the surviving source material is great: Athena Polias at Athens, Demeter and Kore at Eleusis, Hera at Argos, and the Pythia at Delphi. In the chapters that follow, we will take a broader view, tracking the experience of priestesses from across the Greek world. In this, we will look at the collective evidence for priestly costume, votive statuary, ritual duties, perquisites, privileges, authority, and funerary memorials. This dual approach, which combines a focused examination of a few priesthoods from the Greek mainland with a broader overview of disparate material from the greater Mediterranean basin, is meant to make best use of the strengths of the surviving evidence. Specific in-depth investigations of a few detailed cases is methodologically interesting when related to long-term processes. We shall thus combine the microanalysis prescribed by Bourdieu and Adorno with the *longue durée* of Braudel, in an effort to examine the ways in which the general can be found to lie hidden in the particular.[44]

Language and Definitions

A primary obstacle to our understanding of ancient priesthood is the problem of language, particularly that of finding adequate English equivalents for ancient Greek terms. The Greek words that we generally translate as "priest" and "priestess" are based on the root *hieros*, which means "holy." *Hiereus* in the masculine and *hiereia* in the feminine are literally translated "those who are in charge of" or "those who take care of the holy things." These "holy things" can include ritual objects, sacred rites and liturgies, and even religious festivals as a whole. Attested as early as Linear B tablets of the late Bronze Age, the words *hiereia* (written in Linear B as "i-je-re-ja"), and *hiereus* (i-je-re-jo), are found in the *Iliad* and *Odyssey* and in Greek texts right through the Roman period. These words meant different things in different regions for different cults over more than a millennium. In contrast, our word *priest* derives from a contraction of *presbyter*, from the Greek *presbuteros*, meaning "elder." In view of the broad range of responsibilities encompassed by the Greek titles *hiereus* and *hiereia*, the English translations "priest" and "priestess" are wholly inadequate.[45]

Following the practice of women being ordained as ministers in certain Christian churches over the past quarter century, some contemporary writers choose to drop the gender-specific suffix *-ess* when referring to Greek priestesses and call both male and female sacred servants *priests*. This can lead to real confusion.[46] Since priests usually served the cults of male divinities, and priestesses the cults of female divinities, use of the term *priest* for both genders obscures the highly interesting cases in which divinities were served by officials of the opposite sex. I shall maintain the use of the word *priestess*, as it more closely reflects the Greek use of feminine endings and because gender differentiation had real meaning in the ancient society in which these women functioned.

Modern Western theories of priesthood generally define a priest as one who mediates between gods and human beings. But in ancient Greece, all individuals had direct access to their gods. Private people could offer prayers, requests, thanks, and gifts and even perform sacrifice directly to divinities without the intervention of a priest.[47] The historian Herodotos (1.132), writing as an outsider looking at Persian religious practices, found it strange that Persians required the presence of a priest (*magus*) for every sacrifice. This is not to say, however, that sacrifices offered by priests and priestesses may not have had a special status of their own.

Cult hierarchy included a host of religious officials, some of whom had specific duties and others who assumed more general responsibilities. In setting out his "ideal state," Plato (*Laws* 6.75) saw the need for temple attendants (*neokoroi*) as well as priests and priestesses. Aristotle (*Politics* 6.11) distinguished sacred officials who were members of the priesthood from those who were not. The latter group included *hieropoioi*, the "doers of holy things"; *naophylakes*, or "temple guardians"; and *tamiai*, or "stewards of the sacred funds." *Hieropoioi* have been further distinguished from priests and priestesses in terms of their differing relationship to god and state. *Hieropoioi* represented the state in religious affairs, while priests and priestesses acted as servants of the gods.[48]

Titles of cult agents who looked after sanctuaries were often expropriated from household care.[49] This can be observed in our very earliest documentation of sacred offices preserved in the Linear B tablets from Pylos. Here we have thirty women's occupations listed among the workers in service of the goddess.[50] We hear of the wool carders, "pe-ki-ti-ra" (*pektriai*); spinners, "a-ra-ka-te-ja" (*alakateiai*); and weavers, "i-te-ja-a" (*histeiai*). We also have grain grinders or flour makers, "me-re-ti-ri-ja" (*meletriai*), and baking women or grain pourers, "si-to-ko-wo" (*sitokhowoi*). There are also sanctuary sweepers, "ka-ru-ti-je-ja-o," and key bearers, "ka-wa-ri-po-ro." Many of these occupations can be found mirrored in cult titles from the historical period, including key bearers (*kleidouchoi*), worker-weavers (*ergastinai*), and grain grinders (*aletrides*). This is not to argue for continuity in religious practice from the Bronze Age into the Iron Age, but merely to suggest that, over time, much of the activity taking place in and around the sacred precinct was similar to that of household care. Cleaning, weaving, washing, dressing, decorating, grinding, cooking, and feeding can all be seen as the work of women in both house and sanctuary across the ages. It is this powerful analogy between house and temple that provides a critical foundation for female agency in Greek religion.

One of the most characteristic aspects of cult titles is that they reflect the ritual action performed by the attendant. From the sixth century onward, the prefix *hiero-*, or "holy," could be joined to a noun describing a specific function to form a compound title. We find that *hieragogoi* led sacrifice, *hierophoroi* carried sacrifice, *hierarchai* presided over sacred rites, *hieronostoi* searched for holy things, *hierakomoi* took charge of temples, *hieronomoi* were temple managers, *hieroparektes* attended priests, and *hieroskopoi* observed sacrifices and read omens. Some titles reflect specific functions: *hierogrammateis* (sacred scribes), *hierophylakes* (sacred guards), *hierotamiai* (sacred money collectors), and *hieropsaltai* (sacred harpists or singers). Cults could thus create whatever office suited local needs simply by fixing the word *holy* to the action that the agent performed. Emily Kearns has demonstrated how the "language of the sacred" reflects the ways in which Greeks thought about their relations with their gods and gives insight into a two-way process through which words and connotations can direct modes of thought.[51] The sacred language does not merely reflect an objective reality of how things are, but reveals the concepts behind the words and the experience of the society that created and used them.[52]

Religious titles also made use of the *-phoros* ending, combining it with the name of the implement that the sacred servant carried within the ritual. *Kanephoroi* carried the *kana* (baskets), *arrephoroi* brought the *arreta* (secret things), *hydrophoroi* carried the water, and *anthesphoroi* brought flowers. Other titles focus on the action of the servant in tending the cult statue. *Loutrides* washed the statue, while *kosmeteriai* decorated it. The author Harpokration, quoting the fourth-century orator Lykourgos, records that the priestess of Athena Polias at Athens was attended by two helpers called *kosmo* and *trapezophoros*.[53] These words may reflect the roles of the "decorator" and the "table carrier" in performing specific duties within Athena's rites.

The ease with which titles could be invented to suit local needs demonstrates the extraordinary flexibility of Greek religious offices. Some titles are site specific, incorporating the name of the divinity or the location of the shrine: Deliades (handmaidens of Apollo on Delos), Dionysiades (maidens who ran a race for Dionysos at Sparta), Leukippides (virgin priestesses of the daughters of Leukippos at Sparta), and Lykiades (thirty young women who carried water to Lykeion at Sparta).[54] For other cults, groups of girls and women went by names descriptive of the local ritual: *arktoi* (bears of Artemis at Brauron), *melissai* (bees of Demeter at Delphi, Eleusis, and elsewhere), *poloi* (foals of the Leukippides at Sparta).[55]

It has been estimated that there were some two thousand cults operating in Attica during the classical period. With roughly 170 festival days a year in its sacred calendar, Athens hosted a religious hierarchy that was a very crowded arena.[56] The organization and performance of cult activities was a widely shared experience within the citizen body, and a good part of one's life would have been spent preparing for and participating in religious festivals. As cult practice was locally ordained, the number and names used for sacred-service titles across the Greek world were vast and varied. A broad view is, therefore, essential to our full understanding of the dynamics of time and place in shaping ritual practice.

Source Material

Literary Evidence

Literary texts are particularly helpful in reconstructing the religious sentiments behind the practice of service of the gods. This is because they offer longer narratives than do other sources. People served gods because they expected something from them in return. Gods also wanted something from mortals, and usually, this was honor.[57] Women were particularly conscientious in their attention to ritual practice. For priestesses, failure to observe cult requirements represented not just a lapse in duty but a serious crime. It could arouse the wrath of the divinity and cause disorder in the harmonious functioning of the community. It is from Greek literature that we learn much of this in lively accounts of priestly women, their exploits, and experiences.

Homer gives us our first image of a Greek priestess in *Iliad* book 6 (297–310) where the women of Troy go to the priestess Theano to elicit Athena's support against the invading Greeks. Theano opens the doors of Athena's temple, places a beautifully woven robe on the knees of the cult statue, and leads the women in a supplication ritual asking for the death of Diomedes. She then prepares to offer twelve perfect cows in sacrifice to the goddess. Theano's actions can be matched in later historical sources that attest to the role of the priestess as key bearer of the temple, caretaker of the cult statue, leader of prayers, and initiator of sacrifice.

Theano comes to represent the archetype for priestly women. Indeed, her name, based on the very word for "goddess," *thea*, is attested for priestesses in both literary and historical sources. Plutarch tells of a priestess of Demeter and Kore named Theano who famously refused to curse Alkibiades during his trial for profanation of the Mysteries in 415 B.C. (*Alkibiades* 22.5).[58] We hear of a mythical priestess at Argos named Theano, whose dutiful sons Kleobis and Biton pulled her in a cart to Hera's temple on the festival day.[59] The mother of the Spartan king Pausanias was named Theano and served as priestess of Athena Chalkioikos (Polyainos 8.51). During the Roman period, we hear of a little girl named Theano who served in the special cult role of *arrephoros* at Athens.[60] Tradition may have led her family to presume that she would hold religious office one day and the girl may have been named with this in mind.[61]

Greek tragedy presents compelling images of sacred women, but it is not always easy to tell if they reflect the realities of historical priesthood.[62] Aeschylus wrote a tragedy titled *Hiereiai* (*The Priestesses*), for which only a few fragments survive.[63] One can only wonder what an impact this production may have had on the visual arts, particularly on costuming and stage properties used to communicate priestly status. Aeschylus opens his *Eumenides* (lines 1–33) with the Pythia speaking about her role as priestess of Apollo's temple. Dramatic characterizations owe much to the special interests of individual authors. Euripides shows a lively interest in priesthood and focuses on the sacral aspects of his characters Iphigeneia (*Iphigeneia at Tauris*), Kassandra (*The Trojan Women*), and Theonoe (*Helen*).[64] The fragments of Euripides' *Captive Melanippe* will be considered at the opening of chapter 6. In them, he makes clear that it is women who hold the central role in things religious. Euripides is preoccupied with etiological and topographical issues and is a valuable resource for our understanding of foundation myths and the rituals that commemorated them.[65]

Perhaps the most celebrated female character in all of Greek literature is Aristophanes' Lysistrata. Fifty years ago, David Lewis thoughtfully suggested that her character was drawn from the model of a historical priestess named Lysimache.[66] This Lysimache served as priestess of Athena Polias on the Athenian Acropolis for sixty-four years, spanning the late fifth and early fourth centuries. The association of the historical Lysimache with the heroine of Aristophanes' comedy has significant implications for our understanding of name recognition for Greek priestesses, a topic that will be examined in chapter 3. Our corpus of priestly personalities in Greek comedy has recently been augmented by the discovery of a new papyrus preserving the opening scene of Menander's *Leukadia*.[67] This preserves a dialogue between a girl coming to fetch water and the *zakoros* who looks after the temple of Apollo on Cape Leukas.[68]

In historical sources, priestly women are present but not described in great detail. Herodotos's *Histories* is particularly valuable as it includes some sixty-two references to priestesses, roughly half of which concern the Pythia at Delphi.[69] Since Herodotos's accounts were gathered largely from oral sources and assembled from all across the Mediterranean world, some scholars have seen them as relatively free from the prejudices of any one particular state or literary convention.[70] For this reason, Herodotos has been viewed as a particularly valuable source for local traditions.

Herodotos's historical successors are less obliging. Thucydides never mentions priestesses except when he dates the beginning of the Peloponnesian War (Thucydides 2.2.1) to the forty-eighth year of the priesthood of Chrysis at Argos. In this, he employs the historical chronology structured by Hellanikos upon the consecutive priesthoods of Hera at Argos.[71] Plato is more forthcoming and discusses priests and priestesses in the functioning of his "ideal state" (*Laws* 6.759a–c). The fourth-century orator Lykourgos had special insight into priestly offices, having served as priest of Poseidon-Erechtheus at Athens. He was a member of the Eteoboutad clan that controlled the hereditary priesthoods of Poseidon-Erechtheus and Athena Polias. Surely, Lykourgos relied on his firsthand experience when writing his treatise *On the Priestesses* (frag. B 5). Unfortunately, this speech does not survive and is mentioned only in the most general way by antiquarian critics. Both Demosthenes and Plutarch, who served as priest of Apollo at Delphi for some thirty years, provide valuable anecdotal references to priestesses. Among our most informative sources is the second-century-A.D. traveler Pausanias, who gives us a wealth of information on the activities of priestesses at sanctuaries throughout Greece. From him we learn a great deal about local rituals and the role that priestly women played in them.

Epigraphic Evidence

Inscriptions are our richest source of information on ancient priesthoods, providing us with narrowly focused views into the realities of cult organization. How could we have imagined a world in which priesthoods were bought and sold like commodities, bid for at auction, and bequeathed to children? Certainly not from the sketches of Homer's Theano, Aeschylus's Pythia, or Euripides' Iphigeneia at Tauris. Primed with the expectation of seeing women in wholly subordinate positions, readers may be surprised to find inscriptions attesting to the financial compensation of women for their service, the erection of portrait statues in their honor, and their agency in enforcing sanctuary laws. We may never have suspected the broad network of women who passed jealously guarded priesthoods through their family lines generation upon generation, or the benefactions that they proudly lavished on the sanctuaries they served.

Epigraphic evidence thus gives insight into realities unattested in literary texts and focuses on the micrology of the lived experience. It reminds us of the dangers of privileging texts written largely by, for, and about men living in and around Athens during just a few hundred years' time. Above all, inscriptions provide us with the names of historical women who actually held office, allowing us to pursue important prosopographical work. This enables us to reconstruct the roles of inheritance, pedigree, and preparation in the securing and transferring of priesthoods through family lines.

Much work remains to be done in the collection of epigraphic documentation for priestesses across the Greek world. The evidence is uneven, dependent on accidents of survival and the varying epigraphic habits of local institutions. We have relied heavily on a few general collections, as well as on some narrowly focused studies of individual inscriptions.[72] It is not the ambition of this book to provide a corpus of all epigraphic evidence for feminine priesthoods, but rather to present a sampling that helps us make the widest range of points.

Although the late Bronze Age is well outside the parameters of this study, it should be noted that the first attestation of a Greek priestess is found in Linear B texts dating back to the fourteenth century B.C. A tablet from the Mycenaean palace at Pylos preserves for us the name of E-ri-ta, who served as priestess at the local sanctuary. Although the meaning of the text is not entirely clear, it seems that E-ri-ta was a woman in charge of considerable lands and property, that she had legal standing within her community, and that she was assisted in her work by sacred servants.[73] We are certainly not arguing for continuity here, but it must be said that what little we know of E-ri-ta does seem to prefigure the agency of priestesses in the historical period.

Archaeological Evidence

The material culture gathered in this study comes from different sources, technologies, and traditions, reflecting a variety of intentions and serving very different functions. Each category of object has its own distinct language that must be read independently from other source material. Reading these objects and images, internally as a group and externally with regard to local myth, cult, and ritual, enables us to approach an "archaeology of cult" within the broader context of Greek cultural history.[74] Ivory implements, buried deep in foundation deposits at Ephesos, were the very tools used by cult agents in their rituals. In a sense, these instruments can be understood to be extensions of the sacred servants themselves. For this reason, their ornamentation often mirrors the image of the cult attendant, incorporating her face, hand, or whole body into the decorative program (see figs. 5.1, 5.3). The choice of ivory may reflect a communality with sacred servant as well. As we shall see in chapter 5, ivory is a material long associated with the female gender, owing to the quality of its white color and smooth texture. Portrait statues of priestesses erected before and within temples functioned quite differently (see figs. 5.12–14, 5.22–24, 5.26–29; pls. 16–18). These were highly visible, permanent testaments to the prestige of local priestesses across generations of service. The statues became part of the sacred landscape, witnesses to the intimacy of goddess and priestess who shared the ritual space. Funerary markers similarly ensured that priestesses would be remembered always for their agency and give us rare, specific records of the "occupation" that these women undertook in life (see figs. 8.1–2, 8.4–23; pls. 20–25). While inscribed names identify historical women on votive and funerary sculptures, images on cult utensils and in vase painting may be better placed in a mythical past where they depict characters whose actions inspired the rituals observed in historical times.

Iconographic studies of gods and goddesses or heroes and heroines generally rely on attributes, costumes, poses, and narrative contexts to establish identity. But how are we to distinguish images of priestesses from among the many representations of women who moved in and out of priestly status over the course of a lifetime? Everyday life in Greece was full of ritual. Nuptial preparations, funerals, the tending of a loved one's grave, and the departure of a soldier for war—all engaged women in ritual acts that duplicated those performed by sacred officials in public sanctuary settings. As practitioners of household worship and the host of rituals occasioned by domestic life, Greek women assumed the role of "priestess" within their own families. They trained their daughters to perform these rites along with other household duties expected of a good wife and mother. This is why it is so difficult to be certain about identifications of priestly women in the visual repertory, and why we must live with more ambiguity than we may like.

One attribute serves as the preeminent iconographic signifier of priestly status: the temple key. From the late Archaic period on, sculpture and vase paintings show women carrying large, rodlike keys, signifying the function of the *kleidouchos* in communicating priestly status.[75] So powerful is this attribute that, on its own, it can confirm sacral identity for women who appear otherwise unremarkable. The placing of a key in the hand of a young woman, shown on a skyphos in London, endows the generic maiden with priestly status (fig 1.1).[76] It is because of the image of a young man on the reverse side of the vase that the girl has been identified as Iphigeneia, shown in tandem with her brother Orestes in her role as priestess of Artemis at Tauris.

A full repertory of ritual paraphernalia can be manipulated in vase painting to communicate cult activity: libation bowls, wine jugs, baskets, offering trays, lustral branches, and ribbons. Each of these figural elements, what Claude Bérard has called "minimal syntagmata,"

Fig. 1.1
Apulian skyphos, the Sydney Painter. London, British Museum F 127. Photo © Copyright the Trustees of The British Museum.

and Gloria Ferrari has termed "sign-components," can be combined to yield complex configurations through which signification takes place.[77] The ways in which these signs are juxtaposed, combined, and even omitted can be read like a language that transmits the essential acts of procession, libation, sacrifice, and feasting. Setting elements, such as columns, temple facades, altars, lustral basins, and incense burners, can be further employed to communicate the context in which the action takes place: city sanctuary, rural shrine, or household.

A woman depicted on a cup in Toledo, Ohio, neatly illustrates the problems of signification that confront us (fig 1.2).[78] She stands before an altar, manipulating a number of ritual implements, including a sacrificial basket and a large oinochoe from which she pours a libation. Behind her, an incense burner further establishes the sanctuary setting. The combination of sign-components would appear to convey her special agency within the cult action. Can we call her a priestess? We have recognized the maiden on the London skyphos (see fig. 1.1) as a priestess, solely through the presence of a temple key and despite the fact that there are no other ritual indicators to support this identification. In contrast, the woman on the Toledo cup is surrounded by a host

Fig. 1.2
Attic red-figure cup, Makron. Toledo Museum of Art 1972.55. Purchased with funds from the Libbey Endowment, Gift of Edmund Drummond Libbey.

of sacred signifiers, yet, for modern interpreters, she is of uncertain status, because of the absence of the key. The challenge of this study lies in setting parameters within which we can read the signifiers and interpret their meanings. We must guard against narrowing the criteria by which we associate attributes with identity, and allow for some flexibility in our readings. Narrative intent, function of the image, and function of the object that carries the image are but a few of the variables at play in the selection of signs for the communication of meaning.[79] Beyond this, it is likely that there are codes that we simply do not recognize. In addition to searching for patterns among schemata known to us, we must be open to signifiers that have gone previously unrecognized.

Methodological Framework

The diversity of the source material requires a diversity of strategies for coming to grips with it. Therefore, I shall draw upon a number of approaches and modes of analysis to examine multiple aspects of the problems presented. I articulated this multimethodological approach in 1993 in a study focused on narrative intent in Attic vase painting.[80] In this I was, and continue to be, influenced by the contributions of Christiane Sourvinou-Inwood, who has called for the use of "many different approaches and methods as tools . . . to diminish the risk of distortion and illuminate as many aspects as possible."[81] Josine Blok has similarly emphasized the importance of a "pluriformity in methodology" for dealing with the subject of ancient Greek women, as this increases the tensions between traditional and new analytical approaches, yielding optimal results.[82]

The breadth of Sourvinou-Inwood's work, which touches on so many issues of concern to this book—gender, life cycles, ritual, tragedy, visual culture, and theory—has provided a welcome road map for navigating the challenges of disparate sources.[83] Our work is inescapably one of reconstruction, the task of shaping a view into what is fundamentally an alien culture. In meeting this challenge, Sourvinou-Inwood has advised independent lines of inquiry for the discreet bodies of evidence—literary, epigraphic, and visual.[84] She urges neutrality in the examination process in order to avoid prejudices caused by the contamination of one line of inquiry by another. Sourvinou-Inwood's second major methodological guideline is one that encourages the establishment of parameters within which the source material is considered, eliminating, as much as is possible, biases that result from viewing ancient evidence through culturally determined filters.[85] Of course, the process of filtering is complex, and one can never fully escape the perspectives embedded in one's own experience. Nonetheless, the effort to remove filters repays itself and makes us conscious of the forces that shape our questions and, thus, our answers. Before we continue, let us confront some of the most common culturally determined biases that bedevil our view of the Greek priestess and prevent us from seeing her through "ancient eyes."

Romanizing and Christianizing Assumptions

One of the most frustrating aspects of the study of religion is that those closely bound by a shared system of beliefs rarely have cause to write about them in a comprehensive manner. It is from outsiders looking in, as with missionaries and ethnographers, that we get detailed commentaries on religious practice.[86] For Greek religion, with its highly localized character, the situation is even more impenetrable. In the absence of sources that could put the evidence within a broader context, it is easy to rely on that which is familiar and allow Romanizing and Christianizing assumptions to slip in.[87] Our understanding of feminine priesthoods is especially undermined, as, until relatively recently, most religious institutions excluded the possibility of women priests altogether. The first critical step in approaching ancient offices is the elimination of all comparisons with the priests and nuns of the Christian tradition.

Contrary to Christianizing presuppositions, very few priesthoods were held for life. Most cults required women to serve a much shorter period, a year or even a single festival cycle.

Priesthoods with a prerequisite of virginity were held for a short time, after which maidens were free to marry. Priesthoods requiring perpetual celibacy were rare and usually held by older women, who had raised their families, been widowed, and finished with their days of sexual activity. Lifelong priesthoods were typically held by married women leading "normal" lives, complete with husband and children. Greek religious offices were enormously practical, enabling women to serve at each stage in life without sacrificing the full experience of marriage and motherhood.

Unlike the lifelong celibacy practiced by clergy in Roman Catholicism and some other contemporary religions, virginity was viewed as a temporary state for ancient Greek priestesses. Indeed, the Greeks defined virgin (*parthenos*) status quite differently from how we do today. For them, it was the condition of a maiden who had passed through puberty but was not yet married. Emphasis was not focused on a state of intactness, which the modern definition requires.[88] Nonetheless, the example of the Vestal Virgins of Rome has sometimes distorted our view. The Vestals were appointed as girls aged six to ten years old who were committed to virginity, in our modern sense of intactness, for a period of thirty years.[89] At the end of their tenure, they were free to marry, though most elected to stay on as virgins, at this point having forgone most of their child-bearing years. The potency of their state of chastity, the excessive suspicion of any compromise visited upon their purity, and the appalling gravity of punishment by live burial for Vestals who transgressed, make for an extreme case that stands outside the norms of anything known in the Greek world.[90]

A second area of belief that has distorted our view is the anomalous position of the virgin in early Christianity. She was set apart from the rest of society, described as a "sacred vessel dedicated to the Lord," a "human votive offering," and "a royal palace hall."[91] The veneration of the virgin, influenced by Marian devotion, has no parallel whatsoever in the Greek experience, where virginity represented neither a state of perfection nor a guarantee of salvation.[92] On the contrary, Greeks regarded *parthenos* status as a necessary stage through which girls had to pass on their way to full integration into society as wives and mothers. Unlike the Christian virgin, who was subject to "no man but God alone," the Greek virgin priestess remained very much under the control of her male guardian, or *kyrios*, be it her father, uncle, or some other male relative. Greek women were represented by male guardians in all legal and financial affairs. Indeed, their legal and social identities were utterly embedded in familial connections with male members of the *oikos* to which they belonged.[93] Priesthood provided no avenue to social or financial independence from male kin, and virgin priestesses were neither "set apart" and independent, nor venerated as blessed. Focus on virginity not only obscures the full range of possibilities for feminine sacred service, it takes our eyes off married, widowed, and elderly priestesses who were probably much more widespread within the totality of Greek cult.

A third area of popular preoccupation merits only the briefest mention. This is the "myth" of Greek priestesses in the service of sacred prostitution, for which there is no firm evidence.[94] Three cities for which this practice is often alleged—Corinth, Ephesos, and Paphos—were all port towns to which Christianity, and Saint Paul, came very early on.[95] Port cities and their transient populations have characteristic social dynamics in which sailors and prostitutes often figure. But to link what was fundamentally a social and urban phenomenon with local cult practice is a stretch, and most likely the product of negative Christian attitudes toward traditional religious establishments.

"Presentist" Assumptions

The Greek priestess presents something of a dilemma, one that is often misunderstood by those who look to ancient models to find support for contemporary views. Any leap from Greek female priesthood to contemporary claims regarding ancient matriarchy or "Goddess cult" is off the mark and not founded upon hard evidence.[96] Other misconceptions are more subtle and, understandably, emerge from the often-contradictory evidence. It is profoundly true that priesthood offered women a unique opportunity for public life, one in which they played leadership roles equal to those of their male counterparts. But this opportunity is too often described as a vehicle for a temporary "escape" from the private sphere of the household. "To choose to become a priestess meant a choice for becoming extraordinary," writes one scholar, though how much choice a woman had in the acquisition of priesthood remains doubtful.[97] Her family's social status and financial resources were the determining factors in qualifying her for sacred office. She is more likely to have followed a family tradition of priestly service rather than to have schemed for an escape from household life. The equation of priesthood with independence suffers from the distorting effects of modern feminist hindsight.

This "escape" is regularly and wrongly described as one into a marginal position, that of the religious sphere, a place peripheral to the political and economic center of the polis.[98] One common view holds that the dominant patriarchal ideology manipulated a supposed female aptitude for making contact with things dirty, dark, and polluted by assigning to women ritual presidency over transitional experiences, such as mourning and death. This is, by extension, seen as a justification for women's marginalized position within society at large.[99] To be sure, women did oversee the tending of corpses and funerary rites. But while corpses were certainly considered polluting, women themselves were not at all regarded as dirty. The Greek attitude stands in contrast to how women were viewed within some Jewish and Christian traditions.[100] A second common theme is one in which priesthood is understood as part of a strategy by which women, disenfranchised from the social and political life of their communities, could "establish indirect claims to status and attention."[101] We are told that ritual enabled women to vent their aggression and frustration and to negotiate imbalances inherent in their subordinate positions. Ritual confirmed the constraints on women's lives and at the same time provided a release from them, a place where they could "develop a position of dissidence."[102] The tone of these arguments seems to be colored by late twentieth-century political sensibilities. A third approach sees ritual as a respite for the drudgery of women's daily routine, a reward for good behavior in the home.[103] Religious service has been described as one of the few "forms of entertainment open" to women.[104] While there may be some truth in each of these positions, when taken together they leave us with a rather depressing, and not wholly accurate, view of the prospects for female cult agency. They seem to result from a theory of gender oppression that leaves little room for balancing or mitigating factors. The cumulative force of these arguments strips feminine sacred service of a measure of its dignity and discounts the potency of female agency within the totality of Greek cult and culture.

Religious festivals provided women and girls with important opportunities for public exposure and interaction, including the chance to see and be seen by potential candidates for marriage. A position of power in the organization of festivals allowed for increased opportunities to advance family interests. While festival participation has been viewed as an opportunity to satisfy the "male gaze," and surely there was some of this at work, we can recognize a far more complex reality than this.[105] Advancing family interests benefited women as well as men, and the priestesses presented in this study had a real stake in making the system work. One can, of course, take the position that priestly women were simply manipulated by a system that subjected them to the requirements of a male-dominated society. But one can also consider the force of the material evidence brought forward in this book and recognize a world in which women realized genuine accomplishment through their agency within the system. Greek priesthood was a religious, social, political, and economic business and women were indispensable in making this business a success.

Reading the Language of Images

The reading of images as a symbolic system or "language," based on strategies drawn from semiotic theory, has enjoyed real staying power in the study of the visual culture of ancient Greece. Vase painting is ideally suited to this mode of analysis, as it comprises a large body of homogeneous material through which sign-components can be traced and meaning recovered.[106] Scholars at the University of Lausanne and the Centre Louis Gernet in Paris have defined and developed this system from the early 1980s, working in research groups and drawing heavily upon anthropological theory in the analysis of myth and ritual.[107] I shall employ strategies derived from methods developed by the French school, especially in my reading of images from vase painting in chapters 4 and 6.

Among the most significant developments of this approach is a new understanding of the function of ancient images as *mnemata*, or "memorials," for what once was, that is, the legendary days of the distant past.[108] Ferrari has articulated the difficulty in recognizing just how much ancient images reflect reality and how much they describe a world imagined by the artist. She has questioned the traditional identification of "genre" and "daily life" scenes, demonstrating that many of these, in fact, show a mythical or utopian past.[109] Conditioned as we are today by the documentary role of images in capturing the present, we must adjust our way of seeing in order to view them as windows onto the past. My approach will be one that first looks for meaning within a mythological context before considering alternatives. It must be said, of course, that historical experience greatly influenced the ways in which myths were represented. There is, indeed, a powerful dynamic between myth and *realia* in the image-creation process.

Gender, Agency, and Identity

One goal of this study is to collect and evaluate evidence for ancient women so that they can be reinstated into a long-term cultural history. This effort finds its roots in what some have called "second wave" feminism, of the 1970s and 1980s, when women's studies, gender studies, and other newly established fields sought out long-neglected source material.[110] In classical studies, it was philologists, including Mary Lefkowitz, Maureen Fant, Ross Kraemer, and others, who led the way in compiling comprehensive sourcebooks, and Sarah Pomeroy who first put this material into a historical framework.[111] Certain scholars then pushed the boundaries of traditional classical studies, taking up issues of the family, otherness, sexuality, death, time, the household, ownership, and other topics.[112]

We can recognize something of a divide between classicists and classical archaeologists at this point, as archaeologists did not engage with developments in the study of gender until somewhat later on. To be sure, the task of gathering archaeological evidence is slower, since the material culture is so widespread, both geographically and in terms of publication, requiring searches through excavation reports, databases, museum storerooms, and other locations.[113] But the crux of the problem lies with a basic restructuring of the questions asked of the data, approaching an "archaeology of gender."[114] Most archaeological material was not excavated with these new lines of inquiry in mind and requires restudy, from first field reports on. New World and prehistoric archaeologists have been quicker to adopt innovative theoretical frameworks than have classical archaeologists, and many of the strategies that I employ in this book have been borrowed from the former's groundbreaking work.[115]

Lynn Meskell has laid out a useful framework for the phases of feminist analysis that have been experienced within the discipline of archaeology.[116] Separating contemporary feminism from the suffragist movement (1860–1930), Meskell starts with what she calls "first wave" feminism of the 1960s, which focused on women's political, social, and economic liberation from and equality with men. A second wave developed in its wake during the 1970s, bringing new emphasis on the "inherent" difference between men and women and the special bond between women and Nature.[117] The second wave, which continues to this day, tends to view women as a homogeneous, nomothetic group. Meskell defines a third-wave deconstructive feminism, arising in the 1980s and continuing to the present, that has focused its energies on difference, plurality, ambiguity, embodiment, the transitory, and the disruptive.[118]

The approach of this book is influenced by the third wave, insofar as it concentrates on the complexity of the lived experience and the difference, contradiction, and individuality attested in the ancient record. I shall look at the broad structures of organization within the Greek polis, as well as the micrology of lived relations within this system. Central to this work is consideration of the circulation of power within the bureaucracies of cult, the polis, and the "culture industry," as defined by Adorno.[119] Taking his cue, I shall endeavor to move beyond binary constructs and consider a multiplicity of factors, particularly in approaching the long-standing commonplace of visible/invisible for male/female within Greek culture.[120] Adorno's model of "constellation," as appropriated from Benjamin, serves as a guiding framework within which to understand the relationships of the particular to the universal, of the "actor" to the structure.[121] Following Bourdieu, I shall consider the ways in which priestesses used social, cultural, and symbolic capital to propel their agency and to work as effective players within the micropolitics of the Greek city.[122]

It must be said that we stand at an unsettled moment at which there is little consensus as to which phases of which feminisms will survive poststructuralist transformation and critique. The strategies of traditional feminism have been found to lead in directions that are at odds with theoretical movements that have followed in its wake. Judith Butler's questioning of "woman" as a fixed category, in her *Gender Trouble: Feminism and the Subversion of Identity*, of 1990, signaled a fork in the road. She exposed the ways in which traditional feminist constructs decontextualize individuals from their historical, political, and cultural settings and identities.[123] The intervening fifteen years have witnessed a further fracturing of the project into many different feminisms and the rise of theoretical movements focused on difference, multiplicity, performance, and alterity.[124] Writing from the perspective of contemporary human rights law, Janet Halley has now made a case for "taking a break from feminism."[125]

A related methodological force that has contributed to this study is agency theory, developed in the 1990s and still in its early stages as applied to archaeology.[126] While the definition of what is meant by *social agent* varies and, in many cases, still needs to be worked out, this approach is mapping new directions for our understanding of the ancient past.[127] Irene Winter has demonstrated, for example, that the agent/patient model is far better suited to understanding relationships recorded through the lens of Sumerian grammar than is the subject/object construct.[128]

So, too, in art history, the precept of female agency is directing new lines of inquiry into the culturally manipulated circulation of power and ways in which women have claimed it as artists, viewers, patrons, and shapers of aesthetic sensibilities.[129] It was the possibility of female agency, Norma Broude and Mary Garrard tell us, that inflicted the first casuality in poststructuralist gender studies.[130] The idea of a history "consisting of monolithic patriarchal control over women as passive victims, interrupted by sporadic feminist interventions," has been discredited.[131] It must be said, however, that agency theory is not without troubles of its own. Joan Gero has argued against its adoption into feminist dialogue because of its inherent masculinist bias, which implicitly links social action to male agency. Her "Troubled Travels in Agency and Feminism" may mark one more fork in a road that has now spawned a whole network of side streets and deviations.[132]

How does agency theory effect this study? Let us consider the ways in which language colors our understanding of women engaged in cult activity. The designation *sacred servants* conveys an image of dedicated helpers, caretakers of rites and sanctuaries. When we call these same women *cult agents*, a very different image comes to mind, that of active players within the administration of a bureaucracy, invested with power to act and to effect results. This represents not merely a shift in vocabulary but a change in the thinking behind the words and the ways in which we can understand ancient realities. I will use both these designations, in recognition of the fact that there is agency in service and service in agency. The complexity of the lived experience of ancient women leaves room for both truths.

As Henk Versnel has emphasized, ancient women were not an undifferentiated group.[133] The women considered in this book were individuals of privilege, distinguished from others by their class, economic status, or both. Ancient sources tend to be more abundant for the top strata of society than for elsewhere and, in the case of Greek priesthoods, pedigree, wealth, or both were basic requirements for attaining office.[134] Our priestesses may have had more in common with men of the same social and economic standing than they had with women from the lower ranks. We must bear this in mind as we consider the forces that defined their identities and propelled their agency.

These forces can be found in their social, cultural, and symbolic capital, as defined by Bourdieu.[135] Priestly women had significant resources based on group membership, relationships, and networks of influence and support. Kinship, including *genos*, and family unit, as well as collective groupings, including choruses and ritual age-bands, all equipped Greek women with social capital that served them well. Knowledge of ritual practice, local myths, and ancestral traditions invested priestly women with a cultural capital that made them invaluable to their communities. Finally, the accumulated prestige of priestesses, in leading public processions, overseeing polis festivals, sitting in reserved seats at the theater, and having their images erected in sanctuaries, guaranteed them a symbolic capital that must not be underestimated in a world in which status carried long-lasting power. As Bourdieu recognized, it is economic capital that lies at the root of all these other forms of capital. Within the ancient *habitus*, past experience, tradition, and habit joined together with the forces of pedigree and wealth to create the opportunities and constraints that produced Greek priestesses as we know them.[136]

Time, Locality, and Complexity

This study is about time. First and foremost, it is about time in the distant past to which we have access only through fragments left behind. We collect, identify, and attempt to interpret these fragments by searching for patterns and relationships from which we can extract meaning. But it still remains that the fragments are left from a culture that is, in so many ways, foreign to us. Meskell has emphasized the "fundamental difference between women past and present, and between issues which interest us today and which were operative in the past."[137] This is why it is so important to evaluate the evidence on its own terms and within the parameters of the ancient realities in which it was created. Second, this study is about the specific years during which these women lived, their shared histories within a "common time" specific to a unique period, place, and community. The third time to be considered is the "personal time" through which these individuals passed in their life experiences as girls, maidens, women, and old women. As life cycle profoundly affects the ways in which time is experienced, it is a critical lens through which the evidence should be evaluated.[138]

When we turn to locality and the place-specific nature of myth and ritual, the inherent complexity of Greek religion is revealed. Landscape and local geography direct the myth-creation process through which human beings attempt to explain how things came to be. Scores of ancient Greek communities developed their own myths out of their landscapes, along with their own gods, temples, rituals, festivals, and hierarchies of cult personnel to look after them. This complex system of localized cults, flourishing in the absence of a unified "church," made for a vast network of independent constructs. Locality-based worship bound individuals with their landscapes and shared histories under a tightly knit common identity. Multiply this phenomenon thousands of times over, then spread it across a millennium, and the complexity of the Greek religious system begins to emerge. Complexity theory has much to offer the study of Greek worship, just as it has benefited such diverse fields as literary analysis, the social sciences, and architecture.[139] *Where* things happen is central to *how* things happen, and examination of the complex system of localities within Greek worship allows for a fuller understanding of the ways in which cults functioned.[140]

The Greeks themselves had diverse and sometimes contradictory ways of looking at their own religion.[141] But one thing is clear. Theirs was a system in which myth, cult, ritual, and visual images were utterly interdependent and mutually supportive.[142] The process of representation through words and images cannot be separated from the rituals that gave expression to the underlying systemic structure. Ritual fueled the visibility of Greek women within this system. It sent them on daily paths, traversing their cities, as they made their way up to sanctuaries and out to cemeteries. Requirements for the regular visitation of family tombs and the desire for frequent worship in shrines and temples made for a reality in which scores of women crossed their towns daily. If we add to this mix the highly visible roles of women on festival days, the emerging picture is one of far-ranging mobility for women across the polis landscape.[143] Within this landscape, visual culture supported and reflected the dynamic of myth, cult, and ritual agency. It placed images of priestesses in sanctuaries and cemeteries, on painted vases, sculptured reliefs, sacred implements, and statue bases, populating the polis with the mirrored reflections of the women who served.

———

The title *Portrait of a Priestess* is not meant to convey a belief that there is any single image that can be painted for Greek feminine priesthood. As we have seen, the intensely local character of priesthood over such a broad sweep of geography and chronology defies generalization. Instead, the title reflects my focus on visual culture and my desire to respond to a complaint sometimes directed at archaeological research for having produced a history of "genderless, faceless blobs."[144] It is my intention to restore some measure of humanity to the women behind the evidence and to sketch portraits of actual lives lived. I shall bring forward by name the contributions of more than 150 historical women whose lives have been long neglected, slipped between the cracks of the more regularly chronicled accounts of ancient history, politics, and warfare.

A further inspiration for the title is my wish to underscore the narrative quality of the material presented.[145] The fragments of sculpture, paintings, inscriptions, and texts gathered here preserve stories of lived experience. They are not just distant data onto which we can project the concerns and agendas of our own times, but are robust survivors of authentic ancient narratives to which we should, instead, listen. These fragments preserve a rich cultural history of women and status, money and marriage, property and patronage, household and community, that teaches us about what mattered most in the ancient past. They enable us to see the ways in which age, class, gender, family, social institutions, and economic resources shaped the lives of women and affected the circulation of power among and around them. Let us follow these women along the path of priesthood from birth to death and experience the responsibilities, privileges, and agency that distinguished their lives.

CHAPTER 2

Paths to Priesthood
Preparation, Requirements, and Acquisition

In Aristophanes' *Lysistrata*, the women of Athens, protesting the war against Sparta by barricading themselves on the Acropolis, deliver advice to the men gathered at the sanctuary gates. In supporting their right to express their opinion, the chorus of elderly women cites the rituals in which they participated as girls and maidens. The text and punctuation of this passage are controversial but the message, even within a comic context, is clear. The women have a duty to speak on behalf of the city that nurtured them from childhood to maturity in their progressive ritual roles.

> As soon as I turned seven I was an *arrephoros*,
> then, I was an *aletris*; when I was ten I shed
> my saffron robe for the Foundress, being a bear at the Brauronia;
> And once, when I was a beautiful maiden, I was a *kanephoros*,
> wearing a necklace of dried figs.[1]
>
> *Lysistrata 641–47*

Nowhere in Athenian literature is the path through feminine sacred service so explicitly outlined. We see the arrephoros as a seven-year-old child, who grows on to serve as *aletris*, the grinder of sacred grain. Then, as she approaches puberty, she wears a yellow robe in the rites of Artemis Brauronia, the goddess who especially looked after girls in their transition to maidenhood. After the onset of menarche, the maiden assumes *parthenos* status. Now in the prime of her youth and eligible for marriage, she takes on the leading role of basket bearer in the sacrificial procession. All dressed up in a necklace of figs to evoke her fertile state, the maiden leads the public procession and is shown off to the citizenry. This passage has been the focus of lively scholarly debate concerning the ages at which the girls held office and the divinities that they served. Indeed, the entire passage has been dismissed as a fictitious cycle serving the comic needs of the play.[2]

Yet prosopographical work made possible by surviving inscriptions suggests that Athenian girls of citizen families did have the opportunity to hold various ritual offices throughout the course of a lifetime.[3] Of the forty-nine historical basket-bearers for whom evidence survives, ten are known to have held additional cult roles.[4] Eight of these went on to serve as *ergastinai*, the "workers" who had the honor of weaving Athena's robe. During the early first century B.C., Sosandra of Melite served as basket bearer in the Lenaia and the Dionysia, and as a subpriestess of Artemis on Delos. Her sisters, Apollodora and Theodora, were ergastinai at Athens in 99/98 and served as *kanephoroi* at Delphi two years later.[5] The most illustrious sacred pedigree is that of Philippe II, daughter of Medeios of Piraeus, who began her career on Delos, as a basket bearer at the Delia and subpriestess of Artemis during the early first century B.C. Later, she attained the highest office of priestess of Athena Polias at Athens.[6]

It is likely that the obligations of family life, privileges of social status, and busy religious calendar of the polis directed a young woman with priestly potential through a wide range of sacred service roles. Though Roman in date, Plutarch's comparison of a statesman's progress with the stages of female sacred service rings true for earlier periods, as well. Plutarch writes: "Just as at Rome the Vestal Virgins have a definite time allotted them, first for learning, then for performing the traditional rites, and thirdly and lastly for teaching them, and as at Ephesos they call each one of the servants of Artemis, first a novice, then a priestess and, thirdly, an ex-priestess, so the perfect statesman engages in public affairs, first while still a learner and a neophyte and, finally, as a teacher and initiator."[7]

The female experience of progression through sacred service roles is paralleled in the cycle attested for men at Lindos on Rhodes, where they made their way through increasingly distinguished ranks of priestly office. Starting in the 320s B.C., a *cursus* of service can be identified through which a man might first serve as priest of Poseidon Hippios, or Apollo Pythios, or Dionysos, or as a religious official with the title *hierothetes*. Following this, he could move on to a one-year post as a priest of Athena Lindia, and then, if so fortunate, attain the crowning honor of the priesthood of Helios.[8] In this, as in so many aspects of priesthood, the male and female experience was comparable and we can speak of no gendered differentiation.

Modern accounts of ancient Greek priesthoods have often stressed the lack of training or qualifications for officeholders, their part-time status, and the absence of a vocation to direct them in their service.[9] These preoccupations reflect culturally determined assumptions for an expectation that ancient religious offices should look like those we know today. A more useful lens through which to understand Greek cult service is that of the collective groups that defined communality within the polis, groups based on family, gender, age class, and marital status. Social rituals defined communality as well, through activities such as poetic recitations, sacrificial meals, and symposia.[10] For women, it was the female lyric chorus that played the critical role, educating them in Greek tradition and culture, including ritual and the origins of local myth.

Since religion was embedded in all aspects of life, the teaching and learning of ritual practice cannot be separated from it, and there should be no expectation of an "academy" for priestesses. All girls and maidens of the right status were prepared for cult responsibilities as part of their preparations for life in general. It is not as if priesthood came without qualifications, it is just that these are not the qualifications that we might expect today. It was pedigree, wealth, health, and wholeness that qualified ancient Greek women for priesthood. As for worries over the short tenures of sacred office, it could be said that priesthoods had "part time" status because each stage in life through which an individual passes is, indeed, part time. Greek religion reinforced and reflected the identities of women as they progressed through transitions in the human life cycle. Priesthoods mirrored life changes and so offered short-term posts for maidens, both lifelong and temporary posts for married women, and offices requiring perpetual celibacy only for the oldest of women. Recent work in cultural anthropology is helpful here in mapping the ways in which time and age structure social identities and, conversely, the ways in which gender alters one's experience of time.[11]

This is why we shall begin this chapter with a discussion of the cult roles of girls and maidens who were by no means priestesses but whose experiences, collective and individual, provide an important context for our study. We shall see that there was, indeed, a path to ancient priesthood. This path had its origins generations before the birth of the priestess, when fortune favored her ancestors and placed them in a position to pass on the pedigree, wealth, and birthright that enabled her to serve.

Age Class, Sexual Status, and Sacred Service Roles

Ritual functions were divided according to age groups. Certain jobs were appropriate for little girls, others for maidens, others for married women, and still others for women well beyond their child-bearing years. This tiered workforce reflects a hierarchy based on family life in which children assisted with lesser tasks and assumed greater responsibility with age.[12] Cult service provided an opportunity to learn the religious traditions of the polis and, importantly, the hymns that honored local divinities. Feminine sacred service was deeply intertwined with the morphology of female lyric choruses. Among the oldest of formal institutions in Greece, female choruses are attested as early as the seventh century B.C. Claude Calame has shown how these choruses were central to the education and socialization of women from childhood to maturity.[13] Plato himself (*Laws* 672e) maintained that "choral dancing constituted the entirety of education."[14]

Like choruses, the age-tiered groupings of ritual service reflected the collective character of a family model at the core.[15] Each group had a special relationship to the divinity, based on the goddess's own age, sexual status, and characteristics.[16] An image evocative of female choral and ritual groupings is presented on a libation bowl in Boston. Here, we see women joining hands in a circle dance, set to the music of a female flute player (fig. 2.1; pl. 1).[17] Altar and ribbons, the signifiers of ritual, communicate a sacred context, while the wool basket alludes to female virtue in domesticity. While one woman plays the flutes, seven others dance with arms grasped at the wrists to form a chain. The first two women look forward; the second pair look at one another; all wear their hair swept up and bound by fillets, as they move in unison. At the end of the line, two younger maidens with long, flowing tresses look in the same direction, toward the woman who is at the very back. They seem to be students or novices in the choral dance, looking to the older woman for direction. The shape of the vase itself is one with a ritual function. It is a phiale, from which a liquid offering would be poured, perhaps onto a flaming altar such as that shown painted upon it. Women, like those depicted in this choral scene, may have stepped up to such an altar to pour a libation from such a phiale. Thus form, function, and decoration come together in this object that so effectively embodies female ritual action.

Emphasis on the communality of deity and cult attendant is central to the determination of priestly requirements based on age, gender, and sexual status. Virgin divinities such as Artemis were served by virgin priestesses, while matronly goddesses such as Demeter were served by married women.[18] This arrangement can be seen as part of a larger system in which goddesses were helpers in areas specific to feminine needs, including marriage, fertility, and childbirth. Gods similarly assisted male worshippers in their roles as husbands, fathers, warriors, and seafarers. The polytheistic system provided role models with which individuals could identify at each stage in life. Thus, a female worshipper would feel reinforced in her life cycle as a child, maiden, bride, and mother, while male worshippers were supported by gods in their roles as boys, ephebes, soldiers, sailors, husbands, and fathers.

As individuals passed through life and were confronted by new experiences, they had sympathetic divinities upon whom they could rely for understanding. Mirroring the human experience, the Greek pantheon acknowledged the complexities of what it means to be male and female, allowing for sexual ambiguity and plurality, that is, the "maleness" in the female and "femaleness" in the male. To be female was to be a wild, untamed virgin huntress (Artemis), marriageable virgin and daughter (Persephone), passionate seductress (Aphrodite), wife (Hera), mother (Demeter), as well as wise, "malelike" warrior and craftsman (Athena). To be male was to be a craftsman (Hephaistos), warrior (Ares), seafarer (Poseidon), and father and husband (Zeus) as well as to be the "feminine" poet and artist (Apollo) and the sexually active and ambiguous reveler (Dionysos). Recognition of the effectiveness of this system brings us a long way in answering Simon Price's question about why the Greeks so emphasized both genders for their gods. The Greeks developed a religious system based on the human experience and so it both reflected and sustained the human condition in its fullest realization of sexuality, gender, and the life cycle.

Fig. 2.1
Attic white-ground phiale, the Painter of London D12. Boston, Museum of Fine Arts 65.908, Edwin E. Jack Fund. Photo © 2007 Museum of Fine Arts, Boston.

Childhood

From a young age, an Athenian girl of a prominent family could expect to participate in a sequence of sacred service roles. The youngest girls involved in cult duties on the Acropolis were the arrephoroi.[19] They were charged with carrying the "unnamed or secret things," the *arreta*, in rites of Athena and Pandrosos. The girls were aged seven to eleven years old and were elected from members of citizen families, by a show of hands in the Assembly, perhaps in a preliminary round prior to formal appointment by the *archon basileus*.[20] From at least 220/219 B.C., the girls who held the office were honored in dedications made by their families. From these we learn the names of some twenty-one *arrephoroi* who served from the late third century B.C. to the second century A.D. Seventeen girls are known from inscribed bases that held their statues, set up on the Acropolis by their families, or by the Boule and Demos.[21]

Scattered references give some indication of what the arrephoroi did. We know that two of them were involved in the setting up of the warp for the weaving of the sacred robe, the peplos, of Athena during the festival called the Chalkeia.[22] The arrephoroi are said to have performed the rites at the festival of the Arrephoria at the very end of their year of service (Pausanias 1.27.3).[23] In this ritual, the priestess of Athena gave the arrephoroi objects, unknown even to her. They carried these upon their heads out to the sanctuary of Aphrodite in the Gardens and, leaving them there, brought back something else, all covered up. For a time before the feast of the Arrephoria, the girls lived on the Acropolis near Athena's temple. We are told that if they put on gold jewelry, it became sacred.[24]

Having completed a term as arrephoros, a girl might advance to serve as sacred grain grinder, or *aletris*, as suggested by the chorus in *Lysistrata* 642. We are told that the post was held by virgins, who thus met a frequent requirement for the job of food preparation, in which the purity of the preparer is emphasized.[25] We cannot help but remember the special bread baked for the arrephoroi, known as the *anastatoi*, or "risers," and wonder if the work of the *aletris* was not somehow related to these.[26]

At the sanctuary of Artemis Brauronia on the eastern coast of Attica, groups of girls participated in larger, age-classed bands brought together for a broader cult experience. Restricted to daughters of Athenian citizens, participants were selected from each Athenian tribe and organized in classes consisting of members between five and ten years old, safely short of the onset of menarche.[27] The girls were placed under the care of the virgin Artemis, who shepherded them through the dangerous transitional period between childhood and puberty. At Brauron, initiates took the name "bear," in commemoration of a local myth in which a bear was killed after injuring a young girl near Artemis's sanctuary. The goddess was angered by the bear's death and sent a plague that, according to the Delphic oracle, could be stopped only if the Athenians sent their daughters to "play the bear" in local rituals called the Arkteia.[28] Excavations at the site have revealed a temple, a stoa with dining rooms, a stable, and a bridge.[29] Other Attic shrines of Artemis, located at Mounychia in the Piraeus, in Athens, at Halai (Artemis Tauropolos), and in Melite (Artemis Aristoboule), have yielded evidence that may suggest that some girls experienced maturation rites in smaller, localized settings.[30]

A series of images painted on small, two-handled cups called *krateriskoi* have traditionally been viewed as providing evidence for what playing the bear may have looked like.[31] These have been found at Brauron, as well as at all but one of the shrines listed above; are painted in black-figure technique; and date from the late sixth and the fifth centuries. They show girls running in line, some dressed in knee-length tunics and others completely nude. The girls carry crowns, torches, and branches and move past altars and palm trees. Gloria Ferrari has cautioned that these images should not be read as scenes of historical reality but, instead, as representations of a mythical Arkteia set in the legendary past.[32]

Ferrari similarly argues a mythical interpretation for the images shown on three red-figure vases of unknown provenance that have been widely viewed as girls participating in choral performances, footraces, or processions at Brauron.[33] One cup shows little girls interacting with adult women, who have been viewed as priestesses of the cult.[34] A second cup shows older girls completely nude, running in line with their arms outstretched, some clutching wreaths.[35] The image of a large bear appears before a palm tree and one of the running girls looks back at it over her shoulder, as if in distress. Other fragments show a man and a woman, each wearing what appear to be bear masks but that may, instead, show them being transformed into bears. While Lilly Kahil interpreted these figures as a priest and priestess dressed for a ritual drama at Brauron, Erica Simon sees them as characters drawn from the myth of Arkas and his mother, Kallisto, transformed into a bear in punishment for her liason with Zeus.[36]

Quite a different cult experience was open to children who served as "hearth initiates" at the Eleusinian Mysteries. Their job was to offer prayers and sacrifices on behalf of the initiates. Dedications commemorating hearth initiates outnumber all other offerings made at Eleusis. Although the office is known to have existed already in the fifth century B.C., inscribed dedications do not appear until the late second to early first centuries. While only boys are known to have held the post during the classical period, all but one of the named hearth initiates for the Hellenistic period are girls, apparently reflecting a change in the preferred gender for the post.[37] At least from the fourth century on, we know that families annually registered the names of their children as candidates for the office. The *archon basileus* then selected one child by lot from the nominated field. The majority of children who held the office were from distinguished families, many belonging to the Eumolpidae and the Kerykes, which may suggest that only children from established clans could be nominated.[38]

Maidenhood

KANEPHOROI

Having reached the age of puberty, a maiden entered her prime, and a broad range of possibilities for sacred service were opened to her.[39] The most widespread of these was the role of *kanephoros*, which brought with it the highly visible honor of leading ritual processions. This, of course, afforded the *parthenos* an opportunity to be seen publicly in all her marriageable splendor.

33

No wonder *kanephoroi* are characterized in literature as being pretty, dressed up, and wearing white makeup.[40] We are told that when Peisistratos's youngest daughter served in the post, Thrasyboulos fell in love with her, rushed up on the spot, and kissed her.[41] Indeed, to be singled out as leader in a sacred procession presented a girl with an intense social as well as religious experience.[42] The story told of Harmodios's sister illustrates what an honor it was to be chosen as kanephoros and how degrading it was to be excluded. Apparently, the girl arrived at the Panathenaia thinking she was to carry the basket, only to be told that she could not. The tyrant Hipparchos then denied that the girl had ever been asked, thus placing her virtue in question. This humiliation was alleged to have motivated her brother and his lover Aristogeiton to murder Hipparchos during the course of the festival.[43] The agency of the kanephoros was held in such high esteem that the maidens were awarded portions of the sacrificial meat, an entitlement comparable to that of the male officials.[44]

There were many opportunities for maidens to serve as kanephoroi, since nearly every festival required a basket of sacrificial paraphernalia.[45] For Attica alone, we have basket bearers at the Anthesteria, Apollonia, Brauronia, Delia, Diogesoteiria, rural Dionysia, state Dionysia, and Eleusinia and at the festival of Herakles at the Mesogea. Inscriptions list fifty named kanephoroi dating from the fourth century B.C. to the second century A.D. Most of these participated in the three major festivals between 138 and 95 B.C.[46] The maidens who held office came from families of high status, most from the clan of the Kerykes, followed by the Eteoboutadai, Eumolpidai, Apheidantidai, Eupatridai, and Erysichthonidai.[47] The case of the daughter of Miltiades, son of Zoilos, is telling. In the face of a financial crisis, Miltiades took charge of the games at the Theseia in 153/152 B.C., and at the Panathenaia in 142/141, donating large sums of his own money. He then chose his own daughter to serve as kanephoros for the Panathenaia.[48] Here we see a direct correlation between economic capital and the honor of sacred service.

Unlike other cult agents, kanephoroi are immediately recognizable in the visual record through the baskets shown carried upon their heads. These baskets held the implements and offerings necessary for sacrifice: knife, ribbons, garlands, cakes, grains, first fruits, and incense.[49] But since basket bearers were required not just at cult festivals but also at weddings and funerals, care must be taken in distinguishing the contexts in which they are shown.[50] We may differentiate, also, between a kanephoros who leads a public procession, basket carried high upon her head, and a kanephoros who stands alone at an altar, basket held out in one hand. The maiden shown leading a procession at Delphi, on the well-known vase in Ferrara, is distinguished not only by her basket but also by her elaborately woven overtunic, the heavy mantle falling from her shoulders, and her jewelry (fig. 2.2).[51] She is a picture of loveliness, just like the kanephoroi described in literature. Her showy basket appears to be fashioned from metal, perhaps bronze or gold. Cer-

Fig. 2.2
Attic red-figure volute krater, the Kleophon Painter. Ferrara, Museo Nazionale di Spina 44894 T. 57C. Photo courtesy Soprintendenza Archaeologica di Ferrara.

tainly, she is singled out as a special player within the ritual, a *parthenos* who has been honored with a public cult role. In contrast, the more mature woman shown on a lekythos in Paris is dressed simply and holds her basket in one arm rather than up on her head (fig. 2.3).[52] She stretches out her other hand in a gesture of prayer. The column behind her establishes a sanctuary setting. It is unclear whether we are to understand this woman as a priestess or a private individual at prayer, but she does seem to be differentiated from the elaborately dressed maiden kanephoroi who are shown leading processions.

The sprightly kanephoros on the Triptolemos Painter's jug (fig. 2.4; pl. 2) seems to be participating in a festival parade, though she is certainly less solemn than her counterpart on the Ferrara vase (see fig. 2.2).[53] She marches in step with two companions, raising her right hand to steady the big basket upon her head. All dressed up in a pleated underdress and bordered mantle, she is smiling, as if excited by her special role. There may be a correlation here between form and function, as well as with the selection of images used to decorate the vase. The distinctive

Fig. 2.3
Attic red-figure lekythos. Paris, Musée du Louvre CA 2567. Photo M. and P. Chuzeville, courtesy Musée du Louvre.

Fig. 2.4
Attic red-figure oinochoe,
from Chuisi, the Triptolemos
Painter. Berlin, Staatliche Museen
Antikensammlung 2189. Photo
Bildarchiv Preussischer Kultur-
besitz/Art Resource, NY.

Fig. 2.5
Attic red-figure lekythos, the Gales Painter. Boston, Museum of Fine Arts 13.195, Francis Bartlett Donation. Photo © 2007 Museum of Fine Arts, Boston.

Fig. 2.6
Attic red-figure pelike, the Pan
Painter. Newcastle, Shefton
Museum of Greek Art and
Archaeology 203, University
of Newcastle upon Tyne. Photo
courtesy Shefton Museum of
Greek Art and Archaeology.

shape of the vessel may suggest a ritual in which a girl, much like the one depicted, may have
poured a libation from a jug, much like the vase itself.

A lekythos in Boston shows a kanephoros leading a procession in which two men escort
cows to sacrifice (fig. 2.5).[54] Like the maiden on the Ferrara vase, this basket bearer wears a voluminous mantle pinned at her shoulders, falling down in front and back. This is the so-called festival mantle that has been identified as a signifier of the office of kanephoros itself.[55] But these
mantles can be seen worn by men and women alike, and though often seen in festival contexts,
they are also found in nonritual scenes. The festival mantle cannot be used to identify maidens as
kanephoroi, and attempts to do so, particularly for images of maidens who do not even carry baskets, seem off the mark.[56]

The kanephoros shown on a vase in Newcastle is helped in her task by a mature woman
who follows attentively behind (fig. 2.6; pl. 3).[57] As the heavy basket balances precariously on the

girl's head, the matron stretches out her hands, apparently holding something (a necklace?) that might have been shown in paint, which is now faded away. Here, we have a touching visual parallel to the sentiment of Plutarch's text, cited above, in which the priestesses of Ephesos had a time for learning, a time for performing, and a time for teaching the traditional rites to the next generation. On the Newcastle pelike, both teacher and student wear the festival mantle in a scene that effectively depicts the dynamics of feminine age-classed groups in the perpetuation of Greek cult practice.

VIRGIN PRIESTHOODS AND OTHER SACRED SERVICE ROLES

A full variety of priesthoods were reserved for maidens.[58] Many of these had to do with the care and maintenance of the cult statue. Alain Schnapp has articulated the ways in which statues were perceived to be living entities rather than mere representations.[59] They were, thereby, endowed with earthly needs for food, clothing, and shelter. There is much debate over the age and marital status of the maidens called *ergastinai*, or "workers," who wove the peplos for Athena's statue at Athens. Some believe that they were little girls under the age of seven, others believe that they are one and the same as the arrephoroi, and still others hold that they included both married and unmarried women.[60] We first hear of the Athenian ergastinai relatively late, that is, in 108/107 B.C.[61] Inscriptions give the names of around 115 maidens who served in the post, listed according to tribe. Their large number has been seen as comparable to the size of the contemporary ephebe corps of young men.[62] It is possible that the office of ergastina was created or expanded during the Hellenistic period to offer a greater opportunity for daughters of prominent families to be recognized. Groups of maidens chosen as ergastinai would be trained in the art of wool working, just as their male counterparts, the ephebes, would receive military training. On this view, we should understand the age and status of the ergastinai as roughly equivalent to that of ephebic youths, that is, maidens in their teens.

It has been shown that 80 percent of the maidens listed as *ergastinai* came from prominent citizen families experienced in sacred-office holding.[63] Akestion, daughter of Xenokles, was a member of the clan of the Kerykes.[64] Her great-grandfather, grandfather, father, husband, brother, and son each served in the important office of *dadouchos* for the Eleusinian Mysteries. Many of the weaving women are known to have held other cult positions. Xenostrate, daughter of Agias, had served earlier as *errephoros*.[65] We know of three maidens who completed at least two terms as ergastinai: Mikkion, Parion, and Peitho.[66] The fact that they served in 108/107 B.C. and again in 103/102 suggests that ergastinai may have started at a very young age, such as seven or eight, and then had an opportunity to serve once again before marriage.[67] One group of ergastinai dedicated a silver cup to Athena at their own expense and were honored, at their fathers' request, with a public decree.[68]

Another office typically held by maidens was that of the sacred washer, or *plyntria*, who cared for the garments worn by Athena's statue. At Athens, this post commemorated the role of the mythical Aglauros, daughter of King Kekrops, who was said to have been the first to care for Athena's statue on the Acropolis.[69] Upon the princess's death, the statue's garments remained unwashed for an entire year. Thereafter, an annual festival called the Plynteria was established to ensure that this job would never be neglected again. Plynteria festivals were celebrated throughout the Greek world and are known at Tegea, Chios, Paros, Ios, and Thasos, where maiden *plyntrides* assumed responsibility for washing sacred vestments.[70] At Athens, the *plyntrides* seem to have been charged with washing the statue's clothes, while other ritual servants, known as *loutrides*, were responsible for bathing the statue itself.[71] The pattern can be seen outside Athens as well. Nine virgin *agretai*, meaning "the chosen," were selected each year to tend the statue of Athena on Kos.[72]

Evidence for virgin priesthoods increases over time, and extensive epigraphic records from the sanctuaries of Hellenistic Asia Minor attest to a broad range of possibilities for service. A pattern can be recognized through which cults seem to have designated one sacred office as the most distinguished post open to local maidens. At Didyma, this was the office of *hydrophoros*, or "water bearer," who served as priestess of Artemis Pythia. This position came with a tenure of one year and its duties included overseeing the celebration of the Mysteries. It provided a female counterpart to the "prophet of Apollo," a post that was always held by a man. We regularly find the two offices jointly held by a father-daughter team.[73]

At Ephesos, the office of *hydrophoros* was also the top job for maidens. The service of water carriers is recorded in inscriptions listing their names, family backgrounds, and benefactions. We have twenty-six dedications made by *hydrophoroi* of Hellenistic date and another eighty-seven offered during the first three centuries A.D.[74] These inscriptions testify to a wide network of interrelated mothers, daughters, and grandmothers who held the office. At Lagina in Karia, the most esteemed office for maidens was that of *kleidophoros*, or "key bearer." This post was traditionally held by the daughter of the priest of Hekate, on the father-daughter model that we have seen attested at Didyma.

In his travels through Roman Greece, Pausanias hears of many virgin priesthoods, all held for short periods of time. He tells us that Marpessa served as priestess of Athena Alea at Tegea (8.47.2–3) until she reached marriageable age, perhaps reflecting the etiological tale of Auge, whose local service as virgin priestess was brought to an abrupt end when Herakles abducted her. A yearly priesthood at Sikyon was open to a virgin called *loutrophoros*, reflecting the maiden's role as bearer of the wedding bathwater for Aphrodite (Pausanias 2.10.4). She served together with an older woman *neokoros*. At the island sanctuary of Poseidon at Kalaureia, just opposite Troizen, a maiden priestess served until she reached the age for marriage (Pausanias 2.33.2). Artemis was regularly served by virgins, who held her priesthood for a short time, as at the sanctuary of Artemis at Aigeira in Arkadia (Pausanias 7.26.5). The same pattern can be seen at the shrine of Artemis Knagia in Lakonia, named for Knageus, who abducted the priestess of Artemis from Crete (Pausanias 3.18.4). Artemis Triklaria in Patrai had a short-term virgin priestess who was free to marry at the end of her tenure. This arrangement was possibly introduced to prevent repetition of the legend of Komaitho, a local *parthenos* who had entertained her lover Melanippos in Artemis's sanctuary, thereby angering the goddess and bringing plague and famine upon the entire community (Pausanias 7.19.1–3). Komaitho and her lover suffered harsh punishment for their transgression. They were sacrificed to the goddess to appease her wrath.

At the sanctuary of Artemis at Ephesos, virgin priestesses were allowed to move on to a life of marriage and children following their service. Inscriptions from the Imperial period record that many of these priestesses were descended from women who had also held the office, illustrating that virginity was considered a phase rather than a lifelong condition for those who served.[75] Charikleia, the beautiful heroine in Heliodoros's romance *An Ethiopian Story* (1.22.2), fabricates the tale of how she and her lover, whom she here calls her brother, came to be at sea. She recounts: "We belong to the nobility of Ephesos . . . and a tradition calls on such people to undertake divine service. I became priestess of Artemis and my brother here the priest of Apollo. The office is for a year."[76] Although this is a fiction within a fiction, Charikleia's tale may preserve some grain of truth reflecting the reality of priestly service in Roman Ephesos. Here as elsewhere, virgin priesthoods were held for a short term before marriage. When we hear of a true "virgin priestess for life" the model is hardly held up as an ideal but, instead, as a punishment. When Herakles famously had intercourse with forty-nine of Thespius's fifty daughters in a single night, he was insulted and enraged by the one girl who rejected him. He condemned her to lifelong virginity as his priestess, in the cult of Herakles Charops at Thespiai in Boiotia (Pausanias 9.27.6–7).

Maturity

Many of the highest-ranking priesthoods in Greece were held by married women. This is especially true for inherited priesthoods, such as that of Athena Polias at Athens, which relied upon legitimate heirs to keep the priesthood within the clan.[77] The cult of Demeter was one in which married women played a particularly prominent role, not surprisingly, on the model of the archetypal Mother Goddess herself. At Eleusis, the priestess of Demeter and Kore was a married woman, as were the two *hierophantidai* who assisted her, and the priestess of Plouton.[78]

Married women participated in tending cult statues throughout Greece. At Athens, the feast during which the statue was decorated was called the Kallynteria, or "Beautification Day." Similar rites are attested outside of Attica, where they are often known as the *kosmesis* (decoration) and *epikosmesis* (superdecoration).[79] At certain sanctuaries, women designated as *kosmeteirai* were in charge of this work, but at other sanctuaries, such as that of Artemis on Delos, men called *kosmetai* performed the service. At the Heraion at Delos, the job was undertaken by the priestesses, *hiereiai*, while on Thasos, the job was done by the priestess of Demeter and Kore, who went by the title *neokoros*. At the sanctuary of Artemis at Ephesos, the *kosmeteirai* were commemorated with portrait statues. Inscriptions from the bases of these statues record that many women who served came from families that went "far back" and included several generations of women who had held the post.[80] At Sparta, a group of married women wove a himation for Apollo Hyakinthos at Amyklai (Pausanias 3.16.2) demonstrating, once again, the special role of married women in looking after the cult statue.

Demeter's great festival of the Thesmophoria, celebrated throughout the Greek world, was for married women only.[81] It was organized and administered by a hierarchy of women, who left homes and husbands for the duration of the feast. During the first half of the second century B.C., Satyra, a priestess of the Thesmophoria, was honored by her deme, Melite, for piously performing her sacrificial duties and for her benefactions in rebuilding the sanctuaries of Demeter and Plouton.[82] Married women, known as *antletriai*, performed the main ritual at the Thesmophoria, which included bringing up decomposed pigs, long buried in deep pits. These women were required to abstain from sexual intercourse before and during the festival.[83] Two annually elected officials, called *archousai*, appear to have been married women of some means who served as assistants to the priestess. It fell to them to cover the financial expenses of the Thesmophoria, either on their own or with the help of their husbands.[84]

Another cult in which married women played a central role was that of Dionysos, on the etiological model of Queen Agave, who led the maenadic *thiasos* at Thebes.[85] We know of historical maenads at Thebes, Delphi, and Athens and in Macedonia, where Alexander the Great's mother, Olympias, was said to have participated in *thiasoi*.[86] Women known as Thyiades traveled from Athens every other year to join the women of Delphi in celebrating rites of Dionysos on the slopes of Mount Parnassos (Pausanias 10.4.2). Thyiades performed dances at fixed points along the route. Plutarch (*Moralia* 249) recounts a heart-warming tale set in the fourth century at the time of the Third Sacred War. A group of Delphic Thyiades, still in a trance from their revels, wandered into the marketplace at Amphissa and fell asleep. Local women feared that soldiers stationed in the village might mistreat the Thyiades and so formed a circle around them, keeping a silent vigil all through the night.

A development can be observed in the late Hellenistic and Roman East in which married women held office jointly with their husbands. This has been interpreted as a statement of the civic complementarity of men and women, connected to the emergence of women as civic-office holders and benefactresses just at this time.[87] By the middle of the first century A.D., all priesthoods of Imperial cult were regularly shared by a husband-wife team.[88] The practice is exemplified by the case of Flavia Leontis, priestess of Hekate at Lagina during the Hadrianic period.[89] As a maiden, Flavia served as *kleidophoros* while her father was priest of Hekate. Later, she twice held joint priesthoods of Hekate with her husband and also joined him in a priest-priestess team serving the Cult of the Emperors. Flavia simultaneously held the offices of *stephanephoros* and *neokoros* and served as priestess for the festival of Hera no less than four times, and priestess for the Komyria once. Her example is emblematic of the very central role that married women played in the overseeing of cults, marked by an ever increasing number of opportunities for officeholding during the Roman Imperial period.

Advanced Age

Plato believed that sacred offices were best held by mature individuals, and he recommended an age requirement of sixty years for priests and priestesses (*Laws* 759d). Aristotle agreed (*Politics* 1829a). Indeed, the postmenopausal and widowed women who composed the final age-class of cult service enjoyed enormously active roles.[90] Their posts ranged from the prominent celibate priesthoods of Apollo at Delphi, Aphrodite at Sikyon, Artemis Hymnia at Orchomenos, and Sosipolis at Olympia, to a full range of subpriestly positions in which they served alone or in groups. One job routinely assigned to older women was that of keeping sacred fires. This was so at Athens and at Delphi, where widows tended the holy flame.[91]

At Olympia, sixteen elderly women wove a robe for Hera every fourth year (Pausanias 5.16.2–6; 6.24.10). The origin of this was a board of female elders once chosen from sixteen cities of Eleia to settle differences between the towns of Pisa and Elis. The women selected, considered to be "the oldest, the most noble and the most esteemed of all," were highly successful in settling the dispute, making peace between their two cities (Pausanias 5.16.5). On the model of this group, the sixteen women of Elis were charged with supervising the festival of Hera, including girls' footraces and choral dances. At Athens, a college of old, distinguished women known as "the venerable ones" (*gerarai*) were charged with overseeing activities in the cult of Dionysos.[92] This included examining the queen (*basilinna*) before her participation in the sacred wedding (*hieros gamos*) and performing secret rites at the festivals of the Anthesteria, Theoinia, and Iobakcheia. The *gerarai* were required to swear an oath that they had led holy lives and were clean and pure from intercourse with men.[93] At Argos, priestesses of advanced years in the service of Athena were similarly titled *geraraides*.[94] At Hermione, four old women (*graes*) killed the sacrificial cows at the festival of Demeter Chthonia (Pausanias 2.35.4–8). At the sanctuary of Eileithyia at Elis, an old, chaste priestess who wore a white veil was the only one permitted to enter the inner sanctum of the hero Sosipolos (Pausanias 6.20.2–3).

In Greek myth, we see a recurring pattern through which requirements for chastity were transferred from an office, first filled by maidens, to one later designated for old women. This is most famously the case for the Pythia at Delphi. We are told that, in early days, a beautiful young prophetess was abducted and raped by Echekrates. Thereafter, the rules were changed so that the Pythia was selected from women at least fifty years of age who continued to dress in virginal garb in honor of the former prophetess.[95] We hear a similar tale for the sanctuary of Artemis Hymnia at Orchomenos, where a virgin priestess was raped by King Aristokrates, after which the Arkadians changed the rules so that future priestesses were chosen from among women "who had had enough intercourse with men" (Pausanias 8.5.11–13). The older celibate was thus viewed as an appropriate replacement for the young virgin. Perpetual chastity seems to have been a more realistic requirement for an elderly servant than for a young woman in her prime.

These stories may reflect a reality in which cults abandoned the requirement of virginity for young priestesses because it was untenable. The example of Satorneila, priestess of Athena Polias at Miletos, though late in date, is so profoundly traditional in tone as to be instructive here. During the late second or early third century A.D., this well-born lady who had been married and had children was appointed to the virgin priesthood of Athena for life. Apollo at Didyma was consulted for an opinion on this irregular choice and informed the questioners that Athena had, indeed, accepted Satorneila as priestess.[96] The fact that she was from a prominent family with close connections to the Roman Senate probably did not hurt her candidacy. We may detect here some expenditure of social capital in securing this priesthood for Satorneila. Again, a pervasive sense of pragmatism dominated the established structure, allowing for flexibility in the face of individual circumstance.

Requirements for Sacred Office

Pedigree and Financial Status

From the Archaic through the Hellenistic periods, good birth and financial resources had a profound impact on a woman's ability to secure a priesthood. The same can be said for men. A candidate might get away with lack of one or the other, but an individual who was neither well born nor rich would have a hard time attaining high office. At Athens and elsewhere, priesthoods were open only to citizen wives and daughters. Access to certain offices required membership in a specific family group, or *genos*, based on kinship and identified by certain sacral functions.[97] Traditionally, the Attic *gene* have been viewed as politically powerful clans claiming descent from a famous hero-ancestor. More recently, they have been defined simply as family groups that could document themselves over at least four generations.[98] Priesthoods that were specifically controlled by members of these clans are known as "gentilician" priesthoods. Priesthoods open to the entire body of citizen women have been designated as "democratic" priesthoods.[99] Cults had a full range of associations, some linked to groups bound by kinship, others based on geographic location, and still others attached to voluntary groups with common religious interests. This diversity resulted in a wide variety of offices in tribal and family cults; in state and deme cults; as well as in private associations based on personal choice, known as *thiasoi* and *orgeones*.[100]

The *genos* principle can be seen at work in the most prestigious of Attic priesthoods, those of Athena Polias and Poseidon-Erechtheus. The clan of the Eteoboutadai held exclusive right to these inherited offices, one branch providing the priestess of Athena (Aeschines *On the False Embassy* 147) and the other branch the priest of Poseidon-Erechtheus (Pseudo-Plutarch 843E–F). It is surely not by accident that the Eteoboutadai had a special relationship with each of the rival cults that competed in the Athenian foundation myth, the legendary contest between Athena and Poseidon for the patronage of the city (Herodotus 8.55). The exclusive association of the Eteoboutadai with these founding cults confirms that they represent one of the most venerable clans of Attica.

Old families came with impressive economic resources that could be used in financing cults and festivals. Over time, the fortunes of some of these families waned, and, in Hellenized Asia Minor, the sale of priesthoods was introduced to bring in new financing. This allowed for citizen women who lacked pedigree but were rich with cash to purchase priesthoods, taking on the incumbent financial responsibilities and enjoying the related privileges. The long-standing priestly requirements of birthright and finances are vividly articulated by Artemidoros of Ephesos during the Antonine period. Late as his words may be, they paint a picture that was accurate even earlier on: "To dream of traversing the city on a cart is good news for women and girls who are both free and rich, because it means they will get eminent priesthoods, but for a poor woman, riding through the city on horseback predicts prostitution" (*Dream Book* 1.56).

Physical Requirements

We hear of few explicit requirements regarding the purity of priestesses. At Andania, priestesses were required to swear an oath to marital fidelity "in accordance with divine and human law."[101] The priestess of Ge Eurysternos at Aigai in Achaia had to swear that she had been with one man alone in the years before taking up her office. She was even required to drink bull's blood to test her truthfulness (Pausanias 7.25.13). For most priestesses and worshippers alike, it seems sexual abstinence was required for just a few days before entering most sanctuaries, if at all. In comparison to miscarriage, contact with death, deflowering virgins, and childbirth, sexual intercourse seems to have represented a fairly minor pollutant.[102]

Physical defects, however, were serious and could rule out a candidate for priesthood altogether.[103] On Hellenistic Kos, inscriptions that advertise the sale of priesthoods stipulate that the men or women who purchased them had to be "healthy and whole" (*oloklaros*). In the late third century, the priestess of Dionysos Thallophoros was required to be physically healthy, whole, and of sound body, as was the priestess of Aphrodite Pandemos during the second century.[104] The priesthoods of Asklepios, Hygieia, and Epione; of Herakles Kallinikon; and of Zeus Alseios similarly required physical soundness.[105] At Chalkedon, the priest of Asklepios was required to be "whole" in a second-century advertisement for the post.[106] At Athens, priests as well as the *archon basileus* had to undergo physical examinations to determine whether they were unblemished and therefore fit to serve.[107] To this day, Greek orthodox priests are required to have all their digits, and if they lose one, they must ask for special dispensation to stay on in office.

The required "wholeness" of the cult official may be seen as part of a larger dynamic in which divinity and sacred servant share in divine perfection. As the gods themselves are beautiful, so too were those chosen to look after the gods' temples and rituals. Homer (*Iliad* 6.297–310) describes the priestess Theano as "fair-cheeked," idealizing her appearance even though, as wife of a Trojan elder, she may have been beyond the first bloom of youth. The association of beautiful women with sacred office is attested throughout Greek myth; indeed, it is a recurrent theme in stories about the abduction of virgin priestesses. Apollo's priestess at Troy, Kassandra, is portrayed as "the most beautiful daughter" of King Priam (*Iliad* 13.365–66). Her beauty inspired not only the lust of the god but also that of the Lesser Ajax, who pursued her into Athena's temple on the night of the fall of Troy. Auge, the lovely priestess of Athena at Tegea, attracted the attention of Herakles, just as the beautiful Io, priestess of Hera at Argos, inspired the lustful advances of Zeus. Personal names of historical priestesses often reflect their beauty or some other quality that sets them apart from other women: Kallisto (Beautiful), Megiste (Great), Chrysis (Golden), Theodote (God-Given), Aristonoe (Best). While we have no evidence for a "beauty prerequisite" for female priesthoods, we do hear from Pausanias (7.24.4) that the boy chosen to be priest at Aigai was required to be beautiful. In this, again, we see no gendered differentiation in physical requirements for priests and priestesses.

Methods of Acquisition

Four principal paths led to priestly office: inheritance, allotment, election/appointment, and purchase.[108] It must be stressed that these categories are not necessarily exclusive of one another and that they coexisted, combining and integrating various elements. Inherited priesthoods could involve choice by lot from a short list of candidates with the required ancestry. Preselected short lists also played a part in the more "democratic" methods of election and sale. Inheritance is generally believed to be the earliest method of acquisition. At Athens, it continued to play a critical part in the most prominent priesthoods right through the Roman period. Allotment is specifically attested for feminine priesthoods from the second half of the fifth century to the first century. Evidence for the sale of feminine priesthoods survives from about 400 B.C. into the third century A.D. and is geographically restricted to Asia Minor and the islands of the eastern Aegean.

Throughout the centuries, election and selection, by show of hands or otherwise, remained an option for determining sacred office. We cannot speak of a development in which one method makes another obsolete. Inheritance, allotment, election, and sale coexisted, and in some cases, one method did replace another, but in no particular order.

Inheritance

The most prestigious and time-honored feminine priesthoods, including those of Athena Polias at Athens and Demeter and Kore at Eleusis, were passed from generation to generation as carefully guarded privileges within the clans.[109] Inheritance of sacred office hearkened back to the days of the legendary past and was based on alleged family connections to mythical founders of local cults. At Athens, the Eteoboutad clan's claim to the priesthood of Athena was based on descent from a founder, Boutes, who, according to tradition, was one of two sons of King Pandion I. Boutes received the priesthood of Athena Polias and Poseidon-Erechtheus, while his brother Erechtheus became king of Athens (Aeschines *On the False Embassy* 147).[110]

Despite political changes from aristocracy to tyranny to democracy, old and once-noble families held tenaciously to their right of inherited sacred office. We have no fewer than nineteen hereditary priesthoods attested for Attica, eight of which were filled by women.[111] All but two of these priesthoods belonged to Athena or Demeter, divinities whose cults were among the very oldest in the city. Indeed, the priesthoods of Athena Polias and Demeter and Kore were held within the same clans for an astounding seven hundred years. Aristotle tells us that Kleisthenes respected the old clan-based priesthoods and kept them intact despite his political reforms (*Athenian Constitution* 21.6). In reforming the "ideal state," something that Plato supported in his old age, he believed that "priests of temples, or priestesses, who hold hereditary priesthoods should not be disturbed" (*Laws* 6.759a–b).[112] Only for newly organized cults did Plato approve of appointments made partly by election and partly by lot, mingling democratic with nondemocratic methods "to secure friendliness in every rural and urban district." Continuity of cult practice built a bridge with the past, ensuring stability and sustaining Greek tradition.

Surviving epigraphic evidence for the priesthood of Athena Polias hints at how the procedure of inheritance might have worked. One view has the priesthood passed through the eldest Eteoboutad male to his eldest daughter and then, at the end of her service, to her eldest brother's eldest daughter.[113] In the absence of a patrilineal successor, the office could be passed on matrilineally.[114] Epigraphic evidence allows for the reconstruction of the family line of Drakontides of Bate, which shows with certainty that the first six known priestesses of Athena Polias were related. A good case can be made that, in fact, the first ten named priestesses were all part of this same line.[115]

For most cults, such as that of Demeter and Kore at Eleusis, we are left with a limited understanding of the means by which priesthoods were transferred. Since none of the known priestesses of Demeter and Kore are closely related, the priesthood does not seem to have been directly inherited but was passed on to members of the same clan through lot or selection.[116] For the male *dadouchoi* at Eleusis, however, Kevin Clinton has shown a successsion of at least eighteen generations in which the office was passed back and forth between two families.[117] Inherited priesthoods sometimes made use of a form of restricted allotment to determine which of the eligible family members would assume office. Sara Aleshire saw allotment from a preexisting short list as the primary means of filling gentilician priesthoods at Athens from the fifth century to the last quarter of the first century B.C.[118] If *gene* were very large, the number of eligible candidates on the short list may have been great enough to produce results that look as if they were chosen by election. Conversely, if the short list was small, sortition might produce results that resembled those derived from direct or indirect inheritance.[119]

Ancestry that could be traced back to the hero-founder of local cult was an individual's most powerful claim to priesthood.[120] Priestesses serving the cult of Dionysos near Ikaria professed descent from the daughters of Semachos, the legendary founder of the deme and the first in the region to accept Dionysos.[121] In the Hellenistic period, when many new cults were founded, the line of inheritance could begin with a historical individual who initiated the cult. On Thera, a woman named Epikteta founded a sanctuary to the Muses and her own deceased ancestors in about 210–195 B.C.[122] A long text was inscribed on four slabs that made up the base for a statue group showing Epikteta together with her husband and children. The inscription records the legacy she left to her daughter Epiteleia for the establishment of an association dedicated to the worship of the Muses. Epikteta's will ensured that Epiteleia's eldest male descendent would inherit the priesthood. Upon his death, the office was to be passed on through his descendants.

Allotment

Selection by lot was based on the idea that the luck of the draw allowed the gods to choose the winner.[123] Solon himself is said to have introduced the lot for the selection of magistrates years before democracy (Aristotle *Athenian Constitution* 8.1). But this is probably just one example of a fifth-century development that comes to be associated, retrospectively, with the reforms of Solon.[124] Sortition is generally believed to have spread from the civic to the religious sphere under the influence of a new democratic spirit sometime during the first half of the fifth century.[125] But it may have worked the other way around, since the lot was surely in use long before the changes brought on by democracy. We hear of sortition as early as Homer's *Iliad* (15.190–92) where lots are drawn by Zeus, Poseidon, and Hades to divide up the realms of the world. The Achaians used lots to determine who would fight Hektor in *Iliad* 7.175–83. It is likely that sortition was employed to decide inheritance and religious-office holding within families long before it became an instrument of democracy.

We must bear in mind that, as democratic as sortition may seem, it was not without its qualifications. Preselected short lists could severely limit the number of eligible candidates. We have very little evidence for unqualified sortition, open to *all* candidates, a practice that seems to have been used primarily for newly founded cults or those undergoing reorganization.[126] Even then, we cannot be sure just what *all* means. On Kos, sortition was combined with payment for the priesthood of Demeter Antimachia. Women entered a lottery but the winner had to pay an inaugural fee.[127] Thus, the procedure was open to those who could afford to participate.

Although the evidence is not without its problems, allotted feminine priesthoods are attested from the second half of the fifth to the first century B.C. The earliest example is that of the priesthood of Athena Nike at Athens. The date of the Nike Temple Decree, which authorizes that a priestess be established from "all the Athenian women," is much debated.[128] Traditionally, it has been placed at 448/447 B.C. but arguments have been made for lowering the date to 425/424, or even later.[129] The method by which the priestess was selected remains unclear, since there is a lacuna at precisely the place where a critical verb is missing. Most scholars have filled this gap with the words "by lot" and take this to mean that the priestess was selected by unrestricted allotment.[130] Although this is by no means certain, the decree does seems to attest to a change in method through which the priestess will be selected in the future.[131]

The restoration of "by lot" is based on evidence from a late fifth-century funerary stele that commemorates a deceased priestess of Athena Nike who was "chosen from all by lot."[132] Her name is Myrrhine and she was the first to "watch over" the temple of Athena Nike. It has been argued that this Myrrhine is the same priestess whose selection was authorized in the Athena Nike Decree.[133] While this may seem likely, it is by no means certain. The evidence does suggest both a major reorganization of cult space and a change in procedure for choosing the priestess, during the third quarter of the fifth century.[134] The adoption of allotment appears to have been part of this change.

Another example in which sortition was introduced for the reorganization of a pre-existing cult concerns the priesthoods of Aglauros, Pandrosos, and Kourotrophos at Athens.[135] A decree, dated to 363 B.C., responds to an apparent dispute between two branches of the clan of the Salaminioi, one from Heptaphylai and the other from Sounion. A change in procedure was adopted through which the two branches would henceforth enjoy equal representation through selection by lot. This was authorized to begin upon the death of the incumbent priestess. Another example demonstrating a shift in procedure upon the death of a priestess is that of Galato, who served at Pednelissos near Perge during the first century B.C. An inscribed decree states that upon the death of Galato, the city should hold a lottery for the selection of the new priestess.[136]

Election and Appointment

Little is known of the ways in which election and appointment operated. The overall picture suggests that election was used for the more important priesthoods and that appointment was used for lower-level offices.[137] We hear of yearly elections, such as those held for the priestess of Eilithyia at Olympia (Pausanias 6.20.2).[138] We also hear of offices with an elected term of ten years and some with life tenure.[139] While election may seem to suggest democratic values, the practice was not always as open as it appears. The priestess of the cult of the Mother at Minoa on Amorgos in the first century B.C. was elected to her office, but upon winning the election, she was required to pay a fee.[140] Thus, as we have seen earlier, the field of candidates was limited to those who could afford the financial requirements of the office.

The process of appointment also had its restrictions. A decree of 183/182 B.C. authorizes the chief priestess of the cult of the Orgeones of the Mother at the Piraeus, herself chosen by lot, to appoint an assistant, the *zakoros*.[141] Although the decree stipulates that the *zakoros* is to hold office for a term of one year, an amendment was passed just eight years later that allowed the priestess Aristodike to appoint her *zakoros*, Metrodora, to a life term.[142] We do not know the full story of why the rules changed, but someone seems to have exercised influence, and it may well have been Aristodike herself. The economic and social capital of priestly women may have bolstered their ability to have the rules rewritten when necessary. While appointment and election did open the doors to a broader field of candidates, the system was not open in a fully democratic sense that allowed equal opportunity for all.

Purchase

Perhaps the most surprising means of acquisition, to the modern eye, is that of purchase. Sales of priesthoods are attested in the eastern Aegean, in Asia Minor, and at Milesian colonies on the Black Sea. The first case is found in Miletos round about 400 B.C. and the latest dates to the third century A.D.[143] We cannot know with certainty exactly where the practice began. Early evidence for the sales of priesthoods at Miletos and in Milesian colonies may suggest that the practice was encouraged by the oracle of Apollo at neighboring Didyma.[144] However, an inscribed text from nearby Herakleia at Latmos preserves an oracle, probably from Didyma, that advised the city *not* to sell the priesthood but opt for yearly election.[145] This would suggest that the picture is more complex than it might appear at first glance.

Purchased priesthoods usually brought life tenure, but they could be sold before death or bequeathed to a child. We hear of some extraordinarily specific term limits, such as that for the priesthood of Roman Demos and the goddess Roma sold in 130 B.C., which carried a tenure of three years and eight months.[146] We also hear of some remarkably low minimum ages for priesthoods on the island of Kos, where children aged eight, ten, twelve, and fourteen years could qualify for offices sold during the late third to first centuries b.c.[147] It is likely that families bought priesthoods for children in order to exempt them from the certainty of financial obligations and liturgies later in life.

Prices started from modest sums as low as ten drachmas, attested for one of some fifty-seven priesthoods sold at Erythrai in the third century b.c.[148] Elsewhere, prices could be quite high, even very high, if particular privileges such as freedom from military service were being offered by the city in return. On Kos, the priesthood of Adrasteia and Nemesis was bought for the extraordinary sum of 19,800 drachmas in the late first century b.c. The price probably included 18,000 drachmas for the office plus a 10 percent tax.[149]

The sale of priesthoods must be viewed within the broader context of an interconnection between officeholding and financial payment attested in Hellenistic cities outside of Athens. Most cities required certain public services, called liturgies, to be taken on by the wealthiest citizens, compelling them to defray costs arising from festivals, musical and athletic contests, and the maintenance of gymnasia. The purchase of a priesthood could exempt targeted individuals from the constant round of liturgies. In addition, civic offices called magistracies, which required personal rather than financial service, involved the citizen elite in the daily operation of their cities. During the Hellenistic period, we hear of payment in advance for magistracies, just as payment for the privilege of citizenship is known. Within the context of these practices, the payment for priesthood looks far less surprising. Through comparison of numismatic and epigraphic evidence, Louis Robert demonstrated that, in some instances, those who bought a magistracy were also paying for a priesthood.[150]

Unlike magistracies, priesthoods brought the buyer an income. This income could range from parts of the sacrificial animals to the extremely valuable skins and hides of the victims, which could be sold for profit. Hellenistic cities were already familiar with the practice of farming out taxes to bidders, who paid in advance and recouped from the revenue they brought. This precedent made the sale of priesthoods a relatively obvious step. In third-century Kos, the money realized from the sale of at least one priesthood could be put to secular use.[151] We have many anecdotes recalling the strategies of cities and their rulers in times of financial hardship. The sale of priesthoods should be seen as one more example of ingenuity in the face of difficult times.

We might suppose that in some cities, especially the smaller ones or those that had suffered a decline in status, pressure on public finances may have been brought on by a decrease in the number of rich or noble citizens or by a fall in the size of their fortunes or, perhaps, even by general demographic decline. In these cases, the yearly rotation of priesthoods among an available group of suitable officeholders may have been no longer viable. The sale of a priesthood to a rich family for a lump sum would make good financial sense. A practice that began locally in a time of economic struggle could well have spread gradually to neighboring cities, whether or not public finances were under stress. We should not assume that benefit from the sale of priesthoods was completely one sided, representing a total gain for the city selling the office. Such sales did not dispense the city from the continuing need to ensure a certain number of sacrifices for public cults, although most of these could be provided for by magistrates or by prominent citizens acting at their own expense.

In return for payment, a city would offer its priest-buyer privileges over and above the important perquisites of sacrificial meat and valuable hides. We find successful bidders guaranteed specified payments of bread, wine, oil, and ration allowances. By the Roman period, there are cases in which buyers received exemption from a wide range of liturgies, such as sponsoring games, heating baths, and distributing oil. Beyond this, high bidders could even be exempted from the significant requirements of military service and garrison duty. Liturgies varied in expense and burden, and if full exemptions were offered, the bidders for priesthoods would recognize that they were being given a fully balanced bargain. The excellent inscription for the sale of the priesthood of Dionysos Phleos at Priene in the second century B.C. makes the calculation brilliantly clear to us.[152] Exemptions from the cheaper liturgies, those concerning aspects of the festival, athletic contests, the breeding of cavalry horses, official embassies to sanctuaries, and gymnasiarchy, were offered to any bidder who paid from six thousand to twelve thousand drachmas. If the bidding passed the twelve-thousand-drachma mark, the winner was further exempted from even more demanding financial liturgies, including the funding of ships (*trierarchy*), administering of public finances, building of temples, and advancing of money to the city (*proeisphora*). The priesthood was duly sold for 12,002 drachmas, illustrating how attractive the exemptions past the twelve-thousand-drachma level were, at least to one bidder. In this light, one can understand why it made good sense to buy priesthoods for children or to bequeath them to offspring, who would grow up with the certainty of assuming burdensome liturgies in their adult life.

Naturally, the process was open to abuse, and in the mid-first century B.C. it struck the Roman governor Paullus Fabius Persicus as a source of malpractice in contemporary Ephesos.[153] He was keen to reorganize Imperial cult through the regulation of the sale of priesthoods because "men of every sort and kind of family" were buying them. In the Augustan era, the sale of priesthoods was described as mean and imprudent by Dionysios of Halikarnassos (*Antiquities* 2.21.3), writing, in part, for a Roman audience. We should remember, however, that Dionysios was drawing an idealized contrast with a supposed "Golden Age" of early Greek and Roman religion. His particularly harsh view of the practice of selling priesthoods at Ephesos reflects the attitude of Roman outsiders and may not have been fully deserved within the broader context of local tradition.

In the Hellenistic Greek city, the sale of priesthoods did not in itself raise any scruples.

When the citizens of Miletos set up a ruler cult of King Eumenes II, they specified the sale of its priesthood, inscribed details of the procedure on the base of the king's statue, and sent them to the king himself for approval.[154] We see some movement away from sale to election on the inscribed record from Herakleia, mentioned above, dated from 100–75 B.C. to the early first century A.D.[155] The people of Herakleia asked the oracle whether they should sell, with life tenure, the priesthood of their major civic cult of Athena Latmia, or whether they should elect its priests on an annual basis. The god opted for election. The text of the oracle, along with a list of 102 priests appointed in obedience to it, is inscribed on the *antae* of Athena's temple. The long list of names attests to the fact that the new regulations were followed for many years. We cannot be sure in which direction the change of procedure turned, but the query of the Herakleians and the god's reply certainly do not reflect any hesitation about whether the sale would be in some way sacrilegious. Perhaps a scandal or problems with a previous priest or priestly family lay behind the change.[156] The fact that the oracle was consulted reflects, once again, the sentiment that the gods themselves should approve changes that affected the running of civic cults.

Most of the evidence for the sale of priesthoods concerns men rather than women, and this is one area in which we can recognize true gender differentiation between priests and priestesses.[157] The reasons for this difference lie in the legal and contractual nature of the epigraphic evidence, as well as in the nature of exemptions available to men in contrast to those available to women. Surviving inscriptions come largely in the form of advertisements for priestly office (*diagraphes*) in which a civic decree gives conditions and instructions for the sale in introducing the advertisement itself. This is followed by a statement that the priesthood has been sold according to the terms specified, the name of the purchaser, and the price of sale. Since these documents represent contractual records, and since women were not able to enter into contracts without a male guardian, we should not be surprised that the majority of these inscriptions concern men, including husbands or guardians who helped women bid for priestly office.

The practice of selling rests on the presumption that there is something worth buying and that someone has the financial means to buy it. The limits on the independent financial activities of women, as well as the disparity between liturgies and other burdens imposed on men in relation to those imposed on women, made the sale of feminine priesthoods fundamentally less attractive for women and for the cities selling them. To buy one's way out of military service and garrison duty represents an extraordinary dispensation for men. Nothing on the female side could ever equal this perquisite, however attractive it might be for a woman's family to pay a lump sum to absolve her from further financial burdens in life. It has been emphasized that male priesthoods fetched much more money than did female cult offices.[158] Rather distortingly, extreme examples have been used to illustrate this situation. The male priesthood of Dionysos Phleos at Priene, which, we have seen, went for 12,002 drachmas, has been contrasted to the female priesthood of Ge at Erythrai, which went for a mere 10 drachmas.[159] What should be stressed in this comparison is that the priesthood of Dionysos brought with it the impressive list of exemptions from liturgies and military service, while that of Ge is but one of fifty-seven priesthoods sold at Erythrai, many of which went for modest sums, male and female alike. The Erythrai priesthoods were presumably sold to a wide clientele of neither rich nor noble bidders. It is unfair to judge the relative value of male and female priesthoods based on the disparity of these prices and the exemptions that they brought.[160] Variations in price are a result of the nature of the privileges involved rather than the gender of the officeholder.

Examples that we can cite for women purchasing priesthoods are slightly more numerous, and yet more qualified, than has been previously recognized. Cases in which women buy priesthoods are generally embedded in family situations and do not involve women themselves disposing of large sums of money on their own behalves. Instead, it is husbands or male guardians who act for them. The example of the widow Nosso, at Erythrai in the first half of the third century, has often been cited as an example of a woman who purchased a priesthood in her own right.[161] Nosso bought the priesthood of the Dioskouroi for her son Astynous, son of Euthynos. But it was her guardian, Theophon, who acted as guarantor of the purchase. In late third-century Erythrai, the widow Aristagore served as a funnel for passing the priesthood of Aphrodite Pythochrestos from her husband, who was the original purchaser, to her son.[162] Upon the death of her husband, the priesthood was transferred to Aristagore as heiress, so that she could then pass it on to one son, while another son served as guarantor.[163] These examples hardly reflect an independent role for the female purchasers.[164]

A text from Chalkedon dating to the late third century B.C. may give evidence that Aristonike, daughter of Moschion, bought the priesthood of the Mother Goddess without the aid of a guardian.[165] It looks as if Aristonike made this purchase on her own, but we must acknowledge that the inscription is broken at just the place where we might expect the name of her *kyrios* to appear. A Koan inscription of late second- to early first-century date gives rules applying to the priesthood of Dionysos, stipulating that the office cannot be sold to a girl under the age of ten.[166] Mention of the girl's guardian shows that this is yet another case in which a man is acting on behalf of a female bidder. Similarly, during the Roman period at Ephesos, male and female relatives of the virgin priestess were expected to make payment on her behalf because she was too young to do so. In this case, five thousand denarii were paid for the girl's office.[167]

Kos provides us with a relatively large number of inscriptions that deal with the sale of feminine priesthoods.[168] A revised *diagraphe* of late fourth/third-century date for the priesthood of Demeter Antimachaia directs initiates to pay the same fees "as were prescribed before the priesthood became open for sale." This would suggest a change in procedure whereby purchase had recently replaced an older system.[169] Eventually, sale by auction became the most popular method for purchase, though mixed systems in which sortition and purchase were combined continued to be used for certain priesthoods.[170]

During the second century B.C. on Kos, a woman named Kallistrate bought the priest-hoods of Asklepios, Hygieia, and Epione as well as that of King Eumenes II while she also held the annual priesthood of Apollo Dalios and Leto.[171] Kallistrate is typical of those who purchased priesthoods: an individual of high social standing and substantial financial resources who could benefit from the liturgical exemptions accompanying the sale. None of the advertisements for priesthoods on Kos mentions marital status as a requirement and local offices seem to have been open to anyone who could pay the price.

—

The channels through which priesthoods were acquired reflect the pervasive pragmatism of Greek religion. The maintenance of cults and the provision of sacrifice were expensive. Those best able to assume financial responsibility changed over time. Early on, it was the noble families, perceived to be descended from mythical founders, who had the financial resources, the know-how, and the all-important link with the past. In time, changes brought new attitudes about who should be in charge and how those in charge should be determined. Old cults needed to be reorganized in the face of political and economic developments. By the Hellenistic period, stressful economic conditions, the waning fortunes of old families, the emergence of a nouveau riche class, the introduction of new cults, and demographic changes in the populations of Hellenized Asia Minor created a world in which the purchase of priesthoods made good sense.[172] By late Hellenistic times, not only men but also wealthy women took on public liturgies, even those that went beyond areas of female activity, such as provisions for gymnasia. At this late date, exemptions from liturgies were attractive to women looking to buy priesthoods, but the extreme exemption from military service and garrison duty would never be relevant to them.

These developments seem a long way off from the relatively simpler days when Aristophanes' chorus recited their religious résumés, proud of the cycle of sacred service that saw them from childhood to maturity. Indeed, methods through which women attained priesthoods were as diverse, complex, and fluid as Greek worship itself. The paths through ritual agency that women followed were highly individualized; shaped by local tradition; and marked by difference, plurality, and variation. But one thing remained constant across time and space: girls, maidens, and mature and elderly women could rely throughout life on female divinities who especially understood them. These women found fulfillment, learning, and pleasure in serving their goddesses and, in return, gave these goddesses honor and delight.

CHAPTER 3

Priesthoods of Prominence

Athena Polias at Athens, Demeter and Kore at Eleusis,
Hera at Argos, and Apollo at Delphi

The record has left a concentration of evidence for a few mainland Greek priesthoods, in contrast to a paucity of information for the majority of religious offices across the Greek world. In-depth investigation of a few case studies illuminates the localized character of Greek cult service and the diversity of the source material. For the priesthood of Athena Polias at Athens we have a wealth of epigraphic evidence that allows for extensive prosopographical work in naming historical priestesses and reconstructing their family trees. Attic vase painting supplies a wealth of images showing women engaged in cult activity (see fig. 3.1).[1] The priesthood of Demeter and Kore at Eleusis, in contrast, has left few visual images but a considerable corpus of inscriptions concerning the financial and legal aspects of the office. The priesthood of Hera at Argos is notable for its rich repertory of stories from myth. The most famous of all Greek priesthoods, that of the Pythia at Delphi, has left hardly any names of women who held the post and few images to reflect what the prophetess might have looked like. Instead, we have the oracles themselves, the very words that the priestesses are said to have spoken.

Three of the priesthoods examined in this chapter carried the extraordinary privilege of eponymy. The priesthoods of Athena Polias at Athens and of Demeter and Kore at Eleusis were invested with a cultic eponymy by which events were dated according to the personal names and tenures of the women who held the highest post. At Argos, the priestess of Hera enjoyed an even more broadly reaching civic eponymy. The tenure of her service was used to date not only matters of cult but also historical events of the day. In this, the priestess's position was comparable to that of the male archons whose tenures provided dates for historical chronologies at Athens and other cities. Thucydides (2.2.1) used the forty-eighth year of Chrysis's service as priestess at Argos, along with the tenures of the ephorate at Sparta and the archonship at Athens, to date the beginning of the Peloponnesian war.

The names of priestesses were thus among the most widely shared elements of common

Fig. 3.1
Attic red-figure amphora, the
Sabouroff Painter. London, British
Museum E 324. Photo © Copyright
the Trustees of The British Museum.

knowledge across the Greek world. This is striking, in view of the widely held belief that the names of well-born women could not even be spoken aloud in classical Athens.[2] In this, we see a contradiction between what we are told in literature and what we learn from epigraphic sources. The names of priestesses were inscribed on their statue bases and dedications as well as on the statue bases and dedications of individuals who served their cults during their tenures. The practice of sacred and civic eponymy ensured that priestly women, and their contributions, would never be forgotten. As we shall see in chapter 8, the names of priestesses were also inscribed on their funerary memorials. In chapter 7, we shall see the names of late Hellenistic and Roman priestesses inscribed upon their reserved seats within the Theater of Dionysos.

In the face of this evidence, it may be time to reconsider the consensus view that the names of respectable women were to be avoided. While this may have been true for certain orators and in some settings, such as the law courts, the case for muting the names of citizen women has, perhaps, been overstated.[3] A privileging of certain texts fuels this view, such as the funeral speech attributed to Perikles by Thucydides (2.42.2) in which the Athenian war widows are told that the less said about them, the better. As we shall see in what follows, names of respectable and influential women were, in fact, known throughout Athens and elsewhere. We shall return to this subject in chapter 10 but, for now, let us consider four priesthoods of prominence and some of the well-known women who held them.

Athena Polias at Athens

The priestess of Athena Polias held one of the most distinguished offices in the Greek world.[4] Evidence shows that the post was hereditary and exclusively held by members of the Eteoboutad clan. The priesthood was open to married women, and its tenure was for life. It was among the oldest feminine priesthoods at Athens, though we do not know how early the Eteoboutadai's claim to it was established.[5] The fact that one branch of the *genos* controlled the priesthood of Athena Polias and the other held the priesthood of Poseidon-Erechtheus is significant. By 508 B.C., these two branches were geographically separated, residing in different demes (Bate and Boutadai) and belonging to different tribes (Aigeis and Oineis).[6] The central involvement of the Eteoboutad *genos* in the cults of the two competing deities from the Athenian foundation myth suggests that the connection between clan and cult was quite ancient.[7] According to Herodotos (8.55), Athena and Poseidon competed for patronage of the city and Athena's gift of the olive tree won out over Poseidon's sea spring. This contest stands at the heart of the city's charter myth and is celebrated in the sculptural program of the Parthenon's west pediment.[8] The ancestor of the Boutadai was Boutes, who, according to Apollodoros (3.14.8–15.1), was the brother of Erechtheus. When Pandion, the father of these two heroes, died, the kingship went to Erechtheus and the priesthoods of Athena Polias and Poseidon-Erechtheus went to Boutes.[9]

Epigraphic evidence allows for the identification of at least twenty-five priestesses of Athena Polias dating from the end of the fifth century B.C. to the end of the second century A.D.[10] The stemmata proposed by Lewis, and more recently by Turner and Aleshire, for these priestesses and their families show a great deal of intermarriage. In all, priestesses of Athena are known to have come from seven tribes and thirteen demes, indicating that the office was not restricted geographically.[11] It is significant that the priesthood was always held by a woman from Bate (the home deme of the Eteoboutadai) until Penteteris of Phlya in the third century B.C. From then on, the geographical origin of the priestesses is diverse.[12]

The large number of surviving names of women who held the office allows for reconstruction of the network of families and system of intermarriage that enabled the Eteoboutadai to control this priesthood for some seven centuries.[13] It has been speculated that, in early days, the priesthood passed patrilineally through the eldest Eteoboutad male to his eldest daughter.[14] This may be true, though there is no hard evidence for it. The first identifiable priestess of Athena Polias, Lysimache, daughter of Drakontides, had a brother, Lysikles, who was secretary of the treasurers in 416/415. Clearly, this brother-sister team enjoyed particular power and influence on the Acropolis during the late fifth century, one as treasurer and the other as priestess. It has been speculated that Lysikles' eldest son's eldest daughter was the Phanostrate who served as priestess of Athena in 341/340 B.C.[15] Judy Ann Turner reconstructs a stemma through which Lysimache's nephew's son's daughter, Lysimache II (presumably named for her great-great-aunt), served as priestess of Athena Polias circa 300–290 B.C. Again, this is speculation. We do know that Lysimache II's father, Lysistratos, son of Polyeuktes I, was a *prytanis* in 341/340. Her niece, named as [Lysistra]te in an inscription, succeeded her as priestess and married into the very wealthy family of Archestratos II of Amphitrope.[16] Marrying well was something of a tradition for these Eteoboutad heiresses of the priesthood. So attractive was the prestige of the office that influential families were eager to have eligible women enter into their bloodlines. In time, the patrilineal line of succession seems to have worn thin and the priesthood was passed on matrilineally. Such was the case for Penteteris in the third century, Theodote in the second, and a number of later priestesses. It is possible that the old system was changed out of necessity, because of the absence of eligible candidates from the patrilineal line.[17]

An inscribed base for a statue of Philtera, priestess circa 130–110 B.C., boasts of her famous ancestry, including her maternal grandfather, Diogenes, liberator of Athens, and the orator Lykourgos.[18] Turner points out the significance of Philtera's claim that she is of "true Boutad blood" and suggests that the Oineid branch of the family, from which Philtera is descended, may have been considered more authentic than the Aigeid branch, which had supplied many earlier priestesses. Turner also observes that it is likely Philtera was descended from both branches of the family, which seem to have intermarried by her day.[19]

The most stunning example of the staying power of illustrious families in cult affairs is that of Philippe II, daughter of Medeios I, who served as priestess during the late second/ early first century B.C.[20] As the great-great-great-great-great-great-granddaughter of Lykourgos, Philippe could boast of an ancestry that, like Philtera's, included blood from both branches of the Eteoboutad clan. We have noted in chapter 2 that Philippe served as kanephoros at the Delia and as subpriestess of Artemis on Delos before becoming priestess of Athena Polias. Her brother, called Medeios after his father, served as Deliast (a member of the Athenian embassy sent every four years to Delos) and as priest of Poseidon-Erechtheus.[21] Philippe and Medeios are the first known brother-sister pair to hold the two most prestigious priesthoods on the Athenian Acropolis. Like Lysimache and Lysikles of the late fifth century, they held considerable economic, social, and cultural capital in executing their duties and affecting the life of their community.

Sources provide a glimpse of the busy sacred calendar and obligations incumbent on the priestesses who served. At the festival called the Chalkeia, the priestess of Athena Polias was among those who set the warp for the weaving of Athena's new peplos.[22] At the Arrephoria, it was her job to hand the arrephoroi the "secret things" that they carried upon their heads.[23] She probably supervised the Plynteria and the Kallynteria, festivals during which Athena's statue was washed and decorated. At the Skira festival, the priestess walked beside the priest of Poseidon-Erechtheus and the priest of Helios in a procession to Skiron on the road to Eleusis.[24]

Inscriptions attest to the authority of the priestess of Athena Polias. A second-century-A.D. decree stipulates that an Eleusinian official called the *phaidyntes* must inform her of the arrival of the "holy things" at the start of the Eleusinian Mysteries.[25] This special courtesy, which alerted her that the Eleusinian officials had entered Athens, underscores a protocol by which the priestess of Athena Polias held the top position. Her seniority is, in fact, attested much earlier on. Herodotos (5.72) gives us a vivid account of a priestess of Athena who ejected the Spartan king Kleomenes from the Acropolis in 508 B.C. Before the king even got a foot in the door of Athena's temple, the priestess leapt up from her throne and ordered him out. Addressing him as "stranger from Lakedaimon," she cautioned Kleomenes that it was unlawful for a Dorian to enter the holy place.[26] Despite the fact that this account is probably fictitious, a core truth reflects the authority of the priestess in enforcing sanctuary law.

The power of the priestess's voice within her community is emphasized in Herodotos's account (7.142–44) of the evacuation of Athens prior to the battle of Salamis in 480 B.C. The Athenians had consulted the Delphic oracle in the face of the Persian advance. The oracle's response was characteristically obscure: the Athenians must take refuge behind the wooden walls. The citizenry were divided between those who took "the walls" to mean the ramparts of the Acropolis and those who understood them to be the ships of the Athenian fleet. Themistokles urged the Athenians to take to the ships, but evacuation did not take place without the priestess's help. Herodotos (8.41) gives significant credit to her public announcement that the sacred snake had failed to eat its honey cake. This was taken as a sign that Athena herself had left the city, and the populace was thus evacuated more willingly. The power of the priestess to persuade the citizenry to act in accordance with Themistokles' wishes illustrates a collusion between the political and religious spheres of the city and the agency of the priestess in affecting community action.[27]

We learn of rules for the behavior of priestesses, some of which are difficult to comprehend. Strabo (9.1.11) tells us that the priestess was forbidden to eat fresh cheese produced in Attica. Two centuries later, Athenaeus (9.375c) reiterates this regulation and adds that the priestess is also prohibited from sacrificing ewe-lambs.[28] No rule is more elusive than that inscribed in the so-called Hekatompedon decree, dated to 485/484 B.C. though probably representing a copy of regulations composed under Kleisthenes around 508.[29] This set out directions for conduct on the Acropolis. "Sacrificers" were forbidden to set up pots or to kindle fires indoors. The priestesses and the *zakoroi* were not to build storerooms and could not θιπνε[ύεσθαι. If they did, they would be fined one hundred drachmas by the treasurers, and if the treasurers overlooked violations, they would be fined one hundred drachmas as well. This is a heavy penalty when considered against the general fines for the laity of just up to three obols (lines 7–8). It is two hundred times as much as the penalty for worshippers and twice the annual salary of the priestess of Athena Nike.[30] The severity of the penalty suggests that the prohibited acts represented serious transgressions. The meaning of θιπνε[ύεσθαι remains unclear. Proposed translations include "bake bread," "prepare meals," "roast on a brazier," "defecate," and "make love."[31] We cannot know exactly what the violation entailed, but it probably had to do with lighting fires for personal use rather than for authorized ritual activity.

One priestess stands out as a distinct personality among the many women who served. This is Lysimache, the first identifiable priestess of Athena Polias, whose tenure has been placed circa 430–365 B.C.[32] In chapter 5, we will look at the base of her statue found near the south wall of the Acropolis (see figs. 5.9–10). Its inscribed dedication informs us that she was the daughter of Drakontides of Bate and that she raised four children. Restoration of gaps in the damaged inscription allows us to understand that she died at age eighty-eight, having served as priestess for sixty-four years, a number also given by Pliny (*On Natural History* 34.76) writing some four hundred years later.[33]

In 1955, David Lewis boldly suggested that this historical Lysimache served as the model for the leading character in Aristophanes' *Lysistrata*.[34] In this, Lewis followed Papadimitriou, who had earlier associated another character in the play, Myrrhine, with the historical Myrrhine who served as priestess of Athena Nike at the end of the fifth century. Both Myrrhine and Lysimache were priestesses on the Acropolis in 411 B.C., the year in which Aristophanes' play was first performed.[35] We have already met Myrrhine in chapter 2 where we considered sortition in the selection of the priestess of Athena Nike. Myrrhine's grave marker (see fig. 8.1) records that she was chosen "by allotment from all." Papadimitriou's association of this Myrrhine with the Myrrhine of Aristophanes' play is most attractive. When Myrrhine meets her husband at the Acropolis gates (*Lysistrata* 920–50) she produces bedding, which would have been close to hand if she was, indeed, the priestess of Athena Nike, who had special access to the adjacent sanctuary.[36] In associating the character Lysistrata with the historical Lysimache, Lewis had to cope with the change in names. He pointed to the similarity in form and meaning between Lysistrata, "Dissolver (or Disbander) of Armies," and Lysimache, "Dissolver (or Disbander) of Battle (or Strife)." He cited *Lysistrata* 554 as an outright admission of the Lysistrata/Lysimache association. Here, Lysistrata proclaims: "I believe that one day we will be known among the Greeks as *Lysimachai* (Dissolvers of Battle)." Lewis maintained that the ancient audience would have immediately recognized the play on the names.

Over the past fifty years the double association of Lysistrata/Myrrhine has been much debated. The discussion has rarely gone beyond whether or not Lewis was right, and has seldom explored the rich implications of his suggestion for our understanding of the public status of priestly women. Characters from Aristophanes' *Lysistrata* can be seen to embody two models for priesthood current in late fifth-century Athens. The old, inherited, lifelong priesthoods, associated with the gentilician class, were typified by the priesthood of Athena Polias as held by Lysimache. The newly hewn, democratic priesthoods, selected by lot from all, were typified by the priesthood of Athena Nike, as held by Myrrhine. The play intentionally contrasts these two models to great comic effect. When Myrrhine eagerly announces that she wants to be the first to swear the oath, Kalonike stops her, saying: "No, you don't, by Aphrodite, not unless you draw the first lot" (207–8). This reference to Myrrhine and the lottery seems hardly accidental. Not far away is the lucky Myrrhine of the grave epitaph, "chosen by allotment from all," and favored "by divine good fortune."[37]

Aristophanes' use of historical figures for his dramatic characters has long been recognized.[38] Perikles, Alkibiades, Kleon, Socrates, Euripides, and Kinesias are among the many celebrity citizens whom Aristophanes lampooned. If it can be shown that the *Lysistrata* similarly draws upon the lives of historical Athenians, in this case priestesses, our view of the public role of women and their name recognition within the polis can be greatly enriched. Indeed, we might even understand these women to be insiders, part of the "men's club," so to speak, and thus fair game for public comedy. As we have seen above, eponymy ensured that priestesses would have the greatest name recognition, not only among women, but among all citizens. I do not mean to suggest that the characters Myrrhine and Lysistrata were slavishly drawn from their historical counterparts. Instead, I suggest that by invoking the names of two well-known priestesses, Aristophanes supplied a central ingredient for successful comedy: the inside joke.

Centuries later, Plutarch (*Moralia* 534b–c) recounted an anecdote involving a priestess named Lysimache as an example of how to use a joke to deflect unwanted requests from inferior persons. Although we cannot know for certain whether Plutarch was referring to the fifth-century Lysimache, or to a priestess of the same name who served during the fourth century, it is tempting to see this Lysimache as the fifth-century priestess who inspired the character Lysistrata. When the tired muleteers who had brought the "holy things" up to the Acropolis asked the priestess if they could have a drink, she jested that she was afraid to oblige them, lest her action become part of the ritual. Plutarch thus paints a picture of a clever, fun, wisecracking Lysimache. The personality of an individual woman may thus emerge from the sources to provide insight into the impact of an individual priestess within her public arena. So central were priestesses to Athenian society that their names were household words and they were fair game for jokes and for portrayal in theater. Perhaps no greater testimony can be paid to the centrality of priestesses in the society that celebrated them.

Demeter and Kore at Eleusis

The priestess of Demeter and Kore held a unique position, one that bound her to two distinct sanctuaries. In September of every year, she would set out from the great sanctuary at Eleusis and march in procession some eighteen miles to the center of Athens. Accompanied by other priestesses, she carried the *hiera* (holy things).[39] By at least the second century A.D., a corps of ephebes is known to have escorted this procession. The image of the priestess arriving at Athens to signal the start of the Eleusinian Mysteries was a sensational visual event that occurred annually for nearly a thousand years. This spectacle powerfully imprinted itself upon the collective memory of generations of Athenians. Its highly associative symbolism bound initiates and sacred officials together in an intense group experience.

Having arrived at Athens, the *hiera* were housed in the local sanctuary of Demeter, known as the City Eleusinion, at the northwest foot of the Acropolis. Here, they were kept for four days, during which the start of the Mysteries was announced to the general public. Those to be initiated bathed in the sea off Phaleron and washed piglets for the sacrifices that followed. New initiates spent the fourth day secluded indoors and, on the fifth day, processed to Eleusis for induction into the Mysteries. The priestess of Demeter and Kore marched side by side with the priestess of Athena Polias, escorting the holy things safely back home.[40]

The cult of Demeter and Kore was ministered by a host of officials, including men, women, and children. Men held the offices of *hierophantos* (revealer of sacred objects), *dadouchos* (torch bearer), *keryx* (sacred herald), *exegetes* (expounder) of the Eumolpidai, *pyrphoros* (fire carrier), *phaidyntes* (cleanser), altar priest, and others. Boys and girls were hearth initiates.[41] Women served in the posts of the two *hierophantides*, the priestess of Plouton, and the priestess of Demeter and Kore.[42] Of the many cult servants at Eleusis, it was the priestess of Demeter and Kore alone who had the names of both goddesses in her title. She alone participated in the largest numbers of Eleusinian festivals, including the Mysteries, the Eleusinia, the Thesmophoria, the Kalamaia, and the Haloa. It was *her* name that was used eponymously to date the years in which other cult officials served. For these reasons, her office has been viewed as among the oldest in the Eleusinian hierarchy, one that brought with it very great prestige.[43]

It should also be said that this office brought significant financial rewards. Epigraphic evidence suggests that this was the most lucrative of all sacred offices open to Attic women. Payments to priestesses of Demeter and Kore will be examined in chapter 7 but, for now, let us say that we have more than half a dozen inscriptions, dating from the mid-fifth century through the Roman period, that attest to their compensation.[44] These include cash payments made for each initiate inducted into the Mysteries, for carrying out duties at the Eleusinia, and for favorable sacrifices performed. The priestess also received in-kind payments from the harvest of the Rarian field.

The special relationship of the sanctuary of Demeter at Eleusis and the City Eleusinian at Athens has been seen to reflect a bipolar model that connected periphery with center, articulating the relationship of the Eleusinian cult to Athenian state religion.[45] This would support the view that Eleusis and its cult were part of the Athenian polis from the very beginning, rather than having been introduced through annexation later on.[46] The ritual procession of the priestess of Demeter and Kore provided an important visual link between these two locations and reflected the age-old relationship that the two sites shared.

Our earliest explicit evidence for the priestess of Demeter and Kore at Athens dates to circa 510–500 B.C. An inscription, carved on what appears to be an altar of Pentelic marble set up near the Eleusinion, mentions "the priestess" in a law regulating the Mysteries.[47] Fifty years later, Lysistrate, the first priestess of Demeter and Kore whose name is preserved, set up an inscribed base in the entrance porch of the Eleusinion.[48] This shows a rectangular cutting on top to receive a pillar or, possibly, a herm. In the dedicatory inscription carved on front, Lysistrate is referred to as the *propolos*, or "servant," of the "sacred rites of Deo and her daughter."

The priestess of Demeter and Kore had responsibility for a variety of festivals. Evidence attests to her role in the Kalamaia, an agrarian feast celebrated in early summer. A decree dated 164/163 B.C. honors the *demarch* of Eleusis, who "completed the sacrifice of the Kalamaia and organized the procession according to tradition together with the hierophant and the priestesses."[49] The priestess also presided at a festival known as the Haloa, a women's ritual that took place during the season for cutting grapevines and tasting wine. The worship of Dionysos joined that of Demeter for a raucous women's festival in which worshippers enjoyed plentiful food and drink, traded ribald jokes, and spoke freely in a way that women generally did not. It seems that the priestess of Demeter and Kore had the exclusive right to sacrifice at the Haloa, which, by the fourth century, had become a festival chiefly associated with *hetairai*.[50]

Of course, the priestess of Demeter and Kore played a central role in the great women's festival of the Thesmophoria.[51] In Aristophanes' *Thesmophoriazusai*, the choral leader, sometimes labeled "Herald" or "Woman Imitating Herald," and sometimes regarded as the priestess Kritylla, takes a commanding role in overseeing the preliminary ceremonies.[52] She delivers the prose proclamation, the ritual curse, and the motion of the day (295–379). Colin Austin has suggested that this choral leader may have been inspired by the model of a historical priestess of Demeter and Kore.[53] This would provide a parallel case for an Aristophanic character drawn from an actual

Fig. 3.2
Attic black-figure band cup. London, British Museum 1906.12–15.1. Photo © Copyright the Trustees of The British Museum.

priestess, just as we have seen for Lysimache and Myrrhine in the *Lysistrata*. Although this scene is usually read as a parody of the opening of the Athenian Assembly, Austin's closer look at its sacral references may point in a different direction.[54]

Visual images of the priestess of Demeter and Kore are few.[55] A black-figure Siana cup found at Kamiros on Rhodes, dated to the second quarter of the sixth century, seems to show a priestess at a harvest festival (fig. 3.2; pl. 10).[56] She stands behind a flaming altar, holding a winnowing basket (*liknon*), an instrument from which the grain was thrown into the air to separate wheat from chaff. At the far left, the goddess Demeter is enthroned. A line of five dancing women and one man move from the goddess toward the priestess at the altar. Her placement within the composition, counterbalancing the image of Demeter; her proximity to the flaming altar; and her manipulation of the instrument of ritual, the *liknon*, all argue for her identification as the presiding cult agent. Bernard Ashmole interpreted the scene as one showing the Kalligeneia, the third day of the Thesmophoria. Erika Simon has viewed it, instead, as a representation of the Chloia or the Haloa.[57] This cup, to which we shall return to at the end of the chapter, preserves one of our very earliest representations of the priestess of Demeter.

The personal names of some twenty historical priestesses of Demeter and Kore survive, dating from the mid-fifth century B.C. to the Roman period.[58] The office was open to married women with children, a fact that may suggest life tenure, though this is by no means certain. Photios tells us that the *genos* of the Philleidai provided women for the post. Whether or not the Philleidai had an exclusive right to the priesthood has been debated. The fragmentary nature of the evidence does not lend itself to a clear answer.[59] By the Roman period, intermarriage among various *gene* produced a situation in which women eligible for the post belonged to more than one clan. We have seen similar developments for the priesthood of Athena Polias during its later centuries. But unlike the priestesses of Athena, no direct relationships are attested among women who served as priestesses of Demeter and Kore. This would suggest that the office was not passed through direct inheritance but, perhaps, through election or lottery off a short list of eligible candidates.[60]

Several priestesses are known from their inscribed statue bases. Sometime before the middle of the fourth century B.C., a priestess whose name does not survive erected her statue on a base of Pentelic marble in the City Eleusinion. She is identified as the mother of Epigenes from Acharnai. A base found east of the Aeropagus Hill attests to a statue for another priestess of Demeter and Kore, set up during the third or second century.[61] Her name does not survive. Recently, the exciting discovery of an inscribed base for a statue of Chairippe by the master sculptor Praxiteles has added to the corpus of statues known for priestesses of Demeter and Kore. The fame of the artist chosen to carve this commission attests to the importance of the portrait and of the priestess. Her family is well known from a number of other inscriptions. The find spot of the base, some two hundred meters from the City Eleusinion, suggests that it originally stood in the sanctuary where Chairippe served.[62] Mention of an eponymous priestess appears on a small altar dedicated in the second or first century at the City Eleusinion.[63] It shows an incense bowl carved in low relief, a signifier of sacred service.

Habryllis served as priestess of Demeter and Kore around 150–130 B.C. She is known from a base of Hymettian marble found in the west wall of the Church of the Hypapanti near the Eleusinion.[64] The inscription records honors for a girl whose service as hearth initiate is dated to the years of Habryllis's priesthood. The girl went on to serve as kanephoros both at the Pythais festival and at the Panathenaia. Habryllis is known from a second inscription carved on her grave column. We will consider this monument in chapter 8 (see fig. 8.14).[65] Neither the grave column nor the honorific inscription specifies the cult that Habryllis served. She was long assumed to be a priestess of Athena Polias, because of the fact that the girl honored on the inscribed base served as a kanephoros at the Panathenaia. This, combined with the fact that Habryllis's grave marker shows a key adorned with ribbons, symbols that Sara Aleshire associated with the priesthood of Athena Polias, was seen to confirm Habryllis's association with the cult of Athena.[66]

Our understanding of Habryillis has changed in recent years thanks to the discovery of a third inscription, one that specifically names her as the priestess of Demeter and Kore.[67] This was found built into a Byzantine wall within the Roman agora at Athens. It now appears that Habryllis should be added to the list of known priestesses of Demeter and Kore and removed from the roster of priestesses of Athena Polias.[68] This would make sense from the *genos* perspective, as Habryllis was not from the Eteoboutad clan that provided Athena's priestesses.

Habryllis was descended from a very distinguished Athenian family. Her paternal great-great-grandfather, Eurykleides I, and his brother, Mikion II, dominated Athenian politics throughout the second half of the third century.[69] Eurykleides served as treasurer of the military fund (244/243 B.C.) and later as eponymous archon (240/239 B.C.), while Mikion served as *agonothetes* of the Panathenaia (ca. 230 B.C.). In 229 B.C., the brothers orchestrated the liberation of Athens from Macedonian rule and persuaded the Macedonian commander Diogenes to withdraw his troops from Athens.[70] This period saw something of a religious revival at Athens, perhaps in grateful response to the restoration of democracy.[71] Eurykleides and Mikion instituted a new cult of Demos and the Graces, the priesthood of which was passed down through their family line. Eurykleides himself may have served as the first priest of this cult, followed by his son Mikion.[72] The family has been further associated with priesthoods of the cult of Ptolemy Euergetes and Berenike.[73] We know that Habryllis made a significant marriage and, as the wife of Kichesias, gained access to another prominent family and its fortunes. She certainly stands out as a woman with access to a huge reservoir of social and symbolic capital, buoyed by the economic resources of the families into which she was born and married.

A century later, Glauke, daughter of Menedemos of Kydathenaion, served in the post.[74] Her family tree shows the same intersection of wealth and influence that we have seen for others who held sacred office. Glauke's great-grandfather Menedemos I was treasurer of the *prytaneis* at the end of the third century and her grandfather Archon may have served as eponymous archon.[75] Glauke was preceded, or perhaps followed, in her priesthood by Ameinokleia, daughter of Philanthes from Phyle. Ameinokleia's two sons and daughter erected her statue in the sanctuary at Eleusis.[76] Theirs was a distinguished family that could boast an aunt Gorgo who was kanephoros, an uncle Xenon (III) who was archon in 130 B.C. and *epimeletes* at Delos in 118/187, and another uncle Xenon (IV) who was *theoros* to Delphi in 128/127 B.C.[77] The tradition for interfamily officeholding is attested right through the Hellenistic period. Kleokratea, who served as priestess in the mid-first century, was the daughter of Oinophilos from Aphidna, who served as *archon basileus* in 88/87 B.C.[78]

We have the names of nine priestesses who served during the Roman period and whose lives reflect the same interweaving of economic and social capital. Flavia Laodameia, daughter of Kleitos from Phyla, was from a distinguished branch of the Keryx clan.[79] Her husband, M. An-nius Pythodoros, was priest of Delian Apollo in A.D. 113/114–125/126. He was the grandson of the philosopher Ammonios, the teacher of Plutarch.[80] We know Laodameia from a number of inscriptions, including one carved on a statue base that held the image of her great-granddaughter, Junia Melitine. This was erected by Laodameia and her granddaughter, Annia Aristokleia (Melitine's mother), to commemorate the girl's service as a hearth initiate. We know that Melitine went on to serve as a *hierophantid*.[81]

Ailia Epilampsis, daughter of Ailius Gelus of Phaleron, was a well-connected priestess who served to a ripe old age. At the end of the second century A.D., her grandson, the archon Pomponius Hegias, and his sister Pomponia Epilampsis erected a statue of Ailia at Eleusis.[82] Ailia's father had been *strategos* and priest of Olympian Zeus. Her paternal grandfather, one paternal uncle, four male first cousins, her son, and her grandson all held the office of eponymous archon. This broad network of well-placed male relatives reflects the potency of Aelia's social capital, a force that sustained her agency within the system, just as it had done for priestesses of Demeter and Kore over some seven centuries of officeholding.

Hera at Argos

The priestesses of Hera at Argos are known through lively narratives that come down to us from both myth and history. The most famous of these is Chrysis, who, on a summer evening in 423 B.C., set down her torch within the sanctuary and fell asleep. She awoke to a raging fire, ignited by the flame that she had placed too close to the garlands left for the goddess. Terrified of retaliation for her carelessness, Chrysis fled that night to Phlios. We can only imagine the panic of the aged priestess as she ran from the burning temple where she had served for fifty-six and a half years. This was not just an unfortunate accident but a grave dereliction of duty. Such transgressions constituted serious crimes that could unleash the wrath of the goddess on the entire community.

This account comes from Thucydides (4.133), whom, we have seen, used the forty-eighth year of Chrysis's priesthood to date the beginning of the Peloponnesian War (2.2.1). Although the historicity of the Chrysis story is unclear, archaeological evidence shows that the archaic temple of Hera at Argos was, indeed, destroyed by fire.[83] Pausanias (2.17.7) was aware of this fire more than five hundred years later when he chronicled his visit to the Heraion. Above the terrace of the temple that stood in his day were the remains of an older temple that had been destroyed by conflagration. Indeed, archaeological remains show temple foundations, dating circa 650–625 B.C., preserved on the upper terrace. The remains of a second temple, dated to the late fifth century, appear on the level below.[84] Pausanias retells the story of Chrysis, but in his version, the priestess flees to the temple of Athena Alea at Tegea rather than to Phlios.[85] Pausanias claims to have seen a statue of Chrysis standing in front of the burned temple, where, he tells us, her image was set up despite the calamity she caused.

Pausanias also saw statues of priestesses standing before the entrance of the new temple (2.17.3). The women commemorated here may have been members of the long succession of priestesses used by Hellanikos to reconstruct his historical chronology, a list that went back into the second millennium.[86] Assembling the names of priestesses and the number of years that each woman served, Hellanikos presented this list in his *Priestesses of Hera at Argos*, written sometime at the end of the fifth century.[87]

The name of only one priestess, Alkyone, is actually preserved in the fragments of Hellanikos. In his commentary on the fragments, Jacoby has reconstructed a list of twelve Argive priestesses.[88] This catalog is by no means complete and there are large gaps between the names of early priestesses. We are told that, in the beginning, the sanctuary of Hera was hotly contested by Argos and Tiryns. The Tirynthian version of the story holds that the first priestess was Kallithyia, daughter of King Peiras. Argive tradition, however, names Io as the first priestess.[89] At one time, these two women were combined into "Io Kallithyia," but subsequently, they were separated into two successive priestesses. We also hear of Hypermestra (daughter of Danaos), Eurydike (daughter of Lakedaimon and wife of Akrisios), and Alkyone (daughter of Sthenelos) who served in the office, as did Eurystheus's daughter Admete, who later fled to Samos. We hear of Kallisto, who is said to have lived at the time of the Trojan War, and Themisto, who succeeded her. Then comes Kydippe and Theano. Finally, we have the infamous Chrysis, who served in first quarter of the fifth century.

Varying accounts of the tale of Kleobis and Biton name their mother as Theano or as Kydippe. The fact that this priestess had sons suggests that the office was open to married women.[90] Herodotos (1.31) recounts the priestess's dilemma on festival day, when the oxen meant to pull her cart to the sanctuary were delayed in their plowing. Kleobis and Biton came to the rescue, yoked themselves to the cart, and pulled their mother some six miles to the temple. Upon arrival at the sanctuary, mother and sons received the adulation of those gathered for the festival. The priestess then offered a prayer before the image of Hera, asking that the goddess give her boys that which is best for men to have. The goddess complied. After the sacrifice and feasting, when the sons fell asleep in the temple, Hera gave them the best gift of all: death.

Hellanikos lists Io as the second priestess to serve Hera. Versions of Io's story are many, spanning a great number of centuries.[91] Her father is sometimes identified as Inachos, King of Argos, and other times as Peiras, King of Tiryns, who is said to have consecrated the cult statue at the Argive Heraion.[92] Io conforms to the prototype of the virgin princess-priestess who attracts the amorous attentions of a god or hero, in this case, Zeus himself.[93] In order to hide his adulterous intentions from his wife, Zeus disguised Io as a white cow. But Hera was

Fig. 3.3
Attic red-figure hydria, the Agrigento Painter. Boston, Museum of Fine Arts 08.417, Otis Norcroft Fund. Photo © 2007 Museum of Fine Arts, Boston.

not fooled and tricked Zeus into placing the cow under her care. When Hera assigned the watchful eyes of Argos to guard the cow, Zeus sent Hermes to kill Argos and free his beloved Io. The hapless priestess escaped, only to be tormented by an annoying gadfly sent, in turn, by the jealous Hera.

This tale is represented on a red-figure hydria in Boston (fig. 3.3).[94] In the center of the composition we see a running cow, the transformed Io herself. In front of her we see the guard, Argos, with multiple eyes spread across his body, heavily armed with club and sword. He is fleeing from Hermes, who has been sent to kill him. Altar and column set the scene within Hera's temple, and a frightened male and a female bystander run off to the wings at either side. The identity of the female figure standing before the cow is somewhat ambiguous. At first glance, she would seem to be the goddess Hera, identified by her queenly scepter and the setting of the scene within her temple.[95] But what of the temple key that she holds in her hand? Could this indicate that the woman is, instead, a priestess?[96] We shall return to this question at the end of the chapter.

The cult of Hera at Argos has left a wealth of stories from myth but little hard evidence for historical priestesses.[97] A second-century-B.C. sundial from the Heraion, reinscribed during the second century A.D., gives a dedication by a priestess (*hieropolos*) of Hera named Thaleia.[98] A late grave relief, recovered from the staircase of the Church of Saint Constantine in Argos, shows a temple key carved in low relief together with a scepter. It bears a simple inscription [Μυ]ρτία ση(μαιοφόρος) ἀρχαγέτις.[99] As "foundress" and carrier of some sort of "signs," [My]rtia seems to have had a leadership role in what was most likely the cult of Hera, though this is not confirmed. She may well join the long list of names associated with this highly symbolic and distinguished priesthood that can be traced far back into the mythical past.

Pythia at Delphi

We stand at a transitional moment in Delphic studies, when many long-held assumptions regarding the ancient sources for the Pythia are under review. The revisionist approach comes from both the scientific and the literary/historical spheres and calls into question many broadly held beliefs resulting from modern skepticism about the veracity of the ancient source material. From the time of the first excavations at the site, begun by the French in 1892, archaeologists have failed to find evidence for the chasm in the rocks that ancient authors claim to be the source of Delphi's oracular power. Without physical evidence to support ancient claims, modern interpreters have rejected eyewitness accounts of experiences at the sanctuary.[100] But a recent geological survey has revealed that two faults do, indeed, collide at a spot directly beneath the temple of Apollo. This fracture breaks through a bituminous limestone formation from which hydrocarbon gases, including ethylene, could have escaped in antiquity.[101] According to ancient sources, these gases caused hallucinogenic effects first observed in the behavior of goats. Later, shepherds were affected and, eventually, a priestess was set up on a tripod above the chasm from which she breathed in the vapors, entered a trancelike state, and pronounced prophecies.[102] Long dismissed as the stuff of legend, the existence and effects of hydrocarbon gases must be reconsidered, thanks to modern geological investigation.

In addition, the agency of the prophetess herself is under new scrutiny. It has long been assumed that ancient authors exaggerated, or wholly invented, the role of the priestess as the primary agent of oracular pronouncements at Delphi. How could a simple woman from the local peasantry have provided the authoritative voice that answered clients from far and wide? In consequential political affairs, including colonization, tyranny, and war, queries surely were submitted in writing to educated male priests who composed answers and gave them to the Pythia for delivery.[103] Lisa Maurizio has now called this consensus view into question, maintaining that "to deny the Pythia her agency in this religious rite is to render the spectacle of consulting Apollo incomprehensible."[104]

Priests were, of course, at all times absolutely essential to the functioning of the Delphi oracle. Indeed, the foundation myth recounted in the *Homeric Hymn to Pythian Apollo* does not even mention a priestess. The oldest surviving attestation of the Pythia is found in the sixth-century poet Theognis, who refers to her as the priestess (*hiereia*) at Pytho (807–808).[105] The temple hierarchy of male officials at Delphi was large and included the priests of Apollo (*hiereis*); the *prophetai* (prophets or oracle-interpreters); the *hosioi* (holy ones); and, in the tradition of Euripides' *Ion*, a temple boy. Epigraphic evidence suggests that, at least after 200 B.C., there were two priests of Apollo who were appointed for life.[106] It is possible that they were one and the same as those whom the ancient authors call *prophetai*, since the title *prophetes* does not appear in Delphic inscriptions.[107] We learn that there were five holy men called *hosioi* who came from reputable local families, said to be descendants of the legendary Deukalion (Plutarch *Moralia* 292d).[108]

Maurizio has shown that there is much overlap in language used to describe the priestess and the male attendants who surrounded her. The word *mantis* (seer), comes from the root word *men* and describes one who is in a special mental state, what we might call inspiration.[109] The title *prophetes*, by contrast, is based on the root for "to say" or "to speak" and conveys the role of one who proclaims publicly. The prophets have traditionally been viewed as those who wrote down the Pythia's responses. The old model has the Pythia serving as *mantis*, uttering inspired words in an altered mental state, while *prophetai* transformed her babble into intelligible prose. But in reality, things were not so simple. The Pythia is referred to equally in the sources as *mantis*, *prophetis*, and even *promantis*, or "fore-seer."[110] Her active agency within the ritual deserves careful consideration.

The office of prophetess at Delphi is atypical of Greek feminine priesthoods in that the Pythia was chosen from among women who were neither well born nor rich, and who were subject to the extraordinary requirement of perpetual celibacy.[111] In addition, her prophecies were directly inspired by the god rather than indirectly through lots, signs, or incubation, as was the norm at most oracular sites. Early on, the Pythia was chosen from among maidens of the local peasantry, but in time and on account of the rape of one such maiden priestess, the post came to be filled by older women who had passed the age of fifty.[112] Although advanced in years, the women dressed in maiden costume in remembrance of the youthful priestesses from days gone by. The Pythia could have been married and had children, but from the time she took up her post, she was required to remain chaste and live apart from her husband. She held the office until death.

The Pythia was active for just nine months a year, as the oracle closed down for the three winter months, when Apollo was understood to have departed for the land of the Hyperboreans. She gave prophecies only on the seventh day after each new moon. One can only imagine the great queue of questioners on the nine days of the year when the oracle was functioning. It is understandable that, during the classical period when the shrine was especially busy, there were as many as three Pythias working at once on a shift system. Two Pythias would alternate in the mantic sessions and one would serve as an understudy.[113]

Even with these provisions, some inquirers were frustrated by the limited schedule of times for consultation. It was very inauspicious for the priestess to give prophecies on days that were not designated by law. The young Alexander the Great was eager for a consultation before he set out for Asia but had the bad luck to arrive at Delphi on a day when oracles were not being given (Plutarch *Alexander* 14.6–7). When his request for a session with the priestess was rejected, the brash young king tried to drag the Pythia into the temple himself, demanding that she work. Impressed by his passion, the priestess exclaimed, "You are invincible, my son!" and Alexander went away happy with the very words that he had hoped to hear.

When Appius Claudius Pulcher aggressively pressed the priestess Phemonoe for a mantic session, she first tried to put him off (Lucan *The Civil War* 5.130–31). Later, she relented and prophesied that he would have no part in war but find peace in Euboia. Appius was pleased, understanding this to mean that he would win an easy victory. But Phemonoe was, instead, predicting his imminent death. We hear of another impatient male leader, Philomelos, the Phokian commander during the Third Sacred War (Diodorus Siculus 16.27.1). After he seized control of Delphi in 356, he demanded that the Pythia mount the tripod according to ancestral custom. When she refused, saying that it was *not* the custom, he threatened her. The Pythia coolly replied, "It is in your power to do as you please." Philomelos was delighted, understanding that he could carry on with his military plans. He, of course, did not foresee his defeat at the battle of Neon just two years later. On the basis of these stories, one could say that we have a tradition in which calm and composed Delphic priestesses handled impertinent male inquirers with a certain diplomatic aplomb.

We know the personal names of very few women who held the post, and most of these are attested in myth rather than in historical sources. In Aeschylus's *Eumenides* (1–8), the prophetess gives a genealogy for the women who held oracular powers. First it was Earth (Ge) who had the prophetic gift. She passed it on to her daughter, the goddess Themis, who consented for it to be passed on to her sister, the Titan Phoibe. Phoibe, in turn, handed over the oracular seat to Phoibos (Apollo) as a birth gift, also giving him her name. Pausanias (10.5.7) similarly credits Ge with the original prophetic powers, but in his version of the story, Earth passes the gift on to Daphnis, one of the nymphs residing on Mount Parnassos.

There is a widespread tradition that Apollo's first prophetess was named Phemonoe.[114] She is famous for being the first Pythia to have sung in hexameter verse. Phemonoe, which means

"Speaker of Thoughts" or "Thinker of Oracular Speech," became the archetypal name for the Pythia, just as Theano was for priestesses of Athena.[115] When Lucan tells the story of Appius Claudius Pulcher's visit to Delphi in 48 B.C., he names the presiding priestess Phemonoe, though she is a long way off in time from the first Pythia. His Phemonoe is portrayed as wandering aimlessly around the grove near the Castalian Spring, free from her duties, since by then the oracle had fallen silent and the temple was locked shut (*The Civil War* 5.123–127).

Herodotos gives us the names of a few prophetesses who served at critical points in his *Histories*. We hear of a disgraced priestess named Perialla, who was corrupted by Kobon, son of Aristophanes, and dismissed from her office (*Histories* 6.66). When Kleomenes tried to usurp power from Demaratos, he first cast into doubt the legitimacy of Demaratos's succession. Consulting the Pythia on this question, Kleomenes made sure that she had been bribed in advance to give the answer he wanted to hear. "Is Demaratos the son of King Ariston?" Kleomenes asked. Perialla gave the prearranged response: "No." For engineering this false charge of illegitimacy, Kobon was banished from Delphi and Perialla was dismissed from office.

Herodotos (7.140.2–3) tells us that a priestess named Aristonike was consulted by the Athenians prior to the battle of Salamis in 480 B.C. She emphatically urged the Athenians to leave their city: "Why sit, you doomed ones, fly to the ends of the earth!" Pythagoras is said to have studied under a Delphic priestess, Themistokleia, whose name reflects the root "Themis," the goddess who held the oracular powers in early days.[116] We hear of a prophetess named Xenokleia, who refused to give a consultation to Herakles because he was guilty of the murder of Iphitos (Pausanias 10.13.8). Angered by her refusal, Herakles took the tripod out of the temple and carried it away. When he returned the tripod, Xenokleia obliged him, telling him all that he wanted to know.

Epigraphic sources have preserved the name of only one historical priestess of Apollo who served very late in the history of Delphi. Theoneike is referred to as "Pythia of the god" in a third-century-A.D. inscription found on a block built into a Byzantine church.[117] This stone once held a memorial for the priestess's granddaughter, who was also named Theoneike. Her grandfather Hippokrates, husband of her grandmother Theoneike, is named as priest of Apollo. The younger Theoneike married her uncle Phoibianos, who also served as priest.[118] This inscription bears witness to the fact that priestesses of Apollo at Delphi included women who had been married and had children prior to their service. It also suggests that, at least by the Roman period, the privilege of priestly office holding at Delphi may have been concentrated in a few prominent families.

A wide variety of sources inform us on the experience of the Pythia during her mantic sessions. From the third century B.C., authors locate the setting for oracular response at a spot

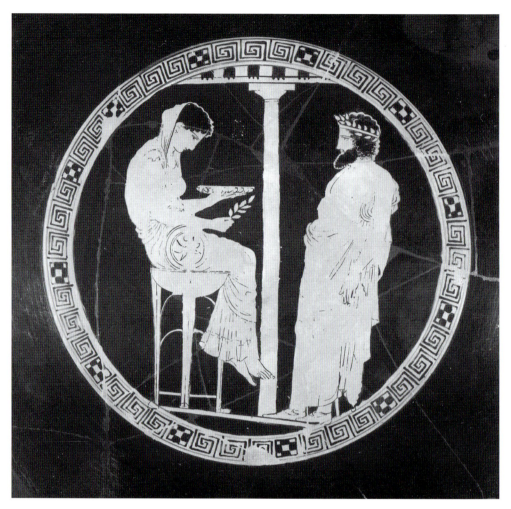

Fig. 3.4
Attic red-figure cup, the Codrus Painter. Berlin, Staatliche Museen Antikensammlung F2538. Photo Antikensammlung, Staatliche Museen zu Berlin, Preussicher Kulturbesitz.

above a crevice in the rocks from which rising vapors escaped.[119] As noted above, the temple of Apollo was carefully positioned atop this geological formation, with its *adyton*, or inner sanctum, placed directly above the fissure. The nearby spring of Kassotis held special powers and its waters plunged underground, reappearing within the adyton of Apollo's temple (Pausanias 10.24.7). The Pythia drank from this spring in preparation for her mantic sessions.[120] In the opening scene of the *Eumenides* (1–30), the Pythia offers a prayer honoring the Delphic divinities before she enters the temple. Plutarch (*Moralia* 397a) tells us that she burned laurel leaves and barley meal upon the altar before mounting the tripod. While giving oracular pronouncements, she wore a crown of bay leaf on her head and held a sprig of bay in her hand, a description consistent with what we see on a red-figure cup in Berlin (fig. 3.4).[121]

Consultation took place within the adyton of the temple, where the stone *omphalos*, or "navel," marked the center of the earth (Pindar *Paean* frag. 52f.17). By several accounts, this is the spot where Zeus's eagles met when they set off in flight in search of the center of the earth.[122] A laurel tree is said to have grown within the adyton, which also housed a gold statue of Apollo and Apollo's lyre.[123] The most distinctive feature of the inner sanctum was the great bronze tripod set above the crevice. Diodorus Siculus (16.26.5) claims that the tripod was actually invented at Delphi for the purpose of holding the Pythia above the escaping gases. The Codrus Painter's cup, dated to circa 440–430 B.C., gives us a rare image of a priestess seated upon the tripod in precisely the manner that the sources describe (see fig. 3.4).[124] She holds a libation bowl in one hand and looks intently into it, as if she were divining some information from its contents. In her other hand she holds a laurel branch, evoking the god Apollo and the laurel tree that grew within the sacred space.

The cup shows the Pythia as we imagine she would have looked performing her mantic duties. Her placement within an architectural setting, complete with Doric column and triglyph/metope frieze, locates the scene within the temple of Apollo. An inquirer stands before her, crowned with laurel and heavily draped in a himation. But this is no generic priestess and no average pilgrim. Painted inscriptions tell us that this Pythia is actually the goddess Themis and the inquirer is King Aigeus of Athens. Without these identifying inscriptions, we surely would have assumed that the images represented a contemporary scene rather than an episode from the mythical past.

We lack sources that describe what normal mantic sessions were like. It is the extraordinary cases that attracted the ancient authors, and such was the motivation for Plutarch's summary (*Moralia* 438b) of an eyewitness account from Nikandros, priest of Apollo. Plutarch himself served as a priest at Delphi and must have been close to Nikandros, to whom he dedicated his essay *On Listening to Lectures*. Plutarch describes Nikandros both as a *prophetes* and as an *hiereus* (*Moralia* 438b, 386b). He recounts that Nikandros was present with some holy men, *hosioi*, when a certain Pythia was forced against her will to give a prophecy.[125] An embassy had arrived from abroad for consultation. Things went terribly wrong at the preliminary sacrifice when the animal victim failed to respond to the first libations. The priests were eager to please the visitors and so further encouraged the animal to respond by giving it a very heavy dousing of liquid offerings. The Pythia disapproved of this intervention and understood the animal's reluctance to be inauspicious. Forced into the adyton for prophecy, she was suddenly filled with an evil spirit. She soon became hysterical and with a terrifying scream ran toward the exit and threw herself down.[126] A few days later she died.

Lucan gives an even more extreme account of a forced prophecy and its disastrous consequences (*The Civil War* 5.65–236). We have already touched briefly on the story of Phemonoe's encounter with Appius Claudius. Having forced the priestess into the closed temple, Appius witnessed a startling sequence of events. He pressed Phemonoe to tell him about the outcome of the civil war and threatened to punish her if she refused to answer. At first, she only pretended to be inspired but soon she was overtaken by Apollo. She raged madly about the cave, with the ribbons and garlands falling loose in her hair. With her head shaking she circled about the temple, scattering tripods in her way, raging with the god inside her. "First the wild frenzy overflowed through her foaming lips; she groaned and uttered loud inarticulate cries with panting breath; next, a dismal wailing filled the vast cave; and at last, when she was mastered, came the sound of articulate speech" (*The Civil War* 5.190–193).[127] Phemonoe did not recover from her possession and died soon thereafter. Just as we have seen in Plutarch's account, forced prophecy could be deadly for a priestess.

These stories have had a lasting effect on the prevailing view of the Pythia as a frenzied, babbling voice box of the god. Simon Price has argued that we should understand these accounts as exceptional rather than as typical.[128] In fact, the Pythia exerted considerable control over the oracles that she delivered. Price points out that for the occasional instances of corruption attested at Delphi, it is the priestess alone who is bribed, not the male priests around her. In addition to Kobon's corruption of Perialla discussed above, we hear that Kleisthenes bribed a Pythia (Herodotos 5.63, 5.66, 6.123) as did the Spartan king Pleistonax and his brother (Thucydides 5.16). These cases suggest that the Pythia was the one who held chief responsibility for the oracles, supporting Maurizio's claim for her primary agency within the ritual.

Ancient sources are also very informative on the experience of the inquirer. Although we are told that the Pythia was interrogated by male clients alone, the reality appears to have been more complex. Plutarch cites a law forbidding women from approaching the temple (*Moralia* 385c). But this contradicts Euripides' *Ion*, in which the chorus of Athenian maidservants ask the temple boy whether it is lawful for them to enter the sanctuary. Ion first answers no, but then adds: "If you have sacrificed the holy cake before the temple and wish to ask a question of Phoibos, go to the shrine. Do not go into the inmost recess without sacrificing a sheep" (*Ion* 226–29).[129] The decree cited at the opening of this book, granting Chrysis priority of consultation at Delphi, suggests that she had direct access to the oracle, despite her female gender. This could be the result of her special status as priestess of Athena Polias or as *proxenos* of Delphi. It is possible that male kin carried the questions of female family members into the adyton. Certainly, there were different rules at different times over the course of the thousand years of activity at the shrine. The fact that many of the surviving questions put to the Pythia pertain to fertility and childbirth argues for the active participation of women in Delphic consultation, even if through male emissaries.

Those seeking an audience with the Pythia had first to perform rites including purification by bathing in holy water and offering a *pelanos* (cake of barley, honey, and meal) upon the altar in front of Apollo's temple. A preliminary sacrifice was offered by the Delphic priests on behalf of all inquirers on regular consultation days. The behavior of the victim, a goat, was carefully watched for signs. If the animal shook itself sufficiently, it was inferred that Apollo approved, and the sacrifice proceeded.[130] The inquirer would then pay a fee and enter the temple, where a final sacrifice was required upon the inner hearth. The local representative of his home city (*proxenos*) would accompany him into the inner chamber. Plutarch (*Moralia* 437c) tells us that those waiting to consult the oracle sat in a room that, at times, was filled with a delightful fragrance floating on air from the adyton "as if from a spring." He likens this fragrance to the aroma of a fine perfume. When the time came for consultation, the client would put his question to the priestess either orally or written upon a tablet.[131]

Just more than six hundred oracular responses survive. These are, allegedly, words spoken by the Pythia. Some texts record authentic, historical responses, while others are clearly drawn from legend, fabrication, or a combination of both.[132] In some cases, oracles seem to be rubber-stampings of decisions already taken.[133] Responses came in the form of prose texts and hexameter verses. There is much discussion of the role of the *prophetai* and poets in putting the Pythia's words into verse.[134] About one-third of the oracles are ambiguous. Categories of inquiry include the personal, the religious, and the political. Plutarch (*Moralia* 386c) gives a wide-ranging list of questions put to the oracle. Will the inquirer be victorious? Will the inquirer marry? Would it be more profitable and better to do this or that?[135] Nearly three-quarters of the historical responses deal with questions of cult, their foundations, festivals, temples, sacrifices, and laws. The majority of the nonreligious responses have to do with public affairs concerning leaders, legislation, the founding of cities and colonies, foreign relations, and war.[136]

Some responses deal directly with questions concerning priestesses. The Parians brought a request to Delphi, asking whether they should execute Timo, *hypozakoros* of Demeter and Persephone (Herodotos 6.135). She had aided Miltiades in his attempt to take Paros and had revealed to him sacred mysteries that were forbidden to men. The oracle responded that the priestess should not be punished, since she had merely contributed to, and not caused, Miltiades' final undoing.[137] A related response concerns the Athenian proposal for a war with Syracuse in 416/415 B.C. Although the question does not survive, the oracle's response does. It advised the Athenians to bring the priestess of Athena from Erythrai or Klazomenai (Plutarch *Moralia* 403b; *Nikias* 13.4).[138]

The model of the Delphic Pythia influenced oracular priesthoods elsewhere. The temple of Apollo Pythios at Argos was supposed have been founded directly from Delphi. Here, a priestess gave prophecies just as at the mother shrine (Pausanias 2.24.1). At the sanctuary of Apollo at Patara, the prophetess was locked in the temple on nights when responses were required (Herodotos 1.182). At a sanctuary of Apollo in Epiros, a virgin priestess oversaw an annual ceremony that included the hand-feeding of snakes (Aelian, *On Animals* 11.2). The Epirotes believed that the snakes were directly descended from the Delphic Python. Pilgrims came from far and wide to watch the spectacle. If the snakes readily ate the food that the priestess offered, the omen was understood to be favorable. While the virgin priestess of Epiros was not strictly speaking a prophetess, her actions did result in signs that portended the future. Herodotos (7.111.2) informs us that, at the shrine of Dionysos among the Satric Bessoi in Thrace, a woman *promantis* delivered oracles "as at Delphi, and nothing more intricate." This observation may reflect the fact that the Pythian model was one in which the prophetess received direct inspiration from the god, rather than through the more widely attested oracular vehicles of lots, signs, or incubation.[139]

Across the Aegean at the sanctuary of Apollo at Didyma, male prophets had given oracles from the early Archaic days of the Branchidai. But by the Hellenistic period, priestesses took over the work of prophecy, presumably under the influence of the Delphic model.[140] An inscription from Didyma dating to the first century A.D. was composed by a *hydrophoros* named Tryphosa, daughter of Melas. Her grandmother, also named Tryphosa, is said to be "the prophetess whom the god appointed in an oracle, when Claudius Charmus the younger was prophet."[141] A second inscription, dating to the first century B.C. or A.D., suggests the presence of female seers at Didyma. It reads: "Gaius, I thank the pretty little prophetess."[142] A third inscription may refer to a prophetess named Kleopatra who served during the second half of the second century A.D., though this depends on extensive restoration of the text.[143]

Sixty-one responses survive for Didyma and show characteristics similar to those from Delphi.[144] Some directly concern priestesses. An inscription carved on the front face of an anta block, dated to the second century A.D., records a response given to Alexandra, priestess of Demeter Thesmophoros.[145] Alexandra was concerned by the fact that since the time she took office, the gods had never before been so manifest in their appearances through maidens and women, men, and children. In response, Apollo assures Alexandra that the manifestations are favorable and advises her that "immortals accompany mortal men . . . and make their will known." The same block preserves an incomplete but related response inscribed on its left side. The text is also addressed to Alexandra.[146] It acknowledges her good service as priestess, praising her for the honor with which she has been "a seeker of the goal of a principled course in life."

From Italy to Egypt and beyond, most oracles were dependent on signs, lots, and dreams rather than on direct inspiration from the god.[147] At Dodona, divination was manifested in the rustling of leaves and the twittering of doves in Zeus's oak tree. We are told that the oracle was established here when two black doves flew out of Thebes in Egypt (Herodotos 2.55). One traveled to Dodona and settled in the oak tree, from which it declared, in human speech, that this was a place of divination for Zeus. The other dove flew to Libya, where the oracle of Zeus Ammon was founded. The priestesses of these establishments were called doves, because they spoke a strange language that sounded like the twitter of birds.[148] Herodotos (2.55) himself visited Dodona and spoke with the presiding priestesses, the eldest named Promeneia, the second Timarete, and the youngest Nikandra. He clearly regarded these women as trustees of sacred knowledge from whom he was eager to learn all he could regarding the origins of the establishment.

The specter of the Pythia loomed large in the ancient world. We learn from Iamblichos, in what is almost certainly an anachronistic invention, that the birth of Pythagoras was predicted by the prophetess herself. When Pythagoras's father consulted the priestess, he was told that his wife would bear an extraordinary son. This is why the boy was named Pythagoras, which means "spoken by the Pythia."[149] When did the priestess of Apollo stop speaking at Delphi? In the fourth century A.D., when the envoy Oribasios was sent to Delphi by the emperor Julian the Apostate, he reported that the spring had fallen still and the Pythia spoke no more.[150] In A.D. 391, the emperor Theodosios issued the famous edict that effectively banned divination and closed all oracular shrines (Theodosian Code 16.10.9). With this, a grand tradition of some one thousand years of prophetic proclamations and the women who spoke them came to a firm and final end.

⁓

In closing, let us examine the varied visual evidence for these priesthoods of prominence and acknowledge just how uncertain our readings of ancient images can be. The four vases considered in this chapter span some 130 years, show black-figure and red-figure technique, and represent shapes that include cups, an amphora, and a hydria. Any comparisons made within this group invite methodological difficulties stemming from chronological, technical, and formal differences. Nonetheless, this exercise usefully engages us with the fundamental problem of the relationship of myth and realia in the image-creation process.

The composition of the scene on the London cup (see fig. 3.2; pl. 10) emphasizes the communality between Demeter and her priestess as they face one another from either end of the picture field. The priestess is surrounded by a combination of sign-components that reinforce her presiding role within the ritual. These include the flaming altar of sacrifice and the winnowing basket, a symbol of the harvest. When this scene is read together with the image on the reverse side of the cup, its meaning is enhanced. Here, a stout man is depicted in the act of plowing, while a younger man follows behind, sowing seeds in the freshly tilled earth. The plowing man has been identified as Bouzyges, the first to yoke an ox and introduce cultivation at Athens.[151] In commemoration of Bouzyges and his important contribution, an annual festival was observed at the foot of the Acropolis called the *hieros arotos*, or "sacred plowing."[152] It fell to the Bouzygai, a clan named for this famous ancestor, to undertake the ritual cultivation each year. If we read the plowing scene as one drawn from legend, that is, as the charter myth upon which the historical ritual was based, should we not then understand the sacrificial scene to show a mythical narrative as well? On this view we can read round the cup, from Bouzyges' first plowing on one side, to the city's first harvest festival on the other. The woman at the altar would then represent a legendary, perhaps first, priestess of Demeter shown presiding over rites that include dancing and sacrifice in thanksgiving to the goddess.

We have already touched upon the iconographic challenges presented by the red-figure hydria in Boston that shows a scene set in Hera's temple at Argos (see fig. 3.3). Here, the mythological character of the narrative is clear, and we can identify with ease the figures of Argos, Hermes, and Io, who has been transformed into a cow. The identity of the woman who stands before the cow is less certain. She is usually recognized as Hera, holding her scepter as queen of the gods. But what about the symbol of priesthood that she carries, the temple key? Alexander Mantis maintains that this is Hera, citing a number of sources that refer to goddesses as *kleidouchoi*, and pointing to images in which Hera holds a key.[153] Erika Simon would disagree, and identifies the woman as a priestess, the successor of Io.[154] There may be a further possibility. Could we, in fact, be looking at Io shown twice within the composition, once as a cow and again as a priestess? This would compress the story of her transformation into a single image in what has been called simultaneous or synoptic narrative.[155] Io is, after all, immortalized as the *kleidouchos* of Hera in Aeschylus's *Suppliants* (291–92) where the chorus asks, "Is there a story told here in Argos that once Io was keeper of the keys of Hera's temple?"[156] Or, perhaps, goddess and priestess are so strongly identified that their images merge into one. This scene beautifully illustrates the difficulties we face in extracting meaning from ancient images.

When we turn to the Codrus Painter's cup, on which a woman is shown seated in the tripod of Apollo, we are surprised to find that our assumptions are not those of the ancient artist (see fig. 3.4). The sacred signifiers, including tripod, laurel branch, libation bowl, architectural setting, and inquirer, tell us that we are looking at the Pythia at Delphi. But added inscriptions inform us otherwise. This is no mortal priestess but the goddess Themis. The inquirer is no earthly pilgrim but the mythical King Aegeus. Without the painted labels we would never have guessed these identifications.

Gloria Ferrari has examined a number of images that similarly appear to show scenes from "everyday life," but, in fact, show narratives from myth.[157] Their identifications are confirmed by the painted inscriptions that label the figures. What looks like a generic symposium scene on a red-figure rhyton in Richmond, in fact, shows mythical kings of early Athens banqueting together.[158] A bell krater by the Dinos Painter seems to present an "everyday" scene of a departing warrior but in fact shows the eponymous heroes Pandion, Akamas, and Oineus.[159] A pyxis in London presents a "domestic scene" with a woman working wool, and others holding an alabastron, basket, and chest.[160] Painted labels tell us that these are no ordinary women but Helen, Klytaimnestra, Kassandra, and Danae. Alain Schnapp and François Lissarrague have encountered a similar phenomenon in their analysis of scenes showing dead heroes. When unlabeled, the images are interpreted as generic battle scenes, but when inscriptions are added, we learn that they portray Ajax carrying the corpse of Achilles off the battlefield at Troy.[161] These case studies caution us to be wary of our assumptions when reading images as snapshots of reality. We must allow for the possibility that they show an imagined world of the past.[162]

Let us conclude with the amphora that shows a woman pouring a libation for Athena, to illustrate the breadth of possible interpretations for its images (see fig. 3.1).[163] The woman wears no jewelry and is shown barefoot. She carries no temple key and wears no fancy dress that might communicate her priestly status. Can her libation bowl and jug, used together as a set, signify her special agency within the ritual? Following the paradigm presented by the Codrus Painter's cup, should we first look for a meaning in the mythical past? Could this woman be Queen Praxithea, first priestess of Athena Polias at Athens, shown serving the goddess who appointed her to office (Euripides *Erechtheus, Pap. Sorbonne* 60)?

When we turn to the image of Athena, a range of possible interpretations presents itself. Athena wears her aegis atop what appears to be a chiton, peplos, and himation, rather than over her traditional costume of a peplos worn alone. She holds a helmet in one hand and, in the other, a scepter rather than her traditional spear. What motivated the selection of signifiers whereby Athena's standard attributes have been exchanged for chiton, himation, and scepter? The dark-trimmed himation falls somewhat improbably from beneath her aegis. Could we be looking at a woman dressed in an "Athena costume" rather than the goddess herself? Is this image influenced by the visual dynamic of ritual theater, in which priestesses took on the likenesses of the goddesses they served?

This line of inquiry will be pursued in the following chapter, in which we shall consider priestly costume and ritual theater. Our efforts to comprehend the roles of myth and realia in the image-creation process are further complicated by the function of mimesis. As we shall see, ancient women engaged in cultic dramas, processions, and feasts dressed in the costumes of goddesses. The vases examined in this review of "priesthoods of prominence" alert us to the obstacles that stand between us and a full understanding of the mentality in which the images were created and received. The challenges that they present repay the efforts of examination, as they engage us so directly with the fundamental dynamics of image and meaning.

CHAPTER 4

Dressing the Part
Costume, Attribute, and Mimesis

Sometime during the second century A.D., Xenophon of Ephesos, a novelist about whom we know nearly nothing, described a fourteen-year-old girl leading a procession in honor of Artemis at his famous hometown. His fictional heroine, Anthia, was an exceptional maiden, selected from all the Ephesian girls to walk first in line. We are told that her natural beauty was enhanced by the adornment of her dress:

> A prodigy of loveliness (who) far surpassed all the other maidens. Her eyes were shining sometimes like a girl's and sometimes severe as of a chaste goddess. Her dress was a frock of purple, her wrap was a fawn skin and a quiver hung down her shoulders. She carried a bow and a javelin and dogs fled at her heels. Time and again when the Ephesians saw her in the sacred procession they bowed down as to Artemis...some of the spectators asserted that she was the very goddess, others declared she was a replica fashioned by the goddess.[1]
> (*An Ephesian Tale* 1.2.5–7)

Anthia did not resemble Artemis by chance. Special care had been taken to costume her in the guise of the goddess whom she honored. Xenophon does not claim priestly status for Anthia, yet she surely had special agency within the ritual as leader of the procession. Xenophon's novel is a work of fiction and is relatively late in date. Nonetheless, the image of divine imitation that he so effectively portrays rings true against earlier evidence from literary and epigraphic texts. His costumed Anthia is typical of sacred dress-up practiced within the context of festivals, particularly those in which priests and priestesses may have reenacted foundation myths.

Were priests and priestesses distinguished by special vestments throughout the calendar year? The question is problematic. Indeed, some scholars have denied the existence of priestly garb altogether.[2] But as we shall see, texts and inscriptions attest that sacred servants were required to wear special attire in particular sanctuaries and on specific occasions.

No text gives a more detailed picture of requirements for ritual dress than does the extraordinary inscription from Andania in the southern Peloponnese.[3] The local Mysteries of Demeter were celebrated just to the east of Messene in the Karnasion grove. A decree dating to 92 B.C. advises participants on appropriate dress, processional order, the setting up of tents, the treasury and its funds, sacrificial animals, woodcutting, water use, bathing regulations, and punishments for violation of rules. The decree's highly specific dress code differentiates appropriate costume for priests and priestesses, male and female sacred officials, male and female initiates and their daughters, female slaves and those who "dress in the manner of the gods." So important were these regulations that the officials in charge of the Mysteries were required to swear an oath that they would enforce them.

The Andanian decree is relatively late in date. But as early as the Homeric epics, we find that individuals about to pray or to offer sacrifice prepared themselves by washing their hands, bathing, and changing their clothes.[4] This symbolized a transition from the world of the profane to the world of the sacred and enabled the worshipper to proceed in a pure state. Although delivered in ridicule, Demosthenes' description of his rival Aeschines' youthful participation in the rites of the god Sabazios is telling. Aeschines' mother was a priestess in this exotic foreign cult, which old-guard Athenians, like Demosthenes, found eccentric. The orator derides his opponent, portraying Aeschines as an acolyte who bathed initiates and helped them into their ritual dress. "At night it was your duty to mix the libations, to clothe the initiates in fawn-skins, to wash their bodies, to scour them with the loam and the bran, and, when their lustration was duly performed, to set them on their legs, and give out the hymn" (Demosthenes, *On the Crown* 259–60).[5] Washing and changing into special costume remained an important component of initiation. As with other cult practices, wearing appropriate costume was meant to please, and prevent offending, the divinities honored.

Within visual culture, the identification of sacred dress can be tricky. Sacred servants were not isolated and distinct from the general population but were private men and women who temporarily took on public religious duties. In vase painting and sculpture, priestesses can be seen wearing the same combination of light undergarment beneath heavy mantle, the chiton and himation, that is the standard dress for all women of the period. It is possible that woven decoration and colors may have communicated priestly status. But pigment rarely survives on marble statuary and indicators that were recognizable to the ancient viewers may be lost to us. We must look to attributes and accessories, as well as to context, in order to establish parameters within which we can recognize priestly costume. Jewelry and royal accoutrements, such as the scepter, can indicate sacred status. But of all attributes, it is the temple key that is the surest signifier of feminine priesthood.

The study of priestly dress is fraught with difficulties common to the study of Greek costume, since so few fragments of ancient textiles survive to show us what clothing of the period looked like.[6] We must cope with secondhand evidence, using texts and images that describe or represent costume, to reconstruct names for garments and the manner in which they were worn. When confronted with images from the visual repertory, we are faced with a fundamental problem of interpretation. Do these represent reality, showing contemporary costume as it was actually worn? Do they show a historical past with costumes from times gone by? Do the images represent a mythical or imaginary world created by the artist?[7] Matching items of clothing named in texts with representations of costume shown in art invites methodological difficulties, as the language of images and the language of texts are not necessarily the same. The task of identifying specific meanings for costume, especially in the case of sacred dress, is even more hazardous, as we are ill equipped to recognize aspects of Greek ritual that would have been immediately understood by the ancient spectator.

Just because it is difficult for us to decipher codes for signification in Greek dress does not mean that they are not there. Those who deny the existence of priestly garb find themselves at odds with long-standing patterns of communication, attested across time and cultures, in which dress and body adornment carry messages about the wearer. The nonverbal power of costume is central to the construction and communication of identity, and to the conveyance of social messages about the relationship of the wearer to the larger group. Clothing, jewelry, hairstyles, cosmetics, body painting, piercing, tatooing, and ornamentation communicate identity and, in turn, shape the identity of those dressed and adorned. Diane Bolger has recently traced the intellectual history of these considerations from phenomenology and perception-theory of the 1960s; through semiology in the 1970s; to their treatment in the fields of sociology, cultural anthropology, and social psychology today.[8] Analysis of dress and body adornment has become a growing theme in archaeological investigation, though it is still more prominent in New World and prehistoric studies than in classical archaeology.[9] It is hard to imagine that Greek priesthood would have escaped this very human means of signification, particularly within a system that was so steeped in tradition and so richly associated with divine, royal, and status-bound symbolism.

Royal and Theatrical Dress

Priestly dress was associated with both royal and divine costume. The scepter is an attribute shared by priests and priestesses, kings and queens, and gods and goddesses alike. As early as Homer, we find the priests Chryses (*Iliad* 1.15) and Teiresias (*Odyssey* 11.91) distinguished by the scepters that they carry. The communality of dress worn by priests and kings is attested in the well-known story told by Plutarch in which Kallias, a *dadouchos* of Demeter at Eleusis, came to the battle of Marathon dressed in his priestly garb (*Aristides* 5.7). Following the battle, some barbarians, "thinking him a king because of his long hair and headband, bowed to the ground before him, took him by the hands and showed him a heap of gold." When it comes to the world of women, literary references to priestly dress are few. Aeschylus's description of Kassandra's oracular garb in the *Agamemnon* (1265–70) gives us one of the few descriptions of feminine sacred costume to survive from classical literature. Arriving at the palace in Argos, the prophetess carries a scepter and wears a prophetic garland (*manteia stephe*) around her neck.[10]

An actual golden scepter, allegedly found in a fourth-century grave in Taras, may be the sacred insignia of a priestess who was buried with the attributes of her service. The scepter, as well as a necklace and a ring said to have been found with it, were acquired by the British Museum in 1871 (figs. 4.1–3; pls. 5–7).[11] As there was no royalty at Taras during the fourth century, the monarchy having ended by at least 473 B.C., it is possible that the scepter belonged to a cult agent.[12] The necklace grouped with it may hold a clue, since two of its pendants show female heads equipped with horns (fig. 4.2; pl. 4). This suggests identification with Io, the priestess of Hera at Argos, whom, as we have seen in chapter 3, was transformed into a cow (see fig. 3.3). Indeed, from the fifth century onward, Io is regularly depicted as a woman with horns.[13] The box-bezel ring associated with this jewelry group shows a seated woman holding what may be a flower, or perhaps a scepter with crowning finial, much like the gold scepter associated with it (fig. 4.3; pl. 6). If this is a scepter, then we may have on the ring an image of a priestess who holds the symbol of her office. Still, we cannot know if this group was truly found together and, if so, whether or not it belonged to a priestess of Hera.[14]

Priestly dress not only resembled royal garb but theatrical costume as well. Athenaeus (1.21e) compares the elaborate vestments of the Eleusinian priest with the costumes that Aeschylus invented for royal characters.[15] An item of dress that often comes into discussion here is the *ependytes*, which means "a garment put on over." The word appears in just three fragments of Attic drama preserved by Pollux, yet the costume that has been associated with it has inspired broad debate.[16] The garment has been identified as an overtunic made from richly woven fabric that falls from the shoulders to just above the knees. In chapter 2, we have seen a fancy tunic worn by the kanephoros on the Kleophon Painter's vase (see fig. 2.2).[17] Here, the fabric features a dark ray pattern at top and bottom, framing bands of meanders, star-bursts, dots, zigzags, circles, and flying birds. This elaborately woven dress may distinguish the maiden as a special agent within the ritual or may simply show that she is wearing her "Sunday best."

Margaret Miller has demonstrated that the so-called *ependytes* was worn not just by

Fig. 4.1 *(top left)*
Gold scepter, from Taras. London, British Museum 2090. Photo © Copyright the Trustees of The British Museum.

Fig. 4.2 *(top right)*
Gold necklace, from Taras. London, British Museum 1952. Photo © Copyright the Trustees of The British Museum.

Fig. 4.3 *(right)*
Gold ring, from Taras. London, British Museum 215. Photo © Copyright the Trustees of The British Museum.

priests and priestesses but also by individuals with eastern associations, including Persians and Amazons. This has led to the view that the garment may have been transmitted to Greece from the East, gaining special popularity in Athens after the Persian Wars. Once in Athens, it may have won significance as an imported luxury item reflecting the wealth of the wearer, whether god or mortal; king, priest, or citizen.[18] It cannot be used to confirm priestly status for the wearer, as it is found across such a broad spectrum of contexts, but it clearly signals status and value.

Sanctuary Laws for Clothing

Laws inscribed on stone and set up in sanctuaries gave explicit guidelines for proper attire.[19] These regulations were intended to prevent worshippers from offending the gods and ensured that rites proceeded in ways that the deities found pleasing and correct. Dress within sacred precincts was a serious matter and there were grave consequences for those who transgressed. A third-century inscription from Patras demands purification if the requirements for female dress were not followed.[20] Women who disobeyed could be cursed.[21] One woman who entered the sanctuary of Apollo Bozenos in improper attire publicly apologized to the god in an inscription.[22] The dress code for the Andanian Mysteries was so strictly enforced that those who turned up in the wrong clothing were not only turned away but could be punished.[23] An official known as the "supervisor of the women" was bound by oath to enforce the regulations. The Mysteries were policed by twenty rod-bearing priests under orders to scourge anyone who disobeyed. Failure to enforce laws could result in the trial, punishment, and dismissal of inattentive rod-bearers.

As we have seen for many other aspects of Greek cult, dress codes were not universal, but locally ordained.[24] From a relatively early date, certain garments and colors were promoted, while others were prohibited. These rules were intended to prevent ostentation that might offend the gods. A fifth-century-B.C. sacred law from Arkadia required all women who wore decorated robes into the sanctuary of Demeter Thesmophoros to leave them there as dedications.[25] Priestesses serving the cult were forbidden to wear fancy dress, anything of the color purple, gold ornaments, or face powder. Some two centuries later, at the sanctuary of Despoina at Lykosoura, also in Arkadia, women were prohibited from wearing purple, flower-decorated, or black garments; sandals; or rings.[26] If any of these items were worn into the shrine they had to be left there as property of the goddess. Worshippers were also forbidden to enter with their hair braided or their heads covered. Sanctuary laws thus served to level social distinctions among worshippers and to promote an atmosphere of communality in which devotion to the deity came first.[27] These prescriptive laws suggest that, far from being "shrinking violets" confined to seclusion at home, women of classical and Hellenistic Arkadia were inclined to dress ostentatiously for public festivals and had to be prevented from doing so.

White has long been associated with a state of purity and was the required color for priestly dress at many sanctuaries. It was worn by all incubants and visitors at healing sanctuaries of Asklepios, such as at Pergamon.[28] Indeed, Asklepios was understood to be a divinity who himself always dressed in white. On Delos, those who entered the sanctuary of Zeus Kynthios and Athena Kynthia were required to be "pure of hand and soul" and to dress in white garments.[29] All persons entering an unnamed sanctuary at Priene were required to wear white.[30] The priest of Athena Nike on Kos was required to wear white at all times. The priests of Herakles Kallinikos and of Zeus Alseios on Kos had to wear purple *chitones*, gold rings, and crowns of leaves when in the sanctuary and while sacrificing. At all other times they were to wear white.[31] The priest of a cult at Pergamon had to wear a white *chlamys*, or "cloak."[32] During the first century B.C. the priestess Epie on Thasos was required to wear "white clothes and the dress prescribed by custom."[33] Harpokration tells us that the Athenian arrephoroi dressed in white, and a decree dating to 108/107 B.C. mentions the girls' white dresses.[34] Pausanias (6.20.2–3) tells us that at the sanctuary of Eileithyia in Olympia, no one was allowed within the inner sanctum but the old priestess of Sosipolis, who was required to wrap her head and face in a white veil.

White was the dominant color worn by all categories of participants at the Andanian Mysteries.[35] Male initiates had to remain barefoot and wear white clothing, while female initiates were to wear nothing transparent or decorated with a stripe more than half a finger wide. First-time initiates were to wear tiaras, to be exchanged for laurel wreaths upon order of the officials. The male officials were required to wear wreaths, while female officials were to wear white felt caps. The board of ten individuals in charge of the officials had to wear purple headbands.

Nowhere is the inscription more exacting than in its prescriptions for female costume. Its provisions established a limit on cost beyond which women could not dress, thus limiting ostentatious display. The fact that the ceiling price was set fairly high suggests that the women who participated in the Mysteries were affluent ladies with an inclination to dress impressively.[36] Women officials were required to wear a long garment of Egyptian origin called a *kalasiris*, a tunic with a fringe along the bottom hem. Alternatively, they could wear an undergarment without colored borders. On top, they were to wear a robe that was not worth more than two minas (one mina equaled one hundred drachmas). Upper limits for the cost of clothing are separately fixed for categories that include female initiates, their daughters, and female slaves. Female initiates were to wear linen chitones and cloaks worth not more than one hundred drachmas, while their daughters could wear an Egyptian *kalasiris* or a *sindonites* (linen tunics) and a cloak worth not more than a mina. Female slaves were to wear the same dress as the daughters, but their clothes could not cost more than fifty drachmas.

Many laws restricted the use of the color purple. This was in keeping with the antiluxury nature of sacred dress codes, since purple dye was one of the most precious commodities in the ancient world.[37] We have seen that from the fifth century onward in Arkadia, priestesses and worshippers of Demeter Thesmophoros and of Despoina were forbidden to wear purple. At Andania, women officials were to sit upon wicker seats with pillows (*potikephalaia*) or round white cushions, neither of which could show any border or purple design.

While purple was forbidden in many cults, priests and priestesses were specifically *required* to wear the color purple at other sanctuaries. The sacred officials of Eleusis famously wore a purple cloak called a *phoinikis*, after the Phoenicians who developed the process for extracting the purple dye from murex shells.[38] Lysias tells us that when the Eleusinian priests and priestesses cursed Andokides for participating in Alcibiades' parody of the Mysteries, they shook their "purple cloaks" at him.[39] The garments worn by Eleusinian priests were highly distinctive. The *dadouchas* Callias made a public display of his office while fighting in the battle of Marathon in full sacred dress.[40]

We also learn that the Eleusinian hierophant and *dadouchos* were distinguished by a special headband made of twisted cloth, called a *strophion*.[41] The binding or laying on of this headband was the culminating act in their investiture as priests of the Mysteries.[42] By Hellenistic times, such headbands were worn by priests of many cults and are attested in white, white with purple stripes, and gold.[43] At Andania, officials were required to wear headbands of purple color.

Ritual dress codes even applied to the selection of footwear. Such laws were chiefly concerned with the use of skins and hides. Female officials at Andania were required to wear shoes made only from felt or the skin of sacrificial animals.[44] At the shrine of Alektrona at Ialysos on Rhodes, worshippers were forbidden to wear shoes or anything made of pigskin.[45] Likewise at Eresos on Lesbos, all footwear and animal hides were banned from the sanctuary.[46] Worshippers consulting the oracle of Trophonios in Boiotia were required to bathe, dress in linen, and put on boots that were made locally (Pausanias 9.39.8–9). Regulations concerning footwear are, at least in part, related to sacrifice and skins of animals that were required, or banned, as victims within the ritual.

The Temple Key

The surest signifier of feminine priestly status in visual culture is the temple key, shown as a large metal bar bent twice at right angles. This type of key would have been inserted through a hole in a door and engaged in the groove of a sliding bolt from behind.[47] The door would be locked by pulling on a strap connected to the bolt, which could then be slipped into place. Such keys are traditionally referred to as "Homeric" keys or as the "keys of Penelope." Traditionally, it was the woman of the house who was responsible for looking after the door keys. In time, keys became the very signifier of marriage. A Roman woman symbolically handed over the house keys upon divorce.[48]

In cult, the key is identified with the function of the *kleidouchos*, or "key bearer," the individual charged with locking and unlocking the temple. Temples functioned as virtual treasuries, filled as they were with precious metal offerings and dedications in other luxury materials. Responsibility for keeping the temple key was no small matter and represents considerable authority within the sanctuary hierarchy. We find bronze and silver keys dedicated by women in commemoration of their cult service. Stratonike, daughter of Antiphon from Myrrhinous, presented a key to Artemis at her sanctuary on Delos during the second century B.C.[49] A bronze key found in the temple of Artemis Hemerasia at Lousoi in Arkadia measures more than forty centimeters in length and bears an inscription that reads: "Of Artemis in Lousoi."[50]

The iconography of the female *kleidouchos* is established by the late sixth or early fifth century B.C. The earliest surviving example is presented in an Archaic terracotta figurine from the sanctuary of Artemis on Kerkyra (Corfu).[51] It shows a draped maiden, holding a bird in her right hand and a key in her left. A second, fragmentary terracotta in the museum at Kerkyra preserves a hand holding what appears to be the shaft of a key with a *taenia*, or "ribbon," dangling from it.[52] A small stone votive statue, once in Monaco but now of uncertain location, shows a draped maiden with a crook-shaped key in her right hand, held up against her breasts.[53] By the second quarter of the fourth century, images of priestesses holding temple keys are carved on Attic funerary reliefs and marble lekythoi (see figs. 8.4–6; pls. 20, 21).[54]

Although we know that men held the office of *kleidouchos*, images of men carrying temple keys are rare.[55] A classical terracotta figurine from Lokroi in South Italy shows a bare-chested male figure dressed in an himation and holding a key with *taenia* high in his left hand.[56] A painted image of a male *kleidouchos* decorates the pediment of the so-called Tomb of the Palmettes, excavated at Lefkadia in 1971.[57] This figure, like the terracotta from Lokroi, has been identified as the god Plouton holding the keys to the underworld. It is more likely that both images show mortal men in their special cult roles as key bearers. The knife of sacrifice, however, is the attribute that comes to stand as the chief signifier for male priesthood. Men were traditionally responsible for the leading and butchering of animal victims within the ritual, and so the sacrificial knife was seen to embody their gendered agency within cult. An Attic gravestone commemorating the priest Simos, dated to about 400 B.C., shows the knife of sacrifice prominently displayed in his right hand (see fig. 8.3).[58]

Key-bearing priestesses shown on fourth-century Attic grave reliefs may well have been inspired by freestanding bronze statuary. While none of these bronze sculptures survive, some idea of what they looked like may be drawn from limestone statues of priestesses, found in sanctuaries of Aphrodite on Cyprus (figs. 4.4–6, pls. 14, 15).[59] The large corpus of original sculptures from Cypriot sanctuaries is rich with works derivative of the late classical Attic mainstream. The conservative nature of Cypriot votive art preserves sculptural types that lag behind stylistic

Fig. 4.4
Limestone statue, from Idalion,
Cyprus. Paris, Musée du Louvre
N3278. Photo M. and P. Chuzeville,
courtesy Musée du Louvre.

changes experienced at the artistic centers of the Greek world.[60] Votive statues from Cyprus may thus give us some idea of the appearance of lost bronze statues of priestesses from classical Greece.

A life-size statue from Idalion, now in the Louvre, shows a woman holding a key under her left arm, close against her hip (fig. 4.4).[61] A smaller statue, about one-third life size, from the sanctuary of Aphrodite at Arsos, shows two temple keys held beneath the priestess's left arm and a flower in her right hand (fig. 4.5–6; pls. 14, 15).[62] Both sculptures date well into the Hellenistic period, probably to the third and second centuries, respectively. The women are dressed alike, with chiton belted high beneath the breasts, sashes tied at the center in a Herakles knot. Their mantles are draped in the familiar fashion, pulled from under the right arm, across the front, and up over the left shoulder. Unlike Attic priestesses, the Cypriot key bearers are veiled. This convention is consistent with the age-old Cypriot practice of showing female worshippers with their heads covered.

The Cypriot priestesses hold their keys together with disk-shaped objects, of uncertain identity. The closest parallels from the local repertory suggest that these are *tympana*, or small tambourines. Classical votive statues from Idalion and Golgoi show women with similar disks suspended from strings tied around their wrists, apparently small tambourines for making music in the ritual.[63] A similar combination of key and drum can be seen on the classical Attic grave relief for the priestess Chairestrate (see fig. 8.8, pl. 22).[64] She cradles her temple key while a young girl approaches her, holding out a large kettledrum. An inscribed epitaph informs us that Chairestrate was the priestess of the "Mother of All Things," a goddess whose worship included the beating of drums.

Although no freestanding statues of *kleidouchoi* survive at Athens, we know that they existed. Pliny tells us that the fifth-century master Pheidias "made a *kleidouchos*, as well as a statue

Fig. 4.5 (far left)
Limestone statue, from
Arsos, Cyprus. Larnaca
Museum 663. Photo J. B.
Connelly.

Fig. 4.6 (left)
Limestone statue, from
Arsos, Cyprus. Larnaca
Museum 663. Photo J. B.
Connelly.

of Athena which Aemilius Paullus took to Rome" (*On Natural History* 34.76). Pheidias's statue has not been recognized in Roman copies, yet some indication of its appearance may be reflected in an honorary relief dated to the second half of the fourth century (fig. 4.7; pl. 13; detail, p. 196).[65] This shows Athena, shield at her side, stretching out her right arm to support a figure of Nike, who crowns a woman, at left. The image of Athena is immediately recognizable as Pheidias's chryselephantine statue of Athena that stood in the Parthenon. Its colossal scale, the placement of the shield, and the Victory held out in Athena's right hand are consistent with copies of Pheidias's famous work, the so-called Athena Parthenos.[66] The woman who is crowned by Nike carries a large temple-key in her left hand and holds her right hand up in a gesture of prayer. She is clearly the priestess of Athena. If the image of Athena represents the well-known statue from the Parthenon, could the priestess figure similarly reflect a *kleidouchos* statue that once stood on the Acropolis?

It should be said here that the woman at the center of the Parthenon's east frieze, positioned just above the door, has often been identified as the priestess of Athena Polias.[67] In considering the figure for inclusion in this book, I was struck by the fact that she is shown without

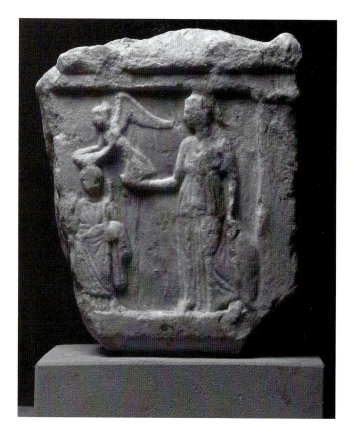

Fig. 4.7 (left)
Marble relief. Berlin, Staatliche
Museen, Antikensammlung K 104.
Photo Bildarchiv Preussicher
Kulturbesitz/Art Resource, NY.

Fig. 4.8 (opposite)
Marble relief. Athens, Acropolis
Museum AM 2758 and 2427. Photo
courtesy Archaeological Receipts
Fund (TAP Service).

a temple key. If this woman was meant to represent a fifth-century priestess, she should have been shown within the parameters of iconographic schemata established for female priesthood, as shown in the Berlin relief (see fig. 4.7) and on classical Attic grave markers (see figs. 8.4–6). This led to my questioning of the identity of the Parthenon figure as a historical priestess, a line of inquiry that resulted in my interpretation of the figure as Queen Praxithea, wife of King Erechtheus and mythical first priestess of Athena at Athens.[68] By omitting the key, the sculptor communicated that this is a priestess from the legendary past, from the days before a temple stood on the Acropolis, from the days before there was a door to be locked or unlocked.

Nothing survives of the inscribed text that could have confirmed the identity of the priestess on the Berlin relief. Yet we do have a second relief, found near the Erechtheion in 1860, that may represent an even earlier tribute to a priestly woman (fig. 4.8).[69] The relief has been dated to the fifth century and, though badly worn, shows a helmeted Athena bending toward a woman who raises her right hand in a gesture of prayer. This figure is very similar to the priestess shown on the Berlin relief and wears an identical costume of himation draped across chiton. In the crook of her left arm, a vertical shaft can be made out; it is the temple key, held in precisely

the same position as that on the Berlin relief (see fig. 4.7). This figure represents our earliest depiction of the *kleidouchos* in Attic sculpture and may derive from the same source as that of the priestess on the relief in Berlin. The common source was, no doubt, a well-known statue type, perhaps from the Athenian Acropolis and, perhaps, carved by Pheidias himself (Pliny *On Natural History* 34.76).

What we lack in evidence for freestanding statuary is more than compensated for in vase painting, where a host of scenes show famous key-bearing priestesses. These images were clearly influenced by dramatic performances. Io is described as Hera's key-bearing priestess in Aeschylus's *Suppliants*, a work that may have influenced her characterization on the Boston hydria (see fig. 3.3). We have noted in chapter 3 that the chorus (291–92) asks whether Io was once *kleidouchos* at the temple of Hera. Euripides calls Iphigeneia the *kleidouchos* of Artemis in his *Iphigeneia at Tauris* (131, 1463), a play that may have provided the inspiration for the image of Iphigeneia seen on the London skyphos, discussed in chapter 1 (see fig. 1.1).

The central role of theater in the creation and dissemination of the *kleidouchos* type should not be underestimated. Actors who played the parts of priestesses probably held large keys as stage properties to communicate their special roles. Three famous priestesses in Greek tragedy, the Pythia at Delphi, Iphigeneia at Tauris, and Theano of Troy, are consistently represented as key bearers in vase painting.[70] Aeschylus's *Eumenides* probably provided the model for the representation of the Pythia, as did Euripides' *Iphigeneia at Tauris* for Iphigeneia as priestess of Artemis. Sophokles' lost *Lakonian Women* may have inspired the representations of Theano as priestess at Troy. The visual "language" is clearly independent from what we find in texts. The Delphic Pythia, for example, is never mentioned as a key bearer in tragedy, but she is routinely shown holding a temple key on Greek vases.

Scenes from theater were especially popular in South Italian vase painting and it is here that we can see the codification of a lasting iconography for female priesthood (figs. 4.9–15). The sacred servant is routinely portrayed as an old woman with white hair and a wrinkled face, usually dressed in a chiton and mantle. Sometimes she is shown wearing the peplos, but whatever the costume, it is always decorated with brightly woven patterns, highlighting the hem or running down the front in a decorative panel. Her fancy dress is complimented with jewelry. The temple key is prominently displayed, usually decorated with a strap or dangling ribbons. One such key is seen on a krater in St. Petersburg that shows the Pythia watching Orestes as he seeks sanctuary at the altar of Apollo (fig. 4.9).[71]

Theano, priestess of Athena at Troy, is depicted with short-cropped white hair and carries a white temple key on an amphora from Paestum, now in Vienna (fig. 4.10).[72] She is surprised by Ajax, who has pursued Kassandra into Athena's temple, where the princess clings to the cult statue for protection. This is one of the most popular scenes in the South Italian repertory and shows Theano in a state of surprise, throwing her hand up and rushing off to the side. Above the head of Theano, the words TPOIO IEPEA, or "Trojan priestess," are painted in white letters.

An old Theano can, again, be seen in flight on a Campanian hydria presenting Ajax and Kassandra at the Trojan Palladion (fig. 4.11).[73] A series of attributes and implements are manipulated here to communicate that the episode takes place within Athena's temple on the night of the

Fig. 4.9 (opposite, top)
South Italian krater, the Group of the Long Folds. St. Petersburg, the State Hermitage Museum 298 (St. 1734). Photo The State Hermitage Museum, St. Petersburg.

Fig. 4.10 (opposite, bottom left)
South Italian amphora, from Paestum, the Boston Oresteia Painter. Vienna, Kunsthistorisches Museum 724 (261). Photo Kunsthistorisches Museum, Vienna.

Fig. 4.11 (opposite, bottom right)
Campanian hydria. London, British Museum F 209. Photo © Copyright the Trustees of The British Museum.

sack of Troy. An owl flies above the priestess, clutching a wreath in its talons and signifying that we are within Athena's precinct. A libation bowl hangs in the background, reinforcing the sacral setting. A wine jug tumbles down in front of the altar, signifying that the priestess has been interrupted in the course of her ritual duties.

The tables are turned for comic effect on a fragment that shows Kassandra assaulting Ajax, rather than the other way around (fig. 4.12).[74] Signed by an artist named Asteas, meaning "witty" or "clever," the iconic image is reversed. Ajax clings to Athena's statue while Kassandra attacks him from behind. Theano is depicted here as a caricature of the priestess type, an old lady with thin white hair and exaggerated wrinkles. Over her left shoulder she carries a large key, while her right hand is thrown open in a highly stylized gesture of surprise. Here, too, inscriptions identify the chief players, and Theano is simply labeled "Priestess." One can only wonder if such reversals in plot were enacted for comic effect on stage, or whether this image reflects the creative humor of the painter.

When Boreas seizes Oreithyia on a krater in London, an old priestess can be seen fleeing from the action, with arms thrown up in the air, temple key and libation bowl falling to the ground (fig. 4.13).[75] We do not know her name, but she is likely to be the priestess of Athena Polias. She may be viewed, along with altar, lustral basin, ribbons, and libation bowls, as just another stage property used to establish the setting upon the Acropolis. The priestess's emphatic hand gestures, expressing heightened surprise, are by now standard fare. We find another nameless priestess on an amphora in Berlin (fig. 4.14).[76] This woman holds a temple key in one hand and a statuette of Athena in the other, identifying the deity whom she serves and indicating her special agency as *xoanophoros*, or "bearer of the cult image." We shall see the role of the *xoanophoros* commemorated in votive statuary and funerary relief in chapters 5 and 8 (see figs. 5.18, 8.12).

Among the many representations of priestesses on South Italian vases, one shown on an amphora in St. Petersburg has inspired particular debate (fig. 4.15).[77] Here, we see an old priestess, holding a key against her shoulder and standing before an altar on which two maidens sit. The priestess is confronted by a bearded warrior, who has drawn his sword. She appears to be defending the girls who have taken refuge within her shrine. A younger man advances from the right, drawing his sword from its scabbard. The sacred setting is established by the altar, with tripod and brazier set on either side of it, as well as by the *boukrania* and votive wheels that hang high in the background. At right, a hydria, probably made of bronze and representing a precious offering, sits upon a tall column.

A Tarentine relief sculpture in the Art Museum, Princeton University, presents a very similar scene (fig. 4.16; pl. 26).[78] This relief is typical of a class of limestone sculptures that decorated small funerary chapels on the east side of ancient Taras, modern Taranto, in South Italy.

Fig. 4.12 (right)
South Italian krater fragment, from Paestum, Asteas. Rome, Museo Nazionale Etrusco di Villa Giulia 50.279. Photo courtesy Museo Nazionale Etrusco di Villa Giulia.

Fig. 4.13 (bottom left)
South Italian krater. London, British Museum 1931.5-11.1. Photo © Copyright the Trustees of The British Museum.

Fig. 4.14 (bottom right)
South Italian amphora, from Paestum, the Boston Oresteia Painter. Berlin, Staatliche Museen Antikensammlung F3025. Photo Antikensammlung, Staatliche Museen zu Berlin, Bildarchiv Preussicher Kulturbesitz.

Fig. 4.15
South Italian amphora. St. Petersburg, the State Hermitage Museum St. 452. Photo The State
Hermitage Museum, St. Petersburg.

Fig. 4.16
Limestone relief, from Taras.
Princeton, the Art Museum
1983–34. Museum Purchase,
gift of the Willard T. C.
Johnson Foundation, Inc.,
and an anonymous donor.

Pottery from graves excavated beneath these structures has traditionally been placed circa 330–150 B.C., though some dates have now been lowered.[79] The Princeton relief would probably have been one of several sculptured panels within a triglyph-metope frieze that adorned the entablature of such a funerary shrine. Both the St. Petersburg amphora and the Princeton relief show two young women seated upon an altar, one of whom holds a lustral branch. Both show an old priestess, wrapped in a mantle and carrying a key over her shoulder. The Princeton priestess has a very wrinkled face with sagging jowls. Her hunched posture emphasizes her advanced age.

Similar iconographic schemata have been observed on at least six South Italian vases that show two maidens seated on an altar and approached by two men, one young and the other mature. These images have been viewed as a group and interpreted in a variety of ways. Some read the subject as the murder of Antigone and Ismene, who have taken refuge at the altar of Hera.[80] Others see the Lokrian maidens at Athena's altar in Troy. Still others identify the scene as one in which the Danaids have been chased by the sons of Aigyptos to the altar of Hera at Argos.[81]

Perhaps the most convincing interpretation is that of Friedrich Marx, who, in 1928, pointed to a story told by the comic poet Dipholos, later adapted by Plautus in his *Rudens*.[82] Here, the maidens Palaestra and Ampelisca are abducted by the pimp Labrax but escape when a storm wrecks the boat in which they have been smuggled, just off the coast of Cyrene in North Africa. Water soaked and frightened, the girls take refuge at the sanctuary of Venus, where a "dear old lady," the priestess, takes them in and bathes them (*Rudens* 350, 403–11). When accosted by Labrax and his comrades, the old priestess defends the girls physically and is "thrown about in all directions in perfectly outrageous fashion" (671–72). Soon, Palaestra's unknowing father, Daemones, and the young Trachalio come to rescue the girls. But first, Trachalio urges the young women to "sit by the altar" (688).

On this view, the Princeton relief could show the old priestess roughed up from her skirmish, while the maidens Palaestra and Ampelisca sit upon the altar of Venus. Ampelisca looks off to her left away from the central action, as if to acknowledge activity in a companion panel, perhaps a neighboring metope. This second panel might have shown Daemones and Trachalio coming to the rescue. Although I cannot cite a parallel in which the subject matter of a funeral shrine's sculptural program is drawn from comedy rather than tragedy, the *Rudens*, or its source, still stands as the best candidate for the inspiration behind the images. The Princeton relief clearly attests to the importance of theater in canonizing and perpetuating a codified image of the priestess with temple key.

We shall see in chapter 8 that, by the second century, funerary markers commemorating Attic and Boiotian priestesses were decorated with a simple key carved beneath the name of the deceased (see figs. 8.14–18; pls. 24, 25).[83] The key was thus elevated over time to stand as the single defining signifier of feminine priesthood. This was in no small part a result of the influence of theater, which needed a conspicuous symbol with which to communicate sacral identity to thousands of viewers. The priestesses shown in the South Italian repertory all belong to the realm of myth, as presented in theatrical performances. In the transformation from words, to mimesis, to painted images of mimesis, the temple key is allocated to certain priestesses who were never known as *kleidouchoi* in myth, or in the dramatic texts. That the key finds its ultimate source within the Greek household, again, underscores the close relationship between house and temple and the agency of the women who cared for both spaces.

Divine Imitation

Beyond keys, *tympana*, jewelry, and fancy dress there is a further range of possibilities for priestly iconography based on the imitation of gods by their cult servants. Ritual dramas were performances in which stories from myth were reenacted in honor of divinities within the context of cult festivals.[84] Inge Nielsen has recently gathered evidence for cultic theaters and sacred dramas from the ancient Near East and Egypt, and throughout the Greek and Roman Mediterranean.[85] Ritual drama was widely practiced across ancient societies and, indeed, mimesis has even been viewed as the very origin of ritual.[86] In the Greek world, hymns played a vital role in the storytelling process but, unfortunately, the Alexandrian School did not regard them as worth preserving.[87] We therefore have lost much of the evidence for what sacred dramas may have involved. Certainly, ritual players memorized songs, reinforced by dance, that recounted etiological myths about the divinity and the origins of local cult practice. At least in certain cults, priests and priestesses seem to have acted out the roles of the deities themselves.

The practice of divine imitation must be viewed within the larger framework of the fundamental intimacy between divinity and worshipper. This relationship is sometimes reflected in restrictions imposed on those entering sanctuaries.[88] Shrines of virgin goddesses were normally open to women alone, as with the sanctuary of Kore at Megalopolis. Men were permitted to enter only one day of the year (Pausanias 8.31.8). At Olympia, men were not allowed to enter the cave of Zeus Sosipolis and Eileithyia, a place sacred to women and childbirth (Pausanias 6.20.2–4). Men who intruded on women's banquets in honor of Demeter at Messene were punished.[89] Similarly, women were excluded from sacrifices to Ares at Geronthrai in Lakonia (Pausanias 3.22.7) and to Poseidon Phykios (Seaweed) on Mykonos.[90] Women could not visit the highest part of the ash altar of Zeus at Olympia (Pausanias 5.13.10). The shrine of the Dioskouroi at Elateia was open to men alone during special periods.[91] Rules for entry to Greek sanctuaries were locally ordained and strictly enforced. A temple attendant, armed with a whip, was posted in front of the shrine of Leukothea at Chaironeia. He was charged with guarding the sanctuary and was required to announce: "No slave, male or female, no Aitolian, male or female, may enter here."[92]

Worshippers sometimes participated in rituals that were based on the reenactment of the experience of the divinity, bringing god and devotee even closer together. Of course, the experience of Dionysos cult brought the worshipper, including women who practiced maenadism, into a union with the divinity, well expressed in the *Bacchae* of Euripides.[93] At the festival of the Thesmophoria, women imitated the progressive ordeal suffered by Demeter in her search for her missing daughter Persephone. This was one of the oldest and most widely celebrated festivals in Greece and was restricted to women who, like Demeter, left home for several days and nights, wandered, mourned, sat on the ground, and refused to eat or speak until coaxed out of silence by obscene, abusive language.[94]

The *Homeric Hymn to Demeter*, dating to the late seventh century B.C., has been viewed as the sacred text (*hieros logos*) for the Eleusinian Mysteries. An even stronger connection can be seen between the *Hymn to Demeter* and the feast of the Thesmophoria.[95] Its ritual of the *aischrologia*, in which obscenities were hurled from woman to woman, finds its source in the story of Iambe, a servant in the palace of the Eleusinian king. When Demeter arrived at Eleusis, distraught at the loss of her daughter, Iambe tried to persuade the goddess to sit down, to eat, and to speak. Finally, Iambe coaxed Demeter out of her silence with a series of mocking remarks that made the goddess smile. Women re-acted this legendary exchange of obscenities at the Thesmophoria, thus sharing in Demeter's ordeal and bringing them closer to the experience of the goddess.

Even more intimate than the relationship between divinity and worshipper was that between divinity and cult agent. We see this connection as early as the *Iliad*, in which the priest of the river Skamander, Eurypylos, and the priest of Idaian Zeus, Laogonos, are said to be honored among the people as gods (*Iliad* 5.77–78, 16.604–5). The obscuring of the line between deity and cult servant is further evidenced in stories of goddesses who disguise themselves as priestesses. Aeschylus presents Hera as a wandering priestess who seeks gifts for the nymphs.[96] Demeter disguises herself as a priestess in Kallimachos's *Hymn to Demeter* (42–44): "Straightaway she likened her to Nikippe, whom the city had appointed as her public priestess, and in her hand she grasped her fillets and her poppy, and from her shoulder hung her key."[97] These references may help to explain the paradox in which divinities played the parts of *kleidouchoi*, roles that would seem to be inherently mortal.[98]

Not only did goddesses impersonate priestesses, but priestesses clearly imitated the goddesses they served. This mimesis may have been part of mystery rites and thereby subject to restrictions of secrecy, leaving us with a paucity of explicit evidence for the practice. When we speak of divine "impersonation" or "imitation" we mean that the cult agent takes on the costume of the divinity in order to play a part in a ritual drama. We do not mean that the priestess "becomes" or "embodies" the goddess. Although textual evidence for divine imitation is relatively late, the cases presented here explicitly attest to cult attendants dressed in divine costume to play parts in processions, dramas, and banquets.

By the Roman period, sacred dress-up seems to have been widespread throughout Greece. At Patras in Achaia there was an annual feast of Artemis called the Laphria. Pausanias (7.18.12) tells of its magnificent procession in which a virgin priestess rode in a chariot drawn by deer, animals sacred to the goddess. At Tegea, the priestess pretended to be Artemis and chased after a man who pretended to be Leimon, son of King Tegeates (Pausanias 8.53.3). According to local myth, Leimon killed his brother Skephros and was, in turn, shot to death by Artemis. The ritual was a reenactment of Artemis's punishment of Leimon in which the priestess and a local man dressed up and played the parts.

A third-century-A.D. novel by Heliodoros tells of Charikleia, the daughter of the queen of Ethiopia, who became a *zakoros* of Artemis (*An Ethiopian Story* 3.4).[99] Charikleia resembled Artemis in her virginity, her beauty, and her taste for hunting. On the great festival day, she marched from the goddess's temple wearing a purple robe woven with gold and carrying a gilded bow and a lighted torch. Dressed in sacred costume, the *zakoros* Charikleia seems to have performed the same role as Anthia of Ephesos, with whom we opened this chapter. Both girls were dressed as Artemis for their local festival processions.

Divine imitation is well attested for priestesses of Athena. Polyainos (8.59), writing in the second century A.D., tells how the priestess of Athena at Pellene was the fairest and tallest maiden in town. It was customary for her to dress in full armor, including a helmet, on festival day. When the Aitolian invaders saw the girl, they thought she was Athena and retreated.[100] A late Byzantine source suggests that the priestess of Athena Polias at Athens dressed in the goddess's *aigis* when she visited newlywed couples.[101] This was part of a ceremonial collection for the *aigis*-sacrifice that followed the Proteleia, the day on which parents brought their daughters to the Acropolis to perform sacrifices before marriage.[102] Although our study concerns priestesses alone, it should be noted that divine imitation is attested for male cult agents as well. At the sanctuary of Ismenian Apollo at Thebes, a boy of noble family, both strong and handsome, was chosen to serve as priest for a year. Called the "Laurel bearer," the boy marched behind the laurel pole and wore his hair long in imitation of Apollo in the great procession for the Daphnephoria festival (Pausanias 9.10.4).[103]

Epigraphic sources, late as they may be, give explicit evidence for ritual impersonation. The first-century-B.C. inscription from Andania that we have considered throughout this chapter specifically refers to a group of people who "must be dressed in the manner of the gods."[104] These individuals are instructed to "wear the clothing that the sacred men [i.e., the officials] specify" (lines 24–25). Apparently, these directives were part of a larger program of reorganization for the local Mysteries of Demeter. The head of the Mysteries, Mnasistratos, set out procedures in which he and his wife would preside at a banquet. There would be a great procession in honor of the goddess, in which Demeter, Hermes, the Great Gods, Apollo Karneios, and Hagna (the pure goddess) would march, probably represented by cult attendants dressed in costume. We learn that a priest and priestess would join Mnasistratos at the head of the procession, followed by the director of the games, the priests of the sacrifice, and the *aulos* (pipe) players. After them would march the sacred virgins, who would pull carts with chests containing the "sacred things of the mystery." The "sacred women" and the "sacred men" would follow behind.

The well-known inscription of the Iobacchoi, found at the sanctuary of Dionysos in Limnai near Athens, similarly gives evidence for the costuming of mortals as divinities.[105] Dated to the second century A.D., this text specifically refers to those who "speak and act the parts" (lines 65–66). The selection process by which players would be chosen to perform the roles is clearly laid out. The cast includes the priest, the antipriest, the *archibacchos* (meaning "leader of the Bacchoi"), the *tamias* (treasurer), the *boukolikos* (shepherd), Dionysos, Kore, Palaimon, Aphrodite, and Proteurythmos (lines 122–25). Clearly, we have a sacred drama here in which ritual agents took on the likenesses of divinities honored.

The performance of sacred theater is similarly presupposed in a Hadrianic inscription from Ephesos.[106] The text gives a long list of roles to be played in the ritual drama: Bromios (Dionysos), Athena Soteira, Homonoia (Concord), the older and younger nymphs, Helios, Kore, Pan, Asklepios, Demeter, the new Dionysos (who is presumably Hadrian himself), as well as a number of less well-known divinities. Of course, sacred dress-up is well attested at Ephesos. Mark Antony's famous spectacle of divine impersonation in 41 B.C. took place within the context of a religious festival that has been identified as the Katagogia.[107] Plutarch recounts: "When he entered Ephesos he was led by women disguised as Bacchai, by men and boys disguised as Satyrs and Pans, and the city was full of ivy, *thyrsoi*, harps, flutes and pipes, and they called him Dionysos Giver of Grace and Gentle."[108] Antony entered both Alexandria and Athens in the guise of Dionysos, just as Demetrios Poliorketes had arrived in Athens centuries before.[109]

The most famous divine impersonator was, of course, Alexander himself. Arrian recounts with some skepticism the popular story of Alexander's march into Gedrosia complete with pipes and garlands, pageantry said to have been devised by the king in imitation of the Bacchic revelry of Dionsysos (*Anabasis* 6.28). Plutarch describes the raucous procession of wagons decked out with purple, embroidered canopies and with tree boughs. Alexander was transported by a team of eight horses (*Alexander* 67), while pipe and flute music mixed with the cries of women, and huge casks of wine flowed freely into drinking cups. Claims by the contemporary Ephippos that Alexander also dressed as Ammon, Hermes, Herakles, and even Artemis may be dismissed as outrageous fabrication.[110] Still, Alexander's well-known devotion and frequent practice of sacrifice placed him in a position of leadership where cult matters were concerned. In this capacity, his adoption of sacred costume may not have seemed so strange. He was simply playing the part of the priest in the ritual at hand. By the Hellenistic period the lines between divinity and mortal became increasingly obscured, particularly with the advent of ruler cult.

How far back in time can we trace the practice of divine impersonation? Herodotos's (1.60.2–5) account of Phye, the woman who dressed as Athena to accompany the tyrant Peisistratos in his return from exile, may be telling: "There was in the Paeanian district a woman named Phye, whose height was almost six feet, and who was altogether comely to look upon. This woman they clothed in complete armor, and, showing her the fashion in which she would appear most becoming, they placed her in a chariot and drove into the city. . . . They of the city also, fully persuaded that the woman was the veritable goddess, worshipped her and received Peisistratos back."[111] Robert Connor has shown that the symbolism of this story reveals patterns deeply rooted in Greek culture.[112] Procession, spectacle, and mimesis were long used as effective tools for communication. There is, of course, no evidence that Phye was a priestess. Nonetheless, this story attests to the power of divine impersonation already in the Archaic period and prefigures the use of sacred dress-up as an effective device within later ritual theater.

By no means am I suggesting that all the cases cited above represent true ritual dramas enacted by true priests and priestesses. I am simply attempting to reconstruct an ancient context in which mimesis played a much stronger role that is generally recognized. As Michael Taussig has shown, mimesis is a necessary part of thinking itself.[113] The wide availability of imagery today, through photography, film, computer modeling, and so forth, separates us from the ancient experience of images, restricted to those that could be drawn, sculptured, or performed. Within this context, mimesis played a vital role in shaping the thought process, as wells as modes of communication, education, and worship. Walter Benjamin observed that the human mimetic faculty plays a decisive role in virtually all our higher functions. Benjamin viewed the human capacity for seeing resemblances as "a rudiment of the powerful compulsion, in former times, to become and behave like something else."[114]

Whatever the force of these suggestions, the collective evidence for divine impersonation in ancient Greece demands a review of images from vase painting that have traditionally been identified as "offering gods."[115] Scholars have long struggled with the interpretation of scenes that show divinities pouring libations and offering sacrifice at altars (figs. 4.17–20; pl. 8). Such acts of worship would appear, at first glance, to be inherently mortal tasks, inappropriate for divinities. Indeed, when Alexander the Great offered to dedicate the temple of Artemis at Ephesos, the Ephesians objected, saying that it was not fitting for a god to make an offering to another god.[116]

Faced with this paradox, scholars have interpreted scenes showing "offering gods" in a variety of ways. The subject is perhaps best known through Erika Simon's classic, *Opfernde Götter*, of

Fig. 4.17
Attic red-figure plate,
the Dish Painter.
Copenhagen, National
Museum 6. Photo
courtesy National
Museum, Copenhagen.

1953.[117] Here, she interpreted the images as scenes from myth, in which gods propitiated other gods, reflecting hierarchical representations of ritual behavior. Himmelmann-Wildschütz saw them as "epiphanies" in which gods show themselves to be divinely self-sufficient, thereby providing a divine prototype for mortal behavior.[118] Fürtwangler was among the very first to take up the subject and thought the images showed an intentional "humanization" of divinities.[119] Others have focused on the libation bowl, shown so prominently in these scenes, as a mediating element between the human and the divine.[120] Recent work by Kimberley Patton reads the images as manifestations of "divine reflexivity" in which gods perform in a "cultic time" that is both parallel and responsive to human cultic observance.[121] The gods, Patton maintains, are not just the objects of cult but the very source of cult, the origin and catalyst for human religious behavior. The Olympians thus reinforce ritual by performing it themselves.

Martin Nilsson is among the very few who have questioned the validity of the designation "offering gods." Focusing on a Roman relief sculpture, traditionally identified as Dionysos making an offering, he argued that it instead shows a priest dressed up like Dionysos, pouring a libation upon the god's altar.[122] Nilsson's views have often been dismissed, but they certainly warrant reconsideration in face of the cumulative evidence for ritual drama within Greek cult practice.

Fig. 4.18
Attic red-figure cup, from Capua, the Euaion Painter. Brussels, Bibliothèque Royale 12. Copyright Royal Library of Belgium.

Our focus is on a series of cups that show women standing before altars, pouring libations from a bowls or jugs, or holding out offerings. Sometimes, the women are identified as a goddesses, because of the presence of attributes, including scepters, spears, or crowns, or because of painted inscriptions that name them outright.[123] But a few of these inscriptions give the name of the goddess in the genitive case. This could suggest that the labels do not identify the divinity but, instead, indicate something that belongs to the divinity, perhaps the sacrifice, the libation, or even a priestess, shown in an act of worship.[124] Scenes of women at altars are regularly found within the tondos of bowls, cups, and plates. This reinforces the relationship of form and function, since the women are shown pouring libations from just such cups and bowls. A red-figure dish in Copenhagen presents a woman at a flaming altar (fig. 4.17).[125] She carries a basket of offerings in her left arm and, with her right hand, holds a small branch toward the fire. She is dressed in a chiton with long overfold and her dark hair is circled with a triple headband. An inscription at upper left reads "Artemis." However, the maiden shows none of the conventional signifiers associated with Artemis: ponytail, high-girded dress, boots, and bow and arrow. In fact, scholars have *not* identified this woman as Artemis, despite the inscription painted above. Why, then, should we expect labels on other cups to identify women shown at altars as goddesses rather than mortal women?

A cup in Brussels invites further scrutiny. Here, a maiden holds a shaft of wheat over an altar (fig. 4.18).[126] She wears a mantle with dark-banded borders and a crown upon her head. Long tresses fall down her back. An inscription at right reads "Demetros." This label, together with the shaft of wheat and the crown, have prompted scholars to identify the woman as Demeter. But why is "Demeter" written in the genitive case? Could this communicate that the offering, the cup, or the woman represented *belongs* to Demeter? We must at least entertain the possibility that we are looking at an image that has been influenced by the experience of ritual drama.

Two white-ground cups by the Villa Giulia Painter show similar images of women sacrificing. One in New York presents the familiar composition in which a woman faces left, holding a libation bowl over an altar (fig. 4.19; pl. 8).[127] She wears an elaborate, tightly pleated chiton with overfold, similar to the dress worn by the maiden on the Copenhagen cup (fig. 4.17). A heavy red mantle is thrown across her shoulders and falls down her back. Double bracelets and a necklace with pendants, painted yellow to resemble gold, adorn her wrists and neck. In her left hand she holds a golden scepter crowned with a starburst finial. Scholars have hesitated to identify this woman, since there are no inscriptions or attributes to signal a specific deity. Those who speculate on her identity most often choose Hera, because of the presence of the scepter, the attribute of the queen of the gods.

The cup in Oxford shows a female figure pouring a libation over one of two altars (fig. 4.20).[128] Her dark ponytail is swept up and bound with a broad band of cloth. She wears a narrowly pleated chiton beneath a bordered mantle and snake-shaped bracelets on her arms. Her scepter has been set aside, propped up behind her. This maiden has been identified as Kore, because of the two altars, one presumably for Demeter and the other for her daughter. This view is supported by Dietrich von Bothmer's reading of the word [K]ores in very faint letters to the girl's right.[129] If Bothmer's reading is correct, we have a second example of the genitive case used in an

Fig. 4.19
Attic white-ground kylix, the Villa Giulia Painter. New York, the Metropolitan Museum of Art, the Bothmer Purchase Fund, Fletcher Fund, and Rogers Fund, 1979 (1979.11.15). Photo, all rights reserved. The Metropolitan Museum of Art.

identifying label. Could this indicate that it is the priestess, not the goddess, who is shown making the offering?

In chapter 1, we considered Makron's cup, on which a woman, surrounded by a full repertory of ritual paraphernalia, sacrifices at a flaming altar (see fig. 1.2). She wears a ponytail swept up on her head, not unlike the woman shown on the Oxford cup, and similarly wears a voluminous, bordered mantle that falls from both shoulders. In one hand, she grasps an elaborate basket and, with the other, pours a libation from a large jug. In costume, action, age, and attribute, she strongly resembles the women painted in cup tondos and regularly identified as goddesses. But the woman on the Toledo cup is not identified as a divinity, because of the absence of an inscribed label or divine attribute. We must ask ourselves whether we are reading the codes correctly, and whether we have placed too much emphasis on a few narrowly defined signifiers.

Fig. 4.20
Attic white-ground kylix, the Villa Giulia Painter. Oxford, Ashmolean Museum 1973.1. Photo courtesy Ashmolean Museum, Oxford.

Similar schemata appear on a jug by the Pan Painter in Munich (Fig. 4.21).[130] Here, a woman pours a libation from a three-footed metal tankard over an altar decorated with an elaborate palmette finial. She is enveloped in a dark-trimmed mantle that covers most of her delicate, dotted dress beneath. Her long hair is bound with a headband. Without a labeling inscription or divine attribute, she has been identified as a generic worshipper. Yet her act of libation at the altar is identical to that undertaken by women who have been recognized as divinities on the cups examined above.

Images traditionally interpreted as "goddesses sacrificing" thus share iconographic and compositional formulas with images that have been traditionally interpreted as ordinary women at worship. We must entertain the possibility that some of these images were influenced by ritual mimesis in which priestesses dressed up like goddesses. The frequency with which images of

Fig. 4.21
Attic red-figure oinochoe,
the Pan Painter. Munich,
Staatliche Antikensamm-
lungen und Glyptothek
2455. Photo courtesy
Staatliche Antikensamm-
lungen und Glyptothek.

women at altars appear on the interior of cups is significant. As these vessels themselves may have been used to pour libations, particularly the fancy white-ground cups, we may have here an expression of the communality of implement and implementor.[131] The agent of ritual who used the cup may be reflected in the image shown within it. But we must also be mindful of the fact that these images may show women from myth, that is, legendary priestesses. Myth, realia, and mimesis may thus come together in producing images of mythical women imitating divinities, informed by the experience of actual ritual dramas in which historical priestesses enacted these same roles.

The concept of divine impersonation is a challenging one that must be considered when approaching the paradoxical representations known as "gods sacrificing." It pushes us to examine the more complex issues of representation, imitation, and likeness in the creation and communication of meaning. Jewelry, scepters, sleeveless tunics woven with rich designs, patterned garments, and heavy mantles pinned at both shoulders all can communicate sacral rank, though they may not confirm it. When details of dress are combined with setting elements that establish a sacred precinct, we can be more certain of the cult identities of the individuals portrayed. A repertory of "sign-components," including libation bowls, jugs, altars, ribbons, incense burners, and *boukrania* can be manipulated by the artist within this ritual space. But no single item communicates feminine priestly status with more certainty than does the temple key. It remains the preeminent signifier of female priesthood across some five centuries.

While sacred costume for priests and priestesses was not universally prescribed, we can have no doubt that it existed. The wearing of sacred dress was so integral to traditional cult that, during its final days, legislation was passed in an attempt to keep ritual costume going. The Caesar Maximin Daia's efforts to promote polytheistic cults in the Greek East included a plan to appoint high priests in each province who were specifically required to wear white. Enforced in A.D. 310, this legislation represents a reenforcement of traditional practices and a final effort to hold on to long-established conventions.[132] Sacred dress was central to this enterprise and ever remained a powerful nonverbal tool in the communication of status, agency, and identity.

CHAPTER 5

The Priestess in the Sanctuary

Implements, Portraits, and Patronage

Philtera, priestess of Athena Polias during the third quarter of the second century B.C., had a pedigree matched by none. Daughter of the distinguished general and defender of Athenian democracy, Pausimachos, she could claim a lineage that went back to the fourth-century orator and politician Lykourgos. Philtera received high honors befitting her priestly service, none more conspicuous than a portrait statue set up on the Athenian Acropolis. The statue was made of bronze and was melted down long ago. But its marble base survives and bears an elaborate metrical inscription celebrating her illustrious ancestry:[1]

> Παλλὰς Ἐρεχθειδᾶν ἀρχαγ[έτι, σὸ]ν κατὰ ναόν
> ἅδε τοι ἱδρύθη Φιλτέρα ἱρ[οπόλ]ος,
> Βουταδέων ἐτύμων ἐξ αἵ[ματος], ἇς γενέτωρ μέν
> ταγὸς ἔφυ στρατιᾶς πεντάκι Παυσίμαχος,
> τοὶ πρόγονοι δ᾽ ἄνθησαν ἐν Αἰγείδαισι Λυκοῦργος
> χὠχθονὶ τιμάεις Ἀτθίδι Διογένης·
> ἐν τῶι μὲ[ν] ῥήτωρ λόγος ἄνδανεν, οὗ δὲ δι᾽ ἔργα
> ἔδρακεν ἀρχαίαν πατρὶς ἐλευθερίαν.
>
> [Εὔ]χειρ καὶ Εὐβουλίδης Κρωπίδαι ἐποίησαν.

Pallas ruler of the Erechtheids, in your temple this Philtera was established as your servant, from the blood of the true Boutads, whose father Pausimachos was the general of the army five times, their ancestors flourished among the Aigeids: Lykourgos and Diogenes, honored by the Attic land. One of these delighted in oratory; through the other's deeds the fatherland glimpsed ancient freedom.[2]

A strong sense of family pride can be detected in this boastful verse that proclaims Philtera to be "from the blood of the true Boutads," a descendant of the mythical royal family of Athens. The reference to the children of Erechtheus associates Philtera with the venerable tradition of the highest elite of Athenian women in the goddess's service.

We are fortunate to have several surviving statue bases from the Athenian Acropolis that once held portraits of priestesses of Athena Polias. We can surmise from the distribution of inscribed bases from sanctuaries across the Greek world that the practice of erecting statues of female cult agents was widespread. By the time that Pausanias traveled through Greece in the second century A.D., he encountered images of priestesses at a host of shrines. He saw them standing in front of the temple of Demeter at Hermione in the eastern Peloponnese (2.35.8). Not far away, he encountered priestess portraits set up "before the entrance" of the sanctuary of Hera at Argos (2.17.3). His tour of the sanctuary of the Eumenides at Keryeneia in Achaia included a viewing of stone statues "of significant artistic workmanship" at the shrine's entrance. He learned from the locals that these represented former priestesses of the Eumenides (7.25.7). Pausanias does not tell us the date of these statues relative to his own time but, as his primary interest was in Greek antiquity, he often neglected to mention contemporary monuments.[3] We might assume from this approach that the portraits he describes dated from before his own day.

The setting up of statues of priestesses in Greek sanctuaries is attested by epigraphic evidence from the early fourth century B.C. on. Surviving documentation increases over time, and by the late Hellenistic period, scores of bases attest to priestess portraits in sanctuaries at Athens, Rhamnous, Aulis, Mantineia, Messene, Thasos, Kyzikos, Pergamon, Sardis, Erythrai, Priene, Knidos, Samos, Kos, Rhodes, Cyprus, and other locations. By the second century, images of priestesses, benefactresses, and women magistrates had become so plentiful in the Greek East that M. Porcius Cato Maior found it necessary to complain publicly about the excessive numbers of female statues crowding cities and sanctuaries (Pliny *On Natural History* 34.31). His protests had little effect, as portraits of priestly and nonpriestly women alike continued to be dedicated in ever increasing numbers throughout the Roman Imperial period.

Let us examine the possibilities for identifying statues of priestesses on the basis of context, that is, from the physical evidence found within the sanctuaries where the women served. During the Archaic period, representations of women frequently appear on ritual implements, including incense burners, libation bowls and cups, water jugs, and other vessels. The relationship of these images to the women who used them will be examined here in view of the communality between implement and implementor. Archaic images of richly draped maidens carved in relief on column drums, and in the round as votive statues, may reflect actual maidens who performed rituals within the sacred space. By the early fourth century, inscribed statue bases provide firm evidence for priestess portraits within sacred precincts. Since religious tradition was one of the most conservative aspects of Greek culture, we might surmise that this practice began much earlier.

The study of representations of women in Greek sanctuaries enables us to better understand the relationship of place and image. The fundamental intimacy of goddess and priestess is central to this discussion. Walter Burkert has observed that large statues in limestone, marble, or bronze were erected by those who were connected with the god in a special way to give "lasting expression of this bond."[4] Statues of priestesses transformed the sacred landscape and became one with it, foresting it with the tangible presence of sacred servants remembered in perpetuity for their ritual actions. These statues may well have become part of a ritual of visitation itself, through which worshippers were educated in local family tradition, shared history, and cult. Shown with their sacred implements, jugs, bowls, and keys, or with their hands raised heavenward in supplication, portrait statues kept the prayers of priestesses alive in perpetuity before the divinity.[5] As Bruit Zaidman and Schmidt Pantel have observed, "It is clearly impossible to study a statue in isolation from the ritual use to which it was put."[6] Let us, then, consider the images within the ritual contexts that reveal so much about their meanings.

Sacred Implements of the Archaic Period

The earliest representations of women in sacred precincts come, not from stone statuary, but from the decorative arts, where they appear on ritual implements made of ivory and bronze. Some of these images have been identified as representations of priestesses because of the cult function of the instruments on which they appear. The foundation deposit of the temple of Artemis at Ephesos has yielded a number of figures carved from ivory and generally dated to the late seventh and early sixth centuries B.C.[7] Francois de Polignac has emphasized that of the ten images found in the deposit, all represent women, suggesting a connection between the female nature of the local divinity, Artemis, and the feminine iconography of the implements dedicated.[8]

One of the most celebrated of the ivories is the so-called Hawk Priestess (fig. 5.1).[9] The young female figure wears a tight-fitting

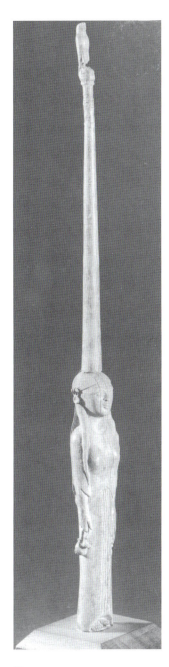

Fig. 5.1
Ivory distaff, from the Temple of Artemis at Ephesos. Istanbul, Archaeological Museum. Photo courtesy Istanbul Archaeological Museum.

Fig. 5.2
Bronze support from Gourizi, Albania. Paris, Musée du Louvre MNB 2854. Photo M. and P. Chuzeville, courtesy Musée du Louvre.

Fig. 5.3
Ivory support, Temple of Artemis, Ephesos. Istanbul, Archaeological Museum 2593. Photo courtesy Istanbul Archaeological Museum.

dress, large "Cypriot" earrings that cap the top of her ears, and tresses that fall well below her shoulders. The ivory object, of which her figure is only the bottom piece, shows a long thin rod surmounted by a hawk. The overall shape is that of a distaff, onto which a ball of thread would have been fixed. The female figure would thus have served as its handle. The maiden is shown holding a wine jug in one hand and a libation bowl in the other, represented with such detailed specificity that they seem to have been copied from actual metal objects. The phiale shows ring-handles suspended from bolsters typical of metal bowls from Phrygia.[10]

A similar combination of oinochoe and phiale are shown held by a maiden on a bronze support from Gourizi near Scoutari in Albania, now in the Louvre (fig. 5.2).[11] The young woman may be seen as a sort of late sixth-century iconographic sister to the Ephesian Hawk Priestess. Like her ivory counterpart, this maiden would have served as a support for a sacred utensil, probably an incense burner. She is shown wearing a high headdress and a tight-fitting garment with richly woven panels, cinched in at the waist with a wide belt. Like the Hawk Priestess, she holds a jug in one hand and a cup in the other, but here lifts them high in the act of pouring from one into the other.

As instruments of ritual, the wine jug and libation bowl form a pair. Wine would be poured from the jug into the bowl, from which a libation could then be poured over an altar or directly onto the ground. The presence of the oinochoe-phiale set in the hands of the Ephesian maiden has been seen to communicate her identity as a priestess.[12] Although some prefer to read this figure as an image of Artemis, none of the attributes associated with the goddess, such as bow, arrow, boots, ponytail, or accompanying animals, are present. Indeed, the maiden may be better identified as a cult agent shown holding the implements of her service. The same pairing of sacred utensils has led to the identification of the Louvre bronze as an image of a priestess as well.[13]

A wealth of representations from Attic vase painting suggests that there may be significance in the pairing of these sacred implements. While divinities are often shown holding a libation bowl, presumably in order to receive a liquid offering, they are less frequently shown holding jugs. Artemis is sometimes shown pouring from a jug into a phiale held out by her brother, Apollo.[14] But we do not see divinities holding phiale and oinochoe as a pair. Used as a set, these vessels are generally found in the hands of women (see figs. 3.1, 6.10–11), or Nikai, the female personifications of Victory so frequently depicted in ritual action.[15] While men and boys are sometimes shown holding jugs, they are rarely shown holding them together with *phialai*.[16] We shall consider this pairing of instruments in chapter 6 when we take a closer look at the representation of ritual action.

Ongoing excavations at Ephesos have shed new light on another ivory statuette from the foundation deposit. This image has long been nicknamed Megabyzos, after the eunuch priest of Artemis known from Xenophon (*Anabasis* 5.3.6–7) and Pliny (*On Natural History* 35.93, 131–32). The figure wears a long, richly decorated robe, broad belt, high headdress, long necklace, and earrings (fig. 5.3).[17] In 1984, the discovery of a new ivory statuette forever changed the traditional interpretation of the so-called eunuch priest.[18] Standing about eight centimeters in height, this figure is a veritable "sister" of Megabyzos, showing the same high headdress, decorated robe, necklace, and earrings. She raises her arms up against what are clearly articulated female breasts and holds two strands of a necklace in her hands. The newly discovered ivory figure so resembles the Megabyzos in costume, shape, proportions, and facial features, that "he" must now be reidentified as a woman. A second surprise came in the discovery that the recently excavated female figure is, in fact, the handle of an ivory double cup. Two shallow bowls found nearby fit neatly into the top of the headdress. On comparison, the tonglike projection atop the head of "Megabyzos" can now be understood to be a dowel for attachment to a vessel (fig. 5.3). It would seem that these ivory sculptures, which served as handles for libation cups, may reflect the appearance of actual women who used them in Ephesian rituals.

The communality between an implement and its user is well attested in Greek cult for which utensils often show a human figure integrated into the overall design.[19] Karyatids serve as supports for libation bowls, *cista*, and incense burners, reflecting the popular taste for anthropo-morphism in the decoration of ritual instruments. The frequent practice of modeling a human hand on the handle of metal vases similarly emphasizes the bond between implement and imple-mentor. Archaic bronze water pitchers that show a woman's face at the handle may give us the image of the *hydrophoros* who carried the vessel in sacred rites.[20] The Ephesian ivories seem to have reinforced such an analogy, emphasizing the agency of the cult attendants who used them. The choice of material may have bolstered this relationship as well. Annie Caubet has demon-strated that ancient texts regularly refer to ivory in feminine terms: translucent, white, and smooth to the touch. Used for erotic, luxury items such as beds, mirrors, combs, drinking cups, and musical instruments, the association of ivory with women's flesh is clear.[21] Indeed, it was the preferred material used for nude female figurines fashioned by Greek artisans on the model of Near Eastern prototypes. Ritual instruments used by female cult attendants in serving a female divinity were therefore carved from the luxurious "feminine" material of ivory. The implements from Ephesos thus underscore the close relationship between material and function, and the gen-dered significance of choices made in the images-creation process.

Archaic Architectural Sculpture and Votive Statuary

The Archaic temple of Artemis at Ephesos was a staggering architectural achievement, vast in size and lavish in decoration. Among its most striking features were the ornately carved figures encircling the lower drums of the columns on the east facade. The surviving sculptures show images of young women draped in rich layers of fabric.[22] One shows a maiden wearing a broad diadem and round earrings; another preserves a fragmentary hand pulling aside a voluminous skirt; yet another preserves a piece of a ruffled overfold, a *kolpos*, peeking out from beneath a heavy mantle. Could these marble maidens reflect the appearance of young cult attendants who served within the sacred space? Let us consider the relationship between ritual movement within the *temenos* and the architectural sculptures that may have mirrored the agents who circu-lated within it.

Sculptured column drums were particularly popular at the great Archaic shrines of Asia Minor. Nowhere do they show imagery more evocative of the living sanctuary than at the Tem-

Fig. 5.4
Marble fragment of sculptured column,
from the Temple of Apollo at Didyma.
Berlin, Staatliche Museen, Antikensammlung
SK 1721. Photo Bildarchiv Preussischer Kul-
turbesitz/Art Resource, NY.

Fig. 5.5
Limestone figure, from the olive tree pediment.
Athens, Acropolis Museum 52. Photo courtesy
Acropolis Museum.

ple of Apollo at Didyma, where nearly life-size reliefs of young women encircled the column shafts of the pronaos (fig. 5.4).[23] These female figures may represent the young women who processed at festival time along the Sacred Way from the Delphinion at Miletos to the altar of Apollo at Didyma.[24] Once there, they may have participated in the ring dances that were so central to Greek female ritual. As opportunities for visibility and display, circle dances in sanctuary settings afforded maidens of marriageable age a chance to be seen by the entire community. Indeed, these were not only sacred rites but also important social institutions.[25] The fragment in Berlin illustrated here (fig. 5.4), preserves the frontal face of an almond-eyed beauty, smiling demurely beneath her veiled headdress, circled with a rolled ribbon or crown.[26] Other fragments show maidens with wreaths resting atop their veils, all dressed up in festival finery. It is easy to imagine them as the sacred servants of the famous oracle, here immortalized in stone.[27]

To the north, at Kyzikos, sculptured column drums similarly adorned the mid-sixth-century temple. Once again, we see a veiled maiden wearing a tight-fitting chiton with deep over-fold, similar to the costume of the Hawk Priestess from Ephesos.[28] She moves between two naked youths, reaching out to take their hands in what may, again, reflect a circle dance. The dance may be set in the mythical past when the first youths and maidens of Kyzikos established a tradition of choral performances that was perpetuated in the historic ritual. Again, the communality between the subject matter of the sculptured column drums and the cult servants who inhabited the sacred space is key. Standing at ground level and nearly life size in scale, the sculptured figures may have reflected the living agents of ritual.

On the Greek mainland, we also find architectural sculpture that reflects ritual action within the precinct. Among the limestone sculptures that decorated small buildings on the Archaic Acropolis at Athens are those belonging to the so-called olive tree pediment (fig. 5.5).[29] Generally dated circa 550 B.C., the sculptures were found just opposite the east end of the Parthenon. They show a building with hipped roof, female figures, an ashlar wall with the leg of a male figure carved against it, and an olive tree incised onto the background, giving the pediment its nickname. Among the figures preserved is a maiden who wears a pad on top of her head, presumably to cushion an object, now lost. Some scholars believe that she once carried a water jug and interpret the building as a fountain house. This allows for the identification of the scene as Achilles' ambush of Troilos at the fountain house at Troy.[30] Alternatively, the scene has been read as one set in Athens, the rape of the maidens at the Enneakrounos fountain on the north slope of the Acropolis.[31] Brunilde Ridgway has offered a different view, suggesting that the cushion on the girl's head indicates her function as an architectural member, a karyatid supporting the roof of the building itself.[32] The structure could then be interpreted as an Archaic predecessor of the fifth-century Erechtheion, famous for its "Porch of the Maidens." The olive tree carved in low relief against the background, according to Ridgway, should be read as a reference to the olive tree of Athena that grew in the courtyard of the Pandroseion, just beside the Erechtheion.

Comparison of the maiden from the olive tree pediment with images from contemporary painting allows for yet another view, one that sees the cushion as an indicator of the girl's role as kanephoros. The maiden has raised her left arm as if to steady something, an action that is duplicated by the young kanephoros on a painted wooden plaque from Pitsa (see fig. 6.3; pl. 3).[33] Here, the girl raises her left hand to balance a basket and extends her right hand to pour a libation upon an altar. Viewed in profile, the maiden from the olive tree pediment shows a remarkably similar pose. She wears a costume like that of Pitsa girl, a peplos with patterned borders beneath a heavy mantle. The kanephoros of the Pitsa plaque wears a red mantle over a blue peplos, while the Acropolis maiden wears a blue mantle over a red peplos. Both wear pads on their heads to cushion the weight of the objects they carry. It is likely that the olive tree pediment showed a ritual scene similar to that of the wooden plaque in which a basket-bearing maiden led a procession into a sanctuary. The kanephoros of the pediment is likely to be from the realm of myth, part of an ancient narrative that provided the basis for rituals observed in the historical period.[34]

That the building represents a predecessor of the fifth-century Erechtheion, perhaps even a mythological predecessor, is possible. The Erechtheion's karyatid porch shows six maidens draped in peploi with heavy mantles pinned at their shoulders (fig. 5.6). Atop their heads, they wear elaborate echinus-shaped pads to cushion the weight of the lintel. Within the context of the holy sanctuary of Athena, the Erechtheion karyatids are likely to reflect the appearance of actual maidens who served as kanephoroi within the sacred space.[35] With libation bowls held low at their sides and dressed in their festival finery, the karyatid maidens are not unlike the women shown on the ivory-handle figure from Ephesos or the bronze support from Gouritzi (see figs. 5.1–2). The visual impact of seeing the burden carried upon the head, be it libation bowl, distaff, incense burner, or lintel block, gives resonance to the image of actual maidens in their ritual work within the sanctuary. The Erechtheion karyatids, set high above ground level, would have looked down upon the processions that passed before them on festival days. On occasions when the *xoanon* of Athena or other sacred relics may have been carried high in processional displays, the karyatids may even have viewed the spectacle at eye level, becoming one with it. Architectural sculpture may thus inform us of ritual movement and circulation within the sacred space and enable us, up to a point, to envision the living sanctuary.

The more familiar category, of course, is that of freestanding stone sculpture. From the very beginnings of monumental stone carving in Greece, life-size statues of women were dedicated in sacred precincts.

Indeed, the earliest surviving monumental freestanding marble statue in Greece was dedicated by a woman, Nikandre, in the middle of the seventh century B.C. This impressive statue, set up in the sanctuary of Artemis on Delos, shows a female figure dressed in a tight-fitting belted peplos, with mantle falling down the back. A metrical inscription carved on her skirt at the left side reads: "Nikandre dedicated me to the far-shooter of arrows, (Nikandre) the daughter of Deinodikos of Naxos, far above others, sister of Deinomenes, wife of Phraxos."[36] Nikandre was clearly a woman of status and wealth, able to offer an expensive gift carved in marble from her native Naxos and dedicated in her own name. It seems likely that she held a position of prominence within the administration of the sanctuary of Artemis, where her dedication was set up. Nikandre's epithet, "far above others," is in keeping with the superlative characterization of priestesses of later date. The listing of male relatives is also typical of later inscriptions that identify priestesses on their statue bases. Nowhere is Nikandre explicitly described as sacred servant, but we will have to wait nearly three centuries before we find the word *hiereia* inscribed on statue bases. It is likely that Nikandre held special agency within the cult of Artemis.

Fig. 5.6 (left)
Karyatid from Erechtheion, Athenian Acropolis. London, British Museum 1816.6-10.128 (Greek and Roman Sculpture 407). Photo © Copyright The Trustees of The British Museum.

Fig. 5.7 (right)
Antenor's kore. Athens, Acropolis Museum 681. Photo courtesy Acropolis Museum.

Although this over-life-size statue is usually interpreted as an image of the goddess, we must hold out the possibility that it could represent Nikandre herself. The holes drilled through her fists, usually interpreted as cuttings for metal attributes, such as bows and arrows or leashes for lions, could just as well have accommodated signifiers of priesthood. One can imagine that the figure held a silver or gold phiale and jug, such as those represented on the ivory statuette from Ephesos and on the bronze *thymiaterion* from Gourizi (see figs. 5.1–2).

Statues of standing young women, dressed in layers of luxurious fabrics and adorned with jewelry, are found in great numbers in the century that follows. Known simply as *korai*, or "maidens," they were offered in sanctuaries from East Greece to the Cyclades, Attica, and the Peloponnese.[37] The meaning of the korai has been much debated by scholars frustrated by the absence of identifying attributes or inscriptions to tell us precisely whom the statues represent. The impressive series of korai from the Athenian Acropolis have received particular attention. Somewhere between 54 and 75 statues of the kore type have been found on the Acropolis where they were set up between roughly 570 and 480 B.C.[38] Only fifteen bases likely to have supported the statues have been recovered. This makes it difficult to know under what circumstances the images were offered and exactly what the dedicators intended their offerings to mean. Over the years, korai have been identified in a wide variety of ways. Some scholars see the images as representations of divinities, particularly as Athena.[39] Others view them as nymphs or as mythical daughters of the early kings of Athens.[40] Another interpretation sees the statues as representations of mortal maidens, worshippers, or special cult attendants, including arrephoroi, kanephoroi, *ergastinai*, and priestesses.[41] Still other scholars regard the statues as representations of anonymous female votaries reflecting aristocratic, and nonaristocratic, values.[42] The korai have even been read as generic female "blanks" that could mean whatever the dedicator wished.[43] It is surprising that, despite intense scholarly attention, the korai have never been examined within the greater context of statues of standing draped women set up in sanctuaries throughout the classical and Hellenistic periods. A diachronic view is most informative, as we learn much from the later statues and their bases, set up at a time when epigraphic habits were much more informative.

Inscribed bases of classical and Hellenistic date confirm the identity of many draped female images as priestesses and other sacred-office holders. Most surviving priestess portraits of Hellenistic date could not be identified as such were it not for the inscriptions that tell us exactly who they are. These statues present no distinguishing attributes to communicate priestly status and show women dressed in the standard chiton/himation costume that was worn by all women of the day. The important factor here is context. What gives a woman the right to have her image set up within the sacred precinct? From the middle of the fifth century, priestesses are known to have had the privilege of setting up *agalmata* within the sanctuaries they served.[44] By the early fourth century, the priestess Lysimache had her portrait statue erected on the Athenian Acropolis.[45] Are we to assume that this practice began suddenly in the classical period, or can we see it as an older tradition, only confirmed in later years when epigraphic documentation became more prominent? It should be noted that korai began to appear on the Acropolis at just around the time of the institution of the Panathenaic festival in 556 B.C. It seems likely that the statues represent young women who were somehow involved in the ritual service of Athena, commemorated in perpetuity for their special roles.

The statue known as Antenor's Kore is one of sixteen korai from the Acropolis that show a metal spike protruding from a maiden's head (fig. 5.7).[46] These spikes have long been associated with *meniskoi*, crescent-shaped objects understood to have functioned as "scarecrows" in keeping birds away from statues in the open air. In Aristophanes' comedy the *Birds* (1114–17), the chorus warns the judges that if they do not vote in the birds' favor, they had better carry *meniskoi* like statues do, to prevent being spattered by bird droppings. Since *meniskos* literally means "crescent moon," most interpreters have envisaged umbrella-shaped metal objects set atop the heads of the statues.[47] Ridgway has offered an alternative explanation and views the rods as attachments for metal headdresses, including crests for helmets or elaborate floral decorations.[48]

I propose a further possibility, one that may be more in keeping with the requirements of votive statuary. The metal rods could have served as attachments for expensive metal baskets, long since stolen away. Treasury records from the Athenian Acropolis attest to bronze, silver, and gilt wooden baskets housed in the Opisthodomos, the Hekatompedon, and the Parthenon itself.[49] We know that some silver baskets weighed more than half a talent and represented enormously precious dedications.[50] Can we see such baskets fixed atop the heads of some of the korai? Envisioned in this way, some of the korai would have functioned much as the female figures that supported mirrors, cups, incense burners, and lustral basins. In fact, temple inventories dating to the second half of the fifth century mention "the *korai* from the baskets."[51] These are usually taken to mean bronze statuettes of maidens stored in baskets, or metal attachments decorated with female images and fixed to baskets.[52] But if we understand the "*korai* from the *kana*" to mean marble statues of maidens that carried metal baskets upon their heads, we can focus anew on the basket as the most precious part of the dedication and the kore statue as a "mere" support for it.[53] Like the statues of the arrephoroi dedicated on the Acropolis by proud parents during the Hellenistic period, at least some of the korai from Archaic times may have represented girls who served in the special cult role of kanephoros. Proud families would have dedicated these statues to commemorate their daughters' service.[54]

Modern favor for the alternative, that the metal spikes held crescent-shaped objects,

Fig. 5.8
Bronze incense burner. Delphi, Museum 7723.
Photo Gösta Hellner, DAI, neg. D-DAI-ATH
1976/509. All rights reserved.

risks missing a level of Aristophanes' humor. Scholars have gone to some pains to reconstruct disks, umbrellas, and even upraised horns on the metal attachments.[55] Yet these objects would not have prevented the birds from dirtying the arms or shoulders of statues. If *meniskoi* are more broadly defined as large crescent-shaped baskets or bowls, like that shown on the bronze incense burner from Delphi (fig. 5.8), we can understand how they may have completely shadowed the figures that supported them, just as Aristophanes describes.[56]

The standing draped maidens from the Archaic Acropolis may thus be viewed as images of cult agents who enjoyed the privilege of having their likenesses set up before the goddess. The precious-metal attributes that some of these carried upon their heads identified their specific function within the ritual and represented the most costly part of the offering.

Classical Votive Statuary

Compared to the wealth of statues of women from Archaic sanctuaries, the classical period has little to offer by way of similar dedications. This has to do with the fact that bronze came into greater use as the preferred material for expensive offerings and was melted down for reuse long ago.[57] This practice is recorded in a late fourth-century Athenian inventory that lists at least twenty-five bronze statues to be melted and recast into new offerings for Athena.[58] Perhaps this was the fate of the sculptures of key bearers, which Pliny (*On Natural History* 34.54, 34.77) attributed to the hands of Pheidias and Euphranor.[59] Langlotz's early attempt to identify the *kleidouchos* of Pheidias with the marble statue of Athena found in the Library at Pergamon has long been rejected.[60] Olga Palagia's association of Euphranor's lost *kleidouchos* with the statue of Hygieia now in the Uffizi Gallery is equally off the mark.[61] Our strongest indication of what statues of classical *kleidouchoi* looked like is provided by the image of a key-bearing woman shown beside Athena's statue on the Berlin relief, discussed in chapter 4 (see fig. 4.7; pl. 13).

We do have an extraordinary survivor in the marble base for the statue of Lysimache, priestess of Athena Polias at the end of the fifth and into the fourth century B.C. This represents the earliest attested statue of a priestess on the Athenian Acropolis. The circular base was found along the south wall of the Acropolis, just to the west of the Parthenon (figs. 5.9–10).[62] It is made of Pentelic marble and is cut on top to support the feet of a bronze statue that would have been roughly two-thirds life size. The inscription has been severely damaged, and much of the text, including the names of the priestess, the dedicator, and the artist, is missing. It reads:

[πατρὸς Λυσιμάχη] Δρακο[ντίδ]ο ἦν [τὸ γέν]ος μέν,
[ὀγδώκοντ᾿ ὀκτὼ δ᾿ ἐ]ξεπέρα[σ]εν ἔτηι
[σύμπανθ᾿ ἑξήκον]τα δ᾿ ἔτη [κ]αὶ τέσσαρ[α] ᾿Αθηνᾶι
[λατρεύσασα γένη τ]έσσαρ᾿ ἐπεῖδε τέκνων.
[Λυσιμάχη--]έος Φλυέως μήτηρ.
[Δημήτριος ἐπό]ησεν.

[Lysimache] daughter of Drakontides and lived for [eighty-eight] years.
[In all for six]ty-four years [she served] Athena and saw four generations
of children.
[Lysimache,] mother of [- - -]es of Phlya.
[Demetrios] made [the sculpture].[63]

Despite the damage, it can be made out that the woman honored was the daughter of a man named Drakontides, that she served as priestess of Athena for a period of time ending in the number four, and that she saw four generations of descendants, one of whom was from the deme Phlya.[64] This is enough to make certain that the woman was the same Lysimache still famous in the first century A.D. when Pliny (*On Natural History* 34.76) wrote that she served as priestess of

Fig. 5.9
Marble base for statue of Lysimache. Athens,
Acropolis *IG* II² 3453. Photo courtesy Acropolis
Museum.

Fig. 5.10
Marble base for statue of Lysimache.
Athens, Acropolis, *IG* II² 3453. Photo
courtesy Acropolis Museum.

Athena Polias for sixty-four years and had her statue sculptured by Demetrios. This Demetrios is generally taken to be Demetrios of Alopeke, a noted portraitist mentioned by Lucian (*Philopseudes* 18–20), whose work can be dated in the first half of the fourth century B.C.[65]

Attempts to find copies of the statue that stood on this base have proved futile. A classicizing head showing a very haggard old woman, known through two Roman copies, one in London and the other in Rome, has sometimes been associated with the lost Lysimache (fig. 5.11).[66] However, it is highly unlikely that Lysimache or any priestess of the early fourth century would have been portrayed as a wrinkled old woman. Even less plausible is the association of a headless statue in Basel, showing a very bent over, decrepit women wearing a peplos, with Lysimache's lost portrait.[67] Surely, a classical priestess would have been commemorated with an image showing her in a dignified, upright posture, standing tall with temple key in hand, just as we see on the grave reliefs (see figs. 8.4–6; pls. 20, 21). While South Italian vase painting may portray elderly priestesses as haggard old crones (see figs. 4.9–15), it represents a very different medium and is from a very different context from that of commemorative portrait statuary on the Athenian Acropolis. The lasting memorials for priestesses of Athena Polias should show them at their best.

Remarkably, a base that once held the statue of Lysimache's *diakonos* (subpriestess), a woman named Syeris, has also been recovered from the Acropolis.[68] Its inscription reads: "Syeris [daughter of ——], *diakonos* of Lysimache." Pausanias actually saw the statue of Syeris during his tour of the Acropolis. The inscribed base that Pausanias (1.27.4) reads gives a more elaborate dedication than the one that has been found:

> Syeris, *diakonos* of Lysimache in the sanctuary
> This portrait image is a clear likeness;
> My deeds, too, and my soul now live
> Clearly before all. For holy fate led me
> to this most beautiful temple of Pallas the revered.
> Where I served the goddess in toil and not unrenowned. . . .
> Nikomachos made it.[69]

Scholars have searched for surviving copies of the lost statue of Syeris. Some point to a bronze statuette in Vienna, showing an old veiled woman, as a miniature copy of the lost portrait, though this is highly unlikely.[70]

How early in the classical period do we find evidence for the dedication of statues of priestesses? In the middle of the fifth century a woman named Lysistrate dedicated an agalma in the entranceway of the City Eleusinion. *Agalma* translates as "pleasing gift," and could mean a statue or some other kind of ornament. The base of Lysistrate's dedication is cut on top to receive what appears to have been a rectangular pillar, possibly a herm. Its inscription reads:[71]

> [ἀ]ρρήτο τελετῆς πρόπολος σῆς, πότνια Δηοῖ,
> καὶ θυγατρὸς προθύρο κόσμον ἄγαλμα τόδε
> ἔστησεν στεφάνω Λυσιστράτη, οὐδὲ παρόντων
> φείδεται ἀλλὰ θεοῖς ἄφθονος ἐς δύναμιν.

> Mistress Deo, Lysistrate, the servant of your, and your daughter's,
> holy rites, set up this gift as an ornament of your entrance way and
> she does not spare her resources but is unstinting to the gods to the
> best of her ability.[72]

Lysistrate is not explicitly called a priestess here but is referred to as a *propolos*, or "handmaiden," of Demeter. This is typical of dedications of the classical period that tend to describe a woman's cult function rather than giving the title *hiereia*. Inscriptions specifically mentioning the title *priestess* did not come into wide use until Hellenistic times. It is likely that Lysistrate was, in fact, a priestess whose office gave her the right to set up an agalma within Demeter's temple.

During the first half of the fourth century, we have firm evidence for a priestess of Demeter setting up her own portrait within the City Eleusion. Although her name is not preserved, we know that she was the mother of Epigenes of Acharnai and that her statue was carved by a sculptor named "[. . .]os, son of Aristeides." We also learn that a priestess of the Thes-

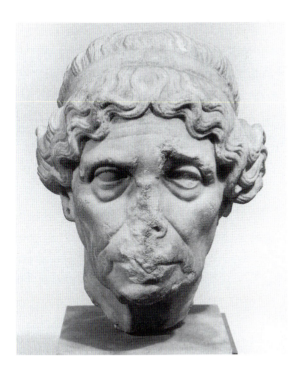

Fig. 5.11
Marble head. London, British Museum
2001. Photo © Copyright the Trustees
of The British Museum.

mophoria named Satyra was given the right to set up a painted portrait of herself in the Eleusinion during the second century B.C.[73] Her deme, Melite, passed a decree that granted her this special right, which, we learn, was "a privilege bestowed on the other priestesses."

Chairippe, priestess of Demeter and Kore in the middle of the fourth century, had her portrait carved by the famed Praxiteles. A block of Hymettian marble, found in the late 1990s during the construction of the metro station at Monasteraki in central Athens, bears an inscription identifying the subject as *hiereia* and the artist. The statue was dedicated by Chairippe's brothers, Aristodemos and Philophron, sons of Philophron of Kephisia. The family is known through other inscriptions. As there are no cuttings on the top of the base, it is likely that Chairippe's statue rested atop a crowning pedestal and was made of bronze. Most likely, it originally stood in the City Eleusinion where Chairippe served, just two hundred meters from the spot where the base was found.[74]

Public portrait statuary had long been a privilege of male politicians, generals, and athletes. Indeed, the best-attested group of classical portrait statues on the Athenian Acropolis are athletic victor portraits.[75] Priestesses seem to represent the first and, one might argue, only category of women to be broadly represented in portrait statuary of the classical period. One of the earliest attested statues of a historical woman may have been that of a Delphic prophetess named Charite. Although the sculpture itself does not survive, an inscribed travertine base that once held it, or its copy, has been discovered at Ostia.[76] This was found together with two similar bases, all bearing inscriptions dated to the first century B.C. Although the bases are late in date, they may have supported original bronze statues plundered from Greece and brought to Italy. They attest to a statue of the comic poet Plato sculptured by Lysikles, an image of the philosopher Antisthenes by Phyromachos, as well as the statue of Charite carved by Phradmon.[77] Charite's inscribed base reads:

Charite, giver of oracles
at Delphi.
Phradmon of Argos made it.

Phradmon's dates are not known with certainty but he is usually placed within the fourth century.[78] From this, we might surmise that Charite served as Pythia sometime during the classical period. Once again, the word *hiereia* does not appear in the inscribed dedication. Instead, we see the descriptive term *themisteuousa*, "one who delivers oracles," used to identify her as priestess.

In the middle of the fourth century near Kephisia in Attica, a woman dedicated an altar to Artemis Agrotera. The dedicatory inscription does not preserve her name but it does preserve her title as *propolos*, or "servant," of the goddess, just as we have seen for Lysistrate, handmaiden of Demeter.[79] The woman also served as *kleidouchos* of the city temple, that is, the shrine of Artemis near the Ilissos River. The fact that she was the mother of Dionysios's children indicates that her office was open to married women. Her choice of an altar for dedication reflects a strong analogy between donor and offering, as sacred servant identifies with cult object.

Representations of sacred women followed the fashions of their day, and by the third quarter of the fourth century, we find an Athenian priestess of Aphrodite Pandemos setting up her image, and that of her son, in a shallow shrine enclosure, or *naiskos*.[80] This architectural form became a very popular votive type for the period. Although the statues of mother and son are lost, the pediment and cornice survive. They were recovered from the sanctuary of Aphrodite on the southwest slope of the Acropolis. An inscription carved on the epistyle tells us that the priestess Menekrateia, daughter of Dexikrates from Ikaria, and her son Archinos dedicated the monument to the goddess. A sculptured frieze preserved above the inscription shows Aphrodite's doves carrying ribbons in their beaks. The word *hiereia* is carved in stone to confirm Menekrateia's office as priestess of Aphrodite.

Across the Mediterranean at Knidos, a woman named Chrysina founded a small sanctuary to Demeter during the middle of the fourth century. She was acting in response to a dream in which Hermes appeared to her and announced that she would become the servant of the goddess.[81] Chrysina's foundation is commemorated in a metrical inscription carved upon a statue base of blue marble, found on the slopes of the Knidian acropolis during the nineteenth century.[82] The dedication, written in mixed Doric and Ionic dialect, reads:

Κούραι καὶ Δάματρι οἶκον καὶ ἄγαλμ' ἀνέθηκε |
Χρυσογόνη[ς] μήτηρ, Ἱπποκράτους δὲ ἄλοχος, |
Χρυσίνα, ἐννυχίαν ὄψιν ἰδοῦσα ἱεράν· |
Ἑρμῆς γάρ νιν ἔφησε θεαῖς Ταθνηι προπολεύειν |

To Kore and Demeter, Chrysina dedicated a temple and a statue,
mother of Chrysogone and wife of Hippokrates, because of a holy
dream Chrysina had at night; for Hermes told her she would become
servant of the goddess in the place named Tathne.

The word *hiereia* is not used in the dedication but instead we have the verb *propoleuein*, "to serve,"
a verb that is related to the word *propolos*, which we have seen used to describe the role of Lysistrate, servant of Demeter in mid-fifth-century Athens. Here on the Knidian acropolis, Charles
Newton found remains of a shrine and a stoa-like building, pits containing terracotta votives, and
twelve bases for statues and other offerings. Inscriptions name women on all but one of the statue
bases, and two of these name priestesses as dedicators.[83] In this same location was found the famous statue of the enthroned "Demeter of Knidos," now in the British Museum.[84] Newton associated it with the blue stone base that records Chrysina's dedication, despite the fact that the base
shows cuttings to receive a standing figure. It is likely that the base held a statue of Chrysina, in
the tradition of priestesses who dedicated their own portraits within the sanctuaries they served.

In summary, we simply do not find the term *hiereia* used in dedicatory inscriptions for
portrait statues until the first half of the fourth century. Here we find it used for a priestess of
Demeter and Kore whose portrait was set up in the City Eleusinion. At mid-century, the word is
used on the base of Chairippe's statue and, later, it is found on Menekreteia's dedication. Charite
is described as the "giver of oracles" at Delphi. Lysistrate of Athens, Chrysina of Knidos, and an
unnamed woman who dedicated an altar to Artemis Agrotera near Kephisia are all described by
some form of the word *propolos*, or "servant." The absence of the term *hiereia* makes it difficult to
know with certainty whether these statues represented priestesses. But the absence of the word
in the epigraphic record does not preclude the possibility that they did. It is likely that these
representations relied on attributes, such as the temple key, to communicate priestly status. Since
we have no surviving statues from the period, we must look to later sculptures that may reflect
earlier, classical conventions.

Hellenistic Votive Statuary

Despite the externally changing conditions of cities and their upper classes, caught between competing kings and the increasingly forceful presence of Rome, a large corpus of Hellenistic statues

Fig. 5.12
Marble statue of Nikeso, from
Priene. Berlin, Staatliche Museen
Antikensammlung SK 1928.
Photo Antikensammlung,
Staatliche Museen zu Berlin,
Preussicher Kulturbesitz.

and statue bases for priestess portraits survives, still to be collected in full. Inscribed texts attest
to the fact that it was priestly women, in particular, who had the privilege of erecting statues
within sacred precincts.[85] The apparent rise in the numbers of such dedications during the Hellenistic period is affected by several factors. First, the title *hiereia* is regularly inscribed on statue
bases, allowing us to know with certainty that priestesses are represented. Second, the widespread
use of marble, rather than bronze, allows for greater chances of survival. Bronze was still used for
the most sumptuous dedications, but a marked increase in marble statuary, particularly at the
shrines of Asia Minor, suggests changes in the societies that produced them. Increases in population, in cults and festival participation, as well as in wealth for a newly widening social group,
allowed for more money, more priestesses, and more statues.

Asia Minor

It is from the great sanctuaries of Asia Minor that we have our earliest and most abundant evidence for the commemoration of Hellenistic priestesses with portrait statues. Priene provides some of the most interesting material, recovered from the sanctuary of Athena Polias and from the shrine of Demeter and Kore. An inscribed base from the Athena sanctuary, dated to the fourth century B.C., records that Menedemos dedicated a statue of his daughter Niko, priestess of Athena.[86] Although no statue was found with the base, a portrait bust of a young girl unearthed in the excavations has been erroneously associated with it.[87] The base is important in its own right, however, as it gives the standard dedicatory formula by which a father sets up a statue on behalf of his priestly daughter.

Priene provides us with the earliest surviving statue of a priestess, Nikeso, found together with its inscribed base. Importantly, the inscription uses the word *hiereia* to describe Nikeso's status as priestess of Demeter and Kore. Her portrait is dated to the first half of the third century B.C. (fig. 5.12; pl. 16).[88] The statue was found at the entrance to the sanctuary of Demeter and Kore, together with two bases. Upon entering the shrine, the visitor would have been confronted with the marble statue of Nikeso on one side, and a bronze statue of Timonassa on the other.[89] Timonassa's bronze statue has never been found. But the marble statue of Nikeso fits perfectly into the cutting atop the base that bears her name. An inscription carved across the front of the block gives a familiar formula in which Nikeso is identified through her male relatives. It reads:

Νι[κ]ησὼ Ἱπποσθένους,
Εὐκρίτου δὲ γυνή,
ἱερῆ Δήμητρος καὶ Κόρης.

Ni[k]eso daughter of Hipposthenes,
wife of Eukritos,
priestess of Demeter and Kore.

Much can be learned from this first certain statue of a priestess. Nikeso is shown dressed in a chiton with an elaborately textured, double-hemmed himation draped across the front (see fig. 5.12; pl. 16). Her left arm is completely swathed in fabric. She wears her hair long, falling down over her shoulders. An attribute may have been held in her right arm, which is now broken away. Scholars have offered a variety of restorations here, including a basket, a water jug, a scepter, and a large torch.[90]

Nikeso's elaborate dress, and the manner in which it is draped, may communicate her sacral status. The shimmering texture of the mantle is unusual and suggests a special silken gar-

ment known as the *Coae vestes*, which originated on the island of Kos.[91] This costume was made up of one layer of light silk atop another of heavy wool, and, indeed, Nikeso's mantle does show two distinct hems along the bottom. The texturing of the cloth suggests a luxurious fabric, appropriate for ritual vestments worn in imitation of the goddess. The swathing of the mantle around Nikeso's arm may have held special significance for the ancient viewer, as a device used to prevent contamination of sacred objects. This convention is well attested in Greek vase painting and on gemstones that show Diomedes, his hands fully wrapped in his mantle as he picks up the sacred Palladion of Athena at Troy.[92] The swathing of Nikeso's arm may have signaled her role as one who handles sacred images and implements. It is the inscription that confirms Nikeso's priestly status for us. But for the ancient viewer, a number of factors may have worked together to establish her sacred identity. These include the exotic fabric of her costume, the enveloping of her right hand in her mantle, her hair worn long in imitation of the goddess, and the very placement of her statue, just before the entrance to the temple and side-by-side with the image of her fellow priestess, Timonassa.

Nikeso's statue shows a standard type used for representations of Hellenistic priestesses in the centuries to come. The temple key, long established as the signifier of feminine priesthood at Athens, is absent from the Hellenistic repertory, with the exception of Cypriot votive statuary (see figs. 4.4–6; pls. 14, 15) and the relief sculpture from Taras (see fig. 4.16; pl. 26). Of course, Cypriot sculptors adhered to Athenian models long after they have gone out of fashion at home.[93] The statue of Nikeso, by contrast, looks forward, and gives us our first view of what will remain the conventional image of the priestess for the following six centuries. Priene also preserves for us inscribed bases from a number of other statues representing local priestesses. Two second-century priestesses of Demeter, Tyrinno and Phrattis, were honored with portraits dedicated by Tyrinno's brother. A second-century priestess of Athena named Zoillis was commemorated with a statue set up by her parents, who also dedicated a statue of her brother, Kydimos, who served as priest of Dionysos.[94]

Up the coast from Priene at Erythrai, a priestess of Dionysos set up her own statue at the turn of the fourth to the third centuries. The metrical text inscribed on its base reads:[95]

[Σ]μὼ τήν[δ' ἔστη]σ[α] γυνὴ Ζωίλου Διονύσωι
[ἱ<ε>]ρέα πρὸ πόλεως Παγκρατίδεω θυγάτηρ,
[εἰ]κ[ό]να μὲ[μ] μορφῆς, ἀρετῆς δ' ἐπίδειγμα καὶ ὄλβου,
[ἀθ]άνατον μνήμην παισί τε καὶ προγόνοις.

[S]imo, wife of Zoilos, [priest]ess of the city, daughter of Pankratides, set up this image of beauty and example of virtue and wealth, for Dionysos, as an eternal memorial for my children and ancestors.

The first letter of the woman's name is not preserved and her name has been restored as either "Simo" or "Timo." The inscription reflects a strong sense of family pride, in which her husband and father are cited by name, and in which both ancestors and children are memorialized. Once again, we see the word *hiereia* used to describe the woman's office. Erythrai preserves for us a number of other bases that held images of Hellenistic women, including priestesses. Zosima, priestess of Demeter, had her statue set up by the Boule and the Demos during the second century B.C.[96]

The venerable sanctuary of Hera on Samos has one of the oldest and most prolific traditions of votive statuary on record. It is not surprising that a priestess of Hellenistic date followed the custom and had her image set up within the sanctuary. Her statue is particularly noteworthy for its unusual costume, which seems to be a tunic over a chiton, or perhaps a very long overfold to the chiton with a kolpos, belted beneath. A mantle falls across the shoulders and down the back (fig. 5.13).[97] The female figure is shown with her arms extended outward, perhaps in a gesture of prayer, or perhaps to hold attributes. To the south, on the island of Kos, eight marble statuettes, six dedicated by women, were found set up along the back wall of the shrine of Demeter near Kyparissi. Two of these were dedicated by a priestess named Leirio, daughter of Ekatonymos. The priestess Pythias offered a dedicatory inscription to Demeter in about 200 B.C. Up on the second terrace of the Koan Acropolis, in the Asklepieion, the base for a statue of the priestess Kallistrate has been unearthed. She served as priestess of Asklepios, Hygieia, Epione, Apollo of Delos, Leto, and King Eumenes at around 190–160 B.C.[98]

To the south on Cyprus, we learn of a number of Hellenistic cult agents from statue bases set up at Idalion, Palaipaphos, and Kition. A Phoenician inscription dated 255/254 B.C. and found at Idalion names Amath'-Osir as kanephoros of Arsinoe Philadelphos at both Idalion and Kition. In the middle of the third century B.C., Phanion Boiskou, the only priestess of Paphian Aphrodite known for Ptolemaic Cyprus, erected a statue of her son Boiskos at Palaipaphos. Eirene Ptolemaiou, priestess of Arsinoe Philopator at various times between 199 and 171 B.C., had her statue set up at Kition by her son Andromachos. Artemo, Theodoris, and Polykrateia, the three daughters of Theodoros Seleukou, administrator of the city of Salamis and strategos of Cyprus (124/123–118 B.C.?) served as eponymous priestesses: Polykrateia's statue was set up in the sanctuary of Aphrodite at Palaipaphos.[99]

Images of priestesses were erected in sanctuaries all across Asia Minor.[100] At Sardis, inscriptions document the contributions made by priestesses of Artemis during the second quarter of the second century B.C. Their benefactions are celebrated on inscribed bases that once held their portraits.[101] At Troy, Meliteia, Pytho, and an unnamed maiden were honored with portrait statues for their roles as kanephoroi during the first century B.C.[102] Hageso, priestess of Artemis on Rhodes, was honored with a portrait statue during the third or second century B.C.[103]

No sanctuary gives us a better sense of the quantity in which priestess portraits were erected than does the great citadel at Pergamon. Here, inscribed bases dating to the second and first centuries B.C. attest to seventeen priestesses of Athena Nikephoros, two priestesses of Demeter and Kore, and two priestesses of uncertain cults.[104] A base of white marble bears a long inscription honoring Metris, daughter of Artemidoros, who served as priestess of Athena during the mid-second century B.C.[105] The Boule, Demos, and Strategoi decreed that Metris be honored with a gold crown and a bronze statue. We learn the names of a host of other priestesses of Athena Nikephoros from the bases that held their statues. These were set up in the Athena precinct, near the Great Altar, on the theater terrace, and were reused in walls from the Upper Agora. We learn of Alexandra, Arsinoe, Asklepias, Bito, Laodike, Lysandra, Metrodora, two women named Moschion, Olympias, and Sosipatra from the statue bases that commemorated their tenures as priestesses of Athena during the second century B.C.[106] For the first century, we have Thale, Theophilo, and a daughter of Diogenes whose name is not preserved, all of whom served as priestesses of Athena Nikephoros, while Phila and a woman whose name is not preserved served as priestesses of the Mother of the Gods.[107]

Scattered marble fragments of priestess portraits have been recovered from across the area between the temple of Athena and the Great Altar of Zeus.[108] No fewer than forty inscribed bases of Roman date attest to portraits that once stood just outside Athena's temple.[109] Interestingly, there is no evidence for statues of men, which may result from the fact that it was women alone who oversaw the cult of Athena Nikephoros. The Pergamene acropolis, crowded with a forest of statues of priestesses from across the centuries, must have strongly resembled the citadel sanctuary that it aspired to resemble, that of the venerable Athenian Acropolis.[110]

At Kyzikos on the Sea of Marmara, honors paid to a priestess named Kleidike during the early first century B.C. give a sense of the exceptional prestige enjoyed by late Hellenistic priestesses. As with many well-born women of her day, Kleidike held multiple priesthoods, including those of Meter Plakiane, Artemis Mounychia, and Demeter and Kore. An inscription records a request made by a group of female religious officials to the Assembly. They asked permission to erect a bronze statue of Kleidike next to the statue of her brother on the monument of her ancestors "in the men's agora."[111] A second decree passed by the Assembly allows for a statue of Kleidike to be set up in a location designated for her within the *parthenon* of the temple of Meter Plakiane."[112] Kleidike's family monument is an early example of what was to become an increasingly popular form in the Roman East: the private family display. Such memorials opened the possibility for female portrait statuary in civic as well as sacred contexts.[113] Kleidike, clearly a member of the elite of Kyzikos, was thus honored with portraits set up in the temple and in the men's agora, commemorating her dual roles as priestess and heiress, privileges borne of her elite status.

The reverence with which Kyzikos regarded the finest of its women is made clear in the extraordinary story of Apollonis, a young priestess of Artemis of the Pythaists who died well before her time during the early first century A.D. She was a member of the privileged class and, most probably, was named for Apollonis, queen of Pergamon, who had been a citizen of Kyzikos before marrying King Attalos I.[114] We will consider the exceptional pageantry of Apollonis's funeral in chapter 8. For now, let us note the remarkable honors that she was granted pertaining to her portrait statues. A posthumous decree instructs that four images be erected for her, one in the sanctuary of the Graces, another in the temple of Aphrodite, and yet another in the temple of Artemis.[115] At the shrine of the Graces, Apollonis's statue was to be crowned by the priestesses at an annual ceremony.

According to the decree, the fourth statue would be set up in a civic building that would take on the newly ordained function of marriage registry office. All couples preparing to wed would henceforth be required to crown Apollonis's statue before the official in charge. Still other portraits of Apollonis were decreed, including a gilded image to be set up in a location chosen by her relatives. The badly damaged text prevents us from knowing the exact placement of all her statues, but it is clear that Apollonis received truly exceptional honors in having her likeness displayed all across the city. Each of the inscribed bases praises Apollonis for her modesty (*sophrosyne*), a virtue that is more typically noted on dedications for portrait statues of men.[116]

Greek Mainland

We began our survey of Hellenistic priestess portraits in Asia Minor, since the surviving evidence is relatively abundant and it preserves at least a few statues together with their inscribed bases. We have traced these sculptures into the Roman Imperial period, noting the longevity and growing intensity of the practice of dedicating priestess portraits in sacred precincts. This has enabled us to examine the broadening of public contexts for statues and other honors given to women, who were increasingly involved in civic-office holding and public benefaction. This long view provides the broader context within which we can now consider the smaller body of surviving material from the Greek mainland. Despite increased opportunities for civic-office holding open to women of Asia Minor, it is through religious posts alone that women of the Greek mainland distinguished themselves. Indeed, no female offices or liturgies other than priesthoods are known for women of mainland Greece during this period.[117]

ATTICA

It is not surprising that practices established early on were continued at Athens, among them the dedication of images of female cult agents on the Acropolis. Unfortunately, none of these has survived to show what the girls, maidens, and women who held office may have looked like. But we do have inscribed bases for seventeen statues of the youngest servants, the *arrephoroi*, whose portraits were set up by proud relatives during the late third to second centuries B.C.[118] The bases record that these images were dedicated to Athena alone or to Athena together with Pandrosos. One statue, of Roman date, was set up for an *arrephoros* called Theano. She was clearly named after Homer's priestess of Athena at Troy, perhaps on her family's presumption that she would one day hold sacred office. The base is inscribed in iambic verse:[119]

ἐρρηφόρον πατήρ με, πότνα, σ[οί, θεά],
Σαραπίων μήτηρ τ' ἔθηκ[ε Χ]ρη[σίμη]
τὴν σὴν Θεανὼ πέντε καὶ [συναίμονες]ι
δὸς δ' οἶς μὲν ἥβην, οἶς [δὲ γηράσκειν καλῶς].

> To you, O revered goddess, my father Sarapion and my mother
> Chresime dedicated me, your Theano, as *arrephoros*, along with my
> five [siblings].
> Grant the latter fair youth and the former graceful old age.

Importantly for us, inscribed dedications sometimes give the names of the priestesses of Athena Polias under whom the little girls served, thus providing an important source of prosopographical data. Inscriptions listing the names of maidens who served as kanephoroi and *ergastinai*, dating to the second and first centuries B.C., similarly provide names of priestesses under whom the maidens performed their duties.[120]

Just a few bases survive from lost statues of priestesses of Athena Polias. These are noteworthy for their identification of the sculptors who carved them, as well as for the elaborately composed dedications they carry, sometimes given in verse. A daughter of Lysistratos of Bate, who held office during the first half of the third century, had her image carved by two well-known artists. The dedication has suffered a great deal but has been restored, to read:[121]

᾿[Ἀθηνᾶς] Π[ολι]άδο[ς] ἱέ[ρειαν]

[--- Λυ]σιστρά[του] Βατῆθεν

--- ος Πο[λυ]εύκτου ᾿Ερ[χιεὺς]

[ἀ]νέθηκε[ν].

[Κηφισόδοτ]ος Τίμα[ρχος] ἐπο[ί]ησα[ν].

[Athena] P[oli]as' pri[estess]

[--- of Ly]sistrat[os] of Bate,

[Lysistrat]os, son of Po[ly]euktos of Er[chia],

  [d]edicate[d].

[Kephisodot]os and Tima[rchos] made it.[122]

The fragmentary state of the inscription has led to dispute over the priestess's name and lineage. Alexander Mantis restores her name as Phanostrate, but David Lewis identified her as Lysimache II, who held office around 270 B.C.[123] This Lysimache would have been the daughter of the son of the nephew of Lysimache I, priestess of Athena Polias at the end of the fifth century, whom we have discussed above.[124] Like the statue of her well-known ancestor carved by the sculptor Demetrios, this Lysimache had her portrait sculptured by artists of some repute: Kephisodotos and Timarchos. As sons of the master sculptor Praxiteles, they achieved their own fame for their portrait of Menander and for the wooden statues of Lykourgos and his sons that they carved for display in the Erechtheion.[125]

Penteteris, daughter of Hierokles of Phlya, served as priestess of Athena Polias around 245 B.C. She was honored with a portrait statue, the inscribed base of which was found on the

143

Acropolis.[126] At the very end of the second century, we find Chrysis, with whom we opened this book.[127] She was honored with two statues on the Acropolis, one of which was dedicated by her cousins:[128]

[ἱέρειαν ᾿ Ἀθ]ηνᾶς Πολιάδος Χρυσίδα
[Νικήτου] Περγασῆθεν θυγατέρα
[Διονύσιος κ]αὶ Νικήτης καὶ Φίλυλλα
᾿[Ἀθηνοβίου] Εὐπυρίδου τὴν ἑαυτῶν
[ἀνεψιὰ]ν ᾿ Ἀθηνᾶι Πολιάδι.

[The priestess of Ath]ena Polias, Chrysis, daugher of [Niketes] of Pergase, [Dionysios a]nd Niketes and Philylla, children of [Athenobios] of Eupyridai, (dedicated) their [cousi]n to Athena Polias.

Chrysis's cousins were distinguished Athenians from a line of prominent public figures about whom we know a great deal. Dionysios and his brother Niketes were Pythian *paides* in 128/127 B.C. and ephebes around 118/117. Dionysios went on to hold the offices of epimeletes of the *emporion* at Delos ca. 100/99 and his brother Niketes was *hippeus* in 106/105.[129] Turner has suggested that Chrysis's mother and her cousins' father were brother and sister, and that Chrysis and her cousins were raised in different demes.[130]

The dedication of honorific statues commemorating priesthood was a very special privilege at Athens. Inscribed decrees attest to occasions on which the city, deme, *genos*, or some other civic or familial body authorized the erection of a statue to commemorate an individual's service. A text from Athens, now lost but copied in a sketchbook during the early nineteenth century, records a decree of the *genos* of the Theonidai concerning a priestess of Nymphe.[131] Only the last two letters of the priestess's name are preserved: [. . .]ra. Eugene Vanderpool suggested several possibilities for restoration, including Theodora, Kleopatra, and Nikephora. A list of honors and privileges granted to this woman includes permission to erect a statue in the sanctuary "at her own expense." This inscription suggests that the setting up of statues was an honor open not just to anyone, but ordained by specific mandate of the *genos*. It also bears powerful witness to the fact that this priestess had her own money and was able to use it as she wished.

The priestly sphere on the island of Delos was intertwined with the religious and political orbits of Athens. Around 120–110 B.C., Medeios of the Piraeus and his wife set up statues of their three children in an exedra on Delos. The pround parents celebrated their daughter Philippe for her service as a kanephoros in the Delia and as a subpriestess of Artemis. They honored another daughter, Laodameia, for her role as a kanephoros at the Delia and at the

Fig. 5.14
Marble statue of Aristonoe, from
Rhamnous. Athens, National Archaeological
Museum 232. Photo Gösta Hellner, DAI,
neg. D-DAI-ATH 1972/457.

Apollonia. Their son Medeios was commemorated for his service as a member of the Athenian embassy for the Delia festival.[132] This very public display of family piety in the great Panhellenic sanctuary on Delos introduced the children of Medeios to a very wide audience. Philippe went on to serve as priestess of Athena Polias at Athens, a post for which she was clearly groomed from a young age.

At the northern border of Attica, the sanctuary of Nemesis at Rhamnous has produced a rare survivor in the marble statue of the priestess Aristonoe, found together with its inscribed base (fig. 5.14).[133] This was set up during the third century B.C. in the smaller of the two temples, found just inside the cella to the left of the door, along with other images, including the well-known statue of Themis. The rectangular base that held Aristonoe's image bears an inscription informing us that her son Hierokles dedicated it. Aristonoe is shown wearing her hair in the fashion of the day, parted down the center and swept back in a roll. She is dressed in a voluminous mantle atop a chiton, just as we have seen for priestess portraits of Asia Minor. We are reminded of the arrangement shown for Nikeso at Priene, whose mantle is drawn from under her right arm, along a diagonal to cover her breasts (see fig. 5.12; pl. 16). Aristonoe's right forearm, found in the excavations and now lost, showed that she originally held a phiale.[134] In this, she joins the images of women of sacred status that we have seen in vase painting and the decorative arts (see figs. 5.1–2, 5.6, 6.7–9).

THE PELOPONNESE

Commemorative portraits ensured that women would be remembered always for their sacred service. They also gave concrete evidence of piety and the fulfillment of vows and promises. At Argos in the third century B.C., Timanthis was honored with a statue set up by her father. The inscribed dedication invokes Aphrodite with her epithet Kypris, reflecting the goddess's birthplace on the island of Cyprus:[135] "Blessed Kypris, take care of Timanthis, whose statue Timanthes set up in fulfillment of a vow, so that someone even afterwards, goddess, visiting this shrine of the promontory, may have a memory of this servant of yours."[136] As we have seen for Niko at Priene, a father sets up a statue of his daughter in the sanctuary of the goddess whom she served. Timanthis is referred to as an *amphipolos*, or "servant," rather than as *hiereia*.

By the late Hellenistic period, women of mainland Greece were making benefactions on a scale comparable to what have seen for the women of Asia Minor. But on the Greek mainland, there was a certain conservatism, which precluded extending civic office to women or tampering with existing cults to open new opportunities for officeholding. At Mantineia in the central Peloponnese, a woman named Nikippa was clearly a central player in the civic and religious arenas during the first century B.C. Yet we have no evidence that she ever held a priesthood. Nikippa was celebrated by the priests of Kore with what seems to have been a painted portrait, for having "generously and zealously" funded the celebration of the Mysteries in the year 64/63 B.C.[137]

An honorary decree tells us that Nikippa conducted the ritual procession, presided over the sacrifice to Kore, presented a peplos to the goddess, and "joined in the adorning" with the priests. This could mean that she decorated the sanctuary, or helped finance its decoration, or even played some role in the regulation of the cult as a whole.[138] We are told that Nikippa performed the rituals and behaved "exactly as was the custom with those who were priests." But since the cult that she served was presided over by male officials alone, Nikippa could not hold an official post. In thanks for her many benefactions and active participation, the priests invited Nikippa to join them for the great feast. Nikippa was clearly part of the "men's club" at Mantineia and participated confidently as an equal among the city's priests, despite the fact that she was not named to office. Indeed, Pausanias (8.9.6) saw a statue of Nikippa when he visited the city some two centuries later, clearly a sign that she was granted every honor befitting a priestess.

We do hear of a full-fledged Mantineian priestess named Epigone, who was honored during the late first century B.C.[139] Her image stood on a base together with a statue of her husband, Euphrosynos. Its inscribed dedication celebrates Epigone as "priestess of every goddess of her own free will" and praises her for her "piety in worshipping the gods" and for "feasting the entire populace."[140] The reference to Epigone's "free will" is striking. This probably refers to her willingness to step up and take financial responsibility for a whole variety of local priesthoods.

The women of Mantineia continued make impressive benefactions right into Roman times. Iulia Eudia was honored during the first century A.D. by the priests of Asklepios and the priests of Zeus. She had made a donation of very sizeable vineyards to their cults. In return for her generosity (*megalopsychia*), the priests granted Iulia the right place her portrait, painted on gilded shields and identified by inscriptions, in the temples of Asklepios and Zeus. Beyond this, she was given the honor of having her birthday commemorated each year with a sacrifice.[141] Like Nikippa before her, Iulia is not known to have held a priesthood at Mantineia and her benefactions were made to cults overseen by men. Nonetheless, she is given all the honors befitting a priestess. While her husband, C. Iulius Strobeilos, is associated with her philanthropies and shares in some of the honors, Iulia is clearly the one who received the most public and permanent distinctions that her city could offer.

The little sanctuary of Artemis Ortheia in the great city of Messene preserves for us a rare and vivid picture of what an active shrine looked like when crowded with statues of female cult agents (figs. 5.15–16).[142] Eleven stone bases, five of which are inscribed, have been found in situ within the cella, deliberately placed in a semicircle spreading out from the cult statue of the goddess. Five life-size statues of girls (four of marble and one of sandstone) can be matched to these bases (figs. 5.17–21; pl. 19), as can three under-life-size marble statues of mature priestesses (figs. 5.22–24; pls. 17–19).[143] The interior of the cella was a space crowded with ritual installations, including the base for Damophon's cult statue of Artemis Phosphoros, seen by Pausanias (4.31.10), an offering table, a stone treasury box for donations, and a forest of statues representing girls and women.[144] Two side chambers were lined with benches, providing seats for participants in the rites that took place within the shrine. Just outside to the east, in the open square, an altar and a high stone pilaster are set along an axis that is aligned with the cella. This was the setting for the shrine's sacrificial activity.[145]

Within the cella, a base set to the cult statue's right hand side preserves a text in iambic verse that gives insight into what these memorials meant to the girls and their families.[146] It can be dated to the first century B.C. and reads:

[Δαμόνικος ----]ς, Τιμαρχὶς Δαμαρχίδα ἱερατεύσαντες
[Μεγὼ] τὰν θυγατέρα.
τᾷ Παρθένῳ τὰν παῖδά σοί με, πότνια
Ὀρθεία, Δαμόνικος ἠδ᾽ ὁμευνέτις
Τιμαρχίς, ἐσθλοῦ πατρός, ἄνθεσαν Μεγὼ
τεὸν χερὶ κρατεύσασαν, Ἄρτεμι, βρέτας
ἄν τε πρὸ βωμῶν σῶν ἔτεινα λαμπάδα·
εἴη δὲ κἀμὲ τὰν ἐπιπρεπέα χάριν
τεῖσαι γονεῦσιν· ἔνδικον γὰρ ἔπλετο
καὶ παισὶ τιμᾶν ἐμ μέρει φυτοσπόρους.

[Damonikos, son of . . .], and Timarchis, daughter of Damarchidas, who served as priests, (dedicate) [Mego] their daughter. To you, the maid, mistress Ortheia, Damonikos and his wife Timarchis, of noble parentage, dedicated me, their child Mego, who have carried your image, O Artemis, in my hand and (they dedicated) the torch which I have held up before your altar. May I also be permitted to give the thanks due to my parents because it is right that children should honor their begetters in their turn.[147]

Mego's parents, Damonikos and Timarchis, held priesthoods and were of noble lineage, a combination that we have seen for priestly families across the Greek world. Their daughter's role in the ritual was very specifically ordained. Mego was charged with carrying the image of Artemis, the *bretas*, and with holding a torch before the altar. At least two sculptured fragments found within the shrine show girls bearing small images, just as is described in the dedication. One fragment

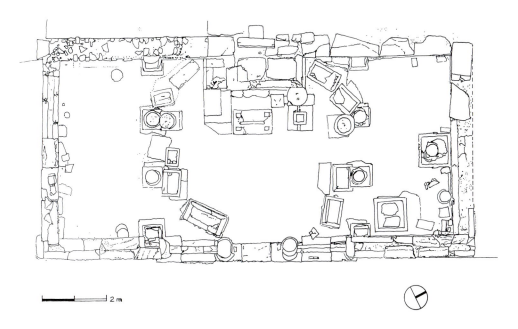

2 m

Fig. 5.15 (top)
Ground plan of sanctuary of Artemis Ortheia at Messene. By G. M. Peters, after H. Chlepa (1987), in Themelis (1996) 110, fig. 12.

Fig. 5.16 (bottom)
Sanctuary of Artemis Ortheia at Messene, interior view from northeast. Photo J. B. Connelly.

Fig. 5.17 (above)
Marble statue, sanctuary of Artemis
Ortheia at Messene. Messene Museum
247. Photo courtesy Prof. Petros Themelis.

Fig. 5.18 (right)
Marble statue of Mego, sanctuary of
Artemis Ortheia at Messene. Messene
Museum 245. Photo courtesy Prof. Petros
Themelis.

preserves a girl's left arm, circled at the biceps and at the wrist with fancy snake bracelets (fig. 5.17).[148] In her hand, she holds a small herm-shaped statue, covered by a cloth and decorated with a shield-shaped boss. On the basis of scale, style, and oxidation of the marble, Petros Themelis has associated this arm with one of the statues recovered from within the shrine (fig. 5.18). He has connected the reconstructed statue, in turn, with the stone base inscribed for Mego.[149]

The reconstructed portrait of Mego, like the statues of girls found with her, dates to the first century B.C.[150] All the girls are shown dressed in a costume typical for adolescents not quite

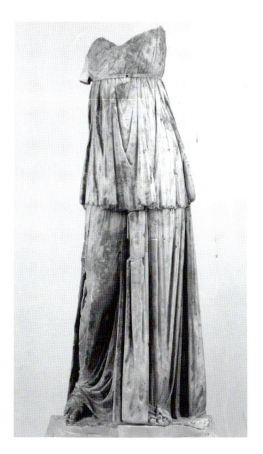

Fig. 5.19 (left)
Marble statue of Timareta, sanctuary of Artemis Ortheia at Messene. Messene Museum 241.
Photo courtesy Prof. Petros Themelis.

Fig. 5.20 (right)
Marble statue of girl, sanctuary of Artemis Ortheia at Messene. Messene Museum 244.
Photo courtesy Prof. Petros Themelis.

of marriageable age: the peplos with long deep overfold cinched with a belt tied high beneath the breasts. Mego's dress is carved with particular attention to drapery folds and delicate creases that represent press lines (fig. 5.18). Two deeply carved columns of drapery fall between her legs and create a strong vertical axis at the center of her figure.

Themelis has associated another statue with the inscribed base of Timareta, because of its size, the shape of the preserved plinth, and the cuttings on top (fig. 5.19).[151] The inscribed dedication reads: "Thiotas and Sopharchis (dedicate) Timareta, their daughter, to Artemis."

The statue shows a girl with elongated proportions characteristic of late Hellenistic style: narrow shoulders, small breasts, a long waist, and full hips emphasized by the broad overfold of the peplos.

A third statue presents a girl, possibly named Theophania, who wears the most elaborate costume of all (fig. 5.20; pl. 19).[152] She is dressed in a peplos that has been carved with great care to show press folds and lined impressions from the fabric that lies beneath. Her dress is cinched with a sash tied in a Herakles knot and terminating in two tasseled ends. No doubt these embellishments were once enlivened with pigment. Theophania further adorns her fancy costume with a circular pendant worn between the breasts. Originally, this boss may have been painted to resemble gold. It is possible that it represents some special item of jewelry associated with the sacred vestments of local cult service.

A fourth statue is different from the others in style and technique and may be slightly later in date (fig. 5.21).[153] This shows a girl wearing a sleeved chiton beneath a heavy peplos, belted with a sash tied in a Herakles knot. The overfold is drawn up under itself to form a heavy pouch, or *kolpos*. The drapery folds are schematically rendered to give a stiff and mannered appearance. From the figure's right hip a rectangular strut projects out to support the weight of her extended arm. Could the strut have given extra support to her arm so that she could hold a statuette, similar to that held by Mego?

We know that Mego was charged with the task of carrying a torch in the ritual and that her parents dedicated this torch in commemoration of her service. Could this suggest that the rites took place at night? A ritual that included nocturnal torch carrying, or even torch racing, would enable the girls to be true *phosphoroi*, "bearers of light," just like Artemis Phosphoros, whose statue stood within the shrine. An inscribed pilaster from an earlier temple of Artemis located on the upper terrace commemorates the gift of a bronze statue offered by Dioskouridas, who had served as *agonothetes*.[154] This confirms that competitions were associated with the festival of Artemis. Of course, footraces were a significant component of girls' festivals across the Greek world, known for Hera at Olympia (Pausanias 5.16.2–4), for Dionysos of Kolona at Sparta (where eleven girls named the "Daughters of Dionysos" competed [Pausanias 3.13.7]), and perhaps for Thessaly and Macedonia as well.[155] The *krateriskoi* from sanctuaries of Artemis Brauronia, discussed in chapter 2, show girls running in what appears to be special rites. Girls' nocturnal torch races would have represented an appropriate ritual for Artemis Phosphoros.

Petros Themelis has articulated a powerful analogy between the statues dedicated in the shrine and the girls' chorus at Sparta, as described in Alkman's first *Partheneion*.[156] Although the poem dates some six centuries before the statues, the archaeological record resounds with imagery established earlier on. The girls of Alkman's poem constitute a self-conscious group that is differentiated from a class of older women who served as their instructors. The girls wore

Fig. 5.21
Marble statue, sanctuary of
Artemis Ortheia at Messene.
Messene Museum 246. Photo
courtesy Prof. Petros Themelis.

fancy dresses and elaborately wrought bracelets of gold, shaped like serpents (lines 66–67). We learn that they carried "the cloak (*pharos*) to Orthria through the ambrosial night" (lines 60–62). The statues set up in Artemis Ortheia's shrine at Messene, in turn, show girls dressed in ornately wrought costumes, made of fancy fabrics, and wearing rings, plus bracelets shaped like serpents.

The statues were deliberately set up as a self-contained group forming a semicircle within the shrine. Could this circle reflect the ring dances that girls, with hands joined, may once have performed for the goddess? We have seen the evocation of ritual ring dancing throughout the visual repertory, from vase painting to the sculptured column drums of the Archaic temples

Fig. 5.22
Marble statue of the priestess
Eirana, sanctuary of Artemis
Ortheia at Messene. Messene
Museum 242. Photo courtesy
Prof. Petros Themelis.

of Asia Minor (see figs. 2.1, 5.4). These dances would have been accompanied by song, perhaps even by singing competitions such as those held in honor of Artemis Orthria in Alkman's *Partheneion*. We have suggested that the ritual at Messene may have taken place by torchlight, just like the nocturnal rites described by Alkman. There is yet another parallel between Alkman's imagery and that of the Messenian sculptures: the herm-statue of Ortheia, hidden beneath the cloth and held in Mego's left arm. Themelis has suggested that this is a *pharos*, such as that described by Alkman, the cloak that the Spartan maidens carried in their nighttime rituals.[157] He has made a convincing case that a small wooden *bretas* was kept in the sanctuary at Messene, probably installed on a base just beside the cult image of Artemis. Themelis has further suggested that, during the ritual, the *bretas* would have been carried from the inner shrine to the open square, where it would be placed on the high base just beside the altar.[158] The ritual movement of

Fig. 5.23
Marble statue of the priestess
Claudia Siteris, sanctuary of
Artemis Ortheia at Messene.
Messene Museum 243. Photo
courtesy Prof. Petros Themelis.

the *bretas*, probably undertaken at night and by torchlight, would have provided an intense sacred
experience for the girl initiates.

Like the maidens of Alkman's *Partheneion*, the young girls at Messene were associated
with and differentiated from a class of older women who oversaw the rites. Three statues of mature priestesses have been recovered, along with the cylindrical inscribed bases that supported
them. A council of elderly men, called the "sacred *gerontes* of (Artemis) Oupesia," dedicated the
statues.[159] Letter forms date the inscribed statue bases to the second and third centuries A.D., ad-
mittedly well after the statues of the younger girls were carved. One priestess, Eirana, daughter of
Numphodotos, is shown in a frontal pose with weight borne on her left leg (fig. 5.22; pl. 17).[160]
Her costume shows a crinkled chiton with buttoned sleeves beneath a heavy mantle. Her himation is pulled high in front to cover her left breast in a doubled-over roll of fabric, a variant of an

Fig. 5.24
Marble statue of the
priestess Kallis, sanctuary
of Artemis Ortheia at
Messene. Messene
Museum 240 and 254.
Photo courtesy Prof.
Petros Themelis.

arrangement we have seen for Nikeso (see fig. 5.12) and Aristonoe (see fig. 5.14). Eirana's left arm is damaged but seems to have extended forward. Two fragmentary left hands found at the site show fingers clutching small incense boxes. On the basis of size and marble type, they can be associated with the statues of priestesses. It is likely that Eirana was shown clutching one of these boxes in her hand, as an emblem of her special agency within the cult.[161]

The arrangement of Eirana's mantle, pulled beneath her right breast and over the left, was a fashion that enjoyed popularity from the end of the fifth century B.C. to the fourth century A.D. It is attested in no fewer than two hundred statues distributed across the Mediterranean.[162] Early on, this arrangement was used for statues of Persephone, Artemis, Isis, Hygieia, and the Muses. By the late Hellenistic and Roman periods, the fashion took on a wide popularity among upper-class women who wished to be shown dressed in the manner of goddesses. Early associations with Persephone and Artemis may account for the use of this type primarily for representations of younger women.[163]

Claudia Siteris wears a more complicated costume than Eirana, with a sleeved chiton beneath a peplos, pinned at the shoulder with fibulae (fig. 5.23; pl. 18).[164] Over this, she wears a heavy mantle, wound into a thick roll and pulled under her right arm and across her left breast. The twisting of the upper edge of the mantle can be seen on statues of Hadrianic date, distributed from Argos in the Greek Peloponnese to Salamis on Cyprus.[165] The schematic V-shaped folds that fall between her breasts and down her abdomen are reminiscent of drapery folds on the very latest of the statues of girl initiates (see fig. 5.21). There is little agreement on the date of the statue of Claudia Siteris, which has been placed anywhere from the first century A.D. to the Antonine period.[166] This uncertainty illustrates just how difficult it is to pin down a type that enjoyed such widespread popularity over so many years.

The priestess Kallis, daughter of Aristokles, is similarly dressed in a chiton beneath a peplos with deep overfold, covered by a himation (fig. 5.24).[167] The mantle shows highly stylized swallowtail folds tumbling down her left shoulder. The effect of this drapery is one of Archaizing stylization that finds its ultimate source in the fifth-century statue of Nemesis at Rhamnous.[168] While the type enjoyed enormous popularity across the centuries, Kallis's statue has been placed in the Antonine period.[169] Her hairstyle, which shows the division of tresses styled into a "melon coiffure," has its origins in the early Hellenistic period, but it was revived by Cleopatra VII and the women of the Augustan age and continued as a popular fashion well into the third century A.D.[170]

BOIOTIA

Let us end our survey of priestess portraits at Aulis in southeastern Boiotia, where the Euripos River empties into the gulf sheltering behind the southern shores of Euboea. Famous in myth as

Fig. 5.25
Temple of Artemis at Aulis, from the northwest, inside adyton facing cella. Photo J. B. Connelly.

the place where Agamemnon sacrificed Iphigeneia to enable the Greek fleet to set sail for Troy, Aulis has long been sacred to Artemis. It is here that the goddess is said to have substituted a deer for Iphigeneia, just before the famous sacrifice took place. Excavations have revealed the foundations of a long, narrow temple, the original date of which is uncertain. Clearly, there were several phases of building and rebuilding during the Hellenistic and Roman periods (fig. 5.25).[171]

Not unlike at the shrine of Artemis at Messene, the cella of the temple at Aulis preserves statue bases in their original placement. As at Messene, proud parents set up images of their daughters in commemoration of their service (see fig. 5.26).[172] But here, the girls depicted are older than those seen at Messene and wear costumes appropriate for maidens of marriageable age, reflecting the age band and status of Iphigeneia herself. Unlike the girls at Messene, the Aulis maidens are full-fledged priestesses, rather than youthful initiates.

One statue was found together with its inscribed base, which identifies it as a portrait of Zopyreina (fig. 5.26). The dedication reads: "Mnason and Atheno (dedicate) their daughter Zopyreina, who served as priestess, to Artemis of Aulis."[173] The statue shows a girl standing with her weight borne on her left leg, her right leg relaxed. She is draped in a voluminous mantle worn atop her chiton. Her right arm is drawn up toward her left shoulder, while her left arm,

Fig. 5.26
Marble statue of the
priestess Zopyreina,
Temple of Artemis at
Aulis. Thebes Museum
BE 66. Photo courtesy
Archaeological Receipts
Fund (TAP Service).

Fig. 5.27 (left)
Marble statue, Temple of Artemis at Aulis. Thebes Museum BE 64. Photo courtesy Archaeological Receipts Fund (TAP Service).

Fig. 5.28 (right)
Marble statue, Temple of Artemis at Aulis. Thebes Museum BE 65. Photo courtesy Archaeological Receipts Fund (TAP Service).

completely swathed in drapery, is held close to her side. The mantle clings to Zopyreina's stomach, circling it in highly contrived concentric folds, while deeply carved tubular folds fall down in stiff vertical lines.

Zopyreina's image conforms to a standard formula known as the Small Herculaneum Woman type, after one of two statues excavated during the early eighteenth century from a well sunk into the theater at Herculaneum.[174] Although the earliest surviving examples of this type come from late second-/early first-century-B.C. contexts on Delos, its origins are much earlier and can be associated with images of the goddess Persephone.[175] The type remains a favorite for statues of elite maidens throughout the Roman era, found in numbers at the Nymphaeum at Olympia.[176] A second statue of the Small Herculaneum Woman type has been found at Aulis, sensitively carved to show a fussy chiton with richly worked drapery folds peaking out from beneath the generously draped mantle (fig. 5.27).[177] As with Zopyreina's portrait, the head of this statue would have been carved separately and set into the cavity carved within the neck.

A third marble figure (fig. 5.28) is under life size and shows a drapery arrangement similar to what we have seen for priestesses at Messene.[178] The mantle is shown doubled over in a thick, cylindrical roll, pulled up over the left breast, reminiscent of that seen for Claudia Siteris (see fig. 5.23). The left arm of the maiden would have been carved separately and doweled into a socket, perhaps enabling it to project forward to hold out a phiale or some other attribute.

One image stands out from the others at Aulis, notable for the quality of its carving (fig. 5.29).[179] The young woman is shown draped in a diaphanous chiton marked with deeply drilled vertical folds, creating the impression of fine fabric revealing the form of the body beneath. The arrangement of the light mantle is similar to what we have seen for some of the priestesses as at Messene (see figs. 5.22–23), in which a roll of fabric was drawn from under the right breast up and over the left. The Aulis priestess's left arm would have been dowelled in separately to stretch forward, and it appears that the right hand might have been extended as well. It is possible, but by no means certain, that the maiden assumed the orans pose, with both hands held out and open.

When Pausanias (9.19.6–7) visited the temple of Artemis at Aulis he commented on two white marble statues flanking the doorway to the cella. One showed a figure carrying torches and the other a figure shooting an arrow. Presumably, these were images of Artemis that dated to well before his time. Pausanias also saw a plane tree that he believed to be the one described in Homer's *Iliad* (2.307) beneath which flowed a spring near the place where the Greeks offered sacrifice. He does not mention the statues of young priestesses that we have discussed here, perhaps because they dated to his own period and therefore did not interest him. It is also possible that they were set up in the years following his visit. Nonetheless, the images of Roman priestesses at Aulis illustrate the longevity of the tradition in which images of priestesses inhabited their sacred space long after their years of service had ended.

—

This survey underscores the centrality of women in Greek cult and the desirability for them to be remembered always in their sacred status. From the Archaic through the Roman Imperial

period, women made expensive offerings as signs of their own wealth, status, and religious responsibilities, with the intent of making lasting memorials for themselves and for their families. Statues of priestesses and the inscribed bases that held them express the self-confidence and pride that these women took in their sacred-office holding. They attest to a well-developed sense of identity and, to a certain extent, to freedom in using their own financial resources to set up their commemorative displays.

The portrait of the priestess must be considered within the larger context of the long tradition of setting up the image of the votary within the temple precinct. This practice is a venerable one, attested at the oldest sanctuaries of the ancient Near East. It is witnessed in the alabaster statues dedicated at the Temple of Abu at Tell Asmar in the third millennium, in the gilded bronze warriors from the Temple of the Obelisks in second-millennium Byblos, and in the thousands of terracotta and limestone votaries offered at the Iron Age shrines of Cyprus.[180] Central to this practice was the understanding that the votary's image gave concrete form to the votary's prayer.[181] Dedication of a statue ensured that the prayer would be repeated in perpetuity before the divinity, long after the dedicator had left the precinct. As priestesses are basically votaries of special rank, the images considered in this chapter are very much part of this tradition. A portrait statue can thus be understood as the concrete embodiment of the priestess's prayers, ritual service, and intimacy with her goddess, entities that lived on long after she had left this world.

Whether draped female statues dedicated in Greek sanctuaries from classical times onward can be understood to be descendants of the Archaic korai cannot be established with certainty. Still, the long history of the type prompts us to wonder whether the Archaic examples might represent cult servants, just as we know from inscriptions that so many of the later statues did. After all, Archaic Greek votive worship was still very much under the influence of the East, where it was the image of the worshipper, not that of the divinity, that was most frequently dedicated in sacred precincts.[182] We should not be quick to identify Archaic draped female figures as goddesses, but allow the possibility that many of them represented worshippers, especially those who held special agency within the sanctuary. Examination of this long sequence of female images prompts new directions for inquiry into questions of gender and space, the communality of divinity and servant, and the analogy of implement and implementor.

Fig. 5.29 (opposite)
Marble statue of maiden, Temple of Artemis at Aulis. Thebes Museum BE 63. Photo courtesy Archaeological Receipts Fund (TAP Service).

CHAPTER 6

The Priestess in Action
Procession, Sacrifice, and Benefaction

And in divine affairs—I think this of the first importance—
we have the greatest part. For at the oracles of Phoibos
women expound Apollo's will. At the holy seat of Dodona
by the sacred oak the female race conveys
the thoughts of Zeus to all Greeks who desire it.
As for the holy rituals performed for the Fates
and the nameless goddesses, these are not holy
in men's hands; but among women they flourish,
every one of them. Thus in holy service woman
plays the righteous role.[1]

The Captive Melanippe frag. 494 K

So speaks a character of uncertain identity in a fragment of a partially preserved drama by Euripides titled *The Captive Melanippe*, performed sometime in the 420s B.C. There is a good chance that these words can be placed in the mouth of Melanippe herself, who is also the focus of a second Euripidean play, *The Wise Melanippe*, in which the heroine is again portrayed as a dynamic woman. The passage cited above stands alone, deprived of the greater context that might have shed light on its function within the drama. Even if it is to be read as a rebuttal of criticism of female roles and, perhaps, as an overstatement of its case, the passage remains a powerful testimony to the central position of women in things religious.[2]

The preeminent position of women within the sacred domain spans geographical and chronological boundaries. Four hundred years after Euripides emphasized women's centrality in religious affairs, the geographer Strabo, writing on the habits of the Getae in Thrace, set forth what he described to be a commonly held belief: "For all agree in regarding women as the chief founders of religion and it is the women who provoke the men to the more attentive worship of the gods, to festivals, and to supplications, and it is a rare thing for a man who lives by himself to be found addicted to these things" (*Geography* 7.3.4).[3] Strabo further quotes from Menander's *Misogynes* or *Woman-Hater* (frag. 237 K-A): "we used to sacrifice five times a day, and seven female attendants would beat the cymbals all round us, while others would cry out to the gods." Women's obsession with sacred ritual is portrayed as an irritant to men, who, if left to their own devices, would not embrace religious practice so enthusiastically. This same sentiment is expressed by Plato, who similarly viewed women as the primary practitioners of cult worship. "Look at what people usually do—all women in particular," he writes, "they dedicate the first thing that comes to hand, they swear to offer sacrifice, and promise to found shrines for gods and spirits and children of gods."[4]

The visual record preserves a large corpus of images showing women engaged in every stage of ritual, from leading processions, to offering prayers and libations, to adorning animal victims, to presiding over sacrifice, to consuming sacrificial meat. Women are not only present in cult scenes, they abound in them. What was the motivation for the popularity of these scenes in visual culture? How can they inform us about the lived experience of women in cult service? In this chapter, we shall consider images of women shown within their sacred precincts, sprinkling incense, pouring libations, and tending to flaming altars. Epigraphic evidence nicely complements these glimpses of ritual action, preserving a micrology of priestesses at work. An advertisement for the sale of the priesthood of Artemis Pergaia on Kos, for example, gives a vivid picture of a sacred servant in action: "Let the priestess . . . open the temple at dawn, burn frankincense in the shrine, and light the fire on the altar."[5] We see the priestess rising at first light, acting as *kleidouchos* in opening the temple doors, purifying the sacred space with frankincense, and starting the fire on the altar.

Women's agency in ritual was not a mere matter of personal piety; indeed, the very cohesion of their communities depended on it. Polignac has pointed to the "blossoming of religious life" toward the end of the Geometric period as the single force that affected the entire social body. Rituals, he maintains, transformed a disparate collection of individuals and groups into a community that was active and solid in its devotion to cult.[6] Over time, rituals reinforced group solidarity, establishing and perpetuating civic, cultural, and religious identities that took strength from a shared and remembered past.[7] Women's centrality in the performance and perpetuation of these rites was essential to the functioning of the city. Priestly women helped link the community with something beyond it, the gods, as well as the ancestors and the ancestral customs through which the gods were honored. As Emily Kearns has stressed, ritual is religion's greatest "authority strategy," one that generates acceptance of the broad structure in which it is located.[8] The two-way communication between deities and humans articulated through ritual allowed for petition and response; praise and blessing; and sometimes, even, request and denial. Although all

Greeks had direct access to their gods, women played a particularly vital and cohesive role in the process through which the gods were honored, as priestesses, wives, mothers, teachers of cult practice, and benefactors of sanctuaries.

As important as it was for a priestess to perform her duties well, it was also necessary for her to meet the financial obligations that accompanied her office. These could range from providing sacrificial victims; to covering the sanctuary's general expenses; to building temples, porticoes, and cisterns; to supplying oil for gymnasia, food for banquets, and entertainment for the populace. As we have stressed throughout this book, Greek cults were utterly pragmatic and tightly bound to the economic fabric of the city. This chapter will conclude with a look at priestly benefactions, since they were just as much a part of a priestess's responsibilities as looking after sacred space and tending to the "holy things."

Procession and "the Hiera"

Priestesses had special responsibility for ritual implements used within the holy precinct. At certain shrines, they had the exclusive right to handle these sacred utensils. Rules prohibiting private use of cult paraphernalia are spelled out in an early Argive inscription, dated circa 575–550 B.C., found at the temple of Athena Polias on the Larisa.[9] These required that an official known as the *damiourgos* should set fines for anyone who damaged the "holy things." An inscription dating to the early Roman Imperial period, found at Athens and concerning a cult whose name is not preserved, required the priestess to maintain an inventory of temple furnishings.[10] Satorneila, priestess of Athena Polias at Miletos around A.D. 200, was called "bearer of the sacred utensils."[11] Clearly, the relationship between implement and implementor was a strong one, as we have already seen in chapter 5 (see figs. 5.1–3).

It was the priestess's responsibility to carry the holy things in sacred processions, which gave visibility, not just to the instruments of worship, but also to the priestess herself. Fritz Graf has elucidated the ways in which ritual movement through the polis landscape served to define the participants and their city. The relationships of cult, divinities, and sanctuaries were articulated through the directions in which processions traversed the cityscape.[12] This movement could be centripetal, marching from the periphery to civic and religious center, or centrifugal, departing from city center and advancing toward places outside of it. Processions provided highly visible, dramatic displays in which leaders and participants understood their roles. Their movements reflected the structures and values of the community. Women who led these processions marched in a spotlight that underscored their agency and highlighted their symbolic capital within the larger group.

Priestesses were celebrated by their communities for carrying out their duties in a

Fig. 6.1
Boiotian black-figure
lekane, the Boeotian
Silhouette Group.
London, British
Museum B 80. Photo
© Copyright the
Trustees of The
British Museum.

pleasing manner. A funerary inscription praises Alkmeonis, priestess of Dionysos at Miletos in the late third or second century B.C., for carrying out her duties in an exemplary fashion: "She led you to the mountain and carried all the sacred objects and implements, marching in procession before the whole city."[13] In chapter 3, we saw that the priestesses of Demeter and Kore led the procession of initiates in the Mysteries from Eleusis to Athens, and back again, carrying the holy things as they marched.[14] So too, priests and priestesses of Artemis Leukophrene at Magnesia on the Maeander were charged with leading the ritual procession. A civic decree dating to the second century B.C. states that the *stephanophoros* (chief magistrate), together with the priest and priestesses, would lead the procession on the twelfth day of the month of Artemision and sacrifice the designated bull.[15]

Scenes of procession in Greek vase painting juxtapose the human escort with the animal victim, producing minimal sign-components for the acts of procession and sacrifice.[16] Let us consider images of women in procession drawn from three very different centers of production: Boiotia, Athens, and Corinth. In each, women are shown carrying holy things upon their heads while leading worshippers toward sacrificial altars. Our first example shows a maiden basket bearer leading a group of men. It is preserved on a cup from Boiotia dated to around 550 B.C. (fig. 6.1).[17] One can make out a low flat basket, which she steadies with both hands, held upon her head, as she approaches a stone-built altar. Upon the altar, a fire has been lit, and a bird, perhaps a raven, has perched itself. Behind the maiden, a man leads a cow for sac-

Fig. 6.2
Attic black-figure lekythos. London, British Museum 1905.7-11.1. Photo © Copyright the Trustees of The British Museum.

rifice, while others march behind, playings pipes and carrying wreaths, a jug, and a lustral branch. Following them, two mules pull a simple country cart carrying four persons. Six men, a goat, and a long-necked water fowl can be seen behind the cart, stretching round the other side of the vase.

Facing the kanephoros from the far side of the altar is Athena, or her statue. She is shown here in what has been called her Promachos or Panathenaic aspect, as a warring goddess, brandishing a spear and raising her shield as if ready for battle. This type is closely associated with an Athenian iconographic model that enjoyed great popularity in the middle of the sixth century B.C. It is repeated on the Panathenaic prize amphoras awarded to victors in the festival contests and may reflect an actual statue set up on the Athenian Acropolis around this time.[18] Since statues were understood to be living entities in Greek antiquity, statue and divinity may be read here as one.[19] Surrounded by a series of signifiers, including the sacred snake, a temple column, and a flaming altar, Athena is clearly positioned within a formalized sanctuary setting. The agency of the kanephoros within this space and the communality she shares with the goddess are emphasized by the placement of servant and deity at either side of the flaming altar. In view of the Boiotian production of the vase, it has been argued that the sanctuary shown is that of Athena Itoneia, near Koroneia.[20]

A similar scene is found on an Athenian black-figure lekythos in London, dated to the early fifth century (fig. 6.2).[21] Here, a female basket bearer leads a procession of two men to a

Fig. 6.3
Painted wooden plaque, from Pitsa. Athens, National Archaeological Museum 16464. Photo courtesy Archaeological Receipts Fund (TAP Service).

flaming altar behind which Athena, or her statue, sits. The first man carries a large oinochoe, the second escorts the sacrificial victim, a bull. The scene presents a kind of shorthand text of essential sign-components, communicating the act of procession with just two marchers. This efficient and economical expression of the sacred rite illustrates how effectively the artist can use a minimum of formal units to capture the larger action of *pompe*. As we shall see in what follows, basket bearers, marchers, jugs, animal victims, flaming altars, and columns can be manipulated to expand, contract, and individualize the representation of ritual.[22]

Similar schemata are presented on the painted wooden plaque from Pitsa near Sikyon in the Corinthia. The *pinax*, dated ca. 540–520 B.C., is a rare survivor of what was a very popular and inexpensive category of votive offering in ancient Greece (fig. 6.3, pl. 3).[23] Here, a maiden basket bearer leads the procession, followed by a young boy who brings a sheep, two older boys who play the lyre and pipes, and two mature women holding fillets and lustral branches. At the back stands a large figure wearing a himation and carrying a branch, possibly representing the dedicator. The young kanephoros at the lead carries a long, flat basket on her head, while she pours a libation onto the altar from a small jug. Within her basket rest two conical oinochoai and a long rectangular box, the instruments of ritual that fall under her care. She dispatches her duties with agility and grace, balancing the basket on a small cushion that rests atop her head.[24] Inscriptions are painted across the top of the plaque in Corinthian script, identifying the nymphs as the divinities worshipped and naming the dedicator (now lost); the artist; and the three women depicted, their names given as Euthydika, Eukolis, and what appears to read "Ethelonche."[25] The personalization of this dedication through inscribed names makes clear that the image commemorates an actual sacrifice made by the individuals represented upon it. Wooden votive plaques thus function much like stone votive reliefs, on which identifying labels make clear that the individuals depicted are from the present, rather than from the mythological past. In this, votive paintings and sculpture differ from vase painting, in which the imagined world of myth and epic take center stage. It is likely that the Pitsa plaque shows a family group engaged in a private sacrifice for which individual members play the roles of kanephoros, animal escort, musicians, devotees, and dedicant.

Iconographic schemata for procession change little over the following century, despite developments in cults and in vase painting, which moved on from black-figured to red-figured technique. The well-known krater in Ferrara, dated to the mid-fifth century, shows a young woman leading a procession past an altar and toward two divinities, or their statues (fig. 6.4).[26] The girl carries on her head a winnowing basket, or *liknon*, covered with a richly woven cloth. The liknon was an implement of the harvest, a broad basket in which wheat was placed after thresh-ing and then thrown against the wind to separate the grain from the chaff. It is associated with fertility and is found in wedding rituals, as well as in cult scenes honoring Dionysos.[27] On the Ferrara krater, the maiden liknon bearer is followed by a troupe of ecstatic dancers who play dou-ble flutes, *tympana*, and castanets. They twist and turn, manipulating snakes in their hands and wrapped round their heads. At the very back of the procession walks a man playing the double pipes, dressed in a richly woven, ungirded, short-sleeved tunic, typical of the costume worn by priests. The placement of the *liknophoros* at the front of the procession and the priest at the back allows them to flank the divinities within the composition and communicates their special agency in the rite.

This enigmatic scene has been interpreted in a variety of ways, ranging from a generic depiction of ecstatic cult, to a specific representation of Orphic-Bacchic worship at Phlya in the Attic countryside.[28] The deities have been variously identified as Dionysos, or Dionysos-Hades, or Sabazios, shown together with Demeter, or Kore, or Semele, or Ariadne, or Rhea Kybele.[29] The liknon bearer has sometimes been identified as the mystic priestess Hipta.[30] We cannot know with certainty the setting of the scene, which may well be drawn from myth rather than from realia. What is significant here is that the image relies on schemata for ritual procession that were established at least a century earlier. Just as on the Archaic black-figure lekythos in London (see fig. 6.2), the divinities sit in an enclosed space articulated by columns, holding their libation bowls out toward a flaming altar and the ap-proaching basket-bearer.

The maiden kanephoroi and *liknophoros* seen in these images are not necessarily to be understood as full-fledged priestesses, though there is the possibility that some of them could be.

Fig. 6.4
Attic red-figure krater. Ferrara, Museo Nazionale di Spina 2897 (T 128). Photo courtesy Soprintendenza Archaeologica di Ferrara.

We have seen in the epigraphic record that some priestesses carried "holy things" and led processions, just as kanephoroi did. In the visual repertory, priestesses and kanephoroi can look very much the same. But we do have images in which the two are clearly differentiated, as on the black-figure band cup (see fig. 6.15; pl. 9), to be considered later in this chapter. Here, a kanephoros approaches an altar, behind which the priestess stands, ready to receive her.

Prayer

When the procession arrived at the sacred precinct, a first responsibility of the priestess could be the act of prayer.[31] Homer gives us two of the best contrasting images of a priestess and a non-priestly woman engaged in prayer, one in public and the other in private.[32] In the *Odyssey* (4.759–67), when Penelope wishes to pray to Athena, she ascends to her upper chamber with her handmaidens. There she washes herself, changes her clothes, and places some grains of barley in a basket. She then invokes the goddess, raising a sacred cry, and asks that her son Telemachos be saved from the suitors. This is an act of private prayer made by an individual directly to a divinity without the intervention of a cult agent and without fanfare in a public setting. In contrast, *Iliad* book 6 (302–11) gives us the priestess Theano, who leads the Trojan women in public prayer before Athena's statue in the city's great temple. At a time of communal crisis, Theano assumes a leadership role in the collective supplication of the goddess. She dedicates a richly woven robe upon the knees of Athena's statue and implores the deity to grant the death of Diomedes. Theano promises to offer twelve heifers if her prayer is answered. At this point, rituals of a fully developed polis are close to the forefront of the *Iliad*'s narrative.

From texts as well as from images, we learn that the standard posture for prayer was one in which arms were raised with palms turned heavenward. The kneeling position was assumed only in special circumstances, and most often by women.[33] Normally, an individual stood tall when praying and held up one or both hands to invoke the gods, to argue a case for intervention, or to send up a petition. In the *Iliad* (1.351) Achilles, brokenhearted and in tears after Briseis is taken from him, sits by the sea and prays privately to his mother, Thetis. He does so with outstretched arms. Later, Briseis is returned by Agamemnon to her father, Chryses. As priest of the Trojans, Chryses leads a public prayer asking Apollo to end the plague that was killing off the Greeks. Chryses lifts his hands to the sky in supplication as he begins his prayer (*Iliad* 1.450). The praying gesture is attested throughout the centuries that follow. In Euripides' *Iphigeneia at Tauris* (267), the herdsman tells Iphigeneia that when Orestes and Pylades were first noticed in the cave by the sea, they were thought to be divinities. One of the oxherds, a god-fearing man, "lifted his hands up in prayer" and called to them for mercy.

The gesture of prayer described in literature can be seen in vase paintings and sculptures that show worshippers holding up one or both hands with open palms. This comes to be known as the orans pose. We have already seen the gesture on the record reliefs in Berlin and Athens on which priestesses of Athena Polias hold their keys in one hand and raise up the other with palm open (see figs. 4.7–8; pl. 13). A two-handed version of the pose is seen on a fragment of a krater found on the Athenian Acropolis that shows two women in an act of worship (fig. 6.5).[34] One woman stands behind an altar and raises her hands. Her left palm is opened outward, and it is likely that the right hand was held in a similar position. At right, the other woman reaches over the altar to sprinkle something (barley corn or incense?) and holds her left hand up, opened skyward. While we cannot say with certainty that these women are priestesses, they clearly show us what priestesses did and how they looked when they did it. The woman who faces us wears her mantle draped beneath her right arm and up and over the left, just like the priestesses whom we have seen in relief sculpture (see figs. 4.7–8). The black border decorating the edge of her mantle may signify that she is a cult official of special rank. Her dominant placement and the arresting effect of her frontality within the composition may further communicate her leadership role as priestess overseeing sacrifice. That this vase was found on the Acropolis could suggest that its subject matter mirrors the ritual activity of priestesses within this sacred space.

Two lekythoi in Oxford similarly show women at prayer. The first presents a female figure standing behind an altar, raising both hands heavenward (fig. 6.6).[35] She wears a mantle draped diagonally over her chiton, leaving her right arm free. Long tresses tumble down her back and a fillet is wrapped round her head. At upper left hangs what may be a pouch for double pipes used in the ritual. The Carlsruhe Painter, who produced this image, was very fond of painting scenes showing women in cult worship. The painter also produced a large repertory of images showing women working wool.[36] As we shall see at the end of this chapter, the choice of these two subjects may be related. Both can be seen to communicate feminine ideals, those of the virtuous woman within the home and those of the pious devotee within the sanctuary.

The second lekythos shows a woman wearing a similar dress, though her hair is bound up in a more matronly fashion (fig. 6.7).[37] She is adorned with a fancy headband or crown, and earrings. She extends a libation bowl in one hand, while raising the other in a gesture of prayer. At right, a bare-chested young man wearing only a short tunic (*exomis*) cradles a basket with high handles and holds a roasting spit for sacrificial meat. All is ready for the culminating moment of the ritual. Dressed in her finery, the woman is the one who leads the prayer and who appears to be very much in charge. The man plays a mere supporting role and, having skewered the sacrificial meat, assists the woman by holding the basket of sacred implements for her to use. Can we call this woman a priestess? It is fairly safe to draw this inference based on her libation bowl,

Fig. 6.5 (top left)
Fragment of Attic red-figured krater.
Athens, Acropolis Museum 752. Photo
courtesy Archaeological Receipts Fund
(TAP Service).

Fig. 6.6 (top right)
Attic red-figure lekythos. Oxford,
Ashmolean Museum 1916.15. Photo
courtesy Ashmolean Museum, Oxford.

Fig. 6.7 (right)
Attic red-figure lekythos. Oxford,
Ashmolean Museum G 300 (V536). Photo
courtesy Ashmolean Museum, Oxford.

gesture of prayer, crown, and dominant placement within the composition, just opposite the handle, as we saw on the other Oxford lekythos (see fig. 6.6).

Libation

Liquid offerings were commonly used to reinforce prayer.[38] Libations could be poured from shallow bowls or wine jugs, either on an altar or directly onto the ground. Liquid offerings were particularly associated with the dead and with the powers of the earth onto which they were poured. Libations were therefore appropriate for funerary rites as well as for rituals honoring gods and heroes. Within votive contexts, libations could take place with or without the offering of animal victims, serving as quick and economical alternatives to full-scale blood sacrifice. When libations accompanied sacrifice, they often punctuated or emphasized specific moments and phases within the ritual.[39] The pouring of a libation onto a flaming altar was particularly effective, as it provoked an intensified flash of fire from the roasting flesh and fat. These flares could be read as responses from the gods in expressing their satisfaction with the sacrifice. Wine was a favorite liquid for libation, but we do hear of rituals for which water, milk, oil, or honey was required.[40]

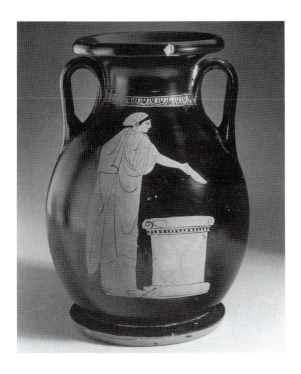

Fig. 6.9
Attic red-figure pelike, the Sabouroff
Painter. Los Angeles, County Museum
50.8.24a, b. Museum Associates/LACMA,
William Randolph Hearst Collection.
Photo © 2007 Museum Association,
LACMA.

A woman holds a shallow bowl above an altar on the interior of a red-figure cup by the
Painter of London E 100 in New York (fig. 6.8).[41] She wears a voluminous mantle over her chiton and her hair is swept up into a *sakkos.* Her placement within the cup's tondo is one that we
have seen used repeatedly for images of women at altars (see figs. 4.17–20).[42] On the Villa Giulia Painter's white-ground cup, also in New York, we saw an elegant maiden standing before an
altar, lifting her phiale high to pour an offering (see fig. 4.19; pl. 8). She is dressed in a fancy red
mantle and pleated chiton with multiple overfolds and carries a scepter, in contrast to the simply dressed woman with a head scarf shown in the tondo of the red-figure cup (see fig. 6.8). Can
we identify the elegant maiden as a priestess performing a public ritual, dressed in imitation of
the goddess, and the second woman, wearing the simple *sakkos,* as a private individual at
worship?

The libation pourer on the red-figure cup in New York (see fig. 6.8) strongly resembles
a female worshipper shown on a pelike in Los Angeles (fig. 6.9).[43] Both women wear identical
costumes of chiton, mantle, and head scarf. Both face right and strike similar poses, in which they
pour libations from bowls held high above altars. Neither wears festival finery, and we may be
meant to understand them as nonpriestly worshippers in a moment of private prayer.

We have seen in chapter 5 that the manipulation of libation bowl and jug as a set might

Fig. 6.10 (left)
Attic red-figure amphora, the Nikon Painter. Boston, Museum of Fine Arts 68.163. Photo © 2007 Museum of Fine Arts, Boston.

Fig. 6.11 (right)
Attic red-figure stamnos, the Achilles Painter. London, British Museum E448. Photo © Copyright the Trustees of The British Museum.

communicate sacred status (see figs. 5.1–2). Such a pairing of bowl and jug can be seen in the hands of a woman on an amphora in Boston (fig. 6.10).[44] She is crowned with a ribbon and wears a peplos with heavy overfold, rather than the usual combination of chiton and himation. She rushes to her right, holding her sacred instruments out from her body in a dynamic pose. The reverse side of the vase shows a herm, garlanded at head and phallus and positioned behind a flaming altar. The woman is clearly about to pour a libation upon this altar in what may well be an act of private devotion.

Libations were poured, not just in cult contexts but also in social rituals performed within the household. They were used to mark critical moments, such as the departure of a warrior for battle. Scenes depicting soldiers taking their leaves regularly show a female family member (mother, sister, or wife) who offers a liquid libation. A vase by the Achilles Painter shows one such poignant scene in which a warrior bids farewell to his father, while his wife or sister stands by, oinochoe and phiale in hand (fig. 6.11).[45] The soldier's loyal hound lingers at his feet. Bérard and Durand have stressed the key role of the woman in this image.[46] She is the agent who prepares and pours the libation, thereby affirming and guaranteeing the permanence of the group, whose bonds are, in turn, reinforced through a sharing of the liquid offering. Each family member will partake in the libation, which will then be poured on the earth, for the gods. This scene illustrates the ways in which the iconographic signifiers are the same for public ritual and private family libation. It is not always easy to distinguish between the two. But one thing is clear. It is the agency of women that guarantees the permanence of relationships, both with the gods and with family members.

Sacrifice

At the very core of Greek worship was the act of animal sacrifice. Once the procession had arrived in the sanctuary, the formal rites of dedication and consecration (*katarchesthai*) took place. These were followed by lustration (*chernips*), the throwing of barley groats (*oulochytai*), and prayer. The culminating moment was the slaughtering of the victim, which was inspected for omens, cut up in pieces, and placed on the altar fire. Divinities and worshippers participated together in the shared feast that followed. Bones and other inedible parts of the victim were set aside for the gods, while the succulent meat and viscera (*splanchna*) were enjoyed by the human participants.[47]

The role of the priestess in sacrifice is powerfully articulated in an inscription from Miletos, dating to 276/275 B.C.:

> [···]·Ν ὅταν δὲ ἡ ἱέρεια ἐπι[τελέσ]ηι τὰ ἱερὰ ὑπὲρ τῆς
>   πόλ[εω]ς
> [ὄργια] μὴ ἐξεῖναι ὠμοφάγιον ἐμβαλεῖν μηθενὶ πρότερον
> [ἢ ἡ ἱ ἐ]ρεια ὑπὲρ τῆς πόλεως ἐμβάληι. μὴ ἐξεῖναι δὲ
>   μηδὲ [lines 5–10 omitted]
> [συη]αγαγεῖν τὸν θίασον μηθενὶ πρότερον τοῦ δημοσίου·
> [····] δὲ τὴν ἱέρειαν γυναῖκας διδόναι Δ ΙΙΗΙΝΛ[-]
> [···τ]ὰ δὲ τέλεστρα {καὶ τελεστ} παρέχ[ειν ταῖς]
> [γυναιξὶν] ἐν τοῖς ὀργί[οις πᾶ]σιν [lines 14–17 omitted]
> ἑκάστην τριετηρίδα·

Whenever the priestess performs the sacrifice on behalf of the city, it is forbidden for anyone to lay down pieces of raw meat before the priestess has done so on behalf of the city, nor is it permitted for anyone to assemble a *thiasos* before the public *thiasos* (has been gathered) [lines 5–10 omitted]. The priestess shall supply the things needed for initiation in all the secret rites [lines 14–17 omitted]. Whenever a woman wishes to initiate (someone) in the rites of

Dionysos Bacchios—whether in the city, in the countryside, or on the islands, she must pay a stater to the priestess at each biennial celebration.[48] (*LSAM* 48.1–20)

This text sets out the rights of the female purchaser of the priesthood of Dionysos Bacchios. The priestess will serve as initiator of sacrifice, organizer of the public *thiasos*, and provider of the implements for initiation. She is also the recipient of a fee paid by those wishing to perform initiation. Importantly, the priestess is portrayed as an active agent who presides over a sacrifice in which she herself handles raw meat.

The role of women in blood sacrifice is a topic of lively debate, as a result of a provocative study by Marcel Detienne.[49] He has argued that women were not only excluded from the slaughter of animal victims but also from partaking in their sacrificial flesh. Robin Osborne has argued that this position is untenable.[50] One great benefit of this scholarly exchange is that our attention has been drawn to a long-neglected subject of importance. The debate is informative not only for what it tells us about Greek sacrificial practices, but also for what it says about modern cultural assumptions and their influence on our understanding of the ancient past.

Central to Detienne's thesis is the suggestion that women were excluded from blood sacrifice because, like animal victims, they themselves bleed, that is, through menstruation. Detienne maintains that as an extension of this gendered physiological function, women were denied access to flesh foods in general. He goes even further and links the exclusion of women from sacrifice to the exclusion of women from the civic and political life of the polis.[51] Detienne's biological explanation for women's lack of political standing is based on the assumption that the ancient Greeks were as preoccupied with menstruation as many writers are today. This position is simply not borne out by the ancient evidence.[52]

Ancient testimonia, in fact, point to the active role of women in all aspects of blood sacrifice, from the selection and decoration of animal victims, to the leading of victims in procession, to acts of butchering and sacrifice, and finally, to the distribution and consumption of meat. As there were no universal laws governing the role of women in blood sacrifice, we must look to individual sanctuaries for which evidence survives. Each shrine had its own regulations for appropriate animal victims; fruits, grains, and other offerings; calendar dates for sacrifice and festivals; and the local policies for exceptions to these rules. Offerings to the gods could include meat, fish, grains, fruits, wine, honey, water, oil, and milk.[53] Aside from the fact that some offerings were more expensive that others, and thereby more precious, there was no privileging of one kind of sacrifice or libation over another.[54] It is not that one type of sacrifice was better than another;

rather, one was more appropriate for the cult requirements. Some cults and some occasions warranted blood sacrifice, while others did not.

Certain tasks within the ritual were appropriate for men, others for women, and still others for youths and maidens. Jobs entrusted to gender- or age-based groups reflected social practice codified within the household. These roles were based on the size and relative strength of family members as well as on traditional gender roles. Girls carried baskets with utensils, boys led animal victims, and men butchered and skewered meat, while women oversaw a host of activities, including the preparation of the victim and other offerings as well as the direction of family members in their duties. In public sacrifice, members of the community played out traditional roles from life in the Greek household. No one job was privileged over another, but each carried a distinct honor within its age band and gender group.

Why, then, do modern commentators privilege blood over nonblood sacrifice and the role of the butcherer over the jobs of other cult agents? The concept that the slaughterer enjoys the highest status is surely a product of Christianizing assumptions that rank the priest at the top, since he reenacts the sacrifice of the body and blood of Christ and serves as the "representative" of Christ on earth. There was nothing like this in the dynamics of Greek sacrifice, for which the presence of a priest or priestess was not even necessary.[55] In the absence of the priest at the Amphiareion at Oropos, worshippers could pray over sacrificial parts and deposit them on the altar themselves.[56] A fourth-century inscription from Kos shows the arbitrariness and relative unimportance of the one who did the butchering: "Let the heralds choose among themselves one to slaughter the ox."[57] A *mageiros*, or "cook," was hired to kill and roast sacrificial victims for the women's Thesmophoria on Delos during the third and second centuries B.C. Osborne points out that the fee this man received was as little as four obols, less than the price of the wood needed to burn the fires.[58] Instead of viewing the butcher as the top-ranking agent and the women in a marginalized position, we should understand the butcher/cook to be the subservient character, a mere hired hand, and a rather poorly paid one at that. The fact that Greek cult practice regularly placed the knife of sacrifice in the hands of men rather than women in no way diminishes the potency of female agency within the ritual.

As a matter of fact, we do have evidence that women handled raw meat and consumed cooked flesh. As early as the second quarter of the fifth century B.C., women who participated in the biennial sacrifice for Athena Patroia on Thasos received a portion of their sacrifice.[59] The priestess of Eileithyia, goddess of childbirth, on the island of Chios round about 400 B.C., was required to consume her perquisites on the spot "along with the women who made the sacrifice."[60] In early third-century Athens, the wives of *orgeones* were given equal portions of sacrificial meat along with their husbands, while their daughters took a portion of no less than half.[61] Detienne would dismiss these examples as extensions of male privilege given over to female family members.[62] But at the great Panathenaic festival in Athens, the unmarried maiden kanephoros received her own portion of the sacrificial meat, an honor that she shared with the city's highest male officials.[63] Winners in the girls' footraces at the stadium of Olympia were awarded wreaths of olive along with a portion of the cow that had been sacrificed to Hera (Pausanias 5.16.3). Detienne would, again, see this privilege as a by-product of the "male" strengths exhibited by the girls, particularly their athletic prowess and speed. But we can identify all sorts of women who had the right to sacrificial meat, including mothers, daughters, and grandmothers, the swift-footed and the slow alike.

The sacred calendar inscription for the deme of Erchia, found at modern Spata in the Mesogeia, gives explicit instructions for the distribution of meat to women on certain festival days. It specifies that the goat sacrificed to Semele, mother of Dionysos, on the sixteenth day of the month Elaphebolion, should be "handed over to the women" and consumed on the spot.[64] Its skin "should be given to the priestess." Similarly, the goat sacrificed to Dionysos on that same day should be given to the women for eating and the priestess should receive the hide. At the temple of Artemis Pergaia in Halikarnassos, the wives of the magistrates were required to prepare the annual sacrifice for which their husbands were responsible.[65] We know that they took a share of the sacrificial victim, since it was decreed that the priestess should receive as much as the wives did. The decree from Miletos, quoted earlier in this chapter, clearly states that the priestess of Dionysos Bacchios performed the sacrifice "on behalf of the city" and that she had the privilege of "laying down pieces of raw meat" before anyone else.[66] This text explicitly places the victim's flesh in the hands of the female sacrificer. An inscription from Kos advertising the sale of the female priesthood of Dionysos Thyllophoros stipulates that it is the responsibility of the priestess "to lay the sacred portions on the altar for those who sacrifice."[67] This widespread evidence for women's active role in blood sacrifice cannot be dismissed as a by-product of their associations with men.

In addition, we have numbers of inscriptions that address situations in which women were *not* allowed to sacrifice, the implication being that under normal circumstances they could. As Osborne rightly argues, these texts should be viewed as presenting exceptions to the rule.[68] A third-century law on mourning from Gambreion near Pergamon stipulates that women who violate the prescribed regulation shall be forbidden to sacrifice to any god for ten years.[69] This would imply that their usual right to sacrifice would be taken away.

When we turn to the literary sphere, we even hear stories of knives in the hands of women, though these are clearly seen to be extraordinary cases.[70] Pausanias (2.35.4–8) tells us of the great summer festival of Demeter Chthonia at Hermione, where the priests led the procession together with the annual magistrates, followed by men, women, and children dressed in white and crowned with wreaths. At the end of the procession, a cow fastened with ropes was held by a group of men, who eventually released it, allowing it to run wild into the sanctuary, where four old women caught it and cut its throat with sickles.[71] Pausanias regards this local

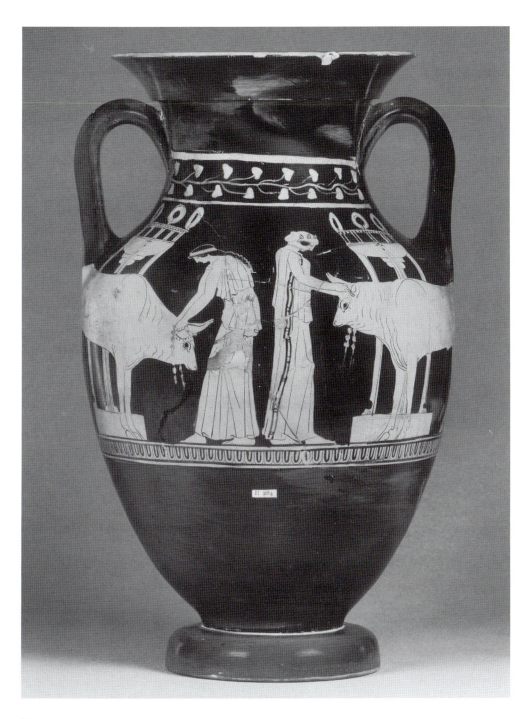

Fig. 6.12
Attic red-figure amphora, the Nausicaa Painter. London, British Museum E 284. Photo © Copyright the Trustees of The British Museum.

ritual as extraordinary and is careful to give evidence that the butchering women really did exist. He saw with his own eyes the raised chairs on which the women sat while waiting for the cow to be brought in.

Pausanias recounts another story in which women with knives are central (4.17.1). When Aristomenes and his troops surprised a group of women celebrating the festival of Demeter at Aegila in Lakonia, the women attacked the men with knives and spits. What is extraordinary here is that the women attacked the men, not that they were encountered in the act of butchering and roasting sacrificial meat. Aristomenes was captured alive, only to be released by the priestess of Demeter, Archidameia, who had fallen in love with him. The priestess was later charged for this crime.

It was within the context of the Thesmophoria that women worshippers at Cyrene castrated King Battos for spying on them during their women-only festival.[72] In retaliation, they carved him up with knives that they had been using to slaughter animal victims. The spectacular part of the story is that the women used their knives for castration, not that they had been butchering sacrificial meat. Read on one level, the message seems to be that women with knives are dangerous. But the same can be said for men. Cases can be cited in which men kill men within the context of religious festivals, as well.[73]

Sacrificing women are abundant in Greek literature. Klytaimnestra orders sacrifices to be offered on altars across the city of Argos in Aeschylus's *Agamemnon* (83). In Menander's *Dyskolos* (261–63), the mother of Sostratos is portrayed as roaming around her deme sacrificing daily to this or that god.[74] The *Fourth Mime* (4.1–20) of Herodas presents the old woman Kynno at the temple of Asklepios making a sacrifice as a thank-offering for a cure. She is embarrassed that her state of poverty allows her to offer only the modest victim of a cock. After the temple attendant pronounces the offering fair and pleasing to Asklepios, Kynno makes arrangements for the distribution of its parts (4.89–95). Epigraphic and literary evidence come together to describe a world in which women were active in the sacrificial sphere, perfectly comfortable while handling raw meat and sharing in cooked parts.

The often-neglected visual record has much to offer this discussion as it places women front and center, decorating animal victims, escorting them to sacrifice, and sharing in their meat (figs. 6.12, 6.13, 6.17). The juxtaposition of sacred servant and animal within the image serves to define their identities as agent and victim.[75] The first step in preparing the victim was its decoration with *stemmata*, or "garlands," signifing its fate as a gift to the gods and as a creature about to die.[76] Sometimes, the horns of animals were gilded with gold, making the offering all the more precious. An amphora in London shows two women adorning cows with *stemmata* (fig. 6.12).[77] They are flanked by large tripods that support cauldrons, communicating a sanctuary setting. Long, flowing locks on the woman at left indicate her relative youth, while a mature woman at

Fig. 6.13
Attic black-figure lekythos, from Vulci. New York,
The Metropolitan Museum of Art, Rogers Fund, 1941
(41.162.255). Photo: all rights reserved, The Metropolitan
Museum of Art.

right wears her hair swept up in a *sakkos*. Both women wear headbands, though that of the older woman is more elaborate and shows the same leaflike adornments as those of the woman's crown on the Oxford lekythos (see fig. 6.7). Both are dressed in peploi, but the older woman's costume is distinguished by dark ornamental bands running vertically down the edge of her dress. Her adornments and mature age may communicate her special agency as the one who oversees the preparation of the animal victims. Here, as in so many images, women are portrayed as being perfectly comfortable in touching animal victims.[78] Are we looking into the realm of myth, at a scene such as that in which the Trojan priestess Theano prepares unsullied cows for sacrifice (*Iliad* 6.297–310)? Or is the image informed by the reality of fifth-century ritual practice, in which women really adorned animal victims? The representation is likely to owe some debt to each of these worlds, as myth, cult, and visual culture come together in a mutually sustaining dynamic.

In her thoughtful study of the representation of sacrifice (*thysia*), Sarah Peirce has argued that images from the so-called komos group should be read as allusions to sacrificial ritual rather than as literal depictions of it.[79] These scenes regularly show women followers of Dionysos escorting cattle in processions that would seem to anticipate sacrifice. A black-figure lekythos in New York shows three women guiding a bull that seems to go willingly to sacrifice in the festive procession (fig. 6.13).[80] Elaborate patterns of lustral branches and background vegetation merge,

Fig. 6.14
Attic black-figure amphora. Berlin, Staatliche Museen Antikensammlung 1686. Photo Antikensammlung, Staatliche Museen zu Berlin, Preussicher Kulturbeitz.

forming a decorative scheme that frames the bull and communicates a setting both wild and cultic. The women wear chitons and heavy mantles decorated with purple bands. They are adorned
with necklaces and wear their hair swept up and bound by purple ribbons. Dressed in festival finery, they convey a celebratory mood and, as Peirce emphasizes, express the emotion behind communal sacrifice and feasting. These women are variously identified as maenads and as nymphs,
ritual participants who transport us to an imagined world. But their portrayal surely reflects
some of the cheerful sentiment experienced in real life in which women took great pleasure in
communal feasting and comradery.

The role of the priestess is vividly portrayed on the name vase of the Painter of
Berlin 1686, dated to the mid-sixth century (fig. 6.14; pl. 12).[81] At the center of the composition, a female cult servant raises lustral branches, sprinkling holy water upon an altar, communicating her leadership position within the ritual. Behind her, men lead a bull for sacrifice,
and before her stands the imposing figure of the Athena Promachos. The goddess's statuelike
image not only establishes the sanctuary setting but also locates the action upon the Athenian Acropolis. It is not the temple key that identifies the woman at center as priestess but, instead, a whole series of sign-components, including her fancy woven dress, the lustral
branches, the altar, the image of Athena, the marchers, and the animal victim. In addition, the
commanding position of the woman at the very center of the composition communicates her
pivotal role. Procession and victim move toward her from the left, while Athena's gaze and
upraised spear focus upon her from the right. All action converges at the center of the picture
field, where the priestess's own dynamic hand gestures dominate, establishing her identity as
the primary overseer of sacrifice.

The image of Athena Promachos can, again, be seen together with the priestess of
Athena on a black-figure band cup in a private collection, dated to just before the middle of
the sixth century (fig. 6.15; pl. 9).[82] The priestess stands in front of Athena and behind the
altar and is approached from the far side by a long and festive procession of worshippers. She
leans over the altar and extends her hand to a man who advances at the head of the *pompe*. He
is followed by the female basket bearer, who raises both hands to steady her *kanoun*, and then
by a line of marchers who lead a bull, sow, and ewe to sacrifice. Behind them is a great procession, complete with two pipers and a lyre player, men carrying branches, hoplites, and
cavalry. All is ready for the sacrifice. The fire has been lit upon the altar and the flames are
rising.

Interpreters have been unable to resist associating this image with the Panathenaic procession and, by extension, with the Parthenon frieze.[83] While we can recognize here certain elements that we would expect to see in a Panathenaiac procession, the image simply cannot be

Fig. 6.15 (above)
Attic black-figure band cup. Private Collection.

Fig. 6.16 (opposite)
Attic black-figure amphora, the Affector. Munich, Staatliche Antikensammlungen und Glyptothek
1441.
Photo Staatliche Antikensammlungen und Glyptothek München, by Renate Kühling.

made to fit descriptions found in texts and inscriptions. Above all stands the problem of the sacrificial victims, the bull, sow, and ewe known collectively as the *trittoia* or *trittys boarkhos* sacrifice. This combination of victims is at odds with the specific requirement for bull and ram sacrifices at the Panathenaia. As early as Homer's *Iliad* (2.546–51), bulls and rams were directly associated with the worship of Athena and Erechtheus, a fact that is confirmed by the epigraphic record.[84] There is simply no way to explain away the conspicuous presence of the large sow in this sacrificial scene.

Perhaps the least interesting thing about this fascinating cup is whether we can prove that it illustrates a Panathenaic procession. What motivated the selection of signifiers used to communicate meaning? The *trittoia* sacrifice is central to the message that the scene conveys. The scale of the sow and ewe has been enlarged to emphasize their importance within the hierarchy of figures. Perhaps the cup commemorates a very special *trittoia* sacrifice, elevated to Panhellenic status by virtue of the manipulation of Panathenaic indicators.

Much more interesting than efforts to match visual elements with a named festival is the recognition of patterns in the way that sign-components are manipulated here to communi-

cate meaning. The flaming altar is a powerful motif. The juxtaposition of a female figure beside the flaming altar endows her with authority and confirms her identity as priestess. In Euripides' *Erechtheus*, Athena grants Queen Praxithea, as first priestess of Athena Polias, the right to make burned sacrifice upon her altar.[85] Euripides may be providing an *aition* for the historical reality in which the priestess of Athena Polias was in charge of fire sacrifice on the Acropolis. As we saw early in this chapter, the priestess of Artemis Pergaia on Kos was charged with lighting the altar fire.[86] Inscribed texts that forbid sacrifice in the absence of a priest or priestess suggest that, at least for certain cults, proximity of sacred servant to altar was essential for the rite to proceed.[87] This band cup compares nicely to the Siana cup that we considered in chapter 3, showing the priestess of Demeter holding a liknon and standing beside a flaming altar (see fig. 3.2; pl. 10). Comparable in date, technique, and design, these two images from early black-figure painting establish sign-components within the visual lexicon that will endure for years to come.

An engaging scene on an amphora by the Affector, from Vulci and now in Munich, shows a woman standing behind a blazing altar, raising her hands in prayer (fig. 6.16; pl. 11).[88] A procession of male marchers approaches her from the left, leading a ram to sacrifice. The men carry wreaths, lustral branches, and a jug. Here, the basket bearer is male and walks in the middle of the line rather than at the front. The officiating woman assumes a position similar to that shown for the priestess on the band cup (see fig. 6.15; pl. 9) in that she stands on the far side of the altar to receive the procession. Her commanding position behind the flaming altar and her conspicuous gesture of prayer establish her identity as priestess. The Affector has made clever use of the available space, placing the diminutive priestess beneath the handle and allowing the procession of much taller men to fill the picture field. The other side of the vase may refer to the cult for which the sacrifice is made. This shows Dionysos with Ikarios, the first mortal to whom the god introduced wine. Form, function, and decoration come together on this amphora, a vessel from which wine may have been poured for participants in a feast honoring Dionysos, just as is illustrated on its belly.

Ritual Feasting

The sacrificial ritual concluded with the sharing of cooked portions of the meat in joyous culmination of religious sentiment in which divinity and participants came together. The thought that women, who have been actively engaged in every step of the ritual process, would be excluded from this culminating moment is unthinkable. Indeed, images show women enjoying feasts with joints of meat held in their hands and giant cups of wine passed between them. A lekythos in Basel shows two pairs of women dining in a vineyard setting, seated on folding stools and leaning across tables filled with meat and cakes (fig. 6.17).[89] The banqueters pass giant "loving cups." One group shares wine from a kantharos, while the other shares it from a skyphos. The large size of these vessels underscores the communality of the feast, in which wine was passed around and around for each woman to drink. This lekythos is one of a group of seven related vases that date to the end of the sixth century, produced by a number of associated painters, including those of the Leagros group, members of the circle of the Sappho Painter, and the Nikoxenos Painter.[90] Most of these vases show scenes set in rustic vineyards with ivy leaves and bowers, but some are set indoors, as indicated by columns.

The interpretation of these images remains a challenge. Some scholars view the women as nymphs shown enjoying a feast in the mythical realm of Dionysos.[91] Others view them as representations of real women enjoying themselves at a historical Thesmophoria.[92] As the most widespread feast celebrated in Greece, the festival of Demeter gathered female worshippers for ritual sacrifice, dining, and drinking, just as is seen on the vases. A third view, offered by Margot Schmidt, reads the images less literally, not as snapshots from a particular festival, or as scenes drawn wholly from myth, but as a visual synthesis of occasions on which women came together for communal dining.[93] Importantly, Schmidt points out that we see no specific signifiers of Demeter

Fig. 6.17
Attic black-figure lekythos.
Basel, Antikenmuseum Basel
und Sammlung Ludwig BS 1447.
Photo Antikenmuseum Basel
und Sammlung Ludwig, by Claire
Niggli.

or the Thesmophoria on these vases. Instead, it is the world of Dionysos that we see, complete with vines and ivy leaves. The absence of satyrs or other mythical characters from the Bacchic circle argues against the identification of the women as nymphs. Schmidt claims that the female figures are exactly what they appear to be: women gathered together for communal feasting.

The collective consumption of meat, cakes, and other offerings marked the final stage in the sacrificial ritual. Dining bound worshippers together in the denouement of the high action of sacrifice, reinforcing common identity through shared experience. These fascinating images show us a world in which women feasted together and, as Sarah Peirce has convincingly argued, illustrate that honors given to the gods brought joy and benefits to worshippers in return.[94]

Gloria Ferrari's insightful analysis of the popular category of images showing women working wool may provide a parallel case through which we can better understand scenes that show women in ritual action. Ferrari has demonstrated that depictions of women spinning and weaving were much more than mere snapshots of "daily life." Indeed, they functioned as emblems of the feminine ideal, reinforcing and perpetuating an exemplar for the female gender.[95] Wool working was not only what a good woman did, it was the enterprise of sweet-smelling, richly dressed, and marriageable maidens.[96] I suggest that images of women shown in ritual action functioned in much the same way. Engagement in cult service was what a good woman did. As with spinning, this exercise was more than just a mark of virtue. It was a signifier of social and symbolic capital, of prestige and desirability, that came together to construct a feminine ideal.

Cult service was inextricably linked to social status, family fortune, health, and wholeness, and thereby set a powerful archetype for female behavior. Maidens chosen as kanephoroi were the most beautiful, well born, richly dressed, and marriageable within the community. Mature priestesses were equally well placed and attractive, exactly the type of women whom men wanted for wives, and children for mothers. The popularity of scenes showing women as active agents in ritual reinforced and perpetuated this model. Again, we can recognize the axis of house and temple at work in the structuring of this ideal for the women who moved between these two spaces.

Benefactions

Priestesses became very attached to the sacred spaces in which they served; indeed, one could say that their very identities were drawn from them. A lasting gift of bricks-and-mortar construction within the sanctuary gave concrete commemoration of sacred service and guaranteed that women would be remembered always in their official status. And, quite simply, these gifts pleased the gods. Financial donations to sanctuaries were as much an expectation of priestly office as was performance of ritual. As first priestess of Athena Polias at Athens, Queen Praxithea took on responsibilities that are clearly spelled out by Athena in her closing speech of Euripides' *Erechtheus* (*Pap. Sorbonne* 90). In what may well represent a charter contract for priestly duties, Athena instructs Praxithea to build and to sacrifice: "For your husband I command the building in mid-city a precinct with stone enclosure. . . . To you, Praxithea, who have restored this city's foundations, I grant the right to make burnt sacrifices for the city on my altars under the title of priestess."[97] Historical priestesses of Athena Polias seem to have been involved in construction and renovation on the Acropolis. In an inscription dealing with the restoration of the statue of Athena Nike, the priestess of Athena is said to be the first to make propitiatory offering to the goddess, which she does on behalf of all the Athenian people.[98]

From at least the classical period onward priestesses made, and were honored publicly for, their gifts to sanctuaries.[99] We have seen in chapter 5 that Lysistrate, priestess of Demeter in the mid-fifth century, dedicated an inscribed base with agalma in the City Eleusinian. The inscription tells us that Lysistrate "does not spare her property but makes abundant gifts to the gods according to her wealth."[100] In the middle of the third century, a priestess of Athena Polias at Athens was praised for "the splendid and munificent banquet which she prepared according to ancestral custom."[101] In the first half of the second century, Satyra, priestess of the Thesmophoria, was honored by the deme Melite for having repaired the temples in the Eleusinion and the sanctuary of Plouton, and for having given from her private means more than a hundred drachmas for the annual sacrifices.[102]

By the Hellenistic period, the benefactions of priestly women had grown to include major public gifts and entire building programs.[103] In third-century Chalkedon, the priestess was to "build."[104] At Halikarnassos in the early second century, the priestess of Artemis Pergaia was authorized to "build the sanctuary wherever she chooses" and also "a treasury for the goddess."[105] Artemisia, priestess of Nemesis at Mylasa in the late second century, dedicated a cult statue and base to Nemesis and the Demos, together with her husband, who acted as her *kyrios*.[106]

During the early first century B.C. on Thasos, a woman named Epie, daughter of Dionysios, stepped forward to cover expenses for the cults of Aphrodite, Zeus Euboulos, and Athena.[107] Having served twice as *neokoros* of Athena, Epie restored the temples and set up statues and votive offerings within the sanctuary. She also built a propylon for the shrine of Artemis Eileithyia, with stone columns, doorways, and an architrave, on which she inscribed a text. When none of the wealthy women in the likely pool of candidates took on the expensive and nonpaying priesthood of Zeus Euboulos, Epie accepted this post as well. She agreed to take on the office and all its financial obligations for life, except in years when someone else could be found to accept the job. Epie is celebrated in a laudatory inscription expounding her high-minded generosity, which went above and beyond what was expected of any single individual.

Phaena Antigonika, a priestess of Demeter at Mantineia in 46/45 B.C., was honored for covering the expenses of the goddess and the other priestesses in a decree that her fellow priestesses set up.[108] In it, they praise her for magnificently entertaining the cult participants before, during, and after her tenure of office, as well as for the munificent testamentary endowment that she left at her death. This gift ensured that her daughter and granddaughter would continue the annual payments to the cult throughout their lives. At the end of the first century B.C., another

Mantineian priestess, Epigone, was honored together with her husband in a long inscription carved on a pedestal that held their statues. We have already considered this statue base in chapter 5.[109] The inscription first describes Epigone's husband's benefactions and his patriotism in traveling with two embassies to the Roman Senate. Then, the "respectable and husband-loving" Epigone, priestess of every deity, is praised for having fulfilled her sacral duties. "Sparing no expense, she piously honored the gods and lavishly feasted the populace" (lines 39–43). Together with her husband, Epigone built a market complex with a covered, heated hall; workshops; porticoes; and a large exedra. She repaired the temples, built banquet rooms, gave treasures, and generally beautified her city of Mantineia.

Nowhere did women give more generously than in Hellenized Asia Minor. More than 160 benefactresses are attested here, mostly dating to the Roman Imperial period. About half of these women are commemorated with inscriptions that honor them alone, without any mention of a male relative or guardian.[110] In first-century-B.C. Priene, Phile, daughter of Apollonios, was the first woman to hold the civic office of *stephanophoros*. In some cities, the office was jointly held with a priesthood; in others, it was not. Whatever the case, the *stephanophorate* always included performing sacrifices and feasting the city's inhabitants. By the Roman period, female *stephanophoroi* are know for some twenty-one cities.[111] Phile focused her energies at Priene on a major public-works program. She financed the construction of an aqueduct and cistern and supplied water pipes for the city "at her own expense."[112] Her benefactions are inscribed publicly for all to see right on the buttress of the cistern that she built.

In early first-century-A.D. Aphrodisias, a woman named Tata, called "Mother of the City," served as *stephanephoros*, revered priestess of Hera for life, and priestess of the Emperors. She is honored in an inscription that says she "spared no expense" in twice supplying oil for athletes.[113] She also held memorable banquets, complete with couches provided for the public, and personally imported "the foremost performers of Asia" for dances and plays to entertain not just the local citizenry but their neighbors as well.

The future and prosperity of cities depended on the ability of priestesses to do their jobs properly. Cult service gave women the responsibility of performing and, in many cases, paying for public rituals. It also brought the prestige of being singled out and recognized for public benefactions. By the late Hellenistic period, holding a priesthood could require laying out great sums of money. Public benefactresses held considerable wealth and influence within their communities and surely functioned as equals to their male counterparts. In many cases their influence must have surpassed that of local men. We cannot know to what extent these women acted alone or under the control of male relatives and guardians. At least in some notable cases, it is clear that women gave in their own right and with their own monies. Texts that commemorate these donations express sentiments of self-awareness and -confidence on the part of women benefactors. These sentiments complement those of joy and well-being that are evidenced for their communal participation in rituals and feasts. On balance, participation in cult activity was a positive force in the lives of Greek women, one that brought with it both a sense of community and a sense of self.

———

Women were so fundamental to the proper functioning of polis religion that priestesses from home cities were sent to carry cults to the colonies. This gave legitimacy to new foundations and ensured that worship would be conducted according to ancestral custom. Pausanias tells of the priestess Kleoboea, who brought the rites of Demeter from Paros to its colony on Thasos (10.28.3). The priestess Aristarcha played a pivotal role in establishing the cult of Ephesian Artemis at the Phokaean colony of Massalia, modern-day Marseilles, in France.[114] Strabo (4.1.4) tells how Artemis herself appeared to Aristarcha in a dream and commanded her to accompany the colonists on their voyage to the new land. Aristarcha was told to take with her a sacred statue of Artemis and to assume the role of local priestess. Once settled in Massalia, the Phokaeans established a temple to Ephesian Artemis, where the goddess was worshipped "as was customary in the mother city." The expertise and authority of transplanted priestesses were critical to the successful transfer of cult and the education of new worshippers in traditional practice.

Euxenia, priestess of Aphrodite at the great city of Megalopolis in the second century B.C., provides a classic portrait of the priestess in action. A woman of noble birth, she seems to have been the granddaughter of Philopoemen, the general of the Achaean League.[115] Euxenia spared no expense in enhancing the sanctuary she served. She built the temple of Aphrodite, and then a sturdy wall around it, and then a house for the public guests. An inscription identifies the motivation for her generosity: "that a woman trades her wealth for good reputation is not surprising, since ancestral virtue remains in one's children."[116] As a bridge between her family's glorious past and its promising future, Euxenia used her wealth to ensure that ancestral virtue was passed to the next generation. Like so many priestesses before and after her, Euxenia served as a channel for transmitting customs, beliefs, and laws to the community that she served. She linked her family and her polis to a shared and remembered past and, by overseeing the repeated acts of ritual, not only maintained the social order but also shaped it.

CHAPTER 7

Priestly Privilege
Perquisites, Honors, and Authority

At the opening of this book, we considered the rights granted by the people of Delphi to the Athenian priestess Chrysis.[1] Far from being mere honorary privileges, these brought concrete financial advantage, legal benefits, and social prestige. Freedom from taxes, the right to own property, priority of access to the Delphic oracle, guaranteed personal safety, and a front-row seat in all competitions were significant privileges that placed Chrysis in a position that was superior, not only to that of the average woman of her day, but also to that of men. The fact that Chrysis could pass these rights on to all her descendents certainly made her one of the most influential members of her family, one to whom future generations would be forever grateful.

Chrysis's privileges perhaps came more from her extraordinary status as *proxenos* than from her rank as priestess. Nonetheless, priestesses across the Greek world enjoyed a wide range of benefits that derived directly from their offices. Payment for cult services came in cash as well as in skins and meat from animal victims, grains, fruits, cakes, bread, wine, oil, and honey. In the case of purchased priesthoods, perquisites may have been of sufficient financial value to remunerate the officeholder for the price paid.[2] By the Hellenistic period, priestesses received public honors that regularly included portrait statues, gold crowns, and reserved seats in the theater.

In this chapter we will examine priestly perquisites and honors, as well as the broader question of authority and influence invested in female officeholders. We shall see that priestesses signed and affixed their seals to documents, argued cases of sanctuary law before the Council and Assembly, appointed sacred officials, gave advice, ejected intruders, and enforced the laws of the sanctuaries they served. This evidence must be considered within the context of our new understanding of the civic character of Greek priesthoods, touched upon in chapter 1. The conventional view that sacred officials were some kind of amateur pseudomagistrates who ran cults in the way that *archontes* administered the secular side of the city has been shown to be not quite accurate.[3] Robert Parker has elucidated the "functional equipollence of magistrates with priests," a dynamic that was absolutely central to the embeddedness of religion within the city.[4] He has advised those searching for religious authority in ancient Athens to look to secular authority.[5]

The fact remains that when it came to religious decision making and the official right to legislate, the powers rested with the Council and Assembly, which gave the orders to priests and priestesses. But while power is one thing, authority and influence may be another. The priestesses who oversaw the business of cult can be understood, in a very real sense, to have been civic leaders with civic authority.[6]

Payment for Priestly Services

Apometra and Hierosyna

Both priests and priestesses received a share of the sacrifices offered under their watch, and in this, there is no gendered differentiation between male and female cult agency.[7] Emoluments are variously called *apometra* and *hierosyna*.[8] Hierosyna are generally understood to be sums charged to the person making the sacrifice and appropriated for the sacrifices themselves.[9] Apometra represent a share paid to the priest or priestess, which could come in the form of cash, a portion of the sacrificial victim, or other offerings. A central question in the discussion of payments to sacred servants is whether these were meant as direct compensation for work, or whether they represented reimbursements or a kind of tax directed to the sanctuary. Sokolowski followed Bannier in viewing apometra as reimbursements paid to sacred servants for the costs of materials used in sacrifice.[10] But Sterling Dow saw apometra as outright income for cult agents, since payments for ritual expenses usually fell under the designation *hierosyna*.[11]

Payments in cash tended to be relatively small in comparison with the more substantial in-kind perquisites that came from sacrificial victims. As early as the mid-fifth century B.C., we find cash apometra of 3 obols paid, along with portions of the sacrificial victims, to a priest or priestess in the Paiania deme.[12] At Athens, apometra are attested in sums ranging from 3 obols to 100 drachmas, while hierosyna are mostly attested in sums ranging from 1.5 obols to 30 drachmas.[13] Emoluments sometimes had a relationship to the cost of the sacrifice and the importance of the divinity.[14] Like so many aspects of Greek priesthood, rates for compensation were locally ordained and each sanctuary determined its own package of perquisites. At the shrine of Aphrodite Pandamos and Pontia on second-century Kos, the collection boxes (*thesauroi*) were opened once a year by the priestess and officials called *prostatai*.[15] The priestess was entitled to half the contents of the box, while the other half was sent to the public bank and placed in the account of the goddess.

Literary and epigraphic sources help us reconstruct levels of compensation for the great female priesthoods at Athens. We learn from the *Oikonomika*, attributed to Pseudo-

Aristotle, that the tyrant Hippias legislated a payment of one day's ration of barley and wheat, plus one obol, to the priestess of Athena upon each birth or death in Athens.[16] If this account is accurate, the priesthood would have guaranteed a nice, steady income. By the fourth century, the male citizen population of Athens is estimated to have numbered some twenty-nine thousand.[17] The total number of annual births and deaths could have been quite high. Borimir Jordan finds it difficult to believe that a female officeholder was compensated on such a level. He sees the fee as a tax paid to the sacred treasury or, perhaps, to the tyrant himself.[18] While it is not clear that this money went into the pocket of the priestess, we must leave open the possibility that it did.

We find further evidence of payments to the priestess of Athena Polias in the Sacrificial Calendar of Athens, dated to 403–399 B.C.[19] Here, her apometra are listed in the amount of ten drachmas. This calendar, which is among our most valuable surviving documents for Greek religion, represents a revision of Athenian law that took place at the end of the fifth century.[20] We shall return to its contents below.

When we considered the Athena Nike decree in chapter 2, our concern was the method by which the priestess was selected. Now we can focus on what this document tells us about her compensation, listed as fifty drachmas per year plus the legs and hides of the animal victims for public sacrifice.[21] A rider carved on the back side of the decree in 424/423 B.C. reiterates that the priestess must be paid the amount stipulated on the front. This suggests that the priestess was not receiving her fair share and underscores the seriousness with which priestly compensation was regarded.

We have a good deal of information about finances concerning the priesthood of Demeter and Kore at Eleusis. A law passed in 460 B.C. mandated that the priestess take an obol from every initiate at the Greater and the Lesser Mysteries.[22] Again, it is not clear whether the priestess kept this payment for herself. On the basis of calculations made from a treasury account from the late fifth century, the number of initiates for the year in question could total some 2,150.[23] Proceeds collected for the priestess would thus amount to more than three hundred drachmas for that year and, by some calculations, could have numbered upward of five hundred drachmas.[24] According to the Sacrificial Calendar of Athens, the priestess of Demeter also received impressive apometra of one hundred drachmas for her duties at the Eleusinia festival.[25] This reflects the very high regard in which Athenians held the Eleusinian cult.

Further payments to the priestess of Demeter and Kore are attested in a number of inscriptions. One, dated to the first half of the fourth century, awards her twenty-two drachmas for favorable sacrifices.[26] Another, dated to 352 B.C., states that the heirophant and the priestess of Demeter received a payment of uncertain amount for performing sacrifices in connection with the Eleusian *orgas* boundary dispute.[27] The Eleusis Sacred Calendar of 330–270 B.C. lists apometra for the priestess in the amount of ten drachmas.[28] Eleusinian financial accounts for 329/328 B.C. inform us that the "priests and priestesses" received portions of the harvest from the Rarian field.[29]

Fragmentary evidence hints at payments to priestesses from a variety of cults. The Sacrificial Calendar of Athens stipulates that a priestess received apometra at the Dipolieia festival. The exact amount is lost.[30] An inscription of early fourth-century date prescribes that deme or tribal priestesses will receive a hierosyna of five drachmas plus three drachmas in lieu of skins that were singed during sacrifice.[31] A decree of 334/333 B.C. states that the priestess of the Thesmophoria in the deme of Cholargos is to receive four drachmas.[32]

Priestesses also collected money for their special services, particularly those concerning fertility and childbirth.[33] The priestess of Athena Polias at Athens presided over the Proteleia sacrifice before marriage and, afterward, took up collections from the brides. Dressed in Athena's *aigis*, the priestess searched out new wives who gave money in hopes of conceiving children.[34] Begging priestesses were also known at Argos. Aeschylus tells us that Hera once disguised herself as a priestess to collect money for the daughters of the River Inachos, nymphs associated with marriage and childbirth.[35] On Kos, a priestess of Artemis begged annually on the first day of the month Artamitios.[36] In third-century Halikarnassos, a decree restricted the number of days on which the priestess of Artemis Pergaia was allowed to beg.[37] This was meant to keep her from abusing the privilege that entitled her to keep the cash collected. We thus hear of a broad range of circumstances in which money crossed the palms of priestesses, reminding us, yet again, of the centrality of economics within the Greek religious system. Cash came from fees charged to those offering sacrifice, through collection boxes, and through direct begging. These payments are relatively small in comparison to the in-kind emoluments of skins, meat, and foods, which often made up the largest part of the perquisite package.

Skins and Hides

The most characteristic perquisite was the skin of the animal victim, a valuable commodity that could be sold on for profit.[38] We have seen that the priestess of Athena Nike was entitled to an annual salary plus the legs and hides of victims from public sacrifices.[39] The fourth-century Sacred Calendar for Erchia stipulates that the skins of goats sacrificed to Semele and Dionysos should be handed over to the appropriate priestesses, while the meat went to women who had made the sacrifice.[40] The priestess of Artemis Pergaia at Halikarnassos was entitled to the thighbone and the parts placed on it and the fourth part of the entrails and the hides for public sacrifices. At private sacrifices, she received the thighbone and parts placed on it and the fourth part of the entrails.[41] The high value placed on perquisites is reflected in the provision that cash would be paid in the event that skins were damaged in the fire of sacrifice.[42] A fourth-century Attic inscription sets out very specific emoluments for the priestesses of Demeter Chloe, Hera, Dionysos Anthios, and others.[43] They are to receive a sum of money, as well as hides, honey, oil, wheat, firewood, and portions of the meat placed upon the offering table.

During the fourth century, the priestess of the *orgeones* of Bendis in the Piraeus was entitled to hierosyna from sacrifices of female animals (or animals sacrificed by women).[44] If an immature animal was sacrificed, the priestess received 1.5 obols plus the skin and the right leg of the victim. For a mature animal, she received 3 obols plus the skin and leg. In the case of cattle sacrifice, the priestess received 1 obol, plus the hide. The male priest of the *orgeones* was given the same cuts from sacrifices of male animals.

Decrees stipulate very specific awards as well as very general ones. During the fourth century on Chios, a priestess (probably of Athena) received various parts of the victim, including one-sixth of the internal organs.[45] At first-century-B.C. Pednelissos near Perge on the southern coast of Turkey, the deceased priestess Galato was given a quarter of the sacrifice.[46] The priestess of Meter at Minoa on Amorgos was entitled to a portion of the sacrifice at the Metroia festival.[47] According to an inscription from the end of the fourth century, pregnant women at Cyrene were obliged to visit the "bride-room" in the precinct of Artemis and to give the priestess, called "Bear," the feet, head, and skin of a sacrificial victim. Women who failed to sacrifice prior to giving birth were required to visit the priestess afterward and give her an even greater perquisite, that of a full-grown animal victim.[48]

Two related decrees, dating to circa 400 B.C., stipulate emoluments for the priestess of Eileithyia on Chios.[49] The first states that whenever the city performed a sacrifice, the priestess was to receive from the *agogos* (leader) a *hemiekteus* of (grain) for a *hemisykteus* of barley groats. A slightly later decree reiterates that the priestess should receive whatever was inscribed on the first stele and, in addition, the head of the animal victim (lines 18–19). Apparently, the priestess was dissatisfied with the level of her first compensation package, since it offered no part of the animal. A punishment clause is added in the second decree (lines 21–23). If the priestess took anything beyond which she was entitled, she would be fined.[50]

Laws and their amendments attest that payments to sacred officials were carefully monitored. Perquisites were spelled out on advertisements for the sale of priesthoods, making clear to the buyers exactly what they were getting for their money. Penalties were imposed on those who failed to pay cult officials their due, and sacred servants could take legal action against those who owed them money. We have seen dissatisfaction with those who failed to pay priestesses, expressed in the rider on the back of the Athena Nike Decree, and in the second Chian inscription dealing with the priestess of Eileithyia. Although some scholars discount these salaries as mere reimbursements for expenditures, the force of the evidence gathered here argues for payments bringing real financial gain to the individuals who earned them.[51] These decrees, and their amendments, mandated that fees be paid and reflect the self-interest of cult agents who were determined to get their fair share.

Access to Sacred Space

The presence of cult statues within sanctuaries rendered them virtual residences for the gods on earth.[52] As servants of these divinities, priests and priestesses enjoyed the special privileges of proximity, sometimes including the right to live within the holy precinct. An official expense account from Eleusis, dated to 329/328 B.C., mentions "the house of the priestess," "the sacred houses of the priestesses," "the sacred house where the priestesses lives," and "the doors of the priestess."[53] This suggests that residential expenses for priestesses fell within the financial responsibility of the cult. Whether these houses were located within the sanctuary is not known, though it seems likely. Pausanias (10.34.7) saw dwellings for cult agents in the sanctuary of Athena Kranaia at Elateia.[54] We know that the Athenian arrephoroi lived on the Acropolis during the year leading up to the Arrephoria festival. We are told that that they even had their own ball court on the sacred rock.[55]

It is clear that some priestesses had a specially designated space within the temple. Herodotos (5.72) recounts how the priestess of Athena Polias jumped up from her throne within the adyton when the Spartan king Kleomenes attempted to enter. This would suggest that a special seat was reserved for her. The Pythia at Delphi had a seat upon the tripod fixed within the adyton of Apollo's temple (see fig. 3.4).[56] The elderly women who killed the cows in the sanctuary of Demeter Chthonia at Hermione had chairs within the sanctuary where they waited for the sacrificial procession (Pausanias 2.35.4).

One wonders if the dedication of marble thrones by Sostratos at Rhamnous during the fourth century might reflect a practice whereby priestesses had special seats within their precincts. Two marble chairs were found in situ set at either side of the door of the smaller temple of Nemesis. One throne was dedicated to Themis during the priesthood of Pheidostrate. The other was dedicated to Nemesis during the priesthood of Kallisto (fig. 7.1).[57] We cannot know under what circumstance Sostratos offered these thrones, whether they were meant to be used by the priestesses named, or whether they were simply votive offerings in the form of seats. Nonetheless, they suggest a tradition in which cult agents had assigned chairs within their sanctuaries just as, we shall see, many had within their local theaters (figs. 7.2–7).

Priestesses had special access to places where others were not permitted.[58] In second-century Eresos, only the priestess and prophetess could enter the temple.[59] The elderly priestess of Zeus Sosipolis at Olympia had exclusive right to the inner sanctum, where it was her job to

Fig. 7.1
Marble throne dedicated by Sostratos to Nemesis in the priesthood of Kallisto, from Rhamnous. Athens, National Archaeological Museum 2673. Photo courtesy National Archaeological Museum.

bring bathwater and barley cakes (Pausanias 6.20.2–3). At the temple of Aphrodite at Sikyon, an older celibate *neokoros* and the virgin *loutrophoros* (bearer of the wedding bathwater) were the only persons allowed to enter the temple.[60] Pausanias tells us of sanctuaries in which no one but the priestess could even look at the cult statue. This was the case at the temple of Hera at Aigion and at the sanctuary of Eileithyia at Hermione (7.23.9, 2.35.11). The special access that priestesses had to cult statues underscored the intimacy of deity and cult servant, bringing with it a symbolic capital that carried real weight in the ancient community.

Public Honors

Crowns

By the Hellenistic period, three standard public honors were awarded to priestesses: gold crowns, reserved seats in the theater, and portrait statues. We have reviewed the evidence for portrait statues in chapter 5 and shall consider *proedria* later in this chapter. Let us now turn to the public crowning, or *stephanosis*, which from the late fifth century was among the highest honors a city could bestow upon an individual.[61] That this honor was extended to priestesses underscores the high regard in which they, and their service, were held.

The first Attic decree that commemorates a public *stephanosis* dates to 410/409 B.C. In it, the Athenians honor Thrasyboulos of Kalydon for his efforts in the assassination of the oligarch Phrynikos.[62] Thereafter, crownings were usually awarded to foreigners, often to kings, until the second half of the fourth century, when, increasingly, they were bestowed on citizens.

Athenian decrees attest to the granting of wreaths of olive, myrtle, ivy, and other plants.[63] While this distinction was at first reserved for political and military figures, priests and *hieropoioi* received this honor by the second half of the fourth century.[64] The nine archons and members of the Council at Athens held "crown-wearing offices."[65] Priests were permanent wearers of crowns, and private persons sometimes wore them, especially for cult rituals.[66]

Among women, crowns were a very rare distinction. It should come as no surprise that priestesses were the first women to receive this honor. Two reliefs discussed in chapter 4 (see figs. 4.7–8; pl. 13) provide exceptional visual evidence for the awarding of crowns to priestesses.[67] They date to the fifth and fourth centuries B.C. Each shows Athena with a female cult agent who holds a temple key in her left arm and raises her right hand in a gesture of prayer. The inscribed texts that would have accompanied these images do not survive to give us the names, dates, and details of the crownings.

Fortunately, we do have some texts that preserve such information for later priestesses. In 255/254 B.C., a priestess of Athena Polias at Athens ([Lysistra]te or [Phanostra]te) received a crown of olive leaves.[68] The *orgeones* of Magna Mater in the Piraeus crowned its priestess, Krateia, with an olive wreath at the end of the third century.[69] This honor rewarded Krateia for exceptional performance of her duties, including the preparation of banquet couches for the festival of Attis (*lectisternia*). We have seen that the deme Melite honored Satyra, priestess of Demeter and Kore Thesmophoroi in the second century, with a myrtle crown and the right to set up her painted portraits in Demeter's shrine.[70] The Athenian *ergastinai* received olive crowns from the Demos and the Boule in recognition of their work during the late second and early first centuries B.C.[71] In 325/324 B.C. a decree passed by the Attic deme of Aixone honored the priestess of Hebe and Alkmene with a crown.[72]

The highest honor of all was that of the gold crown. Such a crown could value five hundred or even one thousand silver drachmas, a very lucrative award, indeed.[73] It could be entirely honorific, awarded by the city to an individual, who was required to return it immediately as a dedication.[74] Numbers of gold crowns were stored in the Parthenon and Erechtheion as part of the sacred treasury.[75] In second-century Pergamon, priestesses of Athena were regularly awarded a combination of gold crown and bronze portrait statue.[76] The practice of priestly *stephanosis* continued well into the Roman Imperial period. A woman named Aba from Histria, in the province of Moesia, was awarded a crown by her city in the second century A.D.[77] She held the priesthood of the Mother of the Gods, among other priesthoods, and was praised for assuming not only liturgies traditionally performed by women, but also those that belonged to men. Aba was granted the extraordinary honor of having her coronation proclaimed at all local festivals.

By the Hellenistic period, elite women who did not necessarily hold priesthoods also received public crownings. At Arkesine on Amorgos during the late third/early second century, Timessa was crowned with a wreath of flowers in recognition of the ransom she paid for fellow citizens captured by pirates.[78] Timessa was also granted a seat of honor at all major festivals of the city. Some 150 years later, the same city of Arkesine awarded a gold crown to another local benefactress, Theodosia, who financed the restoration of the dilapidated agora.[79] We hear of an extraordinary case of a woman from Rhodes who was presented with many crowns, statues, and silver portraits following her victory in a chariot race during the first century B.C.[80] She seems to have been the owner of the winning horse or horses and, from all appearances, had significant control over her own finances.

Proedria

The public honor of proedria granted outstanding members of the community reserved seats at the theater. This brought considerable social prestige and symbolic capital to individuals, who enjoyed high visibility at public performances. Indeed, it was at the theater that the full community of the polis came together as a body. Prominent positioning in the front rows communicated status within the group. The practice of proedria is first attested at Olympia during the first half of the sixth century. Here, a seat was carved with the name of Gorgos, a Lakedaimonian who was *proxenos* of the Eleans (their ambassador in Sparta).[81] We have seen that Chrysis, priestess of Athena Polias, enjoyed this same combination of *proxenia* and proedria at Delphi during the second century B.C. Chrysis's honors followed what was a venerable tradition at Apollo's shrine. We learn from Herodotos (1.54.2) that, during the sixth century, Kroisos, King of Lydia, enjoyed two of the same privileges later granted to Chrysis: proedria and priority in consulting the oracle. It is no small thing that, by the Hellenistic period, a woman held the same awards made to a king some four hundred years earlier.

Reserved seats in the front rows were regularly carved with embellishments to give them a thronelike appearance. This distinguished them from the great semicircle of benches that rose up from behind, constituting the general seating of the *cavea*. Inscriptions identified the dignitary to whom the place belonged. This was usually a civic official or other officeholder, military gen-

Fig. 7.2
Theater of Dionysos, Athens. View southeast looking at section with inscriptions for women's reserved seating. Photo J. B. Connelly.

eral, priest, priestess, other cult agent, or private individual who received the special honor by vote of the Assembly.

The theater of Dionysos at Athens preserves a large number of inscribed seats that give special insight into the practice of proedria (fig. 7.2).[82] While the remains date to the fourth-century Lykourgan building program, names inscribed on seats and benches are mostly Roman in date.[83] A variety of scripts and letter sizes show that the inscriptions were cut at different times and by different hands. We find well-spaced block lettering (see fig. 7.7) as well as smaller, more informal carvings (see fig. 7.5). In some cases, the smaller writing can be seen to overwrite the larger letters. The latest inscribed throne in the theater was reserved for Marcus Ulpius Eubiotus in about A.D. 230.[84]

Some forty-seven seats, mostly located in the front row, were reserved for priests, along with thirteen places for other male religious officials, and eleven for civic officials, including the *strategos* (general), the *keryx* (herald), and the nine archons. Some seats farther up, on the benches of the *cavea*, were reserved for male benefactors of the city. One is set aside for residents of the Kollytos deme.[85]

Among the thronelike seats down front, only one has been recovered that bears the name of a woman: Athenion daughter of Athenios (fig. 7.3).[86] We know from an inscription found near the Propylaia on the Acropolis that Athenion served as priestess of Athena Polias in A.D. 134.[87] Her name is inscribed with her patronymic just below the seat on the front side of the throne. Above, at either side, Gorgon heads are sculptured in low relief. On the sides of the chair, sculptured snakes allude to the snake of Athena that resided on the Acropolis (fig. 7.4). This seat gives concrete evidence that, at least by the second century A.D., the priestess of Athena Polias took her place down front among the priests. Although Athenion's throne was not discovered in situ, it matches the seats found in the front rows in size, type, and decoration.

Inscribed seats for women in the theater of Dionysos date from the first century B.C. through the second century A.D.[88] The broad benches that ascend from behind the front rows are divided into thirteen sections, or *cunei*, separated by twelve aisles leading from the bottom to the top of the *cavea*. From the perspective of standing in the orchestra and looking up, the greatest number of surviving inscriptions are preserved in the sections at the left side of the theater, especially in the third through sixth sections from the left (see fig. 7.2). In contrast, the right half of the theater has suffered a great deal and preserves very few inscriptions. While the state of preservation may distort our impression of seating patterns within the theater, it does appear that the left side of the *cavea* was largely reserved for women. Fourteen inscriptions specifically identify priestesses as the holders of reserved seats here. Nineteen inscriptions give the names of female deities, from which we might infer that the seats were held by representatives of their cults. An additional eight inscriptions assign seats to other female cult agents. In total, we can reconstruct seating for at least thirty-one women on the left side of the theater.

Some inscriptions identify seats by the title of the cult official rather than by a woman's personal name. These include the priestess of Helios (*IG* II² 5093, fig. 7.5), the priestess of Hestia on the Acropolis (*IG* II² 5096, fig. 7.6), the priestess of Livia and Julia (*IG* II² 5096), the priestess of Hestia of the Romans (*IG* II² 5102), the priestess of Demeter Chloe (*IG* II² 5129), the priestess of Ge Themis (*IG* II² 5130), the singing priestess of Kourotrophos (*IG* II² 5131), the priestess of Demeter and Peitho (*IG* II² 5131), the priestess of Hestia of the Romans (*IG* II² 5145), and the priestess of Aphrodite Pandemos and the Nymph (*IG* II² 5149). Other inscriptions give personal names, including "the priestess E[. . .] Antonia" (*IG* II² 5095), "the priestess Kleariste" (*IG* II² 5125), "[. . .] the priestess Oinanthe" (*IG* II² 5133), "Flavia [. . .], priestess of Leto and Artemis" (*IG* II² 5156), and, of course, Athenion, the priestess of Athena discussed above.

Fig. 7.3 (opposite, top)
Marble throne of priestess Athenion, daughter of Athenios. Athens, Theater of Dionysos,
IG II² 5063. Photo J. B. Connelly.

Fig. 7.4 (opposite, bottom)
Marble throne of priestess Athenion, daughter of Athenios. Athens, Theater of Dionysos,
IG II² 5063. Photo J. B. Connelly.

Fig. 7.5 (top)
Seat for priestess of Helios. Athens, Theater of Dionysos, IG II² 5093. Photo J. B. Connelly.

Fig. 7.6 (bottom)
Seat for priestess of Hestia. Athens, Theater of Dionysos, *IG* II² 5096. Photo J. B. Connelly.

Seats are reserved for other cult agents, who are listed by their functions. We find spots for two *hersephoroi* of Chloe Themis (*IG* II² 5098), two *hersephoroi* of Eileithyia at Agrai (*IG* II² 5099), three kanephoroi from the Palladion (*IG* II² 5118), and singers (*IG* II² 5100, 5128). An *olephoros* (the carrier of barleycorn sprinkled before a sacrifice) of Athena Themis (*IG* II² 5103) had her own special seat (fig. 7.7). Some *deipnophoroi* (meat-offering bearers) (*IG* II² 5151), had designated seats, though it is possible that these were male, rather than female, cult agents.

Seats inscribed with the names of female deities were presumably reserved for the women who served their cults. These include those of Aphrodite Epitragia (*IG* II² 5115), Artemis Oinaia (*IG* II² 5116), Demeter Achaia (*IG* II² 5117), Aphrodite Kolias and [. . .] (*IG* II² 5119), Athena Eetione (*IG* II² 5120), Thesmophoros (*IG* II² 5132), Mother of G[ods?] (*IG* II² 5134), Demeter Thesmophoros (*IG* II² 5136), Moirai (the Fates, *IG* II² 5137), [Artemis Ko]lainis (*IG* II² 5140), Artemis in [. . .] (*IG* II² 5146), [Aphrodite] Epitragia again (*IG* II² 5148), Hera in the Harbor (*IG* II² 5148), Hebe (*IG* II² 5150), Kourotrophos Aglauros (*IG* II² 5152), Demeter (*IG* II² 5152), Demeter Kourotrophos Achaia (*IG* II² 5153), Hebe again (*IG* II² 5154), and Demeter Phrearoos (*IG* II² 5155).

Sixteen seats are assigned to individual women without mention of cult or sacred office, some of these "by decree." Several of the women named are known from other sources. One inscribed seat, located five rows back from the orchestra, at the far left side, has been restored to read "Of [Pente]teris [. . .]nas" (*IG* II² 5159). We do know a priestess of Athena Polias from Phlya by the name of Penteteris who served in 245 b.c.[89] But since none of the inscriptions in the theater date to as early as the third century, a connection with this woman is very unlikely.

Of special interest is an inscribed seat in the sixth section from the left, eleven rows back, that reads: "Of Philippe, daughter of Medeios" (*IG* II² 5104). In chapter 2, we met a Philippe, daughter of Medeios of the Piraeus, who served as priestess of Athena Polias during the late second/early first century b.c. This Philippe, presumably named for her, is her niece, the daughter of her brother, also named Medeios, who served as priest of Poseidon-Erechtheus. The Philippe of the younger generation sits right beside her sister, "Ladamea daughter of Me[deios]" (*IG* II² 5123). This Ladamea is also named for an aunt, Laodameia, whom we have seen as kanephoros at the Delia and the Apollonia on Delos.[90] We do not know whether the younger generation of sisters, Philippe and Ladamea, held sacred offices like their aunts. They certainly were from a family distinguished by its cult service and would have had a presumption of ritual agency. What is of interest here is that the sisters lived during the first century b.c., giving concrete evidence that women attended the theater at Athens by the late Hellenistic period.

Finally, we have two seats reserved for Megiste, both "by decree." One Megiste sits right above Philippe, in the sixth section, twelfth row (*IG* II² 5105). A second bench marked for

Fig. 7.7
Seat for *olephoros* of Athena Themis. Athens, Theater of Dionysos, *IG* II² 5103. Photo J. B. Connelly.

Megiste is located two rows up in the same section (*IG* II² 5107). Two priestesses of this name are known: Megiste, daughter of Asklepiades of Halai, priestess of Athena Polias sometime in 27–18 B.C.,[91] and Iounia Megiste, daughter of Zenon of Sounion, who served as priestess of Athena Polias around the middle of the first century A.D.[92] It is possible, but not certain, that these seats could be associated with one or both of these priestesses. It should be said, however, that Megiste was a very common name in Attica.[93]

Both benches marked "Megiste" state that the honor of proedria was given "by decree" (*kata psephisma*).[94] So, too, were the benches designated for Lamidion (*IG* II² 5121) and Alkia (*IG* II² 5124), wife of Atticus Herodes and mother of the famous benefactor of Athens Herodes Atticus.[95] Other benches simply give names of women, without title, cult, or patronymic: Antonia (*IG* II² 5126), Livia (*IG* II² 5161), [. . .]krate (*IG* II² 5162), Theoxene, and Theano (*IG* II² 5164).

From the relatively large number of inscribed female names, we can surmise that women of Roman Athens attended the theater in significant numbers. How early did this practice begin? The debate over whether women were present at the theater in classical Athens is a lively one.[96] Since Greek drama was written, produced, and performed by men and organized by the Demos, a body composed of male citizens only, it has been assumed that the audience watching performances was also exclusively male.[97] But not one ancient source mentions or presupposes the exclusion, or nonattendance, of women. Jeffrey Henderson has collected a number of ancient sources that are best explained if women were, in fact, present at the theater.[98] In Plato's *Laws* (817c, 658a–d), tragedy is referred to as a form of rhetoric addressed to "boys, women, and the whole crowd." The preferences of festival audiences are described as follows: "children like the conjurer, older boys the comic poet, young men, educated women, and the general public like tragedy."[99] Among the often-cited later sources for theatrical anecdotes is one that describes how Aeschylus's *Eumenides* frightened women so much that some who were pregnant miscarried.[100] While no single piece of evidence is conclusive on its own, all sources point in the same direction. The cumulative force of the source material supports the presence of women at the classical theater.[101]

When approaching this question, it must be remembered, above all, that dramatic performances were embedded within the ritual programming of religious festivals. As women participated in the processions, prayers, and sacrifices for these feasts, why should they be excluded from this one piece of the overall cult program? Sourvinou-Inwood has argued persuasively for the full participation of women in the City Dionysia, of which the dramatic performances were just a part. She has shown how the exclusion of women from the theater contradicts "ritual logic," and how modern assumptions regarding this question are influenced by culturally determined biases.[102]

If women were banned from performances during the classical period and then suddenly allowed in during late Hellenistic times, we would expect some comment on this huge change in social practice to be recorded. But not a single ancient source mentions it. We know that Chrysis, priestess of Athena Polias in the second century B.C., was allowed to sit in the theater at Delphi, as stated in the decree cited at the opening of this book.[103] We have seen the sisters Philippe and Ladamea seated on reserved benches in the theater of Dionysos already in the first century B.C.[104]

Indeed, the practice of proedria was widespread in the Greek East. Timessa, benefactress at Arkesine on Amorgos, was granted proedria for the festival of the Itonia and all other festivals of the city during the late third/early second century B.C.[105] At Termessos in Pisidia, near the southern coast of modern Turkey, an inscribed theater seat preserves the name of a chief-priestess who served during the Roman period. Mamastis had her reserved place in section A VII, row 3, seat number 21.[106] Her position was not in the very front, but still was well within the seating space for the community's elite. At Mytilene, the chief-priestess Iulia Potamille, daughter of Sakerdos, and a second priestess, Aur[elia] A[. . .]linne Trophime, were assigned seats just opposite one another, close to the orchestra and near the entrance.[107] Their conspicuous placement enabled them to be seen by all who entered the theater. Celebrity seating catapulted priestly women to a level of visibility that identified them as chief players within their home cities.

Special seating at athletic contests was also a privilege of priesthood. The most conspicuous person at the Olympic Games was the priestess of Demeter Chamyne. She had the unique honor of being the only married woman admitted to the contests.[108] Pausanias (6.20.9) tells us that the Eleans bestowed the office of priestess of Demeter Chamyne on women from time to time as they wished. The priestess was enthroned on a special altar at the very center of the racecourse, just opposite the judges' stand. This altar, built of reused white stone blocks and dated to the second century A.D., stands in situ to this day. It may have been set up for or even by Regilla, the wife of Herodes Atticus. We know that Regilla held the priesthood of Demeter Chamyne at approximately the same time that the altar was erected. We also know that her husband made a number of benefactions to the temple of Demeter at Olympia, including the replacement of the old cult statues of Demeter and Kore.[109] The privileged seating of the priestess of Demeter Chamyne is by no means unique in Roman Greece. Elite female spectators enjoyed reserved seating at athletic contests all across Roman Asia Minor.[110]

Although the epigraphic record preserved in the theater of Dionysos at Athens is mostly Roman in date, it does provide a rare and comprehensive view of the social practice of proedria. It enables us to reconstruct the ancient reality of who sat where, when, and why, within one of the most visible public structures of the city. It also makes clear that, at least by the late Hellenistic period, Greek women did attend theatrical performances. The fact that priestesses were distinguished with reserved seats reflects the esteem in which they were held and gives testimony to their visibility within the community. It has been pointed out that while six thousand men came together in the Athenian Assembly, the Theater of Dionysos brought together some seventeen thousand individuals, including boys, youths, foreigners, allies, metics, prisoners, and, it would seem, women.[111] The theater provided the single setting in which the full community of the polis came together as a body. And it was at the City Dionysia that all the sacred personnel of Athens came together, just once a year, as a group.[112] The symbolic capital afforded priestesses through the public honor of proedria was nothing short of huge, as they took their places of prominence in the very front ranks of their communities.

The Legal Arena

Inscriptions

Priestly business was bound by law. Inscriptions preserve rules that governed the behavior of cult agents and that, in turn, ensured protection of their rights and privileges. Legal cases were brought when these rights were violated or when priestly personnel behaved in ways contrary to law. Penalties for failing to live up to priestly responsibility could be quite heavy. We learn of a priest of Zeus Megistos who was warned he would lose his priesthood and be banned from the sanctuary if he did not act according to the rules.[113] Priests who took more than their allowed perquisites were punished.[114] If a priestess charged a private person more than what was written in the laws, she could be sued.[115] The advertisement for the priesthood of Aphrodite Pandamos and Pontia on Kos warned that the priestess would be fined one thousand drachmas paid to the goddess if she failed in any task to which the contract bound her.[116] If she was found to neglect her duties, anyone who wished could "denounce her according to the law."[117]

Priestesses seem to have initiated and negotiated laws, amendments, and penalties for transgressions. In doing so, they dealt directly with the political bodies of the city's Council and Assembly. Just like other civic officials, priests, and members of the male citizenry, priestesses argued cases before the Assembly.[118] Many of these concerned *asebia*, that is, the violation of ancestral customs and regulations for the ways in which gods, the deceased, and the fatherland should be honored. Sacred institutions needed to be protected, sacrifices had to be offered properly, and illegal foreign gods had to be kept out.[119] It was the duty of priests and priestesses to uphold these ancestral principles; indeed, they were legally bound to enforce sacred regulations.[120]

During the fourth century at Arkesine on Amorgos, the priestess of Demeter came before the Council and the Assembly to make an official report on public sacrifices.[121] She complained that women were entering the sanctuary at forbidden times and asked that a penalty be fixed for those who transgressed. The Council and Assembly passed a decree at the priestess's recommendation. Henceforth, access to the sanctuary was allowed only at times when the priestess was present.

Priestesses were protected by laws that ensured that they received their rightful share. Penal procedures for those denying the priestess of Artemis at Miletos her prerogatives were inscribed in a decree dating to 380/379 B.C.[122] The *kyrios* of the priestess was to submit to the debt officials a list of all who had failed to turn over the required perquisites from sacrifices performed under her watch. While the priestess's male guardian represented her in court, it was clearly her own interests that were safeguarded and defended.

The advertisement for the sale of the priesthood of Aphrodite on Kos, cited above, makes clear that the priestess could exact payment from those who disregarded the laws: "If anyone fails to perform any of the requirements of this document or to sacrifice as has been prescribed, he shall pay to the priestess the penalty specified in each case."[123] If he neglected to do so, the priestess could proceed against him "as if in fulfillment of a legal verdict." The priestess of Aphrodite was also entitled to fines collected from ship captains and merchants who failed to sacrifice to the goddesses before setting out on their voyages. Interestingly, she could lease out her duties to other individuals, who would have "the same power of exacting payment as was prescribed for the priestess." Advertisements for the sales of priesthoods thus set out legally binding contracts that made clear the terms to which all parties were agreeing. These served to protect the interests of the sacred officials as well as the cult that was selling.

Women who worshipped within holy precincts exercised certain decision-making powers of their own. At the sanctuary of Demeter at Myslasa in Karia, women organized the manner in which their nocturnal rites would be celebrated during the third century B.C.[124] A decree from the Piraeus concerning the Thesmophorion reflects the primacy of the priestess within her sanctuary.[125] It states that nobody should perform purifications or approach the altars or enter the megaron without the priestess except during four festivals (the Thesmophoria, Prerosia, Kalamaia, and Skira), and on other occasions specifically sanctioned by ancestral custom. Out of concern for the rights of the priestess, the decree forbids the freeing of slaves, the assembling of *thiasoi*, and the setting up of dedications and private shrines within the sacred precinct.[126] The local demarch was empowered to impose fines on all who transgressed, according to "the laws governing such matters" (lines 16–17).

Literary Evidence

Ancient authors give lively accounts of priestesses embroiled in legal action. A famous case dating to the fourth century concerns a dispute between the priestess of Demeter at Eleusis and the hierophant Archias.[127] Archias had sacrificed upon the sacred altar during the festival of the Haloa, encroaching on a right that was the priestess's alone. He had offered an animal victim brought by the courtesan Sinope. Despite his distinguished Eumolpid background and the lobbying of his prominent family, Archias was convicted of impiety for offering a sacrifice in a manner contrary to ancestral custom. In another late fourth-century case, the priestess of Demeter brought a suit against a hierophant over a purple woolen cloth that he used in cleaning the statues of the goddesses.[128] The disagreement focused on the sole right of the priestess to tend to the sacred images. It is clear from these accounts that priestesses had the authority to take legal action against those who overreached into areas of their control.

Plutarch (*Alcibiades* 22) presents an unforgettable image of the independent-minded priestess Theano in his account of the legal proceedings against Alkibiades in 415 B.C. Alkibiades' alleged mimicking of the Eleusinian Mysteries landed him with an indictment for crimes against Demeter and Kore. He was said to have dressed in a robe similar to that worn by the hierophant and, together with his friends, acted out the roles of various Eleusinian cult officials. As his punishment, Alkibiades was to be publicly cursed by all priests and priestesses. But Theano refused this instruction and proclaimed that she was a "*praying*, not a cursing, priestess." Although Sourvinou-Inwood has doubted the historical veracity of this account, the image of the self-directed priestess was probably influenced by an ancient reality in which priestesses were accustomed to speaking their own minds.[129]

Not only did priestesses bring cases against delinquent cult personnel, but they themselves stood trial as defendants in complex litigations. In a celebrated case dating to circa 332/331 B.C., Aristogeiton falsely filed suit against a priestess of Artemis Brauronia.[130] The priestess's son Hierokles was caught carrying clothes that had been dedicated by worshippers to the goddess. He was subsequently brought before the Assembly on the charge of temple robbery. Aristogeiton insisted that Hierokles be executed without trial but Hierokles defended himself, saying that he had acted on his mother's instructions. The story ends when Hierokles' accuser is fined five talents for bringing false charges against him. Can we detect a certain influence on the part of the priestess in the clearing of her son and the punishment of his accuser?

We also hear tales of wayward priestesses. These must be viewed with a certain skepticism. The case of the priestess Nino, charged and condemned to death during the fourth century, is recounted by a number of sources and later scholia.[131] Apparently, Nino was a leader of a *thiasos* for the foreign god Sabazios, a deity related to the Greek Dionysos, but with roots in Phrygia and Thrace. The Ferrara vase (see fig. 6.4) bears an image that some have associated with the worship of this god. The cult is known in Athens from the fifth century, when it gained popularity among women and was held in contempt by conservative Athenian males.[132] Chief among the old guard was Demosthenes, who artfully manipulated contemporary misgivings about the cult when telling his version of Nino's transgression. Demosthenes was especially keen to place Glaukothea, the mother of his rival Aeschines, at the center of the story. Glaukothea is named as the one who assembled the *thiasoi* that ultimately led to Nino's death sentence (19.281). We learn from Josephus (*Against Apion* 2.37) that it was forbidden, and punishable by death, to initiate people into the mysteries of foreign gods, as Nino had done.

As Nino's infamy spread, so, too, did accounts of her misdeeds. We learn that Menekles accused her of making magic love potions for young men (Scholia to Demosthenes 19.281).[133] Of course, "new religions" are often considered linked to sorcery and magic, not just by the Greeks, but by Romans and Christians as well.[134] It is not surprising that the charges of impiety brought against Nino eventually came to be associated with witchcraft. Nino's story fits into a familiar pattern through which "otherness" is linked with the deviant practice of sorcery and the occult.

A priestess named Theoris from Lemnos was convicted and sentenced to death for practicing magic and for teaching slaves how to deceive their masters.[135] The name of Theoris's cult is not preserved but we are told that she had a servant who supplied drugs and charms to the brother of Aristogeiton. Demosthenes (*Against Aristogeiton* 1.79) called her a "filthy sorceress" and held her in great contempt for her crimes of impiety. The severity of her sentence, which required not only her execution but also that of her entire family, makes plain the gravity of her offenses against sacred law.

In another gripping legal case set in fourth-century Athens, the courtesan Phryne was accused of impiety for holding a revel in the Lykeion, the sanctuary of Apollo Lykeios and site of Aristotle's famous school.[136] The charges against Phryne are recounted in a number of sources, which agree that she introduced a new god (probably named Isodaites), organized illegal *thiasoi*, and participated in some sort of scandalous revelry. According to one account, Phryne performed her own self-defense, with a stunning courtroom spectacle in which she tore open her clothes and bared her breasts to the jury.[137] This action resulted in her prompt acquittal. The tale is, no doubt, a work of fiction, since there is no firm evidence that women ever spoke in an Athenian courtroom.[138]

We hear of a prophetess at Dodona who was accused of giving a false oracle.[139] Her story is set at a time roughly two generations after the Trojan War, during the period of large-scale migrations. The prophetess advised the Boiotians that they would prosper only if they committed a sacrilege. But they suspected that she was intentionally giving them bad advice, under the influence of her Pelasgian kin. Sensing that she wished them harm, the Boiotian messengers took the radical step of throwing her into a fire. They were subsequently brought to trial before the two remaining Dodonian priestesses but protested that it was unlawful for women to act as judges. A trial ensued in which an equal number of men and women served as jurors, who, in the end, acquitted the assassins.

Whether or not these accounts are true or embroidered with the stuff of fiction, it must be said that stories of women in court battles frequently involved priestesses. Their special roles in upholding law and in entering into contracts of service within sanctuaries placed them squarely at the center of legal affairs. This status singled priestesses out from average women of their day and gave them a unique agency in the very public arena of the law. Priestesses were open to scrutiny and accountability; indeed, Aeschines (3.18) tells us that they were subjected to the same public audits as were male officials.

Authority

A tantalizing fragment of Lykourgos's lost speech *On the Priestesses* gives some small insight into the administrative powers of the priestess of Athena Polias at Athens. The fragment reads: "It has been laid down by decree that the priestess also must add her seal to the register."[140] If priestesses had seals and were officially sanctioned to countersign documents, they must have been invested with at least some level of authority within the bureaucracy of the polis. Lykourgos's firsthand experience as priest of Poseidon-Erechtheus must have informed his writing and makes him a reliable source.

Priestesses, like priests, held powers of appointment in the selection of other sacred officials. On Kos, the priestess of Dionysos Thyllophoros was authorized to appoint an attendant (*hyphiereian*) from among women of citizen birth.[141] The priestess was to share with her attendant a legally enforceable monopoly on initiating worshippers in the rites of Dionysos. During the late second/early first centuries B.C., two decrees were passed for the *orgeones* of the Mother at the Piraeus. The first empowered the priestess (herself appointed annually by allotment) to appoint a former priestess as *zakoros* for a term of one year.[142] No woman could be appointed twice as *zakoros* until a full cycle of former priestesses had served once. But an amendment was passed just eight years after the original law, which changed this rule to allow Metrodora, who had served honorably, to continue as *zakoros* for life.[143] One cannot know what powers of influence were exercised in changing this law, but it is possible that the priestess used her authority in having the law amended to advance Metrodora's position.

Herodotos gives us the broadest array of stories in which priestesses exercised authority within their communities. Many of his tales are fanciful inventions but others may reflect some historical truth at the core. We have considered in chapter 3 his account of the priestess of Athena who ejected the Spartan king Kleomenes from her temple in 508 B.C. (Herodotos 5.72). A related story has Kleomenes thrown out of the temple of Hera at Argos (Herodotos 6.81). Here, he reacted by having the temple attendant dragged away and flogged. While these stories are, no doubt, apocryphal, the agency of priestesses in enforcing laws of entry to sanctuaries is surely based on historical reality.

The power of the priestess's voice within her community is emphasized in Herodotos's account (8.41) of the evacuation of Athens prior to the battle of Salamis, an episode considered in chapter 3. By announcing that Athena's sacred snake had failed to eat its ration of honey cake, the priestess signaled that the goddess had left the city and that the Athenians should follow her example. The power of the priestess to persuade the citizenry to act according to Themistokles' wishes suggests a collusion between the political and religious spheres of the city and the singular position of the priestess at the center of these orbits.

Herodotos paints portraits of equally potent priestesses outside Athens. When Miltiades attempted to take the island of Paros, he followed the advice of Timo, *hypozakoros* of Demeter and Persephone (6.134). Following her instructions, Miltiades climbed over the fence that surrounded the precinct of Demeter Thesmophoros. When he reached the doors of the shrine, he panicked and ran back, leaping over the fence and injuring himself. The Parians tried to execute Timo for treason, since she had revealed to Miltiades sacred mysteries forbidden to men. But the Delphic oracle advised against this, holding that Timo had committed no crime, but was a mere instrument in Miltiades' own self-directed downfall. At Pedasa, a place inland from Halikarnassos, we hear of a priestess of Athena who put on an extraordinary visual display when she wished to warn the populace of impending disaster. Herodotos (1.175) tells us that she did this by growing a long beard, which, apparently, happened on three separate occasions. Certainly a fiction, this story does sketch a picture in which all eyes were firmly focused on the priestess and her extraordinary powers to signal imminent danger.

Herodotos recounts no less than sixty-two stories involving priestesses, half of these concerning the Pythia at Delphi.[144] He gives a host of episodes in which the Pythia's word is not only followed but is crucial in shaping the events of the day. The voice of the Pythia must, of course, be understood within the broader context of the wider clerical bureacracy at Delphi. Nonetheless, Herodotos's stories focus on the agency of the prophetess and the seriousness with which her instructions were followed. When Harpagos attacked Knidos during his conquest of Ionia circa 545 B.C., the Knidians devised a clever plan of defense. They would dig a deep trench across the narrow isthmus that attached the city's peninsula to the mainland. In this way, they would create an island city that would be easier to defend. This ambitious project caused a devastating number of injuries. The Knidians then sought the advice of the Delphic oracle. The Pythia proclaimed: "Do not fence off the isthmus; do not dig."[145] The excavations stopped at her order, leaving no option for the Knidians but immediate surrender to Harpagos.

The advice of the Pythia could move scores of people to action. When she encouraged Greeks to cross the sea and dwell in Cyrene, a great multitude emigrated to the coast of North Africa (Herodotos 4.159). She declared that a man from Mantineia must be brought to reform Cyrene's political system (Herodotos 4.161). The Pythia is even credited with having provided Lykourgos with the Spartan system of government (Herodotos 1.65). Her pronouncements could greatly enrich individuals, as when she ordered the Delphians to give Pindar an equal share of all first fruits offered to Apollo (Pausanias 9.23.3). She could also effect religious practice, as when she introduced funeral games to honor the dead Phokaeans at Agylla (Herodotos 1.167). Sometimes, the oracle's advice went terribly wrong, as when the Spartans thought the Pythia was telling them to march against Tegea instead of Arkadia. Carrying chains for Tegean prisoners, the Spartans instead found themselves the ones taken captive (Herodotos 1.66). Whether fact or fiction, these stories emphasize one constant theme: the voice of the Pythia was not only heard but also heeded.

Teaching and Influence

Priestesses were important custodians of local knowledge and cult history. They transmitted to the following generations the proper procedures for the functioning of cult according to ancestral laws. Some priestesses seem to have offered thoughtful consideration and advice; their counsel was not only sought out but held in high regard. When Herodotos (2.55) visited Dodona, he consulted the priestesses Promeneia, Timarete, and Nikandra about the origins of the shrine and its oracular powers. In time, the image of priestess as wise teacher becomes something of a biographical commonplace.[146] Distinguished men corresponded with priestesses and admired them for their learning and intellect. We are told by Aristoxenos that Pythagoras studied philosophy under the Delphic priestess Themistokleia.[147] In Plato's *Symposium*, Sokrates consults Diotima, a religious expert from Mantineia, on the subject of love.[148] The recurring model that finds a philosopher seeking out the authority of a prophetess may suggest that the influence of priestly women was quite real. Plutarch, priest of Apollo at Delphi, dedicated two of his books to a cultured woman named Klea who was leader of the Delphic Thyiades.[149] She was also an initiate in the mysteries of Osiris. By dedicating his books *Isis and Osiris* and *On the Bravery of Women* (*Moralia* 263c) to Klea, a fellow member of Delphic clergy, Plutarch shows a collegiality and respect that appears to be quite genuine. Two centuries later, the emperor Julian wrote to thank the priestess Theodora for sending him books and for her good letters. He speaks of her as a woman who has devoted her life to the god and addresses her as "most revered."[150] Julian also wrote to a woman named Kallixeine, a priestess of Demeter at Pessinus in Phrygia, whom he honored with a second priesthood, that of Kybele the Mother of the Gods.[151] Zosimos of Panopolis (third/fourth century A.D.) wrote to a woman named Theosebeia, who appears to have been among the most influential experts of alchemy in her day.[152] These portraits of priestly women, esteemed for their learning and wise counsel, suggest that female cult agents played significant roles as teachers and advisors to men.

—

Priesthood had its privileges. One of the most basic of these was proximity to the divinity. The intimacy of sacred servant and deity entitled priestesses to special access to holy precincts and to the cult statue. Residency within the sanctuary was a unique extension of this privilege, opening the house of the goddess to cult agents who experienced sacred space in a singular way. Benefits of cash payments and the sacrificial victim's meat and skins brought financial gain. Despite the reluctance of modern interpreters to accept it, there is a real possibility that priestesses were gainfully compensated for their work. The laws governing perquisites demonstrate just how seriously these salaries were taken.

Vivid images show priestesses at work, fixing their seals on official documents, interacting with legislative bodies, negotiating for amendments to sacred laws, appointing sacred officials, and, in short, functioning as legitimate politicians within the polis bureaucracy. They are even portrayed as valued colleagues and confidants to male philosophers. Sacred authority, embedded in secular authority, was very real. As Plato (*Laws* 5.738B) tells us: "No sensible person will try to change whatever Delphi or Dodona or Ammon or some ancient tradition has authorized in any manner . . . on the strength of which people have established sacrifices and rituals." The cult agents who oversaw these rituals were themselves endowed with an authority that "no sensible person" would question.

CHAPTER 8

Death of the Priestess
Grave Monuments, Epitaphs, and Public Burial

In one of the most sensational images to be confected in Greek literature, the heroine Kallirhoe awakens from a blow to the chest to find herself buried alive, having been taken for dead. As she stirs into consciousness, she pushes aside the wreaths and ribbons heaped about her, rattling the gold and silver grave gifts with her sudden movement. The air is heavy with the strong scent of spices, there within her family's well-built tomb where she lies dressed in her bridal clothes. Kallirhoe's spectacular testimonial from within the burial chamber gives a unique perspective of the "deceased" woman experiencing her own funeral rites. We are told that Kallirhoe's body was carried in a great public procession for interment in her family's vault, which was set along the Syracusan seaside. The parade was led by the city's army on horseback, followed by the infantry, members of the Council, magistrates, Kallirhoe's grieving father, her future father-in-law, and all the citizen women dressed in black. Next came her dowry, a great treasure of gold and silver, elaborate clothes and jewelry, together with her fiancé's wealth, transported through the city streets to be deposited in the ancestral tomb. Kallirhoe's magnificent gold-laden funeral bier followed, born on the shoulders of the young men of Syracuse, while the general public marched behind, expressing its grief in loud lamentation.

This scene is the stuff of romance novels. The writer who brings it to us, Chariton of Aphrodisias, is believed to have lived during the first century A.D. Yet he places the love story of *Chaereas and Kallirhoe* back in late fifth/early fourth-century-B.C. Syracuse, in Sicily.[1] Chariton's carefully observed account of Kallirhoe's burial rings wonderfully true against what we hear of public funeral rites for prominent women in the world that Chariton knew best: the Roman Imperial East. Kallirhoe's fictional funeral presents striking parallels to the real-life memorials held for Apollonis, priestess of Artemis of the Pythaists at Kyzikos, during the early first century A.D.[2] An inscribed decree records provisions for Apollonis's funeral, an event that was spontaneously demanded by the populace upon news of her death.[3] The magistrates were directed to prepare an elaborate ceremony and procession, to announce public mourning, to close all temples and shops, and to give the deceased every appropriate honor. On the day of the funeral, Apollonis's corpse was dressed in purple and gold and carried in a procession through the streets. The parade was led by the city's magistrates, priests, and priestesses, while the citizenry marched behind, organized according to gender, age, and status. Boys, youths, male citizens, and other free men were followed by maidens, female citizens, and other free women. All made their way to the monumental family tomb of Apollonis's husband, located within the city walls of Kyzikos along the Great Harbor, which opened onto the Sea of Marmara.

The lavish public funerals for the fictional Kallirhoe and the historical Apollonis give us some idea what burial rites for prominent women might have looked like in the Greco-Roman East. Indeed, in Chariton's hometown of Aphrodisias, we learn of a priestess of the Emperors who was given spontaneous public burial upon demand of the citizens during the second half of the first century A.D.[4] Tatia Attalis seems to have died prematurely, and the stunned populace, reeling with grief, intercepted her funerary cortege on its way to the cemetery. Taking hold of the bier on which Tatia's corpse was carried, the people of Aphrodisias redirected the procession to the ancestral tomb of her grandfather Adrastos, located within the city walls. Here, Tatia received the exceptional honor of burial within the city, just as we have seen for Apollonis. The decree inscribed on the walls of what has been identified as the family tomb of Adrastos preserves for us this spellbinding account of the events leading to Tatia's final honors.

Public burial is among the greatest civic honors an individual could receive in Greek antiquity, one that was usually associated with men who had served their cities as political leaders or military heroes. The public burial of a woman was an exceptional event, and by the Hellenistic period, it was an honor particularly associated with priestesses, benefactresses, and civic-office holders. Much of what we know regarding the celebration of priestesses at death comes from inscribed epitaphs, epigrams, decrees, and literary references of Hellenistic and Roman Imperial date.[5] But a relatively large body of archaeological material, including sculptured grave reliefs, marble funerary vases, and other monuments, attests to the singling out of priestesses at death already in the classical period. This, of course, does not necessarily mean that they received what we would call public burials, but it is nonetheless significant that women were commemorated at death for the sacred offices that they held in life.[6]

On Pausanias's travels through Greece he visited what he believed to be funerary memorials belonging to famous priestesses from the distant past. At Argos, he saw the tomb of a maenad named Choreia, who fought bravely when her bacchantes joined Dionysos in battle against Perseus and the Argives (2.20.4). The maenads were slaughtered in this battle and buried in a common tomb. Choreia, however, was singled out and given a special grave of her own. During his travels to Alexandria in the Troad, Pausanias sought out the local grave of the Sibyl. In the grove of Apollo Smintheos, he was shown the tomb of a Sibyl named Hierophile, identified by an inscribed epitaph (10.12.6–7):

ἅδ᾽ ἐγὼ ἁ Φοίβοιο σαφηγορίς εἰμι Σίβυλλα τῷδ᾽
ὑπὸ λαϊνέῳ σάματι κευθομένα, παρθένος αὐδάεσσα τὸ
πρίν, νῦν δ᾽ αἰὲν ἄναυδος, μοίρᾳ ὑπὸ στιβαρᾷ τάνδε
λαχοῦσα πέδαν. ἀλλὰ πέλας Νύμφαισι καὶ Ἑρμῇ
τῷδ᾽ ὑπόκειμαι, μοῖραν ἔχοισα κάτω τᾶς τότ᾽
ἀνακτορίας. ὁ μὲν δὴ παρὰ τὸ μνῆμα ἕστηκεν Ἑρμῆς
λίθου τετράγωνον σχῆμα.

I, Sibylla, Phoibos Apollo's wise woman,
Under this stone monument lie hidden;
Previously I spoke, a maiden, but now lie silent,
Bound here by strong fate.
But near to the Nymphs and to this Hermes I lie,
Having below a part in the rule I then had.[7]

Of course, by Pausanias's day, many cities claimed the Sibyl for their own and local Sibylline displays could be seen at a whole variety of locations. The author of the *Cohortatio ad Graecos* claims to have seen the Sibyl's remains stored in a bronze urn within a cave, in contrast to the built tomb that Pausanias visited.[8] The final resting places of famous sacred women, whether real or imaginary, were favorite tourist attractions by the Roman period.

Over the years, excavations have unearthed tombs and grave goods that interpreters have associated with deceased priestesses, though none of these can be identified as such with certainty. In the late nineteenth century, two very rich graves of Geometric date were excavated at Eleusis.[9] These yielded sumptuous funerary gifts, including gold, bronze, and iron finger rings; fancy bracelets; bronze, silver, and iron pins; necklaces of gold, amber, and faience; and many ceramic pots. A faience figurine of the Egyptian goddess Isis and two pairs of gold earrings shaped like crescent moons (one found in each grave) were interpreted by the excavator as insignias of priestly office.[10]

More recently, an enormously rich burial has been found at Aigai, the first capital of Macedonia. The large tomb, one in a cluster of nine others, has been dated to circa 500 B.C. In it, the skeleton of a woman in her early thirties was found, adorned with gold from head to toe.[11] The gold strap diadem that circled her brow would originally have been sewn to fabric, together with a wreath of organic material, now disintegrated. Three gold fistulae further adorned her head, along with gold strap earrings. Her dress was fixed with two great gold pins at the shoulders, two gold fibulae lower down, and gold double pins. The purple fabric of her costume was adorned with gold disks, while gold strips trimmed its edges. At her neck she wore a pyramidal pendant and necklace of large gold-ribbed beads. Her arms were circled with gold bracelets terminating in snake heads and her fingers were ringed with gold and silver. Thirteen repoussé bowls, an abundance of *phialai*, a hydria, an inscribed glass unguentarium, gilded iron spits, an iron model of a wheeled cart, a silver and gold tube (a distaff?), and a hollow silver wand were buried with her. Just to the right of her skeleton were found traces of a wooden scepter, adorned with amber and ivory palmette designs.

The richness of this burial treasure, the libation bowls, cart model, and scepter, have led to the identification of the entombed woman as a priestess.[12] In chapter 4, we considered the precious gold scepter, topped with a green glass fruit, that was reportedly found in a tomb at Taras in South Italy (see fig. 4.1, pl. 6).[13] Here, the gold necklace associated with the scepter shows two horned heads of Hera's priestess, Io (see fig. 4.2, pl. 5). This combination of grave offerings led to its interpretation as a jewelry group belonging to a priestess of Hera. A tomb in south Russia has similarly yielded a treasure of gold. Among the necklaces and finger rings were found gold foil appliqués that show the goddess Demeter holding a torch.[14] These images have led to the suggestion that this grave belonged to a priestess of Demeter. Tempting as it may be to associate these burials with women of priestly status, surviving evidence does not allow us to do so with certainty. Nonetheless, this material gives insight into the lavish levels on which women of status were buried across the Hellenized world. It is consistent with the picture presented in the late Hellenistic and Roman Imperial texts considered at the opening of this chapter, where we learned of gold-drenched corpses of priestesses, dressed in purple and buried with treasure.

In so many ways, the care and extravagance with which these women were buried tells us more about those who buried them than it does about the deceased. In recent years, anthropological and archaeological research has focused on the ways in which burial practices inform us about the motives and identities of the living.[15] It has been shown that cognitive processes, ideological constructs, and political motivations of social groups are revealed through the ways in which they acknowledge and commemorate their dead.[16] In the case of Greek priestesses, their lavish burials inform us about the ways in which Greek culture defined and negotiated issues of gender, status, and wealth.

One cannot underestimate the visual impact of the preparation and movement of the adorned corpses of priestly women in funerary processions from city to cemetery. The lasting memorials for priestesses were not just the grave monuments that marked their tombs, but also the collective memory of the communities that buried them through the highly visible process of ritual.[17] As Sourvinou-Inwood has reminded us, the very word that is used for *grave marker* is *sema*, meaning "sign."[18] So, too, the color purple, gold libation bowls, scepters, and jewelry decorated with images of goddesses were all signs that communicated the identity of the dead and the ways in which the living defined them. Let us, then, look at the signs that commemorated the death of the priestess and the bereavement of those who mourned her.

Classical Funerary Monuments

The Stele of Myrrhine

The earliest surviving funerary monument that commemorates a priestess is the inscribed stele of Myrrhine, priestess of Athena Nike at Athens during the end of the fifth century B.C. (fig. 8.1).[19] Found in the Athenian suburb of Zographos during the 1940s, the marble slab stands nearly a meter in height and preserves an inscription that reads:

> Καλλιμάχο θυγατρὸς τηλαυγὲσ μνῆμα, ἣ πρώτη
> Νίκης ἀμφεπόλευσε νεών. εὐλογίαι δ᾽ ὄνομ᾽ ἔσχε
>   συνέμπορον,
> ὡς ἀπὸ θείας Μυρρίν<η ἐ>κλήθη συντυχίας· ἐτύμωσ
>   πρώτε
> ᾽Αθηναίας Νίκες ἕδος ἀμφεπόλευσεν ἐκ πάντων
>   κλήρωι,
> Μυρρίνη εὐτυχίαι.

> Far-shining memorial of Kallimachos's daughter,
> who was the first to watch over the temple of Nike.
> Her name accompanied her glory, as by divine
> good fortune she was rightly called Myrrhine.
> She was the first to watch over the seat of Athena Nike,
> (chosen) from all the Athenians by a fortunate lot, Myrrhine.[20]

Some scholars have rejected this stele as a memorial to a priestess, since the word *hiereia* does not appear in the text.[21] But the word *hiereia* was used only rarely on classical Attic grave monuments, which, instead, employed visual symbols, including the temple key and *tympanum*, to communicate priestly status. Myrrhine is said to have "watched over" or "served" (*amphepoleuo*) the temple and the precinct of Athena Nike. Surely, the woman charged with "watching over the seat of Athena Nike" should be understood as its priestess.

Importantly, the epitaph celebrates the fact that Myrrhine was given a "far-shining memorial," something that was truly out of the ordinary. Christoph Clairmont attempted to reconstruct the original appearance of Myrrhine's grave monument by associating the stele with a large

Fig. 8.1 (left)
Marble grave stele of Myrrhine, priestess of Athena Nike. Athens, Epigraphical Museum 13132. Photo courtesy Epigraphical Museum, Athens.

Fig. 8.2 (above)
Marble grave stele of Myrrhine, priestess, and Eniaton. Athens, Epigraphical Museum 11081. Photo courtesy Epigraphical Museum, Athens.

marble vase found some three kilometers away near Syntagma Square in central Athens.[22] The sculptured lekythos shows a woman led off by Hermes to the Underworld, moving past three figures. Above the image of the deceased woman the name "Myrrhine" is inscribed in large letters. Although she is shown without a temple key or any other attribute of priestly office, Clairmont maintained that she is the same Myrrhine, priestess of Athena Nike, who was celebrated in the Zographos inscription. He reconstructed a single monument composed of not one, but two, marble lekythoi that would have flanked the inscribed slab.[23] There is no way to prove that the stele and vase belonged together and there is no evidence to suggest that the Myrrhine shown on the lekythos was a priestess. Indeed, Myrrhine was a very popular name in Athens and Clairmont's own catalog of classical Attic grave reliefs lists some twelve other markers that commemorate women of this name.[24]

There is, however, an early fourth-century grave stele that is relevant here. Its surface is plain and very worn. It probably once showed painted images of a priestess named Myrrhine, at left, and a man named Enation, at right, whose names are inscribed above the picture field (fig. 8.2).[25] The inscription reads:

> Μυρρίνη ἱέρεα.
> Ἐνατίων.
>
> Myrrhine priestess.
> Enation.

Enation is a rarely attested male personal name. His relationship to Myrrhine is unclear, but it is likely that he was her husband. The cult of this priestess is not mentioned. We have, then, a second priestess named Myrrhine who served during the early fourth century at Athens. This inscription gives us our earliest surviving example of the word *hiereia* used on a grave marker to identify a woman through her sacred office.

Stelai Showing Women with Temple Keys

The corpus of grave monuments assembled here presents an extraordinary group within the larger body of classical funerary markers that commemorate women. Only rarely was a woman distinguished on her grave monument by some specific reference to an activity that she undertook in life. Funerary stelai that single out women for their "professional" activities are truly exceptional. These monuments generally fall into two categories, those that honor priestesses and those that honor nurses.[26] One-of-a-kind examples may be seen for Sanno, the "good tumbler," buried during the second century B.C., and Menophila, the "actress" whose first-century gravestone was found reused in the Athenian Agora.[27] While actresses, tumblers, and nurses were likely to have been slaves or freedwomen, it was priestesses alone among women of citizen families who were singled out for their public roles on grave markers. This allows some insight into the extraordinary esteem placed upon the holding of sacred office.

To be sure, surviving funerary stelai for priests outnumber those for priestesses by nearly two to one. The present count gives twenty-three grave markers for priests compared with only ten or eleven stelai for priestesses.[28] The gravestone of the priest Simos, dated to about 400

Fig. 8.3
Marble grave stele of the
priest Simos. Athens, National
Archaeological Museum 772.
Photo courtesy Archaeological
Receipts Fund (TAP Service).

B.C., shows the standard iconography of male priesthood: a distinctive costume of long, short-sleeved, ungirded tunic and the knife of sacrifice held in the right hand (fig. 8.3).[29] As the consummate signifier of sacred service, the knife is for priests what the temple key is for priestesses.

Three marble grave reliefs commemorating priestesses and dating to the second quarter of the fourth century B.C. show the same shape, design, and iconographic schemata. Each relief presents a female figure carved within in a recessed picture panel. The names of two of the deceased are preserved; "Polystrate" is carved above the figured panel on a gravestone found in the Athenian Kerameikos (fig. 8.4, pl. 20), while "Choirine" is inscribed on a relief from Eleusis (fig. 8.5).[30] Polystrate's gravestone is crowned with finial decoration of palmettes rising from an acanthus plant, very similar to that which we have seen on the stele of Simos (see fig. 8.3). Choirine's marker shows a smooth arch on which a palmette may have been painted. The third stele,

Fig. 8.4
Marble grave stele of
the priestess Polystrate.
Athens, Kerameikos
Museum I 430. Photo
DAI, neg. D-DAI-ATH-
Kerameikos. All rights
reserved.

Fig. 8.5 (left)
Marble grave stele of the priestess Choirine, from
Eleusis. Geneva: Private Collection.

Fig. 8.6 (above)
Marble grave stele of priestess, from Rhamnous. Athens,
National Archaeological Museum 2309. Photo courtesy
Archaeological Receipts Fund (TAP Service).

discovered at Rhamnous in northern Attica, has suffered a great deal and the crowning moulding that might have held an inscribed name is broken away (fig. 8.6, pl. 21).[31] Each relief shows a
woman holding a temple key, identifying the deceased as a priestess. The Rhamnous priestess
faces to the left and holds her key in her left hand, resting it high against her shoulder. Polystrate
and Choirine face right and hold their keys low in their right hands, raising their left hands in a
fistlike gesture that is commonly seen on Greek votive reliefs showing devotees approaching a
divinity.[32]

There is no indication of which cults these priestesses served. It has long been believed
that Choirine was a priestess of Demeter, since her name is related to the Greek word for piglet
(*choiros*), an animal directly involved in Demeter's rites.[33] The stele's find spot near the sanctuary
at Eleusis would favor this identification. May we presume by extension that the priestess of the
Rhamnous stele served one of the local divinities, Themis or Nemesis?[34] As for the relief from
the Athenian Kerameikos, we cannot know which cult Polystrate served. Her name does not appear among the surviving names for priestesses of Athena Polias. The fact that the stelai give no

Fig. 8.7
Marble funerary lekythos. Athens, National Archaeological Museum 6167. Photo courtesy Archaeological Receipts Fund (TAP Service).

attributes or inscriptions that specify cult may suggest that they were produced and purchased as stock types, only personalized later by added inscriptions. While the reliefs show similar iconographic schemata, the technical workmanship with which they are carved is varied enough to suggest different sculptors and workshops. This may strengthen the case for the existence of a standardized "priestess type" among funerary reliefs, one that could be individualized through added inscriptions. The existence of a stock type would suggest that the singling out of priestesses for commemoration at death may have been even more widespread than the surviving evidence attests.

Marble Lekythoi Showing Women with Temple Keys

During the fourth century, large stone funerary vases in the shape of lekythoi, decorated with figures carved in relief, came into vogue as an alternative form of funerary marker.[35] Two of these show women who can be identified as priestesses, because of their temple keys. The women are portrayed, not as the deceased, but as attending family members within the farewell scene. A lekythos in Athens shows a priestess holding a key up against her shoulder, while she shakes hands with an old man who is seated in a chair (fig. 8.7).[36] Behind him stand two mourning women. Although some scholars identify the priestess as the deceased, established conventions for Attic funerary sculpture would point to the seated male as the one who has died.[37] The priestess can then be regarded as the deceased's wife or some other female relative. While the vase commemorates the death of the man, it memorializes his female relative in her sacred status, thus reflecting the value that Greek society placed on the honor of having a priestess in the family. Men clearly participated in the prestige of sacred status achieved by their women relatives, and as husbands and fathers, they may well have covered some of the expense that priestly office brought with it.

A fragmentary marble lekythos from Rhamnous shows a seated man shaking hands with a male figure who is dressed in the long, ungirded tunic worn by priests.[38] At the far right, a woman dressed in chiton and mantle holds a temple key. The relief seems to show a priest and priestess bidding farewell to the seated man. This lekythos was found along the path in front of the peribolos of Hierokles at Rhamnous. In chapter 5, we noted that Hierokles dedicated a portrait statue of his mother, Aristonoe, priestess of Nemesis at Rhamnous during the third century B.C. (see fig. 5.14).[39] It is likely that Hierokles' family was prominent in the local priestly sphere. The very root of his name means "holy" and his father's name, Hieropoios, is used for magistrates who oversaw temples and sacred rites. Clearly, the marble lekythos found near Hierokles' peribolos signals a family desire to display priestly status. It may well commemorate a man who was head of a household that could boast of both a priest and priestess among its own. This family could have been the same one that, a century later, produced Aristonoe, mother of Hierokles and priestess of Nemesis.

Stelai Showing Women with Tympana

We cannot know with certainty which cults were served by the women shown holding keys on Attic grave markers. The examples collected above could represent priestesses of Athena, Demeter, Nemesis, or Themis. There is no such ambiguity for the women shown holding *tympana* in a series of Attic funerary monuments produced during the fourth century. These women were clearly servants of the great Phrygian Mountain Mother, Kybele, a goddess who revels in "the boom of the kettle-drums and castanets and blazing torches."[40] Two grave reliefs from the Piraeus show women with temple key and *tympanum*, confirming their special status as priestesses of Kybele. We know that at least by the end of the fifth century, there was a shrine of the Mother, the Metroon, in the Athenian Agora as well as two sanctuaries in the Piraeus associated with the goddess.[41] Dating to the fourth century, but possibly even earlier, the Piraeus shrines seem to have served as meeting places for private associations devoted to Kybele's worship.[42]

Fig. 8.8
Marble grave stele of the
priestess Chairestrate.
Piraeus Museum 3627.
Photo courtesy Archaeo-
logical Receipts Fund
(TAP Service).

The stele of Chairestrate gives a number of attributes that confirm her priestly status, further corroborated by the epitaph inscribed above (fig. 8.8, pl. 22).[43] The inscription reads:

[Χαιρεστράτη]
[Μεν]εκρ[άτους]
Ἰ[Ι]καριέως [γυνή].

μητρὸς παντοτέκνου πρόπολος
σεμνή τε γεραιρὰ τῶιδε τάφωι κεῖται
Χαιρεστράτη, ἣν ὁ σύνευνος ἔστερξεν
μὲν ζῶσαν, ἐπένθησεν δὲ θανοῦσαν·
φῶς δ᾽ ἔλιπ᾽ εὐδαίμων παῖδας παίδων ἐπιδοῦσα.

Fig. 8.9 (left)
Marble grave stele of Nikomache. Piraeus Museum 217. Photo DAI, neg. D-DAI-ATH-Grabrelief 665. All rights reserved.

Fig. 8.10 (above)
Marble funerary table. Oxford, Ashmolean Museum 1959.203. Photo courtesy Ashmolean Museum.

Chairestrate wife of Menekrates from Ikaria.

The handmaid and august priestess of the Mother-of-all-things is
buried in this tomb, Chairestrate, whom her husband loved while she
was alive and grieved for when she died. But she left the light blessed
in having seen her children's children.[44]

The grandmother Chairestrate is shown seated with her mantle draped over her shoulders. A
ribbon binds her short-coiffed hair. Although it is difficult to make out, her left hand holds the
end of a temple key that rests against her shoulder and rises up from behind her chair. At right,
a young girl who may represent a cult attendant holds out a large drum.[45] Chairestrate's stele
shows such a variety of priestly indicators that it seems to have been made to order. There is,
however, some possibility that it was adapted to order. The awkwardness with which the temple
key has been carved into the background suggests that it may have been added later to reinforce
Chairestrate's status as priestess.

Nikomache, wife of Eukleies, was remembered with a grave marker set up in the Piraeus
at roughly the same time (fig. 8.9, pl. 23).[46] She is shown as a mature woman seated on a chair, extending her hand out to a younger woman standing before her. In her lap, Nikomache cradles a
large *tympanum*. She wears her hair short and bound with a ribbon, just like the young woman
who bids her farewell. In the young woman's lowered left hand, a short, bar-shaped object can be
made out. The sculptor seems to have carved it as an afterthought or, perhaps, stopped carving before it was completed. It is impossible to say whether this object was intended to represent a key
or some other attribute. While some scholars interpret the younger woman as the deceased, I prefer to see the seated Nikomache, the old priestess of Kybele, as the dead. She may be bidding
farewell and, perhaps, passing on the mantle of priesthood to her young successor.[47] The hand-
shake could connote the legal transference of priesthood from mother to daughter, or simply from
outgoing to incoming priestess.

We are told that the annually appointed priestess of the *orgeones* (private society) in the
Piraeus was charged with making collections for Kybele from among nonmembers.[48] In return
for donations, contributors probably received special privileges allowing them to view the mystery
rites or participate in some of the cult activities. It is possible that Chairestrate and Nikomache
were among the priestesses who took up collections for Kybele and who wished to be commemorated at death for this special service.

A marble funerary table in the Ashmolean Museum shows yet another deceased priestess holding a giant tympanum (fig. 8.10).[49] She sits on a stool beneath which rests a lion, Kybele's
favorite beast. The woman lifts her veil in what is known as the "bridal gesture," looking up at a
man who stands before her, most likely her spouse. A similar image is seen on a marble funerary

base of mid-fourth-century date found in the vicinity of the Dipylon cemetery at Athens (fig. 8.11).[50] The female figure is shown seated on a stool and holding a drum in her lap. Her hair is drawn back in a low roll and bound with a ribbon. On top of the base, a circular cutting may have once held a marble lekythos or, perhaps, a *loutrophoros*, the typical grave marker for young women who died before marriage.[51] That the woman was unmarried at the time of her death may be inferred from the fact that she is shown alone, without husband or other family members whom we might have expected to see, bidding her farewell.

Attica was not unique in celebrating priestesses with grave stelai, as examples from Boiotia and the Peloponnese attest. A fragmentary funeral marker from Thebes, dated to the second half of the fifth century, shows a seated woman holding a drum in her lap, similar to what we have seen for Attic priestesses of Kybele.[52] The slab has suffered a great deal and the upper half of the female figure has broken away, yet enough survives to suggest some connection with the Kybele cult. If so, this stele would provide our earliest surviving image of a Kybele priestess depicted with her *tympanum*.[53]

Stelai Showing a Xoanophoros and a Prophetess

Two reliefs, one from Boiotia and the other from the Peloponnese, commemorate cult servants who were singled out for their specific roles within ritual. The grave relief of Polyxena shows the deceased holding a small statuette, presumably the image of the divinity she served (fig. 8.12).[54] Polyxena probably held the post of *xoanophoros*, the cult agent charged with carrying the deity's statue.[55] In costume, style, and pose, Polyxena's figure strongly resembles that of the statuette she holds. This may be deliberate, in order to underscore the intimacy between divinity and cult servant. It has been suggested that the dowel hole, visible in Polyxena's lowered left hand, may have held a metal attribute, such as a key, though this is wholly speculative.[56]

Dated to the first quarter of the fourth century, the grave stele of Polyxena shows features that depart from conventions established at Athens. The deceased is shown in a full frontal pose, unusual by Attic standards. This gives the figure a monumental quality reminiscent of sculpture in the round.[57] In contrast to Attic priestesses, who are regularly shown dressed in chiton and himation, Polyxena wears a woolen peplos. She has pulled its overfold up over her head from behind to create a veiled effect. While Athenian women customarily left their heads uncovered, this is not the case outside Attica. In Thessaly, women are regularly shown veiled, and in Cyprus, votive statues of women worshippers, including priestesses, always show them wearing their mantles over their heads (see figs. 4.4–6).[58]

A large relief from Mantineia in the central Peloponnese presents a woman in a very specific ritual action: she holds a liver in her hands (fig. 8.13).[59] The woman is clearly engaged

Fig. 8.11 (left)
Marble funerary base. Athens, National Archae-ological Museum 3287. Photo courtesy Archae-ological Receipts Fund (TAP Service).

Fig. 8.12 (bottom left)
Marble funerary relief of Polyxena, from Thessaly. Berlin, Staatliche Museen Antiken-sammlung SK 1504. Photo Antikensammlung, Staatliche Museen zu Berlin, Preussicher Kulturbesitz.

Fig. 8.13 (bottom right)
Marble funerary relief, from Mantineia. Athens, National Archaeological Museum 226. Photo Gösta Hellner, DAI, neg. D-DAI-ATH-NM 5912. All rights reserved.

in the act of haruspicy, that is, divination through the reading of animal entrails.[60] The presence of the palm tree in the background evokes the god Apollo and his oracular powers. This relief was found not in a cemetery but within the agora of Mantineia, between the south retaining wall of the theater and the back wall of a temple. This unusual location has led some to believe that it served as a votive relief rather than a funerary marker.[61] Indeed, Pausanias tells us that he encountered many votive tributes in marketplaces throughout the Peloponnese.[62] The stele finds its strongest parallels, however, not in votive art but in funerary sculpture, where it is comparable in terms of size and the high relief of its carving. Cuttings on the sides of the slab may suggest that it was repositioned at some point. It is possible that the relief was moved from an original fourth-century location in a cemetery to its ultimate find spot in the Mantineian agora.[63]

Perhaps the stele was moved so that a very special prophetess could receive public honors. Interpreters have been unable to resist associating this memorial with the famous female prophet of Mantineia, Diotima.[64] The wise and thoughtful priestess, whose teachings on the subject of love were recounted by Sokrates in Plato's *Symposium* (lines 173–209), would be appropriately honored with such an impressive stele in her city's marketplace. This interpretation is entirely conjectural. Many scholars dismiss the very existence of a historical Diotima and view her character as a literary fiction devised by Plato. Nonetheless, the relief from Mantineia stands on its own as an important testament to the role of women in divination and the high value that communities placed on the special agency of these women.

Hellenistic Grave Markers

Over the course of the fourth century, funerary monuments at Athens and elsewhere grew in size and grandeur. Sumptuous *naiskoi* became virtual shrines that housed life-size statues of the deceased, regularly shown with images of family members. This ostentation did not sit well with Demetrios of Phaleron, who came to power as Kassander's handpicked overseer at Athens in 317 B.C. Following the unsuccessful revolt of the Athenians against Macedonian rule after Alexander's death in 323, Antipater installed a garrison of soldiers at the Piraeus.[65] When Antipater died in 319, it fell to his son, Kassander, to appoint a representative to oversee Macedonian interests. He chose Demetrios of Phaleron, described as the most philosophical of all men to ever govern Athens. Demetrios is reported to have studied with both Aristotle and Theophrastos and to have maintained a lifelong interest in learning and writing.

During his years of rule (317–307/306 B.C.), Demetrios introduced significant changes, among them legislation to reduce the extravagance of funerals and tomb monuments.[66] Cicero (*De Legibus* 2.66) records the limits laid down by Demetrios, whom he greatly admired as "eminent in learning" and "a very able citizen in the practical administration and maintenance of government."[67] Demetrios first prohibited burial rites from taking place during the day, restricting them to the hours before dawn. This limited the opportunity for public display of wealth by the city's elite, allowing no individual or group to appear superior to others. He also limited the number of participants who could attend private funerals, weddings, and sacrifices, again restricting the scale on which privileged families could celebrate life's big occasions.

Demetrios established a new group of governmental officials called *gynaikonomoi*, which literally means "supervisors of the women," though we understand that their responsibilities embraced much broader issues than women's conduct alone.[68] These officials oversaw male behavior as well, controlling the number and comportment of men at funerals, marriages, and sacrifices. Athenaeus tells us that the number of men participating at symposia was limited to thirty and that the *gynaikonomoi* actually went around counting heads.[69] Central to Demetrios's innovations was the desire to control what had become large-scale female participation in mourning rituals at funerals and, presumably, their collective display at other events as well. The perceived need for institutional control over these activities suggests that the visibility of women at public events in Athens had become quite extensive by the late fourth century.

Fig. 8.14 (far left)
Marble funerary column of the priestess Habryllis. Athens, National Archaeological Museum 1727. Photo courtesy Archaeological Receipts Fund (TAP Service).

Fig. 8.15 (left)
Marble funerary column of Mneso. Athens, Epigraphical Museum 11144. Photo courtesy Epigraphical Museum, Athens.

Kioniskoi

Among Demetrios's new guidelines were regulations limiting the amount of money that could be spent on funerary monuments. Only three types of memorials would be permitted: the column, the table, and the basin. Of special interest to us are the marble columns, or *kioniskoi*, that were legislated by Demetrios to stand no more than three cubits high.[70] These cylindrical shafts of marble were finished on top with a ring-shaped torus moulding and left unfinished below for insertion into a base (figs. 8.14–17; pl. 24). Actual funerary wreaths were probably laid atop these columns, encircling the shaft and resting on the crowning moulding.

Five Attic *kioniskoi*, dating from the second and first centuries B.C., are known to have commemorated priestesses. Each of these bears an inscription that conforms to a standard formula giving the personal name of the deceased, the name of her father or husband, and the name of his deme. Accordingly, the word "daughter" or "wife" is inscribed where relevant. The all-important temple key, sometimes adorned with broad ribbons, is carved in low relief just beneath the inscribed text.

The earliest of these, the funerary column of Gorgo, has been dated to about 300 B.C., shortly after Demetrios's regulations went into effect.[71] It reads:

Γοργὼ
Φίλωνος Πορίου
θυγάτηρ.

Gorgo daughter of Philon of Poros.

A temple key is carved in low relief just beneath the inscription.

Perhaps the best known of the priestesses who were commemorated with a funerary column is Habryllis, daughter of Mikion, whom we have discussed in chapter 3. Having been long regarded as a priestess of Athena Polias, she is now understood to have served as priestess of Demeter and Kore sometime around 150–130 B.C.[72] Not only did Habryllis come from a very distinguished Athenian family, she made a significant marriage and, as the wife of Kichesias, entered into another great household and its fortunes. Her funerary column was found just north of the Acropolis in 1877 (fig. 8.14).[73] Its inscription reads:

Ἁβρυλλὶς
Μικίωνος
Κηφιέως
θυγάτηρ.

Habryllis daughter of Mikion of Kephisia.

Beneath the text, a temple key with broad ribbons draped at its angles is carved in relief.

A funerary column belonging to Mneso can be dated to the late second or early first century B.C. It shows a simple key decorated with small ribbon (fig. 8.15, pl. 24).[74] An inscription carved above it reads:

Μνησὼ
Κριτοδήμου
Θορικίου
θυγάτηρ,
Ἀσκληπιάδου
Βερενικίδου.

Mneso, daughter of Kritodemos of Thorikos,
wife of Asklepiades of Berenikidou.

Although we know little about Mneso herself, we know that she had a daughter of the same name who apparently served as *ergastine* in 78/77 B.C.[75] Because Mneso's marker shows a key and a ribbon together, just like the column of Habryllis, Sara Aleshire identified Mneso as a priestess of Athena Polias. She maintained that the specific combination of key and ribbon signified the priesthood of Athena Polias.[76] In light of the change in our understanding of Habryllis as priestess of Demeter and Kore, Aleshire's correlation of ribboned key and the priesthood of Athena Polias should be set aside.

Two additional grave columns honoring priestesses of Hellenistic Athens give us the names Theophile and Malthake. Alexander Mantis placed these names, along with Gorgo, Habryllis, and Mneso, in the list of known priestesses of Athena Polias.[77] Aleshire, however, rejected Gorgo, Theophile, and Malthake, since, according to her view, their markers showed a key but no ribbons.[78] Let us look further at the evidence.

The funerary column of Malthake has been dated to the second century B.C. and, indeed, shows a temple key without ribbons (fig. 8.16).[79] Above the key, an inscription reads:

Μαλθά[κη - - -]
Ἁγνου[σίου θυγάτηρ],
Θεοξένου [- - -γυ]νή.

Malthake, [daughter of - - -] of Hagnous,
wife of Theoxenos of the deme [- - -].

Fig. 8.16 (far left)
Marble funerary column of
Malthake. Athens, Epigraphical
Museum 11614. Photo courtesy
Epigraphical Museum, Athens.

Fig. 8.17 (left)
Marble funerary column
of Theophile. Athens,
Epigraphical Museum 11183.
Photo courtesy Epigraphical
Museum, Athens.

The very latest example in our group, the column of Theophile, has been dated to the first century B.C. (fig. 8.17).[80] It shows a temple key and atop it, the barest outline of a ribbon can be discerned, not visible in photographs, but only to the naked eye. Just above the key an inscription identifies the priestess:

Θεοφίλη
Φανοδίκου
Ῥαμνουσίου
θυγάτηρ.

Theophile, daughter of Phanodikos of Rhamnous.

Aleshire did not see the ribbon and thus excluded Theophile from her list of priestesses of Athena Polias. But now, thanks to our new understanding of Habryllis, we know that there is no particular code linking key plus ribbons to Athena's priesthood. We simply cannot know from the available information which cult Theophile served.

Fig. 8.18
Funerary altar of Theomnasta. Thebes, Thebes
Museum *IG* VII 2021. Photo J. B. Connelly.

Funerary Altars

Temple keys are seen on Hellenistic funerary monuments outside Athens at Thebes, Thespiai, and Argos. A second-century-B.C. grave marker for a priestess of Hera at Argos shows the outline of a key together with a scepter.[81] We have seen this same combination of signifiers in chapter 3 when we considered the Boston hydria that shows Hera, or her priestess, with scepter and temple key (see fig. 3.3).

It is in Boiotia that we find the largest corpus of non-Attic grave markers displaying keys.[82] Here we see the second category of monuments allowed under Demetrios's legislation: the funerary altar. These altars take the form of great blocks of white marble or limestone, measuring roughly a meter on each side. They are decorated on the front face with signifiers of priesthood, temple key and wreath, and are inscribed with the name of the sacred servant. Some of these also show *kantharoi*, drinking cups favored by Dionysos, which, together with the ivy wreaths, indicate that the monuments commemorated servants of Dionysos. Of course, the worship of Dionysos was very much at home in Thebes, where the daughters of King Kadmos first embraced the god and promulgated his cult.

Four surviving funerary altars give female names. "Euphantis" is carved, together with a temple key, on an altar from Thebes.[83] A marker from nearby Thespiai preserves the name "Theomnasta" and shows a temple key and an ivy crown carved below the name (fig. 8.18, pl. 25).[84] Another funerary altar from Thespiai gives the name "Sostrate," above which can be seen a temple key.[85] A third altar from Thespiai shows a temple key, but its inscription is no longer legible.[86] The practice of showing temple keys on grave markers continued well into the Roman Imperial period at Thebes, as a marble stele inscribed for Noumenis attests.[87] Her name is inscribed along with her title, "priestess of Demeter," giving us a rare example of the word *hiereia* on a funerary monument. We have not seen this since the early fourth-century Attic grave marker of the priestess Myrrhine, discussed above.

Demetrios's antiluxury legislation served to codify the temple key as an efficient and clear signifier that could stand on its own to communicate the status of priesthood. The preeminence of the key as the symbol for feminine priesthood can thus be seen to endure from the fifth century B.C. right into the Roman period.

Funerary Reliefs of Asia Minor

Demetrios's measures against conspicuous grave monuments at Athens were highly effective, as the absence of sculptured relief markers of Hellenistic date attests. What Athens missed was made up for on the other side of the Mediterranean, where proliferation in figured funerary stelai occurred during the last three centuries B.C. The sculptured grave reliefs of Asia Minor and the islands off its coast are impressive in their quantity, sculptural quality, and adherence to well-defined types.[88] They give us insight into the values, ideals, and enterprises of the local societies that produced them. East Greek grave reliefs conform to established conventions through which the monuments are conceived as architectural frameworks resembling *naiskoi*, with pilasters, attics, and pediments. The deceased is shown standing statuelike within this architectural space (figs. 8.19–20). This is perhaps not surprising for a time when honorific and votive statuary filled cities and sanctuaries with portraits of individuals who were celebrated for their civic and religious contributions. Surely, these same individuals wished to be remembered at death for the prestige and prominence that they enjoyed in life. The deceased are regularly shown accompanied by servants, usually a pair of boys for men and two serving girls for women. There is no interaction between the deceased and their servants; instead, the honored individual stands cold and statuelike, detached from his or her surrounding environment.

Fig. 8.19 (opposite)
Marble funerary relief from Smyrna. Berlin, Staatliche Museen Antikensammlung SK 767. Photo Bildarchiv Preussischer Kulturbesitz/Art Resource, NY.

Fig. 8.20 (left)
Marble funerary relief. Oxford, Ashmolean Museum, Michaelis 149. Photo courtesy Ashmolean Museum, Oxford.

Fig. 8.21 (right)
Marble funerary relief of Akesteime. Oxford, Ashmolean Museum, Michaelis 150. Photo courtesy Ashmolean Museum, Oxford.

The majority of East Greek reliefs date to the second and first centuries B.C., a period in which public display of prosperity, patronage, and finery was widespread among free citizens. Scores of funerary monuments manifesting this desire for display survive from Kyzikos, Pergamon, Smyrna, Odessos, and Phrygia, as well as from the islands of Lesbos, Chios, Samos, Kos, and Rhodes.[89]

At Smyrna, a dozen of some 140 surviving grave reliefs commemorate women who served as priestesses of Demeter and Kore.[90] One of these, now in Berlin, stands more than a meter and a half in height. It constitutes an elaborate architectural construction complete with Corinthian columns, molded entablature, and decorated attic and pediment (fig. 8.19).[91] A wreath in the attic zone indicates that the dead priestess had been honored by her city. She is portrayed in high relief within the *naiskos*, draped in a diaphanous mantle that crisscrosses her chiton, winding round in a broad roll that stretches from hip to hip. The priestess holds her right hand up in a gesture of prayer. Beside her, two diminutive serving girls carry cult attributes: a huge torch is held by the girl at left and a little jug by the servant at right. The torch signifies the cult of Demeter and, together with the crown and the gesture of prayer, communicates that the deceased was a publicly honored priestess. The horn of plenty carved in the background may be a reference to the woman's special generosity as a benefactress of her city.[92]

Apollonis, daughter of Kephisophon, was honored with a similar grave monument, now in Oxford (fig. 8.20).[93] The round-faced priestess raises her right hand to touch a large torch held by a serving girl. At right, a smaller girl holds a ritual vessel. The priestess wears a familiar costume, with the himation twisted in a broad roll that is stretched horizontally across her waist, from which an apronlike flap falls atop her double chiton. The attic zone shows a large wreath with the words Ο ΔΗΜΟΣ, once again communicating that the priestess had received public honors from the People.

The gulf between such impersonal stock figures on grave monuments and the highly personal funerary epitaphs carved upon them has been recognized by several scholars.[94] This apparent disconnect in part results from the mass production of funerary markers, personalized only later by the addition of inscriptions. The grave reliefs from Smyrna are very short on words. But we can glean some individual sentiment for one Hellenistic priestess of Demeter from an epigram attributed to Diotimos.[95] Although we do not know from where the text comes, it vividly evokes the image of two elderly twin priestesses who, apparently, died at the same time:

Αἱ νόμιμοι δύο γρῆες ὁμήλικες ἦμεν, Ἀναξω
καὶ Κληνώ, δίδυμοι παῖδες Ἐπικράτεος, Κληνὼ μὲν
Χαρίτων ἱερή, Δήμητρι δ᾽ Ἀναξὼ ἐν ζωῇ προπολεῦσ᾽·
ἐννέα δ᾽ ἠελίων ὀγδωκονταέτεις ἐπιλείπομεν ἐς τόδ᾽
ἱκέσθαι τῆς μοίρης· ἐτέων δ᾽ οὐ φθόνος, οἷς ὁσίη. καὶ
πόσιας καὶ τέκνα φιλήσαμεν· αἱ δὲ παλαιαὶ πρῶθ᾽ ἡμεῖς
Ἀίδην πρηΰν ἀνυσσάμεθα.

We two old women Anaxo and Kleno the twin daughters of Epikrates were ever together; Kleno was in life the priestess of the Graces and Anaxo served Demeter. We wanted nine days to complete our eightieth year. . . . We loved our husbands and children, and we, the old women, won gentle death before them.[96]

Arkesteime, daughter of Demagoros and wife of Artemidoros, apparently served as priestess of Kybele at Smyrna during the first half of the second century B.C. (fig. 8.21).[97] Her grave monument, now in Oxford, shows her seated on a throne just like Kybele. Arkesteime is attended by two servants: the girl at left carries a box, no doubt for jewelry, and the girl at right holds what appears to be a fan or spindle. In the upper-right corner hangs a kettledrum, and at left, two cymbals or bells can be seen, favorite instruments of the percussion-loving goddess. A bearded snake appears in the background at right, a chthonic symbol evoking the underworld into which Arkesteime has passed.

Again, the stone is silent. But a funerary epigram, composed by Kallimachos and preserved in the *Greek Anthology* celebrates an unnamed priestess of Kybele and the cults of Demeter and the Kabiri.[98] Its words fill in some of the sentiment lacking in the grave relief and give insight into the cursus of priestly office that such a woman may have followed in life. The series of sacred roles that she held brought fulfillment and serenity to the old priestess:

Ἱερέη Δήμητρος ἐγώ ποτε καὶ πάλιν Καβείρων,
ὦνερ, καὶ μετέπειτα Δινδυμήνης
ἡ γρηῦς γενόμην, ἡ νῦν κόνις, ἡ νο . . .
πολλῶν προστασίη νέων γυναικῶν.
καί μοι τέκν᾽ ἐγένοντο δύ᾽ ἄρσενα, κἠπέμυσα κείνων
εὐγήρως ἐνὶ χερσίν. ἕρπε χαίρων.

I, the old woman who am now dust was once the priestess of Demeter and again of the Kabiri and afterwards of Kybele. I was patroness of many young women. I had two male children and closed my eyes at a goodly old age in their arms. Go in peace.[99]

Of particular interest here is the priestess's claim that she served as "patroness" of many young women. This is likely to refer to a role as an advisor or counselor to young women concerning marriage and family life.[100] The wise old priestess thus provided important help in the education and preparation of young women for their domestic roles.

Isias of Laodikea, daughter of Metrodoros, apparently served as priestess of Isis at Smyrna at the beginning of the second century B.C. She is shown on her grave monument with a sweet youthful face and long flowing locks that imitate those of Isis (fig. 8.22).[101] Isias is dressed in the distinctive costume of the goddess, with its characteristic fringed mantle tied in an "Isis knot." In her right hand, she holds a music maker, the sistrum, and in her left a situla, a vessel used to pour libations of water or milk in Egyptian funerary cults.[102] The tree at left places the scene in the rustic outdoors, a favorite setting frequently depicted in Hellenistic relief sculpture.

Fig. 8.22
Marble funerary relief of Isias, from
Smyrna. London, British Museum 639.
Photo © Copyright the Trustees of The
British Museum.

Up above, an olive wreath is carved in low relief around the inscribed words Ο ΔΗΜΟΣ, communicating that the people of Smyrna voted to award Isias a crown. The image of Isias reflects a
prototype that will be used for scores of grave markers depicting initiates in the cult of Isis
throughout the Roman period.[103]

No monument gives greater insight into the esteem in which priestesses were held than
does the grave stele set up for Menophila at the end of the second century B.C. at Sardis (fig. 8.23;
pl. 27).[104] Rarely has a work of art spelled out so explicitly the meaning of the signs and symbols
it employs to communicate meaning. We see a heavily draped Menophila, standing statuelike in
a contemplative pose, flanked in the conventional manner by two servant girls. On a high shelf in
the background three attributes are displayed: a basket, a book, and a lily. Just to the left of
Menophila, the letter "A" is deeply incised into the background. In the pediment we see an olive
wreath. A long epigram inscribed below provides a road map to guide the viewer through the
iconographic sign posts:

Ὁ δῆμος Μηνοφίλαν Ἑρμαγένον
κομψὰν καὶ χαρίεσσα πέτρος δείκνυσι· τίς ἐντι
μουσῶν μανύει γράμματα, Μηνοφίλαν.
Τεῦ δ' ἕνεκ' ἐν στάλα γλυπτὸν ἠδὲ καὶ ἄλφα
βύβλος καὶ τάλαρος τοῖς δ' ἔ<π>ι καὶ στέφανος; --
ἡ σοφία μὲν βίβλος, ὁ δ' αὖ περι κρατὶ φορηθεὶς
ἀρχὰν μανύει μουνόγοναν δὲ τὸ ἕν,
εὐτάκτου δ' ἀρετᾶς τάλαρος μάνυμα, τὸ δ' ἄνθος
τὰν ἀκμὰν δαίμον ἀντιν' ἐληλῖσατο.
κού[φ]α τοι κόνις εἰμὶ· πολλοὶ τοιῇδε θανούσῃ
ᾷ γά[μ]οι οὐδὲ γονεῖς, τοῖς ἔλιπες δάκρυα.

This gracious stone shows a fine woman. Who is she? The letters of the Muses inform us: Menophila. Why then is this white lily and the "one" (*alpha*) carved on the stele? Why the book, the wool basket, and the wreath above? The book is for her intelligence. The wreath tells of her public office (a priestess). The "one" tells she is an only child. The basket is the sign of her well-ordered virtue. The flower is for the bloom that a daimon stole away. Lightly does the dust hover over a person like you, though dead. But woe, without child are your parents, to whom you have left tears.[105]

This poignant farewell resonates on several levels. We are told that the book symbolizes the intelligence of Menophila. Indeed, we are not accustomed to hearing Greek women celebrated for their intellectual strengths. May we infer from the book that Menophila was capable of reading? The wreath, as the inscription tells us, represents her public office. We are told that the wool basket is a signifier of her well-ordered virtue. We have seen the wool basket employed from classical Attic vase painting on, not just as an emblem of domestic virtue, but also as the quintessential marker of femininity (see fig. 2.1).[106] Without the guidance of the epitaph, we might not have guessed that the sculptured lily indicates Menophila's beauty. This extraordinary monument expresses what the people of Sardis valued most about Menophila: her mind, her virtue, her beauty, and her role as public-office holder. Menophila appears to have died young, without husband or children and survived only by her parents.

The grave reliefs of Asia Minor brilliantly attest to the longevity of the practice of honoring priestesses at death. The temple key, the primary iconographic signifier of feminine priesthood on the Greek mainland, is not found in the East Greek repertory. Instead, it is divine at-

Fig. 8.23
Marble funerary relief of Menophila,
from Sardis. Istanbul, Archaeological
Museum I 4033. Photo Turhan Birgili.

tributes, the wreath, and inscriptions that confirm priestly status for East Greek women. Priestesses of Demeter at Smyrna are shown attended by serving girls who carry the great torch of Demeter. Arkesteime, priestess of Kybele, is shown enthroned like the goddess and flanked by Kybele's favorite music makers: drum and cymbals. Isias, priestess of Isis, wears the fringed mantle of the goddess and holds sistrum and situla, instruments of Egyptian ritual. Thus, cult agents are identified through the attributes of the divinities they served. It is the wreath, however, and the words Ο ΔΗΜΟΣ that confirm public office and public recognition for these women at death.

Public Burial

Asia Minor also gives us a valuable corpus of evidence for the burial of priestesses at public expense. An inscription from Magnesia documents the burial of three maenads who had been imported from Thebes to oversee the local Dionysos cult. The proclamation, carved on a marble stele, is a Roman copy of a Hellenistic document recording a Delphic oracle dated to circa

278–250 B.C.[107] The first part of the inscription, written in hexameters, quotes the oracle itself. In it, the Magnesians are instructed to go to Thebes and bring back maenads directly descended from the legendary daughters of King Kadmos. These women are to introduce maenadic rites at Magnesia and to establish local Dionysiac *thiasoi*.

The second part of the inscription gives a prose postscript, documenting that this oracle was fulfilled:

> . . . ἐλθέτε δὲ ἐς
> Θήβης ἱερὸν πέδον, ὄφρα λάβητε
> Μαινάδας, αἵ γενεῆς Εἰνοῦς ἄπο Κα
> δμηείης· αἵ δ' ὑμῖν δώσουσι καὶ
> ὄργια καὶ νόμιμα ἐσθλὰ καὶ
> θιάσους Βάκχοιο καθειδρύσουσιν
> ἐν ἄστει. κατὰ τὸν χρησμὸν διὰ
> τῶν θεοπρόπων ἐδόθησαν ἐκ Θηβῶν
> Μαινάδες τρεῖς Κοσκὼ Βαυβὼ
> Θετταλή, καὶ ἡ μὲν Κοσκὼ συνήγαγεν
> θίασον τὸν Πλατανιστηνῶν,
> ἡ δὲ Βαυβὼ τὸν πρὸ πόλεως, ἡ δὲ
> Θετταλή τὸν τῶν Καταιβατῶν·
> θανοῦσαι δὲ αὗται ἐτάφησαν
> ὑπὸ Μαγνήτων, καὶ ἡ μὲν Κοσκὼ
> κεῖται ἐν Κοσκωβούνῳ, ἡ δὲ Βαυ
> βὼ ἐν Ταβάρνει, ἡ δὲ Θετταλή
> πρὸς τῷ θεάτρῳ.

In accordance with the oracle, and through the agency of the envoys, three maenads were brought from Thebes: Kosko, Baubo, and Thettale. And Kosko organized the *thiasos* named after the plane tree, Baubo the thiasos outside the city, and Thettale the thiasos named after Kataibates. After their death they were buried by the Magnesians, and Kosko lies buried in the area called Hillock of Kosko, Baubo in the area called Tabarnis, and Thettale near the Theater.[108]

Albert Henrichs's thoughtful study of this inscription has underscored its significance as a central document for cultic maenadism during the Hellenistic period. He has shown that the maenads come as a threesome by no accident. They are clearly modeled on the mythical example of the daughters of Kadmos of Thebes: Ino, Autonoe, and Agave.[109] Their claim of direct descent from Ino demonstrates the importance of ancestry in the acquisition of priesthoods. A bloodline that could be traced to the first female followers of Dionysos would be the best possible pedigree for a professional maenad. The establishment of a local cult with such a direct link to the origins of worship would give the Magnesian *thiasoi* authenticity and authority. The Magnesians took responsibility for burying their imported maenads, carefully choosing an appropriate resting place for each. None was buried in the city cemetery, but instead, the maenads were interred at locations closely associated with their life activities. Kosko was buried on a hill for which she became the eponym, a hill no doubt in the vicinity of the plane trees for which her *thiasos* was named. Baubo's resting place in the area called Tabarnis was probably well outside the city and near the place where her revel band gathered. Thettale was buried near the theater, home to Dionysos himself. Henrichs is, no doubt, correct in imagining that the graves of the maenads would have been marked with impressive monuments reminding the Magnesians of their special service to the city.

To the south of Magnesia, at Miletos, another maenad was honored for her service during the third or second century B.C. The inscribed stele of Alkmeonis calls on the local Bacchai to say farewell to their leader, for "this is what a good woman deserves."[110] "Should some stranger ask for her name," the epitaph continues, "it is Alkmeonis daughter of Rhodios who knew her share of the blessings." Evidence for women in the service of Dionysos continues to emerge, as can be seen in the newly discovered epigram of Posidippos that gives testimony to "Niko, the servant of Dionysos who died in the Bacchic mountains."[111]

These women were clearly revered by their communities, and as epigraphic evidence attests, in some cases they were buried by the citizenry in what appear to have been public funerary rites. A remarkable document from Pednelissos near Perge on the southern coast of Turkey spells out in detail directions for the funeral of a priestess named Galato during the first century B.C.[112] The text is fragmentary, but this much is clear: Upon Galato's death, the city would have to choose a successor by lottery from ten candidates. After the new priestess was confirmed, she would be required to give a piglet for a sacrifice to the dead Galato. Presumably, this would enable the new priestess to "purify" her deceased predecessor. Once this was done, all the other priestesses gathered together for the funeral would be required to dress in black and make sure nothing dirty touched Galato's corpse. The fact that Galato's succession and funeral arrangements were provided for in a public document is highly significant. Indeed, there is no mention of her family's role in the burial, and from all appearances, hers would seem to be a thoroughly public funeral.

Inscriptions from Asia Minor thus provide us with an intimate view of the preparation of a priestess for burial: purification of her corpse, funerary sacrifice, selection of final resting place, and setting up of grave monuments. Best of all, we hear the sentiment behind these memorials: "for this is what a good woman deserves."[113] These documents give us an inside look at the process of death, from the loving preparation of the corpse, to sacrifice and purification, to burial and memorial, to plans for succession. It is through ritual that this process is orchestrated and negotiated, and through which the community comes to grips with a passing that belongs not just to the dead but also to the city itself.[114]

By the late Hellenistic and Roman Imperial period, we have full public burials for women of prestige. Although it is late in date, let us conclude our survey with the breathtaking account of Berenikes' public funeral in second/third-century A.D. Syros. Berenike held not only the local priesthood of Demeter and Kore but also the civic office of *archeine*, female counterpart of the eponymous archon.[115] A civic resolution, approved by each branch of her local government, granted her a gold crown and public proclamation at her funeral.[116] It reads:

ἔδοξε[ν] τῇ βουλῇ καὶ τῷ δήμῳ, πρυτάνεως γνώμῃ·
ἐπεὶ Βερνείκη Νεικομάχου, γυνὴ δὲ Ἀριστοκλέους τοῦ
    Εἰσιδώ
ρου, ἀγαθήν τε καὶ εὐσχήμοναν τὴν ἀναστροφὴν
    πεπόηται
ἐν πᾶσιν, ἀρχείνη τε γενομένη ἐκ τῶν ἰδίων ἀφιδῶς
    ἐπετέ
λεσεν καὶ θεοῖς καὶ ἀνθρώποις ὑπὲρ τῆς πατρίδος,
    εἰέρειά τε
κατασταθεῖσα τῶν οὐρανίων θεῶν Δήμητρος καὶ
    Κόρης τῶν
σεμνοτάτων ἁγνῶς καὶ ἀξίως τῶν θεῶν καὶ τῆς
    πόλεως
εἰερ[α]τεύσασα μετήλλαξεν τὸν βίον, ἣ καὶ
    τεκνοτροφήσα
σα· δι᾽ ἃ δὴ δοκεῖ τῇ βουλῇ καὶ τῷ δήμῳ· προεπαινέσαι
    μὲν
τῆς γυναικὸς τὸν προβεβιωκότα χρόνον, στεφανῶσαί
    τε αὐ

τὴν χρυσῷ στεφάνῳ ᾧ πάτριόν ἐστιν ἡμεῖν στεφανοῖν
τὰς ἀγαθὰς τῶν γυναικῶν· ὁ δὲ γράφων ἡμεῖν ἀναγο
ρευσάτω ὑπὸ τὴν ἐκκομιδὴν τῆς γυναικὸς ὅτι "στεφα
νοῖ ὁ δῆμος ὁ Συρίων Βερνείκην Νεικομάχου χρυσῷ
στε φάνῳ ἀρετῆς ἕνεκα καὶ εὐνοίας τῆς εἰς αὐτήν.

The resolution of the prytaneis approved by the Council and the People:

Whereas Berenike, daughter of Nikomachos, wife of Aristocles son of Isidoros, has conducted herself well and appropriately on all occasions, and after she was made a magistrate, unsparingly celebrated rites at her own expense for gods and men on behalf of her native city, and after she was made priestess of the heavenly goddesses Demeter and Kore the most holy and celebrated their rites in a holy and worthy manner, has given up her life—meanwhile she had also raised her own children. Voted to commend the span of this woman's lifetime, to crown her with the gold wreath which in our fatherland is customarily used to crown good women. Let the man who proposed this resolution announce at her burial: "The people of Syros crown Berenike daughter of Nikomachos with a gold crown in recognition of her virtue and her good will towards them."[117]

Berenike is honored for her extraordinary record of public service, as an *archeine* who spent her own funds on behalf of her city, and as a priestess who fulfilled her duties in a holy manner worthy of the goddesses. Berenike is further applauded for her success in raising her children. She clearly attained a central role within civic, religious, and philanthropic orbits of her city. Having managed a successful public career as well as family life, Berenike was celebrated at death by all of Syros. No firmer evidence is needed to show that the burial of a woman could, at least by the Imperial period, be a great public occasion.

CHAPTER 9

The End of the Line
The Coming of Christianity

We are told that in the year A.D. 439, on the evening of December 31, a zealous holy woman known as Melania the Younger breathed out her last in the monastery that she had founded upon the Mount of Olives in Jerusalem. She is said to have been fifty-four years of age when she died, having lived an extraordinary life, from her youth in Rome as a beautiful aristocrat of distinguished wealth and pedigree, to her quiet death as a Christian celibate who had given away her fortune; freed some eight thousand slaves; traveled across the Mediterranean; and built monasteries, a chapel, and a martyrion on the site of the resurrection of Jesus.[1] Her distinguished birth, riches, and impressive social network, which embraced the most potent royal, political, and religious leaders of her day, placed Melania in a position not so very different from that of the influential Greek priestesses of the late Hellenistic and Roman East. Melania's role as patroness of an extensive building program on the Mount of Olives, and as the foundress of two large monasteries, similarly established her as an initiator of bricks-and-mortar constructions at the very center of her chosen world.

Nothing, however, could be more different from the experience of the Greek priestess than the circumstances of Melania's death, which are recorded in a tenth-century Latin codex discovered in 1884 in the Escurial Library in Madrid. As if this discovery were not remarkable enough, a Greek version of the *Life of Melania the Younger* was found in 1900 in the Barberini Library in Rome.[2] Both texts are based on a Greek original, probably written in A.D. 452 or 453 by Gerontius, a monk in Melania's monastery. Upon Melania's death, Gerontius became its director, a position that he held for some forty-five years.[3] He was present when Melania died and gives us a firsthand account of the preparation of her corpse.

> Her burial garments were worthy of her holiness. . . . She had the
> tunic of a certain saint, the veil of another servant of God, another
> garment without sleeves, the belt of another which she had worn

while she was alive, and the hood of another. Instead of a pillow, she
had a hood made from the hair of another saint, which we made into
a cushion and placed under her honored head. . . . She had no burial
cloth, except the linen with which we wrapped her from without.[4]

This is a far cry from the lavish funerals for Greek priestesses, state events in which the bodies of
the deceased were draped in expensive purple and carried through the streets in public funerary
processions. Instead, we see a small group of monastic virgins dressing the body of Melania in
relics, fashioning the hair of a saint into a pillow for her head. No pomp, no pageantry, no public
memorial, but instead, a quiet, modest interment for a woman who gave so much to so many.

Indeed, Melania had a great deal to give. Not only was she born into the immensely affluent clan of the Valerii at Rome, but she married into another branch of the same family.
Thus, a double fortune was compounded into a treasury of riches. When Melania and her husband, Valerius Pinianus, vowed themselves to a life of poverty, so grand was their house in
Rome that no one could afford to buy it. They owned properties throughout the Roman Empire, in Italy (Rome, Sicily, Campania), Spain, Britain, Aquitania, Gaul, Africa, Mauretania, and
Numidia.[5] Their combined family was replete with illustrious public-office holders and attests
to the potent political influence that accompanied their wealth.[6] In this, Melania's pedigree resembles that of the well-connected, affluent priestesses whom we have met throughout the
course of this study.

But Melania's world knew divisions of faith that would have been unthinkable in the
Greek past. Now, some four centuries after the birth of Christ, families often included some
members who embraced Christianity and others who retained a traditional worship of gods and
goddesses. This mixing of faiths within families was a widespread phenomenon in late antiquity
and is particularly well documented among the aristocracy.[7] While Melania's mother, father, and
grandmothers were Christians, one of her uncles, a great-uncle, and a great-grandmother worshipped the Roman pantheon. Indeed, her distinguished great-uncle, Publius Caeionius Caecina
Albinus, served as pontifex, one in the elite college of priests at Rome.[8]

Of great interest are the female role models that influenced the young Melania. A great-
grandmother on her mother's side, Caecina Lolliana, served as priestess of Isis.[9] On her father's
side, her grandmother Melania the Elder was a distinguished Christian ascetic who had re-
nounced earthly possessions, moved to Jerusalem, and founded monasteries on the Mount of
Olives in around A.D. 378–80.[10] It is Melania the Elder who exercised the strongest influence on
her namesake granddaughter, who followed resolutely in her footsteps.

In A.D. 437 in the month of October Melania's illustrious uncle Rufius Antonius Agryp-
nius Volusianus traveled from Rome to Constantinople in order to assist at the wedding of the

western emperor Valentinian III to the eastern princess Licinia Eudoxia.[11] This brother of Mela-
nia's mother was a man with a distinguished political résumé. He served as governor of Africa
Proconsularis when "just a boy," as *comes rei privatae* at Ravenna, as *quaestor sacri palatii*, as a prefect
of Rome, and as praetorian prefect.[12] Melania's uncle Volusian held firmly to his worship of the
Roman pantheon despite the efforts of his family and eminent church leaders, including Saint
Augustine, to convert him to Christianity. Melania's desire to persuade her uncle to embrace
Christianity was so ardent that she traveled from Jerusalem to Constantinople to meet with him
during the royal wedding festivities. Her hagiographer tells us that she made the twelve-hundred-
mile trip in an astoundingly short six weeks, enjoying the enthusiastic welcome of bishops and
clergy along the way.

One should not underestimate the monumentality of such a journey for a woman who
had spent so many years in retreat from the outside world. Indeed, Gerontius tells us that Melania was "zealous to surpass everyone in asceticism" (*Life* 22). We learn that she refused to bathe;
that she wore a haircloth under her cheap, old clothing; that she fasted five days every week; that
she slept just two hours a night, in a sackcloth and in a box that did not allow her to turn over or
stretch out. She spent many nights in vigils upon her knees. For fourteen years she spent the period from Epiphany until Easter in a narrow cell, in sackcloth and ashes, in total isolation but for
a very few visits from her husband, mother, and cousin. At Easter time, when the sack on which
she had been lying for so many months was shaken out, enormous lice dropped from it (*Life* 40).
The image of this abstemious woman approaching the great capital of Constantinople, where she
was to meet with the emperor and members of the imperial family, not to mention a host of
church fathers, is a powerful one. No wonder Melania suffered a crisis of nerves just outside Constantinople at Chalkedon. We are told that only a visit to the shrine of Saint Euphemia gave
Melania the strength to continue her journey. We learn that Saint Euphemia's bones still oozed
blood, and perhaps this was the case when Melania arrived as a pilgrim at the shrine, where the
"Victorious One" provided the necessary inspiration for her to carry on.[13]

When Melania arrived in Constantinople, she made use of her extensive social network,
staying at the palace of her patron, Lausus, in the forum of Augustus Constantine.[14] Lausus was
a prominent figure who had served as grand chamberlain at the court of Theodosios II and for
whom Palladius wrote the *Lausiac History*, which included the story of Melania. Several years before, around A.D. 431, Lausus had given Melania funds to construct a bath at her women's
monastery in Jerusalem. The visual image of a plain, unbathed Melania in a hairshirt as she entered the opulent residence of Lausus must have been enormously striking.

The picture is all the more compelling given that the austere holy woman was a house
guest in close proximity to the portico that sheltered Lausus's exceptional collection of Greek
statuary, an assemblage that included famous sculptures of naked goddesses and robust gods.[15]

The inventory is surprising to the modern reader, who might not expect representations of Greek divinities in the collection of a confirmed Christian. It brilliantly reflects the mixing of traditions that was so widespread in late antiquity, when Christian aristocrats still clung to traditional cultural tastes. The late eleventh-century chronicler George Kedrenos tells us that Lausus's collection included the famous *Aphrodite of Knidos* by Praxiteles, renowned worldwide as the first statue of a female nude.[16] Pilgrims traveled from across the Mediterranean to gaze upon this wonder at the sanctuary of Aphrodite on the southwest coast of modern-day Turkey. The *Amores*, attributed to Lucian, famously recounts a story in which this statue was badly stained as a result of amorous assaults by a young man who crept into the sanctuary at night and attempted to make love to it.[17] One cannot help but wonder if Melania the Younger and the *Aphrodite of Knidos* came face-to-face under the portico of Lausus in what could have been one of the more startling moments in late antiquity. Among the other celebrated images said to have been in his collection was the *Athena of Lindos*, carved in emerald by the sculptors Skyllis and Dipoinos, the *Hera of Samos* by Bupalos of Chios, the *Myokan Eros* by Lysippos, and the *Olympian Zeus* by the master Pheidias. Though these accounts have been regarded as apocryphal, recent scholarship has made the case that Lausus's collection did, indeed, include a remarkable assemblage of authentic original sculptures taken from sanctuaries across the Greek world.[18]

Melania's visit to Constantinople was worth the stress of her travels. Her uncle Volusian fell ill during his stay and Melania managed to covert him to Christianity on his deathbed, an achievement that the rest of her family, and Saint Augustine, had never managed. She thus returned to Jerusalem happy in the success of her mission. The story of Melania and her family reminds us just how long Christianity and traditional cults coexisted and interacted. Not only was there mutual awareness among religions, but also an active practice of conversion within family groups from traditional Greco-Roman cults to Christianity and Judaism, and some transfers back again.[19]

As we conclude our study of Greek priestesses, it is worthwhile to consider them within the broader context of the experience of Christian women of the first centuries A.D. In a changing world bound at the core by the common thread of Hellenism, both Christian women and those who worshipped traditional cults shared certain assumptions based on local experience. This chapter focuses on the archaeological evidence that reflects this shared experience: inscribed gravestones and dedicatory inscriptions recording benefactions. We have seen the importance placed on the identification of Greek priestesses as such on their grave markers. So, too, Christian women were singled out on their tombstones for their special roles in the early church. Grave markers preserve the titles of deacon, deaconess, elder, and prophetess inscribed beside female names.[20] These bear witness to the fact that certain Christian women were singled out and memorialized at death for their leadership roles in the early church. Fascinatingly, tombstones of Jewish women of the same period give leadership titles as well. Bernadette Brooten has interpreted these monuments as evidence for female officeholding within the ancient synagogue.[21]

Christian and Jewish women, as well those of traditional Greco-Roman cults, contributed financially to their religious institutions. The Hellenic system of euergetism had long presumed that elite women would participate in benefactions, including the construction and renovation of buildings, the provision of equipment and goods, the financing of festivals, and the hosting of banquets. The financial security of the community depended on these obligatory and voluntary responsibilities taken on by the privileged ranks, male and female alike. We will consider here the parallel benefactions made by women to basilicas, synagogues, and temples. In this, we can see Christian and Jewish women responding to the immediate social context of their lives within Greco-Roman cities.

The dynamic of conversion from traditional cults to Christianity and Judaism, with some reversals back again, made for very fluid channels of religious influence. The organization of early Christian communities was, in part, inspired by the model of voluntary religious associations developed in the Greek world from the sixth century B.C. on, gaining wide popularity during the Hellenistic period. These associations, known as *orgeones* or *collegia*, provided an important source of identity for increasingly mixed populations of foreigners and citizens. They focused on the worship of a single divinity and, by the late Hellenistic period, are known to have taken up moral and ethical questions.[22] Indeed, most philosophical schools were organized according to their principles. A second source of influence on the early church was the organization of the Greek household.[23] Christians gathered in small groups in private homes, known as house churches (*domus ecclesiae*), for instruction and liturgical services in which food preparation and table service played a central role. Women were vital to the functioning of the house church and, once again, we find the public/private duality at work in defining women's leadership roles. Another source of influence came from contemporary Jewish synagogues. The established organizational model of the Jewish council of elders (*presbyters*) had an impact on the regulation of early Christian worship and social life.[24]

Christian and Jewish communities of the early centuries A.D. responded to the cultures that surrounded them.[25] Synchronic forces shaped the expectations of Christian women, many of whom had converted from traditional Greco-Roman cults. It will be argued here that the broad experience of Hellenism may have provided Christian women with the expectation of leadership roles in their new church. And, indeed, they did enjoy diverse roles in the early ministry. During the fourth through sixth centuries, however, the ever-increasing centralization of ecclesiastical authority within the church edged women out. This process of marginalization made for a world that, by the fifth century, saw women leaders such as Melania opting for lives of extreme asceticism.[26] The process through which Christianity distanced itself from Greco-Roman cult practice, and the conspicuous leadership of women within it, attests to the very potency of Greek feminine priesthoods. They seem to have posed a real threat in the eyes of the early church fathers.

Funerary Monuments

Opportunities for female leadership in the early Christian ministry have long been recognized.[27] Honored places were given to female deacons, elders, widows, virgins, prophets, leaders of house churches, and teachers.[28] Tantalizing references to women as apostles and, perhaps, even as bishops, round out a picture of highly localized patterns of leadership, much as we have seen for Greek cult practice.[29] As early as the first and second centuries, we hear warnings against women teaching and baptizing. Prescriptive texts, canons, and edicts of the fourth and fifth centuries placed limits on female participation and marked the culmination of what had been a gradual process of marginalization.[30]

Inscribed grave markers preserve valuable evidence for the diversity of roles that Christian women played in the Greco-Roman Diaspora. Ute Eisen, Kevin Madigan, and Carolyn Osiek have gathered far-flung epigraphic material that enables us to see patterns of distribution from Sicily to Phrygia.[31] The surviving evidence mostly dates from the fourth through the sixth centuries A.D., when female offices were undergoing critical review. Despite efforts to stop them, some women clearly defied church authority and carried on in their ministries.

One inscription stands out from the others as perhaps our strongest piece of evidence that Christian women were functioning as female priests in fifth-century Salona, modern-day Croatia.[32] It is carved on the lid of a sarcophagus and gives the title "[sac]erdotae" followed by a cross.[33] This single word, meaning "of or to the sacerdotess," the Latin form for "priestess," indicates that the buried woman had served a highly significant official function within the church. Ute Eisen has pointed out that during the second half of the fourth century to the sixth century A.D., the title *sacerdos* was regularly applied to bishops.[34] While we may never know with certainty whether this woman was a bishop, philologically she certainly seems to have functioned as a female priest.

Deaconess

The largest number of inscriptions attesting to Christian women officeholders are those naming female deacons or deaconesses. We have some sixty-one inscribed texts from the East, including thirty-five from Asia Minor, fifteen from Greece, and eight from Palestine, and four texts from the west, including Rome, Gaul, Dalmatia, and Africa.[35] These inscriptions date from the fourth to the seventh centuries, most falling in the later years of this period. Sophia is commemorated with a grave marker, dated to the second half of the fourth century, found below the Tomb of the Prophets on the Mount of Olives in Jerusalem.[36] Her stele shows a Christian cross and a text that reads: "Here lies the slave (*doule*) and bride (*nymphe*) of Christ, Sophia deacon, the second Phoebe, who slept in peace on the twenty-first of the month of March."[37]

Sophia is compared to the prototype for all female deacons: Phoebe, the close associate of Paul. In his letter to the Romans (16:1–2), Paul commends his sister Phoebe, praising her as *diakonos* of the church at Kenchriae, the eastern port of Corinth, and as his *prostasis*, or benefactor. Phoebe is the only deacon of the first century, male or female, for whom we have a personal name. Indeed, this passage gives us our earliest reference to the office of *diakonos*, which, at this stage, shows no gendered differentiation. Phoebe's first-century role as deacon may have looked very different from the later office of deaconess, known in the East from the third century on.

The title of female *deacon* and *deaconess* held different meanings at different times and places across the Christian world.[38] Paul's first letter to Timothy (3:11) states that women deacons must be "serious, not irresponsible talkers, sober, and faithful in all things."[39] By the third century, the ministry of female deacons was directly related to that of bishops, whom they assisted in the baptism of women and in catechism instruction for the newly baptized. This new office is discussed in two documents from Syria, the *Didascalia* (first half of third century) and the *Apostolic Constitutions* (probably late fourth century).[40] We hear of deaconesses traveling with women pilgrims, offering hospitality and protection to socially vulnerable women, serving as monastic leaders, supervising liturgical roles for women, leading prayers, teaching, reading scriptures, and pouring wine and water into chalices.[41]

The *Apostolic Constitution* (8.19–20) deals directly with the issue of the "laying on of hands" (*cheirotonia*), that is, the ordination, of deaconesses. It even gives a prayer to be used at their ordination that exactly parallels that used for male deacons (17–18).[42] The later summary of the *Apostolic Constitution*, the *Epitome* 19–20, has a chapter heading that reads: "About the Ordination (*cheirotonia*) of the Deaconess."[43] Within the threefold leadership structure of the church, the "laying on of hands" was reserved for the installation of bishops, presbyters, and deacons.[44] Whether the ordination of female deacons was seen as a sacrament is a subject of great debate, yet it is clear that in some places and at some times, it surely was.[45]

The post of *diakonos* came under church review during the fifth century. Canon 15 of the Council of Chalkedon (A.D. 451) restricted the office to mature women and specified that "a deaconess should not be consecrated before her fortieth year of life, and even then only after careful examination."[46] But as late as the seventh century, we find younger women who were ordained into the office. A grave marker found at Mahaiy in Moab in Palestine reads: "Here lies Maria, daughter of Valens, deacon, who lived thirty-eight years."[47]

In Asia Minor, evidence for women deacons dates to the fifth and sixth centuries and is distributed across Lycia, Cilicia, Lycaonia, Thrace, Cappadocia, Galatia, Bithynia, and Armenia. At Arachelais in the highlands of Cappadocia, a sixth-century epitaph commemorates Maria, "the deacon of pious and blessed memory who, in accordance with the statement of the apostle, reared children, practiced hospitality, washed the feet of the saints, and distributed her bread to the afflicted."[48] This text replicates the words of 1 Tim. 5:10, in which ideal behavior for the enrollment of a widow is set forth: "she must be well attested for her good deeds, as one who has brought up children, shown hospitality, washed the feet of the saints, relieved the afflicted, and devoted herself to doing good in every way."[49]

At Topallar near Nicomedia in Bithynia, an undated grave marker preserves an inscription that reads: "In memory of the deacon Eugenia we, the poor of Geragathis, have restored the coffin we decorated."[50] The deaconesses of Bithynia are best known from the often-quoted letter of Pliny the Younger, who, in A.D. 112, reported on their activities to the emperor Trajan. Pliny had been sent out to the province to investigate management problems, many of which were blamed on the behavior of local Christians. To advance his research, Pliny tortured two female slaves, whom he called *ministrae*, the Latin word for female deacons, with the hope that they would reveal information on subversive activities. Pliny's efforts were fruitless. He writes: "I found nothing more than a perverse superstition which went beyond all bounds" (*Letters* 10.96.8).

A dozen woman deacons are attested in Greece and Macedonia, dating from the fourth to sixth centuries.[51] In the north, inscriptions found at Bonitsa, Philippi, Edessa, and Volos and on the island of Thasos suggest a local prediliction toward asceticism, with deaconesses living apart from their families as celibates. Here, the title of *deaconess* is often joined with that of *virgin*.[52] To the south, female deacons are found at Patras in Achaia, on the island of Melos in the Cyclades, in Athens, and at Delphi. A stele set up at Delphi is decorated with a Latin cross carved in low relief. Its inscription begins: "The most devoted deaconess Athanasia, who led a blameless life decorously, installed as deaconess by the most holy bishop Pantamianos, set up this monument. Here lie her mortal remains."[53] At this venerable site, world famous for its female prophetess, Athanasia erects her own grave marker in the fifth century A.D., boasting of her installation into office by the bishop himself. The verb *kathistemi*, meaning "installed," is not normally used for ordination and is sometimes used in contrast to it. It may here carry the connotation of appointment.[54]

Very few deaconesses are attested in the west, but what evidence we do have is widely distributed from Gaul, to Italy, to Dalmatia.[55] At Ticini in St. Trinitatis, Gaul, a sixth-century inscription reads: "Here in peace rests the *deaconissa*, Theodora, of blessed memory who lived in the world for about 48 years. She was buried on 22 July 539."[56] Theodora gives evidence of the persistence of women deacons in Gaul despite the attempts to eliminate them. In 396 the Synod at

Nîmes expressed its disapproval of the ordination of women and moved to prevent it (Canon 2). Again, in 441, the Council at Orange (Canon 26) found it necessary to prohibit the ordination (*ordinandae*) of deaconesses.[57] In 517, the Synod of Burgundy held its Council at Epaon, which issued Canon 21, forbidding the consecration (*consecrationem*) of women deacons, a ruling that had to be repeated at the Synod at Orléans (Canon 18) in 533.[58] Theodora's memorial postdates all these official attempts to do away with her office and attests to the determination of women to continue their ministries right into the sixth century.

It is significant that we have no parallel canons prohibiting female deacons in the east. Indeed, when the Holy Synod of the Church of Greece restored the order of the deaconate for women on October 8, 2004, it stated that "the institution of deaconesses established in antiquity and rooted in the Holy Canons was never abolished."[59]

Presbytera

The title *presbytera* is inscribed on grave stelai in early Christian contexts from Italy, Yugoslavia, Greece, and Asia Minor.[60] This distribution suggests a pattern in which provincial Christians, far from the center of authority at Rome, acted with some autonomy, perhaps influenced by the tradition of localized religious practice. The Greek word *presbyteros* means "elder" and gives the root for the English word *priest*. But within the early Christian context, the title carried several different meanings. It could mean individuals of advanced age (Tim. 5:1–2), individuals who were senior in faith (converted first), or those who were members of a respected advisory council.[61] Sometimes the female title *presbytera* could mean the wife of a male *presbyter*, but in other cases, it clearly did not. By the end of the second century A.D., the office of presybter was understood to be one of the three church offices that was conferred by the laying on of hands (*cheirotonia*).

As with other positions held by women in early Christianity, we learn about women *presbytides* largely from the edicts that served to restrict their authority. Epiphanios, bishop of Salamis on Cyprus (ca. A.D. 374–77), railed against groups that ordained women as bishops and *presbytides* in his *Panarion against Eighty Heresies*.[62] He denied that women ever acted as priests and asserted that the only official post ever open to women was that of deaconess. Epiphanios maintained that *presbytera*, *widow*, and *deaconess* were really just different names for the same office, and that *elder* simply meant the oldest of the widows.[63]

By the early tenth century, there was only a distant memory of the women elders of the early church. Atto, the canon lawyer and bishop of Vercelli in the Piedmont, was questioned on the meaning of "female priest" (*presbyteram*) and "female deacon" (*diaconam*). He answered: "just as those who were called *presbyterae* assumed the office of preaching, leading, and teaching, so female deacons had taken up the office of ministry and baptizing, a custom that is no longer expedient."[64] Atto points to Canon 11 of the Synod of Laodikeia (probably held in A.D. 341–81) as the edict that finally closed the door on the ordination of women presbyters. This edict forbade the ordination of presbyterae, from which we might infer that, prior to this, women *were* ordained into the office. Canon 44 of the synod banned the very existence of presbyterae and forbade women from entering the church sanctuary.

A "presbitera" named Leta is celebrated on a gravestone dating to the fourth or fifth century from the catacombs at Tropea, Calabria.[65] The text reads: "Sacred to her good memory. Leta the *presbitera* lived forty years, eight months, and nine days. Her husband made [this tombstone]."[66] At forty years of age and buried by a living husband, Leta hardly conforms to Epiphanios's definition of women elders as the "oldest of the widows." We have evidence that women were, in fact, serving as priests in this very region and at this very time. Pope Galesius I directed a stern letter to fourteen episcopates in the provinces of Lucania and Bruttium in South Italy, and to all of Sicily, in A.D. 494. His epistle (*Epistles* 14) reads: "Nevertheless we have heard to our annoyance that divine affairs have come to such a low state that women are encouraged to officiate at the sacred altars (*ministrare sacres altaribus*) and to take part in all matters imputed to the offices of the male sex to which they do not belong."[67] Leta seems to be exactly the sort of person that Gelasius is concerned about. Just across the straits of Messina in Sicily, we find further confirmation of Gelasius's worries. At the city of Centuripae, a grave inscription dating to the fourth or fifth century commemorates "the *presbyter* Kale, who lived fifty years without reproach."[68]

The earliest surviving evidence for a woman presbyter is on an inscribed grave monument set up at Uçak in Phrygia around A.D. 200–210.[69] Ammion's stele was set up by the bishop Diogas, whose own grave marker, erected by his wife, has also been found. A third stele was dedicated by (presumably the same) Diogas for the bishop Artemidoros, who seems to have been Diogas's predecessor in office.[70] These three monuments, apparently, were all installed together in what seems to have been a cemetery for clergy. There is no mention of a husband or family for Ammion, who assumes her final resting place in the company of two bishops. From all appearances, she seems to have been a highly placed church official.

The location of these three monuments in Phrygia suggests an association with the heretical movement known as Montanism, or the New Prophecy, which arose in a Phrygian village near Hierapolis during the middle of the second century A.D.[71] Montanism was a source of special ire for the church fathers, particularly because it ordained women into the offices of presbyter and bishop (Epiphanios *Panarion* 49.2). Legislation passed by the emperor Justinian I (A.D. 529–65) destroyed the books in which Maximila and Priscilla, the women followers of Montanus, had written down their prophecies. By the time Ammion was buried in the early third century, women presbyters had been banned from mainstream Christianity, yet she clearly continued her ministry in the company of bishops who approved of it, here on the eastern fringe of the heretical stronghold of Montanism.

Prophetess

From Akoluk in Phrygia, in the very heart of the Montanist movement, comes a grave marker for a female prophet of the fourth century.[72] The blue marble stele is crowned by a pediment within which a wreath is carved in low relief. This is reminiscent of the wreaths sculptured on East Greek grave markers for priestesses who had been honored with public crownings (see figs. 8.19–20, 8.22–23). Its inscribed text reads: "The *prophetis(s)a* Nanas, daughter (or wife) of Hermogenes. She implored the Lord who is worthy of all reverence, the Immortal One, with prayers and fervent petitions, with songs and hymns of praise, she prayed day and night. She showed fear of the Lord from the beginning; she had visitation(s) of angels and a mighty (?) voice. Nanas the highly praised, whose tomb . . ."[73] This striking epitaph, like the wreath carved above it, resonates of the Hellenic tradition. Nanas's title, *prophetissa*, gives a suffix that is a popular Greek form. Furthermore, the epitaph is written in the Aeolic-choriambic meter favored by Greek lyric poets, including Sappho and Alkaios almost a thousand years earlier.[74]

Male and female prophets seem to have been an integral part of the church's operations until the second century.[75] Paul placed them as second only to the apostles (1 Cor. 12:28–29). The women prophets of Corinth were especially problematic for Paul, who was bothered, not by their prophetic activities, but by the public manner in which they performed with their heads unveiled (1 Cor. 11:2–16). By the third century we mostly hear of false prophets and the apocalyptic prophecies of the heretical Montanists. The find spot of Nanas's tombstone in Phrygia; its date in the third century; and the ecstatic experience described in her epitaph, complete with visitations by angels, argue for the identification of Nanas as a Montanist prophetess.[76]

Grave Markers of Jewish Women Officeholders

Titles for Christian female officeholders have often been dismissed as "honorary," or as derived from offices held by their husbands or fathers. Leta, the *presbitera* at Tropea in southern Italy, has been viewed as the wife of an elder, rather than as an elder herself.[77] This same pattern in interpretation can been seen for gravestones of Jewish women that show titles indicating their leadership roles within the ancient synagogue.[78] Bernadette Brooten has opened the question of female officeholding in Diaspora Judaism and views these inscriptions as evidence for sacred service that stands well outside the norms prescribed by the rabbis of Palestine.[79] Although this material is not without controversy, it does seem to present a parallel case to the Christian funerary markers discussed above.

Brooten has gathered a corpus of nineteen Jewish grave monuments dating from the first century B.C. to the sixth century A.D., inscribed with Greek and Latin texts that give the names of women and their leadership titles.[80] These include "priestess" (*hierisa, hiereia*), found in Egypt, Rome, Jerusalem, and Bet She'arim; "head of the synagogue" (*archisynagogos/archisyna-*

269

gogissa), found at Smyrna, Crete, and Myndos; "leader" (*archegissa/archegos*), found in Thessaly; "elder" (*presbytera*), found on Crete and in Thrace, Venosa, Tripolitania, Rome, and Malta; "mother of the synagogue" (*meter synagoges*), found at Rome, Venosa, and Venetia; and fatheress (*pateressa*), found at Venosa.[81] Brooten maintains that these leadership titles reflect a form of Judaism practiced among Greek- and Latin-speaking Jews of the Diaspora, in which women were allowed to play much more active roles than in rabbinic Palestine. Her reading stands in direct contradiction to what we find in traditional rabbinic writings, where Jewish women are portrayed as leading restricted lives, wholly separate from the ritual activities of Jewish men.[82]

This material provides a parallel to what we have seen for Christian women of the provinces who carried on in their ministries long after they were banned at the centers of church power. We have met the Christian *presbitera* Leta, who was buried at Bruttium in South Italy. Not far away in Apulia, we find a contemporary Jewish woman named Mannine, whose inscribed grave marker gives her the same title, *presbytera*.[83] Leta the Christian was forty years of age at her death, while Mannine the Jewess was just thirty-eight. Within their shared geographical context of South Italy, Leta and Mannine may have held religious offices that had more to do with local tradition than with the laws of Rome or Palestine. These Christian and Jewish grave markers thus present a fascinating case study in which the archaeological evidence reflects a reality unattested in officially approved texts reflecting the orthodoxy of their faiths.

Benefactions

Women stood out among wealthy converts to Christianity and, from its earliest days, provided much-needed patronage for the new church (Acts 17:4, 12). We hear of several women of means who supported Jesus financially, among them the sisters Mary and Martha and, of course, Mary Magdalene, the faithful disciple and witness to the Resurrection who came to be called "apostle."[84] Saint Paul was also sustained in his ministry by the financial support of women, among them Phoebe, *presbyter* and deaconess at Kenchriae.[85] Paul commended Phoebe to the congregation at Rome as one who had been "a benefactress (*prostatis*) of many and me also" (Rom. 16:2).[86] The designation *prostatis* carried great prestige within the Greco-Roman context in which Paul and Phoebe lived.

Many women patrons owned houses that they opened to believers as meeting places for preaching the word and celebrating of the Lord's supper. These became known as "house churches" and played a central role in the promulgation of the faith in early years.[87] The house church served as both center of worship and of social interaction for Christians, who had no established sacred spaces of their own. Paul names several women, either alone or together with their husbands or brothers, who sponsored churches within their residences. We hear of Apphia, who, together with Philemon and Archippus, had a house at Colossae in Phrygia, where believers met to hear the word (Philem. 1–2). We are told of Nympha, who had a "church in her house" (Col. 4:15). The teachers and missionaries Priscilla and Aquila, dear friends of Saint Paul, had churches in their houses at Corinth, Ephesos, and Rome (1 Cor. 16:19; Rom. 16:3–5; 2 Tim. 4:19; Acts 18.2, 18). At Philippi, a tradeswoman named Lydia, who worked in the profitable purple-dye business, offered her house for the Christian mission (Acts 16:14–15).

The social nexus of the *domus ecclesiae* was a significant factor in the active involvement of women in early Christianity. Tasks associated with communal dining, table service, and social exchange were central to women's work at home, and it was an easy transfer from social practice to religious ritual within the same space. We have recognized this same transfer from house to temple as a dynamic at play in Greek worship and the female priesthoods that oversaw it. The values of Hellenic culture continued to be reflected in the gender roles of sacred service and patterns of patronage in Christian house churches. Such establishments endured into the third century at Rome.[88] But by the fourth century, efforts to centralize church authority made house churches, and the women who ran them, a thing of the past. These were replaced by the architectural form of the basilica and by a dominant male clergy that served within it.

Even then, women continued to contribute financially to their churches, as dedications of great stretches of floor mosaics attest. At Stobi in Macedonia, the exedra of a fourth- or fifth-century Christian basilica shows the names of male and female donors set into the mosaic floor.[89] One inscription reads: "In fulfillment of a vow, Matrona, the most reverend deaconess paved the exedra."[90] At Patras in Achaia, in the northwest Peloponnese, a female deacon named Agrippiane similarly dedicated a floor mosaic in her local basilica. Her offering reads: "The deacon Agrippiane, most beloved of God, made the mosaic in fulfillment of her vow."[91] These deaconesses acted very much in the long tradition of Greek priestesses who beautified the sanctuaries they served.

Like the deaconesses of Stobi and Patras, Jewish women gave great stretches of floor mosaics in the late fourth-century synagogue at Apamea in Syria. Some fourteen of the nineteen floor inscriptions record women donors acting either alone (nine) or with husbands (five).[92] We learn the names of the women donors: Alexandra, Ambrosia, Colonis, Diogenis, Domitila (or Domina, Domnina), Eupithis, Eustathia, Hesychios, Saprikia, and Urania.[93] We also learn that their benefactions were mostly given in fulfillment of vows and for the salvation of the women and of their husbands, children, and households. While the women donors of Apamea gave stretches of mosaic ranging from 35 to 150 feet, a Jewess named Juliana donated a mosaic that filled the entire floor of her synagogue at Hamman Lif in North Africa.[94]

Brooten has collected a corpus of forty-three inscriptions attesting to synagogue donations made by Jewish women acting alone, with their husbands, or through third parties.[95] It is clear that at least some of these women controlled their own property and had sufficient means to make significant contributions. Even if their funds had to be approved by a guardian, these women had no problem obtaining permission to use their money as they wished.[96] Jewish women donors are attested on Delos, at Phokaea in Ionia, at Myndos and Tralles in Karia, at Akmonia in Phrygia, at Apamea in Syria, at five sites in Palestine, in Africa, and at Berenike in Cyrenaica.[97]

No case is more striking than that of Tation, daughter (or wife) of Straton, son of Empedon from Phokaea in Ionia. It was probably in the third century A.D. that she made her gifts to the local synagogue at Kyme. A commemorative inscription tells us that, with her own money, Tation built the synagogue and the colonnade of the courtyard and gave them to the Jews.[98] In return for her generosity, the synagogue granted Tation a gold crown and proedria, the very same honors that we have seen, in chapter 7, awarded to Greek priestesses of the Hellenistic period.[99] It seems that Tation's reserved seat was located in the front row of the synagogue's assembly hall, though this is not explicitly stated. Proedria was a highly unusual award within the Jewish context, even for male officials. But within the local cultural context of Kyme, proedria had long precedent. During the second century B.C., a benefactress of the city named Archippe received the public honors of a portrait statue, a gold crown, and proedria.[100] Archippe's financial contributions to her city are attested in eight surviving inscriptions.[101] She paid for the construction of a new council house and, later, its repairs, as well as for food and wine, and a statue group of her family. Within the local tradition in which women donors received public honors, Tation was simply being treated as a respectable Greek lady, worthy of a crown and reserved seating. Some scholars believe that Tation was not Jewish, based on the wording of the text that says she gave her benefactions "to the Jews." But it is highly unlikely that a nonbeliever would have been given a front-row seat in the synagogue, and we can assume that Tation shared the faith of those who honored her.[102]

The social and cultural forces at work in the Greco-Roman East made for a world in which women wished to be remembered for the contributions they made in life. This desire crossed over religious divisions at a time when individuals were crossing religious barriers themselves, through conversions and through the realities of family life, which saw close relatives worshipping very different gods. The fluidity of movement among religious institutions during the early years of the Christian era, and the strong influence of traditional social practice, shaped the expectations of women who anticipated access to sacred office.

—

At the opening of this chapter we focused on the somber scene of the preparation of Melania's corpse for burial. The church canons of the fourth century, at least in the west, put an end to female officeholding and defined new models for women's service, including the consecrated virgin, the chaste widow, and the celibate wife that Melania became. While Melania's benefactions went far beyond any scale previously known, she never boasted as a self-confident, proud patroness. Instead, her life was one of penitence and quiet denial, far from the world of public accolades.

Excluded from the established structures of the ministry, some women, mostly in the provinces, continued to serve as presbyterae well into the sixth century, in direct defiance of the canons that tried to stop them. But for all practical purposes, the door had closed on priesthood for women in the Christian church. At the end of the sixth century, what was perhaps the last surviving vestige of the vibrant world of Greek female cult practice was, at last, stamped out. Maiden choruses had, from the seventh century B.C., been among the most exalted institutions of Greek worship. They had served a central role in the education of women and the perpetuation of traditional beliefs. The virgin chorus had lived on in the liturgies of the early church. But at the very end of the sixth century, it was replaced by the boys' choir, a fixture of Christian worship that has enjoyed top billing to this day.[103]

CHAPTER 10

Conclusions

Our review of the epigraphic evidence for female officeholding in early Christianity, and in Judaism, reveals a pattern that we have also seen in our study of Greek priestesses. The archaeological evidence bears witness to realities not recorded in the literary texts that have shaped our understanding of ancient women. The Greek texts come down to us, not only through the accident of survival, but also through a selection process made by later scribes and librarians at Alexandria and elsewhere. They do not, therefore, give us a complete picture of the world in which these women lived. Furthermore, they reflect the voice, intent, and experience of the author, determinants affected by the specific contexts in which the authors wrote. The lesson here is that *all* existing evidence must be considered, and its evaluation must take place independently from the prejudices that privileged texts promote.

Other patterns, equally distorting, come to light. These have to do with the conscious or unconscious devaluation, even dismissal, of evidence that does not conform to the consensus view. The leadership titles inscribed beside Christian and Jewish women's names have often been taken to mean "wife of" a male officeholder. While in some cases this may be true, it certainly was not so at all times. Similarly, we see Greek priestesses, especially in the late Hellenistic East, whose offices have been understood to be extensions of their husbands' positions.[1]

As with so many aspects of the interpretative process, individual readings are greatly influenced by one's inclination to embrace the evidence with a "glass is half full" or a "glass is half empty" point of view. The pessimist will see limitations in the same place that the optimist will recognize opportunities. When it comes to ancient women, there has been a long-standing tendency to view the evidence through the "half empty" lens. Fascinatingly, the same position has been reached through very different paths, starting from very different places. Nineteenth-century classicists, projecting the gender ideology of the Victorian elite onto the Greek household, ended up in roughly the same place as twentieth-century feminists who employed a "subordination theory" construct for managing the material.[2] The result is the widely accepted commonplace of silent, submissive, "invisible" women, confined to the privacy of their households and wholly dominated by their men.

The cumulative effect of this long-standing tendency toward pessimism is that women's most visible roles in ancient Greek society have remained veiled, regularly relegated to footnotes advising us: "except in the case of priestesses." But we have seen evidence, fragmentary as it is, that priestesses spoke before Assemblies; fixed their seals on official documents; and, at least by Hellenistic times and maybe earlier, took their honored places in the front rows of theaters. Instead of highlighting the women who led public processions, made dedications in sanctuaries, and stepped forward on festival days to perform rituals and initiate sacrifices, the focus has rested on women locked indoors.

Some of this has to do with what Janet Halley has usefully termed the "prescriptive deployment of theory."[3] One predetermines a lot, and excludes a lot, when one commits absolutely to a single theory or approach. This is why a construct of various methods is so helpful in approaching the subject of ancient women. Like tools in a tool kit, different methods can be used to achieve different results. The multimethodological approach allows for checks and balances, as well as for surprises, opening up new possibilities that could never have been anticipated in advance.

Modern interpreters have tended to read ancient evidence through a political lens rather than through a religious one. In doing so, they mostly see the limitations placed on Athenian women, excluded from the political and military life of the city. We must remember that the right to vote and to join the military were open to women in our own country just in the past century, roughly twenty-five hundred years after the Athenian women in question. The expectation that ancient women would have needed these same twentieth-century rights in order to lead meaningful and satisfying lives seems off the mark. Also, we can no longer say that women were excluded from the political life of the city, as we have redefined *political* to include the religious dimension, so deeply embedded within it. Athenian women did not, of course, have the right to vote. But, as Josine Blok has pointed out, the Assembly met only 145 days a year, in contrast with the 170 annual festival days in the Athenian religious calendar.[4] By a rough estimate, women participated in some 85 percent of all religious activities at Athens. They were in charge of more than forty major cults in the city, not to mention many minor ones.[5] Modern skepticism toward things religious, and the marginalization of the importance of religious offices, have clearly contributed to the "muting" of ancient Greek women and the perception of their powers within the polis.

Even when women are recognized as central players within the religious sphere, we can detect a subtle whittling away of their status and position. Inscribed advertisements for the sale of priesthoods preserve the prices at which sacred offices were sold. It has been stressed that female priesthoods sold for less money than male priesthoods did and, by extension, that female offices were not valued as highly.[6] But as we have seen in chapter 2, prices for priesthoods were directly commensurate with the privileges and dispensations that they brought. Male priesthoods could carry extraordinarily valuable dispensations from military service and garrison duties, burdens with no comparable hardship on the female side. This allowed them to be sold at a much higher rate than that of female offices, but in no way diminished the value that Greek society placed on women's sacred service. Similarly, perquisites paid to priestesses have been interpreted as reimbursements or taxes rather than as compensation for work.[7] While the evidence may be inconclusive, we should be open to the possibility that, at least in some cases, women could keep their pay.

Benefactions from women donors have often been interpreted as gifts from husbands, who are perceived to have been the actual source of the finances.[8] But many dedicatory inscriptions give women's proper names without mention of a husband or father. Indeed, roughly half of the 160 women named in dedicatory inscriptions from Hellenized Asia Minor are listed without any mention of male kin.[9] Some dedications explicitly state that the financing came from the woman's own means.[10] Yet there remains a predisposition to transfer the philanthropy to a husband or male relative. To be sure, most women functioned under the legal and financial guardianship of male relatives. But evidence shows that women had little trouble getting access to funds and directing them as they wished. Scores of female cult agents turned the resources of their *oikoi* toward sanctuaries that held very personal meaning for them.

Perhaps the most extreme example of modern denial of female cult agency is found in the discussion of women and blood sacrifice.[11] The view that women were excluded from sacrifice because, like animal victims, they bleed, is a contemporary construct fabricated on cultural assumptions not shared in Greek antiquity. As we have shown in chapter 6, epigraphic evidence directly attests to women preparing, distributing, and eating sacrificial meat. Women's status within the hierarchy of cult service, in turn, has been qualified by those who view the butcher as the agent with highest rank. This notion is a product of Christianizing assumptions that see the priest as the singular representative of Christ in the reenactment of the sacrifice of Christ's body and blood. The primacy of the priest is a wholly alien concept in Greek worship, where anyone with a knife and victim could offer sacrifice. Women did not usually slit the throats of sacrificial victims because within the gender roles codified in the Greek household, the task of butchery usually fell to men. But this in no way suggests that a priestess's cult responsibilities were regarded as less than those of male priests.

Even the primacy of the most famous of all Greek priestesses, the Pythia at Delphi, has been questioned. As Maurizio has stressed, not one ancient source suggests that anyone other than the Pythia issued oracular responses.[12] Still, modern interpreters persist in denying her the commanding role, shifting the authority for Delphic pronouncements to knowledgeable male priests. When we view the demotion of the Pythia within the broader context of widespread dismissal of female priestly prestige, we see a pattern through which sources are discounted in favor of what makes sense from a modern perspective.

Subtle biases can also be observed in the reading of images. In chapter 5, we considered the so-called eunuch priest from Ephesos, long regarded as a male rather than female figure, under the influence of tantalizing references to Megabyzos in Xenophon and Pliny (see fig. 5.3).[13] The inclination to view the Archaic korai from the Athenian Acropolis as goddesses may reflect a lingering disbelief that real maidens could merit such impressive images of their own (see fig. 5.7). Even the statue of Nikeso (see fig. 5.12; pl. 16), whose inscribed dedication identifies her as the priestess of Demeter and Kore, has sometimes been viewed as an image of the goddess instead. When we do have a certain case in which an inscribed base holds a statue of a priestess, as that of Lysimache on the Athenian Acropolis (see figs. 5.9–10), some interpreters try to reconstruct the lost portrait using a totally unrelated copy of a haggard, old woman (see fig. 5.11). It is highly unlikely that a classical Greek priestess would have her life service on Acropolis represented through anything but a dignified, idealized image.

On the literary side, we see a hesitancy to recognize as "real" a number of women named as key players. Diotima, the wise prophetess of Mantineia whom Sokrates consults on the meaning of love, is regularly dismissed as a product of fiction (Plato *Symposium* 173–209). Yet interpreters are willing to accept any number of male characters in Plato's *Symposium* as reflections of historical men, including Sokrates, Aristophanes, Alkibiades, and Agathon. It is widely accepted that Aristophanes poked fun at the men of his day, Perikles, Alkibiades, Kleon, Sokrates, Euripides, and Kinesias among them. But with the exception of the forward-looking David Lewis, few have understood the profound implications of Aristophanes' choice in putting the historical priestesses Lysimache and Myrrhine on stage.[14]

This brings us to the issue of the naming of Athenian women. From the 1970s, it has generally been agreed that the names of respectable women were not spoken aloud in classical Athens.[15] This avoidance has been seen as part of the general "muting" of women in Athenian society, as reflected in the writings of Thucydides, Xenophon, Demosthenes, and Isaios, among others, and in Greek comedy.[16] Again, we see the privileging of certain texts that support this view. But as we have demonstrated in chapter 3, the practice of sacred and civic eponymy ensured that priestly women, and their names, would never be forgotten. We have seen scores of female personal names inscribed on votive offerings, statue bases, and grave monuments and on dedications in streets, temples, and marketplaces.[17]

In view of the evidence gathered here, it may be time to reconsider this consensus position. Certainly, there were contexts, including legal cases and the speeches of orators, in which women were identified, not by their personal names, but in relationship to their husbands, fathers, or other male relatives. But this could be out of respect or in order to identify them through the *oikoi* that offered them protection. Even today, we can speak of Mrs. Astor and Madonna in a single breath, but this does not mean that Mrs. Astor is being "muted," or that she is without power in the society that identifies her in this way. Nonetheless, the prevailing view has been expressed as follows: "'a woman' was not somebody to respect, but somebody's mother—or sister, or wife, or daughter—that was another matter."[18] I imagine that some of the priestesses profiled in this book would be amazed by this statement. Indeed, we have seen women who were accorded enormous respect in their own rights by the cities and citizens that honored them.

Why is it so important that we adjust our view of the realities of ancient Greek women? For one thing, it has a profound effect on the ways in which we understand what followed. In light of the evidence gathered here, it is surprising that a popular view persists in seeing Christianity as an opportunity through which women escaped their lowly status within the "pagan" system. We hear that "pagan women sometimes held important positions within various mystery cults and shrines." But these institutions are readily dismissed as "relatively peripheral to power within pagan society."[19] In contrast, Christian women who held positions of leadership in the early church are said to have "enjoyed greater power and status than did pagan women."[20] Based on the evidence compiled in this book, we might see the situation the other way around. Indeed, the example of the Greek priestess may have given women of the early church the presumption that they, too, would hold sacred office.

In fact, some measure of the church's motivation in denying the possibility of women priests may have been a desire to distance itself from traditional Greco-Roman cults in which priestesses played such a central role. For Christianity to truly separate itself from "pagan" cult worship it had to abolish one of the most visible and characteristic pillars of Greek religion, the sacred service of women, maidens, and girls. There may be no finer tribute to the potency of the Greek priestess than the discomfort that her position caused the church fathers. Christian monotheism, with its singular vision of an apparently male-gendered god, muted the female divine presence and, thus, the female cult agents who might have served it. Against the backdrop of the two-gendered system of Mediterranean polytheism, there was no longer a place for women priests.

In A.D. 393, the emperor Theodosios issued an edict that called not only for the destruction of all temples and cult images, but also for the cessation of age-old festivals, including the Eleusinian Mysteries, the Panathenaia, and the Olympic Games. With this came the elimination of sacred office and the priestesses who had served the Greek cults for more than a millennium. The only threat to the church now came from schismatic groups within Christianity itself, those that broke away and followed their own prophets and doctrines. The church fathers were particularly enraged by the teachings of the Montanists of Phrygia. This was, in no small part, because some of their sects continued to ordain women as priests.

The bishop Epiphanios of Salamis (A.D. 374–77) sent irate letters condemning the behavior of a series of heretical groups, largely based in Asia Minor but found as far east as

Mesopotamia and Arabia. Among those that angered him the most was a group of women known as the Collyridians, who were said to have originated in Thrace or Scythia. They came to settle in the distant deserts of Arabia, on the easternmost fringe of Ephiphanios's known world. These women persisted in performing a "strange ritual" in honor of the Virgin Mary. On a certain day each year, they decorated a *diphros* (square seat) and spread a linen cloth upon it. They then placed bread on the cloth, offered it in the name of the Holy Virgin Mary, and ate it.[21] The communion rite observed by this community of women enraged the bishop, who railed against their "excessive glorification of the Holy Virgin" as "ridiculous and silly" (*Panarion* 78.23). He proclaimed as "blasphemous beyond all measure" the fact that, in the name of Mary, this group functioned as "priests for women."

Perhaps Epiphanios was also upset that their actions resembled those undertaken by generations of Greek priestesses. Nearly eight hundred years earlier, in the charter myth for the foundation of the priesthood of Athena Polias at Athens, Queen Praxithea had baked wheat cakes destined for the virgin goddess. In a fragment of the Euripidian tragedy named for him, King Erechtheus inquires of his wife: "Since you are dispatching many cakes of wheat meal, oil and honey (*pelanon*) from the house, explain to me these 'moons' made from young wheat."[22] Praxithea's moon-shaped bread cakes were, no doubt, inspired by the waning crescent moon that signaled the arrival of 28 Hekatombaion, the eve of Athena's birthday festival, the Panathenaia. It was beneath this crescent moon that generations of Athenian maidens mounted the windswept Acropolis rock and undertook their annual ritual of singing and dancing the whole night through.[23] And it was Praxithea, whose very name means "one who does things for the goddess," who set a shining example for all that a Greek priestess should be. Born to a noble family, generous beyond measure, she famously placed the communal good of Athens above the lives of her own children. When called upon to make the ultimate sacrifice and offer her daughter to save the city, Praxithea did not waver. Her response was that of a selfless guardian and steadfast citizen: "Our common heritage is at stake and no one will ever obtain my consent to cast out the ancient laws our fathers handed down" (*Erechtheus* frag. 360.43–45).

At the end of Euripides' play, Praxithea stands alone on the Acropolis, having lost her husband as well as all her daughters in the saving of the city. Athena instructs her to build tombs and sacred precincts in honor of her family and to celebrate their memory with annual sacrifices and festivals. Then, Athena grants Praxithea the high honor of her priesthood and the extraordinary right to make burned sacrifice on the great altar. As queen, wife, mother, baker, builder, defender of the city's laws, initiator of fire sacrifice, and guardian of ritual, Praxithea stands as the prototype par excellence for Greek female priesthood. Hers is an ennobling model, one that embraces the selfless altruism that rests at the very heart of the democratic system that made Athens unique in the ancient world.

For at least seven centuries, Athenian women proudly took up the sacred office that was modeled on the ideal of Praxithea's service to goddess and city. Priestesses of Athena Polias, and priestly women like them across the Mediterranean world, assumed responsibilities, performed rites, made benefactions, instructed in traditions, and received substantial honors in return. As we have seen, these tributes included statues, crowns, theater seats, grave monuments, and the collective esteem of their communities. The body of evidence examined in this study has survived by chance across the great distances of time and space that separate us from Greek antiquity. There was surely even more that has been lost to us, at least for now. Yet it is brilliantly clear that priestesses loved their communities, served them well, and were long remembered by them. We can be certain that the contributions of these exceptional women deeply enriched, not just their cities, but also the ancient lives lived in them.

Notes

CHAPTER 1. INTRODUCTION: TIME, SPACE, SOURCE MATERIAL, AND METHODS

1. *IG II²* 1136 = *SGDI* 2685, 106/105 B.C. *Proxenia* is a sort of honorary citizen status, comparable to that of a modern consul. The *proxenos* is a foreigner who represents the interests of the granting city in his or her home state. Chrysis would have represented the interests of Delphi at Athens. C. Marek, *Die Proxenie* (Frankfurt 1984).

2. *IG II²* 3484. Turner (1983) 265–68 argues contra Kirchner (*PA* 10759 and *IG II²* 3484) that Niketes and Philylla are Chrysis's cousins rather than her siblings. The cousins are from a different deme and phyle than those of Chrysis and seem to be related to her through their mother, who may have been a sister of Chrysis's father, Niketes. Turner shows that Dionysios was *epimeletes* of the *emporion* at Delos ca. 100/99 B.C. and that his brother, Niketes, was a *hippeus* in 106/105 B.C. On Niketes (II), Chrysis's great-great-grandfather, see *PA* 10759/*LGPN* 24, and *IG II²* 847, 44. On Protagoras, Chrysis's grandfather, see *PA* 12284/*LGPN* 4, and *IG II²* 950, 6, 27. Turner points out that the lack of a paternal Eteoboutad tie indicates that Chrysis inherited her priesthood matrilineally.

3. Cf. *FD* II 3 145 = *IG* IX 2 for Aristodama of Smyrna, who was granted *proxenia*.

4. The analogy between gender of divinity and sacred servant was particularly strong at Athens. Exceptions can be found for priestesses of Dionysos Anthios (*IG II²* 1356. 9–10), Helios (*IG II²* 5093), Apollo Deiradiotes (Pausanias 2.24.2), Apollo Lykeios (Plutarch *Pyrrhus* 31.7), Apollo Delphinios, Zeus at Dodona, and some cults of Poseidon. The wife of the *archon basileus* at Athens had certain religious duties involved in the worship of Dionysos ([Demosthenes] 59-73-76, 85). Priests are known to have served in some cults of Demeter (*hierophant* at Eleusis), Aphrodite, and Athena (priests of Athena at Lindos on Rhodes, and boy priests for Athena at Tegea). See Holderman (1913) 26–28.

5. Price in *RAW* 303.

6. Price in *RAW* 303.

7. See A. Henrich's important discussion of inscribed texts, ritual authority, and polis religion (2003) 38–58; Turner (1983) vii, 10–13; J. Hooker, "Cult Personnel in the Linear B Texts from Pylos," in Beard and North (1990) 159–74 on cult personnel in Linear B tablets; Garland (1990) 73–91; Price (1999) 67–73; Dillon (2002) 79–106; Parker (2005) 93–99, 133–34, 121 n. 19.

8. We are told that the single most important fact about Athenian priesthoods is their lack of importance for the history of religion. Feaver (1957) 123.

9. Martha (1882), Holderman (1913), McClees (1920); Lewis (1955); Feaver (1957); Clinton (1974); Heiler (1977); Jordan (1979); Turner (1983); Garland (1990); Smarczyk (1990); Kasper-Butz (1990);

Kearns (1995) 188–207; Georgoudi (2003); Aleshire (1994a); Dignas (2002); Goff (2004); Cole (2004); Parker (2005).

10. Turner (1983).

11. Ridgway (1987).

12. Mantis (1990).

13. For Cypriot votive statues of key-bearing priestesses, see Connelly (1988) 21–11, figs. 32–33, and for a Tarentine funerary relief in Princeton, see Connelly in Ridgway et al. (1994) 28–31; for Attic grave reliefs, see Kosmopoulou (2001). Dillon (2002) and Goff (2004) show a few images to illustrate points.

14. Kron (1996) 139.

15. A. Snodgrass, *An Archaeology of Greece: The Present State and Future Scope of a Discipline* (Berkeley 1987) 12–13; Ferrari (2002) 2–3; Sourvinou-Inwood (1991) 7.

16. Padel in Cameron and Kuhrt (1983) 3–19; E. Keuls, *The Reign of the Phallus* (1985) 82–112; W. Schuller, *Frauen in der griechischen Geschicte* (Konstanz 1985); E. Cantarella, *Pandora's Daughters* (Baltimore 1987) chaps. 1–3, 7, 46; Zeitlin (1982) 129; W. B. Tyrrell, *Amazons: A Study in Athenian Mythmaking* (Baltimore 1984) 45; W. B. Tyrrell and F. S. Brown, *Athenian Myths and Institutions: Words in Action* (New York and Oxford 1991) 114–15. Pomeroy (1975) 58–60 summarizes the early history of scholarship on the subject, including F. A. Wright, *Feminism in Greek Literature* (London 1923); A. W. Gomme, "The Position of Women in Athens in the Fifth and Fourth Centuries B.C.," *Classical Philology* 20 (1925) 1–25; M. Hadas, "Observations on Athenian Women," *Classical Weekly* 39 (1936) 97–100; H. D. F. Kitto, *The Greeks* (Harmondsworth 1951) 219–36. See R. Flacelière, *Daily Life in Greece* (London 1965) 55, for view that women never left the house.

17. Xenophon's *Oikonomikos* 7.17–40; [Aristotle] *Oikonomika* 1343b.25ff.; Plato *Laws* 781C2–D2; Thucydides 2.45.2; Euripides *Trojan Women* 645ff.; Aristophanes *Thesmophoriazousae* 397ff., 410, 519, 785–91. See Walcot (1984) 33–47.

18. Gould (1980) 38–59 set the foundation for recent discussion. See Foley (1981b) 148; Graham (1981) 314; Lefkowitz (1986) 112; Just (1989) 105–25; Sourvinou-Inwood (1995a) 111–20; Lefkowitz (1996) 78–91.

19. Cohen (1991) 133–54; Cohen (1996) 3–15. C. B. Patterson, *The Family in Greek History* (Cambridge, MA 1998) 128 follows Cohen, as does Faraone (1999) 167–68.

20. Harris (1992) 309–21; V. Hunter, "The Athenian Widow and Her Kin," *Journal of Family History* 14 (1989) 291–11. I thank Edward Harris for a very helpful conversation on these issues.

21. Foxhall (1989) esp. 32–39.

22. L. C. Nevett, "Separation or Seclusion? Towards an Archaeological Approach to Investigating Women in the Greek Household in the Fifth to Third Centuries B.C.," in *Architecture and Order: Approaches to Social Space*, M. P. Pearson and C. Richards, eds. (London 1994) 98–112; L. C. Nevett,

"Gender Relations in the Classical Greek Household: The Archaeological Evidence," *ABSA* 91 (1995) 363–81; L. C. Nevett, *House and Society in the Ancient Greek World* (Cambridge 1999) esp. 10–20, 173–75; M. Goldberg, "Spatial and Behavioural Negotiation in Classical Athenian City Houses," in Allison (1999) 142–61.

23. Blok (2001) 109.

24. Henderson first made the case (1991) 133–47, followed by Sourvinou-Inwood (1995a) 115 and (2003) 177–84.

25. C. B. Patterson, "*HAI ATTIKAI*: The Other Athenians," in *Rescuing Creusa: New Methodological Approaches to Women in Antiquity*, M. Skinner, ed., *Helios* 13 (1987) 117–73.

26. Blok (2004) 1–26.

27. First questioned by Gauthier (1996) 572 and now fully treated by Parker (2004c) 57–70. The designation *sacred law* was first put forth in Prott and Ziehen (1896–1906) and continued by Sokolowski in *LSAM*, *LSS*, *LSCG*, Cole (1992), Lupu in *NGSL*, and others. See review of *NGSL* by J.-M. Carbon, *BMCR* 2005.04.07. See also Dickie (2004) 579–91; A. Chaniotis, "Negotiating Religion in the Cities of the Eastern Roman Empire," *Kernos* (2003) 177–90; Harris and Rubenstein (2004) 5–7; Harris (2004) 27–34.

28. Bowden (2005) 156.

29. Parker in *RAW* 571.

30. Bremmer (1998) 9–33; Connor (1988) 161–88. Further discussion of "sacred" and "secular" can be found in Kearns (1995) 513; Morris (1993) 23; Sourvinou-Inwood (1990) 304; R. Osborne, *Demos: the Discovery of Classical Athens* (Cambridge 1985) 179; P. A. Butz, "Prohibitory Inscriptions," in Hägg (1996) 71–72.

31. The most comprehensive treatment of these issues are offered by Sourvinou-Inwood (1988a) 270–73, Sourvinou-Inwood (1995a), and Blok (2001) 96–116. See also Parker (1996) 5–7; Bremmer (1988); Cohen (1991) 70–132; M. Jameson, "Private Space in the Greek City," in *The Greek City from Homer to Alexander*, O. Murray and S. Price, eds. (Oxford 1990) 171–95. For broader discussion, see L. Lamphere, "The Domestic Sphere of Women and the Public World of Men: The Strengths and Limitations of an Anthropological Dichotomy," in *Gender in Cross Cultural Perspective*, C. Brettel and C. Sargent, eds. (Englewood Cliffs 1993) 82–92; M. Z. Rosaldo and L. Lamphere, *Women, Culture, and Society* (Stanford 1974).

32. I have benefited greatly from the discussion of public/private in R. Guess, *Public Goods, Private Goods* (Princeton and Oxford 2001). See N. B. Kampen, "Between Public and Private: Women as Historical Subjects in Roman Art," in Pomeroy (1991) 216–48. For theoretical constructs focusing on the house, see J. Carsten and S. Hugh-Jones, *About the House: Levi Strauss and Beyond* (Cambridge 1995); J. Hanson, *Decoding Homes and Houses* (Cambridge 1998).

33. Blok (2001) 97–98; Foxhall (1989) 32–39.

34. Goff (2004) 59–60.

35. Schnapp (1988).

36. I thank Francois de Polignac for helpful conversations about this process.

37. The term *embeddedness* was first used to describe Greek religion by Robert Parker (1986) 265. The highly localized nature of Greek religion was articulated early on by Sourvinou-Inwood *JHS* 98 (1978) 101–21 = (1991) 147–88. See Bremmer (1994) 2–8; Price (1999) 19–46; Kearns (1995) 511–29; Parker in *RAW* 570–71; Henrichs (2003) 40.

38. Bremmer (1994) 2.

39. Chaniotis in *RAW* 320.

40. Strategies drawn from what has been called third wave feminism are helpful here as they stress the necessity for working in spaces outside binary thinking. See O'Neill (1999) 6–8.

41. Meskell and Preucel (2004a); Meskell (2002); Meskell (2001); R. Gilchrist, "Archaeology and the Life Course: A Time and Age for Gender," in Meskell and Preucel (2004a) 142–60; R. Gilchrist, "Archaeological Biographies: Realizing Human Lifecycles, -course and -histories," *World Archaeology* 31.3 (2000) 325–28; M. E. Morbeck, A. Galloway, and A. L. Zihlman, eds., *The Evolving Female: A Life-History Perspective* (Princeton 1999); L. Fedigan, "Changing Views of Female Life Histories," and J. S. Deverenski, "Engendering Children, Engendering Archaeology," in *Invisible People and Processes: Writing Gender and Childhood into European Archaeology*, J. Moore and E. Scott, eds. (London and New York 1997).

42. Clinton (1974); F. Graf, *Nordionische Kulte* (Rome 1985); Schacter (1981); M. Jost, *Sanctuaires et cultes d'Arcadie* (Paris 1985); J. D. Mikalson, "Religion in the Attic Demes," *AJP* 98 (1977) 424–35; Souvinou-Inwood (1991) 147–88; D. Morelli, *I culti in Rodi* (Pisa 1959); Parker (2005); Parker (1996); Bremen (1996); Turner (1982); Heiler (1977) 15–72.

43. Chaniotis in *RAW* 319.

44. A methodological construct called for by Morris (1993) 5; Morris (2000) 4–5. See Bourdieu with Passeron (1990, trans. Nice); Adorno (1966 = 1973, trans. Ashton); Adorno (1984 = 1997, trans. Hullot-Kentor). See G. A. Knapp, "Fragile Foundations, Strong Traditions, Situated Questioning: Critical Theory in German-Speaking Feminism," in O'Neill (1999) 124–25. F. Braudel, *The Mediterranean and the Mediterranean World in the Age of Philip II = La Méditerranée et le monde méditerranéen à l'époque de Philippe II*, 3 vols. [1949], trans. S. Reynolds (London 2000). For discussion of the *longue durée*, see P. Horden and N. Purcell, *The Corrupting Sea: A Study of Mediterranean History* (Oxford 2000) 36–43.

45. See Beard in Beard and North (1990) 3, 7, 9 on the difficulty with the English translation of *hiereus* as "priest." For etymology of the word *priest*, see Garland (1990) 77.

46. Beard and North (1990) 45, where we hear of a "priest of Athena" and "priest of Athena Parthenos" at Athens. There *was* no cult of Athena Parthenos and no cult servant with this title. We are doubly uncertain whether Beard is suggesting that a man or a woman filled this nonexistent post.

47. Dickerson (1991) 66–68. For sacrifice by private persons, see Sourvinou-Inwood (1988a) 266 and Lykourgos frag. B4.1; *LSCG* 69, lines 25–28.

48. Smith (1968).

49. For general discussion of titles of sacred servants in the classical period, see Ferguson (1989) 52–53.

50. Billigmeier and Turner (1981) 1–18; Hooker in Beard and North (1990) 167–79.

51. Kearns (1995) 521.

52. Kearns (1995) citing Connor (1988) 161–88.

53. Harpokration, s.v. *trapezophoros* = Lykourgos frag. 47 C and Istros *FGrH* 334 F9.

54. Deliades: *Homeric Hymn to Apollo* 157; Dionysiades, Leukippides: Pausanias 3.13.7, 3.16.1; Lykiades: Hesychios, s.v. Lykiades korai.

55. *Arktoi*: Scholia to Aristophanes *Lysistrata* 645; *melissai*: Scholia to Pindar *Pythian* 4.106; Kallimachos *Hymn to Apollo* 110; Apollodoros *FGrH* 244 F 89; *poloi*: Hesychios, s.v. *polia*.

56. Blok (2001) 112; J. D. Mikalson, *The Sacred and Civic Calendar of the Athenian Year* (Princeton 1975) 186–204.

57. Lefkowitz (2003) 234–39. I thank Mary Lefkowitz for enlightening discussions of these issues.

58. Sourvinou-Inwood (1988b) 29–39 sees this account as a fictitious invention. Nonetheless, Plutarch's choice, or that of his source, in naming the priestess Theano is significant. The fact that Plutarch gives her patronymic may suggest that she was, in fact, a historical figure.

59. Herodotos 1.31; *Suda*, s.v. Kroisos. Her name is given as Kydippe by Plutarch frag. 133 (Sandbach) and the *Anthologia Graeca* 3.18.

60. *IG* II² 3634.

61. For the naming of Greek women, see Carney (1991) 154–72, esp. 160; Schaps (1977) 323–30; Golden (1986) 245–69; Pomeroy (1984) 9. Nagy (1978/79) 360–62, may count more priestesses named Theano than are attested with certainty. In addition to the priestess of Demeter and Kore named by Plutarch, Nagy includes a woman named Theano who dedicated a garment at Brauron. She is listed among a number of women who make similar dedications and need not necessarily have been a priestess.

62. For discussion of the relationship between women in Greek tragedy and real Athenian women, see Pomeroy (1975) 93–97; Dowden (1995); Lefkowitz (1986); Walcot (1984).

63. *TrGF* vol. 3, Aeschylus frags. 86, 87.

64. Hamilton (1985) 53–73.

65. Sourvinou-Inwood (2003) III.3, 265–500, esp. "Euripidean Tragedy and Religious Exploration," 291–458; Connelly (1996) 80; Kearns (1989) 7.

66. Lewis (1955) 1–12.

67. W. G. Arnott, *Menander*, vol. 2, Loeb Classical Library (1996) 228–29. I thank Colin Austin for this reference.

68. I am indebted to Colin Austin for drawing this to my attention.

69. Maurizio (1995) 84 n. 91.

70. Dewald (1981) 93–95.

71. Hellanikos, *Priestesses of Hera at Argos*, dated between 421 B.C. and the Sicilian Expedition; see Jacoby, *FGrH*, vol. III B Supplement, Hellanikos 323a. The civic and cultic eponymy of the priestess of Hera at Argos will be considered in chapter 3.

72. Lewis (1955); Clinton (1974), Lazzarini (1976); Debord (1982); Mills (1984); Turner (1983); Cole (1992); Osborne (1993); Aleshire (1994a); Bremen (1996); Parker and Obbink (2000); Dignas (2002); Parker (2005); *LGS, LSAM LSS, LSCG, NGSL*. For important overview of the vital role of epigraphy in our understanding of Greek religion, see Henrichs (2003).

73. M. Ventris and J. Chadwick, *Documents in Mycenaean Greek*² (Cambridge 1973) 240–50, no. 114, and 252–58, no. 135; Billigmeier and Turner (1981) 7.

74. For methodological approach, see C. Renfrew, *The Archaeology of Cult: The Sanctuary at Phylakopi* (London 1985) and Morris (2000).

75. Mantis (1990) 28–65.

76. London, British Museum F 127; Mantis (1990) 64, pl. 27.

77. Bérard (1983) 7–12; Bérard and Durand (1989) 25; Ferrari (2002) 23–25.

78. Toledo Museum of Art 1972.55, ca. 490–480 B.C.; K. Luckner and C. Boulter, *CVA Toledo* (Mainz 1976) fig. 34, pl. 53.

79. Connelly (1993) 88–129, esp. 88–90 and 123.

80. Connelly (1993) 88–90.

81. Sourvinou-Inwood (1987); Sourvinou-Inwood (2005). I thank Christiane Sourvinou-Inwood for kindly sharing her manuscript with me before its publication and for her thoughtful insights at every stage of this work.

82. Blok, in Blok and Mason (1987) 44.

83. For gender, see Sourvinou-Inwood (1988c, 1995a); for ritual, Sourvinou-Inwood (1988a, 1990, 1997, 2005); for tragedy, Sourvinou-Inwood (2003); for visual culture, Sourvinou-Inwood (1987, 1988c, 1991).

84. Sourvinou-Inwood (1991) 7–9. Sourvinou-Inwood (1987) 18–20 calls for the separation of iconographic analysis and semantic analysis.

85. Sourvinou-Inwood (1991) 10–13; Sourvinou-Inwood (2004) 141, 146–47.

86. Price (1984) 3.

87. As articulated by Price (1984) 3, 11–15; Sourvinou-Inwood (1995a) 111.

88. Calame (1977) 27; G. Sissa, *Greek Virginity* (Cambridge, MA 1990) esp. 43, 73, 86, 105–23, 170.

89. M. Beard, "The Sexual Status of the Vestal Virgins," *JRS* 70 (1980) 12–27; M. Beard "Re-reading (Vestal) Virginity," in Hawley and Levick (1995) 166–77. A. Staples, *From Good Goddess to Vestal Virgins* (London 1998) 129–56.

90. Plutarch *Numa* 10.4–7.

91. For human ex-voto, see Brown (1988) 260 with n. 6, citing Eusebius of Emesa *Homily* 6 (*De Martiribus*) 18, in É. M. Buytaert, *Eusèbe d'Émèse: Discours conservés en Latin*, I. (Louvain 1953) 162. For "royal palace hall," see Brown (1988) 356 with n. 72, citing Ambrose *De Institutiones Virginis* 12.79: 339B.

92. The Christian practice by which families would consecrate one of their daughters as a "bride of Christ" to ensure the salvation of the household is unthinkable in the ancient Greek context. But it was a very potent force in the teachings of the early church. "In every house of Christians it is needful that there be a virgin, for the salvation of the whole house is that one virgin," wrote Athanasios, *The Canons of Athanasius*, W. Reidel and W. E. Crum, eds. (London 1904) 62–63. See Brown (1988) 264; D. Brakke, *Athanasius and Asceticism* (Baltimore and London 1995) 17–49.

93. Just (1989) 26–39; R. Sealey, *Women and the Law in Classical Athens* (Chapel Hill 1990).

94. See L. McClure in Faraone and McClure (2006) 8–10. M. Rother, "Marriage, Divorce, and the Prostitute in Ancient Mesopotamia," in Faraone and McClure (2006) 21–39; P. Bird, "Prostitution in the Social World and the Religious Rhetoric of Israel," in Faraone and McClure (2006) 40–58; S. Budin, "Sacred Prostitution in the First Person," in Faraone and McClure (2006) 77–92; B. MacLachlan, "Sacred Prostitution and Aphrodite," *SR* 21 (1992) 145–62; S. M. Baugh, "Cult Prostitution in New Testament Ephesos: A Reappraisal," *Evangelical Theological Society* 42.3 (1999) 443–60; H. Conzelmann, "Korinth und die Mädchen der Aphrodite: Zur Religionsgeschichte der Stadt Korinth," *NAG* 8 (1967) 247.

95. B. Winter, *After Paul Left Corinth* (Grand Rapids 2001) 3, 85, 87, 98–100.

96. See N. L. Goodrich, *Priestesses* (New York 1989), esp. 3, 396, 398. The utopian image of a peaceful period of matriarchy and the "Goddess," as presented by M. Gimbutas, has been discounted. See M. Gimbutas, *The Goddesses and Gods of Old Europe 6500–3500 B.C.: Myths and Cult Images* (Berkeley 1982); *The Language of the Goddess: Unearthing the Hidden Symbols of Western Civilization* (San Francisco 1989); and *The Civilization of the Goddess: The World of Old Europe* (New York 1991). For criticism, see L. Meskell, "Goddesses, Gimbutas, and 'New Age' Archaeology," *Antiquity* 69 (1995) 74–86; L. Talalay, "A Feminist Boomerang: The Great Goddess and Greek Prehistory," *Gender and History* 6 (1994) 165–83; Bolger (2003) 15–16, 93.

97. Turner (1983) 411.

98.   Goff (2004) 59.

99.   Padel (1983) 3–17, esp. 5–8, a view that is followed by Goff (2004) 35.

100. We shall see in chapter 6 that rules pertaining to menstruation are all but absent from sacred laws. Among the four hundred surviving texts recording laws for entering sanctuaries, only six mention menstruation, and these are all late, dating to the second century B.C. and after; see Cole (1992) 104. By contrast, heavy weight placed by Jewish law on the polluting effects of menstruating women is extreme. In Leviticus 20:18, we learn that intercourse with a menstruating woman is a crime so serious that it is punishable by death for both parties. Indeed, contact with anything even touched by a menstruating woman is polluting (Lev. 15:19–33). These beliefs seem to have influenced attitudes in the early Christian Church where a menstruating woman's "uncleanness" made her unworthy to receive Holy Communion, and perhaps even to enter a church. During the mid-third century A.D., Dionysios, Patriarch at Alexandria, issued an official exclusion of menstruating women from communion. A century later, another Alexandrian Patriarch, Timothy (ca. A.D. 379–85) adopted the *responsum* of Dionysios, which became canon law in the Byzantine Church, *Patrologia Graeca* 10:1281 and *Patrologia Graeca* 33:1300. The passage of the *responsum* into Canon law was confirmed by the "Quinisext" Council in Trullo at Constantinople in 692. The restriction has endured to this day in the Greek and Russian Orthodox churches.

101. I. M. Lewis, *Ecstatic Religions* (Harmondsworth 1978) 72–117.

102. Goff (2004) 13.

103. Goff (2004) 59.

104. Humphreys (1988) 16.

105. Goff (2004) 5, 91, 93, 108–9.

106. Lissarrague (1990) 9–12.

107. Bérard (1983) 5–37; Sourvinou-Inwood (1987) 1–43; Bérard and Durand (1989); Ferrari (2002) 17–34.

108. Lissarrague, Nilsson Lectures, Swedish Institute at Athens 1995. "La Grèce antique. Civilization I: Fonctions de l'images," *Encyclopedia Universalles-France*² (Paris 1991) 874–77.

109. Ferrari (2002) 17–25.

110. Nicholson (1997); Meskell (1999) 54–56.

111. Pomeroy (1975); Lefkowitz and Fant (1982); Kraemer (1988). The bibliography on ancient women grew steadily throughout the 1980s; representative works include Foley (1981b); Cameron and Kuhrt (1983); C. Mossé, *La Femme dans la Grèce antique* (Paris 1981); J. Peradotto and J. P. Sullivan, eds., *Women in the Ancient World: The Arethusa Papers* (Albany 1984).

112. Humphreys (1988); Foxhall (1989); S. Goldhill, *Foucault's Virginity: Ancient Erotic Fiction and the History of Sexuality* (1995) stand out among many others who took up new and long-neglected areas of study.

113. S. Brown, "Feminist Research in Archaeology: What Does It Mean? Why Is It Taking So Long?" in *Feminist Theory and the Classics*, N. S. Rabinowitz and A. Richlin, eds. (New York 1993) 238–71; T. Cullen, "Contributions to Feminism in Archaeology," *AJA* 100 (1996) 409–14. For studies of women in visual culture see, among others, Ridgway (1987); J. Reilly, " 'Mistress and Maid' on Athenian Lekythoi," *Hesperia* 58.4 (1989) 411–44; Reeder (1995); Ferrari (2002); S. Lewis, *The Athenian Woman: An Iconographic Handbook* (London 2002).

114. For overview of issues in classical archaeology, see Koloski-Ostrow and Lyons (1997), esp. Brown's contribution, 238–71. See also D. Bolger and N. Serwint, *Engendering Aphrodite: Women and Society in Ancient Cyprus* (Boston 2002).

115. For overview, see Brown (1997) 21–24. For approach, see Meskell and Preucel (2004b); Meskell and Preucel in Meskell and Preucel (2004a) 129–31; Bolger (2003); Meskell (2002); Meskell (2001) 187–213; Meskell (2000) 187–213; Meskell (1999); Meskell (1988a, 1988b); I. Hodder, "The 'Social' in Archaeological Theory: An Historical and Contemporary Perspective," in Meskell and Preucel (2004a) 23–42.

116. Meskell and Preucel in Meskell and Preucel (2004b) 129–31; Meskell (1999) 54–56. I am indebted to Lynn Meskell for kindly discussing with me a number of issues raised in this chapter.

117. Meskell (1999) 54–55. The second wave saw the development of women's studies, radical lesbian feminism, ecofeminism, gynocentric feminism, women's spirituality, the "Goddess Movement," and other projects. Gero and Conkey (1991) is representative of the second wave.

118. The leaders of the third wave are queer theorists, lesbian feminists, women of color, postcolonialists, transnationalists, and others who have focused on issues of the body, difference, power, performance, and alterity. The bibliography is large and growing; see Nicholson (1990) and L. Alcoff "Cultural Feminism versus Post-structuralism: The Identity Crisis in Feminist Theory," in Nicholson (1997) 330–55, who argues that there is no such thing as "women" at all. What Meskell defines as third wave is what some others still describe as second wave. It should be noted that, while deconstructive strategies were employed much earlier on in literary analysis and film theory, they were adopted only later in the field of archaeology.

119. Adorno (1991), ed. J. M. Berstein.

120. For overview, see O'Neill (1999) 7. Of course, we need only consider Foucault's "visible invisible" to recognize the inherent difficulties in the binary model, which does not allow for the "strength of the weak," and the micropolitics of power within the contruct; M. Foucault, *The Birth of the Clinic: An Archaeology of Medical Perception* [1973], trans. A. M. Sheridan Smith (New York 1994) chap. 9, "The Visible Invisible." See also M. Foucault, *Discipline and Punish* (New York 1977).

121. Adorno (1966 = 1973) 163. S. W. Nicholson, "Adorno, Benjamin, and the Aura," in O'Neill (1999) 41–65; S. W. Nicholson, *Exact Imagination, Late Work: On Adorno's Aesthetics* (Cambridge, MA 1992); Knapp, "Fragile Foundations," 124, 131; W. Benjamin, *Shriften*, vol. 1, T. Adorno and S. Adorno, eds. (Frankfurt 1955).

122. Bourdieu with Passeron (1990); Bourdieu (1972 = 1977); Bourdieu (1986).

123. Butler (1990) 4–5 and J. Butler, "Gender Trouble, Feminist Theory, and Psychoanalytic Discourse," in Nicholson (1990) 324–40. For helpful overview, see Meskell (1999) 67–69, 103–6.

124. D. Haraway, *Simians, Cyborgs, and Women: The Reinvention of Nature* (London 1991) uses the cyborg metaphor to articulate the mixed values of the present.

125. J. Halley, "Take a Break from Feminism?" in *Gender and Human Rights*, K. Knop, ed. (Oxford 2004) 57–81 and *Split Decisions: How and Why to Take a Break from Feminism* (Princeton 2006).

126. See Preucel and Meskell in Meskell and Preucel (2004a) 31–34; A. Gardner, *Agency Uncovered: Archaeological Perspectives on Social Agency, Power, and Being Human* (London 2004); D. S. Heckman, "Subjects and Agents: The Question for Feminism," in *Provoking Agents: Gender and Agency in Theory and Practice*, J. K. Gardiner, ed. (Urbana 1995) 194–207; M. Johnson, "Conceptions of Agency in Archaeological Interpretation," in *Interpretive Archaeology: A Reader*, J. Thomas, ed. (London and New York 2000) 211–27; J. C. Barret, "Agency, the Duality of Structure, and the Problem of the Archaeological Record," in *Archaeological Theory Today*, I. Hodder, ed. (Cambridge 2001) 304–20. For broader theoretical issues, see A. Gell, *Art and Agency: An Anthropological Theory* (Oxford 1998).

127. Bolger (2003) 184–85.

128. I. Winter, "Agency: An Alternative to Subjectivity," in *Field Work: Sites in Literary and Cultural Studies* M. Garver, P. Franklin, and R. Walk, eds. (London 1996) 202.

129. Broude and Garrard (2005) 3.

130. Broude and Garrard (2005) 1.

131. Broude and Garrard (2005) 3. I am indebted to Norma Broude for kindly sharing part of the manuscript with me prior to its publication. See J. Hoff, "The Pernicious Effects of Poststructuralism," in *Radically Speaking: Feminism Reclaimed*, D. Bell and R. Klein, eds. (North Melbourne 1996) 393–412; Lisa Tickner, "Feminism, Art History, and Sexual Difference," *Genders* 3 (1988) 92–128; D. Fuss, *Essentially Speaking: Feminism, Nature, and Difference* (New York, 1989). S. Brodribb, *Nothing Matters: A Feminist Critique of Postmodernism* (Melbourne 1992).

132. J. Gero, "Troubled Travels in Agency and Feminism," in *Agency in Archaeology*, M.-A. Dobres and J. Robb, eds. (London and New York 2000) 40–50.

133. H. S. Versnel, "Wife and Helpmate: Women of Ancient Athens in Anthropological Perspective," in Blok and Mason (1987) 59–86.

134. A point made by R. Bagnall in "Women, Law, and Social Realities in Late Antiquity: A Review Article," *Bulletin of the American Society of Papyrologists* 32 (1995) 81–82, review of Joelle Beauchamp, *Le statut de la femme à Byzance: 4e–7e siècle*, vol. 1, *Le Droit Imperial* (Paris 1990).

135. Bourdieu with Passeron (1990) 30; Bourdieu (1972 = 1977); Bourdieu (1986) 241–58, esp. 252.

136. Bourdieu (1972 = 1977) chap. 2, "Structures and the *Habitus*."

137.	Meskell (1999) 59. See also Preucel and Meskell in Meskell and Preucel (2004b) 8–11.

138.	Bolger (2003) 186–87; Thomas (1996).

139.	T. Arecchi, "Chaos and Complexity," in *The Post-modern Reader*, C. Jencks, ed. (London and New York 1992) 350–53; C. Jencks, *The Architecture of the Jumping Universe: A Polemic: How Complexity Science Is Changing Architecture and Culture* (London 1997); D. Byrne, *Complexity Theory and the Social Sciences* (London and New York 1998). See also G. Nicolis and I. Prigogine, *Explaining Complexity* (New York 1989); M. Mitchell Waldrop, *Complexity: The Emerging Science at the Edge of Order and Chaos* (New York 1992); S. Kauffman, *The Origins of Order, Self-Organization, and Selection in Evolution* (Oxford 1993); M. Gell-Mann, *The Quark and the Jaguar: Adventures in the Simple and the Complex* (Boston and London, 1994); G. Nicolis, *Introduction to Nonlinear Science* (Cambridge 1995).

140.	A. Cochrane, "What a Difference a Place Makes: The New Politics of Locality," *Antipode* 19 (1987) 354–63; B. Warf, "Postmodernism and the Localities Debate: Ontological Questions and Epistemological Implications," *Tijdschraft voor Economische en Sociale Geografie* 84.3 (1993) 162–68.

141.	Kearns (1995) 526.

142.	Bruit Zaidman and Schmidt Pantel (1989) 228.

143.	Blok (2001) 114 estimates that Athenian women were involved in about 85 percent of all religious events.

144.	R. E. Tringham, "Households with Faces: The Challenges of Gender in Prehistoric Architectural Remains," in Gero and Conkey (1991) 93–131.

145.	With a nod to Henry James.

CHAPTER 2. PATHS TO PRIESTHOOD: PREPARATION, REQUIREMENTS, AND ACQUISITION

1.	Translation by Henderson (1996) 64, with a few slight changes. The punctuation is in dispute; see Parker (2005) 223.

2.	P. Vidal-Naquet, *The Black Hunter: Forms of Thought and Forms of Society in the Greek World* (Baltimore, 1986) 145 reads the passage as a fiction. See Parker (2005) 218–34; Sourvinou-Inwood (1971a) 339–42; Sourvinou-Inwood (1971b) 175; Sourvinou-Inwood (1988b) 35–36; Sourvinou-Inwood (1988c) 138–40; Henderson (1996) 216; A. H. Sommerstein, *Lysistrata, The Comedies of Aristophanes* vol. 7 (Warminster 1990) 83, 188–90; Lloyd-Jones (1983) 87–102; Brelich (1969) 246–59; T. C. W. Stinton, "Iphigeneia and the Bears of Brauron," *CQ* 26 (1976) 11–12; M. B. Walbank, "Artemis Bear-Leader," *CQ* 31 (1981) 276–81; For summary of scholarship on *krokotos*, see Sourvinou-Inwood (1988c) 127–34; (1971a) 340–42; (1988c) 136.

3.	Contra Goff (2004) 246–59.

4.	Turner (1983) 323–42.

5. Sosandra, *PA* 13159, *ID* 1870.3; Apollodora and Theodora, *FD* III 31, *IG* II² 1943. Their father, Sara-pion (*PA* 12564), was *epimeletes* of Delos in 100/99 B.C., and *agonothetes* of the Eleusinia, Pana-thenaia, Delia, and Diasia in 98/97 B.C. (*SEG* 32.218.207–216). Their brother, Diokles, was *kleidou-chos* in the year that his father was *epimeletes* (*ID* 2364). See Turner (1983) 329–30; Mikalson (1998) 240 n. 63; Tracy (1982) 159–63, 215–16.

6. Plutarch *Moralia* 843; *ID* 1869. See Aleshire (1994a) 336, no. 14; Turner (1983) 271–73.

7. *Moralia* 795D–E. Translation by H. N. Fowler, *Plutarch's Moralia*, Loeb Classical Library, vol. 10 (Cambridge, MA 1991) 141.

8. E. Lippolis, "Il santuario di Atena a Lindo," *ASAt* 50 (1988–89) 118–23, esp. 121.

9. Parker in *RAW* 571.

10. For poetic recitation, see J. Svenbro, *La parole et le marbre* (Paris 1975); for female choruses, see Calame (1977); for sacrifical meals, see P. Schmitt-Pantel, *La cité au banquet: Histoire de repas public dans les cités grecques*, Collection de l'École française de Rome (Rome and Paris 1991).

11. Bolger (2003) 186–87; Thomas (1996); C. Gosen, *Social Being and Time* (Oxford 1994); A. Rossi, ed., *Gender and the Life Course* (New York 1983); R. Gilchrist, "Archaeology and the Life Course: A Time and Age for Gender," in Meskell and Preucel (2004a) 142–60.

12. Parker (1983) 80.

13. Calame (1977, and English edition 1997).

14. Translation by Furley and Bremer (2001) 22; see their important discussion of female choruses, 21–23. Nagy (1994/95) 44 has suggested that the most accurate term for describing the experience of chorus members is *paideia*.

15. Calame (1997) 26–33. On chorus and community, see E. Stehle, *Performance and Gender in Ancient Greece* (Princeton 1997); Bruneau (1970) 35–38; Robbins (1994) 7–16.

16. Members of the virgin chorus are referred to as "daughters" of the god, goddess, or community that they served. Homer calls the chorus of nymphs around Artemis the daughters of Zeus (*Odyssey* 6.105), while Kallimachos describes the band of Argive virgins in the service of Athena as the daughters of the Arestorides (*Lavacrum Palladis* 34). The maidens who sing and play the lyre for Artemis at Ephesos are called the daughters of the Lydians (*Autocrates* frag. 1 KA). Examples are gathered by Calame (1997) 31.

17. Boston, Museum of Fine Arts 65.908. P. Truitt, "Attic White Ground Pyxis and Phiale," *BMFA* 67 (1969) 72–92; Lissarrague (1992) fig. 28; Lewis (2002) 49, fig. 3.31.

18. Holderman (1913) 28.

19. By the end of the third century B.C. they are referred to as *errephoroi*. For the two forms of the word, see *GAI* vol., 127–28; F. Adrados, "Sobre las Arreforias o Erreforias," *Emerita* 19 (1951) 127–33; Brulé (1987) 79–98. Mansfield (1985) 268 sees *errephoros* as the earlier form. *Arrephoros* is generally taken to mean "carrier of the secret things"; however, some relationship to the role of *hersephoros* (dew car-

rier) is possible. The following references for *errephoroi* and *hersephoroi* are gathered in Mansfield (1985) 269. Arrephoroi also served in cults of Asklepios (*IG* II² 974 = *SEG* 18.26, lines 18–19, and *IG* II² 1033 = *SEG* 18.29, lines 12–14) and Demeter and Kore (*IG* II² 3729). *Hersephoroi* are known to have served Chloe Themis (*IG* II² 5098), Eileithyia at Agrai (*IG* II² 5099), and the nymph Euboule (*IG* II² 5100b, corrected by W. Merkel, "Notes on the South-Slope Inscriptions," *Hesperia* 16 [1947] 76). See Parker (2005) 219–23; W. Burkert, "Kekropidensagen und Arrephoria," *Hermes* 94 (1966) 1–25; for arrephoroi at Epidauros and Miletos, see 5 n. 3. See also Robertson (1983) 241–88; G. Donnay, "L'Arréphorie: Initiation ou rite civique? Un cas d'école," *Kernos* 10 (1977) 177–205.

20. Harpokration, s.v. *arrephorein*. Burkert (1966) 3–4 believes that a short list of four girls was selected by the demos in this fashion, from which the *basileus* chose two to serve.

21. Turner (1983) 343–50; Mansfield (1985) 296–301; Mikalson (1998) 199; Tracy (1990) 60.

22. Harpokration, s.v. *arrephorein*.

23. Robertson (1983) 241–88, esp. 251.

24. [Plutarch] *XOrat* 839c.; Harpokration, s.v. *arrephorein*, *AG* 1.202.3.

25. Hesychios, s.v. *aletrides*; Parker (1983) 80; Brulé (1987) 114–16. The punctuation is in dispute and the cult title *archegetis* could be read as one for Athena, Artemis, or even Demeter. See Parker (2005) 223 n. 24 and Sourvinou-Inwood (1988c) 140–46.

26. *Suda*, s.v. *anastatoi*.

27. Sourvinou-Inwood (1988c) 67; Parker (2005) 232–48; Kahil (1963); Kahil (1965); Kahil (1977); Brulé (1987) 179–283; Simon (1983) 83–88; Dowden (1989) 9–47; Ferrari (2002) 167–77; Cole (1984) 233–44; S. G. Cole, "Domesticating Artemis," in Blundell and Williamson (1998) 27–43; S. G. Cole, "Landscapes of Artemis," in *The Organization of Space in the Antiquity*, S. G. Cole, ed., special issue *CW* 93 (2000) 470–81; Cole (2004) 198–230; Goff (2004) 105–8, 181–83; Gentili and Perusino (2002).

28. Scholia to *Lysistrata*, line 645 Ravenna MS, *Suda*, s.v. Arktas and Braunoniois. Brelich (1969) 248–49; Parker (2005) 238–39; Lloyd-Jones (1983) 87–102; Hamilton (1989) 449–72; Brulé (1987) 179–86, 200–222; P. Perlman, "Acting the She-Bear for Artemis," *Arethousa* 22 (1989) 111–34; W. Sale, "The Temple-Legends of the Arkteia," *RhM* 118 (1975) 268–84; S. G. Cole, "Domesticating Artemis," in Blundell and Williamson (1998) 27–43; Vernant (1990) 182–84, 201–6. Faraone (2003) 43–68.

29. The Doric stoa, built ca. 430–420 B.C., shows three colonnaded wings, behind which a series of eleven square rooms are preserved, holding eleven wooden couches and seven stone tables each. See Themelis (2002); Themelis (1986); Themelis (1971). For excavation reports, see J. Papadimitriou in *Praktika* (1945–48) 81–90; (1949) 75–90; (1950) 173–87; (1955) 118–20; (1956) 73–87; (1957) 42–45; (1959) 18–20; and A. Orlandos in *Ergon* (1956) 25–31; (1957) 20–24; (1958) 30–39; (1959) 13–20; (1960) 21–30; (1961) 20–37; (1962) 25–39; and J. Papadimitriou in "The Sanctuary of Artemis at Brauron," *Scientific American* (June 1963) 11–20.

30. Simon (1983) 86. Kahil (1981) 253–63; Kahil (1983) 235–37.

31. T. Scanlon, "Race or Chase at the Arkteia of Attica?" *Nikephoros* 3 (1990) 73–120; Dowden (1989) 31. Kahil (1963); Kahil (1965); Kahil (1977); Kahil (1981); Kahil (1983).

32. Ferrari (2002) 175.

33. Dated ca. 430–420 B.C.

34. Basel, Collection of Herbert A. Cahn, inv. no. HC 501. For full bibliography, see Reeder (1995) 322–25. Kahil (1965); Kahil (1977); Kahil (1983).

35. Basel, Collection of Herbert A. Cahn, inv. no. HC 502. For full bibliography, see Reeder (1995) 326–27. Kahil (1965); Kahil (1977); Kahil (1983). For summary of scholarship on *krokotos*, see Sourvinou-Inwood (1988c) 127–34.

36. Kahil (1977); Simon (1983) 88.

37. Dedications in honor of hearth initiates: *IG* II² 3475 + 3476 = Clinton (2005) 244; 3477, 3478 = Clinton (2005) 238; 3480 = Clinton (2005) 270; 3499; *SEG* 33.197. See Clinton (1974) 98–114; Mikalson (1998) 259–60; A. G. Woodhead, *Inscriptions: The Decrees, Agora* vol. 16 (Princeton 1997) 56. 41–42.

38. Clinton (1974) 98–114. Inscriptions preserve the names of fifty-nine hearth initiates, twenty-eight of whom were girls who served between the late second century B.C. and the third century A.D. The girls all came from aristocratic families, some of which set up statues to commemorate their daughters' service. One girl, whose name does not survive, held the post of hearth initiate during the second half of the second century B.C., after which she went on to serve as kanephoros, for the Panathenaia as well as for the Pythia of Apollo, *IG* II² 3477; Clinton (1974) 100, no. 2; Turner (1983) 316.

39. Parker (2005) 224–32.

40. Aristophanes *Lysistrata* 642; Scholia to Theokritos, *Idylls* 2.66–68; Schelp (1975) 18–19; for discussion, see Sourvinou-Inwood (1988c) 53–56; Parker (2005) 225 n. 35.

41. Diodorus Siculus 9.37.1. An alternate version has Peisistratos's daughter serving as arrephoros when the event occurred, though it seems more likely that Thrasyboulos fell in love with an adolescent maiden rather than with a child; see *Papyrus Oxyrrinchus* IV 664, col. i.29–32 (fourth–third century B.C.); Polyainos *Strategmata* 5.14.1. Mansfield (1985) 272–73.

42. In the fragments of *Kitharistes*, a man falls in love with a woman whom he sees in a procession for Artemis at Ephesos.

43. Thucydides 6.56.1–2; Aristotle *Constitution of the Athenians* 18.2.

44. *IG* II² 334.14–15; Lewis (1959). Woodhead, *Agora* vol. 16, 75. Indeed, they were the only female recipients of honorific cuts.

45. Parker (2005) 223–26.

46. Turner (1983) 327–42.

47. Turner (1983) 327–42.

48.   *IG* II² 968.52–53; Mikalson (1998) 258.

49.   Van Straten (1995) 10–12, 162–64.

50.   J. Bazant, "The Sacrificial Basket in Vase Painting," *Acta Universitatis Carolinae Philologica* 1 (1974) 61–68; Roccos (1995); Schelp (1975). See images of weddings gathered in Oakley and Sinos (1993) figs. 71, 75, 93.

51.   Ferrara, Museo Nazionale 44894 (T57 CVP), from Spina. *ARV²* 1143.1; *Addenda²* 334; Durand and Schnapp in Bérard et al. (1989) 52–53; M. Robertson, *The Art of Vase Painting in Classical Athens* (Cambridge 1992) 224, fig. 231; Furley and Bremer (2001) 77–79.

52.   Paris, Musée du Louvre CA 2567; *ARV²* 698.37. Lissarrague in Schmidt Pantel (1992) 186, fig. 29.

53.   Berlin, Staatliche Museen F 2189, from Chiusi. *ARV²* 363.27; P. Sticott, "Zu griechischen Hochzeits-gebräuchen, *Festschrift für Otto Benndorf* (Vienna 1898) 188, fig. 319; Roccos (1995) 653, fig. 13.

54.   Boston, Museum of Fine Arts 13.195, the Gales Painter, said to have been found at Gela in Sicily; *ARV²* 35.1, *Addenda²* 158; Boardman, *ARFV*, fig. 211; Roccos (1995) 642, fig. 1.

55.   Roccos (1995) 646–51.

56.   Roccos (1995) 654–59; at 646 Roccos admits that this mantle is seen "chiefly, although not exclusively, in (festival) scenes."

57.   University of Newcastle upon Tyne, Shefton Museum of Greek Art and Archaeology 203, Pan Painter. *ARV²* 1651 (555.92bis); *Addenda²* 258; B. Shefton, "The Greek Museum, University of Newcastle upon Tyne," *Archaeological Reports 1969–70*, Society for the Promotion of the Hellenic Tradition and the British School at Athens (1970) 59, fig. 12; Roccos (1995) 652, fig. 12; Lewis (2002) 48, fig. 3.29.

58.   Parker (2005) 218–52; Turner (1983) 189 lists twenty-two different offices open to women in sub-sacerdotal roles.

59.   Schnapp (1988) 568–74. See also A. A. Donahue, *Xoana and the Origins of Greek Sculpture*, American School of Classical Studies 15 (Athens 1988) 40–43, 139.

60.   Hesychios, s.v. *ergastinai*. Turner (1983) 193, 359; Goff (2004) 53 thinks they were nine years old; Brulé (1987) thinks that they were girls but that their mothers were somehow involved; Simon (1983) 39 thinks they were maidens and married women; Mansfield (1985) 277–81 has the *arrephoroi* weaving; Parke (1977) 141–43; Parker (2005) 226–27.

61.   *IG* II² 1036. S. B. Aleshire and S. D. Lambert, "Making the "Peplos" for Athena: A New Edition of *IG* II² 1060 + *IG* II² 1036," *ZPE* 142 (2003) 65–86 assign the job of weaving to the *parthenoi* who are mentioned; Tracy (1990) 219. Other lists are found on *IG* II² 1034 (103/102 b.c.) and *IG* II² 1942 (ca. 100 b.c.).

62.   Mikalson (1998) 257–58; Brulé (1987) 98–105; Tracy (1990) 219.

63.   Turner (1983) 193, 359; Mansfield (1985) 279–81.

64. *PA* 468; *IG* II² 1034d.23.

65. *PA* 11264.

66. Around 100 B.C.: *IG* II² 1942.10, 11, and 1; 103/102 B.C.: *IG* II² 1034d.27, 26, and 20.

67. Tracy (1990) 219.

68. *IG* II² 1034 (103/102 B.C.).

69. Photius, s.v. *Kallynteria kai Plynteria*. See Mansfield (1985) 370; Brulé (1987) 105–11; Parker (2005) 474–78; G. S. Dontas, "The True Aglaurion," *Hesperia* 52 (1983) 48–63. The washing of statues is also attested for the cult of Aphrodite Pandemos at Athens, Athena Pronaia at Delphi, and Zeus at Olympia.

70. Brulé (1987) 107; F. Willemsen, *Frühe griechische Kultbilder* (Würzburg 1939).

71. Hesychios, s.v. *loutrides*; Photios, s.v. *loutrides*. Mansfield (1985) 367–68 makes the distinction between the two offices.

72. Hesychios, s.v. *agretai*.

73. Fontenrose (1988) 125–29; Bremen (1996) 90–95, and esp. 90–91, where she discusses the case of Artemon, who, as prophet of Apollo, was joined first by his elder daughter, Batios (A.D. 5/6), and later by his younger daughter, Theodoris (A.D. 10/11), in the prophet/*hydrophoros* father/daughter pairing, *Milet* I 3, 127. See Bremen 90 n. 32 for *I.Didyma* 332.

74. Bremen (1996) 91.

75. *I.Eph.* III 990; Schwabl (1993) 142.

76. Translation by Reardon (1989) 371.

77. Turner (1983) 244–83.

78. Clinton (1974) 70, no. 3 lists the first documented married priestess of Demeter at Eleusis as the mother of Epigenes from Acharnai, dated to the mid-fourth century B.C. Documentation survives for nine known *hierophantides*, most of whom came from distinguished families with extensive priestly connections. Half the inscriptions commemorating *hierophantides* specifically refer to married women. Relatives, including sons, set up statues to honor several of these women for their sacred service, *IG* II² 3585 = Clinton (2005) 371; *IG* II² 3575 = Clinton (2005) 454. See Turner (1983) 218.

79. The cults of Dionysos at Sikyon, Kore at Mantineia, Artemis at Ephesos, and Meter at Kyzikos all celebrated festivals during which the statues were adorned; examples gathered by Mansfield (1985) 527.

80. Mansfield (1985) 544–46, lists thirteen statues with full citations, including *IGSK* 13, *I. Ephesos* 3, no. 989, p. 266, a second-century-A.D. portrait statue for a priestess of Artemis named Oulpia Euodia Moudiana, "whose family, going far back, has included priestesses and *kosmeteirai*," lines 6–8.

81. Burkert (1985) 242; Pomeroy (1984) 49; Brumfield (1981); Zeitlin (1982); Detienne (1989); Versnel (1992) 31–55; Cole (1994) 199–216; Clinton (1996); L. Nixon, "The Cults of Demeter and Kore" in Hawley and Levick (1995) 75–96; Parker (2005) 270–83. U. Kron, "Frauen feste in Demeter Heilig-tumern: Des Thesmophorion von Bitalemi," *AA* (1992) 611–50.

82. Broneer (1942) 265–74, no. 51.

83. Turner (1983) 218; Parke (1977) 83–84; Burkert (1985) 242–43.

84. *IG II²* 1184.18 is a decree passed by the deme Cholargos in the year 334/333 B.C. It mentions two committee women called *archousai* who served under the priestess of the Thesmophoria, assisting her with preparations and paying the bill. The orator Isaios (8.19–20) tells us that these women were "selected" from a number of available candidates who had been previously chosen by the married women of the deme. Broneer (1942) 271–72 takes this to mean that the women were selected "by lot." See Turner (1983) 109–11.

85. Henrichs (1978); Henrichs (1990); R. Kraemer, "Ecstasy and Possession: The Attraction of Women to the Cult of Dionysos," *HThR* 72 (1979) 55ff.; J. N. Bremmer, "Greek Maenadism Reconsidered," *ZPE* 55 (1984) 267–86; Seaford (1996) 30–54; Goff (2004) 214–16, 271–79.

86. Plutarch, *Alexander*, 2.7ff.; Athenaeus, 14.659F60A, 13.560F.

87. Bremen (1996) 114–41. Husband-wife teams are known for the priesthood of Athena Lindia and Zeus Polieus at Lindos from the 40s B.C.: *I.Lindos* 105–6. At Panamara in Karia, the priest of Zeus was joined by his wife (or another female relative) named priestess from the first century A.D., Bremen (1996) 68–73. By the second century A.D., the priest of Hekate at Lagina, who once served on his own, was joined in officeholding by his wife; see *I.Stratonikeia* II 1 nos. 530, 668 discussed by Bremen (1996) 284.

88. Bremen (1996) 114–41, 273–96.

89. *I.Stratonikeia* I nos. 15, 186, 192, 197–99; II 1, nos. 663–64. A. Laumonier, "Recherches sur la chronolo-gie des prêtres de Panamara," *BCH* 61 (1937) 253–59; Bremen (1996) appendix 2, 316, no. 2.

90. J. Bremmer, "The Old Women of Ancient Greece," in Blok and Mason (1987) 191–213.

91. Plutarch, *Numa* 9.11, *The E Temple at Delphi* 385; Parker (1983) 88 n. 58.

92. *Etymologicum Magnum*, s.v. *gerarai*; [Demosthenes] *Against Neaira* 59.73.

93. [Demosthenes] 59.78, as translated and discussed by Cole (2004) 134.

94. Hesch, s.v. *geraraides*.

95. Diodoros Siculus 16.26. By the time Plutarch (*Moralia* 405C) writes in the second century A.D., the Pythia is again chosen from among maidens rather than older women, suggesting a reversal back to the earlier model.

96. *I. Miletos* 484. Fontenrose (1988) 97–98, no. R25 (pp. 199–202); T. Drew-Bear and W. D. Lebek, "An Oracle of Apollo at Miletus," *GRBS* 14 (1973) 65–73; P. Herrmann, *Chiron* 1 (1971) 291–98; Merkel-bach, *ZPE* 8 (1971) 93–95; Bremen (1996) 93.

97. Kearns (1989) 64–77.

98. I. Toepffer, *Attische Genealogie* (Berlin 1889, reprint New York 1973) 3; Bourriot (1976), esp. vol. 1, 526–47, vol. 2, 1043–366; Roussel (1976) 65–88; Parker (1996) 56–66, 284–327.

99. Aleshire (1994a) 326–27; Martha (1882) 33–39; Feaver (1957) 124.

100. For polis cults, see Sourvinou-Inwood (1988a) and (1990) 295–322. For a definition of Athenian state cults, and discussion of gentilician and democratic priesthoods, see Aleshire (1994b) and Feaver (1957) 124. For *gene* and deme cults, see Kearns (1989) 69–102; Parker (1996) 284–332.

101. *LSCG* 65.2–6.

102. Parker (1983) 86–87; see 335 for Cyrene Cathartic Law; Parker in *RAW* 507–9; Cole (1992) 107–11 for summary of most serious pollutants, including miscarriage (forty-four-day waiting period before entering the sanctuary), death of a family member or contact with a corpse (forty-one days), deflowering of a virgin (equal with death), childbirth (two to three weeks for the mother, three days for those who have had contact with her). By comparison, sexual intercourse carries just a one- to two-day waiting period before entering most sanctuaries, and sometimes not at all, if intercourse takes place at night. If intercourse occurs by day, a bath might be enough to purify the worshipper before entering the sanctuary.

103. Garland (1995) 64; Ferguson (1989) 48; Dillon (1995) 48 n. 103.

104. *ED* 216.7–8, ca. 220 B.C.; *ED* 178a(A).6–7; Parker and Obbink (2000); Parker and Obbink (2001); Dillon (1997) 63–66.

105. *ED* 2a.13–14, *ED* 215.8–9. See also *LSCG* 166.8–10 (second or first century B.C.); *ED* 180.15–16; *ED* 182.5–7.

106. *LSAM* 5.11.

107. Anaxandrides frag. 40, 10 K.-A., *PCG* II p. 258. We are told that male citizens who had prostituted themselves were disqualified from holding priesthoods at Athens (*Aeschines* 1.19–21,188).

108. As outlined by Turner (1983): inheritance, 15–51; allotment, 52–119; election and appointment, 120–40; purchase, 141–73. I have relied on Turner, Aleshire (1994a), and *NGSL* 44–49, for the examples cited here, as well as Martha (1882) 24–32. See summary in Goff (2004) 174–78.

109. Turner (1983) 39.

110. Apollodoros *Library* 3.14.8–3, 15.1.

111. Turner (1983) 35–39.

112. Translation by R. G. Bury, Plato, *Laws*, Loeb Classical Library (Cambridge 1968).

113. As suggested by Turner (1983) 249. See also Aleshire (1994a) 332.

114. The case of Theodote (first half of second century B.C.) is discussed in Turner (1983) 254. We hear of other cults in which the priesthood was passed on matrilineally, as with the cult of Mnia and

Ayosia at Epidauros during the fourth century B.C. when the office seems to have passed from mother to daughter; Broadbent (1968) 18–23.

115. Aleshire (1994a) 332. For stemmata, see Davies *APF* 173; Lewis (1955) 7.

116. Clinton (1974) 76; Feaver (1957) 128.

117. Clinton (1974) 52–53.

118. Aleshire (1994a), esp. 333–34.

119. As pointed out by Kearns (1989) 71–72 n. 37.

120. Turner (1983) 29–31. See *NGSL* 45, where Pergamene decree is discussed, *LSAM* 13 (dated to before the death of Attalos III in 133 B.C.). Here, the city grants the priesthood of Asklepios, and other cults at the Asklepeion, to Asclepiades, son of Archias, the original founder of the shrine. The priesthood will pass on to his descendants.

121. Stephanus of Byzantium, s.v. Semachidai; Turner (1983) 29.

122. *IG* XII 3, 330; A. Wittenburg, *Il testamento di Epikteta* (Trieste 1990); *NGSL* 86–87.

123. Plato *Laws* 6.759b–c.

124. P. J. Rhodes, *A Commentary on the Aristotelian Athenaion* (Oxford 1981).

125. See Aleshire (1994a) 334 for date of introduction of sortition in the selection of sacred officials. This problem, she maintains, is "inextricably interwoven with and dependent upon opinions concerning the date of the introduction of sortition for archons." Aleshire (1994a) 334, and Turner (1983) 52–58, date the introduction of sortition to the early fifth century. See also Martha (1882) 29–35.

126. Turner (1983) 69.

127. *LSCG* 175; Turner (1983) 104–6; Dignas (2002) 262–63.

128. *IG* I³ 35 = ML² 44. Mark (1993) 104–7.

129. For problems of chronology, see R. Meiggs, *The Athenian Empire* (Oxford 1972) 497–503; *GHI* I², 108–11; B. Wesenberg, "Zur Baugeschichte des Niketempels," *JdI* 96 (1981) 28–54; Lewis (commentary in *IG* I³) dated the decree to 425/424 B.C.; Mattingly (1996) 461–71, dates the inscription ca. 430; I. T. Kakridis, "Παρατηρήσεις σε αρχαία επιγράμματα" *Ellenika* 12 (1952–53) 143–45 places it as late as 400. See also Aleshire (1994a) 327; S. V. Tracy, "Hands in Fifth-Century B.C. Attic inscriptions 277–82," in *Studies Presented to Sterling Dow on His Eightieth Birthday*, K. J. Rigsby, ed. (Durham 1984) 281–82; Loomis (1998) 76–78.

130. Feaver (1957) 137; Turner (1983) 71–74, 78.

131. Parker (1996) 125–27.

132. *IG* I³ 1330, lines 5–10; J. Papadimitriou (1951) 146; Lewis (1955) 1–3; *GHI*² 109.

133. Clairmont (1979) 103–10.

134. Jordan (1979) 32–33; Turner (1983) 70–71. The Archaic shrine of Athena Nike is located beneath the podium for the fifth-century marble temple; see Mark (1993) 20–30 and 32–34. Remains of a statue base (dated to 600–560 B.C.) and an inscribed altar block (dated ca. 580–530 B.C.) as well as terracotta figurines, establish a sixth-century date for the earliest phase of the sanctuary.

135. *LSS* 19 (= *SEG* 21.527) 12–14. Ferguson (1938) 1–68; Turner (1983) 97; Aleshire (1994a) 327–28, no. 14; Feaver (1957) 129–30. See A. Chaniotis in *RAW* 319; *IG* II (2) 1232, 1237. Parker (2005) 216.

136. *LSAM* 79.

137. Turner (1983) 129–30, 140.

138. For yearly elections, see *SEG* 40.956 (ca. 100–75 B.C. to early first century A.D.) where the oracle instructs people of Herakleia under Latmos to elect each year, from among all the citizens, a priest of Athena Latmia.

139. *NGSL* 46–47. For an elected term of ten years, see *LSCG* 103 B 16–18; for a priest elected to a lifelong tenure, see *LSAM* 78 (ca. 100 B.C.) in which Eirenaios is made priest of Zeus at Tlos.

140. *LSCG* 103B, 16–17, first c. B.C.; Turner (1983) 125–26.

141. *LSCG* 48A, dated to 183/182 B.C.; Turner (1983) 107–8, 133.

142. *LSCG* 48B, 3–8, 14–15; Turner (1983) 134.

143. *LSAM* 44, ca. 400 B.C. On the sale of priesthoods, see Debord (1982) 63–71, with distribution chart for evidence of sale of priesthoods at 65; Parker and Obbink (2000); Parker and Obbink (2001); Dignas (2002) 250–58; B. Dignas, "'Auf seine Kosten kommen'—ein Kriterium für Priester? Zum Verkauf von Priesterämtern im hellenistischen Kleinasien," in H. Heedemann and E. Winter, eds., *Neue Forschungen zur Religionsgeschichte Kleinasiens*, Elmer Schwertheim zum 60, *Geburtstag gewidmet*, *Asia Minor Studien* 49 (Bonn 2003) 27–40; H.-U. Wiemer, "Käufliche Priestertümer im hellinistischen Kos," *Chiron* 33 (2003) 263–310; *NGSL* 48–52. I am indebted to Beate Dignas for kindly allowing me to read select chapters of her dissertation before publication. Evidence for the sale of priesthoods is concentrated on the southwest coast of Asia Minor and in the eastern Aegean Islands, as well as at Milesian colonies on the Black Sea, including Tomoi and Sinope. It is attested for Kos, Chalkedon, Kyzikos, Alexandria Troas, Erythrai, Priene, Thebes at Mykale, Miletos, Ephesos, Magnesia on the Maeander, Hyllarima, Mylasa, Kasossos, Halikarnassos, Proconnesos, Iasus, Chios, Andros, Thasos, Skepsis, Samos, Seleucia ad Calycadmun, and Egypt. See Parker and Obbink (2000) 421 n. 16; Debord (1982) 65 gives map showing distribution of evidence for the sale of priesthoods.

144. Debord (1982) 63–64, believes that the practice originated at Miletos and spread from there.

145. *SEG* 40.956 (ca. 100–75 B.C. to early first century A.D.); Wörrle (1990) 19–58 thinks the oracle is probably from Didyma, though Delphi, Klaros, or Gryneion cannot be excluded. Dignas (2002) 265–66.

146. *LSAM* 49, A 7–10, discussed by Dignas (2002) 256–57.

147. Parker and Obbink (2000) 424, 5. The priest of Zeus Alseios had to be over eight years old (*ED* 215); the priest of Dionysos Thyllophoros first had to be over twelve years old, but later this was lowered to over ten (*ED* 216, *LSCG* 166); fourteen years of age was the minimum age for the priesthood of Asklepios, Hygieia, and Epione (*ED* 2); the priesthood of Korbanthes was to be held by someone over the age of twenty (*ED* 177).

148. *I.Erythrai* II no. 201, *LSAM* 25.68, priesthood of Ge (Earth). Debord (1982) appendix 2, 101–16; Robert *BCH* 57 (1933) 467–80; Sokolowski (1946); Forrest (1959) 513–22; Dignas (2002) 252–53.

149. *LSCG* 161 = *ED* 62; see Parker and Obbink (2000) 426.

150. Robert (1933) 475–81.

151. Parker and Obbink (2000) 425, 14a.

152. *LSAM* 37; Debord (1982) 67 n. 135.

153. *SEG* 4.516 = *I.Eph* 18 b 15–18; F. K. Dörner, *Der Erlass des Statthalters von Asia: Paullus Fabius Persicus* (diss., Greifswald 1935).

154. *MDAI(I)* 1965, 96–117, no. 2b. Wörrle (1990) 44.

155. *SEG* 40.956; Wörrle (1990) 19–58; Dignas (2002) 266–67.

156. M. Segre, "Osservazioni epigrafiche sulla vendita di sacerdozio I," *Reale Instit. Lombardo di Sc. e. Lett. Milano, Rend. Class. di lett. e. sc. morali e stor* 69 (1936) 809–30 for discussion on whether the cause of the change was financial or social.

157. Turner (1983) 148–49.

158. Cole (2004) 125 and (1992) 104–22.

159. Dionysos Phleos: *LSAM* 37 = *I.Priene* no. 174. Ge at Erythrai: *LSAM* 25B68. The purchaser of this priesthood was male, and his name is Polypeithes, restored on the basis of other occurrences of this name in the same inscription.

160. As do Cole (1992) 111–12; Cole (2004) 125; and Dillon (2002) 76.

161. *LSAM* 25.151–54.

162. *LSAM* 25.179–94; Debord (1982) table at 116.

163. It is misleading to view these two widows as independent agents, participating in the bidding equally alongside men (as does Turner [1983] 164–65). These women are, instead, mere channels for the transfer of the priesthood.

164. The husband of the priestess of Artemis Pergaia at Halikarnassos acted on her behalf, *LSAM* 73.

165. *LSAM* 4.26–28; Bremen (1996) 221 n. 53.

166. *LSCG* 166.

167. Schwabl (1993) 142 n. 27.

168. See Parker and Obbink (2000).

169. *LSCG* 175.4–8; Turner (1983) 153.

170. Parker and Obbink (2000) 420.

171. Höghammar (1993) 175 n. 65; S. M. Sherwin-White, *Ancient Cos: An Historical Study from the Dorian Settlement to the Imperial Period, Hypomnemata* 51 (Göttingen 1978) 132–33, no. 266; Parker and Obbink (2000) 426, 19.

172. Turner (1983) 142–44.

CHAPTER 3. PRIESTHOODS OF PROMINENCE: ATHENA POLIAS AT ATHENS, DEMETER AND KORE AT ELEUSIS, HERA AT ARGOS, AND APOLLO AT DELPHI

1. London, British Museum E 324, from Nola. *ARV*² 842.127; *CVA* London, pl. 61, 3. C. Lenormant and J. de Witte, *Élite des monuments céramographiqes*, 1 (Paris 1837–61) pl. 80.

2. Schaps (1977) 323–30; Sommerstein (1980) 395–418; Bremmer (1981) 425–26.

3. Schaps (1977) 323–30.

4. Lewis (1955) 1–12; Garland (1984) 91–94; Jordan (1979) 29–32; Dillon (2002) 84–89; Turner (1983) 244–84; Aleshire (1994a) 330–37; Georgoudi (1993 = 2003).

5. Mentioned by Aeschines *On the Embassy* 2.147.

6. Davies (1971) nos. 4549, 9251; Parker (1996) 290–93.

7. Parker (1987) 198–200.

8. Pausanias 1.24.5; B. S. Spaeth, "Athenians and Eleusinians in the West Pediment of the Parthenon," *Hesperia* 60 (1991) 331–62; J. Binder, "The West Pediment of the Parthenon: Poseidon," *Studies Presented to Sterling Dow on His Eightieth Birthday* (Durham 1984) 15–22.

9. Parker (1996) 290.

10. Lewis (1955) 7–12; Turner (1983) 244–46; Aleshire (1994a) 336.

11. Turner (1983) 247–48.

12. Lewis (1955) 5.

13. The Eteoboutadai carefully guarded their right to priestly inheritance even with the coming of Roman rule. For the last of the identifiable priestesses, Paulleina Scribonia, served ca. A.D. 195 (*IG* II² 3199), see Turner (1983) no. 27. Like so many women who held the office before her, Paulleina was from a family of high-ranking officeholders. Her father was archon of Athens at the end of the second century, *IG* II² 2247.

14. Turner (1983) 249–51.

15. Turner (1983) 252.

16. *IG* II² 776.23–24, 27; see stemma in Lewis (1955) 7.

17. Turner (1983) 254.

18. *IG* II² 3474. Aleshire (1994a) no. 11; Turner (1983) no. 9; Lewis (1955) no. 9. Turner and Lewis iden-tified her with the Phi[l]o[tera] attested in *IG* II² 3473, but Aleshire (1994a) 337, note h, showed that these must be two different priestesses.

19. Turner (1983) 257–58.

20. Aleshire (1994a) 336, no. 14.

21. The genealogy is recorded in Plutarch *Moralia* 843, which is also the source for Philippe and Medeios's priesthoods. See Tracy (1982) 159–65, 210–11; Mikalson (1998) 239–41. *ID* 1869 (120–110 B.C.) commemorates the service of the three siblings on Delos; see Bruneau (1970) 81.

22. Mansfield (1985) 280; Parker (2005) 464–65.

23. Pausanias 1.27.3.

24. Harpokration, s.v. *skiron*; Burkert (1985) 230; Parker (2005) 174–77. This is, perhaps, the site of the mythical battle of Erechtheus and Eumolpos. Skiros, the seer of the Eleusinians, died in the fight-ing and was buried on the spot, giving the place its name. A sanctuary of Demeter and Kore, where Athena and Poseidon were also worshipped, was located nearby and may have been the destination of the procession.

25. *LSCG* 8.16–18 (*IG* II² 1078. 16–22). Clinton (1974) 95.

26. We hear a similar story (Herodotos 6.81) in which Kleomenes was refused entry to the temple of Hera at Argos on grounds that it was unholy for strangers to sacrifice there. Kleomenes had the temple attendant dragged away and flogged before proceeding to make his sacrifice.

27. An inscription found near Troizen (fourth or third century B.C.) may be a copy of the Themistok-lean decree for the evacuation, as recounted by Herodotos, see *GHI* I² R. no. 23. The phrase "priest-esses on the Acropolis" is fully preserved in line 11, although it is not clear what the priestesses are meant to do. M. H. Jameson, "A Decree of Themistokles from Troizen," *Hesperia* 29 (1960) 198–223 restored the text to read that the treasurers and priestesses should remain on the Acropolis and guard the property of the gods, while all others should embark on the ships. Jordan (1979) 78–84 has objected to the placement of the priestesses on the Acropolis during the Persian siege, since this contradicts Herodotos (8.51), who says that the only persons left on the citadel were the treasurers and some poor men. See M. Chambers, "The Significance of the Themistocles Decree," *Philologus* 111 (1967) 166–69. The authenticity of the decree is debated, M. Johansson, "The Inscription from Troizen: A Decree of Themistokles?" *ZPE* 137 (2001) 69–92. N. G. L. Hammond, "The Narrative of Herodotus VII and the Decree of Themistocles at Troizen," *JHS* 62 (1982) 62. A. J. Podlecki, *The Life of Themistocles: A Critical Survey of the Literary and Archaeological Evidence* (Montreal 1975).

28. Jordan (1979) 29 n. 37 points out that the prohibition of ewe-lamb sacrifices contradicts inscriptions that list sheep as offering to Athena (*IG* I³ 246 C.26–27; *LSCG* 18 Δ.15–17, Erchia calendar).

29. *IG* I³ 4. Jordan (1979) 19–23, 36–55. While the text does not explicitly name the priestess of Athena Polias, we might surmise that she was among the priestesses concerned. It is carved on two marble metopes surviving from the so-called H-Temple, a structure that was replaced by a new building, sometime between 510–485 B.C.

30. This is pointed out by Feaver (1957) 142. The salary recorded for the priestess of Athena Nike dates to later in the century; see chapter 2 in the present volume.

31. Jordan (1979) 103–16 devotes an appendix to this word.

32. Lewis (1955) 2–7. Georgoudi (1993 = 2003) 57–196.

33. As restored by Lewis (1955). Cole (2004) 124 restores the number of years that Lysimache served as fifty-three.

34. Lewis (1955) 1–12.

35. J. D. Beazley, "Some Inscriptions on Greek Vases," *AJA* 54 (1950) 319–20 discussed a lekanis lid by the Meidias Painter in the Jatta collection that shows seven women, two of whom are labeled "Myrrhine" and "Lysistrata." Ruvo, Museo Jatta, 1526; *ARV*² 1314.18. See Jean de Witte and Charles Lenormant, *Bull. Nap.* 5 (1857) 280, pl. 1; S. Reinach, *Répertoire des vases peints grecs et étrusques* (Paris 1922) 472; L. Burn, *The Meidias Painter* (Oxford, 1987) M22. Since the Meidias Painter was active in 411 B.C. when the *Lysistrata* was first performed, Beazley associated the names on the vase with the characters in the play. Beazley transcribed the name of the woman to the right of Lysistrata as "Drakontis." Some years ago, I attempted to associate this name with the patronymic of the historical Lysimache, that is, Drakontidou. But firsthand inspection of the vase in Ruvo showed that the label does not read "Drakontis" at all. Instead, it reads "ΑΡΧ . . . ΟΑ" just as Giuseppe Jatta published long ago, G. Jatta, *Catalogo del Museo Jatta* (Naples 1869 = Bari 1996) 834. I thank Signora Jatta for her very kind hospitality in Ruvo in March 2002. I am grateful for having had the opportunity to discuss this vase with David Lewis during the summer of 1992. I am preparing the results of this investigation in a forthcoming article, "Aristophanes' *Lysistrata* and Female Priesthoods in Late Fifth-Century Athens."

36. Mark (1993) 242.

37. *IG* I³ 1330 grave epitaph. Lewis (1955) 3 underlines the tension between the austerity of established cults and the flamboyance of new ones. Lysistrata, who represents the "oldest and best elements in Athenian life," laments that the women of her city jump at the chance to be invited to feasts for the new gods Bacchos, Pan, Aphrodite Kolias, or Genetyllis, (lines 1–3).

38. M. Silk, "The People of Aristophanes," in *Characterization and Individuality in Greek Literature*, C. B. R. Pelling, ed. (Oxford, 1990); D. MacDowell, *Aristophanes and Athens* (Oxford 1995); J. J. Henderson, *Aristophanes: Lysistrata* (Oxford 1987); A. M. Bowie, *Aristophanes: Myth, Ritual, and Comedy* (Cambridge, 1993); M. Vickers, *Perikles on Stage* (Austin 1997). See Faraone in Faraone and McClure (2006) 207–23.

39. *IG* I³ 79 = Clinton (2005) 41, decree concerning bridge over Rheitos, 422/421 B.C.

40. *IG* II² 1078.

41. Clinton (1974) 10–68, 89–114.

42. Clinton (1974) 68–89; Garland (1984) 96–104.

43. Inscriptions concerning Eleusinian cult and dated according to the tenures of priestesses of Demeter and Kore include *IG* II² 3490 for Medeios, exegetes of the Eumolpidai; *IG* II² 3530, dedication to a high priest of Tiberius; *IG* II² 3585 = Clinton (2005) 371, a *hierophantid*; *IG* II² 3586–87 = Clinton (2005) 373–74; hearth initiates. See Clinton (1974) 76; Foucart (1914) 216–20.

44. *IG* I³ 6C.6–20 = Clinton (2005) 19; *IG* I³ 386; *IG* II² 1357, *LSS* 10a.75; *IG* II²1540.57–58; *IG* II² 204.60; *IG* II² 1363 + *SEG* 23.80 A.3–13, B.23; *IG* II² 1672 Col. IIb, 255–62 = Clinton (2005) 177; *IG* II² 1092 B 33–34.

45. An early shrine of Demeter existed on the site of the City Eleusinian from the seventh century, though a formalized architectural complex was not constructed until the very end of the sixth century B.C., Miles (1998) 16–18, 21–23, 25–28. It has been argued that the building of the Eleusinion was contemporary with Solonian laws pertaining to the Mysteries and new building at Eleusis, Sourvinou-Inwood (1997) 132–50, esp. 146.

46. Sourvinou-Inwood (1997) 132–50; R. Padgug, "Eleusis and the Union of Attika," *GRBS* 13 (1972) 144–46; F. R. Walton, "Athens, Eleusis, and the Homeric Hymn to Demeter," *HThR* 45 (1952) 110–13.

47. *IG* I³ 231.13, the *phaidyntes* appears in the next line; Clinton (1974) 69; Miles (1998) cat. 1, no. 39.

48. *IG* I³ 953, Agora I 5484; Clinton (1974) 69; Miles (1998) cat. 1, no. 1.

49. *IG* II² 949.6–10; Clinton (1974) 72. Deubner (1966) 67–68.

50. Scholia to Lucian *Dialogue of the Courtesans* 7.4. Parke (1977) 98–100; Simon (1983) 35–37. Apollodoros *Against Neaira* (= Demosthenes 59) 116; Athenaeus *Deipnosophistae* 13.594b. In chapter 7 we will look at the case of the *hierophant* Archias, who was convicted of impiety for sacrificing a victim brought to the Haloa by the prostitute Sinope.

51. Diodorus Siculus 5.4.7. Clinton (1996) 111–25; Brumfield (1981).

52. A. Sommerstein, *The Thesmophoriazusae* (Warminster 1994) 176 tells us that the speaker of 295–311, 331–51, 372–79, and 380b is labeled "Herald" in the Ravenna manuscript and "woman imitating a herald" by the scholia, but he believes her to be Kritylla, the priestess.

53. Austin, "Le rôle de la Coryphée dans les 'Thesmophoria,'" *Dionisio* 45 (1971–74) 316–25.

54. J. A. Haldane, "A Scene in the *Thesmophoriazusae* (295–371)," *Philologus* 109 (1965) 39–46.

55. K. Clinton, *The Iconography of the Eleusinian Mysteries*, Acta Instituti Regni Sueciae, Series in octavo (Stockholm 1992).

56. London, British Museum 1906.12–15.1; Burgon Group, Siana cup. *ABV* 90.7; *Add.²* 24; *LIMC* IV Demeter 417; Parker (2005) 280–81.

57. B. Ashmole, "*Kalligeneia* and *Hieros Arotos*," *JHS* 66 (1946) 8–10; Simon (1983) 20–21.

58. Clinton (1974) 68–76 and Turner (1983) 284–300, with chronological list and stemmata for several priestesses. Clinton lists eighteen named priestesses to which we can now add Habryllis, daughter of Mikion, making nineteen. If we accept Sourvinou-Inwood's contention that Theano, daughter of Menon, is an invention by Plutarch, then we are left with eighteen priestesses.

59. Photios, s.v. Philleidai. Clinton (1974) 74 argues on the basis of *IG* II² 2954 = Clinton (2005) 379 (first century A.D.) that another clan was involved in this priesthood. Parker (1996) 317 n. 87 points out that the fragmentary state of the inscription permits other interpretations that do not require the involvement of a second clan. See Turner (1983) 285–87.

60. Clinton (1974) 76.

61. B. D. Merritt, "Greek Inscriptions," *Hesperia* 26 (1957) 79–80, no. 25; *SEG* 16.160; Clinton (1974) 70, no. 3; Miles (1998) 188, cat. 1, no. 3, I 5802. *IG* II² 3468.

62. First published by B. Orphanou-Phlorake, "Praxiteles *epoiese*," *Horos* (2000–2003) 113–17, figs. 25–26. Now see A. Ajootian, "Praxiteles and the Priestess Chairippe," Archaeological Institute of America online abstract, Annual Meeting (2006) and A. Ajootian, "Praxiteles and Fourth-Century Athenian Portraiture," in *Early Hellenistic Portraiture: Image, Style, Context,* P. Schultz and R. van der Hoff, eds. (Cambridge 2007). I thank Aileen Ajootian for kindly discussing the inscription with me.

63. B. D. Merritt, "Greek Inscriptions," *Hesperia* 32 (1963) 42–43, no. 48; *SEG* 21.795; see Clinton (1974) 73; Miles (1998) 191, cat. 1, no. 17.

64. *IG* II² 3477. Clinton (1974) 100; Tracy (1990) 179–80; Miles (1998) 208, no. 75.

65. *IG* II² 6398.

66. Aleshire (1994a) 337 note j.

67. This inscription is mentioned in Aleshire (1994a) 337 note i, and Miles (1998) cat. 1, no. 75, where she cites *per litt.* K. Clinton.

68. Miles seems to endorse this view (1998) 208.

69. *PA* 5966 and 10188; Mikalson (1998) 168–203; Habicht (1997) 173–93; Turner (1983) 264.

70. *IG* II² 834.10f. Mikalson (1998) 170f.; Habicht (1982) 79–93.

71. Habicht (1997) 181.

72. *IG* II² 834.25f. and 2798. Habicht (1982) 84–96, esp. 84 n. 32; Habicht (1997) 180ff.; Mikalson (1998) 172ff.

73. *IG* II² 4676 = Moretti, *Iscrizioni storiche ellenistiche* no. 27; Habicht (1982) 107, n. 128.

74. *IG* II² 3475 + 3476 = Clinton (2005) 244, 4690; *AE* (1971) 129–30, no. 25; Clinton (1974) 72, no. 5 and appendix VI; Turner (1983) 288–89.

75. Menedemos I: *IG* II² 912. Turner (1983) 288 identifies her father with the archon listed under *PA* 2568, who was archon in 151/150, 144/143, or 139/138 B.C.

76. *IG* II² 3220, 3495 (dedication); Clinton (1974) 72, no. 6; Turner (1983) 289–91. Ameinokleia's date depends on which Philanthes of Phyle (father or son) we understand to be her father.

77. Turner (1983) 291. One of her cousins, Asklepiades (IV), and her brother Asklepiades (VI) served as Pythaist.

78. *IG* II² 3490, 4704; Turner (1983) 291–92; Clinton (1974) 73, no. 8. Oinophilos: *IG* II² 1714, date according to S. Dow, "The List of Athenian Archontes," *Hesperia* 3.2 (1934) 144–46.

79. Turner (1983) 295–96; Clinton (1974) 74, no. 10.

80. Clinton (1974) 74, no. 10; C. P. Jones, "The Teacher of Plutarch," *HSCPh* 71 (1966) 207–11, stemma at 210.

81. *IG* II² 3546 = Clinton (2005) 43, 3557 = Clinton (2005) 458. (Junia Melitine, cf. *IG* II² 3633), 3558–60, 4753–54. Melitine is no. 9 in the list of *hierophantides* in Clinton (1974) 87; Turner (1983) 296.

82. *IG* II² 3687 = Clinton (2005) 523; Turner (1983) 297–98, with family tree 299; Clinton (1974) 75, no. 16.

83. C. Waldstein, *The Argive Heraeum I* (Boston 1902) I, 73, 110–11; J. C. Wright, "The Old Temple Terrace at the Argive Heraeum and the Early Cult of Hera in the Argolid," *JHS* 102 (1982), 186–201, doubts the association of the burnt stratum found on the site and the fire of 423 B.C.; C. Pfaff, *The Argive Heraion: The Architecture of the Classical Temple of Hera* (diss., New York University 1992).

84. Wright, "Old Temple Terrace," 191 dates the first temple to 650–625 B.C.; P. Amandry, "Observations sur les monuments de l'Heraion d'Argos," *Hesperia* 21 (1952) 222–74, esp. 269, 272, considers it possible that the classical temple was planned or even begun before the fire in 423 B.C. See also C. Antonaccio, "Terraces, Tombs, and the Early Argive Heraion," *Hesperia* 61 (1992) 98.

85. Perhaps the different versions of the story suggest that the Argives used it to explain relationships (friendships and enmities) with nearby cities.

86. F. Jacoby, *RE* 8 (1913), s.v. "Hellanikos," col. 147, lines 24–25.

87. *FGrH* 4 F 74–83; W. McLeod, "New Readings in *IG* XIV, 1285II Verso," *Hesperia* 42 (1973) 411–14. The date of the work is disputed, A. Möller favors 423–421 B.C. in his "The Beginning of Chronology: Hellanicus's *Hiereia*," in *The Historian's Craft in the Age of Herodotos*, N. Luraghi, ed. (Oxford 2001).

88. *FGrH* I commentary, p. 455.

89. McLeod, "New Readings," 413 n. 10, points out that if, as Jacoby argues, Hellanikos kept Io and Kallithyia separate, Io's father's could not have been Inachos (because Inachos was Kallithyia's ancestor) or Peiras (Kallithyia's father). So, in Hellanikos version, Io's father should have been Iasos.

90. Herodotos does not give a name for the mother of Kleobis and Biton, but Plutarch (frag. 133), Dio Chrysostom 64.6, and *Anthologia Palatina* 3.18.2 call her Kydippe. The *Suda* (s.v. Kroisos) lists her as Kydippe or Theano. She is called a priestess only in the *Suda* and *AP* 3.18. Jacoby thinks that Kydippe and Theano must have been listed in Hellanikos as two separate priestesses. Theano had become the archetypal name for Greek priestesses by the time of the lexicographers, as a result of the influence of the famous Homeric priestess of Athena at Troy.

91. Hesiod frag. 124 M.-W.; Akousilaos, *FGrH* 2 F 6; Apollodoros *Library* 2.5.

92. Apollodoros *Library* 2.5 gives three different traditions for Io's lineage: daughter of Iasos, son of Argos and Ismene (daughter of Asopos), e.g., Pausanias 2.16.1; daughter of Inachos, e.g., Herodotos 1.1, [Aeschylus] *Prometheus* 590; daughter of Peiren (= Peiras, Peiranthos, Peirasos, who is a son of Argos in some versions, e.g., Pausanias 2.17.5), e.g., Hesiod frag. 124 M.-W., Akousilaos, *FGrH* 2 F 6. West (1985) 76–77.

93. Aeschylus *Suppliants* 291–92; Apollodoros *Library* 2.5.

94. Boston, Museum of Fine Arts 08.417, said to have been found at S. Maria di Capua in Campania, Italy; *ARV*² 579.84; *Para.* 391; *Add.* 128; *Add.*² 262; *LIMC* IV Hera 486. Mantis (1990) 32–33, pl. 7a.

95. As identified by Mantis (1990) 32–33.

96. As suggested by E. Simon, "Nachrichten aus dem Martin-von-Wagner-Museum der Universität Würzburg," *AA* 100 (1985) 273 n. 251.

97. We hear of a priestess of Hera at Argos named Admete from Athenaeus 15.162a and find the name Admata on a statue base from the Heraion at Argos, *IG* IV 531. See Mantis (1990) 25, n. 41 and 34, n. 92.

98. C. W. Blegen, "Prosymna: Remains of Post-Mycenaean Date," *AJA* 43 (1939) 443–44.

99. *IG* IV 642; *SEG* 14.324 = *MAI* 14 (1951) 317–50. As noted by Mantis (1990) 34. See below in chapter 8.

100. F. Courby, *La terrasse du temple 1* (Paris, 1915) 65–66; Amandry (1950) 215–30; Fontenrose (1978) 196–203. For Delphi, see G. Roux, *Delphes, son oracles et ses dieux* (Paris 1976); M. Delcourt, *L'oracle de Delphes*, 2nd ed. (Paris 1981); Price (1985); R. C. T. Parker, "Greek States and Greek Oracles," in Cartledge and Harvey (1985); C. Morgan, *Athletes and Oracles: The Transformation of Olympia and Delphi in the Eighth Century* B.C. (Cambridge 1990); M. Maass, *Das Antike Delphi: Orakel, Schätze und Monumente* (Darmstadt 1993); Bowden (2005).

101. J. Z. De Boer and J. R. Hale, "The Geological Origins of the Oracle at Delphi, Greece," in *The Archaeology of Geological Catastrophies*, W. G. McGuire, et. al., eds., *Geological Society Special Publication* no. 171 (London 2000) 399–412; J. Z. De Boer, J. R. Hale, and J. Chanton, "New Evidence of the Geological Origins of the Ancient Delphic Oracle (Greece)," *Geology* 29 (2001) 707–10. W. J. Broad, *The Oracle: The Lost Secrets and Hidden Message of Ancient Delphi* (New York 2006).

102. Diodorus Siculus 16.26; Plutarch *Moralia*, "Oracles in Decline," 435d; Pausanias 10.5.7.

103. Amandry (1950) 168.

104. Maurizio (1995) 69–86; Maurizio (1997) 308–35; Maurizio (2001) 38–54. Price (1985) 128–54. See K. Latte, "The Coming of the Pythia," *HThR* (1940) 9–18.

105. *Python* means "snake," and the place is named for the great she-dragon slain here by Apollo.

106. Sources collected by Fontenrose (1978) 218 with n. 29, where he points out that two priests are named in numerous Delphic manumission inscriptions (*Sammlung der griechischen Dialekt-Inschriften* 1684–2342). Euripides *Ion* 369, 413; Plutarch *Moralia* 386; Maurizio (1995) 83–84.

107. Fontenrose (1978) 218 with n. 30, citing Herodotos 8.36.2–37.1.

108. Fontenrose (1978) 219 with n. 32.

109. Maurizio (1995) 70.

110. Apollo himself is called *prophetes* in Aeschylus's *Eumenides*, 19. See Maurizio (1995) 70 for discussion and citations (*mantis*: Aeschylus *Eumenides* 29, 33; *prophetis*: Euripides *Ion* 42, 321, 1322; Plato *Phaedrus* 244b; *IG* XII (3) 863; Strabo 9.3.5; Diodorus Siculus 14.13.3, 16.26.4; Plutarch *Moralia* 414b; Pollux 10.81; Iamblichos *De Mysteriis* 126.4; *promantis*: Herodotos 6.66, 7.111 and 141; Thucydides 5.16.2; Plutarch *Alexander* 14; Lucian *Hermotimos* 60; Heliodoros 4.16).

111. Plutarch, Maximus Tyrius, Aristides, cited by Parke and Wormell (1956) vol. 1, 35 with n. 85.

112. Parke and Wormell (1956) vol. 1, 35 with full citations. For the Pythia as young virgin, see Diodoros Siculus 16.26; as an older woman, see Aeschylus *Eumenides* 38; Euripides *Ion* 1324. For maiden costume of Pythia, see Plutarch 3.405c, 435d, 437d.

113. Plutarch *Moralia* 414b.

114. Strabo 9.3.5; Pausanias 10.5.7. See Fontenrose (1978) 208–10.

115. P. Barratt, *Annaei Lucani Belli Civlis liber V: A commentary* (Amsterdam 1979) at line 126.

116. Diogenes Laertius 8.8 reporting Aristoxenos (= frag. 15 Wehrli).

117. Delphi, Inv. no. 5564, De la Coste-Messelière (1925) 83, no. 10; Amandry (1950) 116 n. 2; Parke and Wormell (1956) vol. 1, 36 n. 90.

118. Which we know from another inscription, *FD* III 2, 118.

119. Fontenrose (1978) 200–203.

120. Sources collected by Fontenrose (1978) 224 n. 37: Scholia on Euripides *Phoinissai* 224; [Kallisthenes] 36 Raabe; Iamblichos *Myst.* 3.11; Lucian *Bis acc.* I.; Oinomaos *apud* Eusebios *PE* 5.28, p. 224a; Gregory Nazianzenus *Oration* 39.5, p. 340 Migne.

121. Kallimachos, *Iambi* 4.26–27; sources collected by Fontenrose (1978) 224 n. 38.

122. Parke and Wormell (1956) vol. 1, 6–7.

123. Parke and Wormell (1956) vol. 1, 29; Price (1985) 135–37.

124. Berlin, Antikensammlung F2538; *ARV*² 1269.5, 1689; *Para.* 471; *Add.*² 356.

125. Fontenrose (1978) cat. H72.

126. Discussed in Parke and Wormell (1956) vol. 1, 37–38.

127. Translation by J. D. Duff, Lucan, *The Civil War*, Loeb Classical Library (Cambridge, MA 1928, reprint 1997) 25.

128. Price (1985) 142.

129. Fontenrose (1978) 217 and n. 26. Translation by D. Kovacs, Euripides, *Ion*, vol. 4, Loeb Classical Library (Cambridge, MA 1999) 341.

130. Parke and Wormell (1956) vol. 1, 30–33.

131. Parke and Wormell (1956) vol. 1, 18–19; Fontenrose (1978) 221–23 (with cat., H21), 226. Divination by lot was a separate rite. We hear of simple yes and no answers given through the display of different colored beans or a choice of urns.

132. Parke and Wormell (1956) vol. 2 collected 615 responses. Fontenrose (1978) organized them according to the historical, quasi-historical, legendary, and fictitious. L. Andersen, *Studies in Oracular Verses: Concordance to Delphic Responses in Hexameter* (Copenhagen 1987) has collected hexameter verse oracles only. Maurizio (2001) 38–54 discusses the ambiguous oracles.

133. See discussion in Goff (2004) 220–26.

134. Plutarch *Moralia* 405c–406d (403e); Bowden (2005) 34–38. Maurizio (1995) 70.

135. Parke and Wormell (1956) vol. 1, 18–19.

136. Fontenrose (1978) 26–28. Delphi's rise has long been linked to its role in influencing colonization, tyranny, and political reforms; see e.g., Parke and Wormell (1956) vol. 1, 49–125; Malkin (1987) 17–91.

137. Fontenrose (1978) cat., Q143.

138. Fontenrose (1978) cat., Q193.

139. Fontenrose (1978) 228–32.

140. Fontenrose (1988) 55–56.

141. Fontenrose (1988) 192, cat., R17.

142. *I. Didyma*, no. 235 B.

143. *I. Didyma*, no. 273.

144. Fontenrose (1988) 179–231.

145. Fontenrose (1988) 196–97, cat., R 22.

146. Fontenrose (1988) 197–98, cat., R 23.

147. Fontenrose (1978) 228–32.

148. H. W. Parke, *The Oracles of Zeus: Dodona, Olympia, Ammon* (Oxford 1967) 62–63.

149. Iamblichos, *Life of Pythagoras* 5; Parke and Wormell (1956) vol. 1, 401.

150. Fontenrose (1978) cat., Q263. Parke and Wormell (1956) vol. 1, 290.

151. *LIMC* II Bouzyges 1. See Parker (2005) 280–81.

152. Ashmole identified this scene with the *ieros arotos*, "*Kalligeneia*," 8–10; Simon (1983) 20–21.

153. Mantis (1990) 32 lists Hades, Hekate, Persephone, and Kybele, all of whom hold keys to the underworld, and Eros, who holds the keys to Aphrodite's love chamber. Artemis is called *kleidouchos* in Aristophanes, *Thesmophoriazusai* 1140 and *adesp. com.* 1147, 27 K-A, *PCG* VIII, p. 480. Mantis points to an image of Hera in a Gigantomachy depicted on an Attic krater in London (British Museum E 469) with what appears to be a key in her hand, and to a krater in the Antikenmuseum in Basel (*ARV*² 1661, *Para* 396) that similarly shows Hera fighting with a temple key in the Gigantomachy, Mantis (1990) 33 pls. 7, 8.

154. Simon, "Nachrichten," 273 n. 251.

155. For synoptic narrative, see A. M. Snodgrass, *Narrative and Allusion in Archaic Greek Art*, the Eleventh J. L. Myres Memorial Lecture, New College, Oxford (Oxford 1982) 5–10, and Snodgrass (1987) 135–57. For simultaneous narrative, see K. Weitzmann, *Illustration in Roll and Codex: A Study of the Origin and Method of Text Illustration* (Princeton 1970). See also N. Himmelman-Wildchutz, "Erzählung und Figur in der archaischen Kunst," *AbhMainz* 2 (1967) 73–101; P. G. P. Meyboom, "Some Observations on Narration in Greek Art," *Meded* 40 (1978) 55–72, esp. 55–56.

156. Translation based on P. Vellacott, *Aeschylus: Prometheus Bound, The Suppliants, Seven against Thebes, The Persians* (London 1961) 62.

157. Ferrari (2002) 17–27.

158. Richmond, Virginia, Museum of Fine Arts 79.100, Triptolemos Painter.

159. Syracuse, Museo Nazionale 30747, the Dinos Painter *ARV*² 1153, 17; *Addenda* 336. The image is still described as a "departure scene " in Reeder (1995) 158–60, no. 20.

160. London, British Museum E 773: *ARV*² 805–5, 89; Ferrari (2002) 18, fig. 2.

161. Lissarrague and Schnapp (1981) 286–97.

162. Ferrari (2002) 19; F. Harvey, "Painted Ladies: Fact, Fiction, and Fantasy," in Christiansen and Melander (1988) 242–54.

163. London, British Museum E 324; *ARV*² 842.127.

CHAPTER 4. DRESSING THE PART: COSTUME, ATTRIBUTE, AND MIMESIS

1. Translation by W. R. Connor (2000) 63.

2. Miller (1989) 319.

3. *LSCG* 65 with bibliography until 1969; Burkert (1985) 279; Meyer (1987) 49–59. A new study is in progress by Laura Gawlinsky. The inscription was unearthed in 1858 and built into the wall of a church in the village of Konstantini in Messenia.

4. Examples are collected by Parker (1983) 19–20: Homer *Iliad* 6.266–68; *Odyssey* 4.750–52; Hesiod *Works and Days* 724–25; Euripides *Electra* 791–94.

5. Translation based on C. A Vince and J. H. Vince, Demosthenes, *De Corona*, Loeb Classical Library, (Cambridge, MA 1926) 189.

6. E. J. W. Barber, *Prehistoric Textiles* (Princeton 1991) xxi tells us that Aegean is one of the worst places for the survival of ancient textiles.

7. Ferrari (2002) 17–22.

8. Bolger (2003) 179–80; see R. Barnes and J. B. Eicher, *Dressing Gender: Making and Meaning in Cultural Contexts* (Oxford 1992).

9. Meskell (2002) 158–63; M. M. Lee, "Deciphering Gender in Minoan Dress," in *Reading the Body: Representations and Remains in the Archaeological Record*, A. E. Rautman, ed. (Philadelphia 2000) 111–23; M. L. S. Sorensen, "Reading Dress: The Construction of Social Categories and Identities in Bronze Age Europe," *Journal of European Archaeology* 5. 1 (1997) 93–116 and *Gender Archaeology* (Cambridge 2000).

10. See E. Fraenkel, ed., *Agamemnon* (Oxford 1950) commentary for lines 1265–70.

11. London, British Museum 2070 (scepter), 1952 (necklace), 218 (ring); Williams (1988) 75–78; R. Engelmann, "Berichte aus dem Britischen Museum," *AZ* 31 (1873) 112. Acquired from Alexander Castellani.

12. Williams (1988) 78.

13. *LIMC* V Io, 34–61.

14. Williams (1988) 78 says that he hopes the group was not chosen and assembled by Castellani himself.

15. We know from [Lysias] *Against Andokides* 51, that the priests and priestesses at Eleusis wore a garment called *phoinikis*; Pollux 4.118 mentions the *phoinikis* as an appropriate costume for a comic actor portraying a young man. See Nielsen (2002) 82–84.

16. Summarized by Miller (1989) 313–29. An often-cited example of the *ependytes* in Greek art is worn by the princess Nausikaa on a vase in the Museum of Fine Arts, Boston, 04.18; *ARV²* 1177.48, *Para* 460, *Add²* 340.

17. Ferrara, Museo Nazionale 44894 (T57 CVP). *ARV²* 1143.1; *Para.* 455; *Add.* 167; *JHS* 95 (1975) pl. 15b.

18. Miller (1989) 327–29.

19. See Mills (1984) 255–65. Rules for entry to the Letoon at Xanthos are inscribed on a large stone dated to late third–second century B.C., *SEG* 36.1221. It was forbidden to carry weapons, *petasoi*, *kausia*, brooches, brass (objects), gold (objects), gold-plated rings, equipment, clothes, or footware into the sanctuary; see *GSL* 16–17; C. LeRoy, "Un règlement religieuse au Létoon de Zathos," *RA* (1986) 279–300.

20. *LSS* 33.

21. *LSS* 32.

22. *TAM* V 238. Found at Kula, transported to Syria, and dating to the Roman period; see Mills (1984) 255–65.

23. *LSCG* 65.25–26, 41–45, 165–70.

24. Mills (1984), 255–65; Dillon (1997) 161–63.

25. *LSS* 32.

26. *LSCG* 68. A. P. Matthaiou and G. Pikoulas, "Ἱερός νόμς από Λυκόσουρα" *Horus* 4 (1986) 75–78; I. Loucas and E. Loucas, "The Sacred Laws of Lycosoura," in Hägg (1994) 97–99; E. Voutiras, "Öpfer für Despoina: Zur Kultsatzung des Heiligtums von Lykosoura, *IG* V² 415," *Chiron* 29 (1999) 233–49.

27. Other examples include *LSS* 28 (Sparta), *LSS* 33 (Patras). See Dillon (1997) 198.

28. *LSAM* 14.9. Dillon (1997) 161.

29. *LSS* 59, Roman period.

30. *LSAM* 35.3–5.

31. *I.Cos*, ED 89 (= *LSCG* 163) lines 8–14. Parker and Obbink (2000) 425, 9.

32. *LSAM* 11.1–2.

33. *SEG* 18.343.33; Salviat (1959) 362–79.

34. Harpokration, s.v. *arrephorein*; *IG* II² 1060 + 1036a (= *SEG* 28.90); see Mansfield (1985) 272.

35. *LSCG* 65, see above, note 3.

36. Dillon (1997) 198.

37. E. Spanier, ed., *The Royal Purple and the Biblical Blue* (Jerusalem 1987).

38. D. S. Reese, "Exploitation of Murex Shells: Purple Dye and Lime Production at Sidi Khrebish Benghazi (Berenice)," *Libyan Studies* 11 (1980) 79–93; F. Bruin, "Royal Purple and the Dye Industries of the Mycenaeans and Phoenicians," in *Sociétés et compagnes de commerce en Orient et dans l'océan Indien*, M. Mollat, ed. (Paris 1970) 73–90; D. S. Reese, "Palaekastro Shells and Bronze Age Purple-Dye Production in the Mediterranean Basin," *ABSA* 82 (1987) 201–06; R. H. Michel and P. E. McGovern, "The Chemical Processing of Royal Tyrian Purple Dye: Ancient Descriptions as Elucidated by Modern Science," *Archaeomaterials* 1.2 (1987) 135–43.

39. [Lysias] *Against Andokides* 51; Clinton (1974) 32–33.

40. Plutarch *Aristides* 5, 6–7; Scholia on Aristophanes *Clouds* 63; Clinton (1974) 47.

41. Clinton (1974) 33, 68.

42. *IG* II² 3592.21–22.

43. White with purple stripes: Plutarch *Aratus* 53.6; gold: *LSAM* 38A.13 and 38B.8 (priest of Poseidon at Priene, second century B.C.). For headbands in general, see Krug (1968) 122–26, 131–40.

44. *LSCG* 65.24.

45. *LSCG* 136.25–26.

46. *LSCG* 124.17; Parker (1983) 52 n. 78.

47. *OCD*³, s.v. "keys and locks"; H. Diels, *Parmenides Lehrgedicht* (Berlin 1897) 117ff., figs. 1–49, and *Antike Technik* (Leipzig 1914) 45–48; Mantis (1990) 28–65.

48. As prescribed in the Twelve Tables. S. Treggiari, *Roman Marriage* (Oxford 1991) 442.

49. *ID* 1442 B56, 1443 B col. I.164, 1444 A fr. a.48.

50. *IG* V 2, 399, Boston, Museum of Fine Arts 01.7515; M. Comstock and C. Vermeule, *Greek, Etruscan, and Roman Bronzes in the Museum of Fine Arts, Boston* (Boston 1971) 435–36, no. 638. Illustrated in Dillon (2002) fig. 3.1; Mantis (1990) 114, pl. 49a.

51. Museum of Kerkyra. Mantis (1990) 36, pl. 5c; H. Lechat, "Terres cuites de Corcyre," *BCH* (1891) 32, no. 12, fig. 4.

52. Mantis (1990) 30, 31, pl. 5a,b. Mantis says that it is not clear that this piece was found on Kerkyra. Lechat, *BCH* (1891) 79, no. 73, fig. 13.

53. Mantis (1990) 31, pl. 6a. See E. Bielefeld, *Wandlungen: Studien zur antiken und neueren Kunst*, Festschriften Homann Wedeking (Waldsassen-Bayern 1975) 53, fig. 7. The torso of a marble kore from Samos shows dowel holes at the breast that have been interpreted as cuttings for the attachment of a key; see U. Kron in *Archaische und klassiche griechische Plastik*, H. Kyrieleis, ed. (Mainz 1986) 61, pl. 25.3.

54. Polystrate's grave marker, Athens, Kerameikos Museum 1430; Choirine's grave marker, Geneva, private collection; Athens, National Archaeological Museum 2309, grave marker from Rhamnous; Athens, National Museum 6167. See Kosmopoulou (2001) 281–319.

55. Nymphodoros, son of Nymphodoros of Marathon, is named *kleidouchos* in an inscription dated to 158/157 B.C., *ID* 2605. In chapter 2, note 5, we met Sosandra, Apollodora, and Theodora of Melite, who served in a series of cult roles in Athens and on Delos during the early first century B.C. Their brother, Diokles, served as *kleidouchos* in 100/99 B.C., the same year that their father, Sarapion, was *epimeletes* on Delos.

56. Lokroi, Antiquarium. Mantis (1990) pl. 6b, identifies the man as Plouton.

57. K. Rhomiopoulou, *Lefkadia: Ancient Mieza* (Athens 1997) figs. 24–26; K. Rhomiopoulou, *AAA* 6 (1973) 87; H. Catling, *Archaeological Reports 1972–73*, Society for the Promotion of the Hellenic Tradition and the British School at Athens, *JHS* 93 (1973) 22.

58. Athens National Archaeological Museum 722; *IG* II² 6902; Mantis (1990) 86, pl. 38a; Clairmont (1993) vol. I.250. For non-Attic evidence for the costume of priests, see P. Stengel, *Die griechischen Kultusaltertümer*, 3rd ed. (Munich 1920) 47–48.

59. For limestone of the Mesaorea Plain of central eastern Cyprus, see Connelly (1988) 2–3.

60. Connelly (1988) 8, 25–29.

61. Paris, Louvre N 3278, A. Hermary, *Catalogue des Antiquites de Chypre: Sculptures* (Paris 1989) 378, no. 768, Ambelliri Collection, acquired by Colonna-Ceccaldi in 1869.

62. Larnaca 663. A. Westholm, "Arsos," *SCE* 3 (Stockhholm 1937) pl. 201 (2); Connelly (1988) 21, 27, pl. 9, figs. 32, 33.

63. Paris, Louvre AM 3063, Hermary (1989) 371, no. 750, Louvre AM 3151; 373, no. 756, Musée du Périgord 1723, from Golgoi; 394, no. 804; A. J. Decaudin, *Les antiquités chypriotes dans les collections publiques françaises* (Nicosia 1987) 222, no. 3, pl. 83.

64. Piraeus, Museum 3627 (ex Athens NM 1030).

65. Berlin, Staatliche Museen K104, ca. 330–320 B.C.; M. Meyer, *Die griechischen Urkundenreliefs*, *AM* Beiheft 13. Meyer (1989) 23, 27, 69, 166, 168, 200–204, 212, 244, 301–2, A 129, pl. 33.1; C. L. Lawton, *Attic Document Reliefs* (Oxford 1995) 151–52, no. 164, pl. 86, with full bibliography. Mantis (1990) 41–42, pl. 12.

66. Importantly, traces of a column can be seen carved in low relief beneath the right hand of Athena where it supports her arm and the Nike held above.

67. Simon (1983) 67; Parke (1977) 40; J. Neils, "'With Noblest Images on All Sides': The Ionic Frieze of the Parthenon," in *The Parthenon: From Antiquity to the Present*, J. Neils, ed. (Cambridge and New York 2005) 204.

68. Connelly (1996) 58.

69. Athens AM 2758 + 2427, Lawton, *Attic Document Reliefs*, 125, no. 91, pl. 48. Mantis (1990) 42.

70. Images are collected and discussed by Moret (1975) and Mantis (1990) 52–65. I thank Oliver Taplin for discussing these images with me, and for his helpful insights.

71. St. Petersburg, Hermitage 298 (St. 1734), the Group of the Long Folds, ca. 370–360 B.C. Moret (1975) 107, 108, 137–39, no. 32, pl. 47/2; Mantis (1990) 57, no. P3, pl. 21b.

72. Vienna, Kunsthistorisches Museum 724 (261); attributed to the Painter of the Boston Orestes, 330 B.C.; *LIMC* VII Theano I 8. Moret (1975) 11, 13–15, 17, 21, 22, 25, 26, 140, 141, 218, no. 13, pl. 11; Mantis (1990) 61, no. Θ8, pl. 26a.

73. London, British Museum F 209; Campanian hydria attributed to a hand close to the Danaid Painter, 330 B.C. Moret (1975) II, 14–17, 19, 21–26, 140, 218, no. 12, pl. 12/2, pl. 13; Mantis (1990) 61, no. Θ7, pl. 25b.

74. Villa Giulia 50279, from Paestum, ca. 350–40 B.C. (*PCG* VIII, no. 66). A. D. Trendall, *The Red-Figured Vases of Paestum* (Rome 1987) 94–95, no. 2/130 (pl. 54b); Moret (1975) II, 14–16, 22, 23, 140, 141, 222, no. 15; Mantis (1990) 62, no. 11 pl. 25a.

75. London, British Museum 1931.5–11.1

76. Berlin, Staatliche Museen F 3025, by the Boston Oresteia Painter, from Paestum; Moret (1975) I, 140, II. Mantis (1990) 62, no. Θ 13, pl. 26b.

77. St. Petersburg, the State Hermitage Museum St. 452, near the Darius Painter (partially repainted); Trendall, *Red-Figured Vases*, 532; see C. Aellen, A. Cambitoglou, and J. Chamay, *Le Peintre de Darius et son milieu* (Geneva 1986) 71–83.

78. Princeton, Art Museum 1983–84. The relief measures 27.5 × 30 cm. See Connelly in Ridgway (1994) 28–31.

79. See J. C. Carter, *The Sculptures of Taras* (Philadelphia 1975). For down-dating, see E. Lippolis, *La ceramica policroma e plastica tarantina: Arte e artigianato in Magna Graecia* (Naples 1996) 493–507.

80. E. Loewy, "Zu griechischen Vasenbildern," *Eranos Vindobonensis* (Vienna 1893) 269–71.

81. Lokrian Maidens: F. Hauser, "Die lokrischen Mädchen," *ÖJh* 10 (1912) 168–73; J. M. Redfield, *The Locrian Maidens: Love and Death in Greek Italy* (Princeton 2003). Danaids: E. Keuls, *The Water Carriers in Hades: A Study of Catharsis through Toil in Classical Antiquity* (Amsterdam 1974) 77–79.

82. *Rudens* 32–33 (= Diphilos, *Poetae Comici Graeci* V, test. 11), probably late fourth–early third century B.C. F. Marx, ed., *Plautus, Rudens* (Leipzig, 1928) 99, 148, 155, 275; Aellen, Cambitoglou, and Chamay (1986) 77–78 include the Princeton relief in their discussion and support Marx's interpretation.

83. These monuments are fully discussed in chapter 8.

84. Versnel (1990) and (1992); Nielsen (2002) 12–19.

85. Nielsen (2002).

86. R. Friedrich, "Drama and Ritual," in *Drama and Religion, Themes in Drama* 5, J. Redmond, ed. (Cambridge 1983) 159–223, esp. 179ff.

87. L. M. Bremer, "Greek Hymns," in Versnel (1981a) 193–215 and Furley and Bremer (2001).

88. Cole (1992) 104–16; P. E. Corbett, "Greek Temples and Greek Worshippers: The Literary and Archaeological Evidence," *London University of Classical Studies Bulletin*, no. 17 (1970) 150–51.

89. *LSCG* 66, second century B.C.; Cole (1992) 105, no. 1.

90. *LSCG* 96.9; Cole (1992) 105, no. 6. See Parker (1983) 85 n. 44 for other instances where women are excluded from the cults of Poseidon, Zeus, and Ares.

91. *LSCG* 82, fifth century B.C.

92. Plutarch *The Roman Questions* 16; Corbett, "Greek Temples," 151 n. 16. Of course, this was more about excluding potential thieves than women. Aitolians, like slaves, were untrustworthy and known, especially after years of terrorizing the Boiotians, to be unreliable around valuables. I thank Jason Governale for this point and for his insight on the Boiotian perspective on Aitolian thieves, pirates, and liars.

93. R. Seaford, "Dionysiac Drama and the Dionysiac Mysteries," *CQ* 31.2 (1981); Seaford (1996) 35–52. Indeed, the Bacchae may be seen as the *hieros logos* for Dionsysiac ritual.

94. Burkert (1985) 242–46; Simon (1983) 18–22; Parker (1983) 81–83; Zeitlin (1982) 129–57, esp. 138–45; Foley (1994) 65–71; Versnel (1990) 234–60; Brumfield (1981); Clinton in Hägg (1996) 111–25.

95. *Homeric Hymn to Demeter* 192–211; A. C. Brumfield, "*Aporreta*: Verbal and Ritual Obscenity in the Cults of Ancient Women," in Hägg (1996) 67–74; Foley (1994) 71–75, 79–104; N. Richardson, *The Homeric Hymn to Demeter* (Oxford 1974) 213–17; Clinton (1988) 71–72.

96. Aeschylus frag. 355 Mette. See Burkert (1985) 101.

97. *Hymn to Demeter* 42–44.

98. Mantis (1990) 32–39 has collected the few images and literary references to gods and goddesses acting as key bearers: Hera is the guardian of the keys of marriage and the house; Hades, Hekate, Persephone, and Kybele hold the keys to the underworld; Eros holds the keys to Aphrodite's love chamber.

99. Reardon (1989) 349–588.

100. Polyainos *Strategemata* 8.59.

101. *Suda*, s.v. *aigis*. Burkert (1985) 101. Mansfield (1985) 189–97; at 190 notes that the text says the priestess is "carrying," not "wearing," the aegis, which would argue against the interpretation of divine impersonation.

102. *Suda*, s.v. *proteleia*. Deubner (1932) 16; Burkert (1985) 221; Mansfield (1985) 194–95. A black-figure krater in Paris shows Athena, or her priestess, dressed in an aegis and waving farewell to a nuptial procession, Louvre cp 10269; *CVA* France 12, pl. 166; Bérard (1989b) 98, fig. 136.

103. Burkert (1985) 97.

104. *LSCG* 65, lines 23–24.

105. *IG* II² 1368. Nilsson (1957) 46, 52, 60, 64.

106. Nilsson (1957) 61.

107. C. P. Jones, "The Bacchants of Pontus," *ECM* 34 (1990) 53–63, esp. 61 with n. 35; J. Keil, "Zum Martyrium des heiligen Timotheus in Ephesos," *ÖJh* 29 (1935) 84–92.

108. *Antony* 24.4, translation by C. P. Jones, "Bacchants," 61.

109. Antony: Velleius Paterculus 2.82.4; Seneca *Suasoriae* 1.6.

110. Ephippos, *FGrH* 126 F5; A. B. Bosworth, *Conquest and Empire: The Reign of Alexander the Great* (Cambridge 1988) 278.

111. Translation by Connor (1987) 42 = (2000) 60, after Rawlinson.

112. Connor (1987 = 2000). Now see J. H. Blok, "Phye's Procession: Culture, Politics and Peisistratid Rule," in *Peisistratos and the Tyranny: A Reappraisal of the Evidence*, H. Sancisi-Weerdenburg, ed. (Amsterdam 2000) 18–48.

113. M. Taussig, *Mimesis and Alterity* (New York and London 1993) 79.

114. W. Benjamin "On the Mimetic Faculty" (Berlin 1933), reprinted in *Reflections* (New York 1986). See also W. Benjamin, "Doctrine of the Similar" (Berlin 1933), translation by K. Tarnowski, *New German Critique* 17 (1979) 65–69.

115. Patton (2006); Simon (1953); A.-F. Laurens, "Intégration des dieux dans le rituel humain? L'exemple de la libation en Grèce ancienne," *Recherches et documents du Centre Thomas More* 12, no. 48. (1985); P. Veyne, "Images de divinités tenant une phiale ou patère," *Metis* 5 (1990) 17–28.

116. Strabo 14.1.22; Nilsson (1957) 103.

117. Simon (1953).

118. N. Himmelmann-Wildschütz, *Zur Eigenart des klassischen Götterbildes* (Munich 1959) 27–31.

119. A. Fürtwangler, "Zwei Thongefässe aus Athena," *AthMitt* 6 (1881) 106–15, esp. 117. K. Schefold, "Statuen auf Vasenbildern," *JdI* 52 (1937) 30–75.

120. H. Luschey, *RE* VII Supplement, VII (Stuttgart 1950) φιάλε, cols. 1026–30; B. Eckstein-Wolf, "Zur Darstellung spendender Götter," *AthMitt* (1952) 39–75.

121. Patton summarizes the history of scholarship and sets out her view of "divine reflexivity" (2006). See also K. Patton, "Gods Who Sacrifice: A Paradox of Attic Iconography" (abstract) *AJA* 94 (1990) 326. I am indebted to Kimberly Patton for kindly discussing this material and for sharing with me her manuscript before its publication.

122. Carl Milles Collection at Lindingö near Stockholm; see Nilsson (1957) 99–106; A. Andrén, *Guide to the Collection of Ancient Sculpture* (Stockholm 1952) no. 74; Ferguson (1989) 53.

123. For attributes and offerings, see Keesling (2003) 144–49.

124. For the use of the genitive case to indicate the divinity to whom an object is dedicated, see, in general, Rouse (1902) 325–26; for its use on vases, see R. M. Cook, *Greek Painted Pottery*, 2nd ed. (London 1972) 256–57; for a full inventory of objects dedicated throughout the Greek world during the Archaic period, see Lazzarini (1976) 241–59.

125. Copenhagen, National Museum 6, from Nola, by the Dish Painter; *ARV²* 787.3, *Add.* 142, *Add.²* 289; *CVA* Copenhagen, pl. 159, 6; Bérard and Durand (1989) 31, fig. 32.

126. Brussels, Bibliothèque Royale 12; *ARV²* 797.134, *Para.* 419, *Add.* 143, *Add.²* 290; *LIMC* IV Demeter 25; H. Metzger, *Recherches sur l'imagerie Athénienne* (Paris 1965), pl. 12; Himmelmann-Wildschutz, *Zur Eigenart*, no. 97, pl. 32.

127. New York, Metropolitan Museum of Art 1979.11.15, ca. 470–460 B.C., Villa Giulia Painter. D. von Bothmer, *Greek Vase Painting* (New York 1987) 56–57, 71, no. 28; *LIMC* IV Hera 145*.

128. Oxford, Ashmolean Museum 1973.1, ca. 460 B.C.; M. Vickers, "A New Cup by the Villa Giulia Painter in Oxford," *JHS* 94 (1974), 177–79, pls. 17–18.

129. Reported in Vickers, "New Cup," 179.

130. Munich, Antikensammlungen 2455, Pan Painter; *ARV²* 558.126, *Para* 387; *CVA* Germany 6, pls. 86.9–10, 92.6.

131. For white-ground cups, see J. R. Mertens, "Attic White-Ground Cups: A Special Class of Vases," *MMAJ* (1974) 91.

132. Lactantius *The Death of the Persecutors* 36.4–5; Eusebios *Church History* 8.4.9, 9.4.2. See Grant (1975) 157–59. In view of the evidence compiled here for white dress in Greek cult, Grant's suggestion that the white dress required by Maximin Daia's legislation was derived from Egyptian practice seems unnecessary.

CHAPTER 5. THE PRIESTESS IN THE SANCTUARY: IMPLEMENTS, PORTRAITS, AND PIATRONAGE

1. *IG II²* 3474; cf. *IG II²* 3473 and 3870 for her service as priestess.

2. Translation by Mabel Lang.

3. C. Habicht, *Pausanias' Guide to Ancient Greece* (Berkeley 1985) 23, 130–37; J. Elsner, "Pausanias: A Greek Pilgrim in a Roman World," *Past and Present* 135 (1992) 3–29; E. L. Bowie, "Past and Present in Pausanias," in *Pausanias historien: Huit exposés suivis de discussions, Fondation Hardt Entretiens sur l'Antiquité Classique*, vol. 41 (Vandoeuvres 1996) 207–30. S. E. Alcock, J. F. Cherry and J. Elsner, *Pausanias: Travel and Memory in Roman Greece* (Oxford 2001).

4. Burkert (1985) 93; V. Siurla Theodoridou, *Die Familie in der Griechischen Kunst und Literatur des 8. bis Jhs. v. Chr.* (Munich 1989) 233.

5. Connelly (1989) 210–18.

6. Bruit Zaidman and Schmidt Pantel (1992) 228.

7. C. Smith in Hogarth (1908) 155–85; P. Jacobsthal, "The Date of the Ephesos Foundation-Deposit," *JHS* 71 (1951) 85–95, esp. 86–87; C. M. Kraay, review of L. Weidauer, *Probleme der früheren Elektronprägung* (Fribourg 1975) in *Gnomon* (1978) 211–13; D. Kagan, "The Dates of the Earliest Coins," *AJA* 86 (1982) 343–60. The debate is nicely summarized by J. B Carter, *Greek Ivory-Carving in the Orientalizing and Archaic Periods* (New York 1984) 225–48.

8. Polignac (1995) 75–77.

9. Istanbul, Archaeological Museum; 10.7 cm high. Smith in Hogarth (1908) 156–57, 172, 175; E. Akurgal, *Die Kunst Anatoliens von Homer bis Alexander* (Berlin 1961) 204–10, figs. 169–73; E. Akurgal, "The

Early Period and the Golden Age of Ionia," *AJA* 66 (1962) 376; R. D. Barnett, "Early Greek and Oriental Ivories," *JHS* 58 (1948) 1–25; Richter (1968) no. 81, figs. 259–62; Mantis (1990) 20–21, pl. 1a, K. Lapatin, *Chryselephantine Statuary in the Ancient Mediterranean World* (Oxford 2001) 49–50. For Cypriot earrings, see Ridgway (1993) 413 n. 935.

10. E. Özgen and I. Özgen, *Antalya Museum* (Antalya 1988) 37, fig. 40 show an example from Bayindir/Elmali.

11. Paris, Musée du Louvre MNB 2854, from Gourizi near Scutari (Skoder); A. De Ridder, *Les bronzes antiques* (Paris 1913) vol. 1, no. 140, pl. 16; C. Rolley, *Les arts mineurs grecs* (Leiden 1967) 7, no. 70, pl. 23; A. Pasquier, *Hommes et dieux de la Grèce antique* (Brussels 1982) 269–81; Richter (1968) no. 177, figs. 557–60.

12. Smith in Hogarth (1908) 172–75.

13. J. Charbonneaux, *Les bronzes grecs* (Paris 1958) 77, 143.

14. London, British Museum E274, from Vulci, *ARV²* 604.53, Niobid Painter. Würzburg 503, *ARV²* 611.32, 1661, *Add.* 131, Manner of the Niobid Painter.

15. Earthly women: see *ARV²* 520.35 (Riehen, C. Granacher collection), *Para* 383; Brauron, Archaeological Museum, *ARV²* 1681, *Para* 447; Syracuse, Museum 22174, *ARV²* 672.1; Paris, Louvre G335A, *ARV²* 652.30; Boston, Museum of Fine Arts 68.163, *Add.* 276, *Para* 402.17bis, 506. *Nikai*: see Providence, Rhode Island School of Design 25110. *ARV²* 556.104, *Para* 388; Providence, Rhode Island School of Design 56.062, *ARV²* 556.106, *Para* 388.

16. Athens, National Museum 2038, *ARV²* 558.142, *Para* 388, the Pan Painter; Oxford, Ashmolean Museum 1931.9, *ARV²* 1069.2, Thomson Painter; New York, Brooklyn Museum 59.34, *ARV²* 604.57, 1701, *Para* 395, *Add.* 130, the Niobid Painter.

17. Istanbul, Archaeological Museum 2593; Akurgal, *Die Kunst Anatoliens*, 198, figs. 158–59; Akurgal, "Early Period," 376, pl. 99, fig.18; Mantis (1990) 20, pl. 1b.

18. Ephesos, inventory number 84/K328. A. Bammer, "Neue weibliche Statuetten aus dem Artemision von Ephesos," *ÖJh* 56 (1985) 39–58, esp. 42–49, figs. 4, 5, 11–13.

19. J. R. Mertens, "The Human Figure in Classical Bronze-Working: Some Perspectives," in *Small Bronze Sculpture from the Ancient World*, M. True and J. Podany, eds. (Malibu 1990) 85–102.

20. Mertens, "Human Figure," 98.

21. A. Caubet, "Pygmalion et la statue d'ivoire," in *Architecture et poésie dans le mond grec: Hommage à G. Roux*, R. Etienne et al., eds. (Lyon 1989) 247–54, citing ancient Near Eastern texts and the Bible.

22. London B 89, B 91, B118, B119, B215 (around 550–540 B.C.); Tuchelt (1970) L 45–51, L 54, 56–57, L 60–61, 64, 71–72, 80–81; Ridgway (1993) 137, 166 n. 4.37, 385–87.

23. Berlin Staatliche Museen, Antikensammlung K 75–81, Tuchelt (1970) 100–222. For reconstruction of temple at Didyma, see G. Gruben, "Das archaische Didymeion," *JdI* (1963) 106–12, 142–47.

24. Karakasi (2003) 49, K 75 and K 76.

25. Maidens dancing in honor of Artemis are attested as early as the *Iliad* 16.181–83, see G. Wickert-Micknat, "Die Frau," *Arch-Hom* III, R (Göttingen 1982) 23, n. 86; O. Rubenshohn, *Das Delion von Paros* (Wiesbaden 1962) 39–46. For Hera at Samos, see G. Köpcke, "Neue Holzfune aus dem Heraion von Samos," *MDAI(A)* 82 (1967) 100–148; H. Kyrieleis, "Der Tänzer vom Kap Phoneas," *MDAI(I)* 46 (1996) 117 on dance and costumes as art forms.

26. Berlin, Staatliche Museen, Antikensammlung SK 1721. Tuchelt (1970) 99–100, K 75–81; *Anadolu* 21, *Festschrift Akurgal* (1978–80, 1987) 195–200; Karakasi (2003) 49, pl. 35.

27. Tuchelt (1970) 217 identified them as priestesses.

28. Base from Kyzikos, Istanbul Archaeological Museum 5370, E. Akurgal, "Neue archaische Bildwerke aus Kyzikos," *AntK* 8 (1965) 99–101; Akurgal, *Die Kunst Anatoliens*, 234; Ridgway (1993) 385–86, 405 n. 9.17; Karakasi (2003) 101, pl. 94; K. Tuchelt, "Die archaischen Skulpturen von Didyma: Beiträge zur frügriechischen Plastik in Kleinasien," *IstForsch* 27 (1970) L 79.

29. Athens, Acropolis Museum 52; T. Wiegand, *Die archaische Poros-Architektur der Acropolis zu Athen* (Kassel 1904) 197–204; G. Dickens, *Archaic Sculpture*, vol. 1 of *Catalogue of the Acropolis Museum* (Cambridge 1921) 69–72; R. Heberdey, *Altattische Porosskulptur: Ein Beitrag zur Geschichte der archaischen griechischen Kunst* (Vienna 1919) 16–28; Langlotz and Schuchardt (1943) 797–807; Richter (1968) no. 44, figs. 151–54; Stewart (1990) 114.

30. E. Buschor, "Der Ölbaumgiebel," *AM* 47 (1922) 81–91; G. Hedreen *Capturing Troy* (Ann Arbor 2002) 127–29 n. 28 summarizes the arguments for interpreting the scene as the ambush of Troilos.

31. Dickins (1912) 71.

32. Ridgway (1993) 290–91, 318–19 n. 7.32.

33. Athens National Archaeological Museum 16464. Van Straten (1995) 57–58; E. Berger, *Das Basler Arztrelief: Studien zum griechischen Grab und Votivrelief um 500 v. Chr. und zur vorhippokratischen Medizin* (Basel 1970) 105, fig. 127; 184 nn. 262–63.

34. Boardman identifies the maiden as a priestess, "Heracles, Peisistratos, and Sons," *RA* (1972) 70–71, and B. Külerich, "The Olive-Tree Pediment and the Daughters of Kekrops" *ActaAArtHist* 7 (1989) 1–21, sees her as a "temple girl."

35. The karyatid illustrated is in London, British Museum 1816.6–10. 128. See Roccos (1995) 659.

36. Athens, National Archaeological Museum 1; Kaltsas (2002) 35–36; Richter (1968) 26, no. 1; G. Kokkorou-Alewras, *Archaische naxische Plastik* (Munich 1974) 1, 12, K1; G. Kokkorou-Alewras, Die archaische naxische Bildhauerei," *AntPl* 24 (1995) 37, 80, K 1, with extensive bibliography; Karakasi (2002) 67, 68, 73, 76, 78; A. A. Donahue, *Xoana and the Origins of Greek Sculpture* (1988) 192, 212, 215, 219. For inscribed dedication of Nikandre, see L. H. Jeffrey, *The Local Scripts of Archaic Greece* (Oxford 1961) 47, 291, 303, 311. While there has been debate over the statue's identity as goddess or mortal, the epigraphic evidence is inconclusive, Kron (1996) 155. Most often, the bow and arrows of Artemis are restored in the woman's hands; see Kaltsas (2002) 35. An alternative view restores the

leashes of two lions, which would have formed part of the original offering; see Ridgway (1977a) 86 and H. Gallet de Santerre, *Delos primitive et archäique* (Paris 1958). Karakasi (2003) 76–77 has re-opened discussion of the possibility that the statue represents Nikandre herself.

37. The most recent comprehensive studies of the type are by Karakasi (2003) and Keesling (2003).

38. Keesling (2003) 85, 97.

39. As Athena, Keesling (2003) 98, 107, 122–24, 201; P. Kastriotis, "Τα εν τω μουσείων της Ακροπόλεως ως αναθήματα τη Αθηνά," *AM* (1894) 491–95; C. Robert, "Miscellen" *Hermes* 22 (1887) 129–35; Rouse (1902) 283–90, 302–6; and in some cases, Ridgway (1990a) 608–12, (1993) 147–79, (1977a) 110; (1997b).

40. E. B. Harrison, "Sculpture in Stone," in *The Human Figure in Early Greek Art*, J. Sweeney, T. Curry, and Y. Tzedakis, eds. (Washington 1988) 54; and Ridgway (1982) 123–27.

41. As young female worshippers, Sourvinou-Inwood (1995b) 241–52; Karakasi (2003) 135–37; Roccos (1995) 647–48; Ridgway (1993) 147–51; M. Steiber, *The Poetics of Appearance in the Attic Korai* (Austin 2001) 135–40. As arrephoroi or other living girls with special cult roles, see Dickins (1912) 32; A. Furtwängler, *Archäologische Studien ihrem Lehrer Heinrich Brunn zur Feier seines fünfzigjährigen Doctorjubiläums am 20 März 1893 in dankbarer Verehrung* (Berlin 1893) 174. As kanephoroi, see Turner (1983) 392–95; Brulé (1987) 248; H. A. Shapiro, "Zum Wandel der attischen Gesellschaft nach den Perserkriegen im Spiegel der Akropolis-Weihung," in *Gab es Griechische Wunder? Griechenland zwischen dem Ende des 6. und der Mitte des 5. Jahrhunderts v. Chr.*, D. Papenfuss and V. M. Strocka, eds. (Mainz 2001) 93–94; M. Steiber, "Aeschylus's *Theorioi* and Realism in Greek Art," *TAPA* 124 (1994) 110–11. As priestesses of Athena, see L. Bruit Zaidman (1992) 411 and Kron (1996) 144. Dickins (1912) 8 suggested that the statues may be donor portraits of proud Athenian women. It should be noted that the Samian *korai* have been read as images of living maidens, H. Kyrieleis, "Eine neue Kore des Cheramyes," *AntP* 24 (1995) 30; B. Freyer-Schauenberg, *Bildwerke der archaischen Zeit und des strengen Stils, Samos 11* (Bonn 1974) 10, 25; F. Brommer, "Gott oder Mensch," *JdI* 101 (1986) 51.

42. As expressions of aristocratic ideologies, see L. A. Schneider and C. Höcker, *Die Akropolis von Athen, Antikes Heiligtum und modernes Reiseziel* (Cologne 1975) 5, 88–95. As anonymous figures of good omen dedicated by artisans, *banausoi*, and other nonaristocrats, see R. Holloway, "Why *Korai?*" *OJA* 11 (1992) 267–74. For anonymous female *agalmata*, see Richter (1968) 3.

43. As generic blanks, see H. Lechat, *Au Musée de l'Acropole: Études sur la sculpture en Attiqe avant la ruine de l'Acropole lors de l'invasion de Xerxès. Annales de l'Université de Lyon X.* (Paris and Lyon 1903) 276–77; Stewart on *kouroi* (1990) 109–10, and on *korai* (1990) 123–24.

44. Lysistrate, priestess of Demeter, set up an agalma in the City Eleusinion; see below, note 71. Athens, Agora Museum, I 5484.

45. See below, note 62.

46. Athens, Acropolis Museum 681, Richter (1968) no. 110, figs. 336–40; Ridgway (1993) 292–96; Keesling (2003) 56–59, 213 dates the statue and its base to 525–510 B.C.

47. J. Maxmin, "Meniskoi and the Birds," *JHS* 95 (1975) 175–80. It must be remembered that the Acropolis korai were not standing on the Acropolis during the time when Aristophanes wrote.

48. Ridgway (1990) 585–89, where she reviews the literature on *meniskoi*.

49. Harris (1995) II.1–4, II.7, II.38, IV.13, V.39, V.40–48, V.214.

50. S. Aleshire, *The Athenian Asklepieion: The People, Their Dedications, and the Inventories* (Amsterdam 1989) 48 n. 3.

51. *IG* II² 1425.380–81. Keesling (2003) 113.

52. Ridgway (1997) 587–88; Schelp (1975) 20.

53. See Vickers and Gill (1994) chap. 2, and p. 106, on the relative values of metals and pottery. A precious-metal basket carried upon the head of an Acropolis kore would have been much more valuable than the marble sculpture of the girl that supported it.

54. We know the names of fifty kanephoroi from Hellenistic dedicatory lists from Athenian Acropolis, Turner (1983) 323–44. For arrephoroi, see Turner (1983) 345–58; Mansfield (1985) 296–301. As noted ealier, only fifteen bases can be associated with statues of korai. At least two of these were dedicated by *banausoi*, artisans unlikely to have had daughters who served in the post of kanephoros. Clearly, not all korai had metal spikes on their heads and not all korai were meant to represent kanephoroi.

55. F. Studniczka, "Antenor der Sohn des Eumares und die Geschichte der archaischen Malerei," *JdI* 2 (1887) 135–48; H. Lechat, "Observations sur les statues archaïques de type féminin du Musée de l'Acropole," *BCH* 14 (1890) 301–62; Maxmin, "Meniskoi," 175–80.

56. Delphi, Museum 7723, fifth century B.C. P. Amandry, "Rapport prélim. sur les statues chryséléphantines de Delphes," *BCH* 63 (1939) 88, fig. 2; *Greek Art of the Aegean Islands* (New York 1979) no. 184, fig. 184.

57. Keesling (2003) 84; T. Linders, "Gods, Gifts, Society," in *Gifts to the Gods*, T. Linders and G. Nordquist, eds., Proceedings of the Uppsala Symposium 1985 (Uppsala 1987) 118–21.

58. *IG* II² 1498–1501A; Keesling (2003) 127.

59. I follow Mantis (1990) 74–75 in viewing the *kleidouchoi* of Pheidias and Euphranor as images of priestesses.

60. E. Langlotz, *Phidiasprobleme* (Frankfurt 1947) 73; Mantis (1990) 74.

61. Florence, Uffizi 214. O. Palagia, *Euphranor* (Leiden 1980) 40–41, pl. 35; A. H. Borbein, review of O. Palagia, *Euphranor*, *Gnomon* 39 (1987) 45.

62. *IG* II² 3453; Lewis (1955) 5; O. Benndorf, "Zur Perieges der Akropolis," *AM* 7 (1882) 47; Ridgway (1981) 186, 231–33; Mantis (1990) 70–74. For extensive bibliography, see Kron (1996) 143 n. 29. For full study of Lysimache, see Georgoudi (1993 = 2003).

63. Translation by Mabel Lang.

64. Cole (2004) 124 reconstructs fifty-six years instead of sixty-four.

65. Lewis (1955) 4–6. *Künstlerlexikon der Antike*, s.v. "Demetrios of Alopeke." See M. L. Lazzarini, "Epigrafia e statua ritratto: alcuni problemi," *AA Pat* 97 (1984–85) 124.

66. London, British Museum 2001; J. Six, "Ikonographische Studien," *RhM* 27 (1912) 83–85 was the first to make the connection; Pfisterer-Haas (1989) 101–5, figs. 164–65. Mantis (1990) 72, pls. 30–31, in turn, has associated the London head with the lost *kleidouchos* of Pheidias. H. Hiller, "Penelope und Eurykleia?" *AA* 87 (1972) 47–67, esp. 55, figs. 7–8, connects the head with the body of an old *peplophoros* in Basel but identifies the figure as Odysseus's old nurse. Zevi (1969/70) 114 connects head and body but identifies the resulting statue as a portrait of Charite, prophetess at Delphi, discussed above. Ridgway (1981) 231–33 rightly points out that the London head is far too late stylistically to be associated with Demetrios's portrait of Lysimache. For a copy in Rome, see B. M. Feletti-Maj, *Museo Nazionale Romano, I ritratti* (Rome 1953) n. 1.

67. Basel Museum BS 202. E. Berger "Die Hauptwerke des Basler Antinkenmuseums zwischen 460 und 430 v. Chr." *AntK* 11 (1968) 68–70; Mantis (1990) 71, pls. 31a, b.

68. *IG* II² 3464; Mantis (1990) 75–76.

69. Translation by A. Stewart (1979) 115. Pausanias's mention of a statue of Lysimache herself seems to have slipped out of his text in a lacuna, Keesling (2003) 220 n. 27.

70. O. Reisch, "Bronzestatuette einer alten Frau im Wiener Hofmuseum," (1919) 296–98; Mantis (1990) 75 n. 318, pl. 32; Keesling (2003) 30.

71. Athens, Agora Museum I 5484; *IG* I³ 953; *CEG* 317; Clinton (1974) 69, no. 1; Miles (1998) 187, no. 1; Maass (1946) 72 takes "Stephano" to be the title of a priestess of Demeter.

72. Translation by Mabel Lang.

73. Agora Museum I 5802, Miles (1998) 188, no. 3, pl. 27; Clinton (1974) 70, no. 3. *Agora* 16, no. 277 = Agora Museum I 5165, Miles (1998) 198, no. 35, pl. 28; Broneer (1942) 265–74, no. 51; Clinton (1974) 71; Clinton (1996) 111–25.

74. The inscribed base was first published by B. Orphanou-Phlorake, "Praxiteles *epoiese*," *Horos* (2000–2003) 113–17, figs. 25–26. A. Ajootian, "Praxiteles and the Priestess Chairippe," Archaeological Institute of America online abstract, Annual Meeting (2006) and A. Ajootian, "Praxiteles and Fourth-Century Athenian Portraiture," in *Early Hellenistic Portraiture: Image, Style, Context*, P. Schultz and R. van der Hoff, eds. (Cambridge 2007). I am indebted to Aileen Ajootian for discussing the statue base with me.

75. Keesling (2003) 170–74.

76. Found in 1969, Zevi (1969–70) 95–116.

77. *EAA*, s.v. Phradmon. Zevi (1969–70) 95–116 associates the head of the old woman in the British Museum (mentioned earlier in association with Lysimache, fig. 5.11) with Phradmon's portrait of Charite; Ridgway (1984) 22; Stewart (1990) 23. For statue of Plato by Lysikles, cf. Plato *test* 18 in *Peg VII* p. 433.

78. Zevi (1969–70) takes as certain that Phradmon was active during the fifth century but B. S. Ridgway, "A Story of Five Amazons," *AJA* 78 (1974) 9 cautions that Pliny's *akme* dates are notoriously unreliable. See also Marcadé (1953) no. 88.

79. *IG* II² 4573; Kron (1996) 154.

80. Athens, Acropolis, in situ, the shrine was reconstructed by L. Beschi "Contributi di topografia ateniese," *ASAtene* 45–46, NS29–30, 1967–68 (1969) 511–36, figs. 7–10. *IG* II² 4596; *CEG* II, 775; Kron (1996) 154–55; Simon (1983) 48–51.

81. For comprehensive discussion of the piece, see Kron (1996) 150–53.

82. London, British Museum 1859.12–2636; Newton (1861) 380, 418, 714, no. 15, pl. 78, 15; *CEG* II, 860.

83. Kron (1996) 153; Newton (1861), no. 13–14, 17–19, 20, 22, 23, 25–27, 80.

84. London, British Museum 1300; Ridgway (1997) 332–34, pls. 79a–c.

85. Gauthier (1985); M. Payne *Areta eneta* (1988); M. Kajava, "Roman Senatorial Women and the Greek East: Epigraphic Evidence for the Republican and Augustan Period," in *Roman Eastern Policy and Other Studies in Roman History*, H. Solin and M. Kajava, eds. (Tvarminne 1987) 59–124; for Hellenistic period, see Höghammer (1993); I. Schmidt, *Hellenistische Statuenbasen* (New York 1995); Bremen (1996); Filges (1997); Eule (2001).

86. *I.Priene*, 160; Price (1999) 70; M. Guarducci, *Epigrafia greca*, III (1974) 91; Eule (2001) 207.

87. London, British Museum 1153; J. B. Carter, *The Sculpture of the Sanctuary of Athena Polias at Priene*, (London 1983) 251–52, 276–78, pls. Xlc–e, XLVIIb. S. Th. Schippreit, "Das alte und das neue Priene," *MDAI (I)* 48 (1988) 193–236, esp. 220–28, pls. 19–21, for heads from Demeter sanctuary. As for the head wrongly associated with the base, the overall shape of the bust, the coiffure of crisp snail curls, and the cold hard features of the girl's face argue for a Roman date; J. Inan and E. Rosenbaum, *Roman and Early Byzantine Portrait Sculpture in Asia Minor* (London 1966) 160 place the head in the Neronian period.

88. Berlin, Staatliche Museen SK 1928; *I.Priene*, 173; Ridgway (1990b) 210–12; Kron (1996) 146–48; Mantis (1990) 98; Eule (2001) 179–80 gives bibliography.

89. Dated to the fourth or third century B.C.; inv. no. 285/286; Kron (1996) 148–49 n. 49, citing T. Wiegand and H. Schrader, *Priene: Ergebnisse der Ausgrabungen und Untersuchungen in den Jahren 1895–1898* (Berlin 1904) 148, fig. 119; Eule (2001) 207.

90. Mantis (1990) 123 restores a hydria; Wiegand and Schrader, *Priene*, 151 restore a *kalathos*; Ridgway (1997) 211–12 restores a scepter; and Kron (1996) 148 suggests a torch. Ridgway has further suggested that the statue may not represent Nikeso at all but, rather, the goddess Demeter. She allows that, if the statue does represent Nikeso, she may be shown with her hair worn long in imitation of Demeter.

91. Ridgway (1997) 212; *RE* 4.127.

92.	South Italian oinochoe, London, British Museum F 366, *RVAp* 177, no. 94; glass-paste gemstone, Vienna, Kunsthistorisches Museen, Inv. XIB 564, F. Cumont, in *Atti della Pontificia Accademia Romana di Archaeologia Memoire* 3 (1933) 93–99. The convention is maintained in Roman Catholic ritual involving the raising of the monstrance, in which the priest cloaks his hands in his vestments before lifting the sacred implement.

93.	Connelly (1988) 8, 25–29.

94.	*I.Priene* 170; inv. no. 284; Eule (2001) 207–8.

95.	*I.Erythrai* 210a; *CIG* II, 858. Translation by Mabel Lang.

96.	E. Pottier and A. Hauvette-Besnault, "Décret des Abdéritains trouvé à Téos," *BCH* 4 (1880) 160, Nr. II-IK, nr. 69; Eule (2001) 200.

97.	Samos, Vathy Museum 87. K. Tsakos, *Samos: A Guide to the History and Archaeology* (Athens 2003) 69, no. 64; Eule (2001) 181, no. 47, dates it to 220–200 B.C., pl. 15, fig. 85.

98.	Höghammar (1993) 56, cat. nos. 84–86; Ridgway (1997) 214–15; R. Kabus-Priesshofen, "Statuettengruppe aus dem Demeterheiligtum bei Kyparissi auf Kos," *AntPl* 15 (1975) 31–64; U. Kron (1996) 149–51, fig. 5. For Pythias, see Höghammar (1993) 56, cat. no. 87. For Kallistrate, see S. M. Sherwin-White, *Ancient Cos* (1978) 132; Höghammer (1993) 175, no. 65; Eule (2001) 202.

99.	For priestesses and female cult agents of Cyprus, see I. Michaelidou-Nicolaou, *Prosopography of Ptolemaic Cyprus*, *SIMA* vol. 44 (Götteborg 1976): Amath'-Osir, 32, no. 24; Phanion Boiskou, 122, no. 4; Eirene Ptolemaiou, 56, no. 2; the three eponymous priestess daughters of Theodoros Seleukou, Artemo, Theodoris, and Polykrateia, 68, no. 13; 45, no. 158; 98, no. 33.

100.	The "statue of Nikokleia" in the British Museum is sometimes regarded as a statue of a priestess (Mantis [1990] 98), but it should be noted that the head, body, and inscribed base assembled to create this composite do not belong together. The headless statue (British Museum 1301; Lullies and Hirmer [1957] pl. 246) unearthed by Newton while digging the sanctuary of Demeter on the Triopion promontory at Knidos in 1858 was later associated with the head of an elderly woman found in a separate location, and with an inscribed base found nearby (London, British Museum GR 1859.12–26.25; *I.Knidos*, 135; Schuchhardt [1968] 793). The dedicatory inscription is dated by letter forms to the late third century B.C. and records that Nikokleia offered (the image) to Demeter (in fulfillment of her) vow. The inscription does not refer to Nikokleia as a priestess. It should be noted that some thirty bases for statues of women have been recovered from the Triopion promontory at Knidos (*I.Knidos*, 131–46).

101.	W. H. Buckler and D. M. Robinson, *Sardis 7.1 Greek and Latin Inscriptions* (Leiden 1932) nos. 90–93; Mantis (1990) 101 n. 436.

102.	Eule (2001) 201. *IK* 3, 15–16.

103.	*IG* XII 1, 66.

104.	Eule (2001) 204–7.

105. *I.Pergamon*, no. 167 (149 B.C.). The inscription is of the "rapport de prêtrise" type, giving praise and thanks for her successful priesthood, L. Robert, *Hellenica I*, "Le prêtre Pausanias de Cyrene" and *Hellenica* volumes in addenda vol. 2 and vol. 7. C. P. Jones, "Diodoros Pasparos and the Nikephoria of Pergamon," *Chiron* 4 (1974) 183–205. I thank John Ma for discussing this inscription with me.

106. Eule (2001) 92–102, 204–7.

107. Eule (2001) 92–102, 204–7.

108. Bremen (1996) 183 suggests that the draped marble statues represent Muses but there is no compelling reason that they should not represent priestesses or other cult servants.

109. *I.Pergamon*, nos. 489–529.

110. H. A. Thompson, "Architecture as a Medium for Public Relations among the Successors of Alexander," *Studies in the History of Art*, National Gallery of Art, vol. 10 (Washington 1982) 173–93.

111. *I.Kyzikos* 1432. CIG 3657.

112. *I.Kyzikos* 1433.

113. Bremen (1996) 173–80.

114. Bremen (1996) 1–3, 170–72.

115. *SEG* 28.953. M. Sève, "Un décret de Consolation à Cyzique," *BCH* 103 (1979) 327–59.

116. Bremen (1996) 3. For honorific portraits, see Gauthier (1985).

117. Bremen (1996) 82.

118. We have the names of twenty-one arrephoroi, most serving late third–second centuries B.C. Most frequently, images are dedicated by father, mother, and brother, but we also find examples in which father, uncle, and mother set up statues, or mother and paternal uncle, or brother together with the Assembly and the deme. Evidence is collected by Mansfield (1985) 296–301; Mikalson (1998) 199 n. 86.

119. IG II² 3634.

120. We have the names of 50 kanephoroi who served mostly between 138–95 B.C. and the names of around 115 ergastinai, first attested in 108/107 B.C., who served in the late second and first century. Turner (1983) 351–69.

121. IG II² 3455; Marcadé (1953) I, 58; Lewis (1955) 8.

122. Translation by Mabel Lang.

123. Mantis (1990). The debate is summarized by Kron (1996) 144 n. 32.

124. Turner (1983) 250–53.

125. Menander: IG II² 3777 (= *test.* 25 K-A, *PCG* VI 2 p. 12). Pausanias 1.21.1 (without naming the sculptor); Lykourgos: [Plutarch] *Lives of the Ten Orators* 843. Mantis (1990) 95–96.

126.	*IG* II² 928; cf. *IG* II² 3470–71 for the name of her father. Tracy (2003) 141. It should be noted that we find a bench in the theater of Dionysos inscribed with the name [. . .]teris, which has been reconstructed to read [Pente]teris. The inscription *IG* II² 5159 gives neither patronymic nor a reference to a priesthood and, with such extensive restoration, no certain identification can be made.

127.	*LGPN* II, Chrysis, no. 5.

128.	*IG* II² 3484.

129.	Athenobios: *LGPN* II, no. 4; Niketes: *LGPN* II, no. 15; Dionysios: *LGPN* II, no. 319. Turner (1983) 268.

130.	Turner (1983) 265.

131.	*SEG* 29.135; Vanderpool (1979) 213–16.

132.	*ID* 1869. Bruneau (1970) 81, 196; Tracy (1982) 159–65, 210–11; Mikalson (1998) 239–41; Turner (1983) 324; Eule (2001) 217.

133.	Athens, National Archaeological Museum 232, *IG* II² 3462; Kaltsas (2002) 274, no. 574; S. Karouzou, *National Archaeological Museum: Collection of Sculpture* (Athens 1968) 181, no. 232; Mantis (1990) 103, 109; Eule (2001) 4–43, 215.

134.	N. Himmelmann, *Die private Bildnisweihung bei den griechen* (Wiesbaden 2001) 7–10.

135.	F. Croissant, "Note de topographie argienne," *BCH* 96 (1972) 137–40; Robert and Robert (1973) 94, no. 181.

136.	Translation by Mabel Lang.

137.	*IG* V 2, 265; Bremen (1996) 178 n. 127.

138.	Bremen (1996) 27–28.

139.	*IG* V 2, 268.

140.	*IG* V 2, 268, lines 40–44.

141.	*IG* V 2, 269 and 270; Bremen (1996) 277 n. 11.

142.	I am indebted to Professor Petros Themelis for kindly providing photographs of the statues and for his permission to publish them here. Themelis (2002); Themelis (1994a) 101–22; Themelis (1993a) 99–109; Themelis (1996) 154–85; Themelis in *Ergon* (1991) 28–30. For excavation of site in 1962-63, see A. K. Orlandos, "Ἀνασκαφή: Μεσσήνη," *Ergon* (1962a) 119–32 and *Ergon* (1962b) 99–112, and *Praktika* (1962) 102–12. G. Despinis, "Ἀνδριάς ἱερείας ἐκ Μεσσήνης," in Χαριστήριον εἰς Α.Κ. Ὀρλάνδον. (Athens 1964) 235–38.

143.	Themelis (1994) 116.

144.	Damophon was famous for having repaired Pheidias's cult statue at Olympia following an earthquake in 183 B.C. He also carved the cult statues for the temple of Demeter and Kore at Lykosoura, and several other images at Messene. Themelis (1994b); Themelis (1996).

145. Themelis (1994) 111; see plans in figs. 1, 10, and 12.

146. *SEG* 23.220; Themelis (1994) 115–16, no. 1032; Orlandos *Praktika* (1962) 110–11; Despinis, "Ἀνδριάς ιερείας εκ Μεσσήνης," 235–38; Eule (2001) 215.

147. Translation by Mabel Lang.

148. Messene no. 247, left arm. Themelis (1994) 116, fig. 19; Orlandos *Ergon* (1962) pl. 117; Despinis, "Ἀνδριάς ιερείας εκ Μεσσήνης," 235, pl. 37.

149. The arm (no. 247) was first associated with the statue (no. 245) and the base (no. 1032) by Orlandos, *Ergon* (1962) 129 and confirmed by Themelis (1994) 116. Ridgway (2002) 118, 135 n. 10.

150. Mego's statue, no. 245. Other life-size statues of girls are Messene Museum 241, 244, and 246. Eule (2001) 215.

151. Inscribed base no. 1034 (*SEG* 23.221) has been associated with statue no. 241 by Themelis (1994) 115–16, fig. 21. Ridgway (2002) 118, 135 n. 10.

152. Messene, no. 244; Themelis (1994) 115–16.

153. Messene, no. 246.

154. Excavated by P. Themelis in 1991 and 1992; see Themelis, *Ergon* (1991) 28–30 and Themelis (1994) 100–102. The inscription (inv. no. 3587, *SEG* 41.365) can be dated to the second half of the third century B.C. Fragments of the bronze statue, a right arm and a right leg wearing high boots, were also found in 1991 and 1992, see Themelis (1994) 29, fig. 42.

155. Junthes in *RE*, s.v. Leibsubungen. See now Posidippus epigram 51 in Austin-Bastianini, *Posidippi Pallaei quae supersunt omnia, Biblioteca Classica* 3 (Milan 2002). I thank Colin Austin for this reference.

156. P. Louvr. E 3320; D. A. Campbell, *Greek Lyric*, vol. 2, Loeb Classical Library (Cambridge, MA 1988) 360–77. Themelis (1994) 116.

157. Themelis (1994) 116, 122. The transporting of the sacred image (*bretas*) was central to the rites at Messene. This is reminiscent of the shrine of Artemis Orthia at Sparta where the wooden image was believed to be that brought by Orestes and Iphigeneia from the sanctuary of Artemis at Tauris on the Black Sea (where Iphigeneia had served as priestess). Many shrines claimed to hold the original *xoanon* but the Spartans maintained that they alone had the true statue.

158. Themelis (1994) 122.

159. Themelis (1994) 111, 117–19 (nos. 1031, 1033, 1027 = *SEG* 23.215–17). Themelis identified these three statues as representations of priestesses and differentiated them from the statues showing the girl initiates (1994) 115–16. He also matched the inscribed bases with their corresponding priestess portraits. The council of old men mentioned in the inscriptions are said to be the descendants of Kresophontes who, according to legend, won Messenia after the Dorian invasion (Pausanias 4.3).

160. Themelis (1994) 118, fig. 23a (Messene, no. 242).

161. Themelis (1994) 117–19, fig. 22. Small spool-shaped incense boxes are shown held in the hands of votaries whose statues were dedicated in the Hellenistic sanctuaries of Cyprus; Connelly (1988) 80, 88, examples from Golgoi and Idalion. The round incense box is held in the fist with thumb pressing down on its lid.

162. A recent study by Filges (1997) has divided these examples into some fifteen subtypes.

163. A variation of this type was used for the image of Poppaea Sabina, wife of Nero, set up within the cella of the temple of Hera at Olympia. See M. Bieber, *Ancient Copies* (New York 1977) 196, figs. 805–6. Poppaea Sabina is shown wearing her mantle in the characteristic arrangement, pulled from under the right breast up and over the left breast. The same stylized bunching of the fabric in a rosette shape can be seen at her left hip. Two other portrait statues from Olympia show even closer parallels to the image of Eirana; these are the works of the Athenian sculptors Eros and Eleusinios; Dittenberger, W. and K. Purgold, *Die Inschriften von Olympia*, 1896–1966 Olympia 5, (Amsterdam 1896–) 659–60, nos. 645, 647. They show the same pose and mantle pulled in a roll up and over the left breast, with bunching of the fabric in a rosette shape at the left hip. These statues represent noble ladies of Achaea who were honored by the Eleans. They can be dated to the second half of the first century A.D.

164. Messene, no. 243, height 0.65 m, Themelis (1994) 118, fig. 23b. Filges (1997) 273, no. 152 (full bibliography), places this within his type Argos/Salamis.

165. Filges (1997) 273, no. 146 (Argos, Museum 182) and Filges (1997) 274, no. 155 (Salamis, found in the gymnasium).

166. Filges (1997) 273 places it in the middle Antonine period and cites Kaltsas as dating the statue to the first century A.D. and H. Meyer (*RE* Supplement XV [1978] 146, s.v. "Messene") as placing it in the Hadrianic period.

167. Messene, no. 240, Themelis (1994) 119, fig. 24.

168. For a work by the master sculptor Agorakritos that George Despinis has reconstructed from surviving fragments, see G. Despinis, "Συμβολή στην μελέτη του έργου ου Αγοράκνιτου" (Athens 1971) 38–40, pl. 49, fig. 2. Despinis dates the statue of Kallis to the early years of Antonine rule.

169. It can be seen in an example from Aptera in Turkey that dates as late as the late Antonine or possibly even early Severan period. Istanbul, Archaeological Museum; Bieber, *Ancient Copies*, 203–4, figs. 839–41.

170. D. B. Thompson, *Troy: Terracotta Figurines of the Hellenistic Period*, Supplementary Monograph 3 (Princeton 1963) 38–39; D. B. Thompson, *Ptolemaic Oinochoai and Portraits in Faience: Aspects of Ruler Cult* (Oxford 1973) 27, 82, 85, 89, 93.

171. Conducted from 1955 to 1961; see Hollinshead (1985) 430–32. Excavation reports by I. Threpsiades, *Praktika* (1956a) 94–104; (1958a) 45, 52, 54; (1959a) 26–29; *Ergon* (1956b) 33–37; (1958b) 53–55; (1959b) 24–26; (1961/62); "Chroniques des Fouilles," *BCH* (1956–62). The temple is unusually oriented along a northwest-southeast axis facing directly onto a nearby spring. Its oblong plan shows proportions that are more at home in the Archaic period and may reflect Boiotian conservatism.

The temple has traditionally been dated to the fifth century on the basis of its polygonal masonry but some see this as a local tendency to use earlier techniques, Hollinshead (1985) 43. n. 61.

172. Thebes, Museum BE 66, statue of Zopyreina; Demakopoulou and Konsola (1981) 80, fig. 27.

173. Thebes, Museum BE 66 (*SEG* 25.542); Demakopoulou and Konsola (1981) 80, fig. 27; Mantis (1990) 103.

174. For full treatment of type, see J. Trimble "Replicating the Body Politic: The Herculaneum Women Statue Types in Early Imperial Italy," *JRA* 13 (2000) 41–68.

175. Trimble, "Herculaneum Women," 68, points out that Roman statues deriving from these types have little to do with the "lost Greek originals" from which they may have ultimately derived.

176. One of these shows the younger Faustina, who was only sixteen when she married Marcus Aurelius in A.D. 146; R. Bol, *Das Statuenprogramm des Herodes-Atticus-Nymphäums, Olympische Forschungen* 15 (Berlin 1984) 179–80, no. 42, pls. 46–47, and inscribed base 114–16, no. 5. Another statue from the Nymphaeum shows Athenais, the youngest daughter of its patron and builder, Herodes Atticus; Bol, *Das Statuenprogramm*, 180–82, no. 43 (pls. 48–50); inscribed base, W. Amelung, *Herodes Atticus* (Hildesheim 1983) II, no. 127; Bol, *Das Statuenprogramm*, 132–34 (fig. 60, pl. 11). The statue of Athenais stood on a base that it shared with a portrait of her brother, Regillus. It is likely that the entire family of Herodes Atticus was originally depicted in this large portrait group. A headless female figure of the Large Herculaneum Woman type found in the Nymphaeum has been identified as an image of Herodes Atticus's wife, Regilla; Bol, *Das Statuenprogramm*, 171–73, no. 36 (pls. 32–33).

177. Thebes, Museum BE 64; Demakopoulou and Konsola (1981) 80, fig. 28.

178. Thebes, Museum BE 65 (height, 0.97 m); Demakopoulou and Konsola (1981) 80; Filges (1997) 277, no. 170 (with complete bibliography) places the statue within his Athens/Thebes subtype.

179. Thebes, Museum BE 63 (height, 1.75 m); identified as Artemis in Demakopoulou and Konsola (1981) 79, pl. 41.

180. Tell Asmar: A. Spycket, *Le statuaire du Proche-Orient ancien* (Paris 1981) 52–75, pl. 37; Byblos: N. Jidejian, *Byblos through the Ages* (Beirut 1968) figs. 74, 76–78. Cyprus: Connelly (1988) 210–18;

181. Connelly (1991) 93–94.

182. In later Greek tradition, the representation of the divinity becomes the more popular dedication, perhaps because of the growing fame and popularity of cult statues from the fifth century B.C.

CHAPTER 6. THE PRIESTESS IN ACTION: PROCESSION, SACRIFICE, AND BENEFACTION

1. Translation by Helene Foley in Fantham et al. (1994) 95–96. H. van Looy, *Euripede VIII 2, Fragments* (Paris 2000) 347–96. While the lines are generally attributed to Melanippe, it is possible that they were spoken by the queen, wife of King Metapontus; see Collard, Cropp, and Lee (1995) 272–74.

2. Fantham et al. (1994) 95–96.

3. Translation by H. L. Jones, *The Geography of Strabo*, vol. 3, Loeb Classical Library (Cambridge, MA 1932) 183.

4. *Laws* 909e–910a, translation by T. J. Saunders, *Plato: The Laws* (Harmondsworth 1975).

5. ED 236.8–11; similar duties have been restored for the priest of Asklepios; see Parker and Obbink (2001) no. 4A.16f. (cf. idem [2001] 425, 10a). First century B.C.

6. Polignac (1995) 152.

7. Sourvinou-Inwood (1990) 30; Lefkowitz (2003) 238.

8. Kearns (1995) 522, citing C. Geertz, "Religion as a Cultural System," *in The Interpretation of Cultures* (New York 1973) 87–125.

9. *LSAG²* 168 no. 8, *SEG* 11.314; ca. 575–550 B.C. C. D. Buck, *The Greek Dialects* (Chicago 1955) 83; Cole (2004) 17–18.

10. *LSS* 127 = *IG* II² 1346.

11. T. Drew-Bear and W. D. Lebek, "An Oracle of Apollo at Miletus," *GRBS* 14 (1973) 65–73.

12. Graf in Hägg (1996) 55–65, with full bibliography for *pompai*. See Connor (1987 = 2001) 56–75, esp. 67; F. Bömer, *RE*, s.v., Pompa; A. Kavoulaki, "Processional Performance and the Democratic Polis," in S. Goldhill and R. Osborne, *Performance Culture and Athenian Democracy* (Cambridge 1999) 293–320.

13. T. Wiegand, *Sitz. Berl. Akad.* 1905, 547. Translation by A. Henrichs (1978) 148, where he discusses this and another inscription (*LSAM* 48) describing the duties of the priestess of Dionysos at Miletos (148ff.).

14. *IG* I³ 79 = Clinton (2005) 41; 422/421 B.C. See Clinton (1974) 14, 69, 88–89.

15. *I.Magnesia* 98, *LSAM* 32. 197/196 B.C.

16. Peirce (1993) 228–29; K. Lenstaedt, *Prozesiondarstellungen auf attischen Vasen* (Munich 1971); van Straten (1995).

17. London, British Museum B 80 (B2), *lekane* of the Boeotian Silhouette Group: *CVA* British Museum 2, III H e, pl. 7:4a–b; C. Scheffer, "Boeotian Festival Scenes: Competition, Consumption, and Cult in Archaic Black Figure," in Hägg (1992) 117–41, and "Why Boeotian? Reflections of the Boeotian Silhouette Group," in *From the Gustavianum Collections in Uppsala* 3, M. Blomberg, ed. = *Boreas* 23 (Uppsala 1993) figs. 7–8; van Straten (1987) 159–60; van Straten (1995) 21–22; Mantis (1990) 26, 27, pl. 4.

18. C. J. Herington, *Athena Parthenos and Athena Polias* (Manchester 1955) associated the attacking Athena type with the Panathenaic prize amphorae. G. F. Pinney, "Pallas and Panathenaia" in Christiansen and Melander (1988) 465–67, refers to it as the "Panathenaic Athena" type and views the Panathenaia as a celebration of victory in the Gigantomachy. See also Shapiro (1989) 27–36; Ridgway (1992) 127–31.

19. Schnapp (1988), esp. 570f.; Connelly (1993) 100–101.

20. Scheffer, "Boeotian Festival Scenes," 119f., "Why Boeotian?" 83.

21. London, British Museum 1905.7-11.1, the Gela Painter (500/480 B.C.). From Vraona near Spata. *ABV* 443.3, 475.29; J. M. Hemelrijk, "The Gela Painter in the Allard Pierson Museum," *BABesch* 49 (1974) 144, figs. 48–49; Durand (1986) 92, figs. 17a, b; van Straten (1995) 18.

22. These same elements are seen also on a loutrophoros from the Acropolis, dating to the second half of the sixth century, Athens Acropolis 1220; *LIMC* I Athena 577; Graef and Langlotz I (1925) pl. 67; Shapiro (1989) 30, pl. 10b. We see Athena Promachos as well as the label "ΑΘΕΝΑΙΑS" (of Athena) painted on the altar. A column stands in front of the goddess. The female leader of the procession faces Athena and pours a libation from a jug held in her right hand; her left arm is raised, presumably to steady a basket, now broken away.

23. Athens, National Archaeological Museum 16464. *SEG* 23.264 (a). D. Amyx, *Corinthian Vase-Painting of the Archaic Period* (Berkeley 1988) 394–95, 604–5; van Straten (1995) 57–58; Hausmann (1960) 15, fig. 4; Mantis (1990) 26, pl. 3a.

24. The absence of tresses falling down the girl's back has been interpreted as a short cropped hairstyle with ritual connotations by Roccos (1995) 651, relying on E. B. Harrison, "Greek Sculptured Coiffures and Ritual Haircuts," in Hägg et al. (1988) 247–54. I believe that we, instead, have the artist's attempt to show the girl's upper body in three-quarter view. As the maiden brings her left arm forward to steady the basket, her hair flows down her back and is thus obscured by the turning of her shoulders. This gives the kanephoros a sense of movement and torsion, distinguishing her from the women who march behind in stiff profile view, emphasizing her privileged role as leader of the procession.

25. *SEG* 23.264 (a). Amyx, *Corinthian Vase-Painting*, 394–95, 604–5 reads the inscriptions in this way, though Heubeck (p. 285) says that the reading "Ethelonche" is not possible. See F. Lorber, *Inschriften auf korinthischen Vasen: Archäologisch-epigraphische Untersuchungen zur korinthischen Vasenmalerei im 7. und 6. Jh. v. Chr.* (Berlin 1978) no. 154A, pl. 46.

26. Ferrara, National Museum 2897 (T 128). *ARV*² 1052.25 and 1680; *Para.* 442, 444; *Add.* 322. *LIMC* III Dionysos, 869. Bérard (1976) 101–14; C. Bérard and J.-L. Durand (1989) 23–25, 29. Carpenter (1997) 70–79; L. Lawler, "The Maenads: A Contribution to the Study of the Dance in Ancient Greece," *MAAR* 6 (1927) 107; I. Loucas, "Meaning and Place of the Cult Scene on the Ferrara Krater T 128," in Hägg (1992) 73–83.

27. Oakley and Sinos (1993) 101, 106.

28. For interpretation as generic ecstatic cult scene, see Carpenter (1997) 79; for representation of Orphic ritual at Phlya, see Loucas, "Meaning and Place," 79–83.

29. Loucas, "Meaning and Place," summarizes the scholarship and argues for the Great Goddess Rhea-Kybele and Dionysos.

30. J. Bérard and J.-L. Durand (1989) 23–25, 29; Loucas, "Meaning and Place," On Hipta in the Orphic tradition, see frags. 199, 211 Kern; M. L. West, *The Orphic Poems* (Oxford 1983) 96.

31. Aubriot-Sévin (1992) 124–45; Pulleyn (1993) 188–95; Burkert (1985) 73–75; Jameson (1988) 963–64; H. Versnel, "Religious Mentality in Ancient Prayer," in Versnel (1981) 1–64; Furley and Bremer (2001); E. Norden, *Agnostos Theos* (Stuttgart 1923) 143–76.

32. A. Corlu, *Recherches sur les mots relatif à l'idée de prière d'Homere aux tragiques* (Paris 1966).

33. Van Straten (1974), esp. 175.

34. Athens, Acropolis Museum, 752. Graef, Langlotz et al. (1925) pl. 64. I thank Francois Lissarrague for drawing this vase to my attention.

35. Oxford, Ashmolean Museum 1916.15; *ARV*² 732.44; Carlsruhe Painter. *CVA*, Oxford, Ashmolean Museum 1, 28, pl. (130) 38.3.

36. *ARV*² 732.32, 732.34, 732.50, 732.51, 733.53, 733.57, 733.59–64, 733.67, 733.69, 734.92, 734.96.

37. Oxford, Ashmolean Museum G.300 (V.536); *ARV*² 714.170; *Add.*² 282; *CVA*, Oxford, Ashmolean Museum 1, 29, pl. 130, 38.9.

38. Jameson (1988) 964–65.

39. Jameson (1988) 965.

40. Graf (1980); Graf in *RAW* 342; Patton (2006).

41. New York, Metropolitan Museum 96.18.75 (GR 596), said to be from Capua, 460–20 B.C. Painter of London E 100, *ARV*² 834.2.

42. Durand (1991) 45–55; van Straten (1992) 247–84.

43. Los Angeles, County Museum 50.8.24 (A5933.50-30), the Sabouroff Painter; *ARV*² 843.134; *Add.* 296; *CVA* Los Angeles, vol. 1, pl. 27.1, 2.

44. Boston, Museum of Fine Arts 68.163. Nikon Painter, ca. 465 B.C. *ARV*² 651, *Add.* 276; *Para.* 402; *ARFV*, fig. 364 (A).

45. London, British Museum E448, Achilles Painter. *ARV*² 992.65, 1677; *Para* 437; *Add.* 311.

46. Bérard and Durand (1989) 45–45.

47. The bibliography on Greek sacrifice is vast. A sampling includes Berthiaume (1982); Burkert (1966); Burkert (1983); Burkert (1985); Casabona (1966); Detienne and Vernant (1989); Durand (1986); Durand (1991); Graf in *RAW* 340–43; B. Grange and O. Reverdin, eds., *Le sacrifice dans l'antiquité, Fondation Hardt Entretiens sur l'antiquité classique*, vol. 27 (Geneva 1981); Peirce (1984); Peirce (1993); van Straten (1987); van Straten (1995); J.-P. Vernant, "A General Theory of Sacrifice and the Slaying of the Victims in the Greek *Thusia*," in *Mortals and Immortals*, F. Zeitlin, ed. (Princeton 1991) 290–302.

48. Translation by Henrichs (1978) 149–51.

49. Detienne (1989).

50. Osborne (1993 = 2000); Henrichs (1990) 264.

51. Detienne (1989) esp. 131 and 147.

52. Dean-Jones (1994) 226–50. Rules pertaining to menstruation are all but absent from the sacred laws that dictate restrictions for entry into sanctuaries. Among some four hundred surviving texts that record sacred laws, only six mention menstruation and these are all late, dating to the second century B.C. and after, as Cole (1992) 104 observes. Menstruating women were required to wait about a week before entering sanctuaries in the few surviving texts that we have: TeRiele (1978) 325–31 (on the seventh day); *LSS* 54.7–8 (nine days); *LSS* 119.13 (seven days); *LSCG* 55.5–6 (seven days); Immerwahr (1971) 235–38 = *LSCG* 99; and *LSS* 91.

53. Graf (1980) 209–21.

54. Berthiaume (1982) 62–70; van Straten (1987) 161–70; Graf (1980); J.-L. Durand, "Greek Animals: Toward a Topology of Edible Bodies," in Detienne and Vernant (1989) 87–105.

55. See Osborne (2000) 307–10. Christianity may not provide the only model that affects our view of ancient sacrifice. There is a clear hierarchy of ritual players in the Spanish bullfight. The privileged status of the matador as the one who kills the bull sets him apart from those who lead, decorate, and exhaust the bull in advance of the culminating moment of death. But even here, there is some flexibility; the matador may choose to play the role of banderillero and participate in the ritual decoration of the victim as well.

56. *LSCG* 69.25–27, fourth century B.C.

57. *LSCG* 151. A.42–44, translation in Osborne (2000) 307 n. 42.

58. *ID* 440 A.32, cf. *ID* 440 A.38. In *ID* 372 A.105, the *mageiros* received more than was spent on wood (three drachmas to one drachma one obol); see Bruneau (1970) 288. For full study of the role of the *mageiros*, see Berthiame (1982).

59. See Osborne (2000) 294–95 and n. 2. Casabona (1966) 349–50.

60. *SEG* 35.923 A.8–10. See Osborne (2000) 308 with n. 45. While this inscription may provide the only *surviving* example of a priestly prerogative that must be consumed on the spot, there is no reason to believe that this is unique.

61. *SEG* 21.530 = *LSS* 20.

62. Detienne (1989) 131f.

63. *LSCG* 33 b 10–15 (335/334–330/329 B.C.).

64. SEG 21.541 (= *LSCG* 18), 144–51 (Semele) and 433–40 (Dionysos).

65. *LSAM* 73, 17–23 (third c. B.C.); L. Robert, *Hellenica* 5 (1948) 64–69; J. Robert and L. Robert, *Bulletin Epigraphique* 55 (1951) 144–45.

66. *LSAM* 48.1–20; Henrichs (1978) 149–51.

67. *I.Cos, ED* 216, B.11–12 (ca. 225 or ca. 175 B.C.). See Parker and Obbink (2000) 425 (10).

68. Osborne (1993) 403.

69. Osborne (1993) 403f. *LSAM* 16 = *Syll.*³ 1219, 23–27.

70. Detienne (1989) 140ff.; Versnel (1996) 191f.

71. According to Aelian (*De natura animalium* 11.4), the cow is led by the priestess of Demeter. Henrichs (1990) 264; Detienne (1989) 141.

72. Aelian frag. 361 Hercher = *Suda*, s.v. Thesmophoros, Sphaktriai; Detienne (1989) 129–31; Versnel (1996).

73. Harmodios pulls the dagger from beneath his myrtle branch in the Panathenaic procession to kill the tyrant Hippias as he passes by (Scholia 893, 895 Campbell).

74. For sacrificial feasts in the *Dyskolos*, see A. Dalby, *Siren Feasts: A History of Food and Gastronomy in Greece* (London 1996) 2–5.

75. Peirce (1993) 225.

76. Peirce (1993) 229.

77. London, British Museum E 284, Nausicaa Painter, 450/440 B.C. *ARV*² 1107.7, *Add.* 330, *Para.* 452.

78. An oinochoe in Laon similarly shows a woman laying her hands between the ears and horns of a bull, as if to adorn the head with fillets, Laon, Musée Archeologique Municipal 37.1044; *CVA*, Laon, 1, pl. 39.5; van Straten (1995) fig. 44.

79. Peirce (1993) 249–50.

80. New York, Metropolitan Museum of Art 41.162.255, from Vulci. *ABL* 247. Peirce (1993) 249–50. A red-figure bell krater in Syracuse, Museo Archeologico 22886, by the Eupolis Painter, shows a woman wearing a crown and carrying two flaming torches as she escorts a bull. The bull similarly seems to go voluntarily with her. Beazley identified the woman as a priestess, *ARV*² 1073.3.

81. Berlin, Antikensammlung F1686; *ABV* 296.4 (550–540 B.C.); *LIMC* II Athena 575; Shapiro (1989) 30, pls. 9c–d. Van Straten (1995) V575.

82. Private collection, ca. 560–550 B.C.; *LIMC* II Athena 574*; L. I. Marangou, *Ancient Greek Art from the Collection of Stavros S. Niarchos* (Athens 1995) 86–93, no. 12, with full bibliography; Shapiro (1989) 18, 29 pls. 9a–b; Shapiro in Neils (1992) 54, 200; Simon (1985) 193, fig. 176; Mantis (1990) 26, pl. 36.

83. H. A. Cahn, *Kunstwerke der Antike*, Münzen und Medaillen 18 (Basel 1958) 27, pl. 22, no. 85, was the first to associate the image with the Panatheneia, but missing the peplos, chose to identify it as the Lesser Panathenaia. Marangou, *Ancient Greek Art*, 90 sees it as the Greater Panathenaia. For correlation of this image with the Parthenon frieze, see J. Neils, "Pride, Pomp, and Circumstance," in

Neils (1996) 181. Van Straten (1995) 14–17 sees no good reason to connect the image with the Panathenaia at all.

84. For bulls, see *LSCG* 31 (= *IG* II² 1146).

85. *Erechtheus* frag. 370 K, 95–97; see Collard, Cropp, and Lee (1995) 175.

86. ED 236.8–11, Parker and Obbink (2001) no. 4A.16f. (cf. idem [2001] 425, 10a).

87. *LSCG* 36 (= *IG* II² 1177, Piraeus, fourth c. B.C., priestess of the Thesmophorion), 1–7; no. 55 (= *IG* II² 1366, second c. A.D., cult of Men), 7–8; no. 119 (Chios, fourth c. B.C., priest of Herakles), 9–12. This also seems to have been the case for the priestess of Demeter and Kore at the Haloa festival, where the hierophant Archias was famously charged for impiety when he sacrificed upon the altar himself. Apollodoros, *Against Neaira* (= Demosthenes 59) 116; Athenaeus 13.594b.

88. Munich, Antikensammlungen 1441, the Affector. *ABV* 243.44, 238, 242; Nordquist (1992) 152–53.

89. Basel, Antikenmuseum BS 1447. Schmidt (2000).

90. A group of six vases was originally identified by Pingiatoglou (1994) pls. 14–17: Munich 1538, from Vulci (*ABV* 395.3) amphora attributed to group of Copenhagen 114, near the Painter of Munich 1519; Villa Giulia 50466, M.439 (*ABV* 366.75) hydria from the Leagros group; Agrigento R 142 (*ABV* 377.235; *CVA* Agrigento Museo Nazionale I. 7) column krater from the Leagros group; Athens National Archaeological Museum 12951, N.948 (*ABV* 380.287) lekythos Leagros group; Art Market, kalpis, *Ars Antiqua* AG Auction I Lucerne May 2, 1959, 41, no. 110; Art Market, lekythos, near the Sappho Painter, *Para* 247, Münzen und Medaillen AG (Basel 1964) no. 79, Sotheby's *Greek Vases from the Hirschmann Collection* (September 12, 1993), no. 21. M. Schmidt (2000) has added a seventh vase, Basel BS 1447, a lekythos related to the Leagros group lekythoi, especially to the Acheloos Painter. This group, minus the kalpis and the addition by Schmidt, is mentioned in Peirce (1998) 80 n. 93.

91. Peirce (1998) 80–81.

92. Pingiatoglou (1994) 49–51.

93. Schmidt (2000) 437.

94. Peirce (1993) 260.

95. Ferrari (2002) 35–60.

96. Ferrari (2002) 56–60.

97. *Erechtheus* frag. 370 K, 90–97, translation from Collard, Cropp, and Lee (1995) 175.

98. *LSCG* 35.17–19.

99. Kron (1996) 142.

100. *IG* I³ 953; Lazzarini (1976) 64; Maass (1946).

101. *IG* II² 776.11–13; Jordan (1979) 30.

102. *Agora* 16, no. 277, I 5165; Miles (1998) 198–99, no. 35, pl. 28. Broneer (1942) 265–74.

103. See important discussion by Bremen (1996) on the prominent role of women elites in Greek cities, particularly in Asia Minor, from the second century B.C. to the third century A.D. Also, Gauthier (1985); Boatwright (1991) 254, 260.

104. Bremen (1996) 29 n. 69: Syll.³ 1015, II 29–33; *LSAM* 4.15.

105. *LSAM* 73.28–30. Bremen (1996) 29, n. 70.

106. *I.Mylasa* 337. Bremen (1983) 220.

107. Fr. Salviat, ed., "Décrets pour Épié, fille de Dionysios: Déesses et sanctuaries thasiens," *BCH* 83 (1959) 362–75; *SEG* 18.343; Bremen (1996) 26–27.

108. *IG* V 2, 266. Bremen (1996) 27–28.

109. *IG* V 2, 268. Bremen (1996) 139–40, 274–75.

110. Boatwright (1991) 258, based on figures from P. Paris, *Quatenus feminae res publicas in Asia minore tractaremit* (1891) 41–77; O. Braunstein, *Die politische Wirksamkeit der griechischen Frau: Eine Nachwirkung vorgriechischen Multerrechtes* (diss., Leipzig 1911); R. Munsterberg, *Die Beamtennamen auf den griechischen Munzen* (Vienna 1911–27) 256; R. MacMullen, "Women in Public in the Roman Empire," *Historia* 29 (1980) 208–18; Plecket (1969) 10–41; W. Eck, "Die Prasenz senatorischer Familien in den Stadten des Imperium Romanum bis zum spaten 3. Jahrhundert," in *Studien zur antiken Sozialgeschichte: Festschrift F. Vittinghoff*, W. Eck, H. Galsterer, and H. Wolff, eds. (Cologne and Vienna 1980) tables I.c 19, 27, 28, 37–39, 51 (292–94); D. Magie, *Roman Rule in Asia Minor* (Princeton 1950) 518–19, no. 50.

111. Bremen (1996) 61. Trebilco counts thirty-seven women who held the post in seventeen cities, Trebilco (1991) 113–26.

112. *MAMA* VIII 492b; *LF²* no. 194; *I.Priene* 208. Bremen (1996) 31, 36, 57.

113. *LF²* no. 432; Bremen (1996) 65, 126, 168 and appendix 2, Aphrodisias, no. 8.

114. See Graham (1981) 303–4, who argues that since religion was of such importance to the Greeks, it may have been taken for granted by ancient authors that individuals who could attend to the religious needs of the colonists would be among the founders. See also Hodos (1999) 66.

115. As suggested by Bremen (1983) 223. The first half of the inscription discusses Euxenia's ancestry but does not say how she is related to Philopoemen.

116. *IG* V 2, 461, lines 7–8, translation by Bremen (1983) 223.

CHAPTER 7. PRIESTLY PRIVILEGE: PERQUISITES, HONORS, AND AUTHORITY

1. *IG* II² 1136, 6–10.

2. Price in *RAW* 303.

3. Price in *RAW* 303; Parker in *RAW* 571; Blok (2004) 21–26. Traditional view is based on Plato *Laws* 758–59 and Aristotles's *Politics* 1299², 14–19; 1319ᴮ, and 1322ᴮ. See Dignas (2002) 247–48.

4. Parker (2005) 7; see larger discussion 89–99.

5. Parker in *RAW* 571.

6. Blok (2004) 18–26.

7. The compensation of a priest is spelled out in the well-known trilingual (Greek, Lycian, and Aramaic) stele set up in the Letoon at Xanthos for the foundation of a cult of Basileus Kaunios and Arkesimas (337 or 358 B.C.). It creates a priesthood that will be passed down through the family of the first elected priest (Simias of Kondorasis) and carries a salary of three and a half *minai. SEG* 27.942; *NGSL* 82; H. Metzger, E. Laroche, A. Dupont-Sommer, and M. Mayrhofer, *La Stele trilangue du Létoon, Fouilles de Xanthos* VI (Paris 1979).

8. For priestly compensation, see Loomis (1998) 76–87, 273–74; E. Puttkammer, *Quo modo Graeci victimarum carnes distribuerint* (diss., Königsberg 1912) 1–16; D. Gill, *Greek Cult Tables* (New York and London, 1991) 15–19; B. LeGuen-Pollet, "Éspace sacrificiel et corps des betes immolées: Remarques sur le vocabulaire desinant la part du prêtre dans la Grèce antique, de l'époque imperiale," in *L'espace sacrificiel dans le civilisations méditerranéennes de l'antiquité,* R. Étienne and M.-T. le Dinahet, eds. (Paris 1991) 3–23; van Straten (1995) 154–55; F. Sokolowski, "Fees and Taxes in the Greek Cults," *HThR* 47 (1954) 153–64; E. Kadletz, "The Tongues of Greek Sacrificial Victims," *HThR* 74 (1981) 21–29; Lambert (2002) 397–98, *NGSL* 164–65. I thank Rob Loomis for his kindness in discussing this material.

9. There are variations in spelling. See *NGSL* 164–65; *LSJ* 823; Threatte *GAI,* vol. 2, 7.03.3d (p. 154). Beata Dignas (2002) 248 has pointed out that the word *hierosyna* is the neuter plural of the adjective formed in an analogous way to *hierosyne,* the very term used for priesthood in so many texts.

10. Sokolowski on *LSCG* 7.17, cf. *LSS* 18 passim.

11. Dow, *HThS* 21 (1965) 35.

12. *IG* I³ 250, A 26–28; Loomis (1998) 76.

13. *IG* I³ 35; Loomis (1998) 86.

14. Loomis (1998) 86.

15. Kos, Inv. AS 14 = Parker and Obbink (2000) no. 1 (ca. 125–100 B.C.), lines 16–20.

16. *Oikonomika* 2.2, 1347a.

17. *CAH*³ VI 566–567 (with bibliography in n. 6), plus some seventy-one thousand citizen wives and children. For Periklean Athens, the estimated figures are forty-five thousand male citizens and one hundred thousand citizen wives and children.

18. Deubner (1932) 16; Jordan (1979) 32.

19. *IG* II² 1357 = *LSCG* 17C; Lambert (2002) 397–98.

20. *LSS* 10.5, who belives that Nicomachos passed these reforms with restoration of the Democracy after the 30. Cf. Lys. 30, 17–25. Isocrates 1, 18.

21. *IG* I³ 35.9–12 and *IG* I³ 36; *GHI* I² 44; Feaver (1957) 137; Loomis (1998) 76–77.

22. *IG* I³ 6C.6-20 = Clinton (2005) 19; Clinton (1974) 69–70.

23. *IG* I³ 386; Clinton (1974) 13 n. 13.

24. Cole (2004) 125.

25. *IG* II² 1357, *LSS* 10a.75. Loomis (1998) 79–80; J. H. Oliver, "The Eleusinian Endowment," *Hesperia* 21.4 (1952) 381–99.

26. *IG* II² 1540.57–58 = Clinton (2005) 137. Loomis (1998) 82–83.

27. *IG* II² 204.60 = Clinton (2005) 144. The amount is restored at thirty drachmas.

28. *IG* II² 1363 + *SEG* 23.80 A.3–13, B.23.

29. *IG* II² 1672 Col. IIb, 255–62 = Clinton (2005) 177.

30. *LSCG* 17a. G. Roux, "A propos d'un livre nouveau: Le calendrier d'Éleusis et l'offrande pour la table sacrée dans le culte d'Apollon Pythien," *AC* 35 (1966) 562–63.

31. *IG* II² 1356, 2–24.

32. *IG* II² 1184.1–7, 15–18; Loomis (1998) 84–85 is inclined to regard this as an emolument rather than a reimbursement.

33. See Dillon (2002) 95–97; for collections, see *NGSL* 44, 81; Parker (2005) 440.

34. *Paroemiographi Supplement* I 65. Burkert (1985) 101; Dillon (2002) 95; Parker (2005) 440.

35. *Xantriai*, frag. 168 Radt, 16–28; Dillon (2002) 96.

36. *I.Cos, ED* 236, 5–8; *LSAM* 47, p. 122.

37. *LSAM* 73.25–28. Parker (1996) 162 n. 32; Burkert (1985) 101; Dillon (2002) 96–97.

38. *NGSL* 71, 72

39. *IG* I³ 35.9–12 (cf. *IG* I³ 36); *GHI* I² 44; Feaver (1957) 137. Discussed in chapter 2 above.

40. For Semele, *LSCG* 18 A, 44–53. S. Dow, "Six Athenian Sacrificial Calendars," *BCH* 92 (1968) 170–86. For Dioynsos, D 33–40. S. Dow, "The Greater Demarkhia of Erkhia," *BCH* 89 (1965) 180–213.

41. *LSAM* 73.9–14, third century B.C., Dignas (2002) 250. Discussed above, chapter 6.

42. *IG* II² 1356, 2–24.

43. *LSCG* 28.

44. *LSCG* 45, second half of the fourth century. Jones (1999) 259–61; Mikalson (1998) 140–43. The priestess is to be given female victims and the priest male victims.

45. *LSCG* 120.9–10.

46. *LSAM* 79.5

47. *LSCG* 103 B.9–10, first century B.C. The exact amount is in lacuna.

48. *LSS* 115 B.15–18.

49. *SEG* 35.923; *NGSL* 20, pp. 303–15.

50. *NGSL* 305. Eran Lupu detects dissatisfaction on the part of cult personnel with the distribution of the sacrificial parts prescribed in the first decree. The document, he maintains, may represent an attempt to deal with possible outcomes of this displeasure, including a priestess taking additional parts to which she was not entitled.

51. Dignas (2002) 45 reminds us that "priesthood is thus about receiving priestly shares." See also Garland (1984) 93.

52. Lincoln in *RAW* 661.

53. *IG* II² 1672.17, 74, 293, 127, 305; see Clinton (1974) 71.

54. The chief of these sacred attendants was a boy priest who had not yet reached the age of puberty and who served for a tenure of five years.

55. [Plutarch] *Moralia* 839b for residency on the Acropolis and the author of the *Lives of the Ten Orators* for the ball court.

56. Diodorus Siculus 16.26; see Burkert (1985) 116.

57. Athens, National Archaeological Museum 2672 and 2673 (= *IG* II² 4638). Shown here is National Archaeological Museum 2673. Mantis (1990) 137–38.

58. J. W. Hewitt, "The Major Restrictions on Access to Greek Temples," *TPAPA* 40 (1909) 83–91; Cole (1992).

59. *LSCG* 124, 18–20, no indication of cult but Ziehen *LGS* II, 117 thinks it might be related to the cult of the Great Mother. A. Chaniotis, "Reinheit des Körper—Reinheit der Seele in den griechischen Kultusgesetzen," in *Schuld, Gewissen und Person: Studien zur Geschichter des inneren Menschen*, J. Assmann and T. Sundermeyer, eds., Studien zum Verstehen fremder Religionnens (Gütersloh 1997) 142–79, esp. 163.

60. Pausanias 2.10.4, see Pirenne-Delforge (1994) 143–45.

61. Blech (1982).

62. *IG* I³ 102 = *GHI* I² no. 85; Blech (1982) 156–57.

63. Blech (1982).

64. *IG* II² 410 (ca. 330 B.C.), priests of Dionysos, Poseidon Pelagios, Zeus Soter, and Ammon (lines 16–22), *hieropoioi* (lines 26–35).

65. Parker (2005) 97 cites Aeschines 1.19, who tells us that the candidates for the archonship had to be sexually uncontaminated since they held "crown-bearing offices."

66. Parker (2005) 97 and n. 27.

67. Berlin, Staatliche Museen K 104; Athens AM 2758 + 2427.

68. *IG* II² 776.24.

69. *IG* II² 1315.20–21, ca. 211/210 B.C.; *PA* 8733.

70. *Agora* 16, no. 277 = I 5165; Broneer (1942) 265–74, no. 51; Clinton (1974) 71; Miles (1998) 198, no. 35, pl. 28.

71. *IG* II² 1034 (98/97 B.C.) and *IG* II² 1036.20–22 (ca. 78/77 B.C.) Cf. *IG* II² 1060 (108/109 B.C.), S. B. Aleshire and S. D. Lambert, "Making the 'Peplos' for Athena: A New Edition of *IG* II² 1060 + *IG* II² 1036," *ZPE* 142 (2003) 68–69.

72. *IG* II² 1199.24–25.

73. Blech (1982) 157 n. 248, 159 n. 255; Feaver (1957) 156; Henry (1983) 24–25.

74. The Assembly dictated how the label on the dedicated wreath was to read, in the case of the Spartokidai of Bosporon, *IG* II² 212 (346/5 B.C.); Harris (1995) 104–5.

75. Harris (1995) Proneas: II.41; Parthenon: IV.57–62; Hekatompedon: V.359–477; Erechtheion: VI.55–66; see discussion at pp. 220–21.

76. *I. Pergamon* 167 (149 B.C.), cf. 223, 226 (dated, respectively, 129 B.C., 113 B.C.).

77. *SEG* 24.1112 = Pleket, *Epigraphica* II, no. 21.

78. *IG* XII 7, 36.17–23; see Bremen (1996) 143 n. 3.

79. *IG* XII 7, 49.26–30.

80. Bremen (1996) 189 n. 166, with text; I. Ringwood Arnold, "Festivals of Rhodes," *AJA* 40 (1936) 432–36.

81. Maass (1972) 80; Jeffery, *LSAG* 199, no. 15.

82. These form the subject of a comprehensive study by M. Maass (1972). See also Parker (2005) 95, n. 17, where it is pointed out that proedria was normal practice in deme theaters; see D. Whitehead, *The Demes of Attica 508/7–ca. 250 B.C.: A Political and Social History* (Princeton 1986) 220. See *IG* II² 1214.23 for proedria for priests in the Piraeus.

83. Kirchner, *PA*, dates all inscriptions to the Roman period.

84. *IG* II² 3700; see Maass (1972) 21 and 101–2.

85. *IG* II² 5084, *Kolly[teon?]*.

86. *IG* II² 5063a; see Maass (1972) 130–31.

87. *IG* II² 3596, cf. *IG* II² 2810, 2776.

88. I thank Victoria Tsoukala for her help in assembling and analyzing this material.

89. Penteteris, daughter of Hierokleos of Phlya, *IG* II² 928, 3470–71. Tracy (2003) 141. Such an identification would raise problems of chronology, since, according to Kirchner, *PA*, all the bench inscriptions belong to the Roman period.

90. *ID* 1869, second/early first century B.C.; cf. Bruneau (1970) 81.

91. *IG* II² 3173 = Lewis (1955) no. 13 = Aleshire (1994a) no. 16.

92. *IG* II² 3283a, 3535–37, 4175–56, 4242 = Lewis (1955) no. 16.

93. Fourteen women of the name Megiste are listed in *LGPN*.

94. On this term, see Maass (1972) 85 n. 54.

95. *IG* II² 5122 = W. Amelung, *Herodes Atticus*, vol. 2 (Hildesheim, NY 1983) no. 63.

96. A. J. Podlecki, "Could Women Attend the Theater in Ancient Athens? A Collection of Testimonia," *AncWorld* 21 (1990) 27–43; Henderson (1991b) 133–47; S. Goldhill, "The Audience of Athenian Tragedy," in *The Cambridge Companion to Greek Tragedy*, P. E. Easterling, ed. (Cambridge 1997) 54–68 and S. Goldhill, "Representing Democracy: Women at the Great Dionysia," in Osborne and Hornblower (1994) 347–69; A. H. Somerstein, "The Theater Audience, the Demos, and the Suppliants of Aeschylus," in C. Pelling (1997) 63–79; M. A. Katz, "Did the Women of Ancient Athens Attend the Theater in the Eighteenth Century?" *CP* 93 (1998) 105–24.

97. Henderson (1991b) 134.

98. Henderson (1991b) 133–47.

99. Henderson, with translation (1991b) 183.

100. A. *Vita* 9; Pollux 4.110.

101. Sourvinou-Inwood (2003) 177–78.

102. Sourvinou-Inwood (2003) 177–84, esp. 182–84; and (1995a) 115.

103. *IG* II² 1136, 6–10.

104. Philippe, daughter of Medeios, *IG* II² 5104; Ladamea daughter of Me[deos], *IG* II² 5123.

105. *IG* XII 7: 36.20–23.

106. *TAM* III 1, p. 872, no. 21 (late second c. A.D.); Bremen (1996) 155.

107. L. Robert and J. Robert, "Bulletin épigraphique," *REG* 74 (1961) 119–268, no. 440; L. Robert and J. Robert, "Bulletin épigraphique," *REG* 83 (1970) 362–488, no. 423. Examples collected by Bremen (1996) 156 (with bibliography in n. 49).

108. Pausanias 6.20.9, where we also learn that virgins were not barred. Earlier at 5.6.7, Pausanias mentioned the exclusion of married women from the Olympic games; see J. G. Frazer, *Pausanias's Description of Greece* (Cambridge 1913) commentary at 6.20.9. M. P. J. Dillon, "Did Parthenoi Attend the Olympic Games? Girls and Women Competing, Spectating, and Carrying Out Cult Roles at Greek Religious Festivals," *Hermes: Zeitschrift für Klassische Philologie* 128 (2000) 457–80.

109. Pausanias 6.21.2; see J. Tobin, *Herodes Atticus and the City of Athens* (Amsterdam 1997) 322.

110. See important discussion by Bremen (1996) 155–56. At Ephesos, a female *theoros* presided at the Megala Olympia held in the city; Bremen (1996) 88; L. Robert, "Les femmes théores à Éphèses," *CRAI* (1974) 176–81 (= *OMS* V, 669–74). The stadium at Aphrodisias shows two seats located toward the back inscribed with female names, though there is no mention of any priesthoods that they held; see Bremen (1996) 155; C. Rouché, *Performers and Partisans at Aphrodisias in the Roman and Late Roman Periods* (London 1993) 88. First inscription: block 10, row Y, Cl[audias] Seleukeias; second inscription: block 11, row U, C. Rouché suggests "Ignatia and Hypsikleis." In the stadium at Didyma, the name of a female *agonothetes* is inscribed on a seat in the third row back; see *I.Didyma* 50. On the duties of an *agonothetes*, see Bremen (1996) 66–68, 73–76.

111. Henderson (1991b) 145. Plato, *Symposium* 175E, speaks of an audience of thirty thousand.

112. Parker (2005) 95.

113. *LSAM* 59.6–7. *NGSL* 314.

114. *LSS* 113; Axos, fifth century B.C., *NGSL* 43.

115. *LSCG* 107.2–5.

116. Kos Inv. AS 14 = Parker and Obbink (2000) no. 1, lines 33–35.

117. Kos Inv. AS 14 = Parker and Obbink (2000) no. 1, lines 32, 35; translation at p. 418.

118. Parker (2005) 93, for priests before the Assembly.

119. Versnel (1990) 123–31.

120. In fourth-century Athens, the priest of Apollo Erithaseos made a public proclamation prohibiting the cutting of wood in the sanctuary of the god "on behalf of himself, the demesmen and the Demos of Athens." His proclamation was inscribed on a marble slab for all to see (*IG* II² 1362).

121. *LSCG* 102.

122. *LSAM* 45. This decree supplements an existing document the sets out the priestly perquisites; see *NGSL* 43.

123. Kos Inv. AS 14 = Parker and Obbink (2000) no. 1, lines 29–32, with translation at p. 418.

124. *LSAM* 61.5.

125. *IG* II² 1177 = *LSCG* 36; Versnel (1990) 122; J. Rudhardt, "La définition du délit d'impiété d'après la législation attique," *Museum Helveticum* 17 (1960) 87–105, esp. 95. Parker (2005) 75; n. 103.

126. Parker (1996) 161–62; Parker (2005) 75.

127. Apollodoros, *Against Neaira* (= Demosthenes 59) 116; Athenaeus 13.594b.

128. [Dinarchos], "Claim-Suit for the Priestess of Demeter, Against the *Hierophant*," frag. XXXV 3 Conomis = Pollux 7.69, s.v. *orthaptou*; see Clinton (1974) 22–23; Foucart (1914) 219.

129. Cf. the account in [Lysias] 6.51. Sourvinou-Inwood (1988b); J. Blok, "Patronage and the Peisistratidae," *BaBesch* 65 (1990) 17–28.

130. Dinarchos 2, *Against Aristogeiton* 12; see I. Worthington, *A Historical Commentary on Dinarchus* (Ann Arbor 1992) 298–99.

131. Well summarized by Versnel (1990) 115–18.

132. See, e.g., J. Bremmer, "Greek Maenadism Reconsidered," *ZPE* 55 (1984) 269 n. 12; S. E. Johnson, "The Present State of Sabazios Research," *ANRW* II XVII 3, 1583.

133. See Parker (2005) 133–34.

134. Versnel (1990) 116 with bibliography, n. 80: see, e.g., A. F. Segal, "Some Questions of Definition," in *Studies in Gnosticism and Hellenistic Religion for G. Quispel*, R. van den Broek and M. J. Vermaseren, eds. (Leiden 1981) 349–75; Brown (1972) 119–46.

135. Plutarch *Demosthenes* 14; Demosthenes *In Aristogeiton* 1.79; Philochoros *apud* Harpokration, s.v. Theoris.

136. See Versnel (1990) 118–22 with bibliography. The ancient sources include anonymous treaty on rhetoric, Baiter-Saupe II, 320; Athenaeus 13.590d; [Plutarch] *Lives of the Ten Orators* 889e; Harpokration, s.v. Isodaites.

137. Parker (1996) 162–63.

138. Goldhill (1994) 352–60.

139. Ephorus, *FGrH* 70 F119 = Strabo 9.2.4.

140. Fr. VI 4 Conomis = *Suda*, s.v. *syssemainesthai*. Cf. Martha (1882) 114.

141. *ED* 216.18ff. (ca. 225 or ca. 175 B.C.); *LSCG* 166.23f. (late second or first century B.C.).

142. *IG* II² 1328 (*LSCG* 48) 16–18 (original decree), ca. 183/182 B.C.

143. *IG* II² 1328 (*LSCG* 48), 21–44 (amendment). *LSCG* 89–90; Jones (1999) 265. *NGSL* 53.

144. Maurizio (1995) 84 n. 91.

145. Herodotos 1.174, translation by A. De Selincourt, *Herodotus*, Penguin ed. (Harmondsworth and Baltimore 1954).

146. Hawley (1994) 72.

147. Diogenes Laertius 8.8, 21 (frag. 15 Wehrli); cf. Hawley (1994) 72.

148. *Symposium* 201d1. Sokrates says that Diotima had previously commanded the Athenians to offer sacrifices that would postpone the plague for ten years. The word for prophet (*mantis*) provides the root for the name Mantineia.

149. *Isis and Osiris*, *Moralia* 351c1, 352c2, 364e1; *On the Bravery of Women*, *Moralia* 242e1; cf. Nilsson (1925) 209.

150. Letters 85–86 Bidez; cf. *PLRE*, Theodora (3).

151. Letter 81 Bidez; cf. G. W. Bowersock, *Julian the Apostate* (Cambridge, MA 1978) 86.

152. See G. Fowden, *The Egyptian Hermes* (Princeton, 1993) 122–26; H. M. Jackson, *Zosimos of Panopolis, On the Letter Omega* (Claremont, CA 1979).

CHAPTER 8. DEATH OF THE PRIESTESS: GRAVE MONUMENTS, EPITAPHS, AND PUBLIC BURIAL

1. The funeral scene is from *Chaereas and Callirhoe*, I 6–9, Reardon (1989) 28–30. Chariton's date is uncertain but Reardon favors the mid-first century A.D.

2. Bremen (1996) 159–60 and 1–3.

3. M. Seve, "Un décret de consolation a Cyzique," *BCH* 103 (1979) 327–59 (= *SEG* 28: 953), see line 59 for the term "of the Pythaists."

4. *REG* 19 (1906) 93–96, no. 9; new edition by J. Reynolds and Roueché in *Hommage à E. Frézouls, Krèma* 17 (1992) 153–60. See Bremen (1996) 156–57. It is of interest that Tatia held no civic magistracies, only the priesthood.

5. See Bremen (1996) 233 for correlation of the rise in wealth in the Greek East with an increase in the number of women benefactors and liturgists during the second century B.C.–second century A.D. Within this context, it is not surprising that we have a good deal of evidence for the commemoration of women as priestesses.

6. N. Loraux, *Tragic Ways of Killing a Woman* (Cambridge, MA 1987) 1–3 draws a strong contrast between the very public funerals for Athenian men who died in battle and the very private funerals of women who died quietly in their beds, with no one to speak of their *kleos* but their own husbands. While this may have been true, in general, for classical Athens, there is a more complex reality for priestesses, especially those of later date.

7. Translation by Brad Cook.

8. A. D. Potter, "Sibyls in the Greek and Roman World," *JRA* 3 (1990) 482.

9. A. N. Skias, "Πανάρχαια Ελευσινιακή Νεκρόπολη" *EA* (1898) 28–122, for Grave A and the Isis Grave, pl. 6.

10. Skias, "Πανάρχαια Ελευσινιακή Νεκρόπολη," 109–10, pl. 6. N. Coldstream, *Geometric Greece* (New York 1977) 78–80, fig. 25b, finds this interpretation attractive but not provable.

11.   A. Kottaridi, "The Lady of Aigai," in D. Pandermalis, *Alexander the Great: Treasures from an Epic Era of Hellenism* (New York 2004) 139–47. She suggests that the deceased is the wife of Myntas I.

12.   Kottaridi, "Lady of Aigai," 139–47.

13.   Williams (1988) 75–78.

14.   B. Segall, *Zur griechischen Goldschmiedekunst des vierten Jhs. v. Chr.* (Wiesbaden, 1966) 17ff., pls. 5, 36–37.

15.   See M. Parker Pearson, *The Archaeology of Death and Burial* (Gloucestershire 1999), esp. chap. 4, "Status, Rank, and Power," and chap. 5, "Gender and Kinship." S. Tarlow, *Bereavement and Commemoration: An Archaeology of Mortality* (Malden 1999); S. Campbell and A. Green, eds., *The Archaeology of Death in the Ancient Near East* (Oxford 1995).

16.   Bolger (2003) offers a thoughtful overview in chap. 6: "Endings: Gender and Mortuary Ritual," 147–82; see esp. the section "Dressing for Death: Gender and Social Identity," 179–80. See Meskell (2002) 178–207.

17.   Anthropological research has stressed that death should be viewed as a process, not an event. For overview, see Bolger (2003) 147.

18.   Sourvinou-Inwood (1995b) 112–13.

19.   *IG* I³ 1330, *CEG* 93, *SEG* 12.80. (Athens, Epigraphical Museum 13132, ca. 430–400 B.C.). First published by J. Papadimitriou (1951) 46–153; Lewis (1955) 1; Clairmont (1979) 103–10; Mark (1993) 111–13.

20.   Translation based on Clairmont (1979) 103–5.

21.   Turner (1983) 85.

22.   Athens, National Museum 4485 (*IG* I³ 1285), *CEG* 93 = Clairmont (1993) vol. 5.150. Found in 1873. Clairmont (1979) did not specify which iconographic attributes led him to this identification. Rahn (1986) 200 points to the bracelet and diadem worn by Myrrhine as "symbols of some public office."

23.   Rahn (1986) 205–7 believes that the lekythos and stele honor the same woman but were not part of the same monument. Instead, he sees the inscribed marker from Zographos and the marble lekythos from central Athens as two separate memorials.

24.   Clairmont (1993) vol. 5.118.

25.   *IG* II² 12200, Athens, Epigraphical Museum 11081. I am indebted to Dr. Charalambos Kritzas, director of the Epigraphical Museum, for discussing this stele with me and for generously providing the photograph. I. Papadimitriou (1951) 151, no. 1, dates the inscription to the end of the fifth century, though the letter forms could be dated to the early fourth century.

26.   Kosmopoulou (2001) 285–99. For the representation of professionals on grave monuments, see E. Berger, *Das Basler Artzrelief* (Mainz 1970) 145–49; Clairmont (1993) vol. 1.220–22; Stears (1995) 123.

27. Sanno: *IG* II² 12583 (= Lefkowitz and Fant 1992, no. 304). Menophila: *Agora* vol. 17, no. 913 (Lefkowitz and Fant 1992, no. 310).

28. Clairmont (1993) 4.147–48; Mantis (1990) 82–96 collects and discusses images of priests in the classical period.

29. Athens, National Archaeological Museum 722; Clairmont (1993) vol. 1.250; Mantis (1990) 86.5, pl. 38a; Connelly (1996) 58–59, fig. 2.

30. Polystrate: Kerameikos Museum I 430, found in 1961 close to the gravestone of Ampharete, Pentelic marble. Scholl (1996) no. 49, pl. 7, 1; Clairmont (1993) vol. 1.248; Mantis (1990) 40, pl. 11a. Choirine stele: Geneva, private collection, removed from Eleusis in 1819 by Admiral E. Halgan, commander of the French navy in the Levant, and later acquired by F. Lenormant, who published it in *Recherches archéologiques à Éleusis* (1862) 356–57, no. 95. Scholl (1996) no. 520, pl. 38, 1; Clairmont (1993) vol. 1.350a; Freyer-Schauenburg (1989). I am indebted to Dr. Freyer-Schauenburg for generously providing me with a photograph of the Choirine stele.

31. Rhamnous stele: Athens, National Museum 2309, found in 1892 in temple precinct at Rhamnous, Pentelic marble (380–370 B.C.). Scholl (1996) no. 206, pl. 38, 2; Clairmont (1993) vol. 1.316; Mantis (1990) 40–41, pl. 11b. The Kerameikos and Rhamnous reliefs are dated by Scholl (1996) to 380–370 B.C., the Geneva relief to 370–360 B.C. These have been studied as a group by Kosmopoulou (2001) 281–319.

32. Athens, National Archaeological Museum 1016, van Straten (1995) fig. 82. Votive statues from Cyprus show clearly that objects held in the fists of worshippers are small spool-shaped incense boxes. A male votary from Golgoi in the Metropolitan Museum of Art (74.51.2465) curls his fingers around such a box and presses his thumb down on top of its lid; see Connelly (1998) 88–89, no. 31, pl. 32. This results in a fistlike gesture, in which the fingers fully encircle the incense box. The gesture appears to have been used as an indication of worship, insofar as it alludes to the burning of incense, a fundamental act of veneration. When this gesture appears on Attic grave stelai for priestesses, it reinforces the sacral status of the deceased, communicated by the presence of the temple key.

33. Lenormant, in *Recherches archéologiques*, 356–57.

34. Scholl (1996) 137.

35. B. Schmaltz, *Untersuchungen zu den attischen Marmorlekythen* (Berlin 1970); A. Proukakis, *The Evolution of the Attic Marble Lekythoi and the Problems of Identifying the Dead among the Figures* (diss., London 1971).

36. Athens, National Archaeological Museum 6167. Clairmont (1993) vol. 4.358; Mantis (1990) 42–43, pl. 13b.

37. Clairmont (1993) vol. 4.358 believes the priestess is the deceased, while Mantis (1990) 42–43 thinks it is the seated male who is the dead.

38. Rhamnous Museum 376 + 143, Pentelic marble. Clairmont (1993) vol. 3.390b. B. K. Petrakos, *O Δῆμος του Ραμνούντος. Σύνοψη των ανασκαφών και των ερευνών 1813–1998, 1. Τοπογραφία* (Athens 1999) 335–413. Parker (2005) 25–26.

39. *IG* II² 3462. Discussed in chapter 5 (fig. 5.14).

40. Pindar, Dithyramb, fr. 70b.9–10, translation by Parker (1996) 188. The following discussion of Kybele is based on Parker (1996) 188–94.

41. Parker (1996) 188 n. 128, 192–93. For worship of Kybele in Attica, see M. J. Vermaseren, *Cybele and Attis: The Myth and the Cult*, trans. A. M. H. Lemmers (London 1977) and M. J. Vermaseren *Cultus Cybelae Attidisque*, II: *Graecia atque Insulae* (Leiden 1982); for worship of Kybele in Piraeus, see J. Petrocheilou, *ArchEph* 131, for 1992 (1993) 21–65.

42. The sanctuary at Moschato has yielded a fragmentary statue of the goddess with her lions. This group may reflect an iconography that was established by the statue of Kybele set up in the Metroon at Athens, a work sculptured by Pheidias or his pupil Agorakritos. Large numbers of votive sculptures showing the seated Kybele holding a drum and flanked by lions have been found throughout Attica and may reflect a common source, probably Pheidias's statue. See J. Travlos, *Bildlexicon* (Tübingen 1971) 288–97; F. Naumann, *Die Ikonographie der Kybele in der phrygischen und der griechischen Kunst* (Tübingen 1983) 162–63, 180–84.

43. Piraeus Museum 3627 (ex Athens National Archaeological Museum 1030), 360–40 B.C.; *IG* II² 6288; *CEG* 566, Scholl (1996) no. 295; Clairmont (1993) vol. 1.495–96, vol. 1.934; Mantis (1990) pl. 13a.

44. Translation by Clairmont (1970) 97.

45. Clairmont (1993) vol. 1.934 suggested that the girl might be a granddaughter who succeeded Chairestrate in some capacity within the cult of Kybele.

46. Piraeus Museum 217, Pentelic marble, 360–350 B.C. Scholl (1996) no. 275; Clairmont (1993), vol. 2.362; Mantis (1990) 50.3, pl. 17a.

47. Clairmont viewed the standing young woman as the deceased (1993) vol. 2.362.

48. Parker (1996) 193; *IG* II² 1328.11, 1329.15.

49. Oxford, Ashmolean Museum 1959.203 (ca. 375 B.C.). It was once used to support a sundial in the garden of Westport House, County Mayo, Ireland. Clairmont (1993) vol. 1.14; Mantis (1990) 49.1, pl. 16a; Boardman, "Archaeological Reports," *JHS* 81 (1961) pls. 13–14. For funerary tables, see A. Scholl, "*Polutalanta mimeia*: Zur literarischen und monumentalen Überlieferung auf wendiger Grabmäler im spätklassischen Athen," *JdI* 109 (1994) 239–71. Kosmopoulou (2002) 93–94, fig. 82.

50. Athens, National Archaeological Museum 3287; Clairmont (1993) vol. 1.13; Mantis (1990) 49.2, pl. 17b.

51. As Clairmont suggests (1993) vol. 1.18.

52. Mantis (1990) 50.4; G. Körte, *AM* (1878) 329, no. 26; Karouzos (1934) 36, no. 117.

53. Mantis (1990) 50.4.

54. Berlin SK 1504. Mantis (1990) 67, pl. 28; Blümel, *Die klassisch-griechischen Skulpturen der Staatlichen Musen zu Berlin* (Berlin 1966) no. 6, pl. 12; Ridgway (1981) 148–49.

55. Mantis (1990) 67.

56. Ridgway (1981) 148–49.

57. The frontal pose is seen outside of Attica at Larisa, where we have a fifth-century-B.C. grave stele similarly showing a woman wearing a peplos (over a chiton) and her veil pulled up and over her head. See H. Biesantz, *Die thessalischen Grabreliefs* (Mainz 1965) K 22, pl. 7; Ridgway (1981) 148–49.

58. Thessaly: Biesantz, *Die thessalischen Grabreliefs*, Cyprus: Connelly (1988) 4, cat. 1–8, pls. 11–14; cat. 13–14, pl. 17; cat. 51, pl. 44; cat. 58–62, pls. 47–49; Cyprus Museum E 516 and Cyprus Museum E 524, pl. 3; Larnaca Museum 654 and Larnaca Museum 653, pl. 10.

59. Athens, National Archaeological Museum 226. Mantis (1990) 51, pl. 18; Ridgway (1981) 141–42, 186, fig. 101.

60. Bowden (2005) 6–8.

61. Ridgway (1981) 141–42 suggests that the relief may be both funeral and honorary. Kron (1996) 142 calls it a votive relief.

62. Ridgway (1981) 142.

63. Ridgway (1981) 142.

64. First by H. Möbius in "Diotima," *JdI* 49 (1934) 45–60 [= *Studia Varia* (Weisbaden 1967) 33–46].

65. Mikalson (1998) 46–74; Habicht (1997) 53–56.

66. The fragments of Demetrios of Phaleron are gathered in F. Wehrli, *Die Schule des Aristoteles* IV (Basel 1968). On his antiluxury legislation, see J. Twele, "*Columnellam aut mensam aut laellum*: Archaeological Remarks on Cicero's '*De Legibus* 2.66,'" *J. Paul Getty Museum Journal* 2 (1975) 93–98; Habicht (1997) 55–56; Mikalson (1998) 59–60; D. Kurtz and J. Boardman, *Greek Burial Practices* (Oxford 1971) 166.

67. Translation by C. W. Keyes, Cicero, *De Legibus*, Loeb Classical Library, series no. 213, vol. 16 (Cambridge, MA 1928, reprint 1959) 453.

68. Athenaeus 6.245a; Philochoros, *FGrH* 328 F65. B. J. Garland, *Gynaikonomoi: An Investigation of Greek Censors of Women* (diss., Johns Hopkins 1981).

69. Athenaeus 6.245a.

70. Cicero *De Legibus* 2.66. Kurtz and Boardman, *Greek Burial Practices*, 166–69.

71. *IG* II² 7244, Mantis (1990) 45.5 (upper) cites the Athens National Museum as the disposition for the object, yet a search could not locate it in the spring of 2005. A further check with the Epigraphical Museum showed that the *kioniskos* is not there either. A. Conze, *AZ* (1862) 297, 11.

72. See discussion in chapter 3, pages 67–68. *IG* II² 3477, after 138 B.C. Habryllis is discussed by Lewis (1955) 9, no. 8; Turner (1983) 261–65; Aleshire (1994a) 336, no. 10.

73. Athens, National Archaeological Museum 1727; *IG* II² 6398; Koehler, *AM* 9 (1884) 301; Mantis (1990) 44.1, pl. 14.

74. Athens, Epigraphical Museum 11144. *IG* II² 6232. Mantis (1990) 44.3, pl. 15b.

75. Turner (1983) 269.

76. Aleshire (1994a) 336, no. 13 and 337, note j. Turner includes Mneso in her list of priestesses of Athena on the basis of Kirchner's remarks at *PA* 10388 (245 n. 1). Neither Lewis (1955) nor J. Töpffer *Attische Geneologie* (Berlin 1889) includes Mneso.

77. Mantis (1990) 414–15.

78. Aleshire (1994a) 337; note j.

79. Athens, Epigraphical Museum 11614. *IG* II² 5271. Mantis (1990) 45.4 (upper), pl. 15g.

80. Athens, Epigraphical Museum 11183. *IG* II² 7356. Mantis (1990) 44.2, pl. 15a.

81. *IG* IV 642; *SEG* 14.324 = *MAI* 14 (1951) 317–50; Mantis (1990) 34, fig. 2.

82. Mantis (1990) 44–45.

83. Thebes, Archaeological Museum 402. Mantis (1990) 45.2 (lower); A. de Ridder, *BCH* 46 (1922) 277, no. 121.

84. *IG* VII 2021; Mantis (1990) 45.1 (lower); R. Foucart, "Inscriptions de Béotie," *BCH* 9 (1885) 405–6, no. 1 identifies it as a statue base.

85. Thebes, Archaeological Museum 400; Mantis (1990) 45.4 (lower); de Ridder, *BCH* 46 (1922), 278, no. 122.

86. Mantis (1990) 45.5 (lower); de Ridder, *BCH* 46 (1922), 278, no. 123.

87. Thebes, Archaeological Museum 37, found in the Church of Zoodokopighi near Thebes. *IG* VII 2676; Mantis (1990) 45.3 (lower). Foucart *BCH* 9 (1885) 406.

88. Zanker (1993) 212–30; Ridgway (2000) chap. 6. Pfuhl and Möbius (1977).

89. Zanker (1993). Pfuhl and Möbius (1977).

90. Ridgway (2000) 194; Zanker (1993) 226.

91. Berlin, Pergamon Museum SK 767. Pfuhl and Möbius (1977) no. 405, pl. 66; Mantis (1990) 100, pl. 45.

92. Zanker (1993) 218; Ridgway (2000) 194–95.

93. Oxford, Ashmolean Museum; Pfuhl and Möbius (1977) no. 409, pl. 67; Mantis (1990) 101.

94. Breuer, *Reliefs und Epigramme griechischer Privatgrabmäler: Zeugnisse bürgerlichen Selbstverständnisses vom 4. bis 2. Jh. v. Chr.* (Cologne 1995), 126; Zanker (1993) 263.

95. Diotimos VI, *AP* 7.733. Third century B.C.

96. Translation by A. S. F. Gow and D. Page, *Hellenistic Epigrams*, Loeb Classical Library, series 68, vol. 2, *AP* 7.733 (Cambridge, MA 1965).

97. Oxford, Ashmolean Museum. Pfuhl and Möbius (1977) no. 898, pl. 134.

98. Kallimachos XLVIII, *AP* 7.728.

99. Translation by A. S. F. Gow and D. Page, *Hellenistic Epigrams*, Loeb Classical Library, series 68, vol. 2, *AP* 7.728 (Cambridge, MA 1965), Kallimachos XLVIII.

100. The Greek word translated as "patroness" is προστασίη. See Gow and Page, *Hellenistic Epigrams*, note to this line; P. M. Fraser, *Ptolemaic Alexandria* (Oxford 1972) 672.

101. London, British Museum 639. Pfuhl and Möbius (1977) no. 376, pl. 61; Walters (1988) 53–54, pl. 1b.

102. Walters (1988) 25, n. 139.

103. Walters (1988) chap. 4, "Style and Chronology."

104. Istanbul, Archaeological Museum I 4033. Pfuhl and Möbius (1977) no. 418, pl. 69; Ridgway (2000) 215f. n. 7. The epigram was first published by W. H. Buckler and D. M. Robinson, *Sardis* VII. *Greek and Latin Inscriptions*, part I (Leiden 1932) no. 111. I thank Christopher Ratté, Orhan Atvur, and Turhan Birgili for their kindness in providing me with the photograph of Menophila.

105. The translation is that of R. R. R. Smith in *Hellenistic Sculpture: A Handbook* (London 1991) 189, except for the last couplet, which follows W. Peek's text in *Griechische Versinschriften aus Kleinasien* (Vienna 1981).

106. Ferrari (2002) 35–60, chap. 2, "The Spinner," esp. 56–60.

107. *I. Magn.* 215(a) 24–41. Henrichs (1978) 127 argues persuasively for the authenticity of the oracle and dates it to 278–250 B.C.

108. Translation by Henrichs (1978) 124.

109. *LSAM* 48, Henrichs (1978) 137ff.

110. Translation by Henrichs (1978), 4 Mil-Ber. 547.

111. In the Milan papyrus "about Nico, the servant of Dionysos who died in the Bacchic mountains" = epig. 44 in C. Austin-G. Bastianini, *Posidippi Pelhei quae supersunt omnia* (Milan LED 2002, p. 55–67). I thank Colin Austin for drawing this reference to my attention.

112. *LSAM* 79.8–14. It is not clear which divinity Galato served. Sokolowski leaves open the choice between the Great Mother and Apollo, while Turner (1983) 112 favors the Great Mother, because the cult personnel mentioned in the inscription are all women and because the name Galato, "Milky,"

has a natural association with the Mother goddess. I am indebted to Mabel Lang for help with this inscription.

113. *LSAM* 48. Henrichs (1978) 48.

114. J. Downs and T. Pollard, eds., *The Loved Body's Corruption: Archaeological Contributions to the Study of Human Mortality* (Glasgow 1999).

115. The *archeine* and the eponymous archon were often a married couple. We find them offering sacrifices together on behalf of the city and feasting the people (e.g., *IG* XII 5: 659 [A.D. 138–61], *IG* XII 5: 660 [A.D. 138–61], *IG* XII 5: 662 [A.D. 166–69], *IG* XII 5: 663 [after A.D. 183]).

116. *IG* XII 5: 655, no specific provenience given, made of white marble.

117. The translation is that of Lefkowitz and Fant (1992) no. 437, with one change. They interpret τῶν οὐρανίων θεῶν Δήμητρος καὶ Κόρης τῶν σεμνοτάτων as "of the heavenly gods and the holy goddesses Demeter and Kore," but I follow *LSJ* (s.v. οὐράνιος) and apply both epithets to Demeter and Kore.

CHAPTER 9. THE END OF THE LINE: THE COMING OF CHRISTIANITY

1. This discussion relies heavily on the work of Clark (1984).

2. The Latin *Life of Melania the Younger* (Escurial a.II.9) was found by the papal nuncio in Madrid, Mariano Rampolla del Tindaro, and is thought to come from Oviedo. The Greek codex (Barberini III.37), dating from the eleventh century, was found by the Bollandists, who published it in 1903 in their *Analecta Bollandiana*. This codex probably came from the monastery of Grottaferrata. In 1905, Rampolla published both texts in his *Santa Melania Giuniore* with commentary and a translation of the Greek text into Italian. These manuscripts are published by Clark (1984) 1–24, with translation, 25–82, and full commentary, 83–152.

3. Gerontios probably wrote the *Life* for an opponent of Juvenal of Jerusalem, possibly his successor the Monophysite bishop of Jerusalem, Theodosios.

4. *The Life of Melania the Younger* 69, translation by Clark (1984) 81–82.

5. Clark (1984) 97–99. The palace of the Valerii on the Coelian Hill was first excavated in 1554.

6. Clark (1984) 83–85. Melania's maternal grandfather, Caeonius Rufius Albinus, was prefect of Rome in A.D. 389–91; her paternal grandfather may have been the Valerius Maximus who served as praetorian prefect in the early 360s. Her father-in-law, Valerius Severus, was prefect of Rome in A.D. 382. According to Paulinus of Nola, Melania's husband's family could be traced back to the first consul of Rome, P. Valerius Publicola.

7. P. Brown, "Aspects of the Christianization of the Roman Aristocracy," *JRS* (1961) 51:1–11 = *Religion and Society in the Age of Augustine* (London 1972) 161–82; J. Vost, "Pagans and Christians in the Family of Constantine the Great," in *Paganism and Christianity in the Fourth Century*, A. Momigliano, ed. (Oxford 1963); A. M. H. Jones, "The Social Background of the Struggle between Paganism and

Christianity in the Fourth Century," in *The Conflict Between Paganism and Christianity in the Fourth Century*, A. Momigliano, ed. (Oxford 1963).

8. Clark (1984) 84 n. 15–16.

9. Clark (1984) 84 n. 14. *CIL* VI 512; *PLRE* I 511.

10. Clark (1984) 94 n. 18, 116. Palladius, *Historia Lausiaca* 46.

11. Clark (1984) 129–40.

12. The *comes rei privatae* was the count of the personal property of the emperor; the *quaestor sacri palatii* (*quaestor* of the sacred palace) was an important legal officer; the prefect was governor of Rome; the *praetorian prefect* was deputy of the emperor.

13. *Life of Melania the Younger* 53. Evagrius Scholasticus, in the sixth century, recorded that the bones of Saint Euphemia still oozed blood (*HE* II.3 = Bidez and Parmentier, p. 41).

14. *Life of Melania the Younger* 55; Constantine Porphyrogenitus, *Book of Ceremonies* I 64, II 1.

15. George Kedrenos (*Corpus scriptorum historiae byzantinae* XXXIV 564). See C. Mango, "Antique Statuary and the Byzantine Beholder," *DOP* 17 (1963) 58.

16. For Kedrenos inventory, see P. Gilles, 1561bis, *Die Bosporo Thracio libri tres* (Lyon 1561) 129–32.

17. *Amores* 15, also mentioned in Lucian, *Essays in Portraiture* 4. See Posidippus frag. *147 Austin-Bastianini, ["on the person who had intercourse with Praxiteles' statue"]. I am indebted to Colin Austin for this reference.

18. S. Basset, *Excellent Offerings: The Urban Image of Late Antique Constantinople* (Cambridge 2004) 98–120; S. Basset, "The Lausos Collection in Constantinople," *ArtB* 82 (2000) 6–25; M. Vickers and E. D. Francis, "The Palace of Lausus at Constantinople and Its Collection of Ancient Statues," *Journal of the History of Collections* 4 (1992) 89–98.

19. J. North, "The Development of Religious Pluralism," in Lieu, North, and Rajak (1992) 174–93.

20. First collected by Eisen (2000), now, more comprehensive treatment by Madigan and Oziek (2005).

21. Brooten (1982).

22. Chaniotis in *RAW* 309.

23. Brown in *RAW* 309.

24. Brown in *RAW* 309; C. A. Bobertz, "Religious Organizations and Bodies: Christianity," in *RAW* 323.

25. P. R. L. Brown, *Authority and the Sacred: Aspects of the Christianisation of the Roman World* (Cambridge 1995); D. R. Edwards, *Religion and Power: Pagans, Jews, and Christians in the Greek East* (New York 1996); A. Brent, *The Imperial Cult and the Development of Church Order: Concepts and Images of Authority in Paganism and Early Christianity before the Age of Cyprian* (Leiden 1999); J. T. Sanders, *Charisma, Converts, Competitors: Societal and Sociological Factors in the Success of Early Christianity* (London 2000).

26. S. Elm, *Virgins of God: The Making of Asceticism in Late Antiquity* (Oxford 1994); J. W. Drijvers, "Virginity and Asceticism in Late Roman Western Elites," in Blok (1987) 241–73.

27. The bibliography is vast: most recently, see Madigan and Osiek (2005); Kraemer (2004); Eisen (2000); M. Edwards, "The Development of Office in the Early Church," in *The Early Christian World*, P. F. Esler, ed. (New York 2000) I.316–29; Cardman (1999) 300–329; Otranto (1982) = Rossi (1991); A. G. Martimort, *Deaconesses: An Historical Study* (San Francisco 1986) = Translation of *Les Diaconesses: Essai Historique* (Rome 1982). B. J. Brooten, "Early Christian Women and Their Cultural Context: Issues of Method in Historical Reconstruction," in *Feminist Perspectives on Biblical Scholarship*, A. Y. Collins, ed. (Chico, CA 1985) 65–91; E. Schüssler Fiorenza, *In Memory of Her* (New York 1983); E. Schüssler Fiorenza, "Word, Spirit, and Power: Women in Early Christian Communities," in *Women of Spirit: Female Leadership in the Jewish and Christan Traditions*, R. Ruether and E. McLaughlin, eds. (New York 1979) 29–70; K. J. Torjesen, "Reconstruction of Women's Early History," in *Searching the Scriptures I: A Feminist Introduction*, E. Schüssler Fiorenza, ed. (New York 1993) 290–310. Earlier important works include R. Gryson, *The Ministry of Women in the Early Church* (Collegeville 1976) = Translation *of Le ministère des femmes dans l'Église ancienne. Recherches et syn-thèse*, Section d'histoire 4 (Gembloux 1972); J. Mayer, ed., *Monumenta de viduis diaconissis virginibusque tractantia* (Bonn 1938). I am indebted to Kimberley Patton and Bruce Beck for their kindness in reading this chapter and offering helpful suggestions.

28. Brown in *RAW* 309.

29. For Junia as woman apostle, Paul *Romans* 16:7; see B. J. Brooten, "Junia . . . Outstanding among the Apostles," in *Women Priests: A Catholic Commentary on the Vatican Declaration*, L. Swidler and A. Swidler, eds. (New York 1977) 141–44 and Eisen (2000) 47–49. Although some read the name of a man, Junius, John Chrysostom (A.D. 344/354–407) is emphatic that we have a female name here, Junia. "It is certainly a great thing to be an apostle," he writes, "but to be outstanding among the apostles—think what praise that is! She was outstanding in her works, in her good deeds; oh, and how great is the philosophy of this woman, that she was regarded as worthy to be counted among the apostles!" Chrysostom *Homily on Romans* 31.2, translation from Eisen (2000) 48. In the *Liturgikon*, a missal of the Byzantine Church used to this day, Junia is honored with fifty-six male apostles, while two other women, Mary Magdalene and Thecla, are designated as "equal to the apostles," Eisen (2000) 48.

30. Cardman (1999) 300–329; Kraemer (1992) 174–90.

31. Eisen (2000); Madigan and Oziek (2005).

32. This text should be considered in view of a second inscription, also found on a sarcophagus lid from Salona, that records the purchase of a tomb by a man named Theodosios. He bought it from "the *matrona* Flavia Vitalia, holy presbyter, for three golden *solidi*." It dates to A.D. 425. Flavia was a freeborn, married woman who seems to have held responsibility for the administration of a cemetery. This business usually fell under the control of presbyters, and Flavia Vitalia would appear to have assumed this duty as part of her priestly office. F. Bulic, "Iscrizione inedita: Salona (Solin)," *Bolletino di Archeologia e Storia Dalmata* 21 (1898) 107–11; Eisen (2000) 131–32, with full bibliography; Otranto (1982) 353–54 = Rossi (1991) 87–88; Madigan and Oziek (2005) 196.

33. *CIL* III 14900; Eisen (2000) 132–33; Madigan and Oziek (2005) 197.

34. Eisen (2000) 132–33, and only very rarely applied to presbyters. P.-M. Gy, "Bemerkungen zu den Bezeichnungen des Priestertums in der christlichen Frühzeit," in *Das apostolische Amt*, J. Guyon ed. (Mainz 1961) 92–109.

35. Madigan and Osiek (2005) 67–96, 143–45; Eisen (2000) 158–98.

36. R. P. L. Cré, "Epitaphe de la Diaconesse Sophie," *RBI* n.s. 1 (1904) 260–62; Guarducci (1978) vol. 4, *Epigrafi Sacre Pagane e Cristiane*, 445, fig. 132; Kraemer (1988) 221, no. 95; Eisen (2000) 158–60; Madigan and Osiek (2005) 90–91, 93.

37. Translation by Madigan and Osiek (2005) 90–91; Eisen (2000) 158–59.

38. Madigan and Oziek (2005) 8.

39. Translation by Madigan and Oziek (2005) 18.

40. Madigan and Oziek (2005) 12–13.

41. Madigan and Oziek (2005) 6.

42. Madigan and Oziek (2005) 114.

43. Madigan and Oziek (2005) 116.

44. R. Gryson, *The Ministry of Women in the Early Church*, translated by J. LaPorte and M. L. Hall (Collegeville 1976) from the French edition (1972) 32; K. FitzGerald, *Women Deacons in the Orthodox Church* (Brookline, MA 1998) 18–19; Cardman (1999) 308–18.

45. Madigan and Oziek (2005) 5–6. They point out that John Chrysostom, Theodoret, and Theodore knew and accepted women deacons and that Origen claimed that it was through "apostolic authority" that women were appointed in the ministry of the church. See Origen, *Commentary on Romans* 10.17 and 16.1–2; *Der Römerbrief kommentar des Origenes*, C. P. Hammond Bammel, ed. (Freiburg 1990–98) 3.832–22.

46. Translation by Eisen (2000) 161.

47. Translation by Madigan and Oziek (2005) 83; Eisen (2000) 160–61; 83; Y. E. Meimaris, "Sacred Names, Saints, Martyrs, and Church Officials in the Greek Inscriptions and Papyri Pertaining to the Christian Church of Palestine," *MELETHMATA* 2 (Athens 1986) 178, no. 888.

48. *SEG* 27.948 A; Eisen (2000) 164–67; translation by Kraemer (1988) 223, no. 100.

49. The parallel is pointed out by Eisen (2000) 165, who gives the translation.

50. *TAM* IV/1 355; Eisen (2000) 172–73 suggests that residents of a poorhouse, presumably owned by one Geragathis, came together to decorate and then restore the coffin of Eugenia.

51. Eisen (2000) 174–82.

52. Eisen (2000) 174–82.

53. Madigan and Oziek (2005) 72–73; Eisen (2000) 176–77; Guarducci (1978) vol. 4, 345–47, no. 4, fig. 99.

54. Madigan and Oziek (2005) 73.

55. Madigan and Osiek (2005) 144–45; Eisen (2000) 174–82.

56. *CIL* V 6467; *ILCV* I 1238; translation by Madigan and Oziek (2005) 72–73; Eisen (2000) 184–88; Martimort (1985) 202, no. 22.

57. Madigan and Oziek (2005) 145–46.

58. Madigan and Oziek (2005) 147.

59. K. K. Fitzgerald, "Church of Greece Restores Diaconate for Women," the Orthodox Christian News Service, January 27, 2005.

60. Eisen (2000)

61. Brown in *RAW* 309; Tabbernee (1997) 67–70.

62. See also *Medicine Box* 49.3–79.4.1; Madigan and Oziek (2005) 165.

63. *Medicine* Box 79.3.6–79.4.1; Madigan and Oziek (2005) 166.

64. *Epistle* 8 (*Patralogia Latina* 134, 114); Otranto (1982) = Rossi (1991). Translation from Madigan and Oziek (2005) 192.

65. *CIL* X.2.8079 = *ILCV* I.1192; Eisen (2000) 129–31, with full bibliography; translation from Otranto in Rossi (1999) 86. Madigan and Oziek (2005) 193–95.

66. Translation by Madigan and Oziek (2005) 193.

67. Otranto (1982) 343–53 = Rossi (1991), translation by Rossi. Madigan and Oziek (2005) 187 point out that the important word here is the enclitic "cunctaque," signalling "and all other things that male presbyters do." This would include administration of the sacraments, liturgical service, and so on. See A. Thiel, *Epistulae Romanorum Pontificium Genuinae* (Brownsberg 1874) 360.

68. Horsley (1981) vol. 1, 121 n. 79; Eisen (2000) 128–29, with full bibliography; Kraemer (1988) 221, no. 93.

69. The stele was found in the ruins of the Church of Constantine and Helen but it no longer survives. Descriptions of the stele tell us that it showed a spindle, distaff, and small box carved in relief. Tabbernee (1997) no. 4, pp. 66–72 with full bibliography and translation; Eisen (2000) 116–17, with bibliography; Kraemer (1988) 221, no. 94.

70. For these two markers, see Tabbernee (1997) nos. 3 and 5, pp. 72–76; E. Gibson, "Montanist Epitaphs at Uçak," *GRBS* 16 (1975) 435–39.

71. E. Gibson, "Montanist Epitaphs," 433–42. For Montanism, see A. Strobel, *Das heilige Land der Montanisten* (Berlin 1980); T. Barnes, "The Chronology of Montanism," *JTS* 21 (1970) 403–8; Kraemer (1992) 157–73.

72. Found in the courtyard of a house, Eisen (2000) 63–64; C. H. E. Haspels, *The Highlands of Phrygia: Sites and Monuments* (Princeton 1971) 215–16, 338–39, no. 107, figs. 630–31; Tabbernee (1997), no. 68, pp. 419–23; A. Strobel, *Das heilige Land der Montanisten: Eine religionsgeographische Untersuchung* (Berlin 1980) 98–101.

73. Translation by Eisen (2000) 63–64.

74. Eisen (2000) 64.

75. Wire (1990); Eisen (2000) 63–87; K. L. King, "Prophetic Power and Women's Authority: The Case of the *Gospel of Mary (Magdalene)*," in *Women Preachers and Prophets through Two Millennia of Christianity*, B. M. Kienzle and P. J. Walker, eds. (Berkeley 1998) 21–41.

76. Tabbernee (1997) 424–25 points to an inscription of a prophet of the cult of Apollo at Laodikeia that is decorated with Christian symbols, presumably as a result of syncretism: *I.Laodikeia* (1969) 6; *BE* (1970) 575. It is dated A.D. 141/142 and shows an Alpha Omega instead of the Chi-Rho. It was found in the Nymphaeum. L. Robert argues in "Bulletin épigraphique," *REG* 83 (1970) 362–488 that this was a syncretic cult of Asklepios and Apollo. L. Antonius son of Zenon Aurelianus is the prophet. Zeno was, according to Robert, politically active in Laodikea, and his son Polemon was a military commander. The family had Roman citizenship.

77. See G. B. De Rossi in *Bollettino di Archeologia cristiana* (1877) 88, pl. 7.4; A. Ferrua, "Note su Tropea paleochristiana," *ASCL* 23 (1954) 9–29, at 11; A. Crispo, "Antichità cristiane della Calabria pre-byzantia," *ASCL* 14 (1945) 127–41, 209–10, at 133–34. Otranto argues for identifying Leta herself as presbyter, in Otranto (1982) = Rossi (1991) 86–87.

78. Horsley (1987) vol. 4, 213–20; T. Rajak, "The Jewish Community and Its Boundaries," in Lieu, North, and Rajak (1992) 22–25.

79. Brooten (1982) 76–83; For support of Brooten's views, see Kraemer (1985) 431–38; Kraemer (1992); Horst (1990) 163–64, n. 59, 64. Levine (2000) 482 shows cautious interest.

80. Brooten (1982). Ross Kraemer has added to this list an inscription from Malta that mentions a women as presbyter and her husband as *gerousiarch*. Kraemer (1985) 431–38.

81. Levine (2000) 482.

82. Kraemer (1992) chaps. 8 and 9, contrasts the picture presented in the rabbinic sources with that emerging from the archaeological and epigraphic evidence.

83. *CIJ* (2000) 590; Brooten (1982) 42–44.

84. In time, Mary Magdalene received the titles of "equal to an apostle" and "evangelist." Her role has been much studied in recent years; see K. King, *The Gospel of Mary of Magdala: Jesus and the First Woman Apostle* (Santa Rosa, CA 2003); M. R. D'Angelo, "Reconstructing 'Real' Women in Gospel Literature: The Case of Mary Magdalene," in Kraemer and D'Angelo (1999) 105–28; A. G. Brock, *Mary Magdalene, the First Apostle: The Struggle for Authority* (Cambridge 2003).

85. R. A. Kearsley, "Women in Public Life in the Roman East: Iunia Theodora, Claudia Metrodora, and Phoibe, Benefactress of Paul," *Ancient Society* 15 (1985) 124–37.

86. Madigan and Osiek (2005) 12–13.

87. F. V. Filson, "The Significance of the Early House Church," *JBL* 58 (1939) 105–12; R. E. Brown, "New Testament Background for the Concept of Local Church," *Proceedings of the Catholic Theological Society of America* 36 (1981) 1–14; H.-J. Klauck, "Die Hausgemeinde als Lebensform im Urchristentum," *Münchener Theologische Zeitschrift* 32 (1981) 1–15; Schüssler Fiorenza (1994) 175–84.

88. J. A. Peterson, "House-Churches at Rome," *Vigiliae Christianae* 23 (1969) 264–72.

89. J. Wiseman, *Stobi: A Guide to the Excavations* (Belgrade 1973) 59–61; Horsley (1988) vol. 2, 194–95, no. 109; D. Feissel, *Recueil des inscriptions chrétiennes de Macédoine du IIIᵉ au VIᵉ siècle* = BCH Supplement 8 (Paris 1983) 231, no. 275 (Matrona); no. 276 (Peristeria); Eisen (2000) 176.

90. Translation by Madigan and Osiek (2005) 84–85.

91. Translation by Madigan and Osiek (2005) 70; Eisen (2000) 175–76; Kraemer (2004) 259.

92. E. L. Sukenik, "The Mosaic Inscriptions in the Synagogue at Apamea on the Orontes," *HUCA* 23 (1950–51) 541–51; Brooten (1982) 158–59; Levine (2000) 240–42. B. Brenk, "Die Umwandlung der Synagoge von Apamea in eine Kirche: Eine mentalitatgeschichtliche Studie," *Tesserae: Festschrift für Josef Engemann*, Jahrbuch für Antike und Christentum. Ergänzungsband 18 (Münster 1991) 1–25; Hachlili, *Ancient Jewish Art and Archaeology in the Diaspora* (Leiden 1998) 32–34, 198–204, 402.

93. *I.Syrie*, 1322–27, 1329, 1332, 1335, 1336; Brooten (1982) 143. The sixteen dedications involving women are listed in Brooten's catalog: 158–59, nos. 7–15; 162–63, nos. 30–34; 164, nos. 39–40. Levine (2000) 240.

94. *CIL* VIII.12457a, Brooten (1982) 161 n. 22; Kraemer (1992) 106.

95. Brooten (1982) 141–44, catalog of inscriptions in appendix (157–65). Kraemer (1992) 106–7, 120.

96. Brooten (1982) 143.

97. Inscriptions recording these benefactions range in date from the first century B.C. to the fifth century A.D. Levine (2000) 485 has shown that of the some one hundred names of donors to synagogues surviving from the Roman Diaspora, approximately 29 percent belong to women. The distribution of benefactions by women is significant, with only 4 percent for Palestine and the great majority coming from Asia Minor, far from the rabbinic center and in regions with long local traditions of benefaction by women to Greco-Roman cults, Levine (2000) 485–88. Levine summarizes Trebilco's findings for the active role played by women officeholders in Greco-Roman cults of Roman Asia Minor, Trebilco (1991) 113–26. Trebilco identifies ten women in six cities who held the title *demiourgos*, forty-eight women gymnasiarchs in twenty-three cities, twenty-eight women *prytanis* in eight cities, thirty-seven women *stephanophoroi* in seventeen cities, eighteen women *agonothetes* in fourteen cities, five women who held the post of *hipparchos*, plus a few women members of a *gerousia*, others who served as *penegyriarch*, still others as *strategos* and *dekaprotos*.

98. *CIJ* 738; Brooten (1982) 157, no. 3. Since the decree states that Tation gave the building specifically "as a gift to the Jews," some infer that she was not Jewish herself, though we cannot know this with certainty; see Kraemer (1992) 119. See also Lifshitz (1967) no. 13; Trebilco (1991) 110–11; T. Rajack, "Jews as Benefactors," in *Studies on the Jewish Diaspora in the Hellenistic and Roman Periods*, B. Isaac and A. Oppenheimer eds., *Te'uda* 12 (Tel Aviv 1996) 31.

99. As we have seen in chapter 7. For combination of gold crown and *proedria* given to priestess at Priene, see *I.Priene* 81.107–30.

100. *SEG* 33.1035–41; public honors enumerated in 1035.5–11 and 1039.32–38; see Bremen (1996) 13–18, 143 n. 3, 157 n. 53.

101. *SEG* 33.1035–41.

102. Levine (2000) 481. L. M. White, *The Social Origins of Christian Architecture*, 2; *Texts and Monuments for the Christian Domus Ecclesiae in Its Environment* (Valley Forge 1997) 325 n. 69.

103. R. T. Rollins, *The Singing of Women in the Early Christian Church: Why It Occurred; Why It Disappeared* (DMA diss., Claremont Graduate School 1988) 98.

CHAPTER 10. CONCLUSIONS

1. For Christian women, see G. B. De Rossi, *Bolletino di Archeologio Christiana* (1977) 88; for Jewish women, see T. Rajak in Lieu, North, and Rajak (1992) 23; for women in Greco-Roman cults of the Hellenistic and Roman East, see Bremen (1996) 116–17, citing D. Maguire, *Roman Rule in Asia Minor, to the End of the Third Century after Christ* (Princeton 1950), who held the view that women's cult titles were only honorary and that their husbands were the real agents of cult.

2. For Victorians, see S. Spencer-Wood, "The World Their Household: Changing Meanings of the Domestic Sphere in the Nineteenth Century," in Allison (1999) 162–89.

3. J. Halley, *Split Decisions: How and Why to Take a Break from Feminism* (Princeton 2006) 5. I thank Janet Hally for helpful discussions of method and approach.

4. Blok (2001) 112, 114.

5. Gould (1980) 50 n. 92.

6. Cole (1992) 111–12, (2004) 125, and Dillon (2002) 76.

7. Jordan (1979) 32.

8. Bremen (1996) 115–16 has demonstrated that most women benefactors of the Greek East in the second century B.C. acted on their own. It is not until the first century A.D. that benefactions of husbands and wives offered together as a couple become more frequent. She cites P. Paris, *Quaetenus feminae res publicas in Asia minore romanis imperantibus, attigerint* (diss., Paris 1891) as an example of an interpretation that sees women benefactors as mere "hangers-on" to their joint officeholding husbands, who are the real agents and donors. She points out (p. 275) that L. Robert's reading of a case

of joint officeholding at Lagina in Caria similarly gives the benefit of the doubt to the husband as primary agent (see *I. Stratonikeia II* 701, in L. Robert *Et.Anat.* 549–50).

9. Boatwright (1991) 258.

10. See priestess of Nymphe, genos of Theonidai, who set up her own statue, "at her own expense," *SEG* 29.135, Vanderpool (1979) 213–16, and Phile of first-century-B.C. Priene, who financed the construction of an aqueduct and cistern and supplied water pipes for the city "at her own expense," *MAMA* VIII 492b; *LF²* no. 194, *I.Priene* 208, Bremen (1996) 31, 36, 57.

11. Detienne (1989).

12. Maurizio (1995) 69–86.

13. Xenophon (*Anabasis* 5.3.6–7) and Pliny (*Natural Histories* 35.93, 131–32).

14. Lewis (1955) 1–12.

15. Schaps (1977) 323–30; Gould (1980) 45.

16. Bremmer (1981) 425. Thucydides 2.45.2; Xenophon *Oikonomikos* 3.12; Demosthenes 30, 39.9, 40, 57.37; Isaios 5.5 8, 7 10.4; for comedy, see Sommerstein (1980) 393–409.

17. See Blok (2001) 116.

18. Schaps (1977) 330.

19. R. Stark, *The Rise of Christianity* (Princeton 1996) 110.

20. Stark *Rise of Christianity*, 110.

21. Similarities have been noted between the ritual of the women in the Arabian desert and the devotion of women in sixth-century-B.C. Judah and Jerusalem who worshiped a goddess called the Queen of Heaven (Jer. 7:16–20; 44:15–19, 25). The prophet Jeremiah condemned these women for baking cakes in the image of the Queen, and for offering libations and burning incense to her. At Kition on Cyprus, the fifth-century Tariff inscription mentions "the two bakers who baked a basket of cakes for the Queen," who in this context means Astarte, Lady of Heaven, Holy Queen; see S. Ackerman, "And the Women Knead Dough": The Worship of the Queen of Heaven in Sixth-Century Judah," in *Women in the Hebrew Bible: A Reader*, A. Bach, ed. (New York 1999) 21–32, esp. 24.

22. *Erechtheus* frag. 350.

23. Euripides *Herakleidai* 777–83.

Bibliography

Adorno, T. W. 1966. *Negative Dialectics*, trans. E. B. Ashton, 1973. London.

———. 1977. *Aesthetic Theory*, trans. R. Hullot-Kentor, 1984. Minneapolis.

———. 1991. *The Culture Industry: Selected Essays on Mass Culture*, J. M. Bernstein, ed. London.

Alcock, S., and R. Osborne, eds. 1994. *Placing the Gods: Sanctuaries and Sacred Space in Ancient Greece*. Oxford.

Aleshire, S. 1994a. "The Demos and the Priests: The Selection of Sacred Officials at Athens from Cleisthenes to Augustus," in Osborne and Hornblower: 326–37. Oxford.

———. 1994b. "Towards a Definition of 'State Cult' for Ancient Athens," in Hägg: 9–16. Stockholm.

Allison, P. M., ed. 1999. *The Archaeology of Household Activities*. London.

Amandry, P. 1950. *La mantique Apollinienne à Delphes: Essai sur le fonctionnement de l'Oracle*. Paris.

Aubriot-Sévin, D. 1992. *Prière et conceptions religieuses en Grèce ancienne jusqu'à la fin du Ve siècle av. J.-C.*, Collection de la Maison de l'Orient Méditerranéen 22. Lyon.

Austin, C. 1967. "De nouveaux fragments de l'Erethée d'Euripide," *Recherches de Papyrologie* 4:11–69.

———. 1968. *Nova Fragmenta Euripidea*. Berlin.

Beard, M., and J. North, eds. 1990. *Pagan Priests*. Ithaca.

Benndorf, O. 1882. "Zur Perieges der Akropolis," *AM* 7:47.

Bérard, C. 1976. "Le Liknon d'Athena," *Antike Kunst* 19:101–14.

———. 1983. "Iconographie, iconologie, iconologique," *Études de Lettres* 4:5–37.

———. 1989a. "Festivals and Mysticism," in Bérard et al. 1989: 109–20.

———. 1989b. "The Order of Women," in Bérard et al. 1989: 88–107.

Bérard, C., and J.-L. Durand. 1989. "Entering the Imagery," in Bérard et al. 1989: 19–33.

Bérard, C., et al. 1989. *A City of Images: Iconography and Society in Ancient Greece*, trans. D. Lyons. Princeton.

Berthiaume, G. 1982. *Les rôles du mágieros: Études sur la boucherie, la cuisine et le sacrifice dans la Grèce ancienne*, *Mnemosyne* Supplement 70. Leiden.

Billigmeier, J.-C., and J. A. Turner. 1981. "The Socio-economic Roles of Women in Mycenean Greece: A Brief Survey from Evidence of the Linear B Tablets," in Foley 1981b: 1–18.

Blech, M. 1982. *Studien zum Kranz bei den Griechen*. Berlin.

Blok, J. 1987. "Sexual Asymmetry: A Historiographical Essay," in Blok and Mason: 1–57.

———. 2001. "Virtual Voices: Toward a Choreography of Women's Speech in Classical Athens," in Lardinois and McClure: 95–116.

———. 2004. "Recht und Ritus der Polis: Zu Bürgerstatus und Geschlechterverhältnissen im klassichen Athen," *HistZeit* 278:1–26.

Blok, J., and P. Mason, eds. 1987. *Sexual Asymmetry: Studies in Ancient Society*. Amsterdam.

Blundell, S., and M. Williamson. 1998. *The Sacred and the Feminine in Ancient Greece*. London and New York.

Boatwright, M. T. 1991. "Plancia Magna of Perge: Women's Role and Status in Roman Asia Minor," in Pomeroy: 249–72.

Bolger, D. 2003. *Gender in Ancient Cyprus*. Lanham, MA.

Bourdieu, P. 1977. *Outline of a Theory of Practice*, trans. R. Nice. Cambridge.

———. 1986. *Handbook of Theory and Research for the Sociology of Education*, J. G. Richardson, ed. New York.

Bourdieu, P., with J. C. Passeron. 1990. *Reproduction in Education, Society, and Culture*, trans. R. Nice. London.

Bourriot, F. 1976. *Recherches sur la nature de génos*. Lille.

Bowden, H. 2005. *Classical Athens and the Delphic Oracle: Divination and Democracy*. Cambridge.

Brelich, A. 1969. *Paides e Parthenoi*. Rome.

Bremen, R. van. 1983. "Women and Wealth," in Cameron and Kuhrt: 223–42.

———. 1996. *The Limits of Participation: Women and Civic Life in the Greek East in the Hellenistic and Roman Periods*. Amsterdam.

Bremmer, J. N. 1981. "Plutarch and the Naming of Women," *AJG* 102:425–26.

———. 1987. *Interpretations of Greek Mythology*. London.

———. 1994. *Greek Religion*, Greece and Rome, New Surveys in the Classics 24. Oxford.

———. 1998. " 'Religion,' 'Ritual,' and the Opposition of 'Sacred vs. Profane': Notes toward a Terminological 'Genealogy,' " in F. Graf, ed. *Ansichten griechischen Rituale*: 9–33. Leiden.

Broadbent, M. 1968. *Studies in Greek Genealogy*. Leiden.

Broneer, O. 1942. "The Thesmophorion in Athens," *Hesperia* 11:250–74.

Brooten, B. J. 1982. *Women Leaders in the Ancient Synagogue*. Chico, CA.

Broude, N., and M. Garrard, eds. 2005. *Reclaiming Female Agency: Feminist Art History after Postmodernism*. Berkeley, Los Angeles, and London.

Brown, P. 1972. "Sorcery, Demons, and the Rise of Christianity: From Late Antiquity into the Middle Ages," in P. R. Lamont, ed. *Religion and Society in the Age of Saint Augustine*: 119–46. London.

———. 1988. *The Body and Society: Men, Women, and Sexual Renunciation in Early Christianity*. New York.

Brown, S. 1997. " 'Ways of Seeing' Women in Antiquity: An Introduction to Feminism in Classical Archaeology and Ancient Art History," in Koloski-Ostrow and Lyons: 12–42.

Bruit Zaidman, L., and P. Schmidt Pantel. 1992. *Religion in the Ancient Greek City*. Translated from French edition 1987. Cambridge.

Brulé, P. 1987. *La fille d'Athènes: La religion des filles à Athènes à l'époque classique, mythes, cultes, et société*. Paris.

———. 2003. *Women of Ancient Greece*. Edinburgh.

Brumfield, A. C. 1981. *The Attic Festivals of Demeter and Their Relation to the Agricultural Year*. Salem.

Bruneau, P. 1970. *Recherches sur les cultes de Délos à l'époque hellénistique et à l'époque impériale*. Paris.

Burkert, W. 1966. "Greek Tragedy and Sacrificial Ritual," *GRBS* 7:87–121.

———. 1983. *Homo Necans: The Anthropology of Ancient Greek Sacrificial Ritual and Myth*. Berkeley.

———. 1985. *Greek Religion: Archaic and Classical*, trans. J. Raffan. Oxford.

Buxton, R., ed. 2000. *Oxford Readings in Greek Religion*. Oxford.

Calame, C. 1997. *Choruses of Young Women in Ancient Greece: Their Morphology, Religious Role, and Sacred Functions*: Lanham, MD. A translation of the French edition, 1977, *Les choeurs de jeunes filles en Grece archaique*. Rome.

Cameron, A., and A. Kuhrt. 1983. *Images of Women in Antiquity*. Detroit and London.

Cardman, F. 1999. "Women, Ministry, and Church Order in Early Christianity," in Kraemer and D' Angelo: 300–329.

Carney, E. 1991. "What's in a Name? The Emergence of a Title for Royal Women in the Hellenistic Period," in Pomeroy: 154–72.

Carpenter, T. H. 1997. *Dionysian Imagery in Fifth-Century Athens*. New York.

Carrara, P., ed. 1977. *Euripide: Erreteo*. Florence.

Cartledge, P. A., and F. D. Harvey, eds. 1985. *Crux: Essays Presented to G. E. M. de Ste. Croix*. London.

Casabona, J. 1966. *Recherches sur le vocabulaire des sacrifices en Grèce*. Aix-en-Provence.

Chaniotis, A. 2004. "Religious Organizations and Bodies: Greece," in *RAW*: 319–21.

Christiansen, J., and T. Melander, eds. 1988. *International Vase Symposium: Proceedings of the Third Symposium on Ancient Greek and Related Pottery, August 31–September 4, 1987*. Copenhagen.

Clairmont, C. 1970. *Gravestones and Epigram*. Mainz.

———. 1979. "The Lekythos of Myrrhine," in G. Köpcke and M. Moore, eds. *Studies in Classical Art and Archaeology*: 103–10. Locust Valley, NY.

———. 1993. *Classical Attic Tombstones*, vols. 1–6. Kilchberg.

Clark, E. A. 1984. *The Life of Melania the Younger*. New York.

Clinton, K. 1974. *The Sacred Officials of the Eleusinian Mysteries*. Philadelphia.

———. 1988. "Sacrifice at the Eleusinian Mysteries," in Hägg, Marinatos, and Nordquist: 69–80.

———. 1996. "The Thesmophorion in Central Athens and the Celebration of the Thesmophoria in Attica," in Hägg: 111–25.

———. 2005. *Eleusis: The Inscriptions on Stone, Documents of the Sanctuary of the Two Goddesses and Public Documents of the Deme*, Archaeological Society at Athens Library no. 236. Athens.

Cohen, D. 1989. "Seclusion, Separation, and the Status of Women in Classical Athens," *Greece and Rome* 36.1:3–15.

———. 1991. *Law, Sexuality, and Society: The Enforcement of Morals in Classical Athens*. Cambridge.

Cole, S. G. 1980. "New Evidence for the Mysteries of Dionysos," *GRBS* 21:223–38.

———. 1984. "The Social Function of Rituals of Maturation: The Koureion and the Arkteia," *ZPE* 55:233–44.

———. 1992. "*Gunaiki ou Themis*: Gender Differences in the Greek *Leges Sacrae*," *Helios* 19:104–22.

———. 1994. "Demeter in the Ancient Greek City and Its Countryside," in Alcock and Osborne: 199–216.

———. 2004. *Landscapes, Gender, and Ritual Space*. Berkeley, Los Angeles, and London.

Collard, E., M. J. Cropp, and K. H. Lee, eds. 1995. *Euripides: Selected Fragmentary Plays*. Warminster.

Connelly, J. B. 1988. *Votive Sculpture of Hellenistic Cyprus*. Nicosia and New York.

———. 1989. "Standing before One's God: Votive Sculpture and the Cypriot Religious Tradition," *Biblical Archaeology* 52:210–18.

———. 1991. "Continuity and Change: The Cypriot Votive Tradition and the Hellenistic Koine," *Cypriot Terracottas: Proceedings of the First International Conference of Cypriot Studies*: 93–100. Brussels and Liège.

———. 1993. "Narrative and Image in Attic Vase Painting: Ajax and Kassandra at the Trojan Palladion," in P. J. Holliday, ed. *Narrative and Event in Ancient Art*: 88–129. Cambridge.

———. 1994. "Tarentine Relief," in B. S. Ridgway et al. *Catalogue of the Greek Sculpture in the Princeton Museum*: 28–31. Princeton.

———. 1996. "Parthenon and *Parthenoi*: A Mythological Interpretation of the Parthenon Frieze," *AJA* 100:53–80.

Connor, W. R. 1987. "Tribes, Festivals, and Processions: Civic Ceremonial and Political Manipulation in Archaic Greece," *JHS* 107:40–50. Reprinted in Buxton 2000: 56–75.

———. 1988. "'Sacred' and 'Secular': ιερά καὶ ὅσια and the Classical Athenian Concept of the State," *AncSoc* 19:161–88.

Daux, G. 1970. "Notes de lecture," *BCH* 94:595–623.

———. 1972. "Stèles funéraires et épigrammes," *BCH* 96:503–66.

———. 1975. "Notes de lecture," *BCH* 99:145–71.

Davies, J. K. 1971. *Athenian Propertied Families*. Oxford.

Dean-Jones, L. 1994. *Women's Bodies in Classical Greek Science*. Oxford.

Debord, P. 1982. *Aspects sociaux et économiques de la vie religieuse dans l'Anatolie gréco-romaine*. Leiden.

de Cesare, M. 1997. *Le statue in immagine: Studi sulle raffigurazione di statue nella pittura vascolare greca*. Rome.

De la Coste-Messelière, P. 1925. "Inscriptions des Delphes," *BCH* 49:61–103.

Delorme, J. 1960. *Gymnasion: Étude sur les monuments consacrés á l'education en Grèce*. Paris.

Demakopoulou, K., and D. Konsola. 1981. *Archaeological Museum of Thebes: A Guide*. Athens.

Demand, N. 1994. *Birth, Death, and Motherhood in Classical Greece*. Baltimore.

Depew, M. 1997. "Reading Greek Prayers," *ClAnt* 16:229–58.

Despinis, G. 1963. "Ἐπιτύμβιοι τράπεζαι," *ArchEph*: 46–68.

Detienne, M. 1989. "The Violence of Well-Born Ladies: Women at the Thesmophoria," in Detienne and Vernant: 129–47.

Detienne, M., and J. P. Vernant. 1989. *The Cuisine of Sacrifice among the Greeks*, trans. P. Wissing. Chicago.

Deubner, L. 1932. *Attische Feste*, reprint 1966. Berlin.

Dewald, C. 1981. "Women and Culture in Herodotus' Histories," in Foley, 1981b: 91–125.

Dickerson, G. 1991. Review of R. Garland, "Priests and Power in Classical Athens," in Beard and North 1990: 73–91, *BMCR* 2:66–68.

Dickie, M. K. 2004. "Priestly Proclamations and Sacred Laws," *CQ* 54:579–91.

Dickins, G. 1912. *Catalogue of the Akropolis Museum I, Archaic Sculpture*. Cambridge.

Dignas, B. 2002. *Economy of the Sacred in Hellenistic and Roman Asia Minor*. Oxford.

Dillon, M. P. J. 1995. "Payments to the Disabled at Athens: Social Justice or Fear of Aristocratic Patronage?" *Ancient Society* 26:25–57.

———. 1996. *Religion in the Ancient World: New Themes and Approaches*. Amsterdam.

———. 1997. *Pilgrims and Pilgrimage in Ancient Greece*. London and New York.

———. 2002. *Girls and Women in Classical Greek Religion*. London.

Dodd, D. B., and C. Faraone, eds. 2003. *Initiation in Ancient Greek Rituals and Narratives: New Critical Perspectives*. London and New York.

Dowden, K. 1989. *Death and the Maiden*. London and New York.

———. 1995. "Approaching Women through Myth: Vital Tool or Self-Delusion?" in Hawley and Levick: 44–57.

Dummer, J. 1977. "Realität des Lebens und Realitätsschwund in der Vasenmalerei," in M. Kunze, ed. *Beiträge zum antiken Realismus: Schriften der Winckelmann, Gesellschaft*, no. 3: 57–62. Berlin.

Dunand, F. 1973. *Le Culte d'Isis dans le basin oriental de la Mediterranée*. Leiden.

Durand, J.-L. 1986. *Sacrifice et labour en Grèce ancienne*. Rome.

———. 1991. "Images sur un autel," in R. Etienne et Le Dinahet, *L'espace sacrificiel dans les civilisations méditerraneanes de l'antiquité*, Actes du colloques à la Maison de l'Orient. Lyon, 4–7 Juin 1988: 45–55. Paris.

Easterling, P. E., and J. V. Muir, eds. 1985. *Greek Religion and Society*. Cambridge.

Eisen, U. 2000. *Women Officeholders in Early Christianity: Epigraphical and Literary Studies*. Collegeville, MN.

Eule, J. C. 2001. *Hellenistiche Bürgerinnen ans Kleinasien*. Istanbul.

Fantham, E., H. P. Foley, N. Kampen, S. Pomeroy, and H. A. Shapiro, eds. 1994. *Women in the Classical World: Image and Text*. New York and Oxford.

Faraone, C. 1993. *Talismans and Trojan Horses*. Oxford.

———. 1999. *Ancient Greek Love Magic*. Cambridge, MA.

———. 2003. "Playing the bear and the fawn for Artemis: female initiation or substitute sacrifice?" in Dodd and Faraone: 43–68.

———. 2006. "The Priestess and the Courtesan: Female Leadership in Aristophanes' Lysistrata," in Faraone and McClure: 207–23.

Faraone, C., and L. McClure, eds. 2006. *Prostitutes and Courtesans in the Ancient World*. Madison.

Feaver, D. D. 1957. "Historical Development in the Priesthoods of Athena," YCS 15:121–58.

Ferguson, J. 1980. *Greek and Roman Religion: A Source Book*. Park Ridge, NJ.

———. 1989. *Among the Gods: An Archaeological Explanation of Ancient Greek Religion*. London and New York.

Ferguson, W. S. 1938. "The Salaminioi of Heptaphylai and Sounion," *Hesperia* 7:1–74.

———. 1949. "Orgeonika," *Hesperia* Supplement 8:130–63. Princeton.

Ferrari, G. 2002. *Figures of Speech: Men and Maidens in Ancient Greece*. Chicago.

Filges, A. 1997. *Standbilder jugendlicher Göttinnen: Klassische und frühhellenistische Gewandstatuen mit Brustwulst und ihre kaiserzeitliche Rezeption*. Cologne.

Foley, H. P., ed. 1981a. "The Conception of Women in Athenian Drama," in Foley 1981b: 127–68.

———. 1981b. *Reflections of Women in Antiquity*. New York.

———. 1985. *Ritual Irony: Poetry and Sacrifice in Euripides*. Ithaca.

———. 1994. *Homeric Hymn to Demeter: Translation, Commentary, and Interpretive Essay*. Princeton.

———. 2001. *Female Acts in Greek Tragedy*. Princeton.

Fontenrose, J. 1978. *The Delphic Oracle*. Berkeley.

———. 1988. *Didyma*. Berkeley.

Forrest, W. G. F. 1959. "The Priesthoods of Erythrai," BCH 83:513–22.

Foucart, P. F. 1885. "Inscriptions de Béotie," BCH 9:405.

———. 1914. *Les Mystères d'Eleusis*. Paris.

Fougères, G. 1888. "Stèle de Mantinée," BCH 12:376–80.

Foxhall, L. 1989. "Household, Gender, and Property in Classical Athens," CQ 39:22–44.

Franklin, S. B. 1902. "Ἐπιτύμβιος κιονίσκος ιερείας," ArchEph: 143–44.

Freyer-Schauenburg, B. 1989. "Zum Grabrelief der Priesterin Choirine," *Festschrift J. Inan*: 59–65. Istanbul.

Furley, W. D., and J. M. Bremer. 2001. *Greek Hymns*, vol. 1. *The Texts in Translation*. Tubingen.

Furtwängler, A. 1893. *Meisterwerke der griechischen Plastik*. Leipzig.

Garland, R. 1984. "Religious Authority in Archaic and Classical Athens," ABSA 79:75–123.

———. 1990. "Priests and Power in Classical Athens," in Beard and North: 73–91.

———. 1995. *The Eye of the Beholder: Deformity and Disability in the Greco-Roman World*. Ithaca.

Gauthier, P. 1985. *Les cités grecs et leur bienfaiteurs* = BCH Supplement 12. Paris.

———. 1996. "La catégorie dite des 'lois sacrées' est un fourre-tout trompeur," *Bulletin Épigraphique: Institutuions*, REG 109:568–74.

Gentili, B., and F. Perusino. 2002. *Le orse di Brauron: Un rituale di iniziazione femminile nel santuario di Artemide*. Pisa.

Georgourdi, S. 1989. "Sanctified Slaughter in Modern Greece: The 'Kourbánia' of the Saints," in Detienne and Vernant: 183–203.

———. 2003. "Lysimachè, la prêtresse," in S. Georgoudi, N. Loraux, and C. Montepaone, eds. *La Grèce au féminin*: 169–213, translated from *Grecia al femminile*, Latertza 1993: 157–90.

Gero, J., and M. Conkey, eds. 1991. *Engendering Archaeology: Women in Prehistory*. Oxford.

Gilchrist, R. 2000. *Gender and Archaeology: Contesting the Past*. New York.

Goff, B. 2004. *Citizen Bacchae*. Berkeley, Los Angeles, and London.

Golden, M. 1986. "Names and Naming at Athens: Three Studies," *EMC* 30:245–69.

Goldhill, S. 1994. "Representing Democracy: Women at the Great Dionysia," in Osborne and Hornblower: 347–69.

Goldhill, S., and R. Osborne, eds. 1999. *Performance Culture and Athenian Democracy*. Cambridge.

Gould, J. 1980. "Law, Custom, and Myth: Aspects of the Social Position of Women in Classical Athens," *JHS* 100: 38–59.

Graef, B. E., H. Langlotz, et al. 1925. *Die antiken Vasen von der Akropolis zu Athen*. Berlin.

Graf, F. 1980. "Milch, Honig, und Wein: Zum Verständnis der Libation im griechischen Ritual," in *Perennitas: Studi in onore di Angelo Brelich*. Rome: 209–21.

———. 1996. "*Pompai* in Greece: Some Considerations about Space and Ritual in the Greek *Polis*," in Hägg: 56–65.

———. 2004. "Sacrifice, Offerings, and Votives: Greece," in *RAW*: 340–43.

Graham, A. J. 1981. "Religion, Women, and Greek Colonization," *Religione e città nel mondo antika, Atti, Centro ricerche e documentazione sull'antichità classica*, vol. II, 293–314, reprinted in 2001, *Collected Papers on Greek Colonization*: 327–48. Leiden.

Grant, F. 1953. *Hellenistic Religion*. New York.

Grant, R. M. 1975. "The Religion of Maximin Daia," in J. Neusner, ed. *Christianity, Judaism, and Other Greco-Roman Cults*: 143–66. Leiden.

Guarducci, M. 1978. *Epigrafia Graeca: I–IV*. Rome.

Habicht, C. 1982. *Studien zur Geschichte Athens in hellenistischer Zeit*. Göttingen.

———. 1997. *Athens from Alexander to Antony*. Cambridge, MA.

Hägg, R., ed. 1992. *The Iconography of Greek Cult in the Archaic and Classical Periods*. Proceedings of the First International Seminar on Ancient Greek Cult, organized by the Swedish Institute at Athens and European Cultural Center of Delphi, *Kernos* Supplement 1. Liège.

———, ed. 1994. *Ancient Greek Cult Practice from the Epigraphical Evidence*. Proceedings of the Second International Seminar on Ancient Greek Cult, organized by the Swedish Institute at Athens. Skrifter Utgivna av Svenska Institutet i Athen 8.13. Stockholm.

———, ed. 1996. *The Role of Religion in the Early Greek Polis*. Proceedings of the Third International Seminar on Ancient Greek Cult, organized by the Swedish Institute at Athens, 16–18 October 1992, Skrifter Utgivna av Svenska Insitutet i Athen 8.24.

Hägg, R., N. Marinatos, and G. C. Nordquist, eds. 1988. *Early Greek Cult Practice*. Proceedings of the Fifth

International Symposium on Ancient Greek Cult, organized by the Swedish Institute at Athens, Skrifter Utgivna av Svenska Institutet i Athen 4. Stockholm.

Hamilton, R. 1985. "Euripidean Priests," *HSCP* 89:53–73.

———. 1989. "Alkman and the Athenian Arkteia," *Hesperia* 58 (1989) 449–72.

Harris, D. 1995. *The Treasures of the Parthenon and the Erechtheion*. Oxford.

Harris, E. M. 1992. "Women and Lending in Athenian Society: A *Horos* Re-examined," *Phoenix* 46:309–21.

———. 2004. "Antigone the Lawyer, or the Ambiguities of Nomos," in Harris and Rubinstein: 19–56.

Harris, E. M., and R. Rubinstein, eds. 2004. *The Law and the Courts in Ancient Greece*. London.

Hatzopoulos, M. B. 1994. *Cultes et rites de passage en Macedoine*. Athen.

———. 1996. *Macedonioan Institutions under the Kings*. Athens.

Hausmann, U. 1960. *Griechische Weihreliefs*. Berlin.

Hawley, R. 1994. "The Problem of Women Philosophers in Ancient Greece," in L. J. Archer, S. Fischler, and M. Wyke, eds., *Women in Ancient Societies: An Illusion of the Night*: 70–87. London.

Hawley, R., and B. Levick, eds. 1995. *Women in Antiquity: New Assessments*. New York.

Heiler, F. 1977. *Die Frau in den Religionen der Menschheit*. Berlin.

Hellstrom, P., and B. Alroth, eds. 1996. *Religion and Power in the Ancient Greek World*. Proceedings of the Uppsala Symposium 1993. Uppsala.

Henderson, J. 1991. "Women and Athenian Dramatic Festivals," *Transactions of the American Philosophical Association* 121:133–47

———. 1996. *Three Plays by Aristophanes: Staging Women*. New York and London.

Henrichs, A. 1978. "Greek Maenadism from Olympias to Messalina," *HSCP* 82:121–69.

———. 1983. "Changing Dionysiac Identities," *Jewish and Christian Self-Definition*, vol. 3, E. P. Sanders, ed. Philadelphia.

———. 1990. "Between country and city: cultic dimensions of Dionysus in Athens and Attica," in M. Griffith and D. J. Mastronarde, eds. *Cabinet of the Muses: Essays on Classical and Comparative Literature in Honor of Thomas G. Rosenmeyer*: 255–77. Atlanta.

———. 2003. "Writing Religion: Inscribed Texts, Ritual Authority, and Religious Discourse of the Polis," in H. Yunis, ed. *Written Texts and The Rise of Literate Culture in Greece* (Cambridge 2003) 38–58.

Henry, A. S. 1983. *Honours and Privileges in Athenian Decrees: The Principal Formulae of Athenian Honorary Decrees*. Hildesheim.

Herrmann, P. 1971. "Athena Polias in Milet," *Chiron* 1:291–98.

Hodos, T. 1999. "Intermarriage in the Western Greek Colonies," *OJA* 18.1:61–78.

Hoffmann, H. 1988. "Why Did the Greeks Need Imagery?" *Hephaistos* 9:143–67.

Hogarth, D. G. 1908. *Excavations at Ephesos: The Archaic Artemisia*. London.

Höghammar, K. 1993. *Sculpture and Society: A Study of the Connection between the Free Standing Sculpture and the Society on Kos in the Hellenistic and Augustan Periods*, Boreas 23. Uppsala.

Holderman, E. 1913. *A Study of the Greek Priestess*. Chicago.

Hollinshead, M. 1985. "Against Iphigeneia's *Adyton* at Three Mainland Temples," *AJA* 89:419–40.

Horbury, W., and D. Noy. 1992. *Jewish Inscriptions of Graeco-Roman Egypt*. Cambridge.

Horsley, G. H. R. 1981. *New Documents Illustrating Early Christianity: A Review of the Greek Inscriptions*, vol. 1. North Ryde, NSW, Australia.

———. 1982. *New Documents Illustrating Early Christianity: A Review of the Greek Inscriptions*, vol. 2. North Ryde, NSW, Australia.

———. 1987. *New Documents Illustrating Early Christianity: A Review of the Greek Inscriptions*, vol. 4. North Ryde, NSW, Australia.

Horst, P. W. van der. 1990. *Essays on the Jewish World of Early Christianity*. Göttingen.

———. 1991. *Ancient Jewish Epitaphs*. Kampen.

———. 1998. *Hellenism, Judaism, Christianity: Essays on Their Interaction*. Louvain.

Humphreys, S. C. 1988. *The Family, Women, and Death: Comparative Studies*. London and Boston.

Jacoby, F. 1949. *Atthis: The Local Chronicles of Ancient Athens*. Oxford.

Jameson, M. H. 1988. "Sacrifice and Ritual: Greece," in M. Grant and R. Kitzinger, eds. *Civilization of the Ancient Mediterranean: Greece and Rome*, vol. 2, 959–80. New York.

Johansen, K. F. 1951. *The Attic Grave-Reliefs of the Classical Period*. Copenhagen.

Jones, N. F. 1999. *The Association of Classical Athens: The Response to Democracy*. New York and Oxford.

Jordan, B. 1979. *Servants of the Gods*, Hypomnemata 55. Göttingen.

Just, R. 1989. *Women in Athenian Law and Life*. London and New York.

Kabus-Preisshofen, R. 1975. "Statuettengrupppe aus dem Demeters Heiligtum bei Kyparissi auf Kos," *AntPl* 15:31–64.

Kahil, L. 1963. "Quelques vases du sanctuaire d'Artémis à Brauron," *AntK* 1:5–29.

———. 1965. "Autour de l'Artémis attique," *AntK* 8:20–33.

———. 1976. "Artémis antique," *CRAI*: 126–30.

———. 1977. "L'Artémis de Brauron: Rites et mystère," *AntK* 20:86–98.

———. 1981. "Le cratérisque d'Artémis et le Brauronion de l'Acropole," *Hesperia* 50:253–63.

———. 1983. "Mythological Repertoire of Brauron," in W. G. Moon, ed. *Ancient Greek Art and Iconography*: 231–44. Madison.

Kaltsas, N. 2002. *Sculpture in the National Archaeological Museum*. Athen.

Karakasi, K. 2003. *Archaic Korai*. Los Angeles.

Karouzos, C. 1934. *To mouseio tes Thebas*. Athens.

Kasper-Butz, I. 1990. *Die Göttin Athena im klassichen Athen*. Frankfurt.

Kassel, R., and C. Austin. 1983. *Poetae comici Graeci*. Berlin and New York.

Kearns, E. 1985. "Change and Continuity in Religious Structures after Kleisthenes," in Cartledge and Harvey: 188–207.

———. 1989. *The Heroes of Attica*, BICS Supplement 57. London.

———. 1995. "Order, Intention, Authority: Ways of Looking at Greek Religion," in A. Powell, ed. *The Greek World*: 511–29. London.

Keesling, C. 2003. *The Votive Statues of the Athenian Acropolis*. Cambridge.

Koenen, L. 1969. "Eine Hypothesis zur Auge der Euripides und Tegeatische Plynteria," *ZPE* 4:7–18.

Köhler, U. 1884. "Grabstein einer Polias Priesterin," *AM* 9:301.

Koloski-Ostrow, A. O., and C. Lyons. 1997. *Naked Truths: Women, Sexuality, and Gender in Classical Art and Archaeology*. London and New York.

Kosmopoulou, A. 2001. "Working Women: Female Professionals on Classical Attic Gravestones," *ABSA* 96:281–319.

———. 2002. *The Iconography of Sculptured Statue Bases in the Archaic and Classical Periods*. Madison.

Kraemer, R. S. 1985. "A New Inscription from Malta and the Question of Women Elders in the Jewish Diaspora Communities," *HThR* 78:431–38.

———. 1988. *Maenads, Martyrs, Matrons, Monastics: A Sourcebook on Women's Religions in the Greco-Roman World*. Philadelphia.

———. 1992. *Her Share of the Blessings*. Oxford.

———. 2004. *Women's Religions in the Greco-Roman World: A Sourcebook*. Oxford.

Kraemer, R. S., and M. R. D'Angelo. 1999. *Women and Christian Origins*. Oxford.

Kriss, R., and H. Kriss-Heinrich. 1955. *Peregrinatio Neohellenika: Wallfahrtswanderungen im heutigen Griechenland und in Unteritalien*. Vienna.

Kron, U. 1996. "Priesthoods, Dedications, and Euergetism. What Part Did Religion Play in the Political and Social Status of Greek Women?" in P. Hellstrom and B. Alroth.

Krug, A. 1968. *Binden in der griechischen Kunst: Untersuchungen zur Typologie 6.–1. Jahr. v. Chr.* Hösel.

Lambert, S. 2002. "The Sacrificial Calendar at Athens," *ABSA* 97:353–99.

Langlotz, E. 1927. *Frühgriechische Bildhauerschulen*. Nuremberg.

Langlotz, E., and W. H. Schuchhardt. 1943. *Archaische Plastik auf der Akropolis*. Frankfurt.

Lardinois, A., and L. McClure, eds. 2001. *Making Silence Speak: Women's Voices in Greek Literature and Society*. Princeton.

Laskares, N. 1923. "Μορφαί ιερέων επί αρχαίων μνημείων," *ArchDelt* 8: 103–16.

Laumonier, A. 1958. *Les cultes indigènes en Carie, BEFAR*, vol. 188. Paris.

Lazzarini, M. L. 1976. "Le formule delle dediche votive nella Grecia arcaica," *MAL* 19:47–354

Lefkowitz, M. R. 1981. *Heroines and Hysterics*. London.

———. 1986. *Women in Greek Myth*. Baltimore.

———. 1993a. "Influential Women," in Cameron and Kuhrt: 49–64.

———. 1993b. "Seduction and Rape in Greek Myth," in A. E. Laiou, ed. *Consent and Coercion to Sex and Marriage in Ancient and Medieval Societes*: 17–37. Cambridge, MA.

———. 1995. "The Last Hours of the Parthenos," in Reeder: 32–38.

———. 1996. "Women in the Panathenaic and Other Festivals," in Neils, 78–91. Madison.

———. 2003. *Greek Gods, Human Lives*. New Haven.

Lefkowitz, M. R., and M. B. Fant. 1982. *Women's Life in Greece and Rome: A Source Book in Translation*. Baltimore.

Levine, L. I. 2000. *The Ancient Synagogue: The First Thousand Years*. New Haven.

Lewis, D. M. 1955. "Notes on Attic Inscriptions (II)," *BSA* 50:1–36.

———. 1959. "Law on the Lesser Panathenaia," *Hesperia* 28:239–47. Reprinted 1997 in P. J. Rhodes, ed., *Selected Papers in Greek and Near Eastern History*: 252–62. Oxford.

Lewis, S. 2002. *The Athenian Woman: An Iconographic Sourcebook*. London and New York.

Lieu, J., J. North, and T. Rajak, eds. 1992. *The Jews among Pagans and Christians*. London.

Lifshitz, B. 1967. *Donateurs et fondateurs dans les synagogues juives*. Paris.

Lincoln, B. 2004. "Epilogue," in *RAW*: 657–67.

Linders, T. 1972. *Studies in the Treasure Records of Artemis Brauronia Found in Athens*, Skrifter Utgivna av Svenska Institutet i Athen 4.19. Stockholm.

Lippolis, E. 1997. *Fra Taranto e Roma: Società e cultura urbana in Puglia tra Annibale e l'età imperiale*. Taranto.

Lissarrague, F. 1987. "Voyages d'image: Iconographie et aires culturelles," *Revue des Études Anciennes* 89:261–69.

———. 1990. *The Aesthetics of the Greek Banquet: Images of Wine and Ritual*. Princeton.

———. 1992. "Figures of Women," in Schmidt Pantel: 139–229.

Lissarrague, F., and A. Schnapp. 1981. "Imagerie des Grecs ou Grèce des imagiers?" *Le temps de la réflexion* 2:286–97.

Lloyd-Jones, H. 1983. "Artemis and Iphigeneia," *JHS* 103:87–102.

Loomis, W. T. 1998. *Wages, Welfare Costs, and Inflation in Classical Athens*. Ann Arbor.

Loraux, N. 1987. *Tragic Ways of Killing a Woman*. Cambridge, MA.

Lullies, R., and M. Hirmer, eds. 1957. *Greek Sculpture*. New York.

Maass, M. 1972. *Die Prohedrie des Dionysostheaters in Athen*. Munich.

Maass, P. 1946. "Στεφανω: Title of a Priestess," *Hesperia* 15:72.

Madigan, K., and C. Osiek. 2005. *Ordained Women of the Early Church: A Documentary History*. Baltimore, London.

Malkin, I. 1987. *Religion and Colonization in Ancient Greece*. Leiden, New York.

Mansfield, J. 1985. *The Robe of Athena and the Panathenaic "Peplos."* Dissertation, University of California, Berkeley.

Mantis, A. 1990. Προβλήματα της εικονογραφίας των ιερειών και των ιερέων στην αρχαία Ελληνική τέχνη. Athens.

Marcadé, J. 1953. *Recueil des signatures de sculpteurs grecs*, vols. 1, 2. Paris.

Mark, I. S. 1993. *The Sanctuary of Athena Nike in Athens: Architectural Stages and Chronology = Hesperia* Supplement 26. Princeton.

Martha, J. 1882. *Les sacerdoces athéniens*, BEFAR 26. Paris.

Mattingly, H. B. 1982. "The Athena Nike Temple Reconsidered," *AJA* 86 (1982) 381–85. Reprinted in *The Athenian Empire Restored: Epigraphic and Historical Studies by H. B. Mattingly*: 461–71. Ann Arbor.

Maurizio, L. 1995. "Anthropology and Spirit Possession: A Reconstruction of Pythia's Role at Delphi," *JHS* 115:69–86.

———. 1997. "Delphic Oracles as Oral Performance: Authenticity and Historical Evidence," *ClAnt* 16:308–35.

———. 2001. "The Voice at the Centre of the World: The Pythia's Ambiguity and Authority," in Lardinois and McClure: 38–54.

McClees, H. 1920. *A Study of Women in Attic Inscription*. Dissertation, Columbia University. New York.

Merrit, B., and J. S. Traill. 1974. *Inscriptions: The Athenian Councillors, Agora* vol. 15. Princeton.

Meskell, L. 1998a. "The Irresistable Body and the Seduction of Archaeology," in D. Montserrat, ed. *Changing Bodies, Changing Meanings: Studies on the Human Body in Antiquity*. London.

———. 1998b. "Running the Gamut, Girls, and Goddesses," *AJA* 102:181–85.

———. 1999. *Archaeology of Social Life: Age, Sex, Class, et cetera, in Ancient Egyptian Life*. Oxford.

———. 2000. "Writing the Body in Archaeology," in A. E. Rautman, ed. *Reading the Body: Representations and Remains in the Archaeological Record*: 13–21. Philadelphia.

———. 2001. "Archaeologies of Identity," in I. Hodder, ed. *Archaeological Theory Today*: 187–213. Oxford.

———. 2002. *Private Life in New Kingdom Egypt*. Princeton.

Meskell, L., and P. Pels, eds. 2005. *Embedding Ethics: Shifting Boundaries of the Anthropological Profession*. Oxford.

Meskell, L., and R. W. Preucel, eds. 2004a. *A Companion to Social Archaeology*. Malden, MA.

———. 2004b. "Identities," in Meskell and Preucel (2004a): 121–41.

Meyer, M. 1987. *The Ancient Mysteries: A Sourcebook*. Philadelphia.

Mikalson, J. D. 1998. *Religion in Hellenistic Athens*. Berkeley.

———. 2005. *Ancient Greek Religion*. Oxford.

Miles, M. M. 1998. *The City Eleusinion, Agora* vol. 31. Princeton.

Miller, M. 1989. "The *Ependytes* in Classical Athens," *Hesperia* 58:313–29.

Mills, H. 1984. "Greek Clothing Regulations: Sacred and Profane?" *ZPE* 55:255–65.

Möbius, H. 1934. "Diotima," *JdI* 49:45–60.

Moret, J. M. 1975. *L'Ilioupersis dans la céramique italiote*. Bibliotheca Helvetica Romana 14. Rome.

Moretti, L. 1967–75. *Iscrizioni storiche ellenistiche*, 2 vols. Florence.

Morris, I. 1993. "Poetics of Power: The Interpretation of Ritual Action in Archaic Greece," in C. Doughery and L. Kurke, eds. *Cult, Performance, and Politics in Cultural Poetics in Archaic Greece*: 15–42. Cambridge.

———. 2000. *Archaeology as Cultural History*. Oxford.

Moulinier, L. 1952. *Le pur et l'impur dans la pensée des Grecs d'Homere à Aristote*. Études et Commentaires 12. Paris.

Muthmann, F. 1975. *Mutter und Quelle: Studien zur Quellenverehrung im Altertum und im Mittelalterum*. Basel.

Nagy, B. 1978–79. "The Naming of Athenian Girls: A Case in Point," *CJ* 74:360–64.

Nagy, G. 1990. *Greek Mythology and Poetics*. Ithaca.

———. 1994/95. "Transformations of Choral Lyric Traditions in the Context of Athenian State Theater," *Arion* 3.1:41–55.

Neils, J., ed. 1992. *Goddess and Polis: The Panathenaic Festival in Ancient Athens*. Hanover, NH.

———. 1996. *Worshipping Athena: Panathenaia and Pathenon*. Madison.

Neumann, G. 1965. *Gesten und Gebärden in der griechischen Kunst*. Berlin.

———. 1979. *Probleme des griechischen Weihreliefs, Tübinger Studien zur Archäologie und Kunstgeschichte*, Band 3. Tübingen.

Nevett, L. C. 1994. "Separation or Seclusion? Towards an Archaeological Approach to Investigating Women in the Greek Household in the Fifth to Third Centuries B.C.," in M. P. Pearson and C. Richards, eds. *Architecture and Order: Approaches to Social Space*: 98–112. London.

———. 1995. "Gender Relations in the Classical Greek Household: The Archaeological Evidence," *ABSA* 91:363–81.

———. 1999. *House and Society in the Ancient Greek World*. Cambridge.

Newton, C. T. 1861. *History of Discoveries at Halicarnassus, Cnidus, and the Branchidae*. London.

Nicholson, L. 1990. *Feminism/Postmodernism*. New York.

———, ed. 1997. *The Second Wave: A Reader in Feminist Theory*. New York.

Nielsen, I. 2002. *Cultic Theaters and Ritual Drama: A Study in Regional Development and Religious Interchange between East and West in Antiquity*. Aarhus Studies in Mediterranean Antiquity, vol. 4. Aarhus.

Nilsson, M. P. 1925. *A History of Greek Religion*. Oxford.

———. 1940. *Greek Popular Religion*. New York.

———. 1957. *The Dionysiac Mysteries of the Hellenistic and Roman Age*. Skrifter Utgivna av Svenska Institut i Athens, 8.5. Lund.

———. 1961. *Geschichte der griechischen Religion*. Munich.

Nollé, J. 1985. "Grabepigramme und Reliefdarstellungen aus Kleinasien," *ZPE* 60:117–35.

Nordquist, G. 1992. "Instrumental Music in Representations of Greek Cult," in Hägg.

Oakley, J., and R. Sinos. 1993. *The Wedding in Ancient Athens*. Madison.

O'Neill, M. 1999. *Adorno, Culture, and Feminism*. London.

Osborne, R. 1993. "Women and Sacrifice in Classical Greece," *CQ* 43:392–405. Reprinted in Buxton 2000: 294–313.

Osborne, R., and S. Hornblower, eds. 1994. *Ritual, Finance, and Politics: Athenian Democratic Accounts Presented to David Lewis*. Oxford.

Otranto, G. 1982. "Note sul sacerdozio femminile nell'antichità in margine a una testimonianza di Gelasio I," *Vetera Christianorum* 19:341–60, trans. A. Rossi, 1991, in "Priesthood and Prejudice: On Recovering the Women Priests of Early Christianity," *JFSR* 7:73–94.

Padel, R. 1983. "Model for Possession by Greek Daemons," in Cameron and Kuhrt: 3–17.

Papadimitriou, J. 1951. "Αττικα I," *ArchEph* (1948–49): 46–153.

Parke, H. W. 1977. *Festivals of the Athenians*. London.

———. 1985. *The Oracles of Apollo in Asia Minor*. London.

Parke, H. W., and D. E. W. Wormell. 1956. *The Delphic Oracle*, 2 vols. Oxford.

Parker, R. 1983. *Miasma: Pollution and Purification in Early Greek Religion*. Oxford.

———. 1986. "Greek Religion," in J. Boardman, J. Griffin, et al., eds. *The Oxford History of the Classical World*: 254–74. Oxford.

———. 1987. "Myths of Early Athens," in Bremmer: 187–214.

———. 1996. *Athenian Religion: A History*. Oxford.

———. 1998. "Pleasing Things: Reciprocity in Greek Religion," in C. Gill, N. Postlethwaite, and R. Seaford, eds. *Reciprocity in Ancient Greece*: 105–26. Oxford.

———. 2004a. "Controlling Religion: Greece," in *RAW* 570–72.

———. 2004b. "Sin, Pollution, and Purity: Greece," in *RAW*: 507–9.

———. 2004c. "What Are Sacred Laws?" in Harris and Rubenstein: 57–70.

———. 2005. *Polytheism and Society in Ancient Athens*. Oxford.

Parker, R., and D. Obbink. 2000. "Aus der Arbeit der 'Inscriptiones Graecae' VI: Sales of Priesthoods on Cos I," *Chiron* 30:415–49.

———. 2001. "Aus der Arbeit der 'Inscriptiones Graecae' VI: Sales of Priesthoods on Cos II," *Chiron* 31:229–52.

Parker-Pearson, M., and C. Richards, eds. 1993. *Architecture and Order: Archaeological and Ethnoarchaeological Studies of Social Space*. London.

Patton, K. 2006. *Religion of the Gods: Ritual, Reflexivity, and Paradox*. Oxford.

Peirce, S. 1984. *The Representation of Animal Sacrifice in Attic Vase-Painting*. Dissertation, Bryn Mawr College. Bryn Mawr.

———. 1993. "Death, Revelry, and Thysia," *ClAnt* 12:219–66.

———. 1998. "Visual Language and Concepts of Cult on the 'Lenaia Vases,'" *ClAnt* 17:59–95.

Pelling, C., ed. 1997. *Greek Tragedy and the Historian*. Oxford.

Pfisterer-Haas, S. 1989. *Darstellungen alter Frauen in der griechischen Kunst*. Frankfurt am Main.

Pfuhl, E., and H. Möbius. 1977. *Die ostgriechisches Grabreliefs*. Mainz.

Picard, C. 1922. *Ephèsos et Claros*. Paris.

Pingiatoglou, S. 1994. "Rituelle Frauengelage auf schwartzfigurigen attischen Vasen," *AthMitt* 109:39–51.

Pirenne-Delforge, V. 1994. *L'Aphrodite grecque*, *Kernos* Supplement 4, Athens and Liège.

Pleket, H. W. 1969. "The Social Position of Women in the Graeco-Roman World," *Epigraphica II. Texts on the Social History of the Greek World*. Leiden.

Polignac, F. de. 1984. *La naissance de la cité grecque: Cultes, espace et société VIIIe–VIIe siècles avant J.-C.* Paris, trans. 1995, *Cults, Territory, and the Origins of the Greek City-State.* Chicago.

Pomeroy, S. B. 1975. *Goddesses, Whores, Wives, and Slaves: Women in Classical Antiquity.* New York.

———. 1984. *Women in Hellenistic Egypt from Alexander to Cleopatra.* New York.

———, ed. 1991. *Women's History and Ancient History.* Chapel Hill and London.

Preller, L. 1846. "Minerva Cliduchus," *AZ* 4:261–64.

Price, S. R. F. 1984. *Rituals and Power: The Roman Imperial Cult in Asia Minor.* Cambridge.

———. 1985. "Delphi and Divination," in Easterling and Muir: 128–54.

———. 1999. *Religions of the Ancient Greeks.* Cambridge.

———. 2004. "Religious Personnel: Greece," in *RAW*: 302–5.

Prott, H. von, and L. Ziehen. 1896–1906. *Leges graecorum sacrae e titutlis collectae.* Leipzig.

Proukakis, A. M. 1971. *The Evolution of the Attic Marble Lekythoi.* London.

Pulleyn, S. 1993. *Prayer in Greek Religion.* Oxford.

Rahn, P. 1986. "Funeral Memorials of the First Priestess of Athena Nike," *ABSA* 81:195–208.

Raubitschek, A. 1949. *Dedications from the Athenian Acropolis.* Cambridge, MA.

Reardon, B. P. 1989. *Collected Ancient Greek Novels.* Berkeley, Los Angeles, and London.

Reeder, E. D., ed. 1995. *Pandora: Women in Classical Greece.* Princeton.

Reinach, S. 1922–24. *Répertoire des vases peints grecs et étrusques,* 2nd ed. Paris.

Richter, G. M. A. 1968. *Korai.* London.

Ridder, A. de. 1915. *Les bronzes antiques.* Paris.

———. 1922. "Monuments figurés de Thespies," *BCH* 46.

Ridgway, B. S. 1970. "Dolphins and Dolphin Riders," *Archaeology* 23:86–95.

———. 1977a. *The Archaic Style in Greek Sculpture.* Princeton.

———. 1977b. "The Peplos Kore, Akropolis 679," *JWalt* 36:49–61.

———. 1981. *Fifth-Century Styles in Greek Sculpture.* Princeton.

———. 1982. "Of Kouroi and Korai: The Attic Variety," in *Studies in Athenian Architecture, Sculpture, and Topography* presented to Homer A. Thompson, *Hesperia* Supplement 20:118–27. Princeton.

———. 1984. *Roman Copies of Greek Sculpture: The Probem of the Originals.* Ann Arbor.

———. 1987. "Ancient Greek Women and Art: The Material Evidence," *AJA* 91:399–409.

———. 1990a. "Birds, 'Meniskoi,' and Head Attributes in Archaic Greece," *AJA* 94:583–612.

———. 1990b. *Hellenistic Sculpture I: The Styles of ca. 331–200 B.C.* Madison.

———. 1992. "Images of Athena on the Acropolis," in Neils: 119–42.

———. 1993. *The Archaic Style in Greek Sculpture,* 2nd ed. Chicago.

———. 1997. *Fourth-Century Styles in Greek Sculpture.* Madison.

———. 2000. *Hellenistic Sculpture II: The Styles of ca. 200–100 B.C.* Madison.

———. 2002. *Hellenistic Sculpture III: The Styles of ca. 100–31 B.C.* Madison.

Ridgway, B. S., et al. 1994. *Greek Sculpture in the Art Museum Princeton University: Greek Originals, Roman Copies, and Variants.* Princeton.

Robbins, E. 1994. "Alcman's *Partheneion*: Legend and Choral Ceremony," *CQ* 44:7–16.

Robert, L. 1933. "Inscriptions d'Èrythrai," *BCH* 57:467–84.

Robert, J., and L. Robert. 1964. "Bulletin épigraphique," *REG* 77:169.

———. 1973. "Bulletin épigraphique," *REG* 86:94.

Robertson, N. 1983. "The Riddle of the Arrephoria at Athens," *HSCPh* 87:241–88.

Roccos, L. J. 1995. "The Kanephoros and Her Festival Mantle in Greek Art," *AJA* 99:641–66.

Rosivach, V. J. 1994. *The System of Public Sacrifice in Fourth-Century Athens*. Atlanta.

Rossi, A. 1991. "Priesthood and Prejudice: On Recovering the Women Priests of Early Christianity," with trans. of G. Otranto, "Note sul sacerdozio femminile nell'antichità in margine a una testimonianza di Gelasio I" ("Notes on the Female Priesthood in Antiquity"), *JFSR* 7:73–94.

Rouse, W. H. D. 1902. *Greek Votive Offerings*. Cambridge.

Roussel, D. 1976. *Tribu et cité*. Paris.

Rousell, P. 1925. *Delos*. Paris.

Ruhfel, H. 1984. *Kinderleben im Klassischen Athen*. Mainz.

Salviat, F. 1959. "Décrets pour Épié fille de Dionysios: Déesses et sanctuaires thasiens," *BCH* 83:362–97.

Schachter, A. 1981. *Cults of Boiotia*, BICS Supplement 38. London.

Schaps, D. 1977. "The Woman Least Mentioned: Etiquette and Women's Names," *CQ* 27:323–30.

Schelp, J. 1975. *Das Kanoun*. Würzburg.

Schlörb-Vierneisel, B. 1968. "Drei neue Grabreliefs aus der Heiligen Strasse," *AM* 83:89–110.

Schmaltz, B. 1970. *Untersuchungen zu den attischen marmarlekythen*. Berlin.

———. 1978. "Zu einer Attischen Grabmalbasis des 4. Jahrhunderts v. Chr.," *AM* 93:83–97.

Schmidt, E. 1931. "Zur Erzplastik des Phidias," in *Corolla Ludwig Curtius zum sechzigsten Geburtstagdargebracht*: 72–80. Stuttgart.

Schmidt, M. 2000. "Rituelle Frauengelage auf einer noch urbekannaen attischen Vase," in P. Linant de Bellefonds, J. Balty, et al., eds. *Agathos daimon: Mythes et cultes. Études d'iconographie en l'honneur de Lilly Kahil*, BCH Supplement 38:433–41. Paris.

Schmidt Pantel, P. 1984. "La difference des sexes, histoire, anthropologie et cité grecque," in M. Perrot, ed. *Une histoire des femmes est-elle possible?* 98–119. Marseille.

———, ed. 1992. *A History of Women in the West*, vol. 1: *From Ancient Goddesses to Christian Saints*, trans. A. Goldhammer. Cambridge, MA.

Schnapp, A. 1988. "Why the Greeks Needed Images," in Christiansen and Melander: 568–74.

Schneider, L. A. 1975. *Zur sozialen Bedeutung der archaischen Korenstatuen*. Hamburg.

Scholl, A. 1996. *Die attischen Bildfeldstelen des 4. Jhs. v. Chr., Ath. Mitt.* Beiheft 17.

Schuchhardt, W. H. 1968. "Eine hellenistische Gewandfigur aus Knidos," in *Festschrift für G. von Lucken, Wissenschaftliche Zeitschrift der Universität Rostock* 17:791–94.

Schwabl, H. 1993. "Ephesiaka: Zu Artemidor I 8 und IV 4," in J. Dalfen, S. Petersmann, and F. F. Schwarz, eds. *Religio Graeco-Romana: Festschrift für Walter Pötscher*, Grazer Beiträge, Supplementband V: 134–43.

Seaford, R. 1981. "Dionysiac Drama and the Dionysiac Mysteries," *CQ* 31:252–75.

———. 1994. *Reciprocity and Ritual*. Oxford.

———. 1996. *The Bacchae*. Oxford.

Segre, M. 1937. "Osservazioni epigraphiche sulla vendita di sacerdozio II," *Reale Instit. Lombardo di Sc. e. Lett. Milano, Rend. Class. di lett. e. sc. morali e stor.* 70:83–105.

Shapiro, H. A. 1989. *Art and Cult under the Tyrants in Athens*. Mainz.

Simms, R. 1989. "The Cult of the Thracian Goddess Bendis in Athens and Attica," *Ancient World* 18:59–76.

Simon, C. G. 1986. *The Archaic Votive Offerings and Cults of Ionia*. Dissertation, University of California, Berkeley.

Simon, E. 1953. *Opfernde Götter*. Berlin.

———. 1978. s.v. "Zeus," *RE* Supplement 15:1414.

———. 1983. *Festivals of Attica: An Archaeological Commentary*. Madison.

———. 1985. *Die Götter der Griechen*, 3rd ed. Munich.

Skias, A. N. 1898. "Πανάρχαια Ελευσινιακή νεκρόπολις," *EA*:28–122.

Smarczyk, B. 1990. *Untersuchungen zur Religionspolitik und politischen Propaganda Athens im Delisch-Attischen Seebund*. Munich.

Smith, D. R. 1968. *The Function and Origins of Hieropoioi*. Dissertation, University of Pennsylvania. Philadelphia.

Sokolowski, F. 1946. "Ventes des Prêtrises d'Èrythrae," *BCH* 70:548–51.

Sommerstein, A. H. 1980. "The Naming of Women in Greek and Roman Comedy," *QS* 11:393–418.

Sourvinou-Inwood, C. 1971a. "Aristophanes *Lysistrata* 641–647," *CQ* 21:339–42.

———. 1971b. Review of A. Brelich, *Paides e parthenoi* (Rome 1969), *JHS* 91:172–77.

———. 1979. *Theseus as Son and Stepson: A Tentative Illustration of the Greek Mythological Mentality*, BICS Supplement 40. London.

———. 1987. "Menace and Pursuit: Differentiation and the Creation of Meaning," in C. Bérard, C. Bron, and A. Pomar, eds. *Image et société en Grèce ancienne: L'iconographie comme methode d'analyse*: 41–58. Lausanne.

———. 1988a. "Further Aspects of Polis Religion," in *Annali Instituto Universitario orientale di Napoli: Archaeologia e storia antica* 10: 259–74. Naples. Reprinted in Buxton 2000: 38–53.

———. 1988b. "Priestess in the Text, Theano Menonos Agrylethen," *Greece and Rome* 35:29–39.

———. 1988c. *Studies in Girls' Transitions: Aspects of the Arkteia and Age Representative in Attic Iconography*. Athens.

———. 1990. "What Is Polis Religion?" in O. Murray and S. Price, eds. *The Greek City: From Homer to Alexander*: 295–322. Oxford. Reprinted in Buxton 2000: 13–37.

———. 1991. *"Reading" Greek Culture: Texts and Images, Rituals and Myths*. Oxford.

———. 1995a. "Male and Female, Public and Private, Ancient and Modern," in Reeder: 111–20.

———. 1995b. *"Reading" Greek Death. To the End of the Classical Period*. Oxford.

———. 1997. "Reconstructing Change: Ideology and Ritual at Eleusis," in M. Golden and P. Toohey, eds. *Inventing Ancient Culture: Historicism, Periodization, and the Ancient World*: 132–64. London.

———. 2003. *Tragedy and Athenian Religion*. Lanham, MD, New York.

———. 2004. "Reading a Myth, Reconstructing Its Constructions," in *Myth and Symbol II, Symbolic Phenomena in Ancient Greek Culture*. Papers from the second and third international symposia on symbolism at Athens, S. des Bouvrie, ed.: 141–80. Athens.

———. 2005. *Hylas, the Nymphs, Dionysos, and Others: Myth, Ritual, Ethnicity*, Skrifter Utgivna av Svenska Institutet i Athen, vol. 8.19. Stockholm.

Stewart, A. F. 1979. *Attika: Studies in Athenian Sculpture of the Hellenistic Age*, Supplementary Papers no. 14, Society for the Promotion of Hellenic Studies. London.

———. 1990. *Greek Sculpture*. New Haven.

Strittmacher, E. J. 1924–25. "Prayer in the *Iliad* and *Odyssey*," *CW* 18:83ff.

Tabbernee, W. 1997. *Montanist Inscriptions and Testimonies: Epigraphic Sources Illustrating the History of Montanism*, North American Patristic Society, Patristic Monograph Series 16. Macon, GA.

TeRiele, G.-J.-M.-J. 1978. "Une nouvelle loi sacrée en Arcadie," *BCH* 102:325–31.

Themelis, P. G. 1971. *Brauron: Guide to the Site and to the Museum.* Athens.

———. 1986. "Brauron, la stoà delle arktoi," *Magna Graecia* 21:6–10.

———. 1994a. "Artemis Ortheia at Messene: The Epigraphical Evidence," in Hägg: 101–22.

———. 1994b. "Damaphon of Messene: New Evidence," in K. Sheedy, ed. *Archaeology in the Peloponnese: New Excavations and Research.* Oxford.

———. 1996. "Damaphon," in O. Palagia and J. J. Pollitt, eds. *Personal Styles in Greek Sculpture = YCS* 30:154–85. New Haven.

———. 2002a. "Contributions to the Topography of the Sanctuary at Brauron," in Gentili and Perusino: 103–16.

———. 2002b. "Messene: Recent Discoveries (Sculpture)," in M. Stamatopoulou and M. Yeroulanou, eds. *Excavating Classical Culture: Recent Archaeological Discoveries in Greece.* Oxford.

Thomas, J. 1996. *Time, Culture, and Identity: An Interpretative Archaeology.* London.

Tracy, S. V. 1975. *The Lettering of an Athenian Mason, Hesperia* Supplement 15. Princeton.

———. 1982. IG II^2 2336. *Contributors of First Fruits for the Pythaïs, Beiträge zur klassischen Philologie.* Heft 139.

———. 1990. *Attic Letter-Cutters of 229 to 86 BC.* Berkeley.

———. 2003. *Athens and Macedon: Attic Letter-Cutters of 300 to 229 B.C.* Berkeley, Los Angeles, and London.

Trebilco, P. R. 1991. *Jewish Communities in Asia Minor.* Cambridge.

Trendall, A. D., and T. B. L. Webster. 1971. *Illustrations of Greek Drama.* London.

Tuchelt, K. F. 1970. *Die archaischen Skulpturen von Didyma: Beiträge zur frühgriechischen Plastik in Kleinasien.* Berlin.

Turner, J. A. 1983. *Hiereiai: The Acquisition of Feminine Priesthoods.* Dissertation, University of California, Santa Barbara.

van Straten, F. 1974. "Did the Greeks Kneel before Their Gods?" *BABesch* 49:159–89.

———. 1987. "Greek Sacrificial Representations: Livestock Prices and Religious Mentality," in T. Linders and G. Nordquist, eds. *Gifts to the Gods: Proceedings of the Uppsala Symposium 1985, Boreas* 15: 159–70.

———. 1992. "Votives and Votaries in Greek Sanctuaries," in O. Reverdin and B. Grange, eds. *Le sanctuaire grec:* 247–84. Geneva.

———. 1995. *Hiera Kala: Images of Animal Sacrifices in Archaic and Classical Greece.* Leiden.

Vanderpool, E. 1979. "The Genos Theonidai Honors a Priestess of the Nymphs," *AJP* 100:213–16.

Vermaseren, M. J. 1977. *Cybele and Attis: The Myth and the Cult,* trans. A. M. H. Lemmers. London.

Vernant, J.-P. 1974 = 1980. *Myth and Society in Ancient Greece.* Paris.

———. 1987. "Mythe et Religion en Grèce Ancienne," in M. Eliade ed. *The Encyclopedia of Religion* 6:99–118. New York and London.

———. 1990. *Figures, idoles, masques.* Paris.

Versnel, H. S. 1981a. *Faith, Hope, and Worship: Aspects of Religious Mentality in the Ancient World.* Leiden.

———. 1981b. "Religious Mentality in Ancient Prayer," in Versnel 1981a: 1–64.

———. 1990. *Ter Unus. Isis, Dionysos, Hermes: Three Studies in Henotheism.* Studies in Greek and Roman Religion 6.7. Leiden.

———. 1992. "The Festivals for Bona Dea and the Thesmophoria," *Greece and Rome* 39 (1992) 31–55. Reprinted in I. McAuslan and P. Walcot, eds. *Women in Antiquity, Greece and Rome* Supplement 3 (1996) 182–204.

———. 1993. *Transition and Reversal in Myth and Ritual Inconsistencies in Greek and Roman Religion II*. Studies in Greek and Roman Religion 6.2.

Vickers, M. J. 1985. "Artful Crafts: The Influence of Metal on Athenian Painted Pottery," *JHS* 105:108–28.

———. 1992. "The Metrology of Gold and Silver Plate in Classical Greece," in T. Linders and B. Alroth, eds. *Economics of Cult in the Ancient Greek World, Boreas* 21:53–72. Uppsala.

Vickers, M. J., and D. Gill. 1994. *Artful Crafts: Ancient Greek Silverware and Pottery*. New York.

Vidal-Naquet, P. 1986. *The Black Hunter: Forms of Thought and Forms of Society in the Greek World*. Baltimore.

Walcot, P. 1984. "Greek Attitudes towards Women: The Mythological Evidence," *Greece and Rome* 33–34.

Walter, O. 1937. "Die Reliefs aus dem Heiligtum der Echeliden in neu-Phaleron," *AE*: 97–119.

Walters, E. 1988. *Attic Grave Reliefs That Represent Women in the Dress of Isis*. Princeton.

Walters, H. B. 1896. *Catalogue of the Greek and Etruscan Vases in the British Museum*.

———. 1915. *Select Bronzes: Greek Roman and Etruscan in the Department of Antiquities*. London.

West, M. L. 1985. *Hesiodic Catalogue of Women*. Oxford.

Williams, D. 1988. "Three Groups of Fourth-Century South Italian Jewellery in the British Museum," *RM* 95:75–95.

Winkler, J. 1990. "'The Ephebes' Song' *Tragoidia* and *Polis*," in J. Winkler and F. I. Zeitlin, eds. *Nothing to Do with Dionysus? Athenian Drama in Its Social Context*: 20–62. Princeton.

Wire, A. C. 1990. *Corinthian Women Prophets: A Reconstruction through Paul's Rhetoric*. Minneapolis.

Wörrle, M. 1990. "Inschriften von Herakleia am Latmos II. Das Priestaertum der Athena Latmia," *Chiron* 20:19–58.

Zanker, P. 1993. "The Hellenistic Grave Stelai from Smyrna: Identity and Self-Image in the Polis," in A. Bullock, ed. *Images and Ideologies: Self-Definition in the Hellenistic World*: 212–30. Berkeley.

———. 1995. "Brüche im Bürgerbild," in M. Wörrle and P. Zanker, eds. *Stadtbild und Bürgerbild im Hellenismus*: 251–63. Munich.

Zeitlin, F. 1982. "Cultic Models of the Female: Rites of Dionysus and Demeter," *Arethusa* 15: 129–57.

Zevi, F. 1969–70. "Tre inscrizioni conferme di artisti Greci," *RendPontAcc* 42: 110.

Index of Monuments

Note: Page numbers in italics indicate illustrations.

Index of Inscriptions

Note: Page numbers in italics indicate illustrations.

Index of Priestesses

Note: Page numbers in italics indicate illustrations.

MYTHOLOGICAL PRIESTESSES

General Index

Judaism, 19, 262–63, 269–72, 275, 290n.100

Julian (emperor), 220

Justinian I, 268

Kabiri, 250

Kadmos, 245, 254

Kahil, L., 33

Kalamaia, feast of (Eleusis), 65

Kalaureia, 40

Kallias, dadouchos, 8

Kallimachos: on Demeter as priestess, 105; on
    priestess of Kybele, 250

Kallisto, 33

Kallynteria, feast of (Athens), 41, 61

Karia, 215, 272

Karyatids, 122, 124–25

Kearns, E. 9–10, 166

Kedrenos, George, 262

Kenchriae, 265, 270

Kephisia, 133, 134, 242

Kerkyra, 93

Keyeneia, statues of priestesses of the Eumenides,
    118

Kioniskoi, 242–44

Klazomenai, 79

Kleisthenes, 47, 62, 78

Kleobis and Biton, 11, 70

Knageus, 41

Knidos, 118, 134–35, 219, 262; *Aphrodite of Knidos*,
    262; *Demeter of Knidos*, 135

Komaitho, 41

Korai, 127–29, 163, 324n.39–43. *And see* Athens,
    City: Akropolis; Sculpture, korai

Kore, cults of: Mantineia, 147; Megalopolis, 104

Koroneia, 169

Kos, 45, 49, 50, 51, 54–55, 118, 140, 181, 182, 189,

198–200, 214, 218, 248; Asklepieion, base for
    statue of Kallistrate, 140; base for statue of
    Pythias, 140; sale of priesthoods at, 45, 50,
    54–55; shrine of Demeter Kyparissi, 140

Kourotrophos, priesthood of (Athens), 49

Kraemer, R., 21

Krateriskoi: as evidence for Arkteia, 32–33, 152

Kroisos, 205

Kron, U., 3

Kybele, 234, 235, 236, 237, 238, 250, 253, 313n.153

Kyme, 272

Kyzikos, 118, 223, 248; funeral of Apollonis at, 141,
    223–24; sculptured column drums at, 124; stat-
    ues of priestess Kleidike at, 141

Lagina, 40, 42–43

Lakonia, 184

Landscape, 24–25; sacred, 119, 125

Langlotz, E., 130

Laodikeia, Synod of, 267

Lausus, sculpture collection of, 261–62

Lefkadia, Tomb of the Palmettes, 93, 317n.57

Lefkowitz, M., 21

Leimon, 106

Lemnos, 216

Lesbos, 248

Leto, cult of, 140

Leukippides, 10

Leukothea, shrine of (Chaironeia), 104

Lewis, D. M., 11, 59, 62, 143, 278

Life cycle, 6, 18, 29, 30, 286n.41. *And see* Time

Limnai, 107

Lindos (Rhodes): *Athena of Lindos*, 262; cursus for
    priests at, 28

Lissarrague, F., 83

Liturgies, 51, 52

Women (*cont.*)
of, 192; "invisibility" of, 3–4, 25, 275–76; legal and social identities of, 18; as magistrates and office holders, 361n.97; naming aloud of, 278–79; public vs. private roles, 5–6, 14, 174. *See also* elderly women; girls; married women; *parthenoi*; priestesses

Wool working, 192

Xenophon: on Megabyzos, 121

Xenophon of Ephesos: on Anthia, 85

Zeus, 30, 33, 48

Zeus, cults of: Euboulos (Thasos), 193; Kynthios and Athena Kynthia (Olympia), 91; Megistos, 213–14; Sosipolis and Eileithyia (Olympia), 104, 202

Zeus, priesthoods of: Alseios (Kos), 46

Zosimos of Panoplis, 220

The display type is Diotima, designed by Gudrun Zapf von Hesse in 1948 and released in 1951. It is named for the prophetess Diotima of Mantineia, the wise teacher of Sokrates in Plato's *Symposium*.